STUDIES IN ACCOUNTING THEORY

Studies in Accounting Theory

Edited by

W. T. BAXTER

Professor of Accounting, University of London

and

SIDNEY DAVIDSON

Arthur Young Professor of Accounting, University of Chicago

1962

RICHARD D. IRWIN, INC.

HOMEWOOD, ILLINOIS

Published in the
United States of
America

by Richard D. Irwin, Inc.

Published in Great Britain by
Sweet & Maxwell Limited of
11 New Fetter Lane London E.C.4

PRINTED IN GREAT BRITAIN BY
THE EASTERN PRESS LIMITED
OF LONDON AND READING

Introduction to the First Edition

WE who study or teach accounts are sadly handicapped by a shortage of good reading. Textbooks we have in plenty; most are sound and many are long. In general they deal competently with the mechanical side of our subject. But gaps exist even here; and when we turn from mechanics to principles the gaps become large indeed. What is more, such material as does exist is not always easy to lay hands on, often taking the form of essays scattered through the old files of British and American periodicals which few of us can readily consult.

Accordingly the Association of University Teachers of Accounting is sponsoring a series of volumes in which useful articles will be reprinted. This, the first, covers general accounting. Later issues may deal with costing and other branches of our subject.

Choosing the articles has not been easy, and I apologise to all authors and readers who feel that I have botched the matter. Many omissions will I hope be readily understood in the light of the preceding paragraphs; my task has not been to compile an anthology of all that is best in accounting, but to fill gaps with material that is hard to come by. Thus the omission of an article does not necessarily mean that I do not admire and recommend it. If it is easy of access, it is disqualified. Happily a good deal of serviceable reading is now coming into better supply, and several much-quoted authors have recently published volumes of their collected writings.

The chosen essays fall into two types. One group deals with professional matters; these will, I think, be of practical service in both classroom and office. But for the most part the essays have a more academic flavour. We start with a few that are concerned with the history of accounting; I should have liked to include more, so that students might see our subject in perspective, and realise that some of its limitations are due to a rather haphazard growth; but the dearth of material is here very striking. Others are intended to give background to studies of company law and management; Mr. Yamey's able contribution on dividend law, written in his very early twenties, may also serve to show students that they need not despair of infusing order into material that obviously baffles their teacher— in Mr. Yamey's case, me. The remaining essays illustrate the basic theory of accounting.

I must plead guilty to one form of bias in making my selection: I have let myself be swayed as much by manner of telling as by content. The warmest admirer of accounting could, alas, scarcely claim that its writings are in general either graceful or sprightly. A most unfortunate tradition has grown up that soundness must be dull. But why? Accounting theory is exciting stuff; and there seems to be no good reason why our writers should suppress their high spirits or turn a deaf ear to style. I have tried to find the exceptions —the men who show that here, as elsewhere, an author should strive to bring out all the life in his subject, and may on occasion give vent to his sense of fun or write with tongue in cheek.

However, it is not merely bad style that renders some of our writing dreary. It is also the absence of scepticism and controversy —without which accounting can never make a good academic discipline. True, if an author is describing the best ruling for a petty cash book, or how to transmute bill of exchange transactions into double-entry, then he has not much scope for spirited debate. Yet as soon as we pass from the elementary and technical parts of our subject we are confronted with countless difficult points of principle —indeed, almost every important branch of accounting still lacks an adequate theoretical basis. Our textbooks never call attention to this intellectual poverty. Nor do they give any hint that, where a step forward has been made, it has often been accompanied by controversies at once animated and entertaining, and on occasion unpleasantly heated. (One might almost risk the assertion that, if an article has not attracted outraged protest, it has not contributed much of merit.) Without such controversies, we are not likely to find the answers to our problems.

The battlefields of conflicting theory provide the best training-ground in abstract reasoning that accounting can offer to students. I have therefore been at some pains to include essays that stress the main points of controversy or adopt unconventional attitudes; in one or two cases, the essays form symposia, in which antagonists set forth the *pros* and *cons* of a debatable issue, and try to demolish one another's cases. It follows that I cannot possibly subscribe to all the views that are voiced. Still less can my fellow members of the Association of University Teachers of Accounting—who have shown their kindness by making helpful suggestions, but have left me complete freedom of choice—be held responsible for contributors' opinions. In some cases indeed the contributors themselves now tell me that time has modified their views; I have however persuaded them that the crude vigour of youth is more likely to stimulate class discussion than the tepid wisdom of maturity. Where the arguments strike me as false or exaggerated, I have assumed that the students' work in orthodox textbooks will supply sufficient corrective, and further that the occasional reading of subversive doctrines is good for the liver.

If the collection may be likened to an art exhibition, I may perhaps claim that it includes sample pictures from all the main modern schools, both extreme and traditional. Can one detect any common note among the artists' somewhat jarring attitudes? I think so. Accounting grew up as a technique for recording what has happened; our figures are histories—records of receipts, payments, and the like. So long as such figures are not asked to do much more than afford evidence of faithful stewardship, they are very adequate. But are they still adequate for more delicate tasks—for determining income, for settling production policies, for measuring the rights of shareholders? Almost all the writers answer " No ! " And this is not merely a pose by our wild young men. The same feeling is to be found increasingly among trusted leaders of the profession; for instance, a talk by Mr. G. O. May includes these remarks:

> If we are going to say that all we can do is just to take the dollars in and out, and that is all there is to it, and if we are not going to interpret the significance of what is happening—then we are resigning ourselves to a position as hewers of wood and drawers of water, and we relinquish the goal that accounting hopes to attain—a position of a highly professional receptiveness to new ideas and a great social usefulness.

One can detect two main causes for the falling prestige of historic figures. First come the ups-and-downs of the price-level, with which a substantial group of essays is concerned. The drop in the value of money during the post-war inflation has been so precipitate that it was bound to affect our thinking. Asset values based on cost may conjure up the best available picture when the price-level is stable, but hardly pass muster when costs have altered substantially. Where such values also affect income figures—and so tax—the repercussions of our concept have been widespread and unpleasant. *The Times* estimates the overstatement of profits in British industry for 1939–49 at no less than £2,500 million—£1,000 million being due to the time-lag error in charging stocks to " production " on a cost basis, and £1,500 million to the same error in the measurement of depreciation.[1] Normally we accountants counter our critics, when we are driven into an awkward dialectical corner, by insisting that the need for caution and prudence overrules all niceties of logic; the post-inflation embarrassments of industry have turned the tables on us and given this cherished argument to our adversaries.

But another attack was already in progress long before inflation came to trouble us. The whole concept of historic cost as a basis of value—even in times of price stability—had already been challenged. At one wing of the attackers was a group of theorists, fresh from their reading in economics, and anxious to demonstrate that value is a function of future benefits rather than past outlays. The other wing was composed of accountants bent on belittling the balance-sheet and elevating the revenue account. Possibly this group of accountants—which includes most of our leading writers—was the more influential in undermining accepted notions. One can readily

---

[1] *The Times*, March 24, 1949.

comprehend their attitude. Their daily work, and especially their negotiations with income tax officials, would predispose them to attach more and more weight to revenue figures. Further, they recognise that a balance-sheet is unlikely to show "values," in the sense of, *e.g.*, a current market value or a subjective value to the owner; and so they tend to dismiss the balance-sheet as a mere appendage of the revenue account—a mausoleum for the unwanted costs that the double-entry system throws up as regrettable by-products. Is this argument sound? If figures for wealth at the beginning and end of a period are meaningless, then can the figures for changes in that wealth—*i.e.*, the revenue account—mean anything? And, if so, what?

It may well be that this dispute is not so formidable as it first appears, and springs largely from differences in the use of words. Some people distinguish sharply between "cost" and "value" (possibly endowing the latter word with a great deal more precision than it can ever in fact possess). Others use "value" as a handy generic term covering a number of allied concepts, such as original cost, replacement cost, current selling price, subjective value, and so on. There seems much to be said in favour of this second attitude. What we seek is a practical measure for wealth. When regard is paid to difficulties of precise definition, to expense and trouble of calculation, to the needs of objectivity and familiarity of concept, then none of the measures can be regarded as perfect; original cost certainly does not get full marks, but its score may well be higher than those of its rivals—provided that its nature is plainly stated, that the price level has not changed much since the expenditure was made, and that the figures are not to be used for purposes for which they are not intended.

In saying this, I am but repeating a commonplace. Most observable phenomena can legitimately be measured in several ways, with widely differing answers. None of these may be "right"—indeed all may suffer from grave defects. But one method may be less unsatisfactory for some given purpose than its fellows. Your skilful statistician is he who shows ripe judgment in selecting the least bad measure for the job on hand.

The critical attitude of the essays may thus, I think, be regarded as reassuring. Accountants are coming to appreciate the limitations of their data, and to suggest alternative methods. The proffered cures take several forms. A number of contributors want us to correct original cost by substituting another "conventional" value, in which original cost is exalted or abased at the tail of some price index. Mr. MacNeal's exhilarating attack sweeps aside any remedy that stops short of wholesale re-appraisal. And Professor Edwards pleads for a forward-looking approach in which the valuations of both capital and income depend on the composite future receipts of the whole firm rather than historic data and separate figures for each asset.

If I were bold enough to criticise the critics, I should try to show that each makes out a reasonable case for using his favourite concept of value in particular circumstances, without explaining fully its limitations in other circumstances. Thus the stock market probably does use the forward-looking approach in arriving at share prices; but I doubt profoundly whether this would be a practical basis for determining income tax assessments or dividend policy; again, somewhat different considerations apply if the just price of munitions is being calculated, or if a firm is paying out the widow of a deceased partner. In short, the *occasion* for making the valuation is all-important. You must not choose a value without first knowing what you are going to use it for.

The essays therefore suggest that the good accountant of the future will be an expert in valuation. I do not for one moment suppose that he will ever be competent to appraise grandfather-clocks or feeding-stuffs or mineral seams; he will be well advised if he continues to leave the appraisal of separate assets—particularly physical assets—to specialists. But, if he is to give his maximum service to his fellow-men, he will have to be ready and able to value much more elusive things: costs, incomes, shares, partnership rights, whole enterprises, and so forth. This implies, I submit, that he must understand the different concepts of value, and know which concept is most serviceable for the task of the hour. He will of course need a much fuller training in theory, particularly economic theory, than most of us have enjoyed in the past.

When the chairman of a meeting does not quite know how to extricate himself from his opening remarks, he usually takes refuge in some such formula as: " And now, ladies and gentlemen, let me no longer stand between you and your speakers." The words have perhaps lost their original freshness, but the idea is as good as ever. An editor, however, cannot very well move a vote of thanks on the last page of his book, and I must do so now. We—readers and sponsors of the book alike—are deep in debt to the authors of the essays, and to the owners of the journals from which they are culled, for granting leave to republish. In not a single case was my request refused, and consent was always ready and courteous. Further, I have as editor been given much help and advice by publishers, contributors, and colleagues (notably Mr. David Solomons and Mr. H. C. Edey); and I am most grateful.

And now, ladies and gentlemen, let me no longer. . . .

W. T. BAXTER.

London School of Economics.
September, 1950.

Introduction to the Second Edition

THE introduction to the first edition of *Studies in Accounting* stressed the shortage of good, readily available reading on accounting topics. This problem still confronts us, though we hope the deficiency has been alleviated, in the areas of costing and the history of accounting, by publication of a volume of *Studies* in each of these fields. In the area of financial accounting, or accounting theory if you will, much that is new and instructive has been published in widely scattered places in the dozen years since the first edition appeared. This second edition is an effort to bring together some of the recent material that we feel is outstanding but not readily available. We also include a few of the essays from the first edition that continue to be helpful; and, where published work did not provide exactly what was wanted, we have commissioned new articles.

Several changes from the general arrangement of the earlier volume seemed desirable. First as to name: *Studies in Accounting Theory* is more aptly descriptive, and also serves to delineate this volume more clearly from the others in the series. The editing has been a joint Anglo-American enterprise. We found it relatively easy to agree on what was worthwhile in accounting writing—which testifies to the similarity of developments on both sides of the Atlantic. Although this was not a criterion in the selection process, it is an interesting fact that there are an equal number of items drawn from American and from British sources.

Perhaps the most significant change in this edition is the increased diversity of source material. Seven of the essays were written specifically for us. Two of them are concerned with the relationship of economics and accounting. Most of the remaining five deal with new developments in related topics that impinge heavily upon accounting theory. In selecting items to reprint, we have ranged further afield than previously; contributions have been drawn from sources that seem far removed from the main stream of accounting thought —the *Political Quarterly*, a U.S. Congressional hearing, and a book on economic planning in Eastern Europe. Journals in accounting, business, and economics furnished the bulk of the other material.

In preparing this volume, we have benefited from the advice and aid of colleagues, contributors and many others. The authors of the essays and their publishers were again uniformly generous in agreeing

to publication.   By their comments—candid, and sometimes brutal—
our colleagues have helped us to winnow the mass of accounting
writing and reduce the size of this volume to its present still rather
bulky form.   We are grateful.   We regret having been forced at times
to make an arbitrary choice between equally attractive articles, and
to leave out much that we admire.   For such omissions, and other
faults, we assume all responsibility.

W. T. BAXTER

SIDNEY DAVIDSON.

London School of Economics.
University of Chicago.

January, 1962.

STUDIES IN ACCOUNTING THEORY

Contents

xiii

THE ACCOUNTANT AND THE COMMUNITY

AUTHORITY

LAW

OUTSIDE THE LAW

PUBLISHED STATEMENTS AND THEIR INTERPRETATION

MANAGEMENT CONTROL

NEW TECHNIQUES

An Historical Defense of Bookkeeping[*]

By Henry Rand Hatfield

Deceased, sometime Professor of Accounting,
University of California.

I AM sure that all of us who teach accounting in the universities suffer from the implied contempt of our colleagues, who look upon accounting as an intruder, a Saul among the prophets, a pariah whose very presence detracts somewhat from the sanctity of the academic halls. It is true that we ourselves speak of the science of accounts, or of the art of accounting, even of the philosophy of accounts. But accounting is, alas, only a pseudo-science unrecognized by J. McKeen Cattell; its products are displayed neither in the salon nor in the national academy; one finds it discussed by neither realist, idealist nor phenomenalist. The humanists look down upon us as beings who dabble in the sordid figures of dollars and cents instead of toying with infinities and searching for the elusive soul of things; the scientists and technologists despise us as able only to record rather than to perform deeds.

We suffer perhaps in silence, even, as Carlyle says, " consuming our own choler as some chimneys consume their own smoke," perhaps in public denying that we suffer at all, but here—in a meeting not of accountants, but of university instructors in accounting—we can admit among ourselves that at times this academic attitude does get under our skins.

The contempt for accounting is not limited to university circles, but is well-nigh universal. It is evidenced by ignorance of the subject, by condescension towards its devotees, by their exclusion from polite literature.

And how abysmal that ignorance! I give two instances. The university speaker who said, " If you do so and so your ledger (speaking figuratively, of course) will show a debit balance." Would he have spoken of an equation with unequal members? And the distinguished writer in the October *Atlantic*,

---

[*] *An Historical Defense of Bookkeeping* originated as a paper read before the American Association of University Instructors in Accounting on December 29, 1923. It was first printed in *The Journal of Accountancy*, April 1924, Vol. 37, No. 4, pp. 241–253.

1

thesaurus of culture, supposedly barred to academic solecisms, who says, " In most sections of America the fact that a man or woman has been divorced . . . is something to be set down . . . on the debit side of the account," ignorant that likely as not a debit (as for instance in the bank account) means the imputation of additional value—which I take it is quite contrary to what Mrs. Gerould intended.

But the contempt for accounting is even more clearly shown by a constantly repeated phrase, a phrase which of all phrases is to me the most exacerbating—because of the combination of ignorance and supercilious condescension. This phrase, which I could quote from uncounted sources, is: " That is a mere bookkeeping entry." One might as well say, " That is a mere algebraic equation," or, " That is a mere statement of discovered fact," or " That is the formulation of a mere axiom." Mere truth, mere fact, mere sanctity, mere virtue. Do you wonder that I lose my temper every time I see the phrase? Of course one may make a misstatement in bookkeeping, just as one may lie either in Greek or in German: but that merits some adjective more individious than " mere."

And remember how accounting has been slighted in literature. The public eye has generally, both in history and in fiction, been turned on the man on horseback, but nevertheless at times there comes upon the stage a more prosaic figure. Great masterpieces have grouped themselves about a scholar as Faust, about a carpenter as Adam Bede, about a manufacturer as in *Les Miserables*, about a sailor as Robinson Crusoe, about courtesans, thieves and beggars beyond recital. Even a horse and a dog have been made the heroes in *Black Beauty* and in *Rab and His Friends*. But never, so far as I recollect, has a bookkeeper been made the hero of novel, play or poem. The bookkeeper is not even honoured by being made a noteworthy villain.

Long ago Sir Roger de Coverley assumed that " little that is truly noble can be expected from one who is ever poring on his cashbook or balancing his accounts." Literature has maintained this attitude ever since, and the bookkeeper has reached his apogee in the gentle and pathetic figure of Tim Clerkenwell. Compare him for a moment with the military hero. The latter appears mounted on a horse, leading, to the music of bugle and drum, his martial columns in charges against the foe, brandishing a reeking sword, and wearing on his brow the victor's wreath of laurel. The bookkeeper too is mounted, but on a quadrupedal stool, he too marshals columns, but of figures to the accompaniment of a clicking Burroughs, his charges are those on the debit side of the ledger, his brow is encircled by a green eye shade, he brandishes only the humble rival of the sword, guiltless doubtless of his country's blood, and incarnadined only with Carter's cardinal ink.

But it is not good for a man's soul always to suffer under the inferiority complex. Let us no longer bear in humility the lash of contumely. Let us face our contemners, be they classicists, philosophers or scientists.

> " No matter if he is a houn',
> They gotta quit kicking my dog aroun'."

Let us boldly raise the question whether accounting, the late claimant for recognition as a profession, is not entitled to some respect, or must it consort with crystal-gazing, sociology, chiropractic, pedagogy and palm-reading.

Three elements, if not conclusively proving, at least presumptively establish, respectability. These are, first, parentage and lineage; second, the company one keeps; and third, the services which one renders the community. Let us examine accounting in these aspects.

Without raising the question as to accounting in antiquity, we look upon the Franciscan monk Paciolo as the father of modern accounting, as his *Summa*, published in 1494, which was the first printed work dealing with algebra, also contained the first text on bookkeeping, a slender tractate entitled *De Computis et Scripturis*.

Not much can be said of Paciolo,[1] aside from his writings, but his academic credentials are flawless. He was an important if not a great mathematician. His first appointment to teach in a university was at Perugia. In less than a year his request for an increase of salary was granted. The reason stated in the official records has a singularly modern sound. It reads: " because he has already taught for two months and has shown himself to be a man of highest learning, and because it appears that he manifestly cannot live on such a meagre stipend." Again in less than six months he was promoted, this time with a more permanent tenure as well as increase of salary. Soon afterward he left the university, probably devoting himself to the study of philosophy and theology. He returned to Perugia in 1487, and while he had previously signed himself " Brother Luke," in his later writings he was wont to describe himself as a " humble

---

[1] H. Staigmuller, " Lucas Paciuolo, eine biographische Skizze," in *Zeitschrift für Mathematik und Physik*, Bd. 34, Historisch-literarische Abtheilung, pp. 81–102, 121–128.

professor of sacred theology." He held many other university positions, at various times teaching at Naples, at Pisa, at Florence, and at Bologna. He ended his career with his highest honour, for in 1514 Pope Leo X appointed him professor of mathematics in the *Sapienza* at Rome, a position in the "university of the highest standing in all Christendom."

In 1496 he was called to Milan by the reigning duke, Ludovico il Moro, whose court was a center of light and learning, and to be established there was a signal honour. Adams in China, Hollander in Porto Rico, Bogart in Persia, Paciolo in Milan—all indications of deserved recognition of professorial eminence—all doubtless to be kept in mind for at least 427 years.

At Milan, Paciolo was brought into contact with many prominent persons, the most significant being Leonardo da Vinci, perhaps the most eminent man of his day. Between the two there grew up an intimate friendship. Da Vinci himself tells that he hastened to buy a copy of Paciolo's *Summa* as it came off the press, and he collaborated with Paciolo on a later book, the *Divina Proportione*, for which Paciolo furnished the text and da Vinci the illustrations. Honour indeed for a university professor! Would not the most eminent mathematician of today rejoice if the greatest man of his time, say Roosevelt or Henry Ford, had hastened to buy one of his treatises (even though it contained the adventitious attraction of some chapters on bookkeeping)? Would not even one so eminent as William James have been flattered if in his psychology the somatic reactions of the emotions could have been illustrated by the master hand of the creator of Mutt and Jeff?

I need not outline to you the nature of Paciolo's treatise, with which you are familiar, at least through Geijsbeek's somewhat paraphrastic translation. Any of you who have not read this will be interested in it, not merely as a piece of technical literature, but because of its quaintness of expression, its naïve attention to detail, its exuberance of piety, its flavour of mediaevalism.

It is seldom the case that a first book on a subject has so dominated its literature as was the case with Paciolo's *De Computis et Scripturis*. It is nearly true to say that for a hundred years the texts appearing in England, France, Germany, Italy, and the low countries were " at the best revisions of Paciolo, at the worst servile transcriptions without even the courtesy of referring to the original author." But further than that many little matters of bookkeeping technique were followed for at least four centuries, merely because they were inculcated by

Paciolo, persisting like buttons on our coat sleeves, long after their significance had disappeared. I need not mention these to you, but may I refer to a peculiar instance relating rather to a matter of general form?

Whether it was because of his churchly connections or because it conformed to the customs of his day, Paciolo's book is replete with gems of moral and religious advice. I know not how it may be in the higher branches, such as sociology or Americanization—but in the elementary textbooks, such as algebra or chemistry, we do not today find the thread of the discourse interrupted by bits of proverbial philosophy or moral exhortation. But in bookkeeping this has continued down until today. I might cite instances from many of the high school texts used today, from practically all used so lately as ten years ago. But let me take a single extreme example. Soule's book is still in vogue in this country. At the foot of nearly every one of his 749 pages, he has a line quite in keeping with Paciolo. The statement in the earlier writer, " Who does nothing makes no mistakes, who makes not mistakes learns nothing," is matched by Soule's " Our greatest glory is not in never falling but in rising every time we fall." " It costs more to make a good merchant than to make a doctor of laws," is matched with " Experience is not a free school, we all pay for our tuition." But even a fifteenth-century monk cannot rise quite to the level of the twentieth-century practical American who tells us " The only amaranthine flower on earth is virtue, the only lasting treasure truth." Bookkeeping was spread throughout the world by a series of plagiarisms and imitations of Paciolo. The habit of imitation became so fixed that in bookkeeping it has persisted throughout the centuries, and even the foibles of Brother Luke are reproduced in the treatises of today.

Let those who vaunt the superior merits of other disciplines remember that this first presentation made by Paciolo was not crude and incorrect but contains the essentials of bookkeeping as we know it today, despite the fact that it was written at a time when chemistry partook of the vagaries of alchemy, biology was a weird collection of errors, and medicine had more in common with the medicine man than it has even today. It may be well to see how this discipline—I do not venture to call it science—compares in its antiquity with the more arrogant natural sciences. In neither case do I go back to the feeble beginnings and adumbrations of learning but compare the position of bookkeeping, as it was first formulated in print by a university professor, with the formulation of natural sciences—not by some dim groper in far-off antiquity—but by the first vice-president of Harvard College. A comparison, thus made, is, I am sure, more than generous to the natural sciences, despite their illiberal attitude towards the social sciences with which, in general, they admit of no kinship.

Charles Morton, who, like Paciolo, was at once distinguished teacher and cleric, was brought to Harvard from England almost two hundred years after Paciolo had formulated bookkeeping. If not professor, he was at least made vice-president, and his work on science was used as a textbook in the college.[2]

But he explained the problem of the migration of birds by saying that each autumn they flew to the moon, 200,000 miles distant, a two months' journey, and in his textbook, earthquakes are explained as follows: " They come from choking up of wind below, fermenting, bursting out, causing trembling and strokes." Or dropping into verse

" In subterranean caverns winds do frolic
When Mother Earth is troubled with the colic."

How marked a contrast to the teachings of the geologist at the University of California. It is told that when he appeared in court as an expert witness, the opposing lawyer foolishly attempting to ridicule his pretension of knowledge, said: " And do you pretend to know what is going on in the bowels of the earth? " To this the geologist replied: " I do not know that the earth has any bowels."

Only two hundred years ago science—in the leading American college—was a futile and ludicrous display of ignorance. More than four hundred years ago, in the very first book published on the subject, bookkeeping was outlined in a form which still prevails around the entire world. Cannot bookkeeping claim an honourable and ancient lineage? Is it indeed an upstart as compared with geology, and chemistry, and landscape gardening, and social psychology, and business English, and olericulture, and otorhinolaryngology, and other cherished subjects of the university curriculum? Founded, like San Francisco, by a follower of St. Francis of Assisi, cradled in mathematics with algebra as a twin, established under the aegis of a great university—surely this is an origin sufficiently academic to give respectability to this our " houn' dog." Perhaps I should adopt the language appropriate to the kennel and speak of book-keeping as having been sired four hundred years ago by a monk,

[2] Authority for the following statements is found in Meriwether, *Our Continental Curriculum*, pp. 188 *et seq.*

and today dammed by thousands of university students, and yet, despite certain questions which the frivolous might raise to a celibate paternity and the extremely puzzling biological enigma of such a multiple maternity, bookkeeping is thoroughly respectable.

But many a house founded by a great man has degenerated and the descendants have been of quite inferior clay. Has the later entourage of bookkeeping been made up of a fair number of respectable persons?

The second book on bookkeeping was also written by a man of distinction, Grammateus or Schreiber. He, like Paciolo, combined algebra and bookkeeping, and his book, dated 1518, was the first work published in Germany dealing with either of these subjects. On the authority of Cantor, he stands, as a mathematician, unquestionably in the front rank of his time.

Almost immediately following Grammateus was Jerome Cardan, that picturesque scapegrace and brilliant scholar, astrologer, physician, scientist, mathematician, professor of medicine first at Pavia, later at Bologna. He, too, wrote a book combining algebra and bookkeeping. This work, says Richard Garnett, marks an era in the history of mathematics, being the first in which the principle of cubic equations was fully explained. Everett says it is one of the most valuable contributions to the literature of algebra. As a physician he was so eminent that he was called to Scotland, no mean journey in those days, to attend an archbishop; he was famous enough as an astrologer to visit the court of Edward VI to cast the king's nativity. But his chief claim to distinction is his general scientific attitude, so far in advance of his times. Says Garnett: " Alike intellectually and morally, Cardan is one of the most interesting personages connected with the revival of science in Europe. He possessed the true scientific spirit in perfection. As a mathematician he effected most important advances, and to complete the catalog of his accomplishments he is no contemptible poet." And to add picturesqueness to his career he became involved in difficulties, was addicted to gaming, imprisoned for debt, banished from Milan, was later deposed from his professorship, imprisoned, released, prohibited from further teaching, but spent his latter years in Rome as a pensioner of the Pope.

Out of the first six writers three are thus seen to be men of eminent distinction—in fields other than that of bookkeeping, as judged by persons who are not themselves particularly interested in bookkeeping. Surely the early days—if not the unknown origin of bookkeeping—are sufficiently respectable so that we need not be ashamed.

Extending somewhat the field of survey we find that Brown lists only 150 names of writers on bookkeeping before 1800. But even the reduced list of those who have reputations in fields other than bookkeeping is too long to repeat in detail. These are not a group of narrow specialists. One finds there authorities on algebra (as is to be expected), on navigation, on optics, a commissioner to settle the foreign exchange, the author of the French code of 1763 (who not only had this great code named after him, the Code Savary, but is perhaps even more distinguished by having had seventeen children who also bore his name), astronomers, a French grammarian, an authority on gunpowder, and the historian of the Baptist church. To find these names in the *Encyclopaedia Britannica* one does not look under accounting or bookkeeping—these articles are scant and unsatisfactory and both contain misstatements concerning the history of the subject—but under the following rubrics; algebra, camera obscura, deaf and dumb, earth figure, fortification and siege craft, gravitation, infinitesimal calculus, insurance, logarithms, mathematical tables, Napier, and navigation.

Perhaps I may be pardoned if I mention more specifically three of the names. There is Simon Stevin. Cantor styles him a Dutch mathematician, but says his claims to fame are varied. He invented a horseless carriage which worked, he was first to solve some problems regarding polyhedra, he proved the law of equilibrium on an inclined plane, he discovered the hydrostatic paradox, he explained the tides by the moon, he devised new forms of fortification, was many times public officer, a soldier and statesman, and the first to introduce decimals. Yet he thought it well worth while, in 1602, to write an extended treatise on bookkeeping for the express purpose of training his royal pupil, the Prince of Orange.

There was Charles Hutton, a colliery boy, who became teacher of mathematics at eighteen and later professor at the royal academy at Woolwich, fellow and foreign secretary of the Royal Society (three others in the brief list were also fellows of that distinguished body), perhaps the most famous for his computation of the density of the earth, an achievement recognized by Laplace and said by various competent critics to show ingenious and important methods, which can hardly be improved upon, author too of a work on conic sections said by Montucla to be a model of precision and clarity, receiver of the Copley medal for his paper on gunpowder, and doctor of laws of

Edinburgh. And yet this man, who could weigh the earth as in a balance, condescended to write a textbook on bookkeeping, a subject which many think worthy the attention only of writing masters and proprietors of business colleges.

There was Robert Hamilton, who after some years' experience as a banker betook himself to teaching, and was professor first of natural philosophy and later of mathematics at Aberdeen; famed, however, more as an economist, for it was he who exposed the economic fallacies of Pitt's policy of the sinking fund. Yet this man, banker, merchant, mathematician, capable of confuting England's master statesman, thought it not beneath his dignity also to write on bookkeeping.

I have limited this survey to writers before 1800. I will mention only two persons since then. Augustus de Morgan, whose eminence needs no description, was so far interested in bookkeeping that one of the best elementary books ever written on the subject acknowledges that it is based on the suggestions of de Morgan. And finally Arthur Cayley, who thirty years ago turned aside from his duties as professor of mathematics at Cambridge long enough to write a most excellent work, entitled *The Principles of Double-entry Bookkeeping*.

I have cited illustrious men who have written on bookkeeping rather than illustrious writers on bookkeeping. I did this merely to establish the argument that bookkeeping is a subject worthy of the attention of able men—not to be relegated to the ordinary business college.

But not all who have attempted to write on the subject have succeeded. He may, like Grammateus, stand high as a mathematician, and yet, as a writer on bookkeeping, " deserve no praise beyond that of being the first German who ventured to write on that difficult subject," producing a book which Row Fogo says is " so confused that it is extremely improbable that he himself knew much about what he was attempting to teach." He may, like Cardan, show originality and genius in science, yet as a writer on bookkeeping be worse than banal. He may, like Collins, hold an honourable position in the Royal Society, yet produce a work on bookkeeping which receives no particular mention by the historian of the subject. He may, like Hamilton, deserve the encomium of McCullough, that he succeeded in the impossible task of opening the mind of the British public on an economic question, and yet have the *Encyclopaedia Britannica* say that his work on bookkeeping is now forgotten. A man of distinction may write on bookkeeping; his work in that line is not necessarily distinguished. Would it be fair to say that it takes a peculiar genius to make a success in that subject?

The third presumptive evidence of respectability is that one performs some important service in the world. Can this be said of accounting? Perhaps this can best be answered by showing that bookkeeping appeared, not as a chance phenomenon, but distinctly in response to a world need. This is true not only of the days of Paciolo, but, as I hope to show, of that more important, almost present-day revival.

It is not without significance that bookkeeping appeared at the end of the fifteenth century, nor that its birthplace was in the Italian republics. We all know of the marvellous awakening of that period, and particularly of the sudden expansion of commerce. Sieveking, one of the few historians who has paid attention to the subject, says that bookkeeping arose as a direct result of the establishment of partnerships on a large scale, a feature of the expanding commerce.

But bookkeeping dozed for several centuries, and it was not until just about four hundred years after Paciolo's book that a startling awakening took place. New works in unheard-of abundance and of a new quality began to appear, and again the universities seriously undertook instruction in a subject which had fallen into academic disrepute.

Why this new prominence in a subject taught before 1500? The answer is so obvious that I offend by explanation. The end of the nineteenth, even more than the end of the fifteenth century was marked by a most extraordinary expansion of business. Then was the period of the organization of the great corporations (ordinarily called trusts), a phenomenon common to America, England and Germany. Then came that new appearance, the billion-dollar corporation, and just then—not a curious coincidence but a necessary response—accountants woke up. Garcke and Fells started the list of works on cost-accounts, Pixley first and then Dicksee began their voluminous writings dealing with the more refined problems of corporation accounts, England chartered the Institute of Chartered Accountants, New York set the example, since followed by every American state, of granting the title of " certified public accountant," the adding machine was invented, logarithms were placed beside the ledger, books were written, conventions were held, accounting was.

In part the new significance of accounting is due to subdivision of ownership and the severance of ownership and control so characteristic of the corporate form of business organization. If the substitution of a small partnership for the individual trader called for improvement in bookkeeping methods, how much more was improvement needed when the partnership was displaced by the corporation with its owners numbered by the tens of thousands.

But still more significant has been the great investment of fixed capital characteristic of modern production and made possible by the organization of corporations. The use of fixed capital on a large scale increases incalculably the difficulty of determining the profits earned in any given year. Paciolo made no serious effort to do this. Business in his day was a congeries of disconnected ventures. A ship went here, a caravan there, a joint venture was undertaken with Messer Juan Antonio in French wool, and a flyer was taken in *ginger michini*. As these ventures fell in, the profit gained in the completed transaction was ascertained, somewhat roughly, it is true, but fairly satisfactorily. But no attempt was made to deal with unfinished operations.

But today business is a continuum. Machinery serves for many years, the factory building stands for a generation, the railroad is built to last for ever. The industrial process is made up of a never-ending stream of raw materials, goods in process and finished commodities. Expenses are incurred in common and not like the expenses of a caravan solely in connection with one parcel of goods. But man is strangely agricultural in his tradition, even though society has become industrial. Time was when the recurring cycle of the year was of immense significance to him, for seed-time and harvest each came in connection with the course of the earth around the sun. And man still thinks that he must reckon results in terms of the accidental period involved in such a circuit. We demand to know how much a concern makes in a year. We must know, because the reciprocal rights of preferred and common stockholders may be altogether changed, depending on whether profit is to be attributed to the month of December or to the following January. We must know in order to satisfy the demands of the income-tax collector. And so accountants are asked to perform the hopeless task of taking this economic continuum, of chopping it up into arbitrary and meaningless lengths called a year, and apportioning to each such year a proper part of the cost of a building which will last fifty years, of a machine which will be used for twenty years, of a blast furnace which will last ten, and of a stock of coal bought in December which will all be consumed before spring again appears.

Progress in the science seems slow. There stand out, however, two contributions of present-day accountants, one of practical, the other of theoretical importance. The first, made by America, consists of innumerable little devices for saving work in the handling of great masses of figures. Cumbersome and needless forms, surviving as tradition from the past centuries in England, and still more on the Continent, have been discarded in America and new forms have been introduced by which results can be obtained with less labor. The other contribution has been the attempt to ascertain the exact cost of producing objects or parts of objects or for carrying on processes in continuous manufacture. Manufacturers now must know not only what it costs to make a machine, but what is the cost of each separate wheel, pinion and screw in that machine; what is the cost not merely of a yard of cloth, but of carding, of roving, of spinning, of weaving, of dyeing, of finishing, of selling that yard of cloth. This has been the characteristic scientific contribution of recent years.

Progress is being made. What better evidence is there than that even lawyers and courts are coming to appreciate that there are such things as accounting principles? No longer is it possible for the Supreme Court of the United States to declare that " the public . . . rarely ever take into account the depreciation of the building in which the business is carried on." [3] Never again, I believe, will the Supreme Court of California repeat the statement regarding depreciation [4]: " The theory is . . . that a sum should be set aside to be handed to the stockholders upon the sad occasion of the company's demise, as an alleviating salve to their sorrow, but such a thing is all wrong. The theory cannot be tolerated for a moment that such a fund is to be stowed away to make glad the hearts of the stockholders."

I have tried to remove the stigma attached to accounting by showing that in its origin it is respectable, nay, even academic: that despite its present disrepute it has from time to time attracted the attention of men of unquestioned intellectual attainment; that it justifies itself in that it has arisen to meet a social need. Its functions are to locate responsibility, to prevent fraud, to guide industry, to determine equities, to solve the all-essential conundrum of business: " What are my profits? "; to facilitate the government in its fiscal operations, to guide the business manager in the attempt to secure efficiency. Are not these efforts worthy of any man's attention? And so I close this paper with quotation from men whom all must respect: Scott, the romanticist,

---

[3] *Eyster* v. *Centennial Board of Finance*, 94 U.S. 503.
[4] *San Diego Water Co.* v. *San Diego*, 118 Cal. 556.

declared the profession of accounting " respectable "; Goethe, the universal genius, speaks of bookkeeping as " one of the fairest inventions of the human mind," and Cayley, scientist beyond question, even more significantly declared " Bookkeeping is one of the two perfect sciences." With these I rest the defence of my houn' dog.

Some Topics in the History of Financial Accounting in England[1] 1500–1900

By B. S. Yamey

Professor of Economics,
London School of Economics.

THIS essay is divided into three sections. The first section describes briefly some examples of accounting records within our period which were not kept on a double entry basis. This serves to illustrate the diversity of types of business records without purporting to provide a comprehensive inventory of them. The second, and largest, section describes major features of double entry bookkeeping in (roughly) the sixteenth, seventeenth, eighteenth and early nineteenth centuries. The description is based on two classes of material, first, some of the numerous treatises or textbooks on accounting or bookkeeping published during the period, and secondly, on ten surviving sets of account-books. These latter include the records of nine substantial business men, namely (in chronological order of the records) Sir Thomas Gresham, Sir William Calley, Sir John Banks, Sir Robert Clayton, Sir Dudley North, Sir Charles Peers, Richard Du Cane, Peter Du Cane and William Braund, and those of an obscure seventeenth-century merchant, William Hoskins.[2] The

---

[1] Nevertheless, some examples of accounting records from Scotland are used as illustrative material; and in Section II there are references to early treatises on accounting published in Scotland.

[2] These records are referred to in Section II by the name of the owner in question. For further information on the records, see:

Gresham: Peter Ramsey," Some Tudor Merchants' Accounts," in A. C. Littleton and B. S. Yamey (eds.), *Studies in the History of Accounting* (London, 1956), pp. 185–201.

Peers: B. S. Yamey, " A Seventeenth Century Double-Entry Journal," *Accountancy*, November 1960, pp. 639–641.

Hoskins, Banks, Clayton, North, the Du Canes, Braund: B. S. Yamey, " Some Seventeenth and Eighteenth Century Double-Entry Ledgers," *Accounting Review*, October 1959, pp. 534–546.

Sir Thomas Gresham needs no introduction. Calley was in the cloth trade, a member of the Company of Drapers and of the Merchant Adventurers. He was knighted in 1629. Banks was a wealthy merchant-financier-landowner, and governor of the East India Company. Clayton, described by John Evelyn as " this prodigious rich scrivener," was Member of Parliament, and also Lord Mayor of London in 1679–80. North was a well-known Turkey merchant and proponent of free-trade doctrine. Peers was a merchant in the Spanish trade, director of the Bank of England, and Lord Mayor of London. Richard Du Cane was a merchant and landowner, Member of Parliament, and director

third and final section of the essay attempts to explain, by historical reconstruction, the changes in accounting practice concerning the calculation of profits which appear to have occurred in the latter half of the nineteenth century, when accounting for joint stock companies came to play a dominant part in the determination of accounting " principles " and conventions.

The essay deals with what may be called " financial " accounting for business enterprises, and excludes specifically the more specialised subjects of cost accounting in business enterprises and the accounting arrangements of the government or government agencies.

I.—Accounts not on Double Entry Basis

The origins of accounting and indeed of written records are probably to be found in the need of an " accounting " officer to render a statement of money and other assets received in his charge on behalf of his employer, or disbursed on his behalf. There was need for a check on the honesty and reliability of subordinates. It has been said of the surviving records and evidence of Greek and Roman accounting: " We must always remember . . . that the whole purpose of ancient accounting was not to measure the rate of profit or loss but to keep accurate records of acquisitions and outgoings, in money and kind, and to expose any losses due to dishonesty or negligence." [3] This statement of the objectives of ancient accounting is also largely true of the system of " charge-and-discharge " accounting which developed on estates in England at least as far back as the early thirteenth century. Each of a hierarchy of officials had to account to his superior for incomings and outgoings on behalf of the owner of the estate; and the form of account tended to conform to a pattern. The accounts were the basis of the periodic audit. Charge-and-discharge accounting survived well into our period;

of the Bank of England. His son, Peter, was director of the Bank and of the East India Company. Braund was merchant, ship-owner, marine insurer, and director of the East India Company and of the Sun Fire Office. Hoskins lived in Cherbourg, and traded on his own behalf and as partner with, or agent of, other merchants.

The dates of the records are: Gresham, 1546–51; Calley, 1600–06; Hoskins, 1655–67; Banks, 1657–99; Clayton, 1669–80; North, 1680–91; Peers, 1689–94; R. Du Cane, 1736–44; P. Du Cane, 1754–58; Braund, 1758–74.

Calley's surviving ledger is the property of Miss J. M. Calley, J.P., of Burderop Park, Swindon, Wilts. (Mr. J. T. Lea, of Salisbury, Wilts, has kindly given me information about this ledger.) The locations of the other account-books are given in the articles referred to, above.

[3] G. E. M. de Ste. Croix, " Greek and Roman Accounting," in Littleton and Yamey, *op. cit.*, p. 38.

and it is known, for example, that some colleges of the two ancient universities were still using the system and its terminology within the last hundred years. The system, somewhat transformed, survives into the present in the guise of the receipts-and-payments account rendered by trustees and by secretaries of sporting, social and other societies.[4]

The system of charge-and-discharge accounting in the estate accounts of the Earls of Northumberland, 1562–1637, has been described as follows [5]:

> The system of accounting which prevails all through the estate organisation appears in its simplest form in the Account of a Reeve of a single manor. This is invariably as follows:
> Arrears
> Rents and Farms
> Other Receipts
>   Total (The Charge)
> Expenses
> Money delivered
>   Total
>   The Balance (Remainder)
>
> . . . We find no attempt to establish whether or not a particular manor shows a profit. . . . The object is rather to establish the liability of the accounting official. Thus arrears are included under the heading of receipts, and " money delivered," *i.e.*, the amount actually paid over to the lord, under the heading of expenses incurred in the running of the manor. The balance between total receipts and total expenses represents the " remainder," the amount for which the accountant stands liable. The form is used not only to establish the liability of such humble officials as manorial reeves, but also of county receivers, and of the Earl's Receiver-General himself. The outline of the latter's Accounts of the revenues proceeding from all the Earl's lands is identical with that of the Reeve of a single Northumbrian manor.

Estate accounts frequently included both receipts and payments of money and receipts and disposals of goods (livestock, grain, etc.), the latter being inscribed on the *dorse* (back) of the account-roll and stated in terms of quantities and not values. There would be cross-entries when some item of " stock " was bought or sold for money.[6]

---

[4] For an early rendering of a steward's account as " an Accompt-Current by way of Debtor and Creditor," see Edward Laurence, *The Duty of a Steward to his Lord* (London, 1727), pp. 133–155.

[5] M. E. James (ed.), *Estate Accounts of the Earls of Northumberland, 1562–1637*, Publications of the Surtees Society, Vol. CLXIII (Durham and London, 1955), pp. xxvi–xxvii.

[6] See, for example, L. F. Salzman (ed.), *Ministers' Accounts of the Manor of Petworth, 1347–1353*, Sussex Record Society, Vol. LV (Lewes, 1955). Thus the entry (translated) for " Pigs " on the dorse of the 1348–49 account runs (p. 29):
" Pigs: And for 43 pigs in hand; whereof, 2 boars and 3 sows. And for

Though the charge-and-discharge accounting system was essentially designed to determine the liability of the accounting official, some great lay estates from as early as the time of Edward I made use of additional records or compilations to give convenient summary views of the profitability of the estate as a whole (or administrative sub-divisions of it) or of its financial position.[7]

The charge-and-discharge system was applicable to non-agricultural as well as to agricultural activities.[8] The accounts of the Stationers' Company in respect of its trading in a group of publications known as the English Stock are particularly interesting.[9] Quarterly accounts were rendered for audit. All the entries are in money terms, a unification which was achieved by entering receipts and stocks of books at their wholesale values (*i.e.*, at the prices charged on the sale of books by the company):

> The Treasurer was " charged," at wholesale prices, with the stock of books in his hands at the beginning of each quarter, with the value of the outstanding debts, with the stock he received during the quarter (also at wholesale prices), with rents collected, with any other money received, and with cash in hand—if any. On the " discharge " side he put payments made for taxes, for dues to the Stock-keepers on the previous account, for general disbursements recorded in the Journal (mainly the cost of producing the books and almanacks), and the values of the stock and debts at the end of the quarter . . . The writing off of stock . . . was shown as a " discharge "; in later years special allowances to booksellers for buying quantities were similarly shown.

It would have been possible for a commercial agent or factor to keep account of his transactions on behalf of his principal on a

---

1 sow from the heriot of Sybil Muleward. And for 1 boar by purchase, *ut infra.*   Total: 45
    Whereof by slaughter for the larder, as below, 22, whereof 1 boar. And sold, *ut infra*, 7, whereof 1 sow from the heriot.   Total: 29
And there remain 16 pigs, whereof, 2 boars and 3 sows."
    The " as below " refers to an entry for " Bacons " from the slaughter of the 22 pigs. The term, *ut infra*, refers to entries on the other (money) side of the account-roll where the purchase of the boar for 3s. 6d. is entered under " Purchases of Stock," and the sale of 7 pigs under " Sales of Stock ": " And for 13s. 6d. received for 7 pigs sold as a lot because sickly, for the larder."

7 See C. D. Ross and T. B. Pugh, " Materials for the Study of Baronial Incomes in Fifteenth-Century England," *Economic History Review*, second series, Vol. VI (1953), pp. 191–193, and the works cited by these authors.
    See also the discussion of sheep accounts in K. J. Allison " Flock Management in the Sixteenth and Seventeenth Centuries," *Economic History Review*, second series, Vol. XI (1958), pp. 98–112, esp. pp. 98–99.

8 For a discussion, with specimens, of accounts kept between 1579 and 1582 for a coal-mine worked for the Earl of Shrewsbury, see Lawrence Stone, " An Elizabethan Coalmine," *Economic History Review*, second series, Vol. III (1950), pp. 97–106. (Accountants may be disconcerted by the author's use of the term balance-sheet.) For specimens of building accounts, see W. Douglas Simpson (ed.), *The Building Accounts of Tattershall Castle, 1434–1472*, Lincoln Record Society Publications, Vol. 55 (Hereford, 1960).

9 Cyprian Blagden, " The English Stock of the Stationers' Company in the Time of the Stuarts," *The Library*, Summer 1957, pp. 167–186, esp. pp. 171–178.

charge-and-discharge basis. Transactions involving the receipt
or payment of money could be recorded separately from those
involving the movement of goods; and summaries could be
made from time to time to satisfy the principal of the proper
management of affairs. There would be no profit calculation,
if only because the factor would not know the cost of goods
supplied to him by his principal or the proceeds of goods
furnished by him to the principal. The parallel between the
reeve and the factor is close. I do not know, however, of any
accounting records kept by factors in the charge-and-discharge
form. In some published expositions of double entry bookkeeping one finds examples where the merchant or bookkeeper
makes purely quantitative entries in the relevant accounts for
activities on behalf of a principal not involving the passing of
money.[10] The relevant accounts recording transactions of a
factor also naturally do not include any calculation of profit.
But there is no known work in English, in our period, which
is devoted exclusively to the description or prescription of an
accounting system designed to serve the needs of a factor. There
is no English counterpart of the manuscript manual written in
the early sixteenth century by Matthaus Schwartz, the head
bookkeeper of the Fuggers,[11] or of Valentin Mennher's *Practique
Briefe pour cyfrer et tenir livres de compte* . . . , published in
Antwerp in 1550. Both these works describe a system of factor's
accounting, involving bilateral accounts with both money and
other quantitative entries, and eschewing any profit calculation.[12]

Merchants, farmers and others frequently kept their accounting
records in forms uninfluenced by the charge-and-discharge model.
Where the double entry system was not employed, the business
man or his accountant was free to improvise a system to suit
his particular requirements or his bookkeeping capacity. Not
recognising any of the rules or restraints more or less implicit
in double entry, each set of records could be arranged and kept

10 Thus Handson described the entry for receipt of goods on consignment from a
principal: " Dr. the Goods received for Accompt of AB, specifying for whose
Accompt: and under that Title naming the particulars of those Goods received
without value, and so they are to have no Creditor to answer that parcel (entry)."
Ralph Handson, *Analysis or Resolution of Merchants Accompts*, 4th ed.
(London, 1669) (a broadside). William Hoskins' ledger (referred to in footnote
2, above) contains non-monetary entries for receipts or transfers of goods on
consignment.
11 A. Weitnauer, *Venezianischer Handel der Fugger* (Munich and Leipzig, 1931).
12 John Browne's *The Marchants Avizo* (London, 1589) was intended for the
guidance of overseas factors. It includes some specimen accounts: but it is
not clear whether these were intended as examples of account-sales presented
in the form of a bilateral account, or as the whole or part of a factor's own
accounting system.

as the owner wished. The following examples do no more than illustrate the variety of possibilities; they are presented roughly in order of increasing sophistication.[13]

The account-book, 1616–1704, of a Kentish estate, which belonged to members of the Toke family, is very largely a chronological record of payments made.[14] It is interspersed with occasional entries for purchases of livestock, even before payment for them had been made. In the early years it also has, at Michaelmas, a statement of the " stocke," listing in detail all the assets in the form of livestock and produce, and, after allowing for debts owing and owed (not listed), ending with what " remayneth cleere to me all men discharged." (One imagines that other account-books must have been kept for debts.) A few pages at the end of the book list some sales in the first five years, and the last entries are several recipes of " drinkes " for cattle diseases.

The " Compt Buik " (1587–1630) of David Wedderburne consists of two parts.[15] The first part is of little interest in the present context, as it is a record of documents relating to properties of the family. The second part, beginning from the rear of the book, is more strictly an account-book, recording transactions of Wedderburne, a burgess of Dundee who carried on the business of a merchant among other activities. The entries are not entirely chronological, because Wedderburne from time to time used up previously empty spaces for later entries. The entries themselves refer to receipts and payments, loans in cash or in kind, purchases and sales, with occasional statements of accounts with particular individuals. There is no money column, no accounting manipulation, and nothing in the way of summary statements. It is essentially a continuous accounting narrative, the only grouping of entries being occasional listings, *e.g.*, of payments, or of the disposition of a particular lot of goods.

Robert Loder's farm accounts, running from 1610 to 1620,

13 For other examples, see Ramsey, *op. cit.*, pp. 186–187. For some American examples, see W. T. Baxter, " Accounting in Colonial America," in Littleton and Yamey, *op. cit.*, pp. 272–287.

14 Eleanor C. Lodge (ed.), *The Account Book of a Kentish Estate, 1616–1704*, British Academy, Records of Social and Economic History, Vol. VI (London, 1927).

15 A. H. Millar (ed.), *The Compt Buik of David Wedderburne, Merchant of Dundee 1587–1630*, Publications of the Scottish History Society, Vol. XXVIII (Edinburgh, 1898).

Philip Henslowe's late sixteenth century account-book is largely in diary form, but with considerably more systematic grouping of similar items than in Wedderburne's book. Henslowe was a theatre-owner and financier of theatrical companies. See R. A. Foakes and R. T. Rickert, *Henslowe's Diary* (Cambridge, 1961).

are more difficult to describe.[16]   His intentions are set out in the preamble which reads (abridged):

> A Bock [for my] Remembrance; what seed wheat and barly I yearly sowe and [how mu]ch I wenow and sell in the same yeare.   Item what h[ay] I ha[v]e yearely growing; . . .   Item how my quite rentes are yearely pay'd me; Item of the valew in some yeares of my aples and cherries.   Item of the quantitie of wolle which I have yearly growing; and how many shep I sheare for it; Item of money owing me; Item what paymentes I pay unto the Kinge; Item how I pay my servauntes theyr wages; Item what my charges in the harvesting and making hay hath bine in some yeares; Item what my horses hath spent me; and what I have payd the smith in some yeares; Item how and what I pay for tieth of my orchardes; Item how much wood I buy; . . . Item how many landes I yearely dounge with the potte, and which are dounged at alle; and o[f] such other remembrances, . . .

His intentions are carried out largely.   It is not a continuous accounting narrative of receipts and payments, etc.   Rather, it sets out, by farming years, the results of various farming activities in considerable detail.   In some cases the account is broken off to make room for estimates of what might have been earned had a different course of action been taken.   These exercises, and the conclusions drawn from them, show deep concern with profit maximisation.   There are also lists of expenditures " written for this end that I might see my divers and manie expenses, and so to prevent them as much as might be."   Finally, for each year from 1613 there is an account (in narrative form, without a money column, as is also true of the rest of the book) of the " wholle summe of cleare Proffites made upon my Farme," " given unto me most unworthy thereof by nature, by my most mercifull God . . .".   The Loder book is interesting not only for its combination of " piety and profits," [17] but also for the combination in it of a primitive accounting form with evidence of keen understanding of economic calculation for business decision-making.   Loder certainly understood the significance of the distinction between avoidable and unavoidable costs, and the relevance of allowing for the costs of capital, matters on which textbooks on cost accounting three centuries later were often unsound.

[16] G. E. Fussell (ed.), *Robert Loder's Farm Accounts, 1610–1620*, Camden Third Series, Vol. LIII (London, 1936).

[17] R. H. Tawney, " The Rise of the Gentry, 1558–1640," reprinted in E. M. Carus-Wilson (ed.), *Essays in Economic History* (London, 1954), p. 187.
    The minute detail of the accounting for profits is exemplified in this entry: " Memorandum yt I kild a cow which when she was kild was worth more unto me than she cost me at spring & then [than] the charge of fatting came to by the full summe of vs. viij d." (p. 157).

The ledger (1492–1503) of Andrew Halyburton is our first example of a ledger in bilateral account form.[18] Halyburton was Conservator of the Privileges of the Scotch Nation in the Netherlands. His ledger consists entirely of personal accounts. Neither the left-hand nor the right-hand side of the accounts is confined exclusively to debit or credit entries. But this feature presumably did not hinder the settlement of accounts, though there is no sign of the striking of a balance in any account in the ledger. There are, however, occasional entries referring to settlements, *e.g.*, " Item 8 day of Apryll anno 95, all thyngis contyt and rakynyt betwix Lorens Tayllyefer and me in hys awan hous in Edynburgh, lyk as it standis in the Jowrnell subscrywit with his awin hand in the 75 layf, and he restis awand me. . . ." Besides references like this to a journal, there are also references to a " lang buk."

The surviving accounting records of Thomas Griggs, an eighteenth-century clothier (who at one time employed about 500 workers mostly on piece-rates) and retail grocer, demonstrate the use of a variety of account-books, specimens of which have survived.[19] There are so-called " cash-books " which contain entries both for cash receipts and payments and also for the movement of bills of exchange. He also had personal ledgers arranged, as the cash books, on a bilateral account basis. There are also books designed to record dealings with the various workers who were issued with materials for processing at their homes. Thus there are books for spinning, weaving and winding, designed to record indebtedness and to control waste or misappropriation of materials. The account-books reveal no systematic calculation of profits or of assets. But there are records of a few *ad hoc* calculations of this sort, as well as some estimates of the cost of certain types of cloths.

A surviving account-book (1616–1664) of Thomas Cullum, " draper, alderman, sheriff, and Restoration baronet," is of interest in providing an example of a regular annual calculation and recording of profits and net assets without benefit of double entry.[20] The surviving book contains only a series of such

[18] C. Innes (ed.), *Ledger of Andrew Halyburton* (Edinburgh, 1867).

[19] K. H. Burley, " Some Accounting Records of an Eighteenth-Century Clothier," *Accounting Research*, Vol. 9 (1958), pp. 50–60.

[20] This account-book provides the basis for A. Simpson, " Thomas Cullum, Draper, 1587–1664," *Economic History Review*, second series, Vol. XI (1958). pp. 19–34.

The account-book is in the Bury St. Edmunds & West Suffolk Record Office. I am indebted to the County Archivist, Mr. M. P. Statham, for his kind assistance; and to my colleague, Miss Olive Coleman, for transcribing the specimen account printed on pp. 22–23, and published by kind permission of the Bury St. Edmunds Borough Council.

THOMAS CULLUM; ANNUAL ACCOUNT, 1648 (see p. 24).

Rest hoped good at Christid 1647	25000	03	00
in debts acompted doubtfull then rest	05005	14	11
Some totall of good & doubtfull then was	30005	17	11
1648 R^d for this whole years sallarie out of all ye excises	01033	00	08
gayned by trade & stock this year to Dec. 30th 1648	02708	10	08
more as Sherife from the Comptor etc.	00063	08	06
Snelson part of 200^li lost last year by him	00100	00	00
[?] pro lease towards that lost by ye Fishmongers	00100	00	00
rent from Christid 1647 to Christid 1648	00101	00	00
4105–19–10			
Some is	34111	17	09

out of wch spent from Dec. 30th 1647 to Dec. 30th 1648			
pd pro dyate bread bear & wine etc.	00444	06	00
pd in extraordinarie expences & rates	00261	19	08
pd rent	00064	00	00
pd wages to my ordinarie servants	00054	00	00
pd pro apparell pro myselfe Children & Servants	00083	10	02
pd pro more housholdstuffe	00014	15	06
pd pro fyring	00012	01	06
pd pro Phisick	00006	18	00
pd pro reparation	00003	07	09
Some spent is	00944	18	07
lost part of that I abated S^rNic.Crisp & S^rGeorg.Strode	01013	03	01
aded more to my desperate debts	00075	06	01
Some totall is	02033	07	09

W^ch being deducted out of that above resteth in debts hoped good monny etc.			
as per Com^te 29120^li.12.00			
in debts acompted doubtfull 02957 .18.00	32078	10	00
besyds desperate debts yet uncast out	03116	08	00

THOMAS CULLUM; ANNUAL ACCOUNT, 1648—*continued*.

Dec 30ᵗʰ 1648	li	s	d
in Cloth as per inventorie as it cost or lesse	02202	02	00
in debts hoped good as per inventorie	24354	15	00
in Monny as per Cashes	00756	06	00
in houses 4 in yᵉ Minories 2 on tower hill	00800	00	00
in leases halfe Moone 700ˡⁱ Key 100ˡⁱ	00800	00	00
in plate 1035 ounces	00260	00	00
Some is	29173	03	00
out of wᶜʰ I owe to the statut against Warner	00052	11	00
resteth hoped good belonging to my proper acco twentie nyne thousand one hundred and twentie pounds twelve shillings I say	29120	12	00
in doubtfull debts as per inventorie	02957	18	00
Some totall of good and doutfull is	32078	10	00

besyds my desperate debts wᶜʰ yet remaine
uncast out being 3116ˡⁱ 8ˢ. not reckoning
any thoushold stuff etc. but plate only for
wᶜʰ and all other his great mercies to me
and myne I humbly thank my God

Tho: Cullum

accounts, though it is clear that other subsidiary records were kept, *e.g.*, of debts. The procedure for the annual reckoning appears to have been as follows (a specimen is shown on pp. 22–23): The value of the opening net assets was introduced from the previous account. The value of the closing net assets was ascertained from a listing and summation of the assets, and deduction of the liabilities. These opening and closing amounts were reconciled to each other by adding to the former a number of items of revenue and then by deducting from this new amount the total of a list of expenditures and losses. The balance was equal to the closing valuation of the net assets. It is apparent that the profit on his trading operations, included among the sources of income, was the balancing item, the amount of which presumably was inserted after all the other figures had been entered. The series of accounts gives special emphasis to debts owing to Cullum. Thus in the list of assets the total of " doubtful " debts is shown separately but nevertheless included in the calculation. Another total, " desperate debts yet uncast out," is mentioned twice in each account, but does not enter into the calculation at all.

The ledger of John Smyth, a leading sixteenth-century merchant in Bristol, shows gropings towards double entry, though it falls short of it.[21] The ledger, which extends from 1539 to 1550 (with some earlier entries), includes both personal and impersonal accounts, and a profit-and-loss account. The entries in the various accounts are by no means fully linked up in pairs as in double entry. Thus there are no indications of cross-references (or counterpart entries in other accounts) for any of the entries in the active account of John Yerbery, clothier, except for the entry of the balance carried forward to another folio: " Item I make hym creditor in folio 233. . . ." The impersonal accounts are goods accounts, voyage accounts and venture accounts— there are no nominal accounts relating solely to particular types of expense or revenue. The goods accounts generally include entries (on the left-hand side of each part of the account) for the quantities involved. The profit-and-loss account was balanced once, in 1543. The entries in the account bring together the results recorded in the various impersonal accounts (with each entry cross-referenced). The penultimate entry is not cross-referenced; it is a debit for £60 " lost by detters & otherwise. . . ."

[21] The Smyth ledger is deposited in the Bristol Record Office (Ashton Court MSS.). I am grateful to the owner, and to Miss Ralph of the Bristol Record Office, for permission to refer to this document. Mrs. J. Vanes has kindly given me access to a transcript of the accounts, and also the benefit of her advice on them. The Historical Manuscripts Commission and the Bristol Record Society are planning to publish the ledger.

The closing debit entry is "for the rest & nete gaynes of this accompt," and is not carried to the credit of any account in the ledger, there being no capital account. A new profit-and-loss account was opened, but it peters out after some entries without being balanced. There are references in some accounts to a " shop boke," probably for recording smaller sales; and, as there is no cash account in the ledger, there must have been a separate cash book.

All the foregoing examples refer to the accounting records of individual business men trading on their own. Some joint stock companies also kept their accounts on bases other than double entry. The Sun Fire Office, founded in 1710, did not introduce the double entry system of bookkeeping until 1890 to take the place of " the ' cash ' system which had prevailed since the office's earliest days." [22] The Capital and Counties Bank, which was merged with Lloyds Bank in 1918, had used single entry: " The process of merging the two great banks was also impeded by the systems of bookkeeping; the Capital and Counties worked on single entry, and this could not give way overnight to the double entry system of Lloyds." [23]

In general, the new " Italian " system of double entry (as distinct from features such as bilateral accounts) probably made slow headway in England during the sixteenth, seventeenth and eighteenth centuries, even after teachers of merchants' accounts and serviceable textbooks on double entry bookkeeping had made their appearance. The widespread adoption of double entry probably took place from the latter part of the nineteenth century onwards, when the development of the accounting profession, the company form of business organisation and the income tax system were major influences.

II.—THE EARLY PRACTICE OF DOUBLE ENTRY (1500–1800)

Early double entry accounting differed in many respects from current practice. The discussion in this section concentrates largely on selected aspects of practice where past and present display differences. This helps to set the stage for the concluding section, which outlines the influence of the joint stock company on the accounting calculation of profit. It is hoped that the reader will nonetheless be able to gain a fairly clear impression

[22] P. G. M. Dickson, *The Sun Fire Office, 1710–1960* (London, 1960), pp. 200–201.
[23] R. S. Sayers, *Lloyds Bank in the History of English Banking* (Oxford, 1957) p. 273.

of the characteristics of early double entry records in the period
ended (roughly) in 1800.

(a) *The account-books*

In many of the earlier expositions of double entry it is taken
as axiomatic that three different account-books are necessary
for a complete set, *viz.*, the waste book or memorial, the journal
and the ledger. Each transaction was first entered, in detail
but in rough, in the memorial, by the person who had handled
the particular piece of business. From time to time the account-
keeper repeated these entries in the journal, but in the special
form appropriate to good " accountantship," and distinguishing
carefully the particular ledger accounts to be debited and credited.
The ledger was then written up from the journal entries. There
were, however, frequent departures, both in didactic books and
in practice, from the simplicity of the tripartite division of
accounting records. The deviations fall into two broad classes.
First, the waste book and journal were merged to form a single
book of original entry. As Ympyn explained in a book published,
in English, in 1547, " many are sufficed with two bokes, and leave
the Memorial." [24] A variation of this economy in books and
simplification of the bookkeeping process was the combined waste
book and journal, which utilised one book for the two successive
stages of initial recording and subsequent and " accomptantly "
journalisation, the " journal " portion occupying the margin of
the page.

The second departure from the classical pattern was more
far-reaching. This involved the use of specialised subsidiary
books, for example, for recording cash transactions, bills transactions or particular types of expenditure. The purpose was to
keep detail out of the journal and also the ledger, so as to avoid
filling them up too quickly [25]; or, collectively, to replace the
journal more or less completely, and to serve directly as posting
media to the ledger.[26] The desire to avoid clutter in the ledger

---

[24] Jan Ympyn, *A Noble and Very Excellente Woorke* ... (London, 1547); an
English version of the original *Nieuwe Instructie* ... (Antwerp, 1543).

[25] According to Malachi Postlethwayt (*The Universal Dictionary of Trade and
Commerce*, 2nd ed., (London, 1757) Vol. 2, pp. 210–211): " To prevent those
books [journal and ledger] filling up, merchants, by experience, find it necessary
to keep other books subservient to them, as a cash-book, book of charges
of merchandise, book of household expences, factory or invoice-book the sale's
book . . . ."

[26] John Weddington in his *A Breffe Instruction* ... (Antwerp, 1567) advocated the
complete dismemberment of the waste-book and the elimination of the journal
(though he wrote that merchants may use a journal as well " yf it please them
to take somiche pains "). This was to allow division of labour in the counting-
house (" because marchantis of great dowingis ought to have many servantes
to helpe them to write ") and also to disencumber the ledger accounts.

accounts and duplication of records, and the special needs of different kinds of business, help to explain the different arrangements of the books of account found in practice. It seems common practice to have had at least a separate cash book, with periodic postings of totals to the cash account in the ledger, with or without a summarised entry in the journal.

The journal originally had only one money column.[27] The double-column journal of today seems to date from the early nineteenth century, and probably owes a good deal to the activities of Edward Thomas Jones. This entertaining character in 1795–96 launched a flamboyant attack on double entry bookkeeping, and invented his " English System," the publication of which initiated, both in England and on the Continent, a protracted and acrimonious debate on the merits of the venerable " Italian " system of double entry. His attack misfired; but his ingenious, if sometimes preposterous, urge to innovate no doubt led to much interest in the reform of the bookkeeping process and was responsible for the design and elaboration of tabular books of account—though these were not unknown before Jones. He also, in his later writings, developed the idea of the use of abstract or control accounts in the ledger.[28] Here, again, he was anticipated by practice. The East India Company, for example, had separate ledgers for different kinds of merchandise (*e.g.*, the Calico Ledger) with summary accounts in the main ledger. And Banks had a separate tenants ledger, which was linked up with the main ledger through its tenants ledger account.[29]

Several of the earlier textbooks refer to the possibility that the owner of a business might wish to keep some accounting information away from his counting-house staff. Several methods were recommended. James Peele in his *The Manner and Fourme . . .* (London, 1553) suggested that the journal pages with the opening entries (of assets and liabilities) should be separated from the rest of the journal and be bound with the ledger; this could then be controlled by the owner or his " keper of the accomptes," leaving it free for the other clerks to write up the journal. In

---

[27] For specimens of early journals, see reproductions in Littleton and Yamey, *op. cit.*, plate VII (Gresham's journal), and Richard Brown, *A History of Accounting and Accountants* (London, 1905), facing p. 158 (Darien Company's journal).

   It will be noted that the former has only simple entries, with one debtor and one creditor only in each case, while the latter has both simple and compound entries. Note also the cross-referencing to the ledger accounts (the fractions), and the " pricking " signs against the cross-references in the latter journal. On this, see my article on Peers, *Accountancy*, November 1960.

[28] On Jones, see my article, " Edward Jones and the Reform of Book-keeping, 1796–1810," in Littleton and Yamey, *op. cit.*, pp. 313–324.

[29] For Banks' and other records referred to in this section, see footnote 2, above.

his later and improved *Pathewaye to Perfectnes* . . . (London, 1569) he went further and suggested the use of a separate secret ledger, already explained two years before by Weddington in his *Breffe Instruction*. . . . Peele advocated and illustrated the use of two ledgers, one for the accounts " in trafique of Marchaundies," and the other for this information and also for " what I have reserved to myne owne secrete knowledge . . ."; there were dove-tailing accounts to link the two ledgers. Richard Du Cane's secret ledger (" livre prive ") is a partial adaptation of the idea of a secret ledger, which does not seem to have been much applied in practice in England.

(b) *Goods accounts*

It seems as if merchants and bookkeepers wished to avoid proliferation of accounts in the ledger [30]: " It is a great Prudence in the general, to make as few Accompts, and to fill them as slowly as may be . . .; because every touch with the Pen is obnoxious to Error; and the more Items, the more liable, and harder to find them out." Yet in both textbooks and surviving business accounts one finds many separate ledger accounts for different categories or lots of goods. Indeed, various goods accounts together with other goods on consignment accounts, goods in partnership (" company ") accounts, and voyage accounts may make up a large part of a ledger. And one would look in vain for a single collective trading account, in which the results of all buying-and-selling activity are brought together for a period, preparatory to transfer to the general profit-and-loss account. One must conclude that many merchants found it useful to have many separate goods accounts, even where there was no question of accounting to partners or principals for the disposal of their goods.

It is possible that merchants wanted separate goods accounts because they were interested in segregating the results of the trade in different commodities. I suggest, however, that the need for an accounting control over stock-in-trade was the more important reason. It was the practice in goods accounts to have additional quantity columns (usually inner columns next to the money columns) in which the movements of quantities were recorded.[31] From such entries in the quantity columns, " a Merchant may, at any time, know what Goods he has on hand . . . without being

---

[30] " A Person of Honour " (Roger North), *The Gentleman Accomptant* (London, 1715), p. 14.
[31] In Calley's ledger there are no quantity columns, but the quantities are recorded in detail in the ledger entries.

put to the Trouble of inspecting his Ware-house, and weighing or measuring the Goods themselves." [32] The goods account could serve as a perpetual inventory record, and provide both information and also a check on subordinates.

Although many merchants seem to have found it useful to sub-divide the " trading " account, others were probably put off by this feature of double entry accounting. Benjamin Booth, a merchant " late of New York and now of London," writing in 1789, partly ascribed the preference of the " bulk of traders " for single entry bookkeeping to the multiplicity of goods accounts in contemporary double entry practice; and he recommended that the ledger, at least, should have only a single goods account.[33] This was to become common practice during the nineteenth century.

(c) *Balancing the books*

The accounting treatises generally give detailed instruction on the balancing and closing of the ledger. Each account is to be balanced carefully (including the quantity columns in the goods account) and any profit or loss carried to the profit-and-loss account. The balance of this account is to be carried to the capital or stock account, after which it is frequently advised to draw up a (closing) balance account, listing all the remaining debit balances on the debit side and the credit balances on the other side (although often the balance account has only two equal and opposite entries, the details being left in two compound entries in the journal). And, much less frequently, it is prescribed that the opening of the next set of ledger accounts should take place by way of an opening balance account in it, which is the previously described closing balance account with debits and credits reversed: " by this manner you shall in Debitor and Creditor lincke, the one great Boke [ledger], withe the other." [34]

In practice, balance accounts, whether opening or closing, appear to have been drawn up less frequently than the closing of the profit-and-loss account and the transfer of any profit

---

[32] John Mair, *Book-keeping Methodiz'd . . .*, 2nd ed. (Edinburgh, 1741), p. 77.
[33] Benjamin Booth, *A complete system of Book-keeping . . .* (London, 1789).
  The multiplicity of goods accounts increased the chances of error. This is illustrated by some surviving records. In 1691 someone drew up a " Supplementall Journall " and ledger to bring order to a set of accounts of a partnership of North and Hampden in the Turkey trade some years earlier. Among the errors brought to light was that some of the cloth accounts still showed debit balances, while others " are just contrary, wh. have credit for a greater number of cloths then the whole parcell was at first." It seems as if some sales had been credited incorrectly to the latter group instead of to the former. (The records are in the Kent Record Office, Maidstone).
[34] Weddington, *op. cit.*

balance to the capital account. This is so even where the closing
of the profit-and-loss account coincided with the introduction
of a new ledger. Opening balance accounts appear to have been
particularly rare in practice in merchants' ledgers. The Bank of
England ledgers of the mid-eighteenth century, however, contain
both annual opening and closing balance accounts, along the
lines recommended in some of the treatises. The opening balance
account, with debits and credits reversed, may well have been
the root of the modern English practice of having assets and
other debit balances on the right-hand side of the balance-sheet.

The textbook writers were well aware that the balancing of
the balance account (or of a trial balance) furnished some proof
of the accuracy of the entries in the ledger: " So that if there is
the least Defect in this Balance, we must conclude there are
Errors in the Accounts; and if it holds, there is very probable
Argument, and, indeed, the best we can have, that all is right." [35]
The textbooks usually give full instructions how to check the
entries in the ledger for completeness and accuracy, either before
the closing procedure begins or after the ledger is found to be
out of balance. In practice, the merchants or their bookkeepers
were not always so scrupulous about discovering the causes of
imbalance and rectifying them before the ledger was closed
finally. In the Hoskins, Banks and Peers records, there are
examples of a single entry introduced into the profit-and-loss
account to get the books to balance; and in one of Braund's
ledgers, there is manipulation of the profit balance for the
same purpose. It was not thought worth the time and trouble to
hunt up the sources of discrepancy [36]; and some textbooks very
humanely gave instruction on what to do on these occasions [37]:
" If there be still a difference, which we do not think it worth
while to make further search for, we may close the books, by
making Profit and Loss Dr. or Cr. for the same."

" Merchants commonly once a-year balance or close their
Ledger, and raise from it the Materials of an Inventory to a new Set
of Books, for the ensuing Year." [38] So wrote John Mair in the
first half of the eighteenth century. A century earlier Richard
Dafforne had written that, apart from special circumstances

---

[35] Alexander Malcolm, *A Treatise of Book-keeping* . . . (London, 1731), p. 97.
[36] " . . . A Person of Estate, who deals, only for himself . . . will not think the
Time and Pains, subducted from his more favourite Pastime, compensated by the
Fruits of Care to prevent, and Industry to find out Errors in his Accompts:
Let them (says he to himself) go, his Loss or Gain will be the same." North,
op. cit., p. 40.
[37] Robert Hamilton, *An Introduction to Merchandise*, 2nd ed. (Edinburgh, 1788),
p. 286.
[38] Mair, *op. cit.*, p. 75.

(the owner's retirement or death), " When the Journall, and Leager are full written; so that there must be New Books . . . Then is a Ballance requisite." [39] To judge from the ten sets of double entry records I have examined, practice was not uniform as to frequency or regularity of balancing, with the emphasis closer perhaps to Daffornc's than to Mair's statement.[40] The Gresham (1546–51) [41] and North books (1680–91) were never balanced. The Calley (1600–06) and Peers (1689–94) books were balanced once, when they came to an end. The Hoskins ledger (1655–67) was closed five times at irregular intervals. The three Banks ledgers (1657–99) were closed thirteen times, at irregular intervals, including twice when an old ledger was replaced by a new one. Richard Du Cane (1736–44) closed his ledger six times. Clayton's ledgers (1669–80) were closed annually, as were those of Peter Du Cane (1754–58) and William Braund (1758–74); the annual closing took place even when new ledgers were not being introduced. The East India Company and the Bank of England closed and balanced their ledgers annually, again without opening new books every year. On the other hand, a surviving ledger of the Darien Company (The Company of Scotland trading to Africa and the Indies) runs from 1696 to 1707 without any trace of a general balance.[42]

The balancing process achieved two objectives. First, it served narrowly bookkeeping purposes. It furnished some proof of the accuracy of the ledgers. It also cleared the ledger of the accumulation of nominal accounts and inactive personal accounts, and made possible the orderly and systematic opening of a new ledger. To adapt a simile used by Mair, the balancing process

[39] Richard Dafforne, *The Merchants Mirror* . . ., 2nd ed. (London, 1651) p. 46.
[40] One cannot know whether more frequent or more regular " balancings " may not have been made without actually giving rise to a balanced profit-and-loss account, capital account and balance account in the ledger. Thus, for example, Malcolm, *op. cit.* p. 87: " If you propose to make an Inventory for the Satisfaction of Knowing the State of your Affairs, without designing a new Leger; then make up your Balance, and Profit and Loss, upon a loose Sheet . . ., without writing any Thing in the Leger . . ."
   See also Richard Hayes, *The Gentleman's Complete Book-Keeper* (London, 1741) Chap. VIII.
[41] The dates in parentheses indicate the period covered by the book(s) in question.
[42] Brown, *op. cit.*, pp. 157–158.
   A surviving volume of the Levant Company (Public Record Office: SP 105–164), divided into two ledgers, covers the years 1710 to 1772. The profit-and-loss account in the first ledger (1710–31) was balanced and closed only once, at the end of the period. In the second ledger (1731–72) the main nominal account balances were transferred to the profit-and-loss account at irregular intervals at first, and then more or less annually. This account was balanced only occasionally, with a single transfer to the capital account when the ledger was closed finally. In both ledgers the balance account has only three entries: one omnibus entry each for debit and credit account balances, and a third for the capital account balance.

harvests the yield sprouting from the farmer's seed (his opening
stock of assets), and this, " being separated from Chaff and
Straw," takes up its former shape of a stock of assets in the
balance account.[43] Second, it provided the owner with two
summary statements in account form—one of profits and losses,
and the other of assets and liabilities. It is my impression that
the former was by far the more important objective, though the
latter is frequently mentioned in contemporary textbooks. This
impression is based on several considerations, which include
the following: the irregularity of balancing in some cases; the
frequent connection between balancing and the replacement of
ledgers; the fact that both the summary accounts (profit and loss
account and balance account) sometimes consist solely or mainly
of two opposite omnibus entries, and in consequence they are
highly uninformative; the nature of the profit-and-loss account
(see below, subsection (d)); and some features of asset valuation
(see below, subsections (e) and (f)). But be that as it may, the
balancing process was the great test of " accountantship "; and
according to Jones [44]: " To balance a set of Books at the First
Trial appears wonderful, and is mentioned with astonishment;
and for the same person to do so two or three years following,
he is considered to possess a portion of infallibility, and is freely
allowed to boast of the exploit as long as he lives—But in how
few Compting-houses hath this been effected! "

(d) *The profit-and-loss account*

The balance of a typical profit-and-loss account in our period
measured the change, from virtually all causes, in the recorded
value of the capital in the business between the opening and
closing dates. With few exceptions, the balances of all nominal
accounts, the recorded profits or losses on all trading accounts
(goods, voyages, etc.), the entries for the owner's additions to or
subtractions from the resources of the firm, and gains or losses
on asset revaluations, were entered in (or cleared through) the
profit-and-loss account. Or, to express it differently, during the
accounting period, or at its termination, all account balances
other than those of assets, liabilities or capital were cleared
through the profit-and-loss account, the balance of which, in
turn, was transferred to the capital account.[45]

It seems to have been the almost invariable practice in this

---

[43] Mair, *op. cit.*, p. 89.
[44] Edward T. Jones, *English System of Book-keeping* (Bristol, 1796) p. 18.
[45] The four surviving Clayton ledgers have no profit-and-loss account. In them,
account balances are cleared straight into a combined capital and profit-and-
loss account called the " general " account.

early period for the owner's personal (non-business) expenses to be carried to the debit of the profit-and-loss account, the practice of carrying them to the capital account in the Braund ledgers being the only exception in the group of ten sets of records examined. On the other hand, it seems to have been more usual for capital transactions (*e.g.*, receipt of legacies or payment of marriage portions) to be recorded directly in the capital account, though several textbooks prescribe clearance through the profit-and-loss account, or, like Dafforne's, allow either alternative. Dafforne noted that both procedures could be used, though he preferred to credit the receipt of a legacy to the capital account: " But all what-so-ever passeth through the Waste-book in time of Trading, I (for uniformities sake) passe unto Profit and Losse. It is but a Ceremony, each his choice." [46]

It seems appropriate to regard the profit-and-loss account primarily as a clearing account, the operation of which facilitated the systematic clearing of the nominal accounts, and of the ledger itself. Of course, it indicated the change in the capital of the firm, and also the " causes " of the change. It seems unlikely, however, that the owner of a business would have examined the typical profit-and-loss account of the period with a view to obtaining some special insight into the operation and progress of his firm. In the typical profit-and-loss account there was no attempt to group or order the entries in a meaningful or helpful manner; and the heterogeneity of entries must have further complicated interpretation.[47] Again, while one must beware of reading too much into the contemporary textbooks, one may note in several of them a tendency to regard nominal accounts (" imaginary " or " fictitious " accounts) as necessary make-weights to supply a debit or credit to preserve the balance in the ledger [48]; the information in these nominal accounts does not seem to have been regarded as useful or necessary in itself. This supports the interpretation that the profit-and-loss account, in which the balances of these accounts were closed ultimately, served a weeding-out process, in which detailed but unwanted information in the ledger was removed.

[46] Dafforne, *op. cit.*, p. 28.
[47] The grouping of entries in the closing accounts in the Peter Du Cane ledgers is exceptional. At the other extreme, the entries in the profit-and-loss accounts in the Braund ledgers are quite uninformative, consisting largely of two omnibus entries, one in debit and one in credit. The entries in the profit-and-loss accounts in the Banks and North ledgers are numerous and unorganised.
[48] See, for example, Malcolm, *op. cit.*, p. 18.

(e) *The valuation of assets*

Three different methods of treating fixed assets and the income from them can be distinguished in seventeenth- and eighteenth-century accounting treatises. First, the asset is carried forward at original cost, the difference between " revenue " payments and receipts (*e.g.*, house repairs and rents received), which generally were entered in the asset account, being transferred to the profit-and-loss account at balancing date. Second, the asset account, containing entries for original outlay and other expenditures and receipts (including receipts from sales of part of the asset) is closed at balancing date, and the difference between total debits and total credits is carried forward as the account balance. There is no debit or credit to the profit-and-loss account. Third, the asset is revalued, upwards or downwards, at balancing date; the revised value is carried forward in the account, and the balancing difference (including the gain or loss on revaluation) is carried to profit-and-loss account.[49]

All three bases of valuation are to be found in our group of accounting records in respect of assets such as stocks and shares, landed property, ships and rights to income. There appears to have been no standard practice. Sometimes different bases were used for different assets in the same ledger, and for the same asset at different balancing dates.[50] As compared with modern practice, there was no inhibition against inconsistency, or against the inclusion of unrealised profits or losses on the revaluation of assets in the calculation of periodic profit, and no serious concern with the maintenance of any distinction between " capital " and " revenue " increments or decrements.

The notion of the systematic percentage writing-down of the cost of fixed assets is not encountered in any of the seventeenth- and eighteenth-century English records or treatises I have examined. The late eighteenth-century accounts of the firm of Boulton and Watt do, however, include annual debits for the depreciation of buildings, at 5 per cent. per annum.[51] Widespread use of modern methods of recording depreciation as an amortisation of a lump-sum outlay seems to have developed only in the second half of the nineteenth century.

---

[49] All three bases are discernible in Malcolm, *op. cit.*, p. 90.
[50] For detailed illustration, see section IV of my article in *Accounting Review* (referred to in footnote 2, above). Revaluations were based on current market valuations (*e.g.*, for investments in East India Stock and Government securities) or the owner's estimate.
  Several examples of the second method of balancing asset accounts are to be found in Ledger I (1750–56) of the East India Company (in the India Office Library, Commonwealth Relations Office, London).
[51] Erich Roll, *An Early Experiment in Industry Organization, being a History of the Firm of Boulton and Watt, 1775–1805* (London, 1930), p. 123.

The account-books examined do not indicate the basis for the valuation of stocks of merchandise. The great majority of the treatises mention that unsold goods should be " valued at the prime Cost." [52] Malcolm was one of the few who refers to other bases: " You may value the Balances of Goods as they cost you, or according to the current Rates." But he preferred the former: " Yet it seems more reasonable to value them as they cost you; for otherwise you bring in Gain or Loss into your Accounts, which has not yet actually happened, and may, perhaps, not happen; because you may not dispose of them at those [current] Rates." [53] This is an early example of the prescription of the *realisation-of-profits* criterion for the recording of gains and losses. We have already seen that this test was not applied in practice in the treatment of fixed assets; and there is therefore little reason to believe that it was generally applied in respect of other assets. The application of the criterion came into its own during the last hundred years or so.

(f) *Bad and doubtful debts*

Debts considered to be worthless were written off against the profit-and-loss account, though in practice this removal of debts from the ledger seems often to have been done sluggishly and belatedly. The need for a record of the debt often seems to have over-ridden the desirability of relieving the ledger of " dead " accounts.[54] These two conflicting considerations could, however, be reconciled by means of an ingenious and interesting procedure, which is sometimes described in the treatises [55] and is employed in the Banks and Peter Du Cane ledgers (in the latter with some modification) and also in early Bank of England ledgers. All the doubtful or " desperate," but not completely hopeless, debts were segregated into a single collective ledger account, descriptively titled as " Desperate Debtors " or the like. This reduced the number of separate personal accounts in the ledger, took up less

[52] Mair, *op. cit.*, p. 77.
[53] Malcolm, *op. cit.*, p. 89. Hayes, *op. cit.*, p. 79, and Postlethwayt (*op. cit.*), also allow either cost or market price.
Hamilton, *op. cit.*, p. 285, is interesting on the valuation of stocks:
  " It is much more proper to value the goods on hand in conformity to the current prices, than at prime cost: For the design of affixing any value is to point out the gain or loss; and the gain is in reality obtained so soon as the prices rise, or the loss suffered so soon as they fall." (By " current prices," he meant " such a value as the owner would be willing at present to buy for.")
[54] Ledger I (1750–56) of the East India Company includes many personal accounts in which there is no entry except the opening balance. To save space, several of these accounts are placed on a single page; it is apparent that they were known to be inactive accounts.
[55] For example, Alexander Macghie, *The Principles of Book-keeping explain'd* . . . (Edinburgh, 1718), p. 30; Malcolm, *op. cit.*, pp. 52–53.

space, and facilitated the closing and opening of the ledgers. In this method, the doubtful debts were not shown at reduced values in the ledger, and there was no debit to the profit-and-loss account until one or more of the constituent debts were judged to be quite worthless. The balance of the desperate debtors' account appeared as a debit balance in the balance account: " And although it introduces the amount of these debts as an article of your stock at the general balance, no great inconvenience follows, because the title by which they are distinguished must lead you to make a proper estimate." [56]

(g) *Prepayments and accruals*

From what has gone before, it is apparent that the business men and accountants in seventeenth- and eighteenth-century England did not keep their profit-and-loss accounts according to any strict concept of periodic profit. Realised as well as unrealised elements of profit or loss, business as well as non-business items, and capital as well as revenue items could be included in the profit-and-loss account, among the " chaff and straw " to be winnowed-out in the balancing process. The arbitrariness of the periodic profit calculation is further illustrated by the treatment of prepayments and of accruals of revenues or expenses.

By and large, little attempt appears to have been made to allocate incomes or expenditures consistently to accounting periods by anything resembling the modern treatment of prepayments and accruals. For example, in both the Banks and the Peers account-books, apprenticeship moneys are credited immediately to profit-and-loss account; no adjustments are made at subsequent balancing dates, even though the fees were to cover a period of seven years. Again, it is unusual to find adjustments at balancing dates for accrued interest or rents. Treatises sometimes specify that interest or rent be recorded at the beginning of the period,[57] or at the end of the period, or when the borrower or tenant actually pays the amount due [58]; there is no hint of adjustment at balancing dates.[59] An exception—anticipating the modern approach—is to be found in Braund's ledgers. He was

---

[56] Hamilton, *op. cit.*, p. 334.
[57] This was done in Gresham's accounts; see Ramsey, *op. cit.*, pp. 197–198.
  Cf.: Hayes, *op. cit.*, p. 24: " If you lend out Money for a certain Time at Interest,

  Dt. the Borrower for the   Ct. Cash for the Money lent.
  Principal and Interest.   Ct. Profit and Loss, or Interest
                                    Account, for the Interest."
[58] Thus there is an entry in one of the Braund ledgers (which were balanced and closed annually): " To Interest on £1017.16.8 for (?) 3 Febry 1757 to 3 Sept 1761 is 4 year 7 m at 5 per cent."
[59] All three methods are mentioned in Malcolm, *op. cit.*, p. 50.

active in marine insurance. Every year he carried down a credit balance on his " account of assurances," reflecting, presumably, an estimate of probable claims on the unexpired portions of policies. By contrast, one of the recommended accounting treatments of loans to shipowners on bottomry bonds was to credit the " profit " (the excess over the amount lent of the amount due if and when the ship should arrive safely at destination) immediately to profit-and-loss account, presumably in order to have a proper record of the amount of the eventual, if hazardous, debt.[60]

Some of the above-mentioned procedures, which are at variance with modern practice, seem to have been dictated by the need to have a record in the ledger of amounts receivable or payable, even when they were not immediately or even unconditionally due. On the other hand, the failure to pro-rate lump-sum apprenticeship fees reflects the fact that no monetary obligation, present or future, arose out of the transaction. In all cases, moreover, considerations of precision and consistency in the calculation of periodic profits appear to have had little weight. The teaching that revenues and expenditures (or appropriate portions of them) should be assigned to accounting periods as precisely as possible, and that " unexpired " portions of receipts and payments should be carried forward as liabilities and assets, belongs to the latter half of the nineteenth century. Indeed, more generally, the problems we associate with the *concept* of profit and the careful calculation of *periodic* profit do not appear to have been problems worrying the early practitioners or teachers of double entry accounting in England. Accounting requirements of business men did not call for any serious concern with these matters.

III.—THE CALCULATION OF PROFIT IN THE ACCOUNTS OF JOINT STOCK COMPANIES [61]

The early profit-and-loss account is probably best regarded as little more than a necessary component in the bookkeeping

---

[60] Dafforne, *op. cit.*, p. 30; Malcolm, *op. cit.*, pp. 42–43. In Ledger I of the East India Company the more conservative method was followed, that is, of taking credit for the gain only when the ship had reached its destination, and the gain had thus materialised.

[61] A number of paragraphs in this section are taken, with little alteration, from my article, " The Development of Company Accounting Conventions," in the September, 1960, issue of *The Three Banks Review*, a publication of the Royal Bank of Scotland, Glyn, Mills & Co. and Williams Deacon's Bank Limited. I am indebted to the publishers of the *Review* for permission to use this material.

process. The role and status of this account increased greatly
during the nineteenth century, when profit calculation came to
dominate the accounting scene. What had often been incidental,
became central. Again, although the early profit-and-loss account
yielded a figure of periodic profit, its determination was in many
ways subordinate and subservient to the statement of asset
" values " in the ledger. This situation, also, was reversed in
the course of the nineteenth century when the primacy of profit
calculation was established. The present section attempts to
explain this major change of emphasis in financial accounting.
It does so in terms of the development of new requirements;
these in turn derive from the rapid growth in importance of
joint stock companies which exercised a dominant influence on
accounting practices and, indeed, on the development of
professional accountancy.[62]

Periodic calculations of a firm's profits and statements of
the value of its assets are of little interest to the businessman
who is closely and continuously concerned with his own business
operations. He has immediate access to the detailed accounts
in his ledger, and it requires no formal calculation for him to
discover from the records, or in other ways, the progress of the
business or the facts of his liquid position or fixed assets. Provided
that he is not accountable for part of his profits to others, whether
these are business associates or the collector of taxes, formal
profit calculation in the accounts is likely to be incidental, and
little thought would be given to the precise definition or careful
and consistent measurement of periodic profit.

Until the coming of general limited liability, it seems that
accounting practices were designed to meet the simple requirements of businessmen actively concerned with the management
of their own enterprises. There had, of course, been many
instances of absentee ownership in industry and trade, ranging
from the small partnership with a sleeping partner to the giant
East India Company. Here accounting records no doubt had
been made to serve as the basis of periodic financial statements
to the absentee owners. But this had no apparent effect on
accounting practice.

[62] For two studies of particular aspects of company accounting, see Harold Pollins,
" Aspects of Railway Accounting before 1868," and H. C. Edey and Prot
Panitpakdi, " British Company Accounting and the Law, 1844–1900," in
Littleton and Yamey *op. cit.*, pp. 332–355 and 356–379, respectively. My
article on " The Case Law relating to Company Dividends " in the present
volume (pp. 428–442) is relevant to some of the points raised in this section.

In company accounting, the periodic profit figure became significant in two respects. First, from an early date it was the practice that dividends to shareholders should not exceed profits. The profit figure set an upper limit to payments to shareholders, and thus acquired direct financial significance. There was, of course, never such a restraint on distributions to partners in an ordinary partnership. Secondly, shareholders were absentee owners who had no continuous or close contact with the operations of their enterprise or with the books of account recording them. To a large extent they had to rely for their impressions of the success and soundness of their company on information made available by the active management. The periodic profit figure not unnaturally came to be regarded as an indicator of the profitability of operations, a summary of the results of the interaction of numerous business decisions and economic circumstances of which the shareholders had no detailed knowledge.

Consider, first, the profit figure as an indicator of the amount available for distribution as dividends to shareholders. As the payment of dividends affects the liquidity of the company, there was a tendency to link the profit figure reasonably closely with the increase in the net current assets becoming available from business operations. Thus changes in either direction in the current value of fixed assets not realised by actual sales were not included in the profit calculation. Unlike profitable sales of the company's output, an unrealised increase in the value of its fixed assets does not improve its liquid position and its financial ability to pay dividends. (It might, of course, enhance its ability to raise money.) Again, an unrealised fall in the value of its fixed assets does not impair its liquidity and its financial ability to pay dividends. Thus, the rule was developed that, by and large, profits or losses should not be recognised in the accounts until they had been realised in the form of cash or its near-equivalent.

But certain fixed assets, notably plant and equipment, do not last for ever, and there is the problem of providing finance for their eventual replacement. Hence it was unwise to treat all the increase in net current assets as being a profit available for distribution. Depreciation of fixed assets was thus to be shown in the accounts even when it was not matched by equivalent current outlays on asset replacement. Accounting for depreciation was essentially concerned with replacement, and not with the revaluation of fixed assets; the connection with the financing of replacement is manifest in company reports and professional

discussions throughout the nineteenth century and also later.
The idea of the regular provision for depreciation by debits in
the profit-and-loss account did not, however, gain rapid or general
acceptance. Precisely because no actual outlay was involved,
there was a tendency in some companies to dispense with
deductions for depreciation especially in years of poor trade.
This enabled a company to report higher profits and pay higher
dividends than otherwise, without necessarily endangering the
company's liquid position. And some companies ignored periodic
accounting for depreciation, and simply debited the profit-and-
loss account for the actual amounts spent from year to year on
replacements or renewals. Gradually, however, it became accepted
practice to provide for the depreciation of fixed assets.[63]

The other important role of the periodic profit figure was that
of an index of profitability, made known to shareholders and
potential shareholders. This role accounted for the tendency to
leave the profit calculation largely unaffected by what were considered to be unusual, non-recurrent or irregular items of profit or
loss. The inclusion of these items, not being " normal," would
disturb and distort the index, and misinform the reader. Thus there
was a tendency for realised as well as unrealised changes in the
value of fixed assets to be kept out of the profit calculation.
Moreover, there was a tendency to prorate or write off certain
expenditures over a series of successive annual profit calculations,
even where there was no question of subsequent replacement
expenditure. For example, the formation expenses associated
with the foundation of a company were commonly not treated
as an expense of the first year of operation. This would have
" distorted " the profit figure. Instead, the total amount would
be spread over the accounts of a number of years.[64]   The
systematic provision for the depreciation of fixed assets in
accordance with a predetermined formula was also often supported on these grounds, more particularly in criticism of the
practices of debiting the profit-and-loss account only in respect
of actual outlays on replacements or of providing for depreciation

[63] The " finance " aspect of company accounting is also apparent in more recent
developments. Since 1945 some companies have begun to re-state the accounting values of their fixed assets from time to time. The need to finance asset
replacements at inflated prices has been among the reasons for this departure
from traditional practice; the writing-up of the book value of the assets facilitates
the debiting of larger annual provisions for depreciation. The unrealised
" gain " on revaluation is not, however, carried to profit-and-loss account as in
eighteenth-century accounting; instead, it is treated as a credit balance which
is not available as profit for distribution to shareholders.
[64] An early example is provided by the records of the East India Company. By
order of the General Court in June 1733, £10,000 p.a. was written off the payment recorded in the account entitled " Prolongation of the Company's Right
to an Exclusive Trade & Perpetuity of their Corporate Capacity."

only in the years when there were profits—these being practices
which were unexceptionable on " financial " grounds.

The book or balance-sheet values of fixed assets resulting
from the application of the conventions were sometimes called
" going-concern values " or "values to the going concern."
It should be apparent, however, that these figures were not the
products of a deliberate process of valuation (as when an appraiser
properly distinguishes the " going-concern " value of plant from
break-up value); rather, they were the consequence of the application of a concept of profit which with some aptness might be
called the " going-concern " concept of profit. The real issues
of asset or enterprise valuation were avoided in the application
of the chosen concept of profit.

Rules and conventions in company accounting would have
been different had the emerging law relating to company affairs
at any stage checked or deflected the course of its development.
But by and large it had little effect. Provision for compulsory
disclosure in accounts moved slowly, and did not touch the
basic conventions. The case law relating to the determination
of profits available for dividends also did not call for any modification in the conventions or in their application. On dividend
questions, the courts, especially after 1889, were unwilling " to
formulate rules for the guidance and embarrassment of business
men in the conduct of business affairs." [65] Provided accounts
were drawn up in good faith in the interests of the company,
and approved by auditors, the British courts were loth to
intervene. In fact, the leading cases pointed to broad legal
principles which were more permissive and lenient than the
accounting conventions in the determination of profit. It was
the accounting conventions and not the legal requirements that
in practice imposed the real restraints on the calculation of
divisible profits—though some of these restraints could, of course,
be broken within the wider limits of the law.

The application of the accepted conventions necessarily left
a fairly wide area of accounting discretion to company managements and auditors. For example, the periodic debits for the
depreciation of a fixed asset call for a decision about the method
of depreciation to be adopted and an estimate of the effective
life of the asset; differences of opinion and of judgment could
properly lead to significant differences in the accounts. The same
is true of the determination of provisions for bad debts and other
contingencies.

[65] Lord Macnaghten in *Dovey* v. *Cory* [1901] A.C. 477.

In practice the exercise of accounting discretion or judgment was conditioned in general by an approved bias towards " conservatism." This meant, by and large, that it was better to err on the side of under-statement rather than of over-statement. Thus asset values in the balance-sheet were to be under- rather than over-stated; and possible losses were to be anticipated rather than deferred in the accounts, while the recording of gains was to be deferred until they had been realised. This attitude is well exemplified in the convention determining the statement of stocks in the balance-sheet; the asset was to be shown at " cost or market value, whichever is lower "—unrealised increases in value to be ignored, while unrealised decreases to be recorded.

The accounting rules and conventions outlined above would have seemed strange to the typical merchant, accountant or textbook writer of a century earlier. The use of *secret reserves* in the preparation of the published accounts of joint stock companies would have seemed even stranger.

The creation of secret reserves, and their resurrection to augment the recorded profits in subsequent periods, were important features of company accounting in the second half of the nineteenth century and for several decades later. The creation or setting-up of secret (or inner) reserves went well beyond the caution characteristic of ordinary accounting conservatism. Provided it was done in good faith and in the interests of the company, the directors could, within wide limits, present final accounts embodying deliberate and material deviations from the application of the accounting conventions. In appropriate circumstances the profits, and hence net assets, could be under-stated, for example by depreciating assets faster than was necessary, by treating capital expenditures as current revenue expenditures, and by providing excessively for contingencies. In this way smaller profits could be disclosed, without shareholders being made aware of the approximate magnitude of the undisclosed reserves; and reinvestment of profits could be made easier.[66] Moreover, if it was considered in the interests of the company, reported profits in later, leaner years could be augmented by drafts on the undisclosed reserves.

The use of secret reserves in company accounting represented the victory of the needs of company management over the developing accent on meticulous accounting calculation (an accent which is seen, for example, in the careful apportionment

---

[66] A prominent company chairman in the 1930s (the late Mr. Arthur Chamberlain) said: " It is better not to show more (profit) and run the risk of exciting appetites."

of prepaid and accrued expenses). It also reflected an attitude taken by company management towards the shareholders; it was deemed axiomatic that, provided they acted in good faith, the management should decide, within limits, what to tell the shareholders in accounting statements prepared for their information.

During the last thirty years the use of secret reserves has been curbed considerably. It remains true, however, that many of the entries in a set of accounts lying behind published company accounts reflect the judgment of those who run the company and of the company's auditors. They do not contain only " hard facts," as was true of the charge-and-discharge stewardship accounts with which our story began. It is interesting to reflect that financial analysts today not infrequently try to convert the data in a balance-sheet and profit-and-loss account into a statement of " sources and uses of funds," a statement which bears a strong family resemblance to the charge-and-discharge accounts of our ancestors.

Economics and Accounting: the Uncongenial Twins

By K. E. Boulding

Professor of Economics, University of Michigan.

ECONOMICS and accountancy are two disciplines which draw their raw material from much the same mines. From these raw materials, however, they seem to fashion remarkably different products. They both study the operations of firms; they both are concerned with such concepts as income, expenditure, profits, capital, value and prices. In spite of an apparently common subject-matter, however, they often seem to inhabit totally different worlds, between which there is remarkably little communication. When I studied economics at Oxford a generation ago, it was not considered necessary for an economist to know any accounting at all. Indeed, as far as I recall, not even the opportunity to study accounting was given. It was no doubt regarded as a pedestrian, commercial, workaday subject, quite unworthy of being admitted to those dignified halls. The situation, I am sure, is better at the newer institutions, both in Britain and the United States. Even in the United States, however, accounting is rarely integrated in any systematic or satisfactory way into an economist's education. The student of economics frequently has to pass a single required course in accounting, and that is the end of it. There is very little intellectual intercourse between economists and accountants at the professional level. The faults here may be more on the side of the economists than of the accountants. It is very rare to find an economist who reads the accounting journals. It is almost equally rare, however, to find an accountant who is well versed in economics.

This situation is all the more deplorable because many of the basic concepts of economics are, in fact, derived from accounting practice, and many accounting practices have been devised in an attempt to answer what are essentially economic questions. The concept of profit, for instance, is essentially an accounting concept. A large amount of the activity of accountants consists in the attempt to measure it. The concept of profit is likewise fundamental to economics. It is supposed to be the great motive power of a market system. It is supposed to account for the behavior of enterprises, and it is supposed to guide the allocation of resources among competing uses. The economist's concept of profit, however, and the accountant's concept often seem to have little in common. We do not, of course, have to have a single concept of profit for all purposes. The concept of profit will quite rightly differ depending upon the purpose for which we need it. The definition of profit for tax purposes, for instance, may differ considerably from the definition which is required for other forms of decision-making. What we need here is not a single definition of profit applicable to all cases, but a spectrum of definitions, in which the relationship of the various concepts is reasonably clear and in which the definition is fitted to the purpose for which it is to be used.

The point where accounting and economics come closest together is in what the economists call the theory of the firm. This is not surprising, as it is with a formalized and abstract description of the history of the firm that accounting is largely concerned, especially if we stretch the concept of the firm to include governmental and non-profit organizations of an economic character. The basic concept here both for accounting and for economics is that of the balance-sheet or position statement. This is essentially a description of the state of a firm or enterprise at a given moment of time. In its simplest form, what might be called the physical balance-sheet of an enterprise consists of a simple list of the values of all variables which are associated with it as they exist at a moment of time. This is a much larger concept, of course, than that of the accountant's balance-sheet. A great many variables which might be significant from the point of view of the state of the enterprise and especially from the point of view of its future, such as the quality of its management, or the morale of its work force, are quite rightly excluded from the accountant's balance-sheet. The accountant is interested in a limited aspect of the state of the enterprise, confined to those items which can be reduced by some rule or other to a value equivalent. What the accountant is doing, that is, when he constructs the balance-sheet, is essentially to make up a list of those items associated with the enterprise which can be valued, and he then proceeds to value them: he replaces the physical quantity of the item by so many dollars, pounds, or whatever the valuation unit may be. This he does by a variety of techniques, the end product of which is all the same—a sum of monetary values.

The ratio of the physical quantity of some item in the physical balance-sheet to the corresponding value equivalent may be called the " valuation coefficient." Frequently, the valuation process is performed by a rule which establishes a valuation coefficient, and then the value of a given physical quantity is obtained by simply multiplying the physical quantity by this coefficient. Thus if an enterprise has a stock of a thousand bushels of wheat, we value this stock at some price or cost per bushel, say $2 per bushel, which is the valuation coefficient, and the total value of the stock is then $2,000. Some confusion may be caused by the fact that certain items in the physical balance-sheet are already expressed as a sum of money, for instance, a loan or a bond. In this case, of course, the valuation coefficient is unity, but it still exists.

The accountant gives some such name as net worth to the total net value of an enterprise. This is the sum of all the value items, both positive and negative (*i.e.*, assets less liabilities). The accountant may not seem to attach much significance to net worth by itself, but he is very interested indirectly in the size of this total, since—as we shall see on p. 49—the size of his profit figure depends on changes in net worth.

The difference in outlook of economists and accountants is perhaps one of emphasis rather than of principle. We may say, however, that accountants are primarily interested in the enterprise as it is now and as it has been in the past. The economist is interested in the " might have beens," as well as the actual situation. The accountant asks himself simply how profitable is the enterprise; the economist asks himself how profitable it might have been if it had done something different, and especially what it would have to do in order to make maximum profits.

Another possible difference, although the accountant might deny this, is that the accountant has a focus of interest in certain aggregates and totals, such as net worth or aggregate profit figures, whereas the economist is more interested in the structure of the enterprises. This interest in structure is admittedly soft-pedalled by many economists; it is a fair criticism of the theory of the firm, as set out in most economics textbooks, that the firm is depicted as acutely concerned with possible costs and revenues, and oblivious of asset structure—as having a profit budget but no balance-sheet.

To put the point in more mathematical language, the economist is interested in the balance-sheet as a vector in *n*-space. The accountant is interested in reducing this *n*-dimensional vector to a simple scalar, that is a single number. Unfortunately, even though rules can be applied, that is principles of valuation, for reducing an *n*-dimensional vector to a single number, these rules are inevitably somewhat arbitrary, and different rules may give entirely different results. This principle can be illustrated in figure 1 in which we take an extremely simple enterprise, which has only two assets which we will call wheat, measured along OW, and money, along OM. A point P in this field represents a position or state of the enterprise, that is, its physical balance-sheet. Thus, the point P represents an enterprise with NP bushels of wheat and VP shillings of money. If, now, we want to represent this position by a single figure, we have to value the wheat. If we suppose NK to be the value of the amount of wheat NP, then the valuation coefficient is $\dfrac{NK}{NP}$, which is the slope of the line KP. The net worth of the enterprise is then ON + NK, or

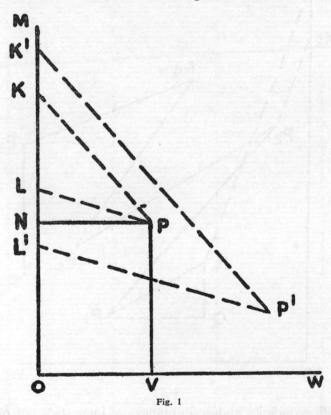

Fig. 1

OK. Consider now, two different positions of the enterprise, P and P¹ (the latter standing for more wheat and less money). The accountant wishes to know which of these two positions represents the larger value or net worth. If the valuation coefficient for wheat is the slope of KP and K¹P¹, then it is clear that P¹ represents the larger value, that is, the larger net worth, as OK¹ is larger than OK. Suppose, however, that we value the wheat at a lower price or coefficient equal to the slope of LP and L¹P¹. Now we see that the point P represents the higher value OL, whereas the point P¹ represents the lower value OL¹. Without knowing a set of valuation coefficients, therefore, we cannot tell whether the point P is " larger " or " smaller " than P¹. This is why the valuation procedure may properly be regarded as the heart of accountancy.

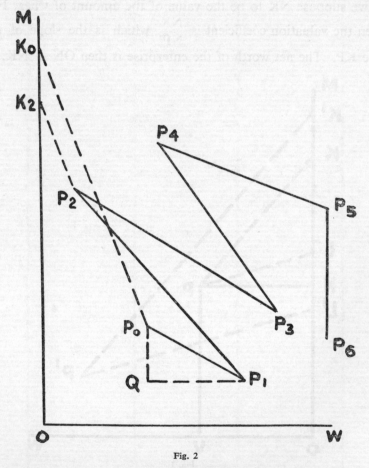

Fig. 2

Both economics and accountancy are interested, not only in the state of an enterprise at a moment, but also in the course of the enterprise through time, that is, the sequence of position statements as they pass from one time period to the next. Suppose, for instance, that in figure 2, in which the axes have the same meaning as in figure 1, the point P_0 represents an initial position of the enterprise. Suppose now that the firm buys more wheat, moving from position P_0 to P_1. This means it gives up an amount of money equal to P_0Q and acquires an amount of wheat equal to QP_1. The price at which the wheat has been bought is $\dfrac{P_0Q}{QP_1}$ which is the slope of the line P_0P_1. Now suppose the firm sells wheat following the line P_1P_2, *i.e.*, at a higher price. It is clear that in some sense a profit has been made. How much profit, depends on the valuation coefficients which are used. P_2 might even indicate smaller profit than P_0, if wheat were valued on both dates at a very high valuation coefficient, such as the slope of K_0P_0 and K_2P_2 (which reduces net worth from OK_0 to OK_2); but the accountant's bias towards conservatism will in general make for low coefficients, and so depress net worth where stocks of goods are high. In the course of successive periods, the enterprise will move to positions such as P_3, P_4, P_5, etc. If its operations have been successful, the result of these various transformations will be to move its position in some sense further " out " in the field. Exactly what constitutes " out," however, depends upon the system of valuation.

Profit can always be defined, in some sense, to mean an increase in net worth. The calculation of profit, that is to say, always involves the calculation of net worth from the position statements of two successive periods.[1] The rate of profit is the rate of increase of net worth in some sense or another. The problem is complicated somewhat by the fact that there may not only be asset transformations in the course of the history of the enterprise, there may also be withdrawals, that is, simple deductions from assets of one kind or another. Thus from the position P_5 in figure 2, we could go directly downward to P_6 indicating a simple withdrawal of money from the enterprise. Yet a third event which may take place during the history of an enterprise is a revaluation—say, a change in the valuation coefficient by which physical assets are valued.

Virtually all events which are of significance to the enterprise can be classified in one of these three categories, either as an asset transformation, a revaluation, or a withdrawal. Asset transformations may be either through production or through

---

[1] This may not be obvious to accounting students trained to draft income statements *before* balance-sheets. But the costs and revenues in the former statement are all implicit in the changes in the latter, and are measured by these changes.

The accountant on occasion isolates some gains, *e.g.*, windfalls may be shown separately from operating profit. But such technicalities do not affect the main argument.

exchange. When a miller grinds wheat into flour, for instance, he diminishes the quantity of wheat (raw materials) in the inventory shown in his position statement, and increases the quantity of flour (finished goods). When he exchanges flour, let us say, for accounts receivable, he diminishes the quantity of flour and increases the quantity of accounts receivable. The most fundamental concept of *cost* is that it represents the transformation ratio in *production*, that is, the ratio in which the input assets are transformed into the output assets. The most fundamental concept of *price* is that of the asset transformation ratio in *exchange*. If wheat costs $1.50 a bushel, this means on the whole that resources or inputs equivalent to $1.50 have to be used up or destroyed in order to increase the stock of wheat by one bushel. If the price of wheat is $2 a bushel, this means that wheat can be transformed into money through exchange at this rate.

Withdrawals may also be of two kinds, positive and negative. A negative withdrawal consists usually of simply putting money into the enterprise. The initial capital of an enterprise represents a negative withdrawal which is usually the first event in its history from the accounting point of view. Interest and dividend payments, of course, represent positive withdrawals.

In accounting practice, revaluations frequently occur at the moment of sale. Inventory, for instance, will be valued at cost in some sense until the moment of sale, when the article is revalued to the sale price. At the moment of sale (that is, in the asset transformation) there is both a change of values from one item in the position statement to another, and an increase in values. The profit-making occurs essentially in the revaluation which takes place at the moment of sale. The fact that revaluation and exchange are bound up in a single transaction has often caused confusion, and it is necessary, analytically, to separate these two essentially dissimilar operations.

Another important difference between the accountant's and the economist's point of view, as we have seen, is that the accountant on the whole is interested in what is or what has been, whereas the economist is interested in what might be. In particular the economist is interested in the problem of what he calls " maximizing behavior." The accountant is interested, primarily, in what has happened to the enterprise in the past and in what is its position today; the economist is interested in the question of whether the enterprise could have done better. In accounting, for instance, price is largely treated as a datum and as a constant. In economics, price is usually treated as a variable. The economist asks himself what would have happened if there had been a different set of prices, exchanges, transformations, or withdrawals from that which actually occurred. Would the enterprise be better off now, or worse off? In particular, the economist is interested in the best pattern of behavior, that is, the pattern of behavior which places the enterprise in a position superior to that which can be reached by any other pattern of behavior. Achieving this best pattern is what the economist means by " maximizing behavior."

A good many of the propositions of price theory are based on the assumption that businessmen do, in fact, maximize profits. This is, of course, a highly dubious assumption. It is not only that there are always things for which businessmen are willing to sacrifice profits, such as security, respectability, liquidity, and so on, which means, of course, that they do not maximize profits. But a more fundamental difficulty is that the information which would enable a businessman to maximize his profits generally is not available to him. The difficulty here is a very fundamental one for the accountant and for the economist. Decisions are always made in the hope of the future, whereas information is always derived from the past. The theory of maximizing behavior assumes implicitly that we know all the possible patterns of the future and that we can select the best out of them. Our knowledge of the future, however, must be derived from our experience of the past, and our experience of the past is highly limited. Our image of the future or of the various possible futures is always dependent on some kind of projection of our past experience. These projections, however, are unreliable and they may be based on a very limited perception of the kind of dynamic system in which the enterprise operates. The basic difficulty here is that the future depends not only on the decision of one person, but on the decision of all the decision-makers of a society. A man can control his own decisions within limits, but he cannot control the decisions of others even though he may attempt to predict them. Because of this, there are bound to be inconsistencies in the images of the future of different individuals, which means that some of them must be falsified. Maximizing behavior, that is to say, is something which cannot be universally applied by its very nature.

In spite of the practical difficulties in the way of maximizing profit, the economist's theory of maximization, which is known usually as the marginal analysis, has a good deal of merit. Its merit lies perhaps in the questions which it raises rather than in the answers which it is able to give. It is always useful to take a given situation and to ask, " Could we have done better? " It is also useful to ask, " What do we need to know in order that we could do better? " It is perhaps because of pressure from the economist that the accountant has in many instances become interested in the concept of what he calls " incremental cost " and what the economist calls " marginal cost." These two concepts are not perhaps identical but they are closely related. The economist looks at a given situation and asks himself " Suppose we did something a little different? Would the increase in revenue be greater than the increase in cost? " If it is, then profits are clearly not being maximized now, and we shall do well to make the change. If, on the other hand, a given change increases revenue less than it increases cost, not only are we very sure that we should not make the change but we have evidence that we should make a change in an opposite direction. Even though, therefore, we can seldom be sure that we are actually at the point of maximum profit, we can frequently tell whether a proposed change is likely to move us toward that point or away from it. The economist recognizes, of course, that marginal costs or receipts are hard to measure. They represent a " might be " rather than an " is " and they are, therefore, not perhaps congenial to the accountant's insistence on the measurement of the actual. It is potentialities, however, rather than actualities which are most significant in the making of decisions, and in so far as we regard the whole process of information collection and processing in the organization as essentially an aid to the making of decisions, these potentialities are even more important than the actualities.

We shall notice also that the accountant himself is not altogether free from the necessity of considering potentialities, and in particular he cannot avoid making certain projections about the future. This is implicit, in fact, in an evaluation process. The act of valuation, Janus-like, has two faces. It faces back into the past and forward into the future. On the one hand, we value assets by past cost, sometimes compounded; on the other hand, we value them as discounted future net receipts. The former is what we can most easily find out; the latter, however, is the truly significant figure. The accountant is wise to take the past accounts as the basis for his evaluations. He may sometimes recognize the uncertainties of the present and of the future by making write-ups or write-downs, as the case may be—periodically adjusting past accounts to the present knowledge of the future. If he does not do this, the stock market will tend to do it for him. A firm, for instance, which has sunk a lot of money into assets in a country undergoing the fervors of a revolution is likely to find that the stock market values its shares on future expectations rather than past costs. In economics, as Jevons once said, " Bygones are bygones." For the accountant, bygones are not bygones without a struggle. It is probably just as well that he struggles. Sometimes, however, the struggle must be abandoned and bygone costs must be written down (or up) in the face of present realities.

The implication of the above is that even the accountant's calculation of profit is essentially based on some expectations about the future. Profit is not simply a matter of past performance; it always has in it an element of future expectation. This is because profit depends upon revaluations, and these revaluations may have to be made in the light of changes in expectations in the future. A firm which suffers a diminution of the value of its assets by a million pounds for whatever reason also suffers a diminution of its current profit—in our fundamental sense—by a million pounds. Profit, therefore, is not merely a matter of trying to sell again at a higher price. Many of the elements of cost in fact involve future expectations. It has been said that we should call no man happy until he is dead; likewise perhaps we should call no firm profitable until it has been finally liquidated. Nevertheless, the accountant must give some kind of an answer to the question " What profits have been earned? " He must do this for legal as well as for decision-making reasons, for the law requires that, to some extent, the behavior of a firm conform to, or at least be limited by, its accounting results, especially for purposes of paying taxes or for distributing dividends.

The economist then looks on the accountant as a man who has to perform an impossible task. He has first to reduce what is essentially a multi-dimensional reality to a one-dimensional figure; and, in the second place, he has to do this on the basis of knowledge about the future which he cannot possibly have. Under these circumstances, it is not surprising that the economist regards much accounting procedure as in the nature of ritual. To call these procedures ritualistic is in no way to deny or decry their validity. Ritual is always the proper response when a man *has* to give an answer to a question, the answer to which he cannot really know. Ritual under these circumstances has two functions. It is comforting (and in the face of the great uncertainties of the future, comfort is not to be despised) and it is also an answer sufficient for action. It is the sufficient answer rather than the right answer which the accountant really seeks. Under these circumstances, however, it is important that we should know what the accountant's answer means, which means that we should know what procedure he has employed. The wise businessman will not believe his accountant although he takes what his accountant tells him as important evidence. The quality of that evidence, however, depends in considerable degree on the simplicity of the procedures and the awareness which we have of them. What the accountant tells us may not be true, but, if we know what he has done, we have a fair idea of what it means. For this reason, I am somewhat suspicious of many current efforts to reform accounting in the direction of making it more " accurate."

I am particularly suspicious of attempts to improve accounting by building into it an explicit recognition of the fact that the price level changes. It is easy to criticize accounting practice— and this is a criticism which economists have frequently made— on the ground that it assumes a monetary unit of constant value whereas in fact the monetary unit fluctuates constantly in purchasing power. The accountant's balance-sheet, it is argued, is reckoned in dollars of different ages, some of them perhaps of the year of the founding of the enterprise and others of last week. In the interim, however, the value of the monetary unit may have changed completely through the large social forces of inflation and deflation. This is almost as if we were trying to add feet to centimeters without reducing them to a common unit of length. A hundred feet plus ten centimeters is certainly not a hundred and ten anythings, and the accountant's balance-sheet total is not much better. It is argued also that because the accountant tends to perform valuation on the basis of historical cost, his measure of profit is inflated in a period of inflation and is correspondingly depressed in a period of deflation. Profits are made by selling things at a price greater than the cost. In an inflationary period, however, if the cost has been incurred at an earlier date, the price will reflect the general rise in prices as well as the relative price of a particular commodity. Hence, profits in accounts will be larger than they should be in terms of a dollar of constant purchasing power. Deflation destroys accounting profits in a similar way. An attempt is made to correct this distortion through valuing inventories by the last-in, first-out method, which is a more sophisticated substitute for the original first-in, first-out method.

The case for " constant dollar " accounting may be a strong one, but it is by no means invulnerable. The profits of inflation and the losses of deflation are not altogether illusory to the individual concern. Inflation, for instance, affects the real distribution of wealth away from those who hold liquid assets towards those who hold assets which are rising in price. Up to a point, the accounting profits of inflation reflect this, although they probably exaggerate it. Similarly, a deflation redistributes wealth towards those who simply sit tight with liquid assets, and the accounting losses therefore of those who trade and indulge in enterprise at such periods, again, arc a partial reflection of this fact. There is something to be said also for a certain naïveté and simplicity in accounting practice. If accounts are bound to be untruths anyhow, as I have argued, there is much to be said for the simple untruth as against a complicated untruth, for if the untruth is simple, it seems to me that we have a fair chance of knowing what kind of an untruth it is. A known untruth is much better than a lie, and provided that the accounting rituals are well known and understood, accounting may be untrue but it is not lies; it does not deceive because we know that it does not tell the truth, and we are able to make our own adjustment in each individual case, using the results of the accountant as evidence rather than as definitive information.

My plea for naïveté, or at least for simplicity in accounting practice, does not preclude the hope that one day we may be able to set the whole information-collecting and processing operation of an organization on a somewhat more rational basis than now exists. At present one suspects that a great deal of information is collected and processed which actually is irrelevant to the making of decisions or the taking of any kind of action. The collection of such information is pure waste from the point of view of the organization even though it may have certain scientific value. Scientific information, however, is much better collected directly than as a by-product of other operations. By contrast, a great deal of information which is highly relevant to the making of decisions is neither collected nor processed. Nobody, to my mind, has yet developed an adequate theory of information collection and processing from the point of view of the decision-making process. When this is done, we may find that both accounting and economics may each lose their life in a larger science and a larger process. Until that day comes, one can only plead for more communication and understanding between the accountant and the economist, for each has much to learn from the other, especially if each recognizes the autonomy of the other. Their concepts are often different because the purposes for which they are used are different. These differences must be borne in mind if fruitful communication is to take place.

What's Wrong with Accounting?*

By Kenneth MacNeal

C.P.A., Philadelphia

ACCOUNTING and bookkeeping used to be twins; today they are fifth cousins once removed—and they live on opposite sides of the tracks. For the most part bookkeeping is a respectable, round-shouldered craft offering a modest living and no prestige. Accounting, on the other hand, has assumed the responsibility of certifying industry's complex bookkeeping figures, and so accountants—specifically, certified public accountants—have become professional men with all the legal and social rewards and penalties that status implies. They have accepted the rewards with easy grace, the penalties with some confusion. This is due largely to the fact that the profession, younger than most of the industries it serves, is getting its first baptism of fire.

There was a time when financial reports were simply certified as correct, and the brief words were accepted at face value. When the signature following was the name of a firm of certified public accountants as standard in the profession as Cream of Wheat is in groceries, it was considered to be a warrant of the contents. Quite naturally the public believed that such reports were based on fact. Quite naturally, also, the public accounting profession did little or nothing to point out the limitations of its work. For any soured finance, Wall Street was the convenient scapegoat. Accountants, the men who certified the figures, were never criticized, since no one thought for a minute they were not acting in the best interest of all parties concerned.

This was particularly apparent during the early years of the great depression, when the mail brought shareholders solvent-looking balance-sheets one month and notices of bankruptcy soon afterward. This didn't make sense, but then nothing did; so why get excited about something that was probably all right and undoubtedly very difficult to understand? In those violent days, when principles of all kinds were dumped overboard, the principles of accounting went unchallenged. The accounting profession's chief concern was about the use and meaning of the

---

* From *The Nation* (New York), October 7–14, 1939.

word " correct " on its certifications. Except for this, the floods
of regulations relating to all financial matters bothered accounting
hardly at all; the S.E.C. rules, directed largely at issuers of
securities, demanded such a mass of additional information
about corporate affairs that the accountants found business very
good in generally very hard times. Any qualms the profession
may have had about New Deal prying were soon allayed, and
the S.E.C. became God's gift to accounting.

Then in December 1938 the fantastic manipulation of
McKesson and Robbins was disclosed. The profession was
chagrined; another huge fraud had not been detected until it
was too late. Accountants generally were critical of Price,
Waterhouse and Company, the fine old firm through whose
fingers the criminal slipped, yet they were also sympathetic for
the good reason that while every accountant exercises all his
vigilance to discover fraud, he knows that fraud on the grand
scale will always exist and not every crook can be caught. Coster
was another Kreuger, they argued. It might have happened to
any of them. But so far as the public was concerned, McKesson
and Robbins was no Kreuger case. The public had been so
enchanted by the role of the match king as an international
swindler, and so agog at all the ramifications, that it didn't get
around to placing blame. But there was no public enchantment
about McKesson and Robbins. Coster had none of Kreuger's
glamor; in the public eye he was a dirty little crook who had got
away with a gigantic swindle. This time Wall Street was not
involved in the public resentment that welled up. The accountants were. Millions of dollars' worth of drugs, crude drugs that
could be weighed and measured and felt, turned out to be fiction.
For the first time the great uninitiated public asked questions it
had never asked before. What occupied the time of the public
accountants who got fat sums for auditing? What was an audit
for if it didn't protect the investor? And what, for that matter,
was public accounting?

A public accountant undertakes, for a fee, to examine the
records of a business and to submit a report of its financial
condition, called a balance-sheet, and a report of the earnings,
called a profit-and-loss statement. Certified public accountants
are the aristocrats of the accounting world. They have passed a
prescribed state examination in accounting, auditing, and business
law, and in consequence have been authorized by the examining
state to append the letters C.P.A. to their names.

Big business does not often employ a certified public accountant to do the actual work of preparing its financial statements,

because these are usually prepared by accountants in its own employ. Neither does it employ him to detect petty dishonesty in its minor employees, because this is covered by internal check and surety insurance. ⌈It employs him primarily to obtain his certificate on its financial statements, in other words, his written assertion that the financial statements are truthful. A business must obtain this certificate in order to retain the confidence of the financial world. ⌉Without it stock exchanges would not continue to list its stock. The Securities and Exchange Commission would refuse to permit it to issue new securities. Bankers would decline to lend it money. A certified public accountant's certificate constitutes an indorsement of the honesty of corporation officials who would otherwise have little or no check on their actions. In many cases it is a stockholder's only outside assurance that the books have not been manipulated to misstate financial condition and earnings, or to conceal major fraud.

But certified public accountants do not work for nothing, and, to keep down the amount of their fees, the scope of their examination is often limited by an officer of the company at the time the accountant is engaged. This officer may feel that a verification of all entries on the books would entail too much expense, and may specify that only a partial verification, or test check, be made. He may forbid the accountant to communicate directly with the company's customers to verify accounts receivable, or he may specify that no physical count of the inventories be taken. If the accountant feels that he has been so restricted in the scope of his audit that he cannot certify all the figures on the company's financial statements, he will qualify his certificate and call attention to this. Otherwise he will sign an unqualified certificate.[1]

Up to 1933 the usual form of unqualified certificate employed by certified public accountants read, with minor variations, as follows: " We certify that the above balance-sheet is, in our opinion, a correct statement of the financial condition of the company as of December 31, 1931, and that the accompanying profit-and-loss statement is correct." This was a forthright statement—something an investor thought he could buy and sell on. Any doubts he might have as to the meaning of " correct " were promptly stilled by Webster's *Unabridged Dictionary*, which defined it in this usage as " conforming to fact or truth."

But in 1933 a Securities Act was passed by Congress, and this Act made accountants legally responsible, together with the

---

[1] The Securities and Exchange Commission now prescribes auditing procedures for companies reporting to it.

issuers of securities, for false and misleading statements which they might make relative to a material fact. The original regulations under which the Act was administered, promulgated July 6, 1933, by the Federal Trade Commission, required accountants to certify that after reasonable investigation they believed their financial statements to be true. This requirement caused great concern in accounting circles, and frantic efforts were made both within and without Congress to have it modified. On April 5, 1934, Senator Hastings of Delaware rose in the United States Senate and declared: " An audit is *not a statement of facts*, and an accountant should not be required to certify that the statements contained in a balance or profit-and-loss statement are true. *Such a certificate is really misleading*."

On April 7, 1934, subsequent to conferences with representatives of the American Society of Certified Public Accountants, the Federal Trade Commission announced that its original regulations had been amended, and that accountants need not thereafter certify to a belief in the truth of their statements. The accounting profession thereupon changed its form of unqualified certificate. After one intermediary version that proved far too candid, the following was evolved: " In our opinion the accompanying balance-sheet and profit-and-loss statement fairly present, in accordance with accepted principles of accounting consistently maintained by the company under examination, its position and the results of operations for the year."

Why was such a complete change of front necessary? The accounting profession is not dishonest. Its individual members probably possess as high a degree of personal integrity as the members of any calling in the world today. Yet upon the passage of a law which would make accountants responsible for material untruths, their profession, without a single important exception, felt impelled to change its form of certificate from one which states that its financial statements are true, to a form of certificate which merely states that such financial statements *fairly present, in accordance with accepted principles of accounting*, the position of a company. Apparently accounting principles and truth do not make good bedfellows.

A complete explanation of accepted accounting principles in all their manifold complexities would constitute a course in accounting, and cannot be attempted here. However, stripped of nice distinctions and minor exceptions, the complicated fabric of accepted accounting practices can be said to be based roughly on five broad principles, as follows:

1. The stated value of assets not held for resale should be based on their cost regardless of their market price.
2. The stated value of assets held for resale should be based on their cost or market price whichever is lower.
3. A mere rise in market price is not a profit, but if the asset is held for resale, a mere decline in market price is a loss.
4. Nothing can bring profits except what has been sold.
5. In general, under-statement is " conservative " and commendable; over-statement is dishonest and reprehensible.

These principles often give rise to figures which are fantastically out of line with the facts, but accountants are invariably ready with a pat justification for each.

Thus when patents worth millions of dollars are exhibited in a balance sheet at a total figure of one dollar, without further explanation of any kind, this is justified as " accounting conservatism." When capital stock to a par value of $1,000,000 is issued for an asset demonstrably worth only $200,000, the additional book cost of $800,000 is exhibited as a balance-sheet asset called " good-will " and is justified by being called an " accounting convention." When stock salesmen's commissions, advertising expenses, and even the early operating losses of a new business are assembled under the caption " Organization Expense," and are exhibited as balance-sheet assets at figures corresponding to their cost, this is justified by the theory that these expenses are expected to produce benefits in the future, and that they should therefore be exhibited as assets to be written off during the period in which the benefits are expected to occur.

When securities instantly saleable for $100,000 are displayed in a balance-sheet at their original cost of $5,000 with their market price shown in parentheses, if at all, this valuation is justified as being in accord with the accounting dogma: " Never anticipate a profit, but provide for all losses." It is this reasoning which causes inventories to be valued at " cost or market price whichever is lower." Accountants vigorously maintain, in defiance of economic principle, that a profit is not a profit until it has been " realized," in other words, until the asset has been sold for cash or for a collectible claim for cash.

Suppose that on January 1 a businessman invests $30,000 in 1,000 shares of General Motors stock at 30. The price of the stock rises during the year, and on December 31 the businessman sells it at 60, duly realizing a profit of $30,000. He then re-invests the entire proceeds of $60,000 in 1,000 shares of International Harvester stock at 60. Accountants who audit the businessman's books as of December 31 will certify that the businessman has an asset of $60,000 represented by 1,000 shares of International Harvester stock, and that he has earned $30,000 during the year. But suppose that on January 1 another businessman had invested $30,000 in 1,000 shares of International Harvester stock at 30. The price of this stock rises during the year, and on December 31 is selling at 60 as mentioned above. The second businessman elects not to sell it, however. Accountants who audit his books as of December 31 will certify that he has an asset of only $30,000 represented by 1,000 shares of International Harvester stock, and that he has earned nothing whatever during the year. Yet it is obvious that both businessmen started with $30,000 in cash and that on December 31 both had 1,000 shares of International Harvester stock. A decline in the price of International Harvester which would wipe out the unrealized profit of the second businessman would also wipe out the realized profit of the first businessman. In fact, there is no difference whatever between them. Yet accountants insist that the realized profit is a profit, and that the unrealized profit is not a profit.

When accountants exhibit land in a balance-sheet at its historical cost of $1 per acre, though the growth of a city around it may have caused it to be worth many hundreds of dollars per acre, their valuation of $1 per acre is justified as " going-concern value." The " going-concern-value " theory holds that the value of a fixed asset is determined originally by its cost to its owner, that this value is based upon the service which the asset is capable of rendering to its owner, and that therefore its original value to a going concern cannot change, regardless of changes in its market value, unless a physical change takes place in the asset itself.

Hence if buildings, constructed at high cost in 1929, become worth only a fraction of that cost in the depressed business conditions of later years, their balance-sheet valuation based on historical cost is justified as " going-concern value." The buildings may be mortgaged for a sum which greatly exceeds their present value, but the balance-sheet will still exhibit a value based on the historical 1929 cost, and will thus indicate that the mortgage is fully secured. That was the reason why so many people unacquainted with the principles of accounting did not understand during the depression why corporations with prosperous-looking balance-sheets were slapped into bankruptcy— there wasn't the slightest chance of renewing mortgages in the shattered real-estate market. But if what accountants said was true, the original owners of the Empire State Building, for example, should have lost nothing.

Behind these theories, which were invented largely to justify the preparation of balance-sheets which exhibit historical costs instead of values, lies the embarrassing fact that the typical certified public accountant of today is, in literal truth, likely to be little more than a graduate bookkeeper. He is not legally regarded as a valuer, nor does he so regard himself. For the most part he simply satisfies himself that the bookkeeping has been properly done, and he then uses book figures with an almost total disregard of how they may fail to reflect indisputable facts. It is this emphasis on book figures rather than on present facts that lies at the bottom of such occurrences as the McKesson and Robbins situation. Here, over many years, huge non-existent inventories and many millions of dollars of fictitious earnings were exhibited in financial statements which were duly certified by a reputable firm of certified public accountants. If these accountants had been concerned more with the assets and less with the books, if they had been concerned more with physical facts and less with documentary evidence, they could hardly have been deceived by such simple expedients as false book entries and supporting vouchers.

From one point of view the evolution of modern accounting practices may be divided into three periods. During the first, which began in medieval times and lasted until the early nineteenth century, the function of early accountants was limited, for practical purposes, to " counting the cost " of individual projects. Thus an Italian merchant might own a ship sailing from Venice to India with Venetian goods to be traded for perfumes, spices and silks. The acquired articles would be brought back to Venice and sold, or the ship might be wrecked and everything on board lost. Each venture was a separate affair, and until its conclusion the chief thing that mattered was its cost to date. By merely recording its cost, the loss or profit from the venture could be determined upon its conclusion, and a new venture embarked upon. The merchant's bookkeeper was employed solely by the merchant, and was responsible only to him. Anyone who might desire to know about the business would have to rely upon his own wits or believe what the merchant told him. Few would deny that the use of original cost as a measure of value was ideally adapted to this era.

But during the first half of the nineteenth century accounting entered its second era, and the picture began to change. The charging of interest by Christians was legalized in England in

1839, and the extension of bank credit gradually became more common. The practice arose of requiring the owner to submit a statement of his financial condition so that the banker might be informed before extending credit. To make sure that he received an honest statement, the banker insisted upon its being prepared by an independent accountant not in the employ of the owner. Thus the profession of public accounting was born.

Obviously an accountant could fulfill his obligation to both the owner and his banker by preparing the sort of financial statement the owner desired, provided that there was no over-statement of earnings or of net worth. The banker was interested only in knowing that earnings and net worth were at least as great as represented. Any under-statement of earnings and net worth merely meant that he had more security than he thought he had, which, of course, was to his advantage. On the other hand, the owner was fully conversant with his own business, and if he desired to understate the value of his own property, this could harm no one.

As a matter of fact, businessmen were quick to see that credit could more easily be obtained were they known to be in the habit of understating their earnings and net worth, exactly as a man is looked up to for being " better than his word." Secret reserves became, and still are, widely approved. Businesses which possessed huge undisclosed assets, and consequently must have made huge undisclosed profits, were looked upon with envy, and still are. Successful bankers carried their land and buildings at one dollar, or omitted all mention of them, and many, including the Bank of England, still do.

With this state of public opinion all around him, let us see how an accountant of fifty years ago reasoned as he prepared a balance-sheet and profit-and-loss statement. First, he was faced with the problem of valuing fixed assets, such as land, buildings, machinery, or equipment. There was probably no ready market for such property. He did not know what it could be sold for, or if it could be sold at all. He did not know what it could be built or bought for. He only knew what it had originally cost the owner. Therefore he was forced to value it on the basis of its original cost to the owner. And to defend this original cost valuation he was also forced to invent his theory of " going-concern value."

Despite this theory, however, the accountant could hardly help knowing that in valuing fixed assets at cost he might be over-valuing them from the standpoint of a creditor. If, therefore, the owner wished to write the value of one of these assets down to a figure below what it had cost, the accountant was quick to commend such " conservatism " and to allow the revaluation. If, on the other hand, the owner wished to write the value of the assct up to a figure above its cost, the accountant was far from quick to approve this. If he allowed such a write-up at all, it was only after having received incontestable proof of the increase in value, and after having done everything in his power to dissuade the owner.

When the accountant faced the problem of valuing current assets such as inventories, he was quite naturally on the alert to prevent their over-valuation. If the inventories had no recognized market, he could value them only at their cost. If the market price of the inventories was below their cost, he valued them at market. If, on the other hand, the inventory were wheat bought at $1 per bushel and if the current market price were $2 per bushel, the accountant would, did, and still does proclaim it to be worth only $1 per bushel, and so value it in the balance-sheet.

During this era accounting practices were fairly well suited to the conditions then existing. The owner was not deceived because he knew his business intimately. The banker and trade creditors disregarded all balance-sheet values except those for current assets, and rested secure in the knowledge that these assets were worth at least as much as represented and perhaps a great deal more. The man who lent the owner money and took a mortgage on the fixed assets disregarded the accountant's valuations altogether and made his own appraisals. The small stockholder or bondholder who might place confidence in the entire balance-sheet and profit-and-loss statement did not exist. Each party looked after his own interest in his own way, and the system worked, after a fashion.

But in the early part of the twentieth century a profound change began to take place in the ownership of business, and accounting entered its third, and as yet unrecognized, era. Businesses grew larger, and many of them became corporations. The owner-manager of such a business ceased to exist, and his place was taken by a multitude of small stockholders on the one hand, and by a hired management on the other. Mortgages on fixed assets were split into bonds and sold in small amounts to people of moderate means. Many mergers and consolidations were made, and corporate security holders grew more and more numerous, until today almost every business of any magnitude is a corporation, literally owned outright by small security holders who know little or nothing about it except information contained in the financial statements sent out by the paid management.

There are now a number of large corporations each of whose stockholders are counted in the hundreds of thousands. It is not unusual for the largest stockholder in a big corporation to own less than 1 per cent. of its stock. Frequently the entire management, including the board of directors, owns only an insignificant fraction of a company's securities. It is reliably estimated that in the United States alone there are not less than twenty million corporate security holders. Accountants now have an obligation to three parties—the small security holder, the management and the creditor; but they still continue to certify financial statements prepared in accordance with practices suited only to conditions existing before the advent of the small security holder.

These financial statements make possible the exploitation of investors on a scale previously undreamed of. Suppose, for example, that a group of financiers decide to make some money through the promotion of a new company. Certain members of the group purchase privately the required fixed assets for, let us say, $1,000,000 in cash. Then others form a corporation which repurchases these assets for $5,000,000 in cash, and a certified balance-sheet is issued exhibiting them at their cash cost of $5,000,000. After this the public is invited to buy $5,000,000 in stock at its book value, whereas it may actually be worth less than one-fifth of this amount. How reliable is the book value? Of what use is the accountant except as a sort of accessory in a confidence game?

Consider the fable of the two investment trusts—which need not be a fable. A group of financiers acquire control of two investment trusts called the " A " trust and the " B " trust. On January 1 each of these trusts is directed to make large identical investments in listed securities. During the ensuing year the market prices of these securities increase considerably, and on December 31 the " A " trust is directed to sell its securities and buy others, and thus realize its profit. The " B " trust, however, is instructed not to sell. Certified profit-and-loss statements are then distributed to stockholders and to the public, showing that the " A " trust made substantial earnings during the year, but that the " B " trust earned nothing at all. After shares in the " A " trust have risen owing to its favourable earnings report, the financiers sell at high prices part of their " A " stock. When shares in the " B " trust have fallen because of selling by disappointed stockholders, the financiers purchase at low prices additional " B " stock.

During the following year the securities market continues to rise, and on December 31 the " B " trust is directed to sell its securities, but the " A " trust is directed not to sell. Certified profit-and-loss statements are then distributed showing that the " A " trust earned nothing during the year, but that the " B " trust made enormous earnings for the year, consisting in reality of the realized appreciation in its securities for two full years. Shares in the " B " trust double in price, and the financiers sell at high prices the " B " stock that they bought a year ago at low prices. Shares of the " A " trust drop sharply owing to selling by disappointed stockholders, and the financiers buy back at low prices the " A " stock that they sold a year ago at high prices.

This sort of thing may go on year after year, but no one will ever criticize the financiers because every one of their financial statements will have been certified by reputable certified public accountants. Yet it is obvious that each year both of the trusts actually earned the same amount, and that the accountants' refusal to regard unrealized profits as profits merely supplied the financiers with a set of legal loaded dice.

Contemporary financial statements, as now prepared, frequently allow the managers and directors of a company to enrich themselves at the expense of stockholders, and to do so in the most comfortable and legal manner. Countless instances have occurred in which a company's land, its plant, or its security holdings have increased in value to a tremendous extent over many years, while this fact has been concealed from stockholders because the assets have been exhibited in the company's balance sheet only at their historical cost, in accordance with accepted accounting principles. As a result, insiders cognizant of the facts misrepresented upon the balance-sheet have been enabled to accumulate the company's stock up to the date when such assets were sold, and an enormous dividend declared. This state of affairs constitutes a vicious, although perfectly legal, defrauding of stockholders, and is exactly the sort of thing that certified public accountants are theoretically supposed to prevent. Yet in actual practice they not only make it possible, but they justify and defend it with their theory of " going-concern value."

Under modern conditions virtually all major fraud must be predicated upon false and misleading financial statements. No officer of a large corporation could walk away with his company's land or its buildings or its inventories. He could not profit by taking its accounts or notes receivable, because he would be unable to collect them. If he tried to pocket its cash or its marketable securities, he would probably be detected immediately, because these items are invariably protected with a complicated system of internal check, and accepted accounting procedure requires their physical inspection at each audit. But with the advent of the uninformed security holder, accepted accounting principles permit new types of exploitation on a scale that makes plain stealing look tame. This exploitation is not crude stealing; it is horse-trading on plush carpets with a background of authentic period furniture; it doesn't give the smartest Indian a chance, nor is it supposed to.

Disclosures following the McKesson and Robbins scandal indicate that Coster's principal purpose was not theft. In fact, it appears that his machinations gave the company itself, as apart from its stockholders, vastly more assets and earnings than it otherwise would have had. Solely on its accounting aspects, what Coster appears to have done was to cause his company's books to record fictitious purchases and sales, and to record that the profits from these imaginary transactions were used to buy additional inventories. The accountants auditing the books were instructed not to make a physical count of the inventories, but were supplied with officers' affidavits and with an incredibly complete mass of forged documentary evidence substantiating both the inventories and the transactions that supposedly created them. Because the accountants were not interested primarily in the actual assets, but were concerned almost exclusively with book figures and supporting vouchers, they were completely deceived— and so was the investing public.

But Coster, by the simple expedient of inventing fictitious transactions, was able to manipulate the profits of his company in any manner that he wished. He was after more than a man can steal; he wanted the power and the riches that come from being the head of a gigantic corporation. By reporting large profits he knew that he could get unlimited financing through the sale of common stock and establish important lines of credit with famous bankers. Then, after he had built his company, it was obvious that a series of fictitious losses would reduce his books to a truthful basis, but still leave him head of a tremendously big corporation.

When caught he was in the first phase of this long-range plan. He had sold stock over a period of years to a multitude of investors, and had formed a connection with the great banking house of Goldman, Sachs and Company. The extra profits had been shown by phenomenal trading in crude drugs, but they were retained in the crude-drug inventory—all paper work which was quite satisfactory to the accountants, and to everyone else, for that matter, except the treasurer. That this incredible scheme came within an inch of succeeding is not half so disquieting as the question of how many times it may have been executed in this country by others, *successfully*. Surely as long as accountants concern themselves solely with the books and do not insist upon examining and valuing physical assets, *there will be nothing in accepted accounting procedure to render it unfeasible*.

It can safely be said that public respect for the accounting profession is now less high than it was a decade ago. It can also be said that this decline in prestige has been caused in large part by a growing realization on the part of the ordinary man that accounting does not talk his language, and that it is quite as apt to deceive as to inform him. The tendency of the accounting profession to ignore the need for changing its methods does nothing to redeem its prestige. On the other hand, its tendency to seek an academic justification of present methods by re-defining the accounting function can only end in its eventual admission that all accounting figures, whether for assets or income, are of little value. When this admission has been made, and when it has been comprehended by the public, accounting prestige will be at low ebb.

The changes in accounting practice being currently proposed as an aftermath of the McKesson and Robbins revelations fall far short of constituting a real remedy for present accounting evils. It has been suggested that accountants be employed by stockholders rather than by officers, and that directors be made full-time salaried employees. But what good would these changes accomplish if the financial statements upon which all must rely continued to be misleading? The simple truth that accountants as well as their critics must face is that an accountant's present knowledge and training do not wholly qualify him to prepare correct financial statements. If accountants would complete their educations, to the end that they might adopt sound accounting principles and become fitted to value those assets whose economic values are not immediately apparent, they would be so qualified. Financial statements purport to exhibit current facts, not accounting conventions or historical data, and they are likely to be useful only to the extent that they do so. They are extremely likely to be mischievous to the extent that they do not do so.

Balance-sheets should be designed to exhibit a complete and

truthful statement of the financial condition of a business on a given date. Profit-and-loss statements should be designed to exhibit, in proper classification, *all* profits and losses incurred during a given period whether capital or current, realized or unrealized. In no other way can stockholders and creditors be placed on an equal footing with informed insiders, and be given a truthful basis of present fact upon which they can base their own estimates of the future.

The main problem is intellectual, not moral. The accounting profession is not corrupt. Its individual members are, on the whole, as honorable as any group of men in the country. The real difficulty lies in the sophistry, illogic and untruth of present accounting principles, which produce figures deceiving accountants, businessmen and the public alike. Not until these principles have been changed will the American public be supplied with realistic, truthful and impartial statements of business facts—needed by it more desperately today than ever before.

The Nature and Measurement of Income *

By Ronald S. Edwards

Professor of Economics, London School of Economics; Chairman, Electricity Council

INTRODUCTION

IT is the function of accountancy to record and present information in a manner calculated to give maximum guidance to those whose interests are involved. It is perhaps a criticism of much accounting literature that it fails to inquire into the *limitations* of statistical technique, and relies with too much appearance of security on the foundations of double entry bookkeeping. A knowledge of the particular method of recording data does not help greatly in deciding what information should be collected and how it should be presented.

Accountancy students are normally taught to regard double entry bookkeeping as the foundation on which the rest of the structure is built. It must, however, be clear that this statistical technique can never add anything to the original data, though it may well present that data in such a way that information becomes available which would not otherwise be disclosed. It is not intended to belittle bookkeeping. On the contrary, " double entry " has a long and honourable career of usefulness and an early association with great seats of learning which other disciplines might envy. Moreover, in the last thirty or forty years, bookkeeping devices have been improved to meet some of the more pressing needs. Yet it seems doubtful whether accountancy as a profession has done all that it is capable of doing in assisting to clarify the *ends* which accounting documents aim at

---

* This essay appeared originally as a series of articles in *The Accountant*, July–October 1938. They were reproduced in full in the first edition of this book. When the second edition was being planned, Professor Edwards offered to let us adapt the articles to current needs; he suggested that their order could, with advantage, be altered somewhat, and that they might be shortened. He kindly gave us *carte blanche* to make these changes. We have availed ourselves of his permission with the usual ruthlessness of editors. Accordingly faults of undue brevity and jerky exposition must be blamed on us rather than Professor Edwards.—*Editors*.

serving. It could reasonably be submitted that we should first decide what it is that we wish to know, and then use double entry as one of several tools for discovering it.

It should perhaps be stressed that, in approaching this subject of income measurement, we are ignoring legal requirements, and therefore no question arises of conventions dependent on company legislation and tax. As S. W. Rowland put it:

> It is possible to preserve respect for the operation of law while not confounding matters which are legal with those which are economic. The relationship of dividend to annual profit is a matter of law; the relationship of profit to industrial and commercial operations is the subject of economic inquiry.[1]

Investment and re-investment

It is difficult to discuss the problem of income measurement without at least a cursory glance at some related matters. The financing of a business involves deflection of resources from the alternative uses to which they might have been put; and the amount of resources employed in any given use will be determined by the competing demand for them for *other* purposes.

To attract purchasing power, a business has to convince the owner of the power that it will yield him *net advantages*[2] if used in this business greater than those offered by any alternative investment. The net advantages of investment in a business will usually include an expected stream of inflowing purchasing power, together with any non-material factors such as pride in a particular trade or dislike of it. To simplify the problem, it will be assumed that the expected money receipts are alone responsible for directing investment into various channels. So the owner of purchasing power has to ask two questions: (a) how much cash does he expect to receive, when and with what degree of certainty; and (b) how does this compare with the alternatives open. Purchasing power will be diverted to the business up to an amount at which it is a matter of indifference to the owner whether an additional pound goes into this particular business or into other investments.

Thus, the first problem in setting up a business is to decide how much purchasing power it should attract. The amount must depend on the expected future receipts from the business, *i.e.*, on long-period budgeting. Such budgets involve immense

---

[1] *Some Modern Business Problems*, ed. Plant, p. 250.
[2] Alfred Marshall used this term because "every occupation involves other disadvantages besides the fatigue of the work required in it, and every occupation offers other advantages besides the receipt of money wages": *Principles of Economics*, 8th ed., p. 73.

forecasting difficulties and much guesswork; nevertheless, any business which buys equipment is either implicitly or explicitly making forecasts.

In deciding how much purchasing power shall be introduced, it is necessary to forecast how it will affect the flow of receipts. Receipts may vary in two ways, either in amount or in the time when they come to hand. Both factors are important—the first because, other things being equal, men prefer to have more rather than less purchasing power, and the second because purchasing power now is preferable to the same amount later, since a price can be obtained in the market for its use. To make comparisons, the influence of time must be eliminated, by discounting all receipts to their worth at a given date, say the date of the investment. Thus, if the owner of the purchasing power is indifferent as between £100 now, £105 in a year's time, and £110 5s. in two years' time, one can say that the *present value* of the two latter sums is £100. This process of discounting must be employed in examining the effect of changes in the amount of investment.

In determining the amount of purchasing power to be invested in a given business, it is convenient to imagine it split up into very small doses, say of £1 each. Each dose added to the total will have an effect on the present value of receipts. Over a certain range each dose may add more than the last to the present value of receipts; but this range will be followed by another in which the additions to the present value get less and less, until a point is reached at which the owner is indifferent as between the addition to present value achieved by a further dose of purchasing power in this business and the alternative ways of using it.

This process of examining differences, additions or margins, whichever term is preferred, should also be adopted in considering the allocation of purchasing power *within* the business. We can visualise a number of competing uses for purchasing power within the business, but as the supply of it is limited, a pound used for the acquisition of one thing (say a machine) involves a pound less on other things. The pound spent in this way should add more to the present value of receipts than if it were spent in the acquisition of any other goods or services. The ideal or optimum distribution of purchasing power involves allocation in such a way that it would be impossible to take a pound from one use and apply it to another without reducing the present value of the receipts.

Re-investment versus withdrawal

Let us now assume that there has been invested in a business the optimum amount of purchasing power, and that this has been laid out in the way most likely to maximise the present value of the receipts to the owner. From this point onward, there is a more or less continuous inflow and outflow of money. The inflow is of two types: first, it includes receipts arising from the business itself, that is receipts from goods and services yielded by the business; secondly, it includes receipts from outside sources, that is, additional purchasing power placed at the disposal of the business. The outflow is similarly of two types. The first represents the expenditure on goods and services for the business, while the second represents purchasing power withdrawn from the business.

Now consider how a person acting rationally decides to dispose of receipts from his business. He will follow exactly the same procedure as he adopted in deciding the amount of the original investment. He will break up the amount available into small units, and will weigh the effect of re-investing each unit upon the present value of the future receipts of the business. As before, he may observe that, over a range of units, each adds more than the last to the present value of receipts; but this process will be reversed sooner or later. Re-investment will not pass the point at which it is found that a further unit will add less to the present value of future receipts than it can earn elsewhere; the units of purchasing power from this point onwards are withdrawn from the business. If it is found that all receipts from the business are re-invested before this point is reached, then the owner should introduce further purchasing power, until the total is brought up to the point at which he is indifferent about a further unit. As prices and conditions are constantly changing, the optimum investment in a business is also likely to vary.

Practical investment decisions must, of course, fall far short of the ideal, the limiting factors being the difficulty of forecasting, the state of our statistical technique and the expense of elaborate records and analysis.

Consumption

Money receipts are desirable only because of the advantages which they confer. Individuals, of course, differ in the extent to which they desire to hold money itself, and they also differ in their preferences when disposing of it. Some get satisfaction from hoarding large amounts of cash, while most of us find it convenient to hold at least a little. Apart from this, cash is exchanged for goods or services, or rights to future purchasing power. There is a wide range of alternatives.

Many outlays result in the acquisition of goods and services which are rapidly exhausted by use or by the passage of time. For example, a seat at a cinema, a railway journey and perishable food are in this category. Others, such as houses and clothing, are more slowly consumed. Individuals with purchasing power have to choose between rapidly exhausted goods and services, and slowly exhausted goods and services; or they may forgo goods and services now in exchange for the expectation of the power to obtain goods and services at some future time or times. That is to say, individuals enjoy freedom of choice between present consumption and future consumption. Some may prefer the expectation of a comfortable old age to a riotous youth, others may feel differently. But most will wish to have information about their power to command goods and services on which to base their judgment. It is the function of accounting to supply part of this information.

No one can foresee the future and, therefore, we have to make guesses about it. Some people prefer to take greater chances, others lesser ones, and the way in which each disposes of his purchasing power will be influenced by this attitude to risk. There are persons and institutions prepared to enter into contracts pledging themselves to make a number of fixed future payments in exchange for a present sum—for instance, governments issue securities whose conditions (annual interest and final repayment) are fixed in terms of so much money. As a result, owners of purchasing power are able, if they so wish, to reduce some at least of the elements of chance (though the result may be to increase other elements, for example, a change in the value of money).

The person who lends his purchasing power under such a contract knows in advance what and when receipts will flow in to him. He can, therefore, arrange his consumption during the contract period in whatever way seems to him best.

Consumption patterns and income measurement

Where there is no guarantee of a series of receipts, the problem of allocating purchasing power between present and future consumption is less simple. Suppose a man pays £100 for a machine, and wishes so to arrange his consumption that he still has £100 of purchasing power, or the equivalent, when the machine is disposed of. Future receipts will be dependent, first, on the ability of the machine to render services, and, secondly, on the price of those services.

If we assume that the machine can be moved without cost, and that there is a perfect market for such machines whether new or not, then at the end of one year it is possible to review the position, taking into account the receipts during the year and the price of the machine at the end of the year. For example, if £15 was received during the first year, at the end of which the machine had a market price of £96, the owner could have consumed goods and services costing £11, and still have been left with the equivalent of £100. If, however, the same sum was received during the next year, at the end of which the machine proved to be worthless, it is clear that no restriction of consumption would be sufficient to maintain an equivalent of £100. But though it may be impossible to make quite sure that the desired end will be achieved, it is nevertheless useful to prepare periodic statements to see what has happened during the intervals; it may be desirable to alter the rate of consumption in the light of experience.

The example of the single machine can hardly be said to present the complicated problems with which accounting is usually called upon to deal. The cash placed at the disposal of a business is normally used to acquire a multitude of different goods and services, and the receipts as they come in are partly or wholly " ploughed back." A business thus presents a constantly changing collection of goods and rights, and a fluctuating cash balance awaiting investment in the business or withdrawal. It is clear that the net balance of receipts is not by itself an indicator by which the volume of consumption can be directed. The owner must pay regard to all the goods and rights possessed.

If the owner's review covers the whole life of the business from original investment to complete and final dis-investment, there is no property and there are no rights to which he must pay regard. The cash book shows how much purchasing power has been received from the business. If the purchasing power advanced to the business is deducted from the purchasing power taken out of the business, the balance may be regarded as the fruit or *income* from the investment; and similarly of course if we add up all the receipts from the sale of goods and services, and deduct all payments for the purchase of goods and services, the resulting balance is the income from the investment.[3] (Because this information is wholly derived from the cash book, some authorities regard this as the central accounting document.)

But a concept of income such as this, which takes account only of the inflow and outgo of cash, has a very restricted usefulness. It applies well enough to those cases where the business owns

---

[3] Income and profit are regarded as synonymous in this article. Loss is negative income.

nothing except cash—all businesses at the date of winding up, but few at any other time. It is, therefore, necessary to have a more workable concept, one which covers all that a business possesses at any moment.

Accounting is a practical attempt to provide such a concept. Our next task must be to study how far it succeeds.

THE ACCOUNTING APPROACH

The accounting concept of income

Because of the interlocking nature of double entry accounts, the essence of accounting income theory (one might suppose) could be sought in balance-sheet valuation. Yet some accountants deny that the accounting concept of income is dependent on valuation. For example, Mr. G. O. May, an accountant of wide experience, argues that "Accounting is not essentially a process of valuation, as some writers on accounting and some economists conceive it to be. . . . Primarily accounting is historical in its approach, with valuation entering into it at times as a safeguard. The emphasis is on cost, though where an asset is intended for sale and its selling value is known to be less than cost, the lower figure may be substituted for cost." [4]

Differences of opinion between accountants are such that one hesitates to attempt any generalisation. Moreover, the rules set down by any one accounting writer are often in conflict with one another, or subject to many exceptions. As Professor Bonbright says, ". . . the rules by which accountants arrive at the annual income of a given enterprise are not self-consistent and could not be derived by deduction from any major premise as to what 'income' means." Professor Bonbright, however, detects, in spite of the variations, a theme which he calls "the prorated-receipts-and-disbursements" concept. This is apparently an attempt to compromise between a view of income which takes account only of receipts and payments during the accounting period, and a view at the other extreme which takes account of variations in capital. To quote Bonbright's own words:

> It still regards cash receipts as the only positive item in the income statement, and cash disbursements (or losses) as the negative item. But it does not treat all receipts as "earned" during the year when they are received, nor does it regard all cash disbursements as deductible from the gross income of the very year when they are made. Both the receipts and the disbursements are spread over a succession of years to which they are deemed "applicable." In this way, what is actually a highly

[4] G. O. May, *Twenty-five years of Accounting Responsibility*, Vol. 2, p. 309.

irregular flow of cash receipts coming to the owner of the business, and of cash payments disbursed by the owner, is artificially converted by various accounting devices into a more regular, standard flow of " net income."

The devices by which cash receipts and disbursements are assigned in part to later years, or are brought forward by anticipation from future years, are numerous, and their exposition would amount to a treatise on accounting. By all means the most important device is that of the property accounts (or " capital accounts "), whereby certain outlays made on behalf of operations that are not closed out during the year are charged at first, not against current income (profit and loss), but against " capital." If, during the year in question, the owner pays $100,000 for a factory building, his net income for that year will not be reported as reduced by this amount. The outlay will first appear in the property accounts; but it will gradually be charged off to income account through the device of a depreciation reserve. What is here called " depreciation," defined as an allowance for falling value, is really no such thing. It is an amortisation of the original cost of the asset, designed gradually to convert this capital outlay into a series of charges against income.[5]

How far this generalisation is borne out by the facts will become clear later. In the meantime, we will proceed with a discussion of the criteria which are adopted in deciding balance-sheet valuations.

Fixed and current

For this purpose the distinction between fixed and floating (or current, or circulating) assets is important.[6] The terms " fixed " and " floating " capital have a long history, and were used by Adam Smith in his *Wealth of Nations*, and afterwards by other economists including Ricardo, Mill and Marshall. The distinction has been discussed not only by economists, but by lawyers and accountants as well. We are, however, still without any completely satisfactory dividing line. Adam Smith regarded fixed capital as that equipment which affords a profit without circulating or " changing masters." Thus he treats a farmer's agricultural implements as fixed capital. By the same test, labour purchased should be treated as fixed capital, for neither the machine's services nor the labourer's services change masters once they have been purchased. Smith, however, maintains that the labour represents circulating capital in spite of the fact that both the machine and the labour derive their value indirectly from the product they combine in producing. It is true, of course, that labour is usually bought in smaller " doses " than machinery,

---

[5] Bonbright, *Valuation of Property*, Vol. 2, pp. 903–904.
[6] The terms floating, circulating and current are used indiscriminately in practice and it will be assumed that they are synonymous.

and that the investment in labour is therefore renewed at shorter intervals than is the case with machinery.

It may be useful to talk of the *investment period* for a particular asset —the period between the date when the asset comes into existence from the point of view of the business, and the date when it ceases to exist from the same point of view. Thus an item of stock comes into existence as an asset as soon as it has been bought or made, and ceases to exist when it is sold. Though the investment periods for all assets of a given type may not be constant, it is reasonable to suppose that some assets *tend* to have a relatively long investment period, and others a relatively short one. Thus assets might be distinguished according to the normal rate of their turnover. Though Adam Smith does not expressly accept this criterion, it seems to be implicit in his argument. It should be stressed that this criterion judges the matter from the viewpoint of a particular individual or business. It is not durability as such which is the test, for if this were so, diamonds would be relatively fixed assets, whereas to a diamond dealer they are likely to be relatively circulating. Ricardo maintains that " according as capital is rapidly perishable, and requires to be frequently reproduced, or is of slow consumption, it is classed under the heads of circulating, or of fixed capital." [7] But Ricardo points out that " wheat bought by a farmer to sow is comparatively a fixed capital to the wheat purchased by a baker to make into loaves." Thus it appears that Ricardo and Smith draw the same distinction, *i.e.*, rate of turnover.

Marshall follows Mill in distinguishing circulating capital " which fulfils the whole of its office in the production in which it is engaged, by a single use," from fixed capital " which exists in a durable shape and the return to which is spread over a period of corresponding duration." [8] The idea of a " single use " appears extremely obscure, but it seems that here the underlying concept is relative durability.

The economists, then, appear to adopt a durability distinction or, from the point of view of individual businesses, an " investment period " distinction. This test must be used with caution if it is used at all, for assets could move from one class to another for various reasons. The amount purchased may change, or the rate at which the services are used up may be varied. Thus a stock of coal expected to last two years may be called a fixed asset, but if expectations are changed and the period is reduced to nine months, then the stock may be called a circulating asset.

[7] Ricardo, *Political Economy* (Gonner's ed.), p. 24.
[8] Marshall, *Principles of Economics*, 8th ed., p. 75.

If this line of reasoning is accepted, a stock of coal in a mine is no different from a stock of coal above ground, and in either case if the stock is expected to last a relatively long while, say ten years, it is a fixed asset.

Accounting literature makes it clear that the investment period test is not the dividing line adopted by everyone. Some writers instead stress the *use* to which assets are put—distinguishing assets which are to be retained and used in the business from those which are to be converted into cash.[9] One can, of course, find many cases in which the investment period test and the function test give the same result; thus by both criteria the ships of a shipping company would normally be fixed capital. Similarly the selling stocks of a department store would be circulating capital. But the two criteria clash at certain points. For example, the coal purchased by a gas company, or the oil purchased by an engineering works, are not held for re-sale, and yet may turn over at frequent intervals. Thus such stocks may be fixed capital, judged by the function test, and circulating by the investment period test.

The importance of asset classification

Economists had their own reasons for making, or attempting to make, a distinction between types of capital equipment, but these reasons do not account for the central position which the classification has achieved in accounting literature. It is true that a series of important cases relating to dividends and the maintenance of capital brought the classification into prominence; but the distinction goes deeper than this.

It seems likely that the classification became important because of the everyday need of accountants to arrive at the profits of an arbitrary period. Recognising the incompleteness of the cash statement as a basis for making decisions, accountants have attempted to provide something more, and have been faced with the problem of asset valuation. This problem was more or less tractable until the growth of " roundabout methods of production " involved a large increase in the employment of specialised equipment contributing to receipts in an indirect manner. The separate selling value of that equipment was rarely a measure of its worth to the business.

At the one end of the scale, a business may possess such assets as bills receivable and book debts, which are relatively easy

---

[9] See, for example, de Paula, *The Principles of Auditing*, 9th ed., p. 74, Dicksee, *Auditing*, 14th ed., p. 201, and R. G. H. Smails, " Economics and Accounting Concepts," *The Accountant*, Vol. XCVII, p. 626.

to value. At the other end, highly specific equipment and monopolistic rights present an impossible problem. The fact that valuation within reasonable limits of accuracy is possible for some assets, but not for others, leads naturally to an attempt at classification. But accountants have gone further and maintained that the " market value " of some assets is important, and in the case of others that it is not important. It happens that a business is more closely associated with and aware of the market price of those assets which it is constantly buying or selling, *i.e.*, those which would be circulating assets under the investment period test. It is also true that under the function test those assets which are to be sold would present less difficulty in valuation than many of the other assets which are to be used. Very broadly, therefore, most circulating assets may present less valuation problems than most fixed assets.

Some meanings of " value "

" Value " or " worth " has many meanings.[10] A brief discussion of some of the concepts may therefore be advisable.

" *Value to the owner* " (or " utility " or " value in use ") means the satisfaction that the given owner expects to derive from his rights to the goods, etc., in question. Its amount is obviously a subjective matter, though comparisons are possible: a rational person presumably does not buy an article unless its utility to him exceeds the utility of the money that he pays as market price; and he will sell it if its utility is less than that of the money obtainable as a price. The worth of financial rights to their owner (with which later parts of this essay are mainly concerned) depends on his estimate of the future cash receipts that they will yield him (*e.g.*, annual dividend and eventual sale price), discounted to allow for time.

In our discussion of accounting practice, however, we are mainly concerned with " *value in exchange* " or market price. Price is the composite result of the bids and offers of all the buyers and sellers in the market.

Current market price can in fact be several different prices for a given person, as he may deal in various capacities or in various markets. Thus the price at which he can buy plant may exceed the price at which he can sell it, owing to factors such as the broker's remuneration; and he may buy his wares at a low price in the wholesale market and sell them for more in the retail market. So we must on occasion distinguish between *buying*

10 See Bonbright, *op. cit.*, Vol. I, *passim.*

price (often " replacement cost ") and *sale price* (or " realisable value ").

All types of market values may become the subject of accounting entries. However, the market does not stand still; current price may soon be higher or lower than when a transaction was enshrined in a firm's records. Accounting is largely based on historical values that may differ greatly from the corresponding current rates. We shall call the historical values *original costs*.

A person measuring business rights has thus a wide range of possible values from which to choose. Part of our task must be to ask which figure is in logic best for a particular calculation— and, in particular, is most useful as a guide to action.

Circulating assets

We must now examine in greater detail the accountant's attitude to the valuation of circulating assets. It is no easy matter to generalise about treatment in practice, as it is difficult to collect an adequate sample. There is considerable unwillingness on the part of many people to disclose information which may be regarded as confidential, while general professional indifference to research of this type makes the collection of data very laborious.

The best way of approaching the problem seems to be to examine the views of those accountants who are generally recognised as among the leaders of professional thought. The *Statement of Accounting Principles*, by Sanders, Hatfield and Moore, though it has been subject to strong criticism, represents at least a considerable section of American opinion:

> The nearest approach to a general rule for the valuation of current assets is that they be stated at (*a*) cost, or (*b*) current replacement values, or (*c*) realisable values, whichever is lowest.[11]

The late Professor Dicksee, discussing stock, book debts and temporary investments, maintained that

> if the accounts are to be upon a sound basis, it is important not to lose sight of the fact that the whole object of the business is to convert these items into cash at the earliest possible moment, or at any moment that may be thought convenient. In every case, therefore, the intrinsic value at the moment is clearly a potent factor, and any shrinkage that may have taken place must consequently be regarded as a loss, if the accounts are to be kept upon a sound basis, and as such it must be deducted from the value of the asset and debited to revenue. *Per contra* appreciations in the value of these floating assets might with equal propriety be credited to revenue; but as, pending realisation, there must always be a doubt as to whether any such appreciation has actually occurred, it is

[11] pp. 70–71.

only prudent to postpone taking credit for the assumed profit until such time as it has actually been earned. A further argument in support of this method of treatment is afforded by the consideration that the proper time to take credit for a profit on the realisation of floating assets would certainly appear to be the time when such realisation is effected.[12]

Mr. F. R. M. de Paula expressed the following view:

Floating or current assets should be valued for balance-sheet purposes upon the basis of their realisable value, as they are held with a view to conversion into cash. These assets, as a general rule, should therefore be valued at cost or the present realisable value, whichever is the lower at the date of the balance-sheet. Upon this principle, therefore, a merchant's stock-in-trade should be valued at cost or net realisable value, whichever is the lower, and in the case of book debts and bills receivable, adequate reserves must be made for bad and doubtful debts.

On no account should floating assets be valued above cost price, as the effect would be to take into account a purely fictitious and unrealised profit.[13]

These statements indicate that cost is normally regarded as the upper limit in valuing circulating assets. This is a trifle muddling, because it is not easy to see what is meant by the cost, say, of a book debt. It will make matters easier if we examine separately the two principal groups of assets which most accountants are prepared to treat as circulating. These are trade debts and stock. The separation will also prove useful in the discussion of the " anticipation " of profit.

Debts

In valuing debts the amount ultimately due is the basic figure and from it is deducted a provision to cover possible losses due to default. However, as there are factors influencing the value of individual debts which are unknown at the time of preparing the accounts, a general provision against all debts taken together is normally deducted, a statistical device of aggregation which works quite satisfactorily.

In many businesses, it is certain that cash discounts will be given in respect of some of the debts. The question arises of whether these cash discounts should be deducted for balance-sheet valuation. Debts are worth such a sum as would, when added to the costs of realisation and interest, equal the amount expected to be realised. This amount is dependent on the proportion of debtors taking advantage of the discount terms.

[12] Dicksee, *Advanced Accounting*, 6th ed., p. 12.
[13] de Paula, *Principles of Auditing*, 9th ed., p. 75.

An approximation can be reached in calculating this figure by comparing the total of debts settled, for, say the previous year, with the cash discounts allowed in that year; if the habits of debtors remain much the same and the discount terms do not vary, this comparison provides an all-round rate for discount. But to get at the balance-sheet value of the debts, a further deduction should be made for costs of collection and interest from the balance-sheet date to the average due date.[14]

In practice it is unusual to find calculations of this type. Often a rough provision is made to cover the expected discount allowable, but it is rare to find accountants deducting an amount to cover interest during the waiting period and costs of collection. It is probably a reasonable defence in most cases to say that the deduction would apply both at the beginning and at the end of the year, and as a result the measurement of a year's income would not be much affected. This is true except in years when turnover is expanding or contracting considerably. If it is claimed that the margin of error is so small as not to warrant the cost of more accurate calculation, then the approximation is justified. But it should be pointed out that profit is being overstated in a very real sense, for additional costs and additional waiting have to be faced before the amount shown in the balance-sheet will be realised; accountants here in fact " recognise profit " as soon as a sale has taken place.

When does profit arise?

But accounting literature in general maintains that no credit should be taken for profit before it is realised. Mr. G. O. May discusses the question as follows:

> What are profits and when do they emerge? is the question most frequently asked of accountants by lawyers, and indeed also by bankers, business men and economists. Now, profit earning is in general a process that is continuous and often drawn out, and the attribution of profits to particular short periods of time, though a practical business necessity does violence to fact and must therefore be arbitrary. The oft-stated rule that a profit should not be taken up until realised, does not altogether meet the case, for not only is there the question, what constitutes realisation, but there is the obvious fact that a profit is usually a balance of a number of items, some positive, some negative, which cannot all be realised simultaneously. The determination of profits is, then, the result of method and opinion, not of logical definition, and the

---

[14] These deductions have to be made in addition to the cash discount, for even if cash discount is granted *immediate* payment is not received. Assume, for example, a debt of £100, subject to 3¾ per cent. if paid within seven days. Even if the full 3¾ per cent. is taken, there will still be seven days of waiting and certain costs of collection before £96 5s. is received. Therefore, the value of the debt is less than this figure.

question arises how method and opinion are to be controlled—the ultimate purpose being, as already stated, to attribute to a particular day, month or year a profit which is the result of inter-related transactions extending over much longer periods of time. The answer is that principles have in fact been evolved which seem in general to work satisfactorily, and that such rules have acquired authority and to some extent the force of law.

H. R. Hatfield, another eminent American accountant, states that it is " a common assumption that profits exist only when the increase in wealth is realised. In this opinion there is rather unusual agreement of many accountants, jurists, and economists." As Hatfield points out, if no profit exists until it is realised, then the expressions realised and unrealised profit are tautological. Presumably what is meant is that certain increases in wealth are not to be regarded as income, while others are.

But does the accountant in fact object to a concept of income which involves any sort of anticipation of cash? Clearly this is not so, for anticipation of cash from realisation of debts is regarded as reasonable. The valuation of a farmer's stocks (which include growing animals and maturing crops) must often cover unrealised appreciation; appreciation on a wine-merchant's stocks is sometimes recognised; and accrued interest and dividends are often treated as revenue if their receipt is tolerably sure.

A concept of income which claims that certain increases in value shall be recognised and others ignored when *all* valuations, however made, involve anticipation of future receipts, requires far more justification than can be derived from the arguments usually proffered. The facts show that it is not anticipation as such to which the accountant objects, though textbooks are full of the contrary assertion.

A second argument against anticipation hinges on the cash position, and the availability of cash for dividends, tax, etc. The accountant sometimes argues that not all increases in net assets can properly be regarded as income because often they could not be withdrawn from the business without paralysing it. This may well be true. But, if our concept of income is in the nature of a mathematical expression (a change or difference between two sums), it cannot very well be made subservient to liquidity or dividend policy. The actual assets themselves are not income and we can scarcely maintain that assets must be of a particular kind before they influence income. Nor would the accountant carry this argument to its logical conclusion, for all asset valuations contribute to income in his sense, whatever the basis of valuation may be. Many a balance-sheet shows a profit that

could not be " withdrawn " without imperilling the liquid position or reducing future income to such an extent that the withdrawal is not worth while. In such cases, consumption may be
increased by borrowing or disposing of other investments.

The valuation of stock-in-trade

We have attempted to show that in the valuation of book
debts there is a deliberate attempt on the part of accountants
to forecast the inflow of cash, that is, to anticipate income in the
sense of estimating its present worth. When we come to stock-
in-trade, we find ourselves face to face with strongly entrenched
opinion that " profit must not be anticipated." To discuss the
meaning which the accountant attaches to this expression, it is
necessary to think of individual items of stock, and not of the
business as a whole. This convention of attempting to trace
profit or loss to particular assets is, of course, arbitrary where
the sale price is the result of several factors. It is, however,
a relic of more simple conditions when business was a series of
more or less separate ventures.[15] Then it was an easy matter
to sterilise, so far as the profit-and-loss account is concerned,
the effect of unfinished operations by bringing in the unsold
stocks at the price paid for them, this figure automatically
appearing on the balance-sheet in a system of double entry
bookkeeping.[16]

If a merchant had in addition to his various stocks nothing
but cash and the house in which he lived and carried on his
business, it would be satisfactory to produce accounts showing
that a series of sales had been completed, leaving a balance of,
say, £500 out of which the rent had to be paid; other assets and
liabilities could be ignored. But if the merchant believed that
the stocks which he had in hand at the end of the period would
require all his energies to sell in the following period at a price
which would scarcely cover their original cost, he would surely
take this into account in deciding his rate of consumption. As
his efforts to sell the stocks in the coming period would yield
nothing more than the sum he had invested, he would reflect
that the present worth of those stocks was less than the price
paid for them. Now an individual merchant with a small business

---

[15] See *e.g.*, H. R. Hatfield, *An Historical Defence of Bookkeeping, ante*, p. 11.
[16] Mr. G. O. May believes that this attitude reflects the philosophy of accounting.
He suggests that the reason for bringing in assets at cost is to sterilise all costs
which do not relate to sales actually made: *Twenty-five years of Accounting
Responsibility*, p. 402. Dickinson, *Accounting Practice and Procedure*, p. 93,
and Leake, *Balance Sheet Values*, 2nd ed., p. 41, also appear to support this
view, though the latter is more doubtful.

could possibly see this for himself without having it embodied
in a set of accounts. On the other hand, in a larger business
where there are several investors and not all of them are acquainted
with every part of the business, it might not be so obvious, and
the facts might well be embodied in the accounts.

But, apart from the convenience or otherwise of treating
uncompleted ventures separately, the fact remains that in a
modern business it is usually impossible to sever such ventures
from the rest of the undertaking. The selling price of stocks has
something to do with advertising policy, display, branding, all of
which involve investment. If we tried to leave in suspense all
unfinished ventures, such as investment in plant and machinery
in a manufacturing business today, we should probably not be
able to draw up a useful statement of income until the business
was sold. We cannot avoid our difficulty by bringing in all
assets at cost, for many of them will have been altered by use and
other influences. There are, however, some accountants who
would still like to value stock-in-trade in this way, though the
more generally accepted view is that this asset should be valued
at " cost or market price whichever is the lower."

Original cost is the upper limit usually accepted by accountants
in valuing stock. Debts and stock are, in fact, regarded as being
on opposite sides of the profit line. Profit is taken to be the result
of a sale. Hatfield suggests that the reason for this test is that

> it offers objective evidence of the correctness of the estimated profit.
> It does not depend merely upon the opinion of the proprietor as to the
> value of his own assets, but the opinion has been corroborated by an
> outsider, and has been manifested by the giving or receipt of cash, or
> by the making of an enforceable contract. It matters not whether the
> amount realised is represented by cash, by the note of the purchaser,
> or by the accounts receivable, provided there is no valid doubt as to
> the real value of the actually acquired asset.[17]

The importance of evidence must not be underrated, and in
the case of a debt there is usually good evidence to go on. In
valuing stock the only evidence of value is a knowledge of market
prices of similar goods; there is in addition the fact that a certain
price was actually paid for each item of stock. If a valuation
can only be made within limits of accuracy, some individuals
may prefer to place more reliance on the lower limit; but in any
case there is no quarrel with the suggestion that, in the measurement of income, reasonably substantial evidence of value should
be required by those responsible for the calculations. It is not
clear, however, that reasonable evidence of profit cannot exist

17 Hatfield, *Accounting*, p. 255.

until a sale has taken place. Professor Paton suggests that " there is reason for holding that in special cases appreciation in some forms is a legitimate supplementary evidence of income realisation." [18] Cropper also admits the possibility of appreciation in market prices being evidence of profit, provided that there is an assurance that the prices will be maintained.[19] Sanders, Hatfield and Moore hold that:

> In general, it is not proper to include in the income statement any profit arising from appreciation of unsold assets. The objection is not overcome, even when it is indicated in the report that such amounts are not available for dividends.
>
> In the case of some commodities, such as grain or cotton, regularly quoted and readily realisable on an organised exchange, it may be the most convenient thing to value inventories on the basis of the current quotations.[20]

However, writers with these views are probably in a minority, and most accountants insist on cost as the upper limit. That is to say, they do not accept the contention that the problem is *merely* one of evidence. Kester, for example, makes the statement that " no refinement of logic can obscure the obvious fact that goods are bought to be sold and that no profit arises until the sale takes place." [21] Yet, in spite of this, practically all accountants agree that:

> Accepted accounting practice requires that unrealised declines in the value of current assets should be reflected in the income statement.[22]

The difficulty of discussing the " cost or market " rule is enhanced because of the quite bewildering differences in practical application. To take one example: the total valuation will depend on whether the cost of all the stock is compared with the market value of all the stock, or, alternatively, individual items are compared. If the lower figure for each item is taken, the total is almost certain to be less than the total cost or total market value of the stock. Then there are the discussions on whether cost should include carriage inwards, and whether it should reflect the fact that cash discount may be taken by the business in paying for the stock.

So far as the writer is aware, the history of this method of valuation has not been traced by research workers. That it is not of recent origin is shown by the fact that it was recognised as a principle at the middle of last century:

[18] Paton, *Accounting*, p. 566.
[19] Cropper, *Higher Bookkeeping and Accounts*, 4th ed., p. 24.
[20] *A Statement of Accounting Principles*, pp. 39–40.
[21] Kester, *Accounting, Theory and Practice*, Vol. 2, p. 227.
[22] Sanders, Hatfield and Moore, *A Statement of Accounting Principles*, p. 40.

The recognised principle that stock should be valued at cost price (unless depreciated in value) and that no profits should be estimated unless realised, much less upon goods only partly manufactured, and subject further to the contingency of a falling market, may be questioned if applicable to the case in question. Upon this plan it would be necessary to value all hides in process of tanning, and the produce thereof, at their cost price, to which would be added the cost of tanning material consumed, the proportion of wages disbursed for the attendant labour, and a sum for rent and expenses. But, *apart from the insuperable difficulties attending this*, there are reasons why a tanner is justified, to some extent, in estimating a profit upon goods in process of manufacture, and in connection with which his time, skill, capital and labour have for a period of six months been brought into requisition.[23]

Thus, even in those days the rule did not pass without challenge. More recent criticism comes from Professor Paton. In discussing the cost or market rule, he states that " the practice, imported from Europe, did not make marked headway in this country (U.S.) until the advent of the Federal income-tax programme." [24] In Britain, too, it may be supposed that the rule has become the more firmly established because it is accepted by the Inland Revenue in computing income for tax purposes. Its effect is to delay liability, and for this reason it is bound to be popular.

Professor Paton commences his criticism in the following terms:

No writer has ever been able to find a single definite point supporting the proposition that " cost or market, whichever is the lower," is a sound accounting rule, while the array of clear-cut objections is overwhelming. In general, the recognised concepts and procedures of accounting are entirely out of harmony with this device; by implication it is constantly under the fire of the professional accountant himself.[25]

He goes on to level the charge that the rule is inconsistent, and is employed with the utmost crudity. He maintains that the business world is concerned with market values at all times and not merely when these values bear a certain relationship to earlier values.[26]

This charge of inconsistency is sometimes rebutted by an appeal to the requirements of " conservative finance." Such an appeal, however, strikes at the very root of accounting as a subject concerned with accurate measurement. It may well be argued that absolute accuracy in measurement is out of the question,

---

[23] J. Sawyer, *Bookkeeping for the Tanning Trade*, 2nd ed., 1862. (Our italics.)
[24] *Journal of Accountancy*, March 1938, p. 201.
[25] Paton, *Journal of Accountancy*, March 1938, p. 202.
[26] It appears that Professor Paton would prefer valuation at original cost, but if any other method is adopted such as replacement cost he desires it to be adopted *consistently*.

having regard to the data available; however, the best possible estimate should be made, not one designed merely to deter the investor from consumption. It is not, we presume, the function of the accountant to invent methods of curing improvidence.

It may be important for reasons other than income measurement to know the amount and value of stocks on hand. For example, a department store may wish to compare the efforts of its different buyers and for this purpose may wish to compare sales and purchases of stock for each department every month or year. The question then arises as to the valuation of the stock when a new buyer takes over, or at the end of any accounting period. It is likely that the buyer, if he were free, might not invest in some of the goods in stock at the price which was paid for them; on the other hand, he might be prepared to pay more for other items of stock than they had actually cost. He would not in any case be prepared to pay more than the replacement cost, as he could acquire similar goods on the market at this figure. It would be just worth while for the buyer to take the stock at a valuation equal to such a sum as would leave a difference between the valuation and the expected selling price of the stock, wide enough to cover (a) the avoidable costs [27] involved in the holding and selling, and (b) a contribution or margin at least as great as could be obtained from investing the sum in other goods. Clearly, goods ought not to be bought if they will not yield a margin wide enough to cover the costs which would not be incurred if they were not bought. Moreover, if they survive this test, but other goods are available which would also survive it and make a better contribution to " overhead " and profit, those other goods should be bought instead.

Thus, compare the following:

	Article A	Article B
Purchase price	40	37
Add Avoidable costs ..	4	6
	44	43
Expected selling price ..	51	51
Contribution to overhead and profit	7	8

[27] Avoidable cost is the difference between the total cost of the business if it takes over and sells the stock and the total cost if it does not.

It would seem that if article A is in stock at the end of an accounting period, while B would have to be bought, the maximum price which the new period could be charged for A would be £39, because after deducting from the expected selling price of £51 the costs which still have to be incurred, namely, £4, there would be available £47, thus leaving a margin of £8, which is the same as the contribution which would be yielded by the purchase of B.

One criticism that can be expected is that of impracticability. It might be suggested that no one could value on the basis of contribution to overhead cost and profit. Yet this is exactly what a buyer in a department store, for example, is doing all the time; he is choosing out of an almost unlimited market those goods which will pay him best. To the various alternatives available we add one more, the stock in the business, and adjust the valuation thereof to such a point that the buyer would, of his own free will, acquire these goods rather than any others which are on offer. It will, of course, be clear that the valuation cannot exceed replacement cost, otherwise the buyer would take the similar, but cheaper, goods from the market.

This valuation may not be the value of the stock to an outside buyer. It is merely the value to certain officials of the business. Their judgment, moreover, is conditioned by many other factors relating to the business—such as the existence of adequate selling facilities and personnel. They can appraise the one type of asset—stock—only against the background of all the other assets, and not *in vacuo*. Much the same argument can be applied in turn to every type of asset. This raises the fundamental question of whether we can measure capital and income by summing separate asset values, instead of treating the firm as a whole, a question to which we return later.

Those who discuss the cost or market rule do not appear to be in agreement on the meaning of market value. Some adopt replacement cost, while others prefer to take the expected selling price of the goods if disposed of in the ordinary course of business, even though this is higher than replacement cost. It seems to the writer that any valuation above replacement cost must result in a misleading income statement. Valuation at selling price seems to be over-valuation in the sense that costs must still be incurred in disposing of the stock, and the next accounting period is robbed of its chance of earning income on the investment it takes over.

Stocks in a manufacturing business

The problems of an industrial concern are usually more complex than those of a trader. Let us take, for example, replacement cost of finished goods in a firm which makes one branded article. If we asked the manager to state the price at which he would be just prepared to take the existing goods rather than manufacture a fresh stock, his answer would be conditioned by the rest of the assets of the business and its commitments. The worth of the stock to the manager would be equal to the addition to his total costs which would be necessitated by the increase in the rate of manufacture if he had to re-build the stock. These additional costs would, for one thing, depend on how quickly he needs the stocks. He may need them immediately to avoid a penalty clause in a contract for delivery by a certain date; in which case the additional cost may be much higher than if production could proceed slowly.

The valuation difficulties are much more evident when we turn to work-in-progress. The accountancy profession has never evolved a satisfactory technique for the valuation of work-in-progress. The discussion of the problems in most of the accepted works on accounting is conspicuous by its absence. Mr. de Paula, however, has stated his views on the subject in the following terms:

> It is submitted that the process stocks should be taken as a whole and valued at current standard cost, and also at the net realisable value, *i.e.*, the sale price of the finished product, less allowances, costs of selling, distribution and cost of completion of manufacture. If in total the net realisable value is below the standard cost value, then the lower valuation should be adopted.
>
> The standard cost would cover raw materials, direct labour and normal works overhead applicable to the partly manufactured goods. No addition should be made for selling, distribution, administration and financial charges.[28]

This statement seems subject to several criticisms. In the first place, current standard cost including normal works overhead is based partly on arbitrary allocations. In view of this it cannot be regarded as a satisfactory figure on which to base income calculations. The obvious objection to net realisable value, is that it assumes that the next period shall complete and dispose of the stock without having the opportunity of earning any remuneration for so doing; it anticipates income as no provision is made for interest on the valuation figure or on the costs of completion. Mr. de Paula, apparently, holds the opposite

[28] de Paula, *The Principles of Auditing*, p. 114.

view, for he says, " It will be appreciated that there is no question of anticipating profit by the adoption of this principle, as the net realisable value is only adopted *if it is below cost* and, therefore, there cannot be any profit in the valuation." [29] This view appears to depend on the separation of profits for each asset.

The same problems of separate valuation will be found in connection with raw materials. Here again most accountants accept the view that original cost should be the upper limit, but the alternative of replacement cost which is often adopted, if less than original cost, is criticised. Rowland, for example, suggests that replacement cost is irrelevant:

> Coming to raw materials, here again it may be suggested that cost of replacement need not enter the argument. The question to be kept before the mind is whether our undertaking can ultimately sell the finished goods at a price which will more than cover direct and indirect costs. If we can cover a cost based on the price we actually gave for our raw materials, then no loss will occur, and it seems to be a piece of pedantry to depress the profit of this year just because we did not do as well as we might have done in ideal circumstances. On the other hand, there is here an obvious case for writing down if the net expected price of realisation is not such as to yield a profit.[30]

To the present writer it appears that replacement cost must at least provide an upper limit to value. If a dental mechanic uses gold in the manufacture of artificial teeth, he would actually be ignoring plain facts if he said that his gold stock was worth more than other gold stocks which he could acquire in the market. Valuation at net realisable value, *i.e.*, at such a figure that as far as can be estimated " no loss will be incurred in the succeeding year upon the sale of the corresponding finished product," [31] seems to deny the following year the possibility of making a profit while saddling it with the job of making and disposing of the goods.

The manufacturer's valuation of stocks, even more than the merchant's, depends on possession of the other assets. For instance, the valuation of work-in-progress must assume the existence of the plant necessary for its completion. Considered separately, the assets in a factory cannot satisfy an adequate theory of income.

Information for the investor on stocks

It may not be out of place to point out some items of information which might be useful to investors. In a merchant business

[29] *Op. cit.*, p. 114.
[30] *Some Modern Business Problems*, ed. Plant, pp. 268–269.
[31] de Paula, *op. cit.*, p. 110.

they might like to know the original cost of stock-in-hand, its replacement cost, and the price which the buyer would be prepared to pay for it at the date of the balance-sheet. In a manufacturing business, the original cost and replacement cost of raw materials would be useful information. For finished stock, in addition to quantities, it would be useful to know the expected selling price, and the rate of turnover, and possibly certain items of cost, such as materials and labour at current prices. In the case of work-in-progress, information about quantities and the current cost of direct materials and labour would be helpful. Such information, while making no pretence at valuation for income purposes, would help the investor, or his professional advisers unacquainted with the actual running of the business, to form some views about the near future.

Fixed Assets

Most accounting authorities emphasise the importance for valuation of the distinction between fixed and circulating assets. We have seen that, so far as circulating assets are concerned there is little agreement on definition or method of valuing. Now what of fixed assets—assets " fixed " either by the concepts of function or rate of turnover? In discussing these, Dicksee says:

> The justification for thus ignoring fluctuations in the value of capital assets is that these assets have been acquired, and are being retained, not with a view to their eventually being realised at a profit in the ordinary course of business, but with a view to their being *used* for the purpose of enabling trading profits to be made in other ways. For example, there is no fixed connection between the realisable value of a ship and its earning capacity; and in the case of a factory, its value to the undertaking depends merely upon the accommodation that it offers, and is entirely irrespective of any speculative rise or fall that may have taken place in the value of land or building materials. Similarly, the value of machinery to a business depends upon the amount of work that can be turned out, and not upon the market price of iron or steel at that particular time. For practical purposes, therefore, these fluctuations may fairly be said to be of no account, and in any event it is quite an open question whether, pending a realisation (which is not contemplated), any more reliable basis of value could be adopted than the actual cost in the first instance—subject, of course, to due provision for depreciation.[32]

Elsewhere he says:

> The points to be borne in mind here are that depreciation may reduce their value, and that fluctuation may increase or reduce their value. So far as depreciation is concerned, inasmuch as use has directly

[32] *Advanced Accounting*, 6th ed., p. 12.

contributed to the profit earned, it is clearly an expense with which profit may fairly be charged. The only question is " How ? " which will be considered in full under the head of depreciation. On the other hand, fluctuation is something altogether apart from trading profit and loss, being merely an accidental variation (owing to external causes) in the value of certain property owned but not traded in; to carry the amount of such variation to profit and loss account would be to disturb and obscure the results of actual trading, and so render comparison difficult, if not impossible.[33]

We will comment only on one or two points which seem to beg the facts. The suggestion that there is no fixed connection between the realisable value of a ship and its earning capacity seems to ignore the point that the realisable value of a ship *as a ship* depends *entirely* on its earning capacity. Secondly, the value of machinery to a business depends on the expected earnings of the business which are themselves dependent on many factors, one of which will be the price which the business and its competitors have to pay for new machinery, which price is related to the market for iron and steel. Another point is that depreciation appears to be regarded as a function of *use* only. It seems a curious and detached view of business which suggests that it will obscure the results of trading if we include as losses the effects of those unforeseen changes which Dicksee calls " external." In any case, external and internal influences can rarely be disentangled for the purpose of separately assessing their effects.

It would take far more space than is available to pick our way through the many and conflicting statements that have been made about the accounting valuation of fixed assets, but on one point practically all accountants are agreed: the separate selling value of fixed assets is irrelevant for balance-sheet purposes.[34]

The truth of this is very obvious in the case of some assets— for example, the possession of an organisation which runs smoothly is partly acquired by expensive trial and error for every business. In so far as this is the case, it is clearly impossible to separate completely this asset from the rest of the business; it has no existence except as part of the organisation, and no separate market price. Preliminary expenses offer similar difficulties. This, however, is part of the general conceptual problem of defining a separate asset: its value depends on the extent to which we assume that the equipment of the business is to be broken down and sold to separate buyers. Thus the difficulty

---

[33] *Auditing*, 14th ed., p. 199.
[34] Except presumably for those fixed assets which the business has decided to dispose of.

which is present in all separate asset valuation for income measurement is particularly obvious with fixed assets. The separate selling prices of pieces of equipment do not necessarily indicate their influence on the income of the business except, of course, to the extent that they might suggest the minimum contribution to receipts.

In the case of second-hand machinery, even if we exclude the important element of indeterminacy arising from the difficulty of estimating the amount and type of use which it has received, there are also costs of movement, setting up and taking down. The business had to pay the costs of carriage and setting up. If the asset is sold to someone else, not only are the results of these costs of no further value, but the equipment has to be dismantled and carried somewhere else, thus involving further costs which reduce the net selling price.

Thus there has been due recognition of the fact that net selling price is of little assistance to valuation for income purposes. There has, on the other hand, been an insistence on the importance of original cost. The importance of original cost and the unimportance of selling prices are often brought together. Mr. de Paula, for example, says:

> Fixed assets will appear in the balance-sheet at cost, less the depreciation written off to date, and this represents the present value of such assets to the particular undertaking as a going concern, or, in other words, the value of such assets to the proprietors of the particular business. Current realisable value and break-up value are disregarded as these do not affect the working lives of the particular assets at all.[35]

There is wide acceptance of the view that fixed assets are brought into the balance-sheet at their *going-concern* value. So far as the writer is aware, this expression has never received at the hand of an accountant a formulation which could be regarded as logically satisfactory. One might assume that the value of an asset to a going concern is the difference between the value of the concern with this asset and its value without it, subject to an upper limit of replacement cost since the asset cannot be worth more than this sum. But this method of valuing would give curious results. If we assume that two assets working together will produce a certain stream of receipts, we can place a value on these two assets together. Now let us assume that either asset has no value at all unless used in conjunction with the other. It follows that each is worth to the going concern the whole of the expected receipts, for the difference between the

[35] de Paula, *The Principles of Auditing*, 9th ed., pp. 74–75.

value of the business with and without either asset is the difference between all the receipts and no receipts at all. It follows that if we sum the going-concern value of the assets, we get in this case a total of twice the value of the business, or the total replacement cost of the assets, whichever is the lower. It can be shown that by taking away from the business each piece of equipment in turn and examining the difference to the value of the business made by the subtraction, we obtain a series of values which, if summed, give the value of the business only under assumptions relating to divisibility of equipment, which accountants would be the first to agree rarely exist in the real world.

The expression " going-concern value " is unfortunate in that it is misleading. Accountants, when valuing fixed assets, do not look at the value of the asset to the going concern. This, however, does not make it any easier to say what they do look at without going through the mass of literature on depreciation.

The nature of depreciation

The physical state of equipment may be one factor governing its value. This is so because the physical state influences either future receipts or payments, or both. If a machine is wearing out, then the value of the future expected receipts arising from the machine gets smaller and smaller. Alternatively, the flow of receipts, so far as it is dependent on the working of the machine, can possibly be maintained by repairing and renewing parts of the machine or the whole of it. This has the effect of increasing the present worth of future payments. But the future receipts and payments of the business are also dependent on the way in which prices move—the price of the product and the prices of replacing and repairing the equipment. To attempt to eliminate the effects of price changes and to have regard only to physical condition may possibly make the job of accounting an easier one, but it is to be doubted whether it makes it a very useful one.

Yet this seems to be the deliberate intention of at least one eminent accountant. P. D. Leake states that going-concern value is " based upon the unexpired original capital outlay on plant computed by deducting from historical cost, less estimated scrap value, an equal annual instalment in respect of each year of the estimated efficient life which has expired." [36] From this it appears that one has to make an assumption relating to the number of years during which the plant is expected to be retained, and then to assume that the services rendered by the plant each year will

[36] *Balance Sheet Values*, 2nd ed., p. 11.

be of equal value. As the value of the services rendered by the plant will depend on the demand for the product, and as the years of service will depend *inter alia* on this factor, on current cost of similar equipment and on changes in technique, the assumptions which are implied seem to have little to recommend them except simplicity. Leake, however, holds that " the appropriate balance-sheet values of [tangible wasting assets] should be computed strictly on the basis of unexpired cost to the present owner, apart altogether from considerations of future profits or annual value expected to arise out of their application to industrial purposes." [37] Elsewhere he says:

> The going-concern values of material wasting assets, being always equal to the owner's unexpired cost, are not affected in any way by considerations as to the probable cost of replacement, or as to whether the undertaking happens to be earning a small or a large percentage of profit on the real capital employed or by any considerations whatever based on the estimated amount of future earnings.[38]

It seems fairly clear from this that going-concern value is not the value of the equipment to its owner or to any alternative user—it is merely original expenditure adjusted in an arbitrary manner. But Leake is not alone in his advocacy of valuation at original cost less straight-line depreciation. His views find wide acceptance both in the United States and in this country. To the present writer many of the arguments advanced in favour of it appear to be groundless even if we suppose that separate asset valuation is possible and useful. For example, Professor R. G. H. Smails compares this procedure with an attempt to adjust the valuation in the light of new knowledge. He supposes that an asset which is being written off on the straight-line basis is revalued, and is found to be worth 800 dollars as against the book figure of 1,600 dollars remaining after two years' operation. He then says:

> Is income of the third period to be stated at 800 dollars less and the entrepreneur to be urged or forced to restore to his business the amount " overdrawn "? Periodical income computed in this way would fluctuate so widely as to be a useless concept for the formulation of a personal standard of living or for the conduct of day-to-day financial affairs. Surely the artificial concept of the accountant with its constant depreciation charge based on the original estimate is superior to this theoretical alternative, in spite of the abrupt valuation adjustment that may be involved in the final period, *i.e.*, the period in which the fixed asset becomes valueless? [39]

[37] *Ibid.*, p. 21.
[38] *Ibid.*, p. 60.
[39] Smails, " Economic and Accounting Concepts," *The Accountant*, November 6, 1937, p. 627.

This outlook on trouble seems to be similar to that of which we accuse the ostrich. Surely a rational personal standard of living does not depend on ignoring the future. A person may, of course, decide to save nothing for the future quite deliberately, but he does not want to do so accidentally because of the inconvenience of giving recognition to his expectations of future income. He does not want to put his head in the sand and refuse to believe that what he possesses has gone down in value by 800 dollars. Moreover, the question of whether the entrepreneur is to be forced to restore the amount " overdrawn " is an example of a notion which often colours accounting pronouncements. The view is implicit that investors *ought* to keep their capital intact. Why should they?

This view possibly accounts for a certain amount of misunderstanding which results in many arguments about the nature of depreciation. One often hears the merits of this or that method of calculating depreciation discussed from the point of view of the provision of funds for replacement of assets. One hears it said that depreciation should be calculated on the basis of the expected replacement cost of a given asset in order that money *should be available* for replacement. In the same way one hears people compare the merit of investment of depreciation quotas inside or outside of the business in the light of the need for funds at a future date for renewal of assets.

Now depreciation, in so far as it affects the measurement of income, is in no way related to financial exigencies. The expected replacement cost of an asset is important for valuation purposes not in order to ensure a sum of money in the future, but because, assuming the asset is worth replacement in the light of alternative investments, the present value of this future expense is a factor reducing the present value of the business. The present value of the business will be greater or less according as the discounted value of the replacement cost of the equipment is less or greater (provided that this replacement was assumed in estimating the flow of future receipts). Thus, if replacement cost rises, the present value of the business will be reduced thereby, but against this must be placed the fact that the receipts from the product of the business may also be increased by the rise in the replacement cost of equipment. The two influences may or may not cancel out; one must know all the other influences to decide the net result. One thing is certain—the argument as to whether depreciation of equipment should be calculated on original or replacement cost is, taken by itself, practically devoid of meaning for income measurement.

The other question, *i.e.*, the disposal of depreciation quotas, is from the point of view of the investor purely a matter of comparing net advantages. As each £1 becomes available, it is necessary to ask whether if ploughed into the business it will add more to the present value thereof than the present value of the receipts which could be obtained by investment elsewhere.

The last point which we shall have space to deal with concerns the different bases of calculating depreciation, *i.e.*, the straight-line, reducing balance, and annuity methods under which annual depreciation charges remain constant, fall or rise respectively. All of these are over-simplifications of a complex problem arising from an artificial segregation of factors. If we assume all prices are constant, we have only to take into account the fact that the time for replacement is brought nearer, either because of use or the mere passage of time. Depreciation is the present value of the difference between providing for the sum needed for replacement at, say, the end of nine years instead of ten. Both the straight-line and reducing balance methods ignore the process of discounting which is necessary in arriving at *present* cost. The annuity method takes this into account, but ignores other factors—for example, mounting outlays on repairs. If we exclude all price changes and assume the technical efficiency of the equipment is maintained at a constant level, then the annuity principle, taking into account and discounting all future payments, is satisfactory.

Obsolescence

The term obsolescence usually implies a fall in value due to causes other than physical wear and tear. Most people would agree that a reduction in the value of existing equipment resulting from invention is obsolescence, while many would accept the view that a fall in the value of equipment because of a fall in the demand for the product is also obsolescence.

At this stage there are two points which must be emphasised. For income measurement depreciation, however caused, is a factor to be considered. The other point is that obsolescence is not necessarily an influence which cannot be foreseen. A businessman may forecast correctly that his sales will fall off in the course of a few years, he may even guess fairly accurately how long it will be before a given type of machine will be superseded by a better; every businessman has to attempt such forecasts in order to decide whether a given investment will be worth while.

Many accountants believe that, in setting a term to the life of equipment for the purpose of calculating a depreciation rate, obsolescence should be taken into account. Carter, for example, says:

> In certain businesses, the possibility of *obsolescence*, *i.e.* machinery being rendered obsolete by the later and better inventions which will do the same work more quickly and more cheaply, is a very important factor, and influences largely the " rates " of depreciation. If the loss sustained by obsolescence is unexpected and very large, it is not carried to profit and loss at once, but written off gradually over a number of years; but where such obsolescence can be foreseen, it should be provided for in anticipation.[40]

We might comment in passing on the curious practice of not " recognising " a large amount of obsolescence merely because it is large. It is a strange view of the function of accounting which suggests that we should pretend that we have assets which do not exist merely because we might pull in our belts if we were acquainted with the facts. Yet this is not an uncommon notion; the writer has seen the cost of a fire, not covered by insurance, suspended in the balance-sheet as an asset and written off over the five years following the fire! This, of course, involves deliberate overstatement of current income and understatement of future income.

Mr. de Paula [41] seems to consider that expected obsolescence should be taken up in the depreciation rate, and that in addition there should be a contingency reserve for unexpected obsolescence. This brings us to another view sometimes expressed by accountants, namely, that obsolescence should be regarded not as a charge in calculating profits, but as an appropriation of them.

Let us first discuss the attempt to anticipate obsolescence and incorporate it in a rate of depreciation. This seems sensible if it does not imply rigidity. A decision to write off a particular asset over a period of five years may be the best estimate possible at the time of purchase. But with the passage of time further information will become available. At the end of each accounting period, surely, management should revise estimates; the depreciation rate will change. It is useless to object that this may mean a variable charge for depreciation each year. Of course it may; obsolescence arises because of changes in values and, if obsolescence is to be dealt with at all, then it seems reasonable to deal with it as accurately as possible, even though this involves a variable charge. Why should the attempt to measure income be nullified because forecasts have proved incorrect? Indeed, failure to record obsolescence promptly must lead eventually,

---

[40] Carter, *Advanced Accounts*, revised edition, 1937, pp. 645–646.
[41] de Paula, *Principles of Auditing*, 9th ed., p. 125.

in grave cases, to a sweeping adjustment sometimes associated with capital reorganisation. Often these reorganisations are held over either because the loss is not certain, or because it is inconvenient to recognise it. Lack of certainty applies to almost every valuation; anyone who attempts to measure income must face this fact. Those who have to make plans are better off with information whose accuracy is certain only within limits, than if they have no information at all.

Next, consider the view that obsolescence should be ignored in measuring current profit, and dealt with by retaining some part of profits in anticipation of future obsolescence. This must lead in some years to the overstatement of current profit, and so nullifies (to quote Professor Paton) " the best efforts of the accountant to develop the art of periodic reporting on a significant basis. Actually we do have good years and bad years in business, fat years and lean years. . . . It may be that in some situations the year is too short a period through which to attempt to determine net income . . . but if this is the case, the solution lies not in doctoring the annual report, but in lengthening the period." [42]

In short, if the obsolescence reserve is designed to deal with obsolescence which has taken place, then it represents a reduction of capital and of the income of the year in which it takes place. If the obsolescence has not taken place, then the reserve represents saving (possibly fixed saving) on the part of the owners; it is an addition to capital and should be shown as such or as a *general* reserve.

Intangibles

The lack of settled practice relating to the so-called intangible assets is a result of two things—separate asset valuation and attempts to avoid the recording of fluctuations. Hatfield's comment on the usual definition is interesting:

> Intangible assets are defined as meaning patents, copyrights, secret processes and formulas, goodwill, trade-marks, trade brands, franchises and other like property. The phrase is not particularly appropriate and, except by enumeration, the separation between tangible and intangible assets is not easily made, accounts receivable are considered tangible assets, although literally there is nothing tangible about them. Real estate is considered typically tangible, a franchise intangible. But there is no real difference between them as regards tangibility, materiality, or realness. Real estate represents a right, tracing ultimately back to

---

[42] *Journal of Accountancy*, 1938, p. 199. Some large companies today, instead of writing off depreciation and obsolescence in a predetermined way, charge a lump sum each year which varies fairly directly with the success of operations in that year.

the sovereign power which permits an individual to make use of a portion of the earth's surface. The uses to which it may be put are many, but not unlimited. The owner may not, for instance, erect a glue factory in a residential district, nor, even before 1921, locate a saloon within a given distance of church or school. A franchise is similarly a right granted by the sovereign power permitting an individual to make certain restricted uses of a portion of the earth's surface. It is an important but not an essential difference that the uses are even more restricted than in the instances cited above. It is certainly not an essential difference that the portion of land is a long narrow strip rather than a square forty-acre tract. While the term intangible assets is without etymological significance, it is still of use as a collective term, in general embracing the items given in the definition just quoted.[43]

It is clear that the separate valuations of these assets is likely to be difficult or impossible. The accountant, however, is faced with the fact that, if expenditure has taken place, he must charge it to profit and loss or carry the whole or part of it forward, disclosing it on the balance-sheet. He cannot, therefore, escape the problem by merely ignoring it—some action is necessary. As a result, we get arbitrary charges to profit and loss. Let us take, as an example, expenditure on registration and flotation of a limited company. Cropper says that the usual practice is " to spread the expenditure over the first three or five years of the company's trading." [44] Heavy initial advertising is treated in the same way. Other expenses like the cost of experimentation in forms of organisation are often completely ignored in valuation. Now it may be that preliminary expenses, advertising and experimentation have no influence on the value of the business at the end of the accounting period. If they have, however, that influence cannot satisfactorily be isolated from the rest of the flow of future receipts and future payments. As a result, there is a great deal of question-begging in connection with this type of asset. Accountants will sometimes say that the expenditure carried forward is merely " deferred revenue expenditure " or a " fictitious asset," [45] terms which seem to the writer almost meaningless. The expenditure is not deferred, for it has already been made, and if it is revenue expenditure, as most accountants use the term, then it should not be carried forward. To say that the expenditure is merely " held up " also fails to avoid the issue, for it is necessary to decide how much to hold up, and this decision affects the income for the year. What right a " fictitious asset " has in the balance-sheet the writer does not know.

---

[43] Hatfield, *Accounting*, p. iii.
[44] Cropper, *Higher Bookkeeping and Accounts* (4th ed., 1930), p. 36.
[45] See Cropper, *op. cit.*, p. 94.

Some accountants believe that intangibles should be completely eliminated from the industrial balance-sheet:

> ... exchangeable property consists of two clearly distinguishable kinds of value, *i.e.*, first, material things which our senses tell us actually exist and which are proper subjects for industrial accounting, and, second, mere rights to profits and other value expected to arise in future years, falling mainly under the head of commercial goodwill. The appropriate values at any time, of all actually existing material things applied to industrial production, can always be ascertained, without much room for doubt, with the aid of simple and logical accounting rules. While, on the other hand, the constantly fluctuating exchangeable values of mere rights depending upon the probability of earning, in years still to come, profits over and above ordinary competitive profits, do not affect real profit and loss, and moreover they cannot be computed because there are, and can be, no accounting or any other rules capable of being applied.[46]

It is not difficult to think of industrial concerns whose principal asset consists of the right to a name; the ignoring of changes in the value of this name when measuring income would seem to restrict unduly the usefulness of accounting concepts. Moreover, we should be curious to know the simple and logical accounting rules for valuation of material assets, for Leake's going-concern value is not a valuation at all, but merely a statement of original cost from which is deducted each year a sum which depends on an estimate made when the asset was bought.

Moreover, Leake's use of the term " competitive profits " is unfortunate. It is possible for a business which has invested in intangibles to earn only the competitive rate on its total investment—but this does not mean that the intangibles are valueless. The notion arises, from what is called the super-profits theory of goodwill, which is an attempt to give a rather grand title to quite a simple notion.

Goodwill

When a business changes hands, the purchaser or his advisers try to estimate the future receipts which it will yield and the future payments which will be necessary to produce those receipts. The evidence will include the accounts for past years. The buyer then decides what sum he is willing to give for this stream of future receipts less payments, having regard to the risks. If the vendor is prepared to accept this sum or a lower one, the deal goes through. The accountant to the purchaser is then faced with the fact that he has to credit cash and debit some

---

[46] Leake, *Balance Sheet Values: The Limitations of Industrial Accounting*, 2nd ed., pp. vi–vii, Preface.

other account or accounts. For some of the assets, he will have separate valuations culled from one source or another; but the balance of the purchase-price he has to call something, and he calls it goodwill.[47]

One of the things on which nearly all accountants agree is that this sum must not be written up—even if it is clear beyond all reasonable doubt that the value of the business has risen. Original expenditure is the upper limit to valuation. But what do accountants say about depreciating this figure? Hatfield summarises the position:

> Among accountants favouring the writing off of goodwill are Bell, Leake, Pixley, Webner and Wildman, while Cole, Couchman, Dicksee, Finney, Kester and Montgomery hold that it is unnecessary or even improper. Even among those advocating writing off of goodwill, there is a strange difference as to the circumstances in which this should be done. The more general opinion is that, if done at all, it should be done when the company has enjoyed unusual profits which can be appropriated for that purpose. But some, on the contrary, say that it is when profits are below the expected amount that goodwill has declined, and hence it is then that it should be marked down. As Couchman has cleverly expressed it, " to put it briefly, if you can write it down, you need not; if you cannot, you should ! " [48]

Goodwill then is merely the difference between the value of the business at a moment of time, *e.g.*, date of purchase, and the valuations, however made, of certain of the assets which are separately stated in the balance-sheet. Thereafter those separate assets will be subject to adjustments which will be reflected in the income account, while the balance or goodwill is subject to an upper limit, but may be reduced according to the way the accountant or his employer feels about it.

Capital versus *revenue expenditure*

We are told that the " proper distinction between capital and revenue as regards both receipts and expenditure, is one of the *fundamental* principles of correct accounting. It is very essential in all cases that this distinction should be rigidly observed, and amounts rightly allocated between capital and revenue. Failure or neglect to discriminate between the two will falsify the whole of the results of the bookkeeping." [49] But when we inquire how we should distinguish, we are given definition by extension, or we are told that capital expenditure results in the

---

[47] The super-profits theory is dependent on the rather obvious fact that if there are valuable intangibles, the market rate of interest on the value of the tangible assets will not exhaust the income.

[48] Hatfield, *Accounting*, p. 123.

[49] Carter, *Advanced Accounts* (revised edition, 1937), p. 251.

acquisition of assets. It might be pertinent to ask whether any expenditure is incurred other than with a view to the acquisition of assets. What is meant, we suppose, is that capital expenditure results in the acquisition of an asset the value of which is not exhausted within the accounting period under review. This, however, renders useless the definition by extension. For example, a week's labour purchased during the accounting period is usually regarded as revenue expenditure, but if the labour is engaged on the last day of the accounting period it becomes capital expenditure. Presumably a machine which is expected to be held for two years is capital expenditure *ex ante*, but if it is scrapped within the accounting period it is revenue expenditure *ex post*. Such rough-and-ready language ought not to be accorded an important place in theoretical analysis.

If that part of expenditure which benefits future periods is capital expenditure, then one must measure the benefit which future periods are to receive. But how is this done? The answer at present is that one takes an arbitrary proportion of what was paid and carries it forward via the balance-sheet—which brings us back to the subject of valuation, which some accountants say has nothing to do with the future at all.

Railway accounts illustrate the problem well. Mr. Newton, an authority on railway accounting, tells us that:

> Capital expenditure represents the outlay in acquiring and equipping an undertaking. The cost of land, buildings, rolling stock, permanent way, machinery, and plant (plus law and Parliamentary expenses) comes within this category.
>
> When the undertaking is fully equipped, further capital expenditure is not incurred until such time as any improvement or extension is necessary. . . .[50]

It is the last part of the quotation which is important. What are improvements and extensions? Mr. Newton says only that they increase the " revenue-earning capacity " of the undertaking. But every payment which a railway makes is intended to increase its capacity to earn revenue. It will pay the wages of train drivers next week because it needs their labour—its revenue will be greater if it has their labour than if it has not. You cannot distinguish the cost of a new tunnel from the cost of a driver's hire on these lines. But the expression " increase its capacity to earn revenue " in practice implies more than this. One thinks of the undertaking becoming more *valuable* than it was at some given previous time—that is, one compares its total values *at different accounting dates*; expenditure which increases its value is capital expenditure,

[50] C. H. Newton, *Railway Accounts*, pp. 164–165.

while expenditure which merely succeeds in maintaining its value
is revenue expenditure.

But, even if all the expenditure for the year was charged to
revenue, it still might not succeed in reducing the net revenue
to a figure which would link the capital value of the undertaking
at the beginning of the period with that at the end. An additional
station and the opening of a new line would be charged to capital,
and yet they might be necessary merely to counteract a fall in
the value of the whole undertaking. The electrification of sub-
urban lines may be required to prevent a fall in value that would
otherwise ensue because of loss of traffic to the roads. Yet
some part, if not the whole, of the electrification is almost certain
to be charged to capital account.

Even the renewal of existing assets may raise insoluble problems
of expense allocation and once again show the danger of looking
to individual assets when considering income measurement:

> In the interval that elapses between the original purchase and the
> date of the renewal of the asset, it is probable that the progress of science
> and invention has provided an improved type better able to do the work
> required, and consequently it would be futile to replace the asset by one
> identical with the original design.
>
> The renewed asset is, generally speaking, not only of better type, but
> probably also capable of increasing output. It is " better " than the
> original and the value of the difference between the two assets, *i.e.*,
> *betterment*, must be assessed when renewal is effected.
>
> " Betterment," therefore, is the difference between the estimated
> *replacement* cost of the displaced asset and the cost of the new asset.
>
> " Betterment " is, strictly speaking, properly chargeable to capital
> account, but, in practice, it may be charged to revenue account.[51]

Now we will pass over the facts that replacement cost may
be high because of changes in the price level, or because the
asset is obsolete and so could be replaced only if it were specially
made. But we cannot pass over the fact that the more expensive
asset may do no more than keep, or may not even succeed in
keeping, the undertaking at its original value. Individual assets
may be getting " better," but the whole may be declining in value.
Is the measurement of income to ignore the value of the business?

Capital gain and loss

One often comes across the expressions *capital gain* and
capital loss. Now it is possible, at least in theory, to distinguish
between that income which was anticipated and that addition to
or deduction from expected income which results from the fact
that expectations have been falsified. The results of these

[51] Newton, *op. cit.*, pp. 175–176.

unexpected changes are sometimes referred to as capital gain or loss. This distinction, which aims at dividing up income according to its *causes*, is one which we have not introduced into our consideration of the subject. This, however, is not to imply that it is unimportant to examine the causes of income; it is however something to be done after income has been determined, and the latter is the problem to which we have confined ourselves.

There is little doubt that these expressions, capital gain and loss, are often used in accounting to describe changes in income other than those which result from uncertainty. They are, for example, sometimes employed to stress the distinction between " abnormal " and " normal " transactions (*e.g.*, gains on sale of fixed assets), and where the actual value and balance-sheet value have parted company by such a wide margin that an adjustment is felt to be necessary. This margin may have been due to nothing more than the valuation technique adopted, and not to any unexpected change.

A summary of accounting practice

We have now examined (very sketchily, it is true) the attitude of accountants towards valuation. The object of this survey was to throw some light on the accounting concept of income.

It has been argued by certain accountants that the balance-sheet is less important than the income account. Whether this is true or not depends on the purpose for which such documents are prepared. Double entry bookkeeping is such that receipts and payments which are not " closed off " to the income account are carried forward, and if they are carried forward they appear in the balance-sheet. Hence the decision on what to disclose in the balance-sheet is essentially the same as the decision on what to put in the income account. It follows that, for income measurement, we cannot distinguish between the importance of the two documents:

> Every profitable transaction must automatically result in an increase of the profit shown by the profit and loss account, and in an exactly corresponding increase in the net amount of assets which the concern holds. Where, on the other hand, a transaction results in a loss, the profit shown by the profit and loss account is diminished, and to a corresponding extent net assets disappear. These statements are so thoroughly true that it would be feasible to measure profit by ascertaining the net surplus of assets over liabilities at successive points of time and (after adjusting introductions of and withdrawals of capital) taking the difference between the two results to represent the profit or loss of the intervening period.[52]

[52] Rowland & Magee, *Accounting* (Part I), p. 281.

Since profit depends on the valuation of assets, no excuse is needed for reviewing accounting technique in this matter.

Most accountants would probably agree that value can only be measured by the purchasing power which could be commanded directly *or indirectly* as a result of the possession of the asset or assets to be valued. Now the collection of rights which make up a business can normally be disposed of in a number of different ways, one of which will result in a greater value for the collection than any other disposition. The business should be valued on the assumption of this disposition, because we presume that, other things being equal, people prefer more rather than less purchasing power. This disposes of a bogy which worries some accountants, namely, the separate valuation of assets which have been bought for use rather than sale. They jump to the conclusion that valuation of an asset must imply its separation from the business and disposal to another user to whom, for obvious reasons, its value may prove less than its value as part of the present group of assets. The separated worth of an asset disposed of to another user is at best only a test of its minimum worth; accountants who condemn any attempt to use this value for income measurement are justified, but they are starting at shadows of their own making.

Let us now try to summarise accounting procedure. First, assets are sorted into two broad classes, fixed and circulating —which, for purposes of income theory, is unsatisfactory since accountants have not stated precisely the dividing line.[53] Second, fixed assets must not be valued at a figure exceeding original cost, but depreciation must be written off. No generalisation of the principles of writing off is possible owing to the confusion of views.

When cost as the upper limit of asset value is defended on grounds of conservatism in accepting evidence, it is possible to understand the argument while not necessarily agreeing with it. But when it is defended on more fundamental grounds concerning the nature of income and its " anticipation," there is nothing to be done except to seek a generalised statement of the underlying concept, and this we have been unable to discover.

The " function " distinction between fixed and circulating assets leads to the curious result that income depends on the *object* of the concern. The profit of a man who owns and farms

---

[53] Not all accountants take this distinction very seriously. Mr. S. W. Rowland, for example, refers to the " mumbo-jumbo on the distinction between fixed and circulating assets " found in existing law and traditional accountancy: *Some Modern Business Problems*, ed. Arnold Plant, p. 254.

land differs according as we regard him as a farmer or a land speculator. It is not clear what the profit is if the farmer is a shrewd person with an eye to land values as well as agricultural prices. It must be even more difficult to make a decision in the case of a complicated organisation.

For circulating assets, most accountants agree that valuation has some reference to existing conditions, though even here the upper limit of original cost may be applied to such assets as stock-in-trade. We have seen that this is often defended on the ground that profit does not " arise " until an asset is sold. The inadequacy of this argument is patent, and it is, in fact, subject to a string of exceptions; in addition, impending loss is usually recognised—a major inconsistency.

Now in the actual job of measuring income it is likely, almost certain in fact, that different men will disagree in weighing up different factors. This we must face, but what is not excusable is the absence of any agreement on the object. Accounting at present lacks an income concept. It is useless to say that income is the figure we arrive at after applying our valuation rules, when the rules themselves are not agreed.

This brings us back to the attempted generalisation by Professor Bonbright—the " prorated-receipts-and-disbursements " concept. Readers who care to refer back to it [54] will agree that it is broadly true as a description of accounting practice. But it still leaves us with our problem. Why do accountants act in this way? It is not sufficient to say that the irregular flow of cash cannot form a basis for consumption decisions, and that therefore this flow is converted into " a more regular, standard flow of ' net income.' " How large and how regular is this net flow to be? Is it determined by the view that the business must go on for ever? How is the rate chosen, seeing that accountants are deliberately abandoning the process of looking forward in favour of looking backward? The question is one of some seriousness in an economy in which absentee ownership is very important.

The Increased-Net-Worth Theory of Income

Our review of accounting practices suggests that they are, from the standpoint of income measurement, inadequate and confused. What then can the critic offer instead? The approach that best satisfies theoretical requirements has been clumsily termed " the increased-net-worth theory of income."

[54] p. 76.

This theory involves the assumption that it is possible to discover the *worth* of the business to the investors at a given date, and depends on the view that this worth is equivalent to purchasing power. If we call the worth of the business to the investors at one date C_1 and the worth at any later date C_2, and if drawings by the investors (in money or money's worth) from the business are D, then income$= C_2 - C_1 + D$. Thus a comparison is made of money value at one date with money value at another. Whether it is possible to discover the worth of property and rights we shall discuss in due course. There are clearly two reasons for attempting the task from time to time, namely the desire to reconsider consumption policy, and the need to compare alternative investments.

A particular right or piece of property is valuable because there are people willing to pay for the future services which it will yield. These services may be consumed by the owner, or may be sold; if it is expected that they will command a price (although they may not actually be sold) the right or property yielding them will be valuable. The value will depend on the money price of the services, and when they are expected to be received. More distant receipts are of less value than similar receipts which will fall in at an earlier date, because the earlier loan of purchasing power commands a price. If this price, namely the rate of interest, rises, then the present or discounted value of future services (receipts) will fall. Thus present value is determined by the market's expectations of the quantity of services, their future prices, and the rate of interest. The owner of the property or right has to decide whether his view of future events is such that at the market price he prefers to hold or to sell. If getting information were costless, such an investigation could be made continuously, but where the property is a whole business the expense is such as to make it worth while only at intervals.

We can summarise by saying that, whereas the receipts less payments concept of income covers satisfactorily those cases where all the receipts and payments are in the past, the increased-net-worth concept attempts to handle those cases where some of the receipts and payments are still in the future, and, therefore, have to be anticipated and discounted. It is a " forward-looking " or *ex ante* approach.

Net worth a synonym for capital

In discussing the meaning of " net worth " we must start by separating a business from those who have advanced purchasing power (or the equivalent) to it. The business thus separated has at any moment of time various rights and perhaps some cash, all of which we can refer to as *assets*. Assets are sources of future services, and in so far as these services are expected to be valuable, the right to them will command a present price, which price is the worth of the asset. The whole beneficial interest or equity in these assets belongs to one or a number of persons or institutions, since the business as a separate entity is merely in the position of a trustee.

When we here use the expression " net worth," we mean the worth of the business to the investors. The investors are a given group who have yielded up purchasing power to the business in exchange for rights whose value is the capital of the investors. Thus net worth and capital are synonymous.

People who sell goods on credit to a business are, of course, investors in a sense, but accounts are not usually necessary to determine their rights. Similarly, debenture-holders in a company are investors, but their rights are usually defined precisely, and the rate of interest they are to receive is stipulated in the contract. The income account of the business deals with the rights of a particular group, whose share of the inflowing receipts is what is left after satisfying all other rights. The net worth with which we are in practice concerned is, therefore, a residue. The obligations which are fixed in amount, and hence easily determined, are not the ones for which we need elaborate accounts; it is for the measurement of those which are flexible in amount that we require statistics.

The owners of such rights have been called by various names (*e.g.*, " proprietors " or " equity-holders ") to distinguish them from the owners of other rights. Where liabilities end and proprietorship begins has been discussed by many writers, and various tests have been suggested such as the amount of direct control exercised, the amount of risk undertaken, predominance in value of rights. None of them appears wholly satisfactory.

Capital, then, consists not of assets themselves, but of particular rights in those assets, and the next problem is to find a way of valuing these rights.

Net worth and separate assets

We have repeatedly stressed that the value of a business cannot normally be approached by summing the separate values of assets, because these separate values are themselves derived from the value of the business as a whole. The receipts of the business, on which its value depends, are derived from the combination of the various factors of production which have been, or will be, acquired. *Before* each unit of a factor of production is bought, it is required to show that it can be expected to add to the present value of receipts an amount not less than the amount which it adds to costs. Once the unit has been acquired, its purchase price loses significance. Original cost has no bearing on current value, which is dependent on future prospects.

The value of a business to investors is the present worth of all its future receipts less the present worth of its future payments. (Receipts of new capital from the investors, and withdrawals, must be excluded from the calculation.) How (if at all) do existing asset values affect our forecast of these cash flows?

A given asset may be of potential service to a number of users and for a number of purposes; some users may esteem it more highly than others. A machine, for example, once it has been set down in a factory, can be used in that factory as part of the equipment for manufacturing some product. On the other hand, it can be sold to somebody else who will take it away and use it for a similar or different purpose, *e.g.*, for breaking up and sale as scrap metal.

The investor is interested in the course in which the machine gives the highest return. If there are several machines which go to make up the business, and the worth of these machines as scrap metal exceeds the discounted value of the product that they could together produce, then it would pay the investor to scrap them. We can assume, therefore, that if a business is running, the present value of future net receipts from its products is expected to exceed that of the receipts from the sale of the assets separately. From this it follows that for valuation purposes the separate selling prices of all the assets are important as a measure of the worth of the business only at the time when the business should be closed down. They represent a *minimum*.

In estimating net worth for the purposes of measuring income, we usually have to deal with a group of assets which are not going to be sold immediately, but which will be used or sold in the ordinary course of business. Particular assets will be disposed of from time to time, and their market price at sale is revelant to the present value of the business as a whole, because that price represents part of the inflow of receipts. In this somewhat indirect way, separate assets affect cash budgets and therefore net worth.

Moreover, replacement cost of all assets may in some circumstances provide an *upper limit* to the present value of future net receipts. No one would pay more for a business than the price at which it could be duplicated. Exact duplication may not be possible owing to the possession by the business of monopolistic rights conferred by the state, such as patents and trade marks. Or it may be impossible because one of the attributes of the business inheres in a person. Imperfect competition, or monopoly which results from such qualities as these, may also exist temporarily merely because knowledge itself is imperfect. A business may be very profitable because very few people know that it is profitable. In this case, too, exact duplication is impossible—for the introduction of another producing unit reduces the expectation of future receipts for all producers, and a business with different expectations is a business with a different value. This explains why someone buying up the shares of a competitor will often pay more for the shares than the reproduction cost of all the assets.

Thus, for one reason or another, the replacement-cost test of individual assets does not determine precisely the maximum value of the business as a whole—unless the business operates under conditions of perfect competition. These conditions are never realised, but in certain industries they are approached fairly closely. In such industries, the replacement cost of all the assets is a guide to the value of the business, provided that it is possible to make an allowance for the fact that the existing assets are no longer new. But even then it is merely an upper limit—it may well be that future expected receipts would not warrant replacement of the assets.

We may summarise this section by saying that the replacement cost of all the assets, and their selling price, will (after deduction of the rights of creditors) provide upper and lower limits to the capital of the investors. As, however, exact reproduction may for one reason or another be impossible, the upper limit is not often effective. The only way of estimating the value of the business as a whole is to estimate future receipts and future payments, and discount them; separate assets affect that value only so far as they affect the cash budget.[55]

Valuing anticipated net receipts

In most cases, then, income measurement by the increased-net-worth method involves the following steps:

1. Net worth at the beginning of an accounting period is computed. This is done by estimating anticipated future

---

[55] The first edition of these *Studies* (p. 241) includes a statement of the conditions in which the whole product can be imputed to individual assets, by the marginal approach. It concludes that this can be done only under very rare conditions, and that there is no reason for attempting such allocation.

cash receipts and payments, and then discounting these sums. (Surplus cash-on-hand may also be included in the total.) The arithmetic is in principle the same as that by which an actuary finds the present value of an annuity; but, as the sums at stake may well be highly variable and uncertain, the practical difficulties are greater.

2. Net worth at the end of the period is computed in the same way.

3. The difference between net worths at beginning and end, adjusted for any money or money's-worth paid in or withdrawn by the owner during the period, is the period's income.

Thus income is seen as the *appreciation* of the owners' rights, measured in terms of the cash that will become available to the owners as dividends or otherwise, and regardless of individual assets. Receipts during the past period may, of course, form part of closing net worth; but the income may be quite a different amount,[56] and does not depend on realisation.

Practical difficulties in the approach

Our attempt to justify the logic of the increased-net-worth theory of income does not imply any failure to appreciate the difficulties involved in the actual attempt to forecast and discount future receipts and payments, or in the selection of the appropriate interest rate. It is, in fact, so difficult that one wonders sometimes whether people would ever buy businesses, or shares in businesses, if they stopped to think of the valuation complexities implied in their act, let alone the chances of their anticipations not being realised. However this may be, when a business changes hands its valuation is a fact—it has been sold at a certain price.

It is, however, a very different matter to expect an accountant in the ordinary course of his duties to estimate the value of a business. Such a task cannot be within the province of the accountant, for it requires besides shrewd judgment, which he may possess, considerable technical knowledge of conditions in a particular firm, which he could not be expected to have. A business is not like a bushel of wheat, something which can be

---

[56] Just as the sum received under an annuity is not all income, but can be apportioned between income and return of capital—income being the interest (*i.e.*, appreciation) on the capital at the beginning of the year.

This should dispose of the charge that the increased-net-worth theory involves double counting of revenue items (when they are first anticipated, and again when they are actually received). The *discounted* value is counted at first anticipation; thereafter only the " discount " earned during a period is treated as that period's income.

easily graded and for which there is an easily ascertainable market price. And, if the accountant cannot be made responsible for finding net worth, then *he is not responsible for calculating income in our sense*.

Thus a corollary of the increased-net-worth theory is that the estimation of income depends on the owner himself. The main factors are too subjective to permit delegation. Doubtless many owners will not in fact attempt detailed calculation (any more than when buying an investment); they may be content with round numbers, or even mere " feelings " about the progress of the business.

However, the accountant should certainly try to supply information upon which the owners can base intelligent judgment. We shall later try to suggest what information is suitable.

Conceptual difficulties in the approach

The increased-net-worth theory relies on the fundamentals that govern buyers and sellers whenever a sale is freely made. It satisfies logic better than any other approach. Nevertheless it involves conceptual as well as practical difficulties. Those who make decisions about future consumption and like matters will have to bear in mind many relevant forces. For example, money is not stable in its power to command goods and services. If the value of the pound sterling in terms of all goods and services falls during the year, and the investor's net worth was £1,000 at January 1, and the same figure at December 31, he would have to realise that although his income was nil, his power to command goods and services had actually fallen.

Or suppose interest rates fall. This will increase the value of a given expectation of receipts. This rise is income in our sense. Suppose, when the interest rate was 5 per cent., a man bought for £1,000 a right to receive £50 per annum in perpetuity. Suppose at the end of the first year the interest rate fell to 4 per cent. and so the capital value rose to £1,250. Then income under the increased-net-worth concept would, for that year, be £50 + £1,250 − £1,000 = £300. If this £300 were *consumed* either by selling part of the investment or by borrowing £250 and paying interest at the market rate, then *future* net receipts would be only £40 per annum, a sum equal to the market rate of interest on £1,000. The concept might, therefore, be criticised on the ground that it could lead to a rate of present consumption which would involve lower future consumption, *i.e.*, £40 per annum instead of £50.

There is, we believe, an adequate answer to this criticism.

Future consumption is a question of individual preference, and no income concept could take into account all matters which might affect it. For example, the rate at which any person discounts future receipts may change from time to time, and be influenced by all kinds of factors. Again, not all people are affected in the same way by particular price changes, because some of these changes may not influence their behaviour.

Income in our sense provides persons with *one* piece of information which must influence their decisions; but these will also depend on all sorts of other factors, some of which it may be the function of the accountant to disclose, and others of which he may know nothing.

The test of any definition of income is twofold. First, does the definition yield information that is important for behaviour? Secondly, can we state it precisely and in a way that can be clearly understood? It is believed that the increased-net-worth concept satisfies these conditions.

SOME SUGGESTIONS

Let us now consider what improvements might be feasible in practice. We shall deal mainly with the reports of public companies.

Lack of agreement on concepts

It has to be admitted that accountants are not agreed on the way in which income is to be defined. It follows, therefore, that even if there were no deliberate manipulation, an outsider (including most shareholders) cannot know the principles on which the figure is calculated. What information is he given? First, a profit-and-loss account that need not be complete, and tells us little about cash receipts and payments. This is supported by a statement called a balance-sheet, which those writers who are wisest call " a list of ledger balances," but which nine members of the public out of ten think is a statement of assets, liabilities and capital bearing some relationship to the worth of the business. The figure of income, given without explanation, is dependent on the figures in the balance-sheet, some of which are related in a definite way to current prices, others less definitely; a third group are mere statements of money paid; and, worst of all, some of the figures may represent payments less deductions whose amounts are not disclosed.

Serious consequences follow from the lack of agreement on the definition of income and capital maintenance. First, let us think of the shareholder who pays no attention to market prices. He usually believes that every dividend he gets is " income," and probably assumes in a muddled sort of way that the company does not pay a dividend unless its capital is " intact " in some sense, a faith in which he is strengthened by the fact that the balance-sheet discloses net " assets " more than equal to the subscribed capital. If the company fails and is reconstructed, shareholders are probably rudely shocked when the book value of their shares is cut down perhaps by 90 per cent. It is small satisfaction to tell them that balance-sheet values are not in any sense real, and are independent of future demand conditions. These shareholders have probably " consumed " their dividends because they were lulled by accounting documents into a false sense of security. The form of these documents, and the fact that they are certified by an auditor, have created an unwarranted atmosphere of safety, instead of emphasising the risks attendant on investment.

Other shareholders, with less trust in accounting documents and more sense of the changeableness of financial matters, will keep an eye on the market values of their securities, as these give an indication of other people's opinions on the prospects of the company, and some of these other people have sometimes more information than the particular shareholder. In any case, his actions will probably be influenced not only by the dividends which come to him, but also by the so-called capital gains or capital losses which result from changes in the price of the share. But what causes these changes in price? Obviously one cause is change in opinion on future prospects, and this cause we cannot eradicate, at least in our type of economy. But although we cannot eradicate change of opinion about the future, we can feed that opinion on facts rather than leave it to rumour and obscure documents. The *facts* that we can supply relate, of necessity, to the past and the present, but the publication of those facts, and in particular their publication *at frequent intervals* would result in more informed buying and selling of stocks and shares; and investors would, as far as is possible, be safeguarded from adopting for long periods a consumption policy different from that which they would adopt if they knew the available facts.

Merchanting businesses

The problem of reporting the affairs of simple trading concerns does not present much difficulty. Where debts, stock-in-trade, and, perhaps, a building, are the principal assets, the sum of their market prices will give at least some guide to the worth of the business. Individual asset valuation can be made a reasonable test of total value, and income can be calculated without a wide margin of error by comparing one balance-sheet with the next. Current methods of presenting the balance-sheet would need little adjustment, though valuation technique would have to escape from its slavish attachment to original cost and conservatism. Supporting documents should include a detailed statement of receipts and payments (with disclosed adjustments to take account of any time lag due to credit terms).

The problem of reporting gets progressively more difficult the greater the extent to which the value of the business depends on trade names, organisation, specialised equipment, and similar elements. That is why accounting for industrial concerns presents so many more complications, and why the present methods of reporting are unsuited thereto.

Industrial businesses

The writer looks back with regret to the " double account " system of published reports, formerly prescribed by statute in Britain for many types of public utilities, but now rare. In these undertakings, the futility of ascribing separate values to assets of a highly specialised nature (such as tunnels and cuttings) was so patent that a form of annual statement was adopted which avoided any appearance of so doing.

Under the double account system, the balance-sheet is in two parts, the first of which is called the Receipts and Expenditure on Capital Account. The merit of this document is that it is a plain statement of receipts and expenditure. Not even a layman could mistake it for anything different from what it purports to be. There is no attempt to value assets, and this is perfectly clear. Those accountants who are always protesting that the ordinary form of balance-sheet does not attempt valuation could prevent all doubt about the matter by adopting statements such as this one.

The receipts shown in the account consist of shares, loans and debentures, increased by premiums and reduced by discounts; the expenditure is analysed under a considerable number of headings. Both receipts and expenditure are in three columns, showing the totals up to the beginning of the year, the amounts for the year, and the grand total to the end of the year. The expenditure is not, of course, the whole expenditure, but only that part which is classified as capital expenditure.

The second part of the balance-sheet starts with the balance of the receipts and expenditure on capital account, and then proceeds to set out certain "floating" assets and (on the other side) credit balances. The former consist of cash, securities, stocks and shares, debts and stores on hand; the credit balances comprise sums due by the company, besides several so-called funds and reserves for renewals, insurance, improvements and contingencies.

The other main group of documents is concerned with so-called revenue receipts and expenditure. Considerable detail is furnished in connection with each branch of the work, which is summarised in an account for the whole undertaking. The balance on this account is the net revenue for the year.

It is suggested that all industrial firms might with advantage adopt certain features of the double account system for their published reports. The main documents should consist of receipts and payments accounts with certain adjustments. It is difficult to see how the details of the classification could be settled by statute, though this has, of course, been done for railways and some other undertakings. It seems best that legal control should be limited to requiring certain important headings of receipts and payments to be shown separately, the auditors being given power to report on any features of the accounts which in their view are obscure. For example, full details of sales should be obligatory.

Conflicting rights to capital and dividends

Should the receipts and expenditure accounts be grouped into capital and revenue? This does not seem to matter unless certain contracts depend on a particular division. If such a classification is adopted, the reason for it should be quite clear, and the dividing line made as definite as possible. Of course, it may be retorted that unless you have such a division you cannot decide on dividend policy, even apart from different classes of rights. Today the whole position relating to dividend policy is obscure. We have discussed earlier the factors which *should* determine the withdrawal of cash from the business. This amount is not dependent on an income concept, but is simply related to the question of maximising the return from capital, *i.e.*, of maximising the present value of future receipts less payments. In some types of business this is, of course, well recognised, and dividends are not related to a concept of income. Dividends from mining companies often represent inflowing receipts without any deduction for the fall in value of the mine consequent on depletion of the ore. If we had perfect foresight, the value of a share in a mine at the end of an accounting period, plus the dividend for that period, less the opening value of the share, would represent interest. In the real world, perfect foresight is absent, and, as a result, the closing market value of the share, less opening market value, will usually (after adjustment for the dividend) fail to equal the interest. New technical facts may be discovered about the quantity or quality of the ore reserves, the price of the metal may change, the rate of interest may alter. All such factors influence the market value of the shares in the mine, and must be weighed by shareholders in determining their consumption policy, and in deciding whether to retain or sell their holdings. In such cases, dividend policy consists of the distribution of funds which the concern no longer requires for the prosecution of the enterprise—the distribution can hardly be identified with an income concept which could be stated in general terms. The distribution may, of course, be influenced by the private interests of paid officials with jobs to keep.

Dividends from other industrial and commercial concerns are usually related more closely to some concept of capital maintenance. There is a long, complicated and obscure series of legal precedents relating to dividends and capital. The general result is to leave directors pretty free in the matter of dividend policy—subject to the articles and memorandum. However, a general feeling exists that, despite the *minimum* requirements of the law, capital ought in some sense to be maintained intact. As a result, cash is retained and re-invested in ways that may or may not be economically justified.

It seems important to destroy the implied link between cash distribution and the notion of income. The increased-net-worth concept does not require the maintenance of a given company's resources at a particular level, measured either in physical or value terms.

There is, of course, no problem where a contract for a payment of a fixed annual sum of money exists, as is the case with debentures. There would, however, be some difficulty in cases where there are preference and ordinary stocks, and particularly where the former have no cumulative rights. Preference stockholders are at present in an anomalous position, for the dividends to which they are entitled depend on the way in which income is calculated, and they cannot know when they make their contracts what the attitude of the directors will be to this matter. If the directors took the view that they ought to distribute all funds which they could not employ for the shareholders as profitably as the shareholders could employ for themselves, the position of preference shareholders might become more insecure. At present, their dividends often depend partly on reserves which have been built up in the past, and if these were not built up some of their security might go. Nevertheless, anything which brought to a head the consideration of such contracts would not be a bad thing; it is amazing how ignorant many preference shareholders are about their dependence on directors' decisions, and how readily they swallow specious arguments for writing off their rights if these have proved burdensome to the directors and ordinary stockholders.

But it is surely not beyond the wit and ingenuity of man to devise contracts whose terms are reasonably clear. We do not have to agree to obscure income concepts for the purpose of making contracts with people who wish to take different degrees of risk in investing their money.

Other data

What statements of assets and liabilities should be made available? First, there should be statements of capital, debentures and loans, with their rights. Second, there are the debts owing to and by the company; their nominal amounts should be disclosed, and then any desirable adjustments for bad debts and discounts.

Lists of assets should be given. But no attempt at all should be made to place values on assets unless those values mean something; one can conceive of cases where details of replacement cost or selling price would be helpful. Thus no " going-concern " value would be placed on plant; on the other hand, marketable securities should be set out with details of the purchase price and the current market value for the purpose of comparison.

It would be necessary to support the financial information with other statistical data on matters relevant to a consideration of the ability and success with which the concern is being run, and of its future prospects. Quantitative details of stocks carried, and relevant financial information, might be supplied. For example, current replacement cost of raw material might be stated, and the expected selling price of finished stocks. Inventories of equipment in use (in broad classes) and details of freehold and leasehold property should also be available. Quantitative data on turnover during the year should support the financial figures of sales, so that movements in the latter could be weighed in the light of price changes.[57]

---

[57] It might not be possible to set out the financial report with the arithmetical precision of the balance-sheet, both sides of which agree so happily. In which case, the classic beauty of double entry would not be demonstrated in the final accounts.

The agreed income tax computation should be made public. This would be very useful because, although the basis of income tax is arbitrary, we do know between fairly close limits what the relevant conventions are.

If directors were compelled to go as far as this in the matter of disclosure, they might in some cases care to go a step further and comment on various matters of opinion. For example, they might indicate the extent to which they believe changes in particular price levels are important for their business.

The auditors should be responsible for certifying so much of the report as deals with money matters; on them would fall the duty not only of checking fraud, but of seeing that the receipts and expenditure were set out under headings which could not mislead a normal person with a reasonable training in financial matters. They would be responsible for showing clearly how the valuations of any assets which are valued are arrived at.

In the case of small companies at least, detailed information might not be necessary more than once annually. On the other hand, figures of turnover could be made available at intervals of three months, or even one month, without imposing any heavy cost on the companies concerned. Such frequent information, with any warning comments which the directors cared to attach, would help to prevent some mistakes which would otherwise be possible.

The principal object of the above plans is to distinguish matters of fact from opinion, and to make available as much information as is *reasonably* possible—information that will form a basis for weighing up the ability of the administration and also for considering the future prospects of the various classes of capital. Any information which can be reduced to documentary form and assists the achievement of these aims should be disclosed. It would still be a matter of very great difficulty to assess the worth of ordinary stocks and shares, which must depend on an estimate of future receipts less outgoings, including payments on prior capital, but it would be less difficult than at present. Investors' income calculations would be better informed.

Objections to disclosure

Detailed disclosures of the type suggested are sure to be opposed by the majority of managers, who would naturally resent such interference. But what are the solid arguments against disclosure?

The first objection might relate to the rights of the individual, and those of the state to interfere with him. If an investor chooses to trust managers and forgo safeguards, is he not entitled to do so? Our answer might well be Yes if the case rested merely on the rights of individuals to bargain with one another. But the case does not rest here. The issue is much bigger. The existing system of property rights is not in any sense *natural*; it is man-made. We have the strongest reasons for wanting to know how it is working. Individuals wish to know how best to invest. The community as a whole needs to know how well or badly different classes of people and various types of enterprise are faring, and how these results are affected by particular property rights. It needs to know because it is interested vitally in the machinery of production and distribution; to avoid mistakes in either, it must have information. This, and not the protection of the individual from himself, seems to be the important reason for forcing the disclosure of information about business.

The community would gain very greatly from the disclosure of more information. There would be less wastage of resources than at present, since market calculations would be better informed. New capital is directed into those channels where it is expected to earn most. These expectations should be founded on detailed reports, and not on rumour or on profit figures whose underlying assumptions are unknown. Obscure accounting documents can be responsible for much avoidable wastage. Society is entitled to know the facts.

Next we must consider arguments based on the welfare of the company concerned. The question of cost needs to be considered. Since the bookkeeping would not require to be adjusted in any material way, the extra cost would be confined to the preparing of the statements and their publication. This would be trivial. So cost is not the factor likely to stand in the way of sweeping changes; other matters carry much more weight. Profit may be damaged by the disclosure of detailed figures. If the business is doing well, competition may be attracted, and its enterprise will not be rewarded. It will however have the advantage of a start; moreover, though success resulting from administrative or technical ability would be evidenced by disclosed accounts, it does not necessarily follow that the *cause* of such success would be obvious or easily imitable. Administrative genius would still command a high price.

The disclosures that attract competition to a flourishing company will repel them when it is doing badly, and so are a protection. A sick company might indeed be deprived of credit as a result of disclosure; but it cannot surely be sustained that the community is better off if people lend to a business when they would not lend if they were acquainted with its real financial condition.

Another argument sometimes advanced is that disclosure of bad trading conditions may result in a general fall in confidence, and hasten forward the slump. This assumes that boom and slump are questions of oscillating confidence and can be cured by preventing people from knowing the facts. The validity of the assumption is open to considerable doubt; in any case, it is a sad view of humanity which acts on the assumption that to improve the welfare of the people you must keep them ignorant. It is the creed of the totalitarian state.

This brings us back to another important social argument. There is much dissatisfaction with the way in which our economy works. But how can remedies be suggested if the facts are not known?

Accounts of private firms

In deciding his consumption policy, and whether to keep or dispose of an investment, the owner will take into account its market price, where there is one, in addition to his own views and those of his friends relating to the future prospects of the investment.

One of the principal objects of company reports is to assist this weighing of prospects. We have suggested that the normal functions of the accountant should not include estimation of income in our sense; he should merely provide as much significant data as he can. One can conceive of situations arising in which it is obvious to the directors or accountants that the market, in its calculations, has failed to take account of an important factor which, in the view of the directors, makes the market valuation seriously wrong. On such occasions the directors, acting perhaps on the advice of the accountants, might feel it their duty to draw attention to the particular factor.

In private firms, on the other hand, valuation is not put to the test of the market, and as a result there is no ready way by which the investor can calculate his income.

The relationship between the accountant and the owner of the small business is, of course, much more intimate than that between the accountant or the auditor of the large company and its shareholders. But the work of the accountant is coloured, to a very large extent, by the requirements of income tax. In any case, there is probably little accounting change necessary in a simple merchant's business, except in the attitude of accountants to market values. The difficulty of measuring the income of industrial businesses is much greater. But the industrialist, as much as the merchant, has to have regard to the future in deciding his rate of consumption and also in deciding whether to keep or sell the business. In this connection, the more he realises the artificiality of balance-sheet valuations, the better it will be for everyone concerned. Accounts should avoid any appearances which are likely to lull the businessman into a false sense of security. When a small manufacturer is told that his drawings are either less or more than his net profits, he should be made to understand clearly that net profit is not, according to ordinary accounting conventions, attached to some definite concept of capital maintenance.

If there were a change in the type of documents presented to company shareholders, there is little doubt that it would have its effect on accounting for private businesses. One would not, of course, present to the owner of a one-man business exactly the same information which one would present to shareholders, for the reason that he would probably already know most of it. But one would attempt to summarise the operations of preceding accounting periods, in receipts and expenditure accounts, drawing attention to significant changes. The accountant, particularly if he is acquainted with economic and statistical science, can provide the businessman with much that is worth paying for besides the accounts for income tax.

CONCLUSION

Published accounts should have as their object the provision of information for a judgment of net worth. The clearer and more relevant this information, the easier it is for the shareholder to calculate his income.

The accountant should try to provide the information on which the net worth judgment is based, but cannot normally be expected to make this judgment himself. As we find out more about the ways in which investors reach decisions—and this is very much a job for the research worker in accounting—we shall learn how to develop the methods and forms of reporting that are most likely to help.

Income Measurement in a Dynamic Economy *

By Sidney S. Alexander

Professor of Industrial Management,
Massachusetts Institute of Technology.

Revised by David Solomons

Professor of Accounting,
University of Pennsylvania.

CONTENTS

---

* Professor Alexander's monograph was originally written for the Study Group
on Business Income, organised by the American Institute of Accountants (now
the American Institute of Certified Public Accountants) in 1948. It was given
a limited circulation as one of the Group's *Five Monographs on Business Income*.
The present version, revised by Professor Solomons, differs importantly from
the original in that the section on " variable income " has been substantially
recast, and what appeared to be an inconsistency in the original discussion
has been removed. Various small changes have also been made in the interests
of clarity.

SUMMARY

A YEAR'S income is, fundamentally, the amount of wealth that a person, real or corporate, can dispose of over the course of the year and remain as well off at the end of the year as at the beginning. The arbitrary choice of a time period of one year raises certain difficulties in income accounting because many transactions relate to several different years. The elaborate developments of the art of accounting are principally designed to handle the problems raised by the attempt to assign to each year a share in the flow of income which is associated with the activities of many years. With these difficulties connected with the attempt to decompose the income of a corporation's entire life into the income of individual years, the present monograph has little to do.

Another set of problems, which concern the question of what is meant by " as well off at the end of the year as at the beginning," is the principal subject of the present monograph. It is here argued that in a dynamic economy, when values are changing both because of changes in prices and changes of expectations of future earning power, there is no unique well-defined ideal concept of income against which can be compared the actual practice of income measurement. Instead, many variant concepts can be conceived, each of which has certain advantages for a particular purpose. Consequently, in any dispute over how income should best be measured, it is only rarely that the question can be settled by appeal to the fundamental income concept. More frequently, the several different methods of income measurement under consideration are all consistent with the basic concept of income, but each puts a different interpretation on the elementary notions of which the basic concept is composed. In particular, important variations in the practice of income measurement are related to different interpretations of what is meant by a person's being as well off at the end of the income period as at the beginning.

Because different interpretations are possible, and because any concept of income can be justified only by reference to the use to which it is put, the only criterion by which a choice may be made among various methods of measuring income is the relative effectiveness of the different methods in serving the purposes for which the concept of income is to be used. But the concept is in fact used for many different purposes, so it is only natural that the measure of income best for one purpose should not be well suited to another. That means that either a compromise measure must be devised, fairly suitable to several purposes but ideal for none, or a different measure has to be constructed for each purpose. Both these lines have been followed in practice.

Choice among various concepts of income is not governed only by considerations of which measure best serves the ends in view. Another very powerful factor operating on the development of accounting methods has been the attempt to minimize the accountant's responsibility for the human judgments which must be made in passing from a consideration of the accounts to the conduct of business affairs. This desire to avoid responsibility has led accountants to set up two requirements for sound accounting that somewhat limit the choice of methods. These are the requirements of objectivity and conservatism. To the extent that accountants have achieved objectivity and conservatism they have made the measurement of income safer but they have also made it yield a result that only partially achieves the end sought. Anyone using the accountant's measure of income, particularly the businessman, must then make it accord with reality by himself making the subjective judgments which the accountant has avoided.

This division of function is probably well justified; the formation of the subjective judgments necessary for a final evaluation of income is more in accord with the activities and responsibilities of the businessman than with those of the accountant. It is certainly not suggested that the accountant should assume these responsibilities. But it should be recognized that income, as measured by the accountant, does fall short of the ideal appropriate to any particular purpose because the necessary subjective judgments have been left out.

The economist's concept of income is designed primarily to fit the case where the future is known with certainty. Strict application of that concept would mean that a corporation which each year paid dividends equal to its income would always have the same level of income. Year to year variations of income are inconsistent with the economic concept of income under conditions of certainty. When the future is reasonably certain as in the case of a bond or annuity, the accountant shares the economist's point of view, but in the measurement of business income that viewpoint is abandoned, presumably because of the uncertainties inherent in business operations. In order to make a meaningful comparison between the economist's and the accountant's concept of income, the economist's concept must somehow be extended to the case of uncertainty concerning the future. This can be done by the introduction of the concept of variable income which is elaborated in Chapter V. Variable income can be taken to represent the economist's concept of income as applied to conditions of uncertainty and it can be contrasted with income as conventionally measured by accountants.

The principal respect in which the accountant's measure of income departs from the economist's concept arises from the quest for objectivity. The accountant's practice consists of matching historical costs against historical revenues. It deals therefore in recorded events, and the only difficulties are the traditional accounting problems of just how to match up those recorded events in relation to any particular time period. Changes in goodwill or going value, which are not recorded events but judgments of the future course of events, are not in general permitted to enter the income records of accountants. From the economist's point of view, however, changes in going value should be counted in income since they do influence the amount that a person can dispose of while remaining as well off after the change as he was before. Furthermore, most of the purposes for which income is measured would be better served by the inclusion of changes in going value. Its exclusion in practice can be justified by the need for objectivity, but, it is here argued, attempts to justify the exclusion of changes of going value from income on grounds of principle are ill-founded.

A second characteristic which distinguishes the accountant's concept of income from one more nearly in accord with the viewpoint of economic theory is that the accountant accepts the money measure of values, while economic reasoning most frequently runs in real terms, *i.e.*, in terms of what the money can buy. It should not be thought that there is a body of economic doctrine that says it is wrong to measure income in money value when price levels are changing. But the whole orientation of economic reasoning is towards dispelling the money illusion and encouraging measurement in real terms. The most hotly contested points of dispute in the measurement of income depend fundamentally on whether income is to be measured in money terms or in real terms. In particular, the issue of whether depreciation should be charged on the basis of historical cost or of replacement cost hinges on whether income is to be measured in money or in real terms.

Since the ultimate criterion governing the definition of income is the purpose to be served, choice between the real and money measures must depend on what purpose is in view. The question of which procedure to use cannot then be settled on the basis of principle, but only on the basis of which procedure works best for the purpose in hand. One method is superior to the other if it works better, and an appeal to general principles may obscure the issues of social philosophy or practical expedience which govern the choice. Income for any purpose must be so defined as best to serve the general welfare and the interests of those concerned. When those interests are in conflict the issue must be resolved by a comparison of the merits of the various claims and interests, and not by recourse to a " true " concept of income, independent of the ends served by the use of the income measurements.

Another unsettled question is whether capital gain should be counted as income. This question can be somewhat clarified by breaking capital gain into two parts; one, like the gain in value of a bond issued at a discount and gradually approaching redemption at par, can clearly be recognised as income; another, like a change in market value of an asset, is more debatable. The second component of capital gain may be called unexpected gain. The principal argument for its exclusion from income is that an unexpected gain is not a measure of how much better off a person has become, but is merely a revision of a valuation of how well off he is and has been. Even if this argument is accepted, however, it means that at some time in the past an asset was acquired that is now recognised to be worth more than was then believed, and what is more to the point, is worth more now than it cost then. Consequently, the unexpected gain must be counted as income of some period, and the principal respect in which it differs from other types of income is in the difficulty of associating it with any particular period within the time during which the asset has been held.

The two questions, should income be reckoned in real or money terms, and should a capital gain be counted as income, are both embodied in the controversy over whether depreciation should be based on original or on replacement cost. Current accounting practice, which bases depreciation on original cost, implies that income is to be measured in money terms and capital gains on assets used in the business are to be counted as income. That is, the difference between the current year's income as based on historical cost depreciation and as based on replacement cost depreciation can be regarded as the capital gain in money terms on that part of fixed plant and equipment which has been charged against the current year's revenues. If the principle is to be adopted that capital gains should not be included in income, then replacement cost should be used as the basis of the depreciation charge. If a real rather than a money measure of income (even including capital gain) is to be used, then the depreciation charge should be adjusted for changes in the general price level, rather than in the replacement cost of the specific assets owned. If, however, it is desired to include capital gains in income, and to use a money measure of income, then the current practice constitutes an elegant and automatic way of distributing the money-measured capital gain on a depreciable asset over the useful life of the asset.

I. THE BASIC CONCEPT OF INCOME

Use of the income concept

The determination of income is the principal task of the business accountant. The final result of his calculations is used in a variety of ways with important consequences for the individual firm, the business community and the economy as a whole. In particular, income is used as the basis of one of the principal forms of taxation. It is used in reports to stockholders or the investing public as a measure of the success of a corporation's operations and as a criterion of the availability of dividends. It is used by rate regulating authorities in investigating whether those rates are fair and reasonable. It is used for the guidance of trustees charged with the responsibility of distributing the income from property to one person while preserving the capital for another. Probably the most important use of income is, or should be, as a guide to the management of enterprise in the conduct of its affairs.

Because of the practical importance of the measurement of income in so many everyday affairs, extensive and complicated rules for the determination of income have been developed. These rules have come from academic and practising accountants, from courts of law, from tax authorities, and in the United States from regulatory bodies such as the Interstate Commerce Commission or the public utilities commissions of the several states, and from supervisory agencies such as the Securities and Exchange Commission.[1] It should not be surprising that rules emanating from so many different authorities should be at variance with one another, since each has used income for purposes of its own and has adjusted its concept of income in accord with that purpose. All concerned, however, have looked to the accountant for the basic formulation of the rules for income determination.

---

[1] The position in Great Britain is notably different. Most public utilities have been nationalized, and the statutes under which this was done do not contain any rules for the determination of income: nor does the Companies Act lay down rules for private enterprises.

The accountant in his turn has tried to eliminate the element of subjective judgment from the determination of income. He has tried to establish as nearly as possible hard and fast rules of calculation in order to eliminate the guesswork and to ensure precise measurements. But in a dynamic world subject to unforeseen changes of prices and business conditions, it is not possible to avoid guesswork in the determination of income. To the extent that the accountant can eliminate guesses, he is substituting something else for income. That something else will be a good approximation to income in a fairly static situation when prices and business prospects are not changing very much; in a dynamic situation when prices and business prospects are fluctuating violently, the approximation will be a poor one.

It is the purpose of this study to analyse the income concept from a purely theoretical point of view and to compare the results of that analysis with income as conventionally measured by accountants. The object of the analysis will be to clarify what happens to income as actually measured in periods of changing prices or changing prospects.

In his quest for certainty, the accountant has come to assume certain values as constant which are in fact variable. In particular, the value of the monetary unit has been regarded as constant and the measure of all other values. No increase in value of any other asset has, in general, been recognized until its credentials have been validated by " realization," *i.e.*, exchange for money. Such unquestioning faith in the monetary unit must indeed have been shaken by the great rise of prices in almost all countries during and after World War II. In some countries, where at various times the currencies have declined catastrophically in value, a rejection of the local monetary unit has been common and accounts have been kept in gold or in foreign monetary units. In English-speaking countries, no serious attempt to reject the monetary unit has been made, but numerous suggestions have been directed toward adjusting income computations to take account of changes in the price level.

The procedures of accounting are everywhere permeated by the assumption that the monetary unit is the only reliable measure of value. Once that assumption is thrown into doubt, it is not possible to repair the theoretical structure by superficial adjustments of money values according to changes in price levels. A complete re-examination of the income concept is required, therefore, a re-examination that may serve as a guide to the interpretation of figures derived from conventional accounting operations, and possibly as an aid to those accountants who are trying to bring their practices into closer accord with a unified theory of income.

In the present study, the subject will be approached from the viewpoint of economic theory. Many studies of the same subject have been made from the viewpoints of the accountant and of the lawyer.[2] One disavowal must be made immediately. Economic science has no single universally accepted body of doctrine that need only be translated into non-technical language in order to tell the layman what " the economist " believes. Different economists believe different things and use different concepts, frequently with the same names. That is the basis of many a great controversy, and the subject of income and capital has been especially rich in controversy among economists. It would accordingly be arrogant for anyone to present " the economist's view of income." What is here presented is, at best, a personal view.

Nevertheless, the approach of most economists to the concepts of income and capital differs from that of most accountants in several important respects. The economist is accustomed to thinking of income in real terms while the accountant usually measures income in terms of money. Secondly, the economist usually considers an asset value as measured by the present worth of the asset's future net receipts, while the accountant has come to value assets largely in terms of historical costs adjusted for that part of original cost already charged to past operations. Finally, and most important of all, the economist regards income as the change in the recipient's entire command over goods and services over a given period. The accountant singles out certain transactions and confines his attention to the profit and loss on these transactions: he does not measure the net change in the income recipient's entire command over goods and services. There are, of course, exceptions to these rules, but they do broadly hold and so we must expect a difference in income and capital as conceived by the economist and by the accountant respectively.

It is no mere accident that these differences exist. The most perplexing and perhaps insoluble problems in defining and measuring income and capital arise out of the economist's attempt to take account of changes in the values of assets or in the purchasing power of money. So long as the accountant can avoid these problems he can operate with relative confidence in a world of certainties. But to ignore the world's uncertainties does not

---

[2] For a bibliography, inevitably far from complete, see *Changing Concepts of Business Income: Report of Study Group on Business Income* (New York: The Macmillan Co., 1952), pp. 147–160.

get rid of them and to the extent that the real value of money does change and it is necessary to revalue assets, the accountant will be presenting a false and misleading picture. Faced with a choice between precision of operation and precision of concept, the accountant has chosen the one, the economist the other. That is, the accountant has chosen a concept of income which permits precise measurements but which yields misleading results under conditions of fluctuation and uncertainty. The economist has sought to construct a concept that would stand up under fluctuating conditions but such a concept cannot easily be applied in practice.

If prices did not change, and if the cost of an asset, adjusted for depreciation, were generally more or less equal to the present value of its future stream of receipts, there would be no difference between the economist's and the accountant's concept of income and capital. But when prices do change and when historical costs are out of line with present values of future receipts, there will be a divergence between income and capital as measured by the economist and as measured by the accountant. An examination of the nature of that divergence and of the consequences of the use of one concept rather than the other are the principal objects of the present study.

The study will be complicated by the fact that the economist has bitten off more than he can chew. Those conceptual problems which the accountant, ostrich-like, avoids by burying his head in the sands of monetary measurement and historical costs cannot easily be solved. Perhaps they cannot be solved at all. But something may be gained by considering rather than ignoring them.

The concept of income

Income is a familiar notion in everyday life. But as in the case of many other familiar objects, it is not customary for those who use the notion to get down to its fundamentals. For most people, certain simple rules of calculation suffice to guide the measurement of income for all practical purposes, and it is not necessary to inquire further as to what income really is or should be.

Since the widespread practices of income determination are very seldom referred back to a fundamental concept of income, it is almost certain that all the practices cannot be consistent with a single basic concept of income. Each man conceives of income as he is accustomed to measure it, and there may be no common concept that governs all practices. We may begin, however, by trying to infer from the general practices of income determination what fundamental ideas are implied, and then, after refinement of these ideas, we may use them as a basis of criticism of the very practices from which they were, in a sense, abstracted.

Two notions in general use may be considered as lying behind the income concept. One is a man's income for a year, the other is a businessman's profit from a particular operation. These two are certainly inter-related. Indeed, we may presume that the second was a stage in the determination of the first. But since the two different basic approaches lead to concepts of income which differ in practical applications, we may consider them separately.

Income for a year

A man's income for any year is generally recognised to denote roughly the amount which has become available for his expenditures during that year. It may be distinguished from his wealth, which is defined as the total amount available for his expenditure or consumption at any given time. Wealth is a stock of value, income is a flow of value. That part of a man's income that he does not spend, he saves, that is he adds it to his wealth. In general terms, his wealth at the end of any period is equal to his wealth at the beginning of the period plus or minus the difference between his income and his consumption.

These rough notions are suitable for the loose conversation of everyday life, but they are too vague for precise analysis. They do serve, however, to illustrate the essential nature of the income concept. The basic notion involved is that each man desires certain experiences which are afforded him by the use of material objects or by actions performed by himself or by other people. We may call the desired experiences satisfactions. Material objects whose use affords satisfactions are called goods, actions affording satisfactions are called services. If we could measure a man's satisfactions, we might then immediately define his total income for a given year as the amount of satisfactions over which he has gained command during the year. A man may be said to have gained command over satisfactions when he has gained the legal right to receive the goods or services which can afford the satisfactions.

If we call a man's command over satisfactions at a given moment his well-being at that moment, then we can define his total income for a given year as the net amount of well-being over which he has acquired command during that year. The word " net " is introduced here in order to take account of any element of well-being which has been given up in exchange for another element of well-being.

When a man actually enjoys some of the satisfactions at his command, he may be said to consume the good or service which affords the satisfactions. His command over the satisfaction is exercised, and his well-being is then reduced by a corresponding amount.[3] Therefore, the net change in his well-being over any year is his income minus his consumption. We can turn this obvious statement around to get an alternative phrasing for the definition of income; a man's income in any year is equal to his consumption plus the net change in his well-being.

In order to make the picture complete, we might conceivably take account of unpleasurable experiences (dissatisfactions) undergone during the year. In particular, account might be taken of the work the man has had to do to gain the well-being he has acquired during the year. This is not usually done, however, in the determination of income.

There is then an asymmetry in the concept of net income, as between the treatment of the exchange of one good or service for another and the treatment of the exchange of unpleasurable activity for a good or service. Thus if a man sells his car for $1,500 and uses the proceeds to take a trip abroad his income, as usually measured, is unaffected by this transaction. If, however, he sells an extra month's work for $1,500 and spends the proceeds on a trip, then we say that both his income and his consumption are the larger by $1,500. The surrender of the motor-car must be set against the satisfaction of the trip abroad. The surrender of a month's leisure is not taken into account. This is a peculiarity of the concept of the income of an individual that does not carry over to the case of a business enterprise.

The foregoing definition of income is put forward to indicate the basic ideas that lie behind the concept of income. This concept may be approached in theory, but cannot be attained in fact because of the impossibility of providing an objective measure of satisfactions and hence of well-being. A second approach might then consist of defining a man's income and well-being, not in terms of satisfactions, but in terms of goods and services that afford these satisfactions. The goods and services need not be measured in common units, so that a man's income could be thought to consist of the difference between two collections of goods and services. From this point of view, a year's income would equal the collection of goods and services consumed over

---

[3] Strictly, we should except from this generalization the enjoyment of unperishable consumer goods such as works of art.

the year plus the goods owned and the services commanded at the end of the year minus the goods owned and services commanded at the beginning of the year. If the catalogue of goods and services were complete, this definition of income would closely approach the basic concept of income; but it would probably not be useful for any of the purposes for which a measure of income is desired. Those purposes require the measurement of income not as a complex relationship of heterogeneous objects and actions, but as a single measure in a well defined unit.

In order to achieve such a measure, it is necessary to do further violence to the concept of income and to eliminate from our definition those goods, and more particularly those services, which are not usually exchanged for money. Command over the remaining class of goods and services customarily exchanged for money may be called wealth, which is the *economic* component of well-being. A man's wealth may be defined as the aggregate of those goods and services at his command which are " directly capable of a money measure." [4] Because the elements of wealth are capable of a money measure, the aggregate of wealth is also capable of a money measure. It is this fact which, in practical operations, leads us to use wealth rather than well-being as the basis of income measurement.

It is probably obvious to most people that market value is the appropriate measure of well-being associated with each item of wealth in a man's possession. If one man feels that some of his possessions mean more in terms of his well-being than their market value, and others less, he is free to buy more of the first type of goods and sell some of the second type until market values and well-being are matched so far as he is concerned. [5] A man's economic income, as distinguished from his total income, can accordingly be defined as the net increase in the wealth available for his consumption in a given period. An equivalent definition of a man's economic income in a given year is his consumption of wealth during that year plus his wealth at the year's end minus his wealth at the end of the previous year.

According to this line of thought, the essence of the income concept is the amount that a man can consume over the income period and be as well off at the end of the period as at the beginning. For practical purposes, the phrase " as wealthy " is substituted for the phrase " as well off " and a corresponding change

---

[4] Alfred Marshall, *Principles of Economics*, 7th ed. (London: Macmillan, 1916), p. 57.
[5] For exceptional goods and services it may be possible to buy but not to sell, or vice versa, but these are complications which need not concern us here.

is implicitly made in the concept of consumption. The latter is no longer to be regarded as the sum of all satisfactions enjoyed by the income recipient in the period under consideration, but as the value of money-measurable goods and services used up in affording those satisfactions which did result from the destruction of wealth in consumption.

The foregoing concepts are highly academic; but they will help us when we come to discuss more practical questions than those concerning the nature of well-being or of wealth. It is important to note that economic income measured in terms of wealth is only a rough approximation to a more fundamental but unmeasurable concept, income in terms of well-being. The most troublesome problems in the measurement of income arise when the measures of wealth we are using can no longer be regarded as sufficiently close approximations to the concept of well-being. In particular, in periods of shifting price levels, the money measure of wealth may be a poor basis for the determination of income.

Once we have limited the income concept to wealth, we need no longer confine our attention to the income of an individual. We can now speak of the income of an asset. Any particular piece of property of an individual represents a certain amount of his wealth. If further accessions of wealth are connected with his ownership of the asset, we may call such accessions, net of any change in the value of the asset, the income of that asset. A business or a corporation may be regarded as an asset and indeed the growth of the business corporation was probably the major factor leading to a clear distinction between income and capital.[6]

Taking our cue from the definition of income for an individual, we may, as a first approximation, say that the income of any asset is equal to the net accession to the value of the asset over the period considered, including in that accession all receipts attributed to the asset. If we needed the income measure only for the determination of the income of the individual who owns the asset, we could refine the definition by reference to considerations governing the concept of income of the individual. Thus, for example, a change in the market value of the asset in exact proportion to a change in the general price level could not be regarded as an accession to the well-being of the individual, and therefore might be excluded from the concept of income.

Since the concept of income of that most important type of asset, the corporation itself, is used for so many purposes other than reporting its income to its stockholders, it may not always

---

[6] See Littleton, A. C., *Accounting Evolution to 1900* (New York: American Institute Pub. Co., 1933), p. 206.

be desirable to apply the rules appropriate to the measurement of an individual's income to the income of a corporation. For example, we may better serve some purposes for which corporate income is used if gains from changes in the general price-level are included in income. This question will be investigated in detail later.

Because we are interested primarily in business income, we can avoid some of the problems in the determination of income that arise from the personal equation of the individual as a human being. We may define the income of a corporation in a given year as the amount the corporation can distribute to the owners of equity in the corporation and be as well off at the end of the year as at the beginning. For a corporation to be as well off at the end of the year as at the beginning must mean that the value of the owners' equity at year's end equals the value at the beginning of the year. This is usually expressed as " maintaining capital intact." The problem of measuring income is, accordingly, inseparable from the problem of measuring changes in the value of equity or of capital.

From the starting point of the income of an individual for a given year, we have approached the income of a business enterprise as the difference between the net worth of its equity at the beginning and end of the period, any distribution of wealth to equity holders during the year being added back into year-end equity. This general type of income concept we may call an equity-change concept so emphasising the importance of the valuation of assets and liabilities at the beginning and end of the period. Such periodic valuation is necessary in order to find out how well off the equity owner is at the end of the period compared with the beginning and so to determine how much he could consume during the period and still be as well off at the end as at the beginning, in accordance with the basic notion of the income of an individual for a given year.

Profit from an operation

Another approach to the basic concept of income stems from the analysis of the profit or loss on operations performed during the year. Thus, a merchant might inquire what profit his sales for a given year have brought him. To answer this question he must determine the cost of the goods sold. Once he has done this to his satisfaction, then by deducting the costs from the revenues he can compute his profit from the sales of a given period. This suggests another general type of approach to the determination of income, namely, the operating profit approach. That approach, in counter-distinction to the equity change approach, proceeds by matching costs against revenues or against the products of a specified operation.

We have used sales as a particular example of the sort of transaction which can be used as a strategic point in the conduct of a business at which profit can be measured, but other types of operation might conceivably be chosen. For example, production rather than sales might be the basis of computation of an operating profit. From the value of the product of the operations performed in a year there could be deducted the cost of those operations, and the result would be a profit on goods produced. In that case, inventories of finished goods would be valued at market rather than at cost,[7] and operating profit would be reported on goods produced but not sold.

II. VARIANT CONCEPTS OF INCOME

A simplified example may help to clarify the differences between the two approaches to the income of a corporation which have just been distinguished, as well as to illustrate some of the all too many different concepts of income. The complexity of this highly oversimplified case may serve as an excuse for the unrealistic assumptions made, since greater realism could be achieved only at the cost of overwhelming complications.

The Neverlose Manufacturing Company is engaged in the manufacture of gadgets. At the beginning of 19x5, it was expected that throughout all future time the company would manufacture a hundred thousand gadgets a year and sell them for $100,000 at a total cost of $90,000 including all charges,[8] so affording an annual profit and an annual dividend of $10,000 indefinitely into the future. The current long term interest rate is 5 per cent., and so the value of the equity in the company is $200,000, the present value of $10,000 a year indefinitely into the future.

During 19x5, however, the company actually manufactured 130,000 gadgets at a total cost, including all charges, taxes, etc.,

---

[7] Allowance should, of course, be made for any additional costs that must be incurred in selling the finished goods.

[8] These costs are assumed to have been determined according to accepted accounting practice, except that in addition to the items normally charged to " cost of goods sold," interest charges, income taxes and other charges normally deducted in the process of obtaining net income after taxes have also been included. No charges for revaluation of fixed assets or inventories are assumed entered into " cost of goods sold," except to the extent such factors enter into predetermined allowances for depreciation, obsolescence, bad debts, etc.

of $104,000, or $0·80 each, the cost of inputs being measured (on the usual accounting basis) as of the time of *purchase*. Under prices as of the time of *manufacture*, it would have cost $117,000 or $0·90 each, to produce the 130,000 gadgets.

In 19x5 the company sold 107,500 gadgets at $1·00 each (leaving 22,500 units in finished goods inventories). The cost of goods sold was thus $86,000; under conditions as of time of sale, it would have been $96,750.

The company paid dividends of $21,500 on December 31, 19x5.

Appraisal of tangible assets and liabilities at beginning and end of 19x5 by an independent appraiser shows an increase of tangible net worth (before dividends were paid) of $25,000 when year-end inventories of finished goods are valued at historical cost, $27,500 when they are valued at his estimate of replacement cost, or $30,000 when they are valued at his estimate of market. These appraisal figures can be accepted as reasonable, even where they do not agree with the company's records.

As of January 1, 19x6, it is expected that in future the company will sell 120,000 gadgets a year at $1·00 each, and will produce 120,000 gadgets a year at an annual cost of $109,000. The whole of the $11,000 profit will be distributed at the end of each year. Therefore the year-end value of equity after dividends is the present value, at 5 per cent. interest, of $11,000 a year indefinitely into the future, or $220,000.

As shown below, there are many possible measures of the company's income for 19x5. They fall into four major categories:

Equity-change concepts

1. Mixed economic income (see p. 142)
    (= comprehensive equity-change) $
        Year-end equity change $20,000
        Dividends   21,500
                                                         ————   41,500
    Divisible into:
        (a) Pure economic income $11,500
        (b) Unexpected gain   30,000

2. Tangible equity-change income
        (a) If finished goods inventories are valued at
                historical cost   25,000
        (b) If finished goods inventories are valued at
                replacement cost   27,500
        (c) If finished goods inventories are valued at
                market   30,000

Operating profit concepts (see p. 144) $

3. Accounting income

    (= mixed profit on sales)   21,500

    Divisible into:

        (a) Pure sales profit $10,750

        (b) Price gains on items charged to cost of

                 goods sold   10,750

4. Mixed profit on production   26,000

    Divisible into:

        (a) Pure production profit $13,000

        (b) Price gains on items charged to cost of

                 goods produced   13,000

Each of the four major types of income, and some of the sub-types, have a claim to be considered for the title " The Income " of the corporation. There are many other possible concepts, some of which we mention below, but we must be content to investigate only those listed above. These should give us sufficient variety.

Mixed economic income is the most simple and direct form of the equity-change approach to the concept of income. It is simply the change in the corporation's equity over the year after adding back any dividends paid during the year.

In the case of the Neverlose Company the year-end net worth is $220,000 after dividends, and $241,500 before dividends. Year-beginning net worth as estimated at January 1, 19x5, was $200,000, so that the company's mixed economic income for 19x5 is $41,500. This is the amount the corporation might have paid out in dividends (assuming it to be legally permitted) without reducing year-end net worth below what it was believed to have been at the beginning of the year.

But it might be objected that, should the Neverlose Company actually pay a dividend of $41,500, it would be worse off thereafter than it really was at the beginning of the year. For the beginning-of-the-year valuation of the equity at $200,000 was too low. From what is known or believed at the end of the year, the beginning-of-the-year equity can be revalued. In fact, it should equal the end-of-the-year equity of $241,500 discounted back to the beginning of the year. That is to say, on December 31, 19x5, the company's equity is judged to be worth $241,500. A fair value of the equity on January 1, 19x5, would then be such a sum as would amount to $241,500 by December 31, 19x5, if it earned 5 per cent. interest over the year. That value comes to $230,000.

From this point of view, the company's income in 19x5 was $241,500 minus $230,000, or $11,500. That amount may be called the pure economic income of the Neverlose Company in 19x5. It is the difference between the year-end net worth and the year-beginning net worth, both valued according to the knowledge and beliefs current at year's end. Pure economic income is also the amount that could be paid out in dividends this year with the expectation that in all future years an equal amount can be paid annually. Thus, if this year $11,500 had been paid out in dividends, the remaining $10,000 of the $21,500 actually paid out might have been invested, presumably at 5 per cent., and so would yield $500 per year. This $500 plus the $11,000 expected annually from operations would lead to the expectation of a dividend potentiality of $11,500 a year.

In paying out a dividend of $21,500, the company has impaired capital relative to the beginning of the year, at least from this point of view, for net worth has been reduced from $230,000 to $220,000. The fact that net worth was, on January 1, 19x5, believed to be only $200,000 is beside the point, it may be argued; the difference between the $230,000 we now believe the equity to have been worth at the beginning of the year and the $200,000 we then believed it to have been worth is merely a correction of an estimate. From this viewpoint, it should not be regarded as income. It may be given a special name of its own, say " unexpected gain."

Given the rate of interest and the equity as valued at the beginning and end of the year, mixed economic income can always be broken down into pure economic income and un-expected gain. Whether the unexpected gain should or should not be counted as income is a controversial question we shall discuss later.

The definition of tangible equity-change income is formally quite similar to that of mixed economic income but the concept is markedly different. Tangible equity-change income is the change over the year in the value of the corporation's equity exclusive of the capitalised value of its own expected future earning power (going value).[9] In subsequent discussion we shall use the term " going value " to denote the difference between the capitalized value of the future dividend payments and the

[9] In order to preserve the subsequent discussion from undue complications, intangible assets other than going value are ignored. The expression " tangible assets " or " tangible equity," unless qualified to the contrary, will in subsequent discussion refer to assets or equity exclusive of going value. Going value is here defined as simply the difference between the tangible equity of the corporation and the capitalized value of its future disbursements to owners.

tangible equity however measured. That is, once someone has specified a measure of tangible equity, we can find the corresponding going value as the difference between the capitalized value of future dividends and the specified tangible equity.

The fact that future prospects of the Neverlose Company have improved over the year 19x5 is not taken into account in the measurement of tangible equity-change income unless the changes in prospects are reflected in the valuation of physical assets. This concept of income thus requires some method of appraising the value of the corporation's assets other than by future earning power. Market values are the most likely basis for the appraisal of some of the assets, but more mystical bases are used for others.

However little theoretical justification there may be for excluding intangible asset changes while including tangible asset changes, the practical reasons for doing so are very powerful. Accountants and business men would be surprised and shocked to find a business carrying an increase of going value to income account. We shall later consider how well founded such an attitude is. For the present, we may note merely that tangible equity-change income can be computed in a manner that is conceptually simple. It is merely necessary to appraise the tangible equity at the beginning and end of the year, and take the difference. The result, plus any dividends paid out during the year, is tangible equity-change income.

Since there are many different ways of appraising assets, there are many different ways of estimating tangible equity-change income. Of these many ways, three have been entered in the table above. The first, 2 (a), includes finished goods valued at historical cost. The third, 2 (c), includes finished goods valued at market prices minus expected selling cost. The difference between these two concepts is very similar to the difference between profit from sales and profit from production to be considered below.

Accounting income is the income that would conventionally be reported for the corporation for most purposes. It is the profit gained on this year's sales, computed as $21,500 by deducting from the proceeds of this year's sales, $107,500, the total historical cost of goods sold including all charges, $86,000. Any item of cost that entered goods sold was valued at the price paid for it at the time of acquisition of the item by the company. Had costs been based on the prices of raw materials and other cost items as of the time of sale, the cost of goods sold would have been $96,750. Costs so based may be broadly termed

" replacement costs," and we have used this term in the foregoing illustrations.

The accountant's income can accordingly be broken down into two components, pure sales profit and price gain respectively. Pure sales profit is the difference between sales revenue and cost of goods sold when both costs and revenue are valued at prices prevailing at time of sales. The difference between sales profit as usually measured (mixed sales profit) and pure sales profit is the element of price gain contained in mixed sales profit. That price gain is equal to the difference between the value of the items of cost charged to sales at prices ruling at time of sale and the corresponding value at prices ruling at the times of acquisition of the various items of cost—the difference, that is to say, between replacement costs and historical costs.

In brief, accounting income, here identified with mixed profit from sales, is composed of the difference between sales revenue and replacement cost at the time of sale plus the profit or loss from the changes in the value of cost items between time of acquisition and time of sale.

The concept of mixed production profit is formally similar to accounting income except that it is applied to production rather than to sales. Certain specified actions performed by people connected with the business enterprise may be designated as production. Usually the actions so designated are considered the principal business of the enterprise. Just as it is possible with some degree of arbitrariness to assign all costs incurred by an enterprise to the sales of various time periods, so it is also possible to assign all costs to the production of various time periods. Then the mixed production profit of any time period, say a year, will equal the value of the year's production minus the costs assigned to the year's production.

For the Neverlose Manufacturing Company mixed production profit for 19x5 may be computed as $26,000, the difference between $130,000, the sale value of goods produced, and $104,000, the total historical cost of that production. Just as mixed sales profit can be broken down into pure sales profit and price gain, so can mixed production profit be broken down into pure production profit and price gain on cost items charged to production. Pure production profit, $13,000, is the difference between the sale value of goods produced, $130,000, and the total cost of goods produced at current prices, *i.e.*, replacement costs, $117,000. The price gain component of mixed profit on production, $13,000, is the difference between the replacement cost of production, $117,000, and the historic cost of production, $104,000.

If each year's entire production were sold in the same year, we should expect mixed profit from sales (accounting income) and mixed profit from production to be equal. Similarly, pure profits from sales would equal pure profits on production, and the price gain components would also be equal. Differences arise to the extent that sales in a given year may be made partly from the production of other years, and the product of this year's operations may be sold partly in this year and partly in other years.

All these different measures of income are measures of money income. To each there corresponds a measure of real income which takes account of the fact that the value of the monetary unit has changed in purchasing power as between the beginning and the end of the year, and as between time of acquisition of cost items and time of use or sale. It is not necessary to investigate in detail the manner in which the money income measures can be adjusted to obtain real income measures. But it would not, in general, be appropriate to try to convert any of the money measures into real measures merely by dividing by the price index. For each measure is the difference between two money quantities. To get the corresponding real measure each of the two money quantities must first be converted into real quantities by dividing by the appropriate price index, and then the difference may be taken. To take the money difference first and then to deflate by the price index produces a misleading result.

The operating profit approach to income is more narrowly limited than the equity-change approach in that equity can change either as a result of operations or for other reasons. But that does not necessarily imply a superiority of the equity-change approach over the operating profit approach. For some purposes the equity-change methods may include more than is desired. Similarly for some purposes the pure operating profits may be more useful than the mixed operating profits which include price gains. No one of these concepts can be proclaimed as the *true* concept of income. Each has certain advantages and disadvantages. Furthermore, even the advantages and disadvantages cannot be clearly identified because that which is good for one purpose may be bad for another. We want to use a measure of income for several different purposes, and it should not surprise us to find that a measure which is good for one purpose is not good for another.

III. Income Under Conditions of Certainty

Of all the variant concepts of income mentioned above, that which we call economic [10] is the one most immediately related to the notion of income as the amount that the recipient can consume and remain as well off at the end of the period as he was at the beginning. For the corporation, equity is the appropriate measure of well being. Mixed economic income is the amount that can be paid in dividends while keeping the value of equity intact. But other concepts of income satisfy the same condition, at least formally, provided equity is defined and valued appropriately. Thus, if equity is valued on the basis of original cost, accounting income will also correspond to the basic notion of income. Some question may be raised, however, as to how good a measure of well being is equity based on original cost. In any case, the essential feature of economic income is to be found in the way in which equity is valued under that concept. The basic tenet of economic income is that equity is an asset of its owner, and it should therefore be valued according to the principles applied to other assets.

The value of an asset

The value of any object can usually be explained in terms of supply and demand, an explanation which is useful only to the extent that we can actually describe the operation of the factors which govern supply and demand. Supply, at least of reproducible objects, is governed by the cost of production, or more fundamentally, by the circumstances influencing those costs. Demand for an object is governed by different factors depending on whether the object is desired for consumption or for procuring other objects. Demand for consumption goods is governed by consumer preference backed up by purchasing power. But in the case of capital assets, as we may call those assets held not for consumption but for eventual use in procuring other assets, the demand is governed by what the assets are expected to procure in the future.

The very nature of capital assets involves an evaluation of future receipts. Such an evaluation is complicated by three serious difficulties. First, and most important, the future receipts are not known, but can only be estimated. Secondly, a dollar in the future is not worth a dollar today even if its purchasing

---

[10] In the previous section a distinction is made between pure economic income and mixed economic income. That distinction is appropriate only under conditions of uncertainty. In the present section, in which uncertainty is assumed away, we need refer only to economic income.

power should remain constant; this is reflected in the phenomenon of interest. Finally, the purchasing power of money does not remain constant. It is from these three circumstances that the interesting and important problems in the measurement of economic income and the corresponding concept of capital arise. We may first make some simplifying assumptions that will permit us to see how the value of capital may be measured when these difficulties do not plague us.

Let us assume that the future receipts associated with the asset are known with certainty, that we have a set of rules for determining the present value of a sum of money to be received at any specified future date, and that the general price level remains constant. Then it is quite easy to measure the value of the asset. It is the sum of the present values of the future receipts.

For brevity, we may call that very important set of rules which we use to convert future receipts or payments into present values " the rate of interest." It must be recognised, however, that we are dealing with a whole set of rates of interest, one for each possible time span. The way in which the structure of interest rates is determined is very complicated and remains highly controversial. Fortunately, we need not concern ourselves with that problem. We may take the rate structure as given, determined by market forces. Then, to measure the value of any asset, we need merely capitalize its future net receipts; that is, find the sum of the present values of those future net receipts.

The value of equity

The simple and obvious method of valuing owner's equity in a corporation would seem to be to take the difference between the aggregate value of the corporation's assets minus the corporation's liabilities. If this were done in the conventional manner, the result would be inappropriate for our present purposes since there would be no guarantee that owner's equity as so measured would equal the present value of future payments to ownership. The conventional measurement of balance-sheet items does not aim toward that end. That is why a corporation's economic income cannot appropriately be measured by the changes entered on the balance-sheet.

Even though we could measure the value of almost all the assets and liabilities of the corporation independently of the value of the corporation as a whole, that would not help us in the determination of the net worth of the equity. For the corporation has a going concern value different from the sum of the values of its assets that can be independently measured.

This difference can itself be expressed as an asset called " going value " or goodwill but that asset cannot be valued independently of the total value of the corporation as an entity. So if we substitute a value of equity obtained by addition of independently valued assets and deduction of liabilities, then we are misstating equity from the economist's point of view. This is recognised every day by business men and investors who ignore book values in valuing a corporation, and look rather to future receipts.

Only if an appropriate value is entered for goodwill can owner's equity be measured from the balance-sheet in accord with the view that equity is an asset of the owner. To enter any increase of goodwill as a part of income would shock most accountants, yet the goodwill is the one asset which most clearly embodies the economist's concept of asset value since it most clearly represents capitalised earning power.

From the economist's point of view, the owner's equity in a corporation may be valued like any other asset as the present value of the stream of future net receipts. There are many possibilities open to the management of a corporation of varying purchases and sales and operations. To each possibility there can be associated certain time patterns of disbursements to the owners of equity throughout the future. Each of these time patterns may be considered to stretch forward endlessly, though from some particular time onward in each pattern receipts and disbursements may be steadily zero.

By identifying the corporation's income with the change in the stockholders' equity, we are not guilty of confusion between the income of the corporation and the owners' income from the corporation, as may at first sight appear; for so long as we maintain our present assumptions that the directors of the corporation have perfect foresight and act both rationally and in the best interests of the stockholders, then with any one pattern of net receipts to the corporation there can be associated only one pattern of disbursements to stockholders—that pattern which has the maximum present value. The directors are free to withhold dividends and plough back profits only if they have the expectation of getting a normal return on the amount ploughed back and of paying out correspondingly higher dividends at a future date, so leaving the present value of stockholders' equity still at its maximum. We are justified, therefore, under our assumptions, in regarding the corporation's income and the stockholder's income from the corporation as uniquely tied together, given, of course, that the appropriate rate of interest for the firm is the same as the rate appropriate for the stockholders.

It will now be seen why it is enough to take account of the corporation's disbursements to stockholders, while ignoring what is left in the corporation. For whatever is left in the corporation must either some day result in a disbursement to ownership or else it should not be counted in equity, for the present value of a dollar now invested which will never be paid back is zero. Only if a definite length of time is taken and broken off at some future date, say five years from now, must we take account of what is left in the corporation. For then the value of equity must be defined as the present value of disbursements over that five years plus the present value of equity five years hence. But the value of equity five years hence must depend on the future disbursements as of five years hence and forever after.

A definition which requires knowledge of all future circumstances is obviously of little practical use. It is presented here for conceptual clarification only. It is interesting to note that most of the concepts of accounting are not required for this definition. Neither costs nor revenues, assets or liabilities as such, or depreciation, are mentioned. All that is needed to determine the present value of equity is the present value of future disbursements to ownership. If this were actually known, however, and future rates of interest were known, the equity of the corporation at all future dates would also be known, and hence the future income of the corporation would be known for all time to come as well.

Is our definition circular?

It may be objected that we have now involved ourselves in a circular definition. Income has been defined as the amount that can be disposed of in a given year while leaving the recipient as well off at the end of the year as at the beginning. Stockholders' income so defined has been declared equivalent to the net change in value of owner's equity over the year. But owner's equity is from the owner's point of view an asset and it must be valued by reference to future receipts like any other asset. If those receipts were themselves income, we should be engaged in formulating a circular definition, for we should be saying that the stockholders' income was equal to the increase in their equity, and their equity was to be valued by reference to the income which it produced. But fortunately for our purposes the receipts need not be income but can be a mixture of income and return (or reinvestment) of principal. The objection of circularity is based on a confusion of receipts with income. In order perfectly to measure this year's income we need to know all future receipts, we do not need to know all future incomes. The latter can be computed from the former, if the rates of interest are known. Given all future receipts and rates of interest, we can calculate present and future income.

Thus, suppose we are valuing the equity of a very simple corporation whose net dividends are expected to be $103·00 next year, $106·09 two years from now, and $109·27 three years from now with no further dividends thereafter.

If the appropriate rate of interest is 3 per cent. the present value of each of these annual instalments is $100 and the present value of the equity is $300. This can be computed directly from the scheduled receipts without first distinguishing income from return of principal. Capital can be measured from the antcipated inflow of receipts and then the measure of capital so obtained can be used in the determination of income. Therefore there is no circularity in our definition of income.

Pure economic income

In the above example, at the end of the first year the owner of the asset can expect $106·09 one year later and $109·27 two years later. It may easily be computed that the asset is then worth $206 which in addition to the $103 cash just received makes $309. So by our definition income of that year is just $9 or 3 per cent. of the $300 value of the asset at the beginning of the year. Income is $9·00, $6·18 and $3·18 in the first, second and third years respectively.

It is no coincidence that the income so determined shows a yield on the value of the asset just equal to the rate of interest. The process of calculating the present value of an asset consists of breaking down a stream of present and future receipts into two parts, income and return (or continued investment) of principal, in such a way that income in any period will represent a yield on principal still invested just equal to the rate of interest. It is always possible to do this by a simple mathematical procedure and so there is no circularity in our definition of income.

But this same reasoning then implies that unless there is a change in the interest rate, income from a given amount of capital will remain constant so long as that capital remains intact. Therefore, we may now formulate a rather odd definition of income which is equivalent to that previously formulated. This year's income is the amount that can be disposed of in the year with the expectation that an equal amount can be disposed of each year indefinitely in the future so long as the rate of interest remains unchanged. Ideally defined then, if a firm did not reinvest earnings, its income would be constant except for changes in the rate of interest.

Similarly, the income of an individual, if properly measured, must, under the assumed conditions of certainty and stability of interest rates, be constant over his lifetime except to the extent that he consumes or builds up capital.

A conclusion so contrary to the practice of income determination deserves further study. In the conventional measurement of a person's income, no account is taken of the capital value of the person's earning power. Suppose a man receives $10,000 salary this year, but can expect to receive only $5,000 a year henceforth into the future. Is it then appropriate to say that the man's income this year is $10,000 or something less? This question can be translated into the question whether, if the man spends $10,000 this year, he will be as well off at the end of the year as at the beginning. The conventional accounting answer would be, " Yes, he can spend the $10,000 he receives and he need not cut into his capital at all." The answer of economic theory is " No." The prospect of receiving $10,000 this year is part of the man's capital. His income is an amount such that, if it is consumed this year, he will be left with the prospect of consuming an equal amount in the future. Let us suppose that for $4,500 the man can purchase an annuity of $500 for the rest of his life, excluding the current year. Then the income of this and each subsequent year may be calculated at $5,500. The $10,000 he received this year should be considered as $5,500 income and $4,500 return of capital. If the $4,500 return of capital is reinvested in the annuity, it will increase his annual income in future by $500 a year, and this with his salary of $5,000 will give him $5,500 a year. If the $4,500 is consumed, then he is consuming part of the capital represented by the capitalised value of his future earning power as of the beginning of the year.

The contrary conclusion of conventional accounting shows that it is not customary for individuals to use the economic concept of income but rather a tangible equity-change concept or an operating profit concept.

It makes little practical sense to apply the economic concept to a man, since as a general rule no one is interested in changes in the capitalised value of a man's earning power. The contrary is true in the case of a business enterprise, however. A corporation that earns $10,000 this year and $5,000 in all subsequent years (according to conventional accounting) can quite appropriately be said to have had income of less than $10,000 this year. Suppose there are a thousand shares of common stock in the corporation, these constituting the entire issued stock. Suppose that each year the corporation pays dividends equal to earnings as reported by the accountant. Then a share of stock will receive $10 this year and $5 per year in each subsequent year. Given a 5 per cent. rate of interest and perfect certainty as to the future, such a share would be worth about $105 at the beginning of this year and $100 ex-dividend at the end of the year so that the net income from the share will be the $10 dividend minus the $5 decline in capital value or about $5 this year, and the income will continue to be $5 a year in succeeding years.

We might, of course, say that the income from the share was $10 but that there was also a $5 capital loss when the market value declined from $105 to $100. But this merely raises the question to be discussed later of whether a capital gain or loss should be treated as income. It would certainly seem that if the owner of a share of the stock is intent on preserving his capital intact he should consider as income available for consumption only $5 of the $10 received.

The economic concept of income then does make sense in the case of a business enterprise because in that case a great deal of importance attaches to the capitalized value of future receipts. The fact that accountants do not measure economic income but something closer to operating profit is one of the important points of divergence between the accountant's concept of income and that of the economic theorist.

As a matter of fact, when economists get into the actual business of measuring income as in the measurement of national income, they follow the practice of businessmen and accountants rather than the dictates of economic theory. Measures of national income are certainly not based on the economic income concept as here defined. In large part this is inevitable because the national income estimate must be built up from private income reported by businesses and individuals. These are based on a concept much closer to tangible income than to economic income. But more fundamentally it is doubtful that economists want to measure national income on a capitalised basis which would mean that each year's income as currently reported would be adjusted for changes in the present value of future receipts. As will be indicated below, the economic income concept tends to gloss over the particular causes of variation of receipts from year to year that are sometimes the principal object of interest in income measurement.

We may now briefly summarize the nature of economic

income under conditions of certainty of future receipts, interest rates and constant prices.

Given a specified stream of future receipts and a set of interest rates, it is always possible to compute for each period:

(1) The income of the period, and
(2) A receipt or payment on account of capital,

such that:

(a) The period's receipts equal income plus the receipt on account of capital or minus the payment on account of capital,
(b) The receipt or payment on account of capital is equal in amount to the change in the capitalized value of future receipts over the period, but is of opposite sign,
(c) The income of the period is equal to the receipt of the period plus or minus the change of capitalized value of future receipts over the period,
(d) The income of the period is equal to the capitalized value of future receipts at the end of the previous period, multiplied by the rate of interest.

Income so defined is economic income.

We may illustrate the difference between an accountant's and an economist's concept of income under conditions of certainty by a simple example. Suppose it is known that, according to the best rules of accounting, a certain corporation's future profits will be zero and $10,250 in alternate years forever into the future. Assume that a dividend is accordingly paid of $10,250 on December 31 of every second year and no dividend is paid in the intermediate year.

If the appropriate rate of interest were 5 per cent. an economist would disagree with the accountant and say that the income was $5,000 and $5,250 in alternate years rather than zero and $10,250 as reported by the accountant: for immediately after the payment of a dividend, the equity is worth $100,000 (which sum, at 5 per cent. compound will yield $10,250 in two years' time and every second year thereafter), while a year later it is worth $105,000 (this being the sum which will yield $10,250 in one year's time and every second year thereafter). So in a year of no dividend, the income is equal to the growth of $5,000 in the equity; while in a year in which $10,250 is received as dividend, the income is $5,000 less than this (that is, it is $5,250) by reason of the fall in the value of the equity.

Furthermore, if equity of the corporation was originally acquired for $100,000, the accountant would presumably continue to carry it at a value of $100,000 since all profits earned are paid out in dividends. The economist, however, as we have just explained, would say that on January 1 of alternate years the corporation was worth $100,000 and $105,000 respectively. If the owner were thinking of selling, he would be well advised to go by the economist's rather than the accountant's valuation. For at the end of the year of zero receipts, the owner of the corporation according to the accountant has an asset that will pay off $10,250 at the end of the year and will be worth $100,000 after the payment. To sell such an equity for $100,000 when interest is at 5 per cent. would indeed be foolish.

If the asset under consideration were an annuity, not a corporation, however, the accountant would come round to the economist's point of view. What is the explanation of this remarkable double standard of action? The accountant will agree with the economist in valuing the annuity, for in that case the accountant is willing to grant the assumption of knowledge of the future. But in measuring the income of a corporation, he is not willing to act as if the future were known and for very good reasons.

To those accustomed to the accountant's concept of income, the idea that variations in a corporation's income from year to year may represent errors of measurement may come as a shock. One year's income of a corporation is frequently compared with another's as a gauge of the skill and success of management. This comparison lacks justification from the viewpoint of economic income. Why then does the accounting concept of income differ from the economic concept in such a way that variations in income regarded as normal from the accountant's point of view must be considered errors of measurement from the point of view of the economist?

The accountant's basic concept of income is similar to the economist's. A year's income is the amount of wealth that could be distributed to the owners of equity over the year and still leave equity at year-end equal to equity at year-beginning. But this basic concept lies so far behind the accountant's operations that it is frequently lost from sight. More immediately there is substituted another concept of income which is equivalent to the economic concept, only under highly special circumstances. Instead of basing income on the difference in the value of assets, accountants usually base it on matching costs and revenues.

It would be possible so to define costs and revenues as to insure that the difference between the two would equal economic income as defined above. If, for example, revenues were defined as any increase in assets (or decline in liabilities) and cost as any decline in assets (or increase in liabilities), then the difference between revenues and cost would be the net change in equity, provided going value is included among the assets annually revalued.

But accountants do not try to keep accurate account of all changes in the value of assets and liabilities. Only those increases of assets which are specially secure are counted as revenues; and costs are counted, not as actual changes in the value of assets, but as the results of matching certain past or future payments with particular sales receipts. In both cost and revenues, primary emphasis is given to money payments. Gains are frequently not recognised as such until they are realised, that is, until they are converted for however short a period into money. Costs, too, are usually based on the money given for the resources used, but here exceptions are sometimes made, as in valuing inventories at the lower of cost or market.

The principal difference between the accountant's and the economist's approach to income, then, is the accountant's refusal to take account of certain changes of value of the assets held by the corporation as they accrue. Only some of the gains and losses accrued but not realised are recognised by the accountant. On the other hand, the economic definition of income requires that all accrued gains and losses be recognised, even gains and losses of going-concern value. The difference is principally a difference in timing, for eventually accrued gains and losses will be realised as the relevant assets are disposed of either through direct sale or through use in the production of goods and services which are eventually sold. Over the long run, therefore, the two measures will tend to yield the same results, but over short and intermediate periods there will be considerable differences. Even in the long run, however, so long as the business is not sold, increases of going value will not enter into accounting income.

In the following discussion, it is frequently desirable to contrast an economist's definition of income with that of an accountant. This contrast is, at times, fairly complicated, and it would be unduly so if a complex set of accounting rules were to be reviewed at each step. Accordingly a strict historical cost concept of income will be used as representative of the accountant's point of view. This is, of course, a caricature of accountancy. In actual practice revaluation of assets by market value and other modifications of historical cost methods may enter into accounting practice. But, for simplicity, such modifications will in general be ignored.

Income based on historical costs, or more briefly, historical income, might be computed as follows. The value of all assets except cash and receivables at the beginning and the end of the year can be measured by the cost of their acquisition in cash or its equivalent, minus such portion of that cost as has already been charged to operations. The value of cash is its face-value. Receivables can be valued at what they are expected to realise in cash. Liabilities can be measured or estimated directly from the books of the company. Equity can be computed as the difference between assets and liabilities. The change in equity so measured from year-beginning to year-end represents historical income, or as we shall call it, " accounting income."

An alternative method, and that usually used, is to start with revenues. In the simplest case revenues may be the proceeds of sales. Costs can be matched to these revenues according to established rules in such manner that all costs incurred can be assigned to those periods deemed most appropriate. Accountant's income for any period is the revenue of that period minus the costs assigned to that period.

Of course, in practice, great problems arise under this method as to how much of the costs incurred in the past, or expected in the future, is to be charged to this year's operations. But these problems, the traditional problems of accounting, do not concern us in this investigation. We need merely know that this method does provide some formula for assigning all costs to operations of particular periods. Such a method will be contrasted with the economic concept. In applying that concept we need not try to measure costs and revenues at all but we must compare equity at year-beginning with that of year-end in terms of future receipts rather than past expenditures. Roughly speaking, the historical cost method values an asset (except cash and receivables) at what it cost to acquire it minus that part of past cost that has already been charged to operations; the method of economic theory values an asset at the present value of what it can expect to receive in the future. The two methods would be equivalent only if the cost of an asset not yet charged to operations should always just equal the present value of its future receipts.

Accountants seldom attempt to charge to the costs or receipts of any year changes in going value. This follows first from the general accounting practice of charging a change in an asset's value to revenue or cost only as it is disposed of by use or by sale. In rare cases, usually when it has been purchased for cash or the equivalent, goodwill or going value may be charged off as a cost in annual instalments. But never is a year-to-year variation in the value of goodwill or going value permitted to enter a sound income account. This means that accounting income approaches tangible income rather than economic income as defined above.

Accounting income then differs from economic income in two important respects: it excludes gain or loss on going value and it excludes gain or loss on those tangible assets not entering directly or indirectly into the current year's sales.[11] Tangible equity-change income (or more briefly tangible income) accordingly lies halfway between economic income and accounting income. Like accounting income, it excludes gain or loss on goodwill and going value, but unlike accounting income, tangible income includes gain or loss on tangible assets accrued but not realised through the period. Differences between the three concepts can then be expressed in the following relationships.

Under conditions of certainty:

Economic income=any change over the period in the capitalised value of dividends of this and future periods.
Tangible income=economic income – change in value of goodwill over the period = total change in the value of tangible equity.
Accounting income=tangible income – change in value of tangible assets not realised in this period+changes in value of tangible assets accrued in other periods and realised in this period=proceeds of all assets sold – costs assigned to these assets.

The choice between the economic concept and the accounting concept of income must depend principally on whether or not it is appropriate to include going-value change in income and whether it is better to count gains and losses as they accrue or as they are realised.

Going value change as income

There may be some question as to how going value (goodwill) can change under conditions of certainty. There is a good deal of merit in the question, since uncertainty is one of the most important factors leading to changes in going value. But even under conditions of certainty, going value can vary as it is, in a manner of speaking, realised. We may illustrate this by a simple example.

Consider a corporation with tangible equity valued at $100,000, and with dividend payments expected with certainty of $10,250 at the end of the current year and $5,000 a year thereafter. Given

---

[11] On this point, accounting practice is far from uniform. Some revaluations are occasionally carried to surplus, sometimes through earnings, sometimes directly (see George D. Bailey, " Concepts of Income," *Harvard Business Review*, Vol. XXVI, No. 6, November 1948). In any case it is not accountant's practice to revalue assets annually in conjunction with the determination of the year's income.

a 5 per cent. interest rate, the present value of equity in this corporation (*i.e.*, the capitalised value of future dividend payments) is $105,000 and going value is therefore $5,000. After this year's dividends of $10,250 are paid, the capitalised value of future payments will be $100,000. If the value of tangible equity is maintained at $100,000, then going value has been reduced to zero. Economic income for the first year is $5,250, the remaining $5,000 paid in dividends being only a repayment of that part of the capital represented by going value. The tangible and the accounting income in this case would be $10,250. We may then say that the difference between the accounting income and the economic income in this case is that economic income takes account of the $5,000 decline in going value while the accounting and tangible income ignore this decline.

Since the treatment of going value is one of the most important respects in which accounting income differs from economic income, it is necessary to go into considerable detail in investigating why it is included in one and excluded from the other. It is particularly important to find out whether the exclusion by the accountant is based on principle or on practicality. For if it is based only on practicality then we need to remember that in interpreting the accountant's measurement of income, we must make allowance for its deviation from what it should be in principle. In short, we must find out whether economic income is an ideal from which accounting income differs only to the degree that the ideal is practically unattainable, or whether economic income is inappropriate even if it could conveniently be measured.

IV. A Critique of Accounting Income

The exclusion of going value change

Why does the economist include the net change of going value in income while the accountant excludes it? It is easier to explain the economist's behaviour than the accountant's. The economist's concept of the value of any asset is based on capitalized earning power, and that is in particular true of the equity in a corporation. To say this does not, of course, answer the question but just pushes it one step further back, from the income statement to the balance-sheet. Why does the economist in valuing equity insist on measuring the capitalised value of its future receipts? Why can he not accept a value which has regard only to the value of the net tangible assets? The economist's reply is that such a measure of value is unacceptable because it simply isn't what the equity is worth. The owner would be foolish to sell the equity for its tangible value if the capitalized value of future earnings were higher. A purchaser would be foolish to buy at tangible value if capitalised future earnings were lower. After all, an object's value is supposed to represent what the object is worth.

The accountants grant that the capitalised earning power is the only proper basis for valuing equity for purchase or sale and the courts apparently have also come to accept this view. If then it is universally agreed that the proper basis for valuing equity when buying or selling it is capitalized earning power, that must also be the proper basis for maintaining equity intact. If accountants use a different basis they must, in measuring what they call the income of a corporation, be interested in something other than in determining the amount which can be distributed as dividends while preserving equity intact.

Fortunately, the accountants can speak for themselves in this controversy. In the *Accountants' Handbook* [12] are set out the arguments supporting the " General Accounting Rule," which implies the exclusion from accounting income, except for the amortisation of the cost of intangibles actually acquired by purchase or exchange, of changes in going value and related intangibles. Paton expresses the rule as follows:

> Goodwill and other intangibles should not be recognised except where they are supported by costs actually incurred, in terms of transactions between essentially independent parties, and then only to the extent of the cash or equivalent cost. Intangible value so recognised should never be appreciated, but should be amortized as circumstances indicate.

We may examine in detail the supporting arguments adapted by Paton in part from Yang.[13]

> 1. It is the *function of accounting* to show as assets the costs incurred in acquiring plant and other necessary elements (adjusted to allow for the effect of operation and passage of time) and to show as income, when realised, the earning power, in the particular setting of such assets. To set up the capitalized value of an estimated element in earning power is inconsistent with this general function and tends to obscure the actual situation, from the standpoint of the owners of the particular enterprise, rather than to clarify it. On the other hand, where a special investment is made by the present owners in estimated future earnings, as in the purchase of goodwill, it becomes entirely consistent with the purposes of accounting to recognise such investment as an intangible asset, an asset on which, in the case of a perpetual earning

---

[12] W. A. Paton, ed., *Accountants' Handbook*, 3rd ed. (New York: Ronald, 1947), p. 841.

[13] J. M. Yang, *Goodwill and Other Intangibles* (New York: Ronald Press Co., 1927).

power, the special element in earnings, as it materialises, is a return or which, in the case of a terminable earning power, is recovered or liquidated through the realization of such earnings.

2. While it is recognised that the validity of the book values of typical tangible assets, particularly specialized fixed assets, depends in considerable degree upon the presence of *earning power*, most of the tangible assets have some market value apart from their use in the business, whereas the intangibles have as a rule no economic significance except in terms of the going concern as a whole. Further, the tangible assets are in general more determinate in amount, stable in value, and realisable than the intangibles. These considerations make the general measurement and accounting recognition of intangibles, where not specifically purchased, impracticable.

3. Recognition of non-purchased intangibles is unnecessary from the standpoint of *managerial purposes*. Aside from the question of the sale of the enterprise as a whole, there is no question of managerial policy to be affected by such recognition. Setting up estimated intangibles does not affect cost of production in the strict sense, creates no basis for a shift from one method or policy to another, bears no relation to general planning and budgeting. In this connection, it is worth noting, the case for the recognition of appreciation of fixed tangible assets is much stronger than the case for the recognition of intangibles.

4. Since the value of intangibles is merely an expression of differential earning power, such value, if recognised, would require *continuous adjustment* up and down, as earning power fluctuated over a period of years. Further, the fluctuating surplus created by capitalization of estimated differential earning power would in no sense be true surplus and might constitute a misleading and improper figure in the balance sheet.

5. Earning power should in general be expressed in terms of *return on investment* or cost values, not such values plus the capitalized value of an estimated element in earning power itself. For example, to capitalize *proprietary skill* and efficiency, often a factor in building up goodwill, is illogical and confusing from the standpoint of the owners, as it means the placing of objective costs and implicit elements, which are validated commercially only by the appearance of superior earning power itself, in the same category. Hence the capitalization of intangibles, without purchase, tends to create an improper relationship between balance-sheet and periodic income report.

6. *Rational comparisons* between enterprises, far from being promoted by a general attempt to set up estimated intangibles as assets, would be rendered more difficult. Carried to a logical extreme it would mean that in a particular field no concern would show a rate of return on asset values in excess of the normal or representative rate—which would be an absurd situation. In other words, it would create, artificially, a dead level of earning rates in the particular industry below which individual concerns might fall but above which it would be impossible for any enterprise to appear. Likewise comparisons between periods in a single enterprise would be made less satisfactory by such a process of capitalization.

7. Capitalization of an intangible, aside from purchase, assumes that it is possible to impute the effect of an element of earning power to one or more intangible factors. In view of the composite nature

of business income such an *imputation*, in the absence of the commercial test of actual cost incurred, is sheer hypothesis. Further, setting up a reservoir of intangible value to express the difference between capitalized estimated earning power and the conventional book values of other assets, as has sometimes been advocated, involves the unwarranted assumption that the book values of such other assets, as factors in income determination, are correctly stated.

8. Adoption of a policy of estimating and recording intangible values from period to period would not only obscure important relationships and run counter to the essential purposes and functions of accounting, but it would tend to encourage juggling and misrepresentation and would result in balance-sheet totals little if any more significant and stable than those which might be obtained by the continuous introduction into the statements of capitalized values as shown by the market for outstanding securities.[14]

Let us examine these arguments point by point.

1. It is the *function of accounting* to show as assets the costs incurred in acquiring plant and other necessary elements ... and to show as income, when realised, the earning power, in the particular setting, of such assets. To set up the capitalized value of an estimated element in earning power is inconsistent with this general function. ...

Whether or not it is the function of accounting to show as assets the (adjusted) costs incurred in acquiring necessary assets is itself an open question which can hardly be used as the basis for settlement of the matter at issue. Whether the accountant should, in the balance-sheet, carry assets at adjusted cost rather than at economic value is by no means clearly settled in principle in favour of cost. There may be strong *practical* considerations in favour of the use of cost, but this establishes no *principle* that it is the function of accounting so to do. Are there then independent reasons for carrying assets at adjusted costs so strong that they can be extended to require exclusion of going concern value from the balance-sheet (except as acquired by incurring costs) and changes therein from the determination of income?

This question sends us back in the *Accountants' Handbook* to the discussion of the "Case for Adherence to Cost" as the basis of accounting. Paton here quotes with slight modifications from Paton and Littleton, *Introduction to Corporate Accounting Standards*:

Recognition of inadequacy of recorded cost (or cost less accrued depreciation) as a continuous expression of market value should not lead to (the) conclusion that accounting based on cost is unsound and should be replaced by an accounting for values. The primary purpose of accounting is the measurement of periodic income by means of a

[14] *Accountants' Handbook*, 3rd ed., pp. 841–843.

systematic matching of costs and revenues. Substitution of estimated current market values for recorded cost factors on the way to assignment to revenue would constitute a radical change in the standard scheme of income determination; periodic net income would then include the effect of all write-ups and write-downs of cost factors involved.

There seem to be no convincing reasons for the assumption that accounting would more adequately meet the needs of the parties concerned if estimated replacement costs or other evidences of current values were regularly substituted for recorded dollar costs. Costs are objectively determined data, current values are largely matters of opinion and for some types of cost factors are very unreliable. Hence a shift from costs to estimated values would generally mean the presentation of less dependable income figures. Such a shift, moreover, would result in income reports less satisfactory from the legal point of view—a matter of importance in connection with income tax determination, dividend policy, security retirements, etc.[15]

The defensive tone of this argument hardly seems consistent with the contention that " it is the function of accounting " to use the cost basis and therefore going concern value should be excluded. It seems rather that current values would in principle be preferable to cost as the basis for accounting, but that practical reasons militate against this improvement in principle. These practical reasons are that there would be a change in the scheme of income determination, a subjective element would be introduced, and the results would be less satisfactory from the legal point of view. These are certainly arguments of expediency, not of principle.

More fundamental is the contention that " there seem to be no convincing reasons for the assumption that accounting would more adequately meet the needs of the parties concerned if estimated replacement costs or other evidences of current values were regularly substituted for recorded dollar costs." This last statement furnishes the key to the whole problem. For it implies that whether costs or current values are to be used as the basis of accounting depends on which serves best the purposes for which a measurement of income is required. That makes the question of whether or not income should include change of going concern value anterior to the consideration of whether to use cost or current value as the basis. Clearly if the primary function is to determine income, we must first agree on the nature of income. Then we can decide whether a cost or current value basis is the more appropriate. The accountant's first argument against inclusion of going concern value by an

[15] *Accountants' Handbook*, 3rd ed., pp. 805–806; Paton and Littleton, *Introduction to Corporate Accounting Standards* (American Accounting Association, 1940), p. 123.

appeal to the " function of accounting " puts the cart before the horse. We must decide directly from the use to which the income concept is to be put whether or not income should be based on going concern value. The use of cost by accountants cannot be appealed to as an argument for the exclusion of going concern value, as that use of cost is itself dependent on the question at issue.

2. The argument that tangible assets alone have determinable values and that they have value apart from their earning power in the business may be granted as one of practicality, which may be compelling to the accountant's practice, but it does not affect the question of principle. In any case the argument is rather trivial because the considerations mentioned are irrelevant to the determination of income for the business. This is shown by the fact that accountants avoid using the values which the tangible assets have for purposes outside the business and carry them at another conventional figure, their adjusted costs. The argument that tangible assets have some outside value which is objective but irrelevant to the determination of the corporation's income hardly serves to dismiss the use of going concern value from the determination of income.

> 3. Recognition of nonpurchased intangibles is unnecessary from the standpoint of *managerial purposes.*

This statement may be challenged. Capitalized present value of the concern is not only a consideration for management, it is *the* consideration. Suppose the manager of a large corporation knew that by undertaking a certain deal he could add a million dollars to his tangible equity, *i.e.*, to his profits for this year as measured by the accountant, but that the corporation would then have to go out of business. He would certainly be justified in setting the prospective loss of going value against the prospective gain of tangible value: indeed, it would be a dereliction of duty not to do so. It is management's duty to weigh any opportunity to increase tangible assets against any possible adverse effect on earning power. The usual statement that it is the duty of management to maximize profits is true of economic income but not of accounting income. Management must consider the effect of any action on future as well as present profits. That is exactly what is meant by being long-sighted. But the future profits are precisely the content of going concern value. A dollar's worth of tangible assets is neither more nor less valuable than a dollar's worth of going concern value.

The case for recognition of appreciation of fixed assets mentioned in this context by Paton is not stronger than that for capitalized earning power. For if capitalized earning power is recognized, it is not only unnecessary to recognize changes in tangible fixed assets, but it is unnecessary to recognize explicitly even revenues from sales or costs of those sales.

That is, it is not necessary to match costs against revenues at all. Merely measure dividend distribution this year and the change in the capitalized value of future distributions. It is true that proceeds of sales and costs are relevant to the estimation of what dividends can in fact be paid this year and in the future, but this is a basic task of business management. The essence of the task is the budgeting of prospective receipts and outlay, and to this the accountant's complicated matching procedures have little relevance.

> 4 .... the value of intangibles ... if recognised, would require continuous adjustment ... the fluctuating surplus created ... would in no sense be true surplus. ...

The adjustment required would be of two sorts. One would be the result of changes of expectations of future earnings. This sort of adjustment will be considered in detail later when we come to discuss income under conditions of uncertainty. But, under conditions of certainty the only adjustment required in the capitalized value of future receipts (or dividends) is the difference between this year's receipts and this year's income.[16] It is true that in measuring going concern value an adjustment is necessary for the difference between change in the capitalized value of future receipts and the change in tangible assets.

That either of these adjustments is required is not a defect of the concept of going concern value. The concept is useful precisely because it introduces the corresponding adjustments into income. The fluctuating surplus resulting would, the economist argues, be the only true surplus and the accountant's is the false one. For the economist's surplus represents the difference between the admittedly true present value of the equity and the stated capital. The accountant's figure for surplus is the difference between a conventionalized book value of equity and stated capital. That book value is out of touch with any value that we would be well advised to call the true value of equity. The adjustments are accordingly desirable although perhaps impractical.

> 5. Earning power should in general be expressed in terms of *return on investment*. ...

---

[16] This point was illustrated on pp. 158–9 above.

The way in which earning power is best expressed for various purposes is no doubt a matter of selecting some one or more productive factors and relating earnings thereto. But this has little bearing on the way in which earnings themselves are best measured, and in our view their measure must certainly include as one of its major elements the change in the present value of future net receipts. For some purposes, (*e.g.*, the control of public utilities and other monopolies) it may be useful to express earnings, so defined, as a rate of return on the historical investment, though more often than not this is a matter of antiquarian interest only.

> 6. *Rational comparisons* between enterprises . . . would be rendered more difficult.

Far from being more difficult, rational comparisons between enterprises would have more significance on a capitalized earning basis than on historical cost book value. For to compare two enterprises, it is sufficient for almost all purposes to know the present value of the future earnings of each. It is true that it would be circular to compute rates of return on capitalized earnings—the result would be the number you first started with, namely the rate of interest used for capitalization. But by the same token, for most purposes, there is no need to compute a rate of return at all, for capitalized value gives you the same information.

If it is desired to compare the success which different corporations have had in making the most of their investment, then the ratio of present value of equity to capital funds invested is quite as good as (and equivalent to) the return on capital funds invested.

A dead level of earning rate on capitalized value would indeed be created, and if " badwill " (the negative of goodwill) be permitted, where that is appropriate, individual firms would neither fall below nor rise above that level. That just means that the rate of return would lose significance if the denominator is to be capitalized earnings. Taitel has found that there is sufficient revaluation of book values in actual practice to rob the rate of return on book value of any validity for long term comparisons of success in exploiting investments.[17] He was forced to make large adjustments to book value in order to estimate actual investment.

It is true that, under conditions of certainty, comparison of the income of different periods would lose interest if equity were valued as capitalized earnings. For then income would be

[17] Martin Taitel, *Profits, Productive Activities and New Investment*, Monograph No. 12, U.S. Congress, T.N.E.C., (Washington, 1941), Chap. III.

constant from year to year except as the value of investment in the business, or the rate of interest, changed over time.

But under conditions of uncertainty comparisons between periods would be just as significant when equity is based on capitalized expected earnings as when equity is based on historical cost. However, a different concept of economic income, to be discussed in the next chapter under the name of variable income, would be appropriate for such year to year comparisons.

7. Capitalization of an intangible ... assumes that it is possible to impute the effect of an element of earning power to one or more intangible factors.

In capitalizing future dividends no imputation of earning power to particular factors is necessary, nor is it even necessary to value the tangible assets at all. If, by any process whatsoever, the accountant does value the tangible assets, then the economist can, conceptually at least, keep the picture straight by computing going concern value as the difference between the value of total equity (capitalized dividends) and tangible equity as measured by the accountant. The assumption that the book values of assets other than going concern value are correctly stated as factors in income determination is indeed unwarranted, and so far from its being implied by the use of going value, it is more accurate to say that the use of going value is motivated precisely by the fact that book values do not represent the earning power of assets, so a residual item is thrown in to make the sum total of assets correct even though the individual elements are not correctly valued on the basis of their earning capacity.

8. Adoption of a policy of estimating and recording intangible values from period to period would not only obscure important relationships and run counter to the essential purposes and functions of accounting, but it would tend to encourage juggling and misrepresentation ...

The argument that use of intangible values would obscure important relationships and violate the fundamental purpose of accounting has been answered under points 1 and 6 above. The encouraging of juggling and misrepresentation is a practical difficulty which we need not evaluate here since we are interested in whether there is justification in principle for the elimination of intangibles or whether that is based solely on practical considerations. The significance of introducing intangibles has been amply discussed above. The instability has been discussed in point 4. The reference to marketable securities raises the question of great variability of capitalised earning power under conditions of uncertainty which we will discuss later.

A fallacious argument frequently levelled against the inclusion of changes in the capitalised value of future earnings as income is that to do so is double counting. It is time, the argument runs, to count the future receipts when they are received, but they should not be counted twice. Hatfield argued, for example:

> An orchard of trees as it increases in growth from year to year un-doubtedly becomes more valuable, but it is more valuable primarily because the larger trees yield a larger supply of fruit. The increasing yield is a cause of larger income. It in itself constitutes the larger income and this income can be distributed or divided or conserved by the owner. The increased value of the orchard as such is a reflection of this increased income but practically it is the crop income which is available as dividends and not the increased value of the orchard ... Indeed to consider both the increased receipts and the capitalization of the receipts as available for dividends to a certain extent is giving double recognition to a single factor.[18]

A simple illustration will expose the fallacy in Hatfield's example. Suppose that an orchard acquired at a cost of $1,000 will just meet expenses for the first year and thereafter can be expected to yield $52·50 per year over expenses forever into the future. Hatfield implies that the income available for dividends should be zero the first year. Given a 5 per cent. rate of interest the orchard is worth $1,050 at the end of the first year, this being the value of a perpetuity of $52·50 per annum. Hatfield would deny that the $50 increase in capitalized value of the orchard's earnings should be considered as available for dividends. Actually, we are here arguing that the $50 should be considered as income retained in the business. Theoretically a small part of the orchard might be sold for $50 and the proceeds distributed as dividends. The remainder of the orchard would presumably yield $50 a year thereafter. Or $50 could be borrowed in perpetual loan at 5 per cent. interest so that $50 could be paid as dividends (after paying interest on the loan) in this and all succeeding years. If no dividends are paid the first year, it is not double counting to say that income the first year is $50 and that this is reinvested in the business. Income in subsequent years will be $52·50 or $2·50 more than if that $50 first year's income had not been reinvested in the business.

Hatfield's argument is an exact parallel to that advanced against the alleged double taxation of savings. If income is taxed and $100 is earned and reinvested to earn $5 a year, not only will the original $100 be taxed, but the $5 a year will also

---

[18] H. R. Hatfield, *Accounting* (D. Appleton & Co. 1927), p. 252, quoted by Paton in *The Accountants' Handbook*, 3rd ed., p. 122, in support of what he describes as "the usual position that treating unrealised increase in capital assets as income is objectionable."

be taxed so there will, it is said, be a double tax on savings. This argument ignores the fact that the $5 annual interest is additional to the $100 and not just a repayment of the $100. It would indeed be unfair to tax as income all of a fifteen year annuity of $10 a year purchased for $100. Part of each year's receipts would then be return of principal. But in the case of a perpetual bond the purchaser was $100 better off for originally earning the $100. He is in addition $5 a year better off for investing the $100 rather than having consumed it when earned. Any time that he wants to sell his bond for $100 he can do so, consume $100 worth of goods as well as having consumed $5 worth annually paid for from the interest payments during the time he held the security. The point is that the annual income is additional to the increase of the capital value rather than a repetition of it.

On the other hand, it is argued that the man in the year he received the $100 net of taxes has a choice of consuming $100 worth of goods immediately or contracting to receive $5 a year indefinitely, which would permit a consumption of $5 a year indefinitely. Since the interest rate is assumed to be 5 per cent., these two choices represent equivalent value. Yet if he chooses the $5 a year he will subsequently have to pay taxes which he will not have to pay if he chooses to spend the $100 immediately. In this sense then, the taxation of savings is a double taxation. One of two otherwise equivalent choices is burdened by taxation while the other is not.

Similarly, in this sense there is some double counting in the concept of income but this double counting is not peculiar to a case of change in the capitalized value, but is characteristic of all income. That is, it might be argued that in purchasing a perpetual bond paying $5 a year a man exchanges $100 right now for its equivalent value—$5 a year in perpetuity. There is accordingly no accession to his wealth as he receives the $5 annually, and the $5 should no more be considered income than should a suit of clothes, bought and paid for in one period, when it is delivered in the following period. The $5 a year has similarly been bought and paid for in a previous period and represents nothing more than payment for value received. Adoption of this point of view would destroy the income concept completely. Any set of receipts over time that we should be tempted to call income can be capitalized to a certain value at an arbitrarily chosen initial point of time, and then can be regarded as deliveries over time of the value of the stream of receipts so capitalized. Consequently all income payments could come to be regarded as a sort of return of capital, it being understood that the equivalent value of sums of money at two different times is to take into account the rate of interest.

Suppose, for example, that we accept the doctrine that the purchaser of the perpetual bond of $5 annually should not count the annual $5 payments as income, but should count them as repayment of capital. If he is to maintain his capital intact he would have to reinvest his annual payments, and so the current money value of his capital would grow at 5 per cent. a year. As a result of the adoption of this concept of income, we should be forced to conclude that in order to maintain capital intact it must grow at the going rate of interest per year! This would destroy the phenomenon of income completely.

Our conclusion must be that no valid principle has been advanced to warrant the exclusion of going value from the determination of income. One possible exception is the argument that inclusion of going value obscures comparisons between periods. The only fundamental question remaining then is: do we want an income concept that shows changes in our wealth from period to period or one that measures how much the events of a particular period contributed to our wealth? The difference will be discussed below as the difference between economic income and sales or production profit, which is here called activity profit.

Accrued versus realised gains and losses

Implicit in the historical cost approach to income is the refusal to recognise any gains other than realised gains. For if unrealised but accrued gains were recognised, an appreciating asset would no longer be carried at cost of acquisition but rather at value at the time of revaluation. However the structure of assets is transformed, no profit is deemed to arise under the accountant's rules for income determination until an asset is exchanged for cash or a claim to cash (*i.e.*, a receivable). That is, all assets except cash and receivables are assumed to be worth what the corporation gave for them. Cash and receivables, on the other hand, have a face value. So these assets have the unique characteristic of not being valued by historical cost, *i.e.*, by the value of the asset that was given for them, and so profit can creep in only in a transaction in which an asset is exchanged for more cash or a claim to more cash than the asset cost.

The refusal to recognise a gain until it has been realised reveals the accountant's prejudice in favour of cash over other assets.

The economist argues that a man is better off as of the moment when his asset gains in value and not as of the moment it happens to be sold. The accountant might grant the validity of the economist's point. But an accrued but unrealised gain is uncertain and cannot be objectively measured. It can be estimated only after an appraisal, and different appraisers might give different results. Therefore it seems best, the accountant argues, to wait until the asset is sold before taking account of any income from its appreciation. If the asset is not sold directly, but is used in the productive operations of the corporation, the gain will be realised as part of the difference between the asset's cost and the proceeds of the sale of the object in which it is embodied.

Economists count gains when accrued, accountants usually count gains when realised by sale of the asset on which the gain has been made. However, accountants are frequently, if not always, willing to accrue costs and losses in agreement with economists. This difference in the treatment of gains and losses is exemplified in the widespread practice of valuing inventories at cost or market whichever is lower. The effect of this rule is that a decline of inventory values is immediately charged against income, while an increase of inventory value is counted only at the time of sale of the appreciated item or the product in which it is embodied. This dual standard indicates that the treatment of accruals is not dictated by the nature of the income concept used but rather by practical considerations summed up in the term " conservatism." Conservatism in accounting consists principally of counting gains only when realised but anticipating costs and losses as soon as possible. But conservatism is rarely carried so far as to charge declines in value of fixed assets (other than those associated with depreciation and obsolescence) to current income. That is, there is no standard treatment of fixed assets similar to the " lower of cost or market " treatment of inventories.

In spite of the conspicuous exception in the case of inventories, we may say that in general accountants do operate on a realised gain basis. " Among accountants the rule that ' profit belongs to the period of sale ' is almost axiomatic." [19]

Why do economists insist on accrual and accountants on realisation? Once more we may ask if the difference is one of principle or practicality. Economists' insistence on accrual stems from the fundamental idea of income as a difference between wealth at two different points of time. If a corporation has more valuable assets at the end of the period than at the beginning

[19] W. A. Paton, *Accountants' Handbook*, 3rd ed., p. 111.

this is an increase in wealth, whether a sale has taken place or not. The accountant may reply that he cannot be sure the gain has been made until the sale has taken place. " Making of the sale furnishes objective evidence of the profit. That is, after the sale has been effected, the profit no longer depends merely on the opinion of the proprietor; it is manifested by an enforceable contract." [20] Furthermore, " The sale is generally considered to be the most decisive and significant event in the chain of transactions and conditions making up the stream of business activity." [21]

There are then two principal arguments for the accountants' practice of counting income on realization rather than as it accrues. The first, that sale affords an objective measure, is an argument of convenience. This argument would be consistent with the view that in principle income is earned as accrued, but in practice it is more convenient to measure it as realized, otherwise we must depend on the proprietor's opinion rather than on the judgment of the market. The objective nature of sale as contrasted with the subjective estimation of accruals constitutes a practical argument for the use of realized rather than accrued profits.

The second argument, that sales are the most significant events in the operation of an enterprise, may have greater theoretical weight. For if selling is the major difficulty facing an enterprise, so that an item produced but unsold cannot, in view of the uncertainty of sale, be valued at anything over the cost of production, then there would seem to be strong arguments for waiting until the sale is made to count the profit. But then there is probably some error in carrying the product at cost, for if it is sold at prevailing prices, there will be a profit, but if it proves unsaleable, there will be a loss.

Of course, the economist does not argue that the product should be carried at sale price. From the point of view of economic income, there is no need whatsoever to value individual assets. Only the change in the total equity need be valued and that depends only on the corporation's current and future net receipts.[22]

If in fact the sale is a critical stage in achieving a profit from the operations of an enterprise, it would seem appropriate to recognise this in the process of accruing value to the product. Part of the difference between cost and selling price could be

[20] Hatfield as quoted in *Accountants' Handbook*, 3rd ed., p. 111.
[21] W. A. Paton, *Accountants' Handbook*, 3rd ed., p. 111.
[22] Or current and future dividend payments. On the equivalence of the present value of dividends and net receipts, under our present assumptions, see above, p. 149.

accrued during the period of production and another part in the period of sale. In practice, however, this would be very difficult, and it is doubtful whether any useful end would be served thereby. It is much more convenient to confine the profit to the period of sale. This argument applies to ordinary operating profit, but not to gain in value of asscts held in the business.

Although the accountant's use of realized rather than accrued gain is based principally on convenience, there is some justification for it in principle to the extent that sales are the main limitations on profits. But the application of the realization criterion is far broader than could be justified by this consideration. We must conclude that the realization rule is based principally on the tenet that only money gains should be counted, a tenet itself based on the accountant's search for objectivity.

Fluctuating versus stable income

Although the accountant's departures from the economic concept of income are motivated principally by practical considerations, they are so basic as to constitute a different type of income concept. This is vividly illustrated by the frequently stated requirement that a measure of income should be useful in comparing one year's operation with another's. Under conditions of certainty, such a requirement is clearly antithetical to the concept of economic income, which, starting from a fluctuating set of receipts, breaks them down into a relatively stable stream of income and a fluctuating sequence of capital receipts.

A year to year comparison of the success of a company's operations under conditions of certainty requires a measure of operating profit rather than of economic income. Because the phrase " operating profit " has a meaning for accountants somewhat different from what we mean by it, we shall reluctantly abandon that phrase and use instead the phrase " activity profit."

Activity profit is the difference between the value of the results of certain specified operations performed over the year and the costs of those operations. It may be contrasted with economic income, which is the net increase of the owners' equity in the corporation over the period other than that arising from additional investment by the owners. The economic income concept is attached to the given year in that it deals with differences between beginning and end of the year. The activity income concept is attached to the year only in that the transactions selected for inclusion are those that reached a specified stage during the year. The transaction as a whole may contain other stages which were reached either in the same or in other years.

Economic income is then related to comparison of net assets at two different times, activity profit to the matching of revenue or output on the one hand with cost on the other. The basic question behind economic income is " How much better off has the corporation become over the period? " The basic question behind activity profit is " How much better off is the corporation for having performed certain activities which are somehow associated with the period? "

The accountants' rejection of going value as an element of income is consistent with the concept of activity profit, but inconsistent with the very essence of the economic concept of income. For, having eliminated going value, accountants no longer measure changes in the value of equity, if the latter is to be defined as the present value of future net receipts or dividend payments. The accountants' use of time of realization as the criterion of the period to which a gain is to be assigned implies that sale rather than some other operation is to be the critical activity for the measurement of activity profit. That is, the adoption of the realization rule implies that accounting income will be the same as profits from sales. The relative merits of sales profits as against economic income as *the* income concept can be judged only on the basis of what need the concept must satisfy. We may postpone consideration of that fundamental question, however, until after we have considered these measures of income under conditions of uncertainty. It suffices for the present to point out that a concept of income which serves as a measure of the success of a particular year's operations as compared with other years is, under conditions of certainty, inconsistent with the definition of income as a net change in equity over the period. For, under conditions of certainty, equity at the beginning of the period is equal to the discounted value of the corporation's exactly predictable net receipts. The net change in wealth over the period, therefore, always equals interest on equity at the beginning of the period. Under conditions of uncertainty, however, it may be possible to bring the two concepts of activity profit and economic income closer together.

V. Income under Uncertainty

Objectivity versus relevance

So far we have assumed stable price levels and interest rates, and perfect certainty as to future net receipts. Let us drop the assumption of perfect certainty. This makes no difference for accounting income; that concept does not depend on future receipts but only on past costs and current sales. It is true that in estimating certain costs such as depreciation, obsolescence and amortisation of deferred charges, accountants do have to make some judgments of the future, but this is done on a rule of thumb basis rather than as a genuine prediction. The error introduced into accounting income by basing depreciation on a necessarily fallible estimate of the useful life of the equipment will be infinitesimal compared to the error introduced into economic income by the uncertainty of future net receipts.

The very basis of economic income is the present value of future net receipts. Since these are uncertain, economic income is uncertain. In practice, equity must be valued as the capitalisation not of the actual future net receipts but of *expected* future net receipts. But whose expectations are to be used? Each person in valuing equity must, of course, use his own expectations so that the valuation process becomes subjective, a condition abhorrent to accountants.

The non-objective character of economic income under conditions of uncertainty is not alone sufficient basis for its rejection in favour of some more objective standard. For the fact is that expected future net receipts although unknown are the most important determinants of the value of an asset, and so the most appropriate basis for the determination of income. Original cost is advocated as a substitute method of valuation largely because original cost can be objectively measured. Unfortunately it is an objective measure of the wrong thing.

When any decision has to be made on the basis of a corporation's income, it will always be wiser for the decision maker to base his judgment on the best estimate of economic income he can make, however subjective that judgment may be, rather than to rely on the perfectly objective measure of income based on historical cost, which is irrelevant except as an approximation to economic income or as a subject for idle curiosity. It is better to act on the subjective evaluation of the relevant factors. An example was given above of the folly of acting so as to increase accounting income while decreasing economic income. For a reduction of economic income means a reduction of wealth and it is foolish to try to increase operating profit if in so doing one reduces one's wealth.

Changes of expectations

The non-objective character of income based on expectations is, however, only the beginning of the difficulties we meet in applying economic income to conditions of uncertainty. Since future prospects are uncertain, we may from time to time change our expectations. Each such change implies a change in our valuation of equity, the capitalised value of expected net receipts. Economic income has been defined under conditions of economic certainty as the change in equity over the period. Is it appropriate to include in income a change of equity resulting from a change in expectations?

The economic concept of income so far developed can give no answer to this question. That concept is based on the criterion of being as well off at the end of a period as at the beginning. We are now facing the problem that arises when at the end of the period we have changed our opinion as to how well off we were at the beginning of the period. Under such circumstances which valuation shall we use, that of the end of the period, that of the beginning of the period, or some mixture of the two?

If, as in the example of the Neverlose Manufacturing Co. above, expectations change so that an owner's equity valued at $200,000 at the beginning of the year is valued at $241,500 at the end of the year, should we say that the owners are $41,500 better off at year's end, or that they just didn't know how well off they were at the beginning of the year?

One point of view was mentioned above, according to which only $11,500 of the $41,500 should be considered income. This figure was obtained by subtracting from the year-end value of the equity of the Neverlose Co. the hindsight value of equity at year-beginning. The hindsight value of equity at year-beginning is calculated by discounting the year-end value of equity back to the beginning of the year. Income computed as the difference between equity at year-end and hindsight value at year-beginning may be called pure economic income. It equals the current rate of interest on hindsight value of beginning-of-year equity.

The difference between the hindsight value of year-beginning equity and year-beginning equity as valued at the beginning of the year may be termed "unexpected gain." We must choose between the alternatives of considering unexpected gain as an actual increase in wealth or as a mere revision of an estimate of wealth. As an actual increase of wealth, it should be included in economic income; as a revision of an estimate, it should be excluded.

The first viewpoint is based on the assumption that a man is as well off as he thinks he is, and not as well off as someone with superior knowledge either now or later may know him to be. If he owns a plot of agricultural land originally believed to be worth $1,000, which upon the discovery of oil beneath it is then believed to be worth $100,000, he is according to this view $99,000 wealthier for the discovery of the oil. This $99,000 could accordingly be spent for consumption, leaving him with $1,000 or just as well off as he considered himself at the beginning of the period. Therefore the $99,000 unexpected gain is income.

The second view is that the land was really worth about $100,000 at the beginning of the year; the owner simply did not know it. Upon discovering the oil, the owner should merely revise his estimate but should not regard the revision as available for consumption. If he consumes any of the value of the land, say $10,000 worth, then he will be worse off at the end of the year than at the beginning of the year by that amount, for at the beginning of the year he held an asset actually worth $100,000, whatever he may have thought it was worth. Now, if he holds an asset worth only $90,000, he has consumed $10,000 of his capital. Because a man has changed his mind as to what his capital is worth does not justify his consuming part of the capital.

We obviously cannot use the definition of economic income to settle this argument since the difference concerns the meaning of a phrase in that definition. The two views disagree on what is meant by " as well off at the end of the period as at the beginning " under conditions of uncertainty. The issue must be deferred until we examine in detail the purposes for which an income measure is needed. Then we may consider which of the two points of view serves those needs best.

For the present then, we may merely distinguish pure income and unexpected gain as two components of what we must now call mixed economic income.

The concept of variable income

There is one possible approach to economic income under uncertainty which comes a great deal closer to accounting income than does pure economic income. We may introduce this approach by some rather bizarre examples.

Suppose that in a certain country where the long term interest rate is 5 per cent. the government has issued a perpetual bond sold for $100 with the following arrangement. Each year a coin is tossed. If heads appear the bondholder is paid $10; if tails appear no payment is made for that year.[23]

---

[23] As a matter of fact this example is hardly more bizarre than the British premium savings bonds which, while securing the investor's capital, pay no interest in the ordinary sense, but offer the chance, after a qualifying period of three months, of a prize in a monthly lottery. The amount of the prize fund is determined by calculating interest, at a rate prescribed from time to time, on the bonds eligible for the draw.

Under this arrangement the income will be variable without affecting the principal. So long as the interest rate remains unchanged at 5 per cent., the bond should be worth $100 on January 1 of each year. Consequently, whatever is received as payment each year can be counted as income even though an equal amount cannot be expected in each future year. This example certainly comes closer to the actual facts of business than does the assumption of perfect knowledge of the future.

In any case, it would be highly inappropriate to say that such an asset each year earns income equal to interest on the capital value. It has an expectation of such income, but the expectation will sometimes be exceeded and sometimes disappointed.

There is some question of whether in a year in which $10 is paid, part of that $10 might not be considered unexpected gain. In general, unexpected gain arises whenever an asset is found to be more valuable than it was previously thought to be. In a year in which $10 is paid, the bond will have been found at year-end to have been worth at the beginning of the year about $5 more than it was valued at that time. But the bond was at the beginning of the year correctly valued because there was then only half a chance of getting the $10.

Now suppose that another sort of security is on sale in our mythical country. Like the first bond this pays either $10 or nothing at the end of the year, depending on the toss of a coin. But it is good only for twenty years from issue. In this case the security declines in value each year so that the net income of each year is either $10 or zero minus the appropriate deduction for loss of value of the asset.[24] This arrangement begins to look more like an asset as assets really exist.

Finally, consider another arrangement which yields each year a payment which may be anything within a fairly wide range depending on some game of chance. Any particular part of that range may be deemed to have a certain probability, but these probabilities are not well known and can only be roughly estimated. If it is not believed that the probability distribution of payments varies from year to year, the payment actually made in any particular year may be considered income for that year. The application of these considerations to business income may be illustrated by yet another example.

Suppose, in a period of stable prices, a retailer sells only one type of product, say candy at $1·00 a box. He buys the candy for $0·75 a box, rents a store for $1,000 a year and pays a clerk

---

[24] That appropriate deduction varies from year to year. In the nth year it is equal to $5/(1·05)^{21-n}$ on the assumption that the interest rate is 5 per cent.

a salary of $4,000. He has no other expenses. He averages $40,000 sales a year with considerable fluctuations from year to year.

The accountant would report his income as varying according to sales volume so that when he sold $60,000 worth of candy, his income would be $10,000. When he sold $20,000 worth, his income would be zero. Can we not reformulate our economic definition of income so as to agree with the accountant at least in this simple case and still not sacrifice our basic economic principles? This can be done if we follow the procedure just applied to the perpetual bond whose payments depend on the toss of a coin.

We may say that this candy dealer has an expectation of sales of $40,000 a year, and therefore of $5,000 net receipts per year. Here we may define net receipts as the difference between aggregate receipts and aggregate costs paid out. Furthermore, we may add that this expectation is not altered by the experience of any particular year. If the interest rate is 5 per cent., his business is worth $100,000 year in, year out. In any year in which he sells $60,000 worth of candy and has net receipts of $10,000, he is well justified in counting that $10,000 as income even though in subsequent years he can expect net receipts of only $5,000 annually. For at the beginning of the year he had an asset worth $100,000. At the end of the year he still has an asset worth $100,000 plus $10,000 cash from his net receipts.

Once we have abandoned the fiction of certainty of future receipts, it no longer seems reasonable to impute hindsight values to beginning-of-year equity as is done in computation of pure economic income. Yet if hindsight values are not imputed, an inconsistency apparently arises. For given an asset worth $100,000 at the end of the year just after the owner has received $10,000 as this year's dividend, the interest rate being 5 per cent., it seems inconsistent to say that the asset was worth only $100,000 at the beginning of the year. Surely, it now seems, one would have been well advised to pay more for it at that time. But at that time, this year's receipts as well as the value of the asset ex-dividend at the end of the period were uncertain. In view of the uncertainty, it may be maintained, $100,000 was indeed the correct value of the asset as measured by the then present value of expected future receipts.

The existence of uncertainty, therefore, breaks down the rigid relationship between the beginning-of-period value of equity and end-of-period value of equity plus receipts. Once we regard each year's net receipts as a quantity subject to chance fluctuation we are justified also in regarding each year's income as subject to chance fluctuation.

The concept of income which is suggested by this line of thought may be called " variable income." Subject to one important reservation referred to below, it is equal to the net receipt from an asset over the period, plus or minus a pre-determined adjustment factor, namely, the expected change in the ex-dividend value of the asset between the beginning and end of the period on the basis of the expectations current at the beginning of the period.

If we apply this definition to the perpetual bond paying $10 on heads, zero on tails, we can say that there is an average expectation of receipts of $5 a year, and this expectation holds from year to year. If in a particular year $10 is received, then this sum is the variable income of the year. Similarly in the case of the candy merchant, in the year in which his net receipts were $10,000, his variable income was $10,000 as well.

It must not be inferred from these examples that variable income is always equal to net receipts. Consider the bond mentioned above that pays either zero or $10 a year for twenty years, depending each year on the toss of a coin, and after the twentieth year the arrangement terminates. The expectation of receipts each year is $5, but the expectation of income is somewhat less, because the security is losing value from year to year as the arrangement runs out. At issue, the security is worth $62·31, assuming an interest rate of 5 per cent., this being the present value of a twenty-year annuity of $5 a year. One year later it is worth $60·43 (the present value of a nineteen-year annuity) and two years later $58·45. If in the first year heads appear and the second year tails, then variable income for the first year is $8·12 (a receipt of $10 minus the fall in value of the security of $1·88) and in the second year it is −$1·98 (a loss).

In most practical cases, no particular receipts are expected from an asset or a collection of assets, but rather any value in a whole range may be expected with a different probability for each part of that range. It is accordingly appropriate to approach the problem of asset valuation not in terms of *expected* receipts but in terms of *expectation* of receipts. Such an expectation is the average of the various possible values expected, each weighted by its probability. When, as is usually the case, these probabilities are not formulated exactly, the expectation may nevertheless be formulated directly on the basis of the owner's or investor's judgment. An investor may judge that a certain corporation has the expectation of earning net receipts of $100,000 a year even though he would not wish to estimate whether this expectation was made up of an even chance of $200,000 or nothing or of $150,000 and $50,000.

It is unfortunate that the concept of variable income depends so heavily on expectations. The reason for this dependence is the necessity of getting beforehand an appropriate adjustment to receipts as they appear. The objection to considering the entire amount of these receipts as income is that they may be related to some change in value of the asset itself. If, for example, a large receipt for this year reduces the value of the asset, it is inappropriate to consider the receipt entirely as income; part of the receipt must be regarded as repayment of principal. Exactly the same is true of payments made in connection with operating the asset—some of these may increase the value of the asset and cannot therefore be regarded as negative income. If now we conceive of the net receipts as fluctuating according to chance circumstances or to skill of management and we wish to include these chance fluctuations in income, we must have some method of distinguishing between that part of the net receipts which is the result of the chance fluctuation that does not affect capital value and that part which is associated with a change in capital value. The solution to this problem embodied in the concept of variable income is that an adjustment factor for a period is determined at the beginning of the period. When net receipts of the period fluctuate, variable income will be those net receipts plus or minus the pre-determined adjustment.

This procedure is justified, however, if and only if a larger than average receipt in one period is not at the expense of a receipt of a later period. If part of the receipt for this year is at the expense of a receipt of a future period, it is appropriate to count into income only the excess of what is gained this year over the discounted value of what is sacrificed from the expectation for future years. Conversely, a restriction in a receipt this year (or a larger than average payment) may be the cause of larger receipts in the future, and in these circumstances, it would be appropriate to include in income not only the year's small net receipt but also the discounted value of the increment in net receipts expected in the future.

This qualification to the clear-cut definition of variable income which was given above will be seen to be of particular importance when we come to consider the measurement of business income in practice. For what the qualification implies is that where the variation in the size of the year's receipts leads to a *consequential* change in expectations between the beginning and end of the year, we cannot ignore such a change in expectations in arriving at variable income. The same thing is true of a change in expectations attributable to the activity of the firm during the year.

Variable income and unexpected gain

Changes of expectation which occur during a period introduce serious difficulties into the concept of variable income. Provided we can distinguish a given period's receipts from the main body of the asset, as we can when we are dealing with income from securities, we can separate variable income from a correlative concept of unexpected gain which, for want of a better term, we shall call variable unexpected gain.

Suppose a perpetual bond that pays either $10 or nothing depending on the toss of a coin in a particular year is, at the close of the year, voluntarily modified by the issuer so that in the future it will pay $12 or nothing depending on the toss of a coin. If the interest rate is 5 per cent., the value of the bond will have been increased from $100 to $120. If in this year tails appear, the variable income of the bond is zero, while the variable unexpected gain is $20.

The sum of variable income and variable unexpected gain is equal to the total change in the value of the equity from the beginning to the end of the period, including in the end-of-period equity any disbursement to ownership over the period. But this total is exactly the same as mixed economic income, which in turn is the sum of pure income and pure unexpected gain. So the difference in the two concepts, pure income and variable income, can be explained in terms of the sort of unexpected gain that is eliminated from mixed economic income. If from mixed economic income we subtract the unexpected gain as measured by comparing actual beginning-of-period value of equity with hindsight beginning-of-period value, then pure economic income is the remainder. If from mixed economic income we subtract unexpected gain computed as the difference between the value of the asset at the end of the period and what that value was expected to be as of the beginning of the period, the remainder is variable income.

We may illustrate these relationships by reference once again to the candy merchant. Suppose this year that there is an improvement in the market. During the year, his sales are $50,000, netting $7,500 over cost. He expects in the future to average $44,000 sales a year and so make $6,000 a year net. All the relevant facts relating to his situation are set out below, using the notation V_0 and V_1 to represent the value of equity, excluding the year's receipts, at the beginning and end of year 1, with the additional subscripts a and e to indicate respectively actual values and expected values. Actual receipts are represented by R_a and i is the rate of interest.

At the beginning of the year he expects recurrent net receipts of \$5,000 a year. At that date, therefore, assuming an interest rate of 5 per cent., the value of equity (V_{0a}) is \$100,000, and the expected value of year-end equity (V_{1e}) is also \$100,000.

During the year he actually nets \$7,500 (R_a).

At the end of the year his expectation for the future is that he will average recurrent net receipts of \$6,000 a year. On this basis, with a capitalisation rate of 5 per cent., the actual ex-dividend value of year-end equity (V_{1a}) is \$120,000.

If we make the simplifying assumption that withdrawals from the business can only be made at the end of each year, we can compute the hindsight value (at year-end) of year-beginning equity,

$$\frac{1}{1+i}(V_{1a} + R_a), \text{ as } \$127,500 \times \frac{1}{1\cdot05}, \text{ or } \$121,428.$$

Then the merchant's mixed economic income can be expressed as:

$$V_{1a} \quad - \quad V_{0a} \quad + \quad R_a$$
$$\$120,000 - \$100,000 + \$7,500 = \$27,500$$

This can now be split up in two ways. We can split it into pure income and pure unexpected gain, thus:

Mixed economic income	=	Pure income	+	Pure unexpected gain

$$V_{1a}-V_{0a}+R_a = \frac{i}{1+i}(V_{1a} + R_a) + \frac{1}{1+i}(V_{1a} + R_a)-V_{0a}$$

$$\$27,500 = \frac{\cdot05}{1\cdot05}(\$127,500) + \frac{1}{1\cdot05}(\$127,500)-\$100,000$$

$$= \$6,072 + \$21,428$$

Or we can split it into variable income and variable unexpected gain, thus:

Mixed economic income	=	Variable income	+	Variable unexpected gain

$$V_{1a}-V_{0a}+R_a =(V_{1e}-V_{0a}+R_a) +(V_{1a}-V_{1e})$$
$$\$27,500 =(\$100,000-100,000+7,500)+(\$120,000-100,000)$$
$$=\$7,500 +\$20,000$$

If, in any period, net receipts match expectations and expectations of future net receipts do not change, then in that period variable income, pure income and mixed economic income will all be identical. The principal difference between variable and pure income is that whereas the full amount of any excess of the current period's net receipts over expectations are included in variable income, only interest on the excess is included in pure income.

Measurement of variable business income

The application of the notion of variable income to the affairs of the candy merchant will have suggested certain serious short-comings of the concept, in its simple form, when we try to apply it to business income. So long as we are attempting to measure the income from securities only, the concept is reasonably free from difficulties. We normally have no difficulty in separating the owner's receipts (dividends) from the main body of the security; and changes in the owner's expectations during the year cannot usually be said to be the result of any activity of his own, so that the separation of variable income from unexpected gain rarely presents difficulty.

As a matter of fact, even in the case of stock, the identification of variable income may not be entirely straightforward. Suppose a share of stock is purchased at the beginning of the year for $100 in the expectation that it will pay a $5 dividend and be worth $100 at the end of the year. This valuation is based on the expectation of a $5 annual dividend indefinitely into the future. Suppose the stock actually pays $3 this year but rises to $103 on the expectation of $5·15 dividend indefinitely into the future (we assume a 5 per cent. rate of interest). If the fact that the dividend had been cut from $5 to $3 was the reason for the expected increase in future dividends, it would be inappropriate to say that variable income was only $3 and that the $3 rise in the value of the security was all unexpected gain.

But it is when we come to measure the income of a business (whether incorporated or not) that really serious complications arise. In a business enterprise, there is no clear distinction between the main body of the enterprise itself and the receipts and payments made during the year. Some assets are being realised, and others are being acquired or added to, all the time. Separation of those net receipts which give rise to income from those which merely result from changes in the composition of the assets is a task which occupies a good deal of the accountant's time.

More serious still is the difficulty of knowing what to do about changes in expectations as between the beginning and the end of a period. In so far as these arise because of extraneous events quite outside the control of the managers of the enterprise, it is appropriate that the changes in valuation associated with these changes in expectation should be regarded as unexpected gains. But to the extent that changes in expectations are the result of skill in directing the enterprise during the year, or are otherwise internally generated within the firm, it is not reasonable to exclude the resultant changes in valuation of the enterprise from variable income, if variable income is to serve at all satisfactorily as an index of the result of managerial activity. Valuation changes which are the result of managerial effort are just as much income as was the appreciation in value of the share of stock which resulted from the restriction of current dividends to stockholders.

Unfortunately we do not have any objective means of separating an appreciation in the value of an enterprise that has been internally generated (whether as the result of forbearing to distribute income or of special skill on the part of management) from an appreciation that is the result of an externally generated favourable change of expectations, for it is usually impossible to say what is the result of skill and what is the result of luck in business. If we are willing to deal with mixed economic income, we can escape the necessity of having to make this distinction; but if, for certain purposes, we require an income concept that is free of unexpected gain, then we must do the best we can, while realizing the intractable nature of the difficulties involved. We cannot eliminate the unexpected without specifying what is expected.

An appropriate conceptual device for measuring variable income for a corporation is as follows:

(1) Find the change in tangible equity (before dividends).
(2) Add to it the change in value of goodwill and other intangibles excluding any part of the change which is attributable to changes of future expectations not resulting from this year's actions.

That is, the variable income of a corporation is equal to the change in tangible equity (before dividends) plus any increase or minus any decrease in goodwill and other intangibles which has been internally generated.

In the practical measurement of business income, it is frequently possible to make an assumption that greatly simplifies the determination of variable income. That assumption is that if the value of the net tangible assets of the corporation is maintained intact, the corporation's earning power will be maintained.

If it is assumed that the going value of an enterprise will be maintained provided the value of its net tangible assets (*i.e.*, the value of its tangible equity) is maintained intact, then the task of measuring variable income is made very easy. Income of any period will be equal to the value of the tangible equity (before dividends) at the end of the period minus its value at the beginning of the period. This assumption, that the going value of the enterprise is not subject to change except by externally induced changes of expectations so long as net tangible assets are unchanged, lies behind most practical measures of income. Where the assumption is true, tangible income will equal variable income.

To recapitulate, under conditions of uncertainty the variable income concept seems to be the most useful economic income concept that excludes unexpected gain from income. For a business enterprise, variable income equals the change in net tangible assets plus the change in the going value minus any part of these changes attributable to externally induced changes in expectations of future receipts. If we assume that so long as tangible equity is maintained going value will be unchanged, then variable income is equal to tangible income.

Three observations are called for. First, if the computation of income is to be based in principle on variable income, but in practice on tangible income, the validity of the procedure depends on the basic assumption that going value will not change. Therefore, special adjustments will have to be made whenever that assumption is not valid. In particular, if going value is built up at the expense of net tangible assets, or net tangible assets are built up at the expense of going value, then account must be taken of these changes in going value, since without this adjustment tangible income will not equal variable income.

Secondly, in comparing the value of tangibles at different times, it is necessary to take account of changes in value associated with the passage of time or the rate of use of the tangibles. Our basic assumption can be turned around to be used as a guide to depreciation policy. That is, in so far as we are free to choose a depreciation policy, let us choose that one which goes farthest to make the basic assumption true. In accord with this view, the annual depreciation allowance should be reckoned as the amount that would have to be reinvested to keep the going value of the concern constant in the absence of changes of expectations.

Thirdly, we have to choose a rate of interest at which to discount expected net receipts in arriving at going value. This rate will be determined by the market. It will be equal to the rate of return yielded in the market by enterprises considered to be equally risky. This rate will change from time to time, of course, with fluctuations in the capital market, and each change of rate will bring a change in going value. Since such changes in interest rates are, in most cases, unexpected and in all cases externally induced, the changes in going value to which they give rise must be regarded as unexpected gains or losses.

It may be that profit on sales is interesting in its own right, that there are some uses for which it is to be preferred to an income concept that is based on the notion of maintaining capital intact. But before going into that question, let us see under what conditions profits from sales will agree with variable income.

If all prices remain constant, and if an enterprise which maintains the value of its tangible equity can be expected to maintain its earning power, then profit from production will equal variable income. Under these circumstances variable income will differ from profit on sales only by the difference between profit on sales and profit on production. That difference is one which need not concern us here. It will in general be small, and where it is large, as in the construction industry, business practice will usually be found to make some special allowance in valuing work-in-process, and accountants will adjust the concept of income accordingly.

Under what circumstances in actual practice will profits from sales be a poor measure of variable income? We will postpone discussion of the effect of price changes and we may regard the difference between profit on production and profit on sales as generally of little importance. The really important possibility of divergence between sales profit and variable income arises when the firm's activity of a given year has affected the sales profit to be expected in future years. Thus, if in a given year certain expenditures, say for advertising, charged as costs of the current year's sales, will in fact have the effect of boosting sales in subsequent years, the current year's variable income will in truth be larger than the sales profit by the present value of the future sales profit attributable to this year's action. Conversely, if some of this year's sales are achieved at the expense of customer goodwill, such that future sales profit will be lower than if sales had not been pushed so far or hard this year, then sales profit for this year will be greater than variable income.

We may conclude that under constant prices, sales profit is an acceptable approximation to variable income except where:

(1) There is a significant change in going value either as a consequence of some action in this period or of an expected change in the enterprise's future selling position, as through

the approaching expiry of a franchise. An unexpected change should, of course, result in an unexpected gain or loss rather than an increase or decrease in variable income.

(2) There is a material divergence between profit on production and profit on sales owing to a difference in timing of production and sales, with a consequent build-up or run-down of inventories of finished goods.

VI. CHANGES IN PRICES

Real income

Occasionally tremendous changes in the general price level demonstrate the instability of the monetary measure on which business accounts are based. In extreme cases of inflation the maintenance of capital intact in money value becomes a ludicrous preoccupation. If income is to be defined as the amount a man can dispose of and yet be as well off at the end of the period as at the beginning, it is clearly inappropriate to use money value as a measure of well being in a period during which money's command over goods and services is shrinking rapidly.

Under such circumstances it is appropriate to substitute a " real " measure of well being for the money measure. The simplest way to convert a money measure into a real measure is through an accepted index of the general price-level. No perfectly satisfactory index of the general price-level exists, nor can one be conceived. It is not only that price indexes are imperfect because of poor price reporting and inadequate coverage, but even in theory it is impossible to construct a perfect price index no matter how much information one has.

Since all prices do not move together it is necessary to use an average of different price movements. The average must be weighted, and the appropriate weights change as between the beginning and end of the period over which price change is being measured. Because of this difficulty, one leading contemporary economist has rejected the income concept entirely in advanced theoretical analysis.[25] But for practical purposes, the theoretical imperfection of index numbers need not worry us too much. We are willing to use a price index as a general measure of the purchasing power of money in many important affairs in spite of the fact that different indexes give different results, no one of which can clearly be said to be superior to the others.

The deflation of money wages by a price index to obtain a

[25] Hicks, J. R., *Value and Capital* (Oxford: Oxford University Press, 1939 and 1941), p. 180.

measure of real wages is a familiar operation. Unfortunately a corresponding deflation of money profits by a price index does not yield a measure of real profits as it would be sensible to define them. Suppose that this year the net worth of a certain corporation which has paid no dividends during the year increases from $1,000,000 to $1,100,000 so that the money measure of mixed economic income is $100,000. Suppose that during the same period the general price-level rises from 100 to 110. In measuring the real income of the firm for the year, it would not be sufficient to deflate the money measure of income ($100,000) by the price index (110) to get about $90,000 as the measure of real income. That procedure will not indicate by how much the real value of owner's equity has changed over the year. In order to measure real income it is necessary to put both year-end and year-beginning equity into terms of dollars of equal purchasing power. If we compare them in terms of dollars of year-end purchasing power then the year-beginning net worth in current dollars (assumed to be $1,000,000) must be adjusted to the year-end price-level (110 per cent. of the year-beginning price-level). That is, in year-end dollars the year-beginning net worth was $1,100,000 while year-end net worth in year-end dollars is also $1,100,000. The corporation has accordingly earned no real income over the year; the real value of its net worth was at year-end just equal to the real value of its net worth at year beginning.

For most of the many possible concepts of income, there are several different ways of defining a corresponding real income concept. It would be a bewildering and thankless task to consider them all. We may confine our attention to a few of the more important concepts of real income. These are: real economic income, real variable income, contemporaneous sales profit, and pure sales profit. With each of these there will be associated a correlative concept of gain not counted as income.

It is most convenient to express any real measure of income in terms of monetary units of purchasing power as of a specified time. In what follows, unless otherwise stated, the real income of any year will be expressed in dollars of purchasing power as of the end of the year.

Real economic income of an enterprise is the real value of its equity at year-end minus the real value of its equity at year-beginning plus the real value of dividends paid over the year. That is, in comparing year-end net worth with year-beginning net worth, account is taken of the change of purchasing power of the money unit. It is thus quite possible that a firm which has earned money economic income has suffered a real economic loss. That merely means that although the money value of equity rose, it rose less than the general price-level so that its real value declined.

A real pure income could be defined, but since we will have no need for this concept, which implies conditions of certainty, we may pass on to the concept of real variable income. As before, that depends on net receipts and expectations thereof. An adjustment to the current year's net receipts can be computed, the adjustment having two components, namely:

(a) the difference between the present value of the stream of net receipts expected as of the beginning of the year and what, at that date, it is expected to be worth at the end of the year after this year's expected net receipts are taken out. This part of the adjustment is to be expressed in money units of beginning-of-year purchasing power.

(b) the change in the going value of the enterprise brought about by changes in expectations resulting from entrepreneurial activity within the firm during the year. This change is appropriately expressed in money units of end-of-year purchasing power.

Either part of the adjustment may be positive or negative and so, of course, may the total adjustment. Real variable income is the sum of the real value of this year's net receipts and the real value of the adjustment. The variability is introduced by the variation between actual net receipts and expected net receipts, and also by the internally generated change in going value.

Correlative to this there is an unexpected gain equal to:

(a) the real value of the future stream of net receipts as expected at year-end minus the real value of that stream as expected at year-beginning, minus

(b) the real value of any internally generated change in going value.

The sum of real variable income and the correlative measure of unexpected gain is real economic income.

We shall consider two different ways of translating money profit from sales into real terms. We may call these contemporaneous sales profit and pure sales profit respectively.

Contemporaneous sales profit is so called because it is based on matching revenues and costs in money units of the same purchasing power. That is, against the sales revenue of a given year is matched the costs of those sales with each item of cost revalued according to the movement of the general price-level between the incurrence of the cost and the time of the sale. Thus a raw material purchased for $1·00 when the price level was 100 is charged to cost at $1·10 if the price level is 110 at the time of sale of the product to which it is charged.

The measure of contemporaneous sales profit so obtained may be contrasted with pure sales profit, with which it is sometimes confused. Pure sales profit is equal to sales revenue minus cost, priced according to the particular prices of the cost items prevailing at date of sale. Only if the prices of the cost items used by a firm have on the average moved in strict proportion to the general price-level will contemporaneous sales profit and pure sales profit be the same. In general the two will differ according to the degree by which the price movements of the firm's cost items have diverged from the movement of the general price-level.

In brief, pure sales profit is based on replacement cost valuation of cost items, contemporaneous sales profit is based on general purchasing power valuations of cost items. For inter-year comparisons, it would be appropriate to deflate each year's contemporaneous or pure sales profit by that year's general price index just as wage payments are deflated to measure real wages.

Correlative to contemporaneous sales profit is the time-lag gain on sales. It is so called in order to indicate that it is that part of total money gain which is attributable to the fact that costs and revenues are not simultaneous. It is the difference between mixed sales profit and contemporaneous sales profit. It is equal to that part of mixed sales profit which is attributable to the change in the general price-level.

Similarly, the difference between pure sales profit and mixed sales profit may be called the price gain on sales. It is equal to the difference in value of the cost items as between time of acquisition and the time they are charged against sales revenue.

To illustrate, suppose a merchant, A, buys goods for $1000 when the index of general prices stands at 100. He sells them some time later for $1300 at a time when the general price index stands at 110 and the specific price index for the goods in question has risen by 15% since they were purchased. Then:

Mixed sales profit   = $1300 − $1000   = $300

This is divisible into:

Contemporaneous sales
    profit   = $1300 − $1100   = $200
Time-lag gain on sales   = $1100 − $1000   = $100
                                           $300

Alternatively, it is divisible into:

Pure sales profit   = $1300 − $1150 = $150
Price gain on sales = $1150 − $1000 = $150

$300

The relative merits of the various measures of income will be discussed after consideration has been given to the broader issues of whether a real or monetary measure is to be preferred for each important use. That issue is truly fundamental. Once it has been settled, the problem of which measure of real income or of money income should be used is largely one of practical convenience.

Real versus money income

If we start with a general notion that income is the amount that can be freely disposed of while leaving capital intact, we must now inquire whether it is money value or real value of capital that is to be kept intact.

In the elementary use of the income concept by an individual the real value is the most appropriate, for money is merely the measure of what it can purchase. So, if a man buys an asset for $100 at the beginning of the year and sells it for $200 at the end of the year, and meanwhile the price-level doubles, he has made no real gain on the transaction. His $200 will buy no more at the end of the year than his $100 would have bought at the beginning of the year. It would clearly be a delusion to believe that he had really gained by the operation. Yet just this delusion does enter into conventional income accounting, which takes no heed of changes in the general price-level.

For certain purposes, however, there is some justification for ignoring changes in the general price-level. Under the trust fund theory of the capital of a corporation, that the creditors are entitled to protection against any reduction in the value of owner's equity below a stated amount, it is appropriate to use a money measure of capital rather than a real measure. For under this doctrine, the creditors have a right to demand that a certain money amount of capital be preserved in the business. If the money value of the assets increases, the creditors can have no objection to the distribution to the owners of the equity of part or all of the increase in value, since what is left will afford as much protection as before in money terms and the creditors' claims are of certain amounts of money rather than for a specified real value.

Correspondingly when the price-level declines, the creditors can justifiably object to any attempt to reduce the money value of capital which must be maintained intact for their protection. From this point of view a money measure of capital is clearly appropriate, since a claim fixed in money terms is being protected.

For the purposes of taxation, as well, there is some justification for the use of a money measure. Consider the man in the previous example who worked up $100 worth of material into $200 worth of product while the price-level doubled. Contrast him with the man who deposited $100 in the bank at the beginning of the year. In real terms the first man is just as well off at the beginning of the year as at the end of the year. The second man has only 50 per cent. of the real value that he deposited at the beginning of the year. To tax the first man on his $100 money gain is in fact a capital levy in real terms but any tax on money income less than 100 per cent. leaves him better off than the man holding cash or a bank deposit. A general price rise is a capital levy on those holding money or claims to money. It may be more equitable that the increase of money value of any asset be subject to a tax since this makes the burden of the price rise more evenly spread.

Of course, it would be more equitable still if a real rather than a money measure were used throughout the economy. Then the man with the $100 bank deposit might claim a 50 per cent. loss on that account to be deducted from his other income for tax purposes. Such a procedure has, in principle, greater merit than the taxation of money rather than real profit. But it may be deemed impractical to carry the real income concept so far as to allow a deduction for loss on all assets whose values have not increased in proportion to the general price-level. If the holders of money and of government bonds are not to be indemnified for their real loss brought about by the rise in prices, then those property owners who have escaped that loss by owning assets whose prices have risen may equitably be taxed on their money gain.

The issue is not whether real or money capital shall be maintained. There is general agreement that for the social good, real capital should not only be maintained, but expanded. The question is quite a different one of whether such maintenance of real capital should be allowed for in the determination of income. For it is quite possible to hold that income should be computed on a money basis while real capital can be maintained or increased largely out of reinvestment of income so computed.[26]

[26] This is the view held by the principal bodies of accountants both in the United States and in Great Britain. Thus the Committee on Accounting Procedure of the American Institute of Certified Public Accountants, in a letter issued in October 1948 and re-affirmed in 1953, stated: " The Committee ... has

This is in fact what has been happening in the United States and in Great Britain in the past few years. Under these circumstances, money income is greater than the corresponding amount of real income but part of the reinvestment of money earnings helps maintain the real value of capital intact.

Since pure profit from sales (defined as the excess of sales revenue over the cost of resources used up, priced as at the date of sale) seems usually to be granted by business men as the true measure of profits, we may infer that it is the concept most acceptable to the business man. The reason is not far to seek. The business man is inclined to think of maintaining or of expanding the physical volume of his operations—the idea of obtaining a constant money volume of sales in a period of rising prices is repugnant to him. Although he is unaccustomed to thinking in real rather than in money terms in contemplating general economic developments, he is keenly aware of changes in the cost of replacing inventory or capital assets. It is usually left to economists and a few accountants to suggest that if, for a particular firm, its own costs, selling prices, and volume remain unchanged while there is a movement of the general price-level, an adjustment should be made in its income for changes in the general price-level.

This attitude of business men, that they wish to maintain physical volume intact, with perhaps some expansion or at least some upward adjustment for increasing efficiency and size of the market, indicates that for the internal purposes of the corporation, and perhaps for reports to stockholders and for directors' decisions on dividend policy, a real measure of profit seems appropriate. Such a real measure might be based on the prices relevant to the corporation rather than on general purchasing

reached the conclusion that no basic change in the accounting treatment of depreciation of plant and equipment is practicable or desirable under present conditions to meet the problem created by the decline in the purchasing power of the dollar. ... The immediate problem can and should be met by financial management, ... When prices have risen appreciably since original investments in plant and facilities were made, a substantial proportion of net income as currently reported must be re-invested in the business in order to maintain assets at the same level of productivity at the end of a year as at the beginning." (*Restatement and Revision of Accounting Research Bulletins*, 1953, Chap. 9, pp. 68–69).

The views of the Council of the Institute of Chartered Accountants in England and Wales are very similar. It recommends that : " Historical cost should continue to be the basis on which annual accounts should be prepared and, in consequence, the basis on which profits shown by such accounts are computed. ... The Council also recommends to members . . . that they should draw attention to the desirability of: (a) setting amounts aside from profits to reserve in recognition of the effects which changes in the purchasing power of money have had upon the affairs of the business, particularly their effect on the amount of profit which, as a matter of policy, can prudently be regarded as available for distribution. . . ." (No. XV of the Institute's Recommendations on Accounting Principles, issued May 1952).

power. That is to say, pure profit rather than contemporaneous profit seems to be the one thought of as ideal by business men. This is a matter of choice for those concerned. If the stockholders and officers of a corporation wish to have some measure of the funds available for disposal while yet leaving capital intact, they can choose the meaning to give to the phrase " capital intact " which best serves their own particular purposes. The use of pure profits from sales in this connection seems to accord well with the aspirations and preconceptions of business men and investors.

Pure profits versus mixed income

Although business men are interested in an approximation to pure profits from sales primarily as a basis of a dividend and taxation policy that will permit them to maintain their place in the market, they are also interested in mixed profits from sales (*i.e.*, the excess of sales revenue over historical money costs). As between two corporations or as between two time periods a more reliable measure of success is furnished by mixed profit than by pure profit, for it is certainly an important function of the business man to buy and sell wisely. So if one firm has in a given year a greater pure profit from sales than another, but a lower mixed profit, then the first has not done so well as the second.

Of course, either one of these concepts is inferior to the mixed economic concept (*i.e.*, total equity-change) as a measure of how well the firm has done. Sometimes the pure profit on sales is regarded as superior to mixed profit on sales because there is an expectation of the recurrence of pure profits in the future, but the price gain component of mixed profits, it is argued, cannot be expected to recur. Whether there is anything in this argument depends on the facts of each particular situation. Sometimes price gains can be expected to recur, sometimes pure profits on sales are more likely. If a measure of profit is desired that will take account of expectations of the future, surely it should be so designed as to take explicit account of such expectations rather than to bring them in by the back door.

It is more sensible to value a corporation on the basis of expected future net receipts rather than on a mechanical projection of past profits, however measured. It may be true that a measure of pure profits from past sales furnishes more useful information on which to base a projection of future net receipts than does a measure of mixed profits from sales. But it would be folly to project past pure profits into the future in the face of any information which shows that changes in the profit level are to be expected. If no such information exists and current profit levels can be expected to continue into the future, then there will be no difference between pure profits and expected future net receipts, and aggregate pure profits will be identical with mixed economic income.

There is no escape from the necessity of using expected net receipts as the basis of a sound evaluation of a corporation. Any attempt to avoid the subjective nature of such expectations through the exclusive use of some objective measure of profit on past operations is likely to do more harm than benefit to anyone relying on the valuation. A valuation must be based on a judgment of the future, it cannot be both sound and objective at the same time in a world of uncertainty.

In any case, as between two companies one with and the other without price gains, each with the same pure profit from sales, the one with price gains can generally be considered to have done better. We say generally rather than always because account must be taken of the effect of this year's activities on future earning prospects. That is, for inter-firm comparison, mixed profits from sales are superior to pure profits from sales but both are inferior to mixed economic income.

Should unexpected gains be counted as income?

Business and taxation practice has long distinguished between capital gains and income. One type of capital gain, the appreciation of an asset that corresponds to an interest payment, as in a bond redeemable at a premium, can clearly be recognised as income. Such capital gains are expected gains. That part of any capital gain over and above appreciation in lieu of interest or similar payment is an unexpected gain, since if it were generally expected it would disappear. Thus an asset which is expected to be worth $105 one year from now will be worth about $100 now if the interest rate is 5 per cent. If after a year it should be worth $115, then $10 of the $15 appreciation may be considered unexpected gain, the other $5 as expected gain in lieu of interest or dividend payment.

As argued above, the expected gain should certainly be considered as income; should the unexpected gain be so considered as well?

Naturally, that depends upon the purpose for which the particular measurement of income is being made. For taxation purposes it certainly seems that the beneficiary of an unexpected gain is thereby better able to bear taxation than one who has had no such gain. In some countries capital gains are not subject to taxation as income. In the United States, however, taxes are imposed on realized capital gains. The practise of capital gain taxation has varied over the years but currently capital gains on assets held longer than six months are taxed as the equivalent in income of only 50 per cent. of their amount with a maximum rate of 25 per cent. The principal justification of such differential treatment of capital gains relates principally to the concentration in time of the realization of capital gains. If capital gains were handled on an accrued basis or somehow spread over the period during which the asset has been held, there would be less justification for treating them differently from income of other sorts. In short, the doctrine that gains are to be counted only when realized leads to the concentration of a capital gain into the time period in which the asset is sold, and so, with a progressive tax, would lead to an excessive tax burden in that period.

Even if spread over the holding period, a capital gain, or the unexpected portion thereof, differs from ordinary income in its nature as a revision of an estimate. Nevertheless there are strong arguments for considering capital gains as similar to other types of income, problems of timing aside. Even if we should agree that an unexpected gain is not income in the period when it is recognized but is merely a revision of an estimate of wealth, that implies that an equivalent income was earned and unrecognized in an earlier period.

Thus suppose a man bought some land for $1,000 at the end of 19x2, and received during the year 19x3 $100 in rental therefrom over all expenses and sold the land at the end of 19x3 for $2,000, the interest rate being 5 per cent. We may reasonably claim that his 19x3 income should be unaffected by this sale since the unexpected gain is merely a revision of the estimate of his wealth. But then we must also grant that he bought in 19x2 for $1,000 an asset that was really worth $2,000. Therefore even if we agree that the capital gain realised in 19x3 should not be counted as income, we must also admit that a gain of $1,000 accrued in the previous year when an asset worth $2,000 was purchased for $1,000.

It is obviously inconvenient to tax capital gains as they accrue. There is, however, justification for the taxation even of unexpected capital gains because they partake of the nature of income according to the fundamental definition of income as the amount that can be consumed while leaving the income recipient as well off as before. The problems surrounding the taxation of capital gains are accordingly not basically problems of principle but problems of practical convenience. It is impractical to tax capital gains as they accrue, at least the unexpected component, and if they are taxed when realized in the same manner as any other income, an inequity may result under a system of progressive income taxation.

Present methods of taxation do lead to the spreading of taxation of one very important class of capital gains over the period during which the asset is held and used. If depreciable assets used in the conduct of a business gain in value, this will be reflected in increased receipts from the sales of the products in whose production the assets are used. If the depreciation is based on original cost the profit as measured by the accountant will then contain each year part of the capital gain on the asset. Therefore basing depreciation on original cost will, in the case of assets which have increased in value, lead in effect to a steady inclusion of part of the capital gain in each year's reported profits until the asset is retired. That is, each year's reported profit, computed in accordance with the standard practise of basing depreciation on original cost, will include not only pure profits on sales but also price gains on that part charged to this year's costs of any asset which has appreciated in value.

The accountant's procedure in matching costs of one period against revenues of another automatically includes in income the capital gains or losses on those cost items charged to the current year's operations. If, then, depreciation were to be based on replacement cost, it would be necessary either to tax the capital gain accrued in the revalued assets or to let this capital gain escape taxation. The capital gain will not be realized through sale but through the use of the more valuable assets in the conduct of the business. Under the present system, such capital gains appear as a component of ordinary income. If depreciation were based on replacement cost, such capital gains would not appear as any component of income subject to tax unless a specific tax was levied on the revaluation of the assets on which increased depreciation was claimed. This, of course, would defeat the purpose of claiming increased depreciation based on replacement costs, except possibly for timing considerations.

A distinction must be drawn here between an asset that appreciates more than the general price level and one that merely appreciates along with the general price level. In the first case there is a capital gain in real terms, in the second in money terms only. The considerations discussed in the previous section on the real versus money measure of income apply to this case as well.

Of course, similar reasoning applies to capital losses on assets whose value is charged to cost. If an asset suffers an unexpected decline in value, and depreciation continues to be based on original cost, then reported sales profit will be lower than pure sales profit and accordingly some tax allowance is automatically made for the capital loss suffered.

Conclusions

The principal differences among the bewildering number of concepts of income that may be conceived can be narrowed down to three major issues. These are the real versus the money measure of income, inclusion versus exclusion of capital gains, and accrual versus realization as the criterion for timing of a gain or loss. If agreement were reached on these three major issues, almost every one of the many controversial points concerning the measurement of income could be settled, and most of the differences which separate accountants and economists in this area would disappear. But income is used for so many different purposes that a set of decisions on the three major issues appropriate to one use of a measure of income may very well be inappropriate to another.

A period of changing prices especially urgently poses the issue between the real and the money measure of income. If a real measure of values were used throughout the economy, strong arguments could be made for a real measure of income. But in an economy in which many contractual relations are expressed in money terms, certain inequities would be introduced by measuring business income in real terms while government obligations, corporate bonds, and bank deposits were still fixed in money terms.

The accountant's rejection of accrued income, which implies, among other things, the exclusion from income of changes in going value, is based primarily on the practical necessity of making income, as far as possible, an objectively measurable concept. But subjective valuations are inherent in any useful concept of income so that the user must make his own adjustments to the accountant's measure.

Capital gains can be recognized as a form of income, but a form which requires separate treatment from the point of view of most of the users of income. The accountant's procedures do lead to the separate treatment of capital gains on operating assets sold outside the normal course of the business, but capital gains on inventories and on other assets which are eventually charged to cost ultimately get mixed up with normal income, and lose their separate identity.

Business Valuation, Goodwill and the Super-Profit Method*

By H. C. Edey

Reader in Accounting,
London School of Economics

The super-profit formula

The purpose of this essay is to examine the significance and usefulness of the procedure known as the super-profit method of valuing business goodwill.

Goodwill in the economic sense is another word for organisation. Its value is derived from the economic benefits that a going concern may enjoy, as compared with a new one, from (a) established relations in all the markets in which it is accustomed to deal—not only in its sales markets, but also in the markets for all the goods and services it buys, including the labour market, the markets in which it buys its raw materials, the market for finance, and so on; (b) established relations with government departments and other non-commercial bodies with which it has negotiations; and (c) the personal relationships that grow up among people working together in a business, and the fund of knowledge and the habits that are built up, all of which will in favourable circumstances make for smoother and more effective working than could be expected in a new business. These things cannot be separated from the business and sold as can such assets as plant and machinery.

The formula for calculating the value of a business by this method, as it is generally stated, can be written:

$$V = A + \frac{P - rA}{j}$$

where:

V is the value to be found [1];

A is the value of the net tangible assets;

P is the expected annual return;

r is the normal annual rate of return appropriate to the business, expressed as a fraction (that is, 10 per cent. is written ·1 or 1/10);

---

* Based on an article in *Accountancy*, January and February, 1957.
[1] But see p. 210 below for the case where V is less than A.

$P - rA$ is the super-profit;

j is the appropriate rate for capitalisation of the super-profit, also expressed as a fraction;

$\dfrac{P - rA}{j}$ is the value of the goodwill, which we may write as G.

We shall now discuss possible interpretations of this formula.[2]

The net tangible assets

The tangible assets are those assets that could be sold separately.[3]

For the time being we shall avoid the complication introduced by the existence of loan capital or preference shares by assuming that apart from current liabilities the business to be valued is financed entirely by equity capital.

We shall assume initially that the value of the tangible assets is defined as their estimated saleable value as individual assets in the best market available. To arrive at the net value, the amount of the current liabilities is deducted, so that A is an estimate of the break-up value of the business. Later, the alternative assumption of basing the value of the tangible assets on their market replacement cost will be examined.[4]

The dividend expectations

The annual return, P, expected from the business will be taken, for our purpose, as an estimate of the annual dividend distribution that can be maintained in the future by the use of the assets, organisational structure and management that are to be handed over to the purchaser. The assets in question, so far as these could be sold separately, are those of which the value is included in A.[5]

The future level of dividends will depend partly upon whether new capital is paid into the business at a later date. This possibility must be taken into account in any valuation. This point is usually ignored in texts and here we shall simplify the problem by assuming that no further capital is to be paid in.

Another determinant of the level of dividends after any given point of time is the level of dividends before that time. The lower,

---

[2] One of our problems is the vagueness of textual discussions of this method of valuation. This makes it necessary for us to consider what interpretations, if any, are likely to make this method a useful valuation procedure.

[3] We shall later make certain qualifications to this definition.

[4] Original cost valuations cannot be relevant. I assume this need not be discussed.

[5] Income from assets which are not to change hands, or which are to be valued separately from the business (*e.g.*, marketable securities), must be excluded from the estimate.

for example, earlier dividends are in the period after the valuation, the higher should later dividends be, for the lower level of earlier dividends will leave more resources in the business and these should add to earnings: restricting dividends has the same effect as paying additional capital into the business. This, too, is a question that is usually ignored in texts; again we shall simplify the problem by assuming that the business will be so run as to maintain dividends at a maximum constant level.[6]

These simplifying assumptions can be made because we are concerned, not with problems of valuation in general, but with relative merits of a particular valuation procedure. We shall show that even on simplified assumptions such as these, the super-profit method is not a very useful tool of valuation. Textbook expositions of the method do not explain how the formula could be adapted to deal with more complicated cases; but the argument that follows suggests that in such cases the method is not likely to be more satisfactory than in simple cases.

An important feature of our definition of P is that we have not identified it with profit. The future dividend level is the fundamental concept, for it is the dividend distribution that determines what can be spent by the owner or owners of the business; the profit reported for a given period is at best a rough indicator of the dividend stream to follow.[7] A series of dividends are cash receipts: a profit figure is only an accounting measurement of a highly approximate character.[8]

The normal rate of return

We now turn to r, the normal annual rate of return appropriate to the business.

Some textual discussion of the super-profit method seems to require that r be defined as the long-run rate of return an investor would expect to receive on an investment equal in amount to A, in a business of the type that is being valued, having regard to current market yields on other possible investments, and on the

---

[6] In principle, that pattern of dividend payments, capital investment (and capital repayments if any) will be planned which maximises (so far as can be seen) the value of V.

[7] Or, possibly, in exceptional circumstances, of the liquidation value later: a dividend in liquidation is a special case of a future dividend, and is equally important as a factor in the valuation.

[8] It is, we suspect, because the usual discussions of valuation in accounting textbooks and treatises have been based on the explicit or implicit assumption that profits will be fully distributed, so that they are identical with dividends, that profit is often spoken of as the fundamental factor in valuation. The valuers have really been setting a value on expected future dividends; but they have described this process as a capitalisation of profit. It is true that undistributed funds may be realised by selling the business interest; but this is only because the immediate or ultimate buyer expects dividends sooner or later.

assumption that A is the break-up value of the business. Presumably r will then be above the current market yield on irredeemable Government stocks.[9] It will presumably be less than the average rate which an investor would require on his whole investment in the business where this is greater than the break-up value A, since the risk can be presumed to be less: if the investment does not exceed the break-up value, the ultimate loss, should the venture prove unsuccessful, may well be less than if it does, even though the possibility exists that bad management will dissipate the whole of the assets.

Some idea of current rates of return in different kinds of business can be obtained from published financial data, the rate in each case being expressed as the ratio of the current dividend to the market value of the relevant security. However, these statistics can at best be no more than rough-and-ready guides, even for valuations not based on the super-profit method. In the first place the conditions of one business are seldom reproduced closely in a second: a rate of return that an investor would think appropriate for one business may well be inappropriate for another; but there is no way of determining the adjustment necessary to the first rate in order to approximate the second: this is for the individual investor. This affects all valuation methods and is not peculiar to the one we are discussing.

Secondly, the observed ratio between a current dividend and the market value of the share does not tell us the relation that is generally expected by the market to exist between *future* dividends and that price. This can only be estimated, and the estimates of different investors will vary. Hence no unique measure of the expected rates of return upon market prices for other investments is available; a valuer must be content with rather general impressions and must in the final analysis make up his own mind what rate is appropriate.[10] This, too, is a problem common to all valuations, whether by the super-profit method or otherwise.

[9] Strictly speaking these should be described as stocks redeemable only at the discretion of the Government: " one-way-option " or " undated " stocks, such as $2\frac{1}{2}$ per cent. Consols.

[10] This raises an interesting question. In the conventional theoretical economic model we assume that a valuation is carried out by capitalising a given estimated future flow of cash receipts at a given rate of interest. In passing from this model to the world of experience, both the capitalised flow and the capitalisation rate acquire a certain fuzziness, in that it seems an investor or a valuer is likely to apply, consciously or unconsciously, explicitly or implicitly, a correction for uncertainty to both. He may cut down his first estimate of the dividend flow in order " to be on the safe side "; and then he may increase the first estimate of the right capitalisation rate for the same reason, or perhaps reduce it because the future of the company seems rosy. There is thus a functional relationship between the estimates of the dividend flow and of the capitalisation rate.

Finally, there is the problem that the market prices of investments cannot be identified with the net tangible assets of the super-profit method. The market prices of other investments include, for each other investment examined, the value of goodwill—the amount which we are attempting to measure in relation to the business to be valued. The reported yields on other securities—in each case the ratio of dividend to market price—cannot therefore be identified with *r* in our formula, which is the rate the investor would think appropriate on that part of the purchase-price invested which is equal to the saleable value, *A*, of the net tangible assets. This problem arises only when we are using the super-profit method.

This is a serious difficulty, for even in principle it does not seem possible to calculate the value of the equivalent of *r*, as we are at present defining it, for other investments. The values of the net tangible assets of other investments can perhaps be found, even though there are practical difficulties; but it is not possible thence to arrive at a dividend to net tangible asset ratio, since we cannot determine what part of the dividend is return on net tangible assets and what part is return on goodwill. The most we can do is ascertain this ratio for any investments whose market value is known not to exceed the saleable value of the net tangible assets. Hence, even if it cannot be said that this difficulty renders our interpretation of the super-profit method invalid, it certainly raises doubts. It would be surprising if those who have used the method have in fact had access to the figures of *r*, as we have defined it, for alternative investments. If these cannot be obtained we are left with little objective guidance in assessing *r* for the investment to be valued.

It can indeed be argued that all *ex ante* assessments of economic values are subjective; and that such an assessment of *r* need not involve a greater subjective element than the *ex ante* assessment of any capitalisation rate, that is, of any minimum required return. There is, however, a difference between *r*, as defined above, and an average capitalisation rate expressing the relation required between expected dividends and the total amount invested. In principle, whether the latter has been received can be checked *ex post* if we consider the whole life of the business. There seems no way of checking *r*, even *ex post*, since this involves the splitting of the dividends received into a part attributable to use of the net tangible assets and a part attributable to goodwill.

However, let us assume that this definition of *r* is acceptable as a procedure that a prospective investor may find useful.

Capitalisation of the super-profit

We have now provisionally defined A and r. From these we obtain the product rA. This is, by definition, the annual dividend which would satisfy the investor on the assumption that he invested a sum A in the purchase of the business. The quantity $P - rA$ is the super-profit. It will pay the investor, when he calculates his maximum offer price for the business, to add to the sum A any amount up to the present value he sets on $P - rA$. This addition is the value of the goodwill. The formula assumes that he capitalises $P - rA$ at a rate j, so that the value of the goodwill is

$$\frac{P - rA}{j} = G.$$

We now have to consider, therefore, what meaning should be attached to j.

Again there is little help in the texts. Given the above interpretation of r, we may reasonably assume that the investor would set j sufficiently above r to reflect the greater possibility of loss in buying an expectation of future dividends unbacked by saleable tangible asset values. One would also expect j to be assessed having regard to alternative investment opportunities. It is only possible to calculate the value of j for a similar business opportunity, however, after the value of r has been determined for that opportunity, for until that is done we do not know how much of the dividend on that other investment is super-profit; if then we estimate the value of A for that investment, the value of j can be obtained from our formula (by inserting the known market value as V and solving for j). But, as we have noted, r is in general unknown for other investments. It seems then that all we can say of j is that it is assessed by the potential investor as some figure higher than r and higher than the average minimum rate of return he would accept on the total investment.

Alternative definitions of r

These difficulties are reduced if we define r as the market yield on undated Government stocks or the average market yield on debentures or preference shares, or some approximation to this; rA would then represent a fixed interest return available to the investor if the net tangible assets were disinvested. This would still leave the problem of calculating j for other possible investments in order to assess the alternatives available. In principle, however, this would be possible, as we have just seen, by estimating the value of A for each other investment; since we know V, its market value, and r is now given, j can be calculated from our formula.

This definition has the advantage of precision. It also gives a fairly clear-cut meaning to rA, as the fixed interest return that could be obtained by investing the break-up value of the business: if P is not greater than this there is certainly no point in continuing the business. On the other hand, it may still not be worthwhile to continue the business even though P is greater than rA: something better than a fixed interest rate is to be expected from an equity investment, even when fully represented by tangible assets. Furthermore, there is the practical difficulty in assessing the value of j, where r is a low rate, that (especially where the assets happen to be very specific so that A is low) the numerical value of $P - rA$ may be high, and a relatively small, possibly arbitrary, alteration in j may make a large difference to G, and therefore to V.

A third possible interpretation would be to take j as equal to r, both being defined as the estimated market rate of return appropriate to the whole investment being valued, including the value of goodwill. This would be to define r and j as we should define the capitalisation rate used when the method of valuation is the direct capitalisation of expected dividends.[11] In the simplified case we are discussing this method is described by the formula

$$V = \frac{P}{r}$$

where P has the meaning given above. If r and j are so defined, the two formulae are algebraically identical since

$$A + \frac{P - rA}{j}$$
$$= A + \frac{P - rA}{r}$$
$$= \frac{rA + P - rA}{r}$$
$$= \frac{P}{r}.$$

This interpretation raises no difficulties in ascertaining r (and therefore j) that would not arise in a valuation by direct capitalisation, at a single rate, of the future expected net cash flow.

On the other hand, the first possibility we have discussed, namely that r should be rather below this rate and j rather above

[11] I shall call this the *dividend capitalisation* method.

it, has the attraction that it draws specific attention to the greater uncertainty that probably attaches to the " top slice " of the value. It is true that there is less guidance from market data in the assessment of r and j; but after all the assessment of a direct capitalisation rate rests to a large extent on personal temperament and judgment. Certainly yields on other securities that at least look as if they were direct capitalisation rates are published daily, while the equivalents of r and j are not. But as we have pointed out above, the former are not true alternative yields to that obtainable on the business to be valued: they are at best only rough guides or indicators.

Significance of break-up value

It may be helpful at this point to take a numerical example. In a given business let the net tangible asset valuation, A, be £1,000, let the value of the expected maintainable dividend, P, be £120 per annum, let the value of r be 10 per cent. per annum and let j be 20 per cent. per annum. Then we have

$$V = 1,000 + \frac{120 - \cdot 1 \times 1,000}{\cdot 2}$$

$$= 1,000 + \frac{20}{\cdot 2}$$

$$= 1,100 \ ^{12}$$

The first point we note is that the use of the formula demands the calculation of the break-up value of the business, and thus draws attention to this figure and to its relation to the total value of the business. The break-up value is an important figure for three reasons. First it is the minimum value of the business. A seller would be foolish to sell at a lower figure; and it would always be worthwhile to buy a business at a figure below its break-up value (allowing, of course, a tolerance for the uncertainty of a break-up estimate). Secondly, as has already been implied in the above discussion of r, the break-up value is of significance in relation to the risk of investment, in that it gives some indication of the possible salvage value if the worst comes to the worst. True, bad management or misfortune may result in this salvage value being dissipated as time goes on; but at least this value is available when the investment is first made. Finally, the break-up value

[12] This gives the same valuation as would have been obtained from the direct capitalisation of the expected dividend at a capitalisation rate of about 11 per cent. Let i be the dividend capitalisation rate. Then

$$i = \frac{120}{1,100}$$

$$= 10 \cdot 9 \text{ per cent. approximately.}$$

gives the minimum liquidity available to the owner, subject again to the size of any losses incurred after the investment is made.

Net tangible assets and goodwill: further considerations

At this point, however, we must introduce a qualification. This arises from the difficulty of defining the tangible assets clearly. Among the assets that could often be sold separately from the business as a whole we must include such things as patents, unpatented knowledge, and the like, which are probably specific to the type of business being valued, but might be bought by another business in the same line. If our concept of A as the break-up value of the business is to be preserved, we must include in A an assessment of the value of such assets. There is no doubt, however, that both textbooks and practical valuers tend to regard the value of such assets as too doubtful for inclusion in A, and regard their value as part of the value of G. This may not be unreasonable, in that it restricts the break-up value to be included in A to that part of the net realisable value concerning which there is less doubt. It does, however, mean that our definition of the tangible assets will not always hold. Possibly it would be better to avoid the use of the term " tangible assets " in this context and merely define A as the best estimate of the current break-up value of the business that can be made.

The next point to be noted is that an excess of the total business value over the break-up value, given by a positive value of

$$\frac{P - rA}{j} = G$$

can be due to several causes. The business may possess goodwill as it is defined on page 201 above: that is, it is expected to produce a higher dividend stream than a new business similar in all other respects because the former is well organised. Secondly, the tangible assets may be specific, so that their break-up value included in A is significantly lower than their replacement value, even when new. If this is the case we cannot regard G as the value of goodwill only; it may include an element of value attributable to the contribution of the specific assets (though it will normally not be possible to say how much). If no break-up value has been assigned to such assets as patents and the possession of confidential knowledge (as is likely in view of the uncertainty of such valuations), G will include the value of these. G will also include the value, if any, of any other advantages that cannot be assigned a break-up value, such as the possession of a non-transferable licence, the services of particularly valuable staff at salaries favourable to the business, and the advantages of favourable location where these are not reflected fully in the rental paid.[13] Finally G will include any value derived from absence of competition.[14]

Clearly there are many possible factors operating here, the relative contributions of which will not be given by the formula and indeed, in general, will not be susceptible of estimation. The significance to be attached to G will vary with the relative importance attached to these factors. It may be argued that, as the division of the value V into two elements, A and G, may draw explicit attention to the break-up value, so it also draws explicit attention to the need to explain G and therefore to the possible effect on future returns of the presence or absence of these factors.

It is possible for the value of G to be negative where the value of P is less than the return, at the chosen rate of interest r, on A. This is an indication that the value invested in the assets can be put to better use by liquidating the business and investing elsewhere, at any rate in the view of the purchaser or valuer who assesses A and r. In this case the valuation must not be taken as V but as A, provided that A is the full break-up value.

Temporary super-profits

A special case arises when the value of P is likely to fall after a given period of time.[15] The business may enjoy profitable advantages that are expected to disappear at some foreseeable time in the future, such as the services of men or property in return for a payment below what will be demanded in the longer term (for example, when the contract under which the services were enjoyed terminates), or the temporary enjoyment of absence of competition.

In the numerical example above, the tangible asset valuation was £1,000, the net maintainable dividend was £120, r was 10 per cent. per annum and j was 20 per cent. per annum. These figures gave a super-profit of £20 which, capitalised at 20 per cent. per annum, gave the goodwill a value of £100. Now suppose,

[13] Where the site is owned, however, the value of location would presumably be included in A as part of the value of land and premises.

[14] Strictly we should say, not that the value of each of these things will be included in G, but that G will be greater or less as these factors are present or absent. This is because the value of G is partly determined by the values of r and j; and as we have seen different definitions of these are possible; and moreover the numerical assessments, given the definitions, may contain a substantial subjective element.

[15] This possibility is mentioned because it receives a good deal of attention in texts dealing with the super-profit method. Possible explanations of this may be found in Appendices I and II.

instead, that after six years the total profit was expected to fall from £120 to £115 because the lease of the premises occupied by the business would then have expired, and the competitive rental that would then have to be paid would be £5 higher than at present, so that the super-profit would be £20 for six years, then falling to £15. The longer term super-profit of £15 should presumably be capitalised separately from the £5, which will be received for only six years. The valuation would then be given, in £'s, by:

$$V = 1,000 + \frac{115 - \cdot1 \times 1,000}{\cdot2} + 5 \times \left[\frac{1 - \dfrac{1}{(1 \cdot 2)^6}}{\cdot2} \right]$$

$$= 1,000 + 75 + 17$$

$$= 1,092$$

the term in square brackets being the present value of a terminable six-year annuity of £5 per annum.[16]

However, had the direct capitalisation of dividends method been used the same problem could have been dealt with quite simply by capitalising separately (a) the net maintainable profit of £115, and (b) the six-year annuity of £5. The super-profit formula seems to offer no particular advantage in this situation.

Replacement cost of net tangible assets

Earlier we deferred consideration of the possible significance of the super-profit method where A is defined not as the break-up value, but as the replacement value of the net tangible assets, that is, the estimated cost of replacing the tangible assets in their condition at the date of the valuation,[17] less liabilities. At first glance it might seem that significance could be attached to A, so defined, as the maximum value that a purchaser should pay for the business, since for this amount he could acquire a similar collection of assets and liabilities. If, for example, the replacement cost of tangible assets is £500 and the capitalised value of super-profit is, say, £100, giving a total of £600, the correct value of the business, it may be said, is nevertheless £500, for no one is likely to pay more for a business than the cost of creating a similar one.

However, this argument conceals a fallacy. An upper limit to the value of a business is indeed set by the fact that no sensible

---

[16] The actuarial symbol for this term is a_n. Values for this can be found, for different periods and rates of interest, in actuarial tables.

[17] In the case of assets of a specific type, for which there is no good second-hand value, this concept can be interpreted as the current cost of new assets of the same kind less an allowance for depreciation calculated on the replacement value.

purchaser would pay more for it than the amount he would need to set up a similar business yielding the same expected return, less an allowance for the extra trouble and risk and for the amount in the early years by which the dividends would probably fall short of the required level. It is indeed desirable, in principle, to estimate the full cost of creating a similar business to that being valued in order to set an upper limit on the value V.[18] But this upper limit is, in general, a different figure from the replacement value of the tangible assets *less* the liabilities.

In the first place, the productive methods that would be used if a new business were established may well be different from that of the business being valued. New and improved assets and methods may be available. Secondly, it can happen that mistakes were made in the business to be valued that would be avoided in another business: the wrong assets may have been acquired. Thirdly, the upper limit includes, in principle, outlay that would not be covered by the valuation of the tangible assets. In order to set up a similar business it may well be necessary to spend money on such matters as development of productive methods and markets, and very likely to accept a zero dividend in the early years of the business, or a dividend below the estimated longer term competitive rate. It is, indeed, the fact that such expenditure or sacrifices have been made that may account for the emergence of valuable goodwill, in the sense of an excess of V over the value of the net tangible assets.

We must, I think, conclude that where A is defined as the replacement cost of the net tangible assets it is difficult to attach such significance to the super-profit method as to make it a useful valuation method.

Capital gearing

We must now consider the problem of capital gearing. Where there are prior interests in the form of loan capital or preference shares, some expositions of the super-profit method suggest that the value of the equity interest can be arrived at by first finding a value for V that includes the value of the prior interests, *i.e.*, by estimating V as if the business were financed wholly

---

[18] This procedure is valid, even if the potential purchaser is not in a position to set up a business for himself, for it gives the maximum figure that a potential competitor would have to spend in order to enter the trade or industry. It would obviously be dangerous to pay substantially more than this sum for an established business merely because earnings were in excess of a market rate of return thereon, in view of the possibility of competition likely to be induced by such a level of earnings. Of course, if it was not possible to reproduce the business (*e.g.*, because it possessed a legal monopoly) the replacement cost in this sense would become infinite.

by equity capital, and then deducting from the value of V so found the liquidation value of any loan or preference capital. Interest and dividends on such loan and preference capital are, in consequence, not deducted in computing P. This method ignores two relevant facts.

First, the total value of a business financed wholly by equity capital is not necessarily the same as that of the same business financed partly by fixed interest or dividend capital. It is a matter of experience that it may be possible to raise the total value of a business by altering its capital structure. Indeed the concept of an optimum gearing that will give the maximum value to a particular business is one that reflects experience. For some business interests, where uncertainty is high, the optimum gearing may be zero. But, in general, some element of gearing can be expected to raise the total value. Hence a valuation that ignores the effect of gearing may be less than the possible maximum.

Secondly, the current market value of such prior interests as debentures and preference shares is not necessarily equal to their liquidation value unless, indeed, liquidation is expected to take place in the near future. It may in fact be greater or less, depending upon the interest or dividend expectations, the degree of uncertainty attached to these, and current market rates of interest, such interests normally being valued by the dividend capitalisation method.

It seems therefore that if the super-profit method is to be relevant it must be applied to the equity interest and it must be assumed that the optimum capital gearing possible will be adopted,[19] so that V, A, P, r and j all relate to the equity interest, not the whole business (except where these are the same). In the calculation of the break-up value, A, the amounts payable on liquidation to the holders of prior rights must be deducted. P must be defined as the dividend that can be paid on the equity interest after meeting interest or dividends on loan or preference capital. The total value of the business must then be reached by aggregating V with the value found separately for the loan and/or preference capital.[20]

---

[19] Where the interest to be valued is not a controlling interest in the business, the owner will not be able to affect the gearing; even so, market forces, such as the threat of take-over bids, may sometimes bring about an adjustment where this is possible. The possibility of change in the capital gearing will, of course, depend in all cases upon the existing capital structure and upon who holds any prior interests. In some cases it might be worthwhile to offer existing holders of loan or preference capital a consideration for a change in their rights.

[20] This implies, in principle, a trial and error process. It may be necessary to estimate the effect, on the overall value, of different possible capital structures, as it is necessary to estimate the effect of different possible business policies. That gearing and policy will be assumed, within the range of possibility, that give the maximum overall value to the business.

Usefulness of the super-profit method

What has been said above suggests that the super-profit method of valuation has little to commend it, even when it is possible to give a significant interpretation to the formula.

It is true that if *A* is computed as the break-up value of the equity, the formula does draw express attention to the greater uncertainty that may attach to any excess value. This will not always be of great practical significance, but it is undoubtedly a factor which most valuers would wish to consider. There seems no particular advantage in using the super-profit formula, however, in order to gain this advantage. It is just as effective to carry out the valuation using the direct dividend capitalisation formula and to estimate separately the break-up value of the equity as the lower limit to the valuation. Similarly, the upper limit can be obtained from an estimate of the replacement value of the business as a whole, including in this figure an allowance for any estimated extra outlay or lower dividends likely during the early years of a new business.

Certain legal valuations are required to take goodwill into account.[21] This requirement is a way of drawing attention expressly to the fact that the full value of the business is required, not merely the value of the net tangible assets. Such a requirement does not, however, imply that a specific valuation of goodwill need be made by using the super-profit method. A valuation by the capitalisation of expected dividends will necessarily include the value of goodwill (which can be obtained separately, if desired, by subtracting the assessed value of the net tangible assets).

Our discussion has been based on the assumption of simpler conditions than will normally be met in practice. In particular a valuation must take into account the possibility of a varying dividend pattern over time (the most usual expectation being a more or less steadily rising dividend), the possibility of additional capital payments into the business by the future owner or owners, and the possibility of special capital distributions. The super-profit formula is not well adapted to deal with these complications. It may be argued that they are not usually taken expressly into account in the dividend capitalisation formula. It is true that in the analysis of investment opportunities on the organised securities market the usual starting point for discussion is the simple formula

$$V = \frac{P}{i}$$

21 See, for example, section 59, Finance Act, 1940.

where P is the current dividend (or possibly an estimate of next year's dividend) and i is given the heavy task, not only of representing the return on alternative opportunities, but of reflecting all the hopes and fears of the investor or his adviser, including the expectations of rises (or falls) in the dividend, of calls for more capital and the possibilities of return of capital. Those, however, who wish to take expressly into account the logical implications of the points we have mentioned, can do so, without departing from the direct dividend capitalisation principle, by substituting for the above formula the more general formula for the present value of any future cash stream, positive or negative:

$$V = \frac{P_1}{(1+i)} + \frac{P_2}{(1+i)^2} + \frac{P_3}{(1+i)^3} + \cdots$$

where the P's are the estimated net cash receipts, considered separately, for each future year 1, 2, 3, . . . ; the receipts may be negative in years when the owner pays in funds, and may include both dividends and capital repayments; i is a rate of return which reflects current alternatives foregone. This formula can be made even more general by giving i a time suffix, that is, by assigning to each separate year its appropriate rate of interest.

This concludes our survey. In the two appendices that follow we shall discuss, respectively, a possible theoretical basis for the super-profit method, and the application of the method to the valuation of professional practices.

APPENDIX I

Theoretical Basis for the Super-Profit Method

In my view the super-profit formula represents a brave but unsuccessful attempt to apply certain concepts of abstract economic theory to an important business problem. It can be given significance in the following way. Assume a world with conditions approaching those of perfect competition. Assume that resources have little specificity, and that there is little technical change. The saleable value of an asset approximates closely its replacement value. Rates of return on investment and interest rates tend to a standard level.

We can then define A as the market value of the business assets and r as the standard rate of return. In such conditions, profits (equal to dividends) will deviate little from the standard rate of return on the market value of the assets; that is, P will usually approximate to rA. The existence of super-profit will be exceptional. Should P be found to exceed rA, this will imply a disequilibrium that is unlikely to persist. The present value of the super-profit will therefore be that of a short series of receipts capitalised at rate r. If we set j equal to $\dfrac{1}{a_n}$, this valuation of the super-profit can be represented by the simple capitalisation formula

$$\frac{P - rA}{j}$$

instead of the more usual form $(P - rA)\, a_n$, (a_n being the present value of an annuity of 1 for n years at $100\, r$ per cent.)

APPENDIX II

The Value of Professional Practices

IT is typical of professional practices that the earnings from them are largely due to the personal qualities and exertions of the practitioner. The assets used in such a practice are likely to be relatively few and low in value in relation to net earnings as compared with trading and manufacturing businesses. Profit is fairly clearly defined.

An incoming practitioner buying a practice from a retiring practitioner will in general be prepared to pay the market value of the practice assets, corresponding to A in the super-profit formula, and a further sum in consideration of the fact that he will probably enjoy the full benefit of the connection his predecessor has built up instead of having to build up his own practice over a period of some years. This corresponds to G, the value of goodwill, in the super-profit formula.

Suppose we take the average net profit which the outgoing practitioner has been able to withdraw annually from the practice in recent years as P in our formula, and rA as the return attributable to the investment in the practice assets; r in this case might reasonably be the overdraft rate of interest. $P - rA$ is then the net personal earnings. Suppose, too, we assume

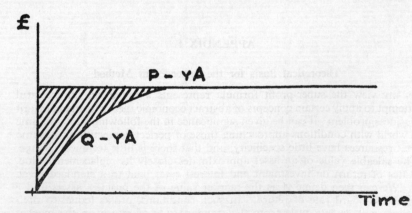

that the incoming practitioner would have been able to build up his net fees to P in three or four years if he had started a new practice. If he acquires the established practice as a going concern the net fees will be at this figure from the beginning.[22] Let us now plot the level of $P - rA$ on a graph, of which the y axis measures money value and the x axis time from the date of purchase. On the same graph we plot a curve $Q - rA$ which we assume measures the net fees, Q, that the new practitioner would earn if he started his own practice, less rA, the interest on the money he would in that case have to invest in second-hand assets like those in use in the existing practice. We then have the pattern shown by the diagram on page 216.

The shaded portion shows the maximum the new practitioner would be prepared to pay for the goodwill of the practice, subject to a discounting factor to bring it to a present value. If the present value of the shaded portion $P - Q$ turned out to be roughly equal to three times $P - rA$, the value of the practice would be given by the formula

$$V = A + \frac{P - rA}{j}$$

where j was $33\frac{1}{3}$ per cent.

This is not an unreasonable approach to professional practice valuation, provided that the full significance of each term in the formula is borne in mind in assessing the value to be assigned to it. If one can assume there is some uniformity in the time it takes to build up a practice to its normal level, we might expect j to take a fairly standard value.[23] On balance, however, it would seem simpler, and less likely to lead to error, to recognise the problem as simply that of determining the present value of an annuity of the difference between the net fees to be expected in the practice and the net fees that would be earned by an average practitioner in a new practice.

The use of the super-profit formula may be explicable historically in terms of this approximation for the professional firm, however.

---

[22] If the outgoing practitioner has specially outstanding personal qualities it may of course be that part of his fees will be permanently lost as soon as he goes. We should then take P net of this loss.

[23] Another approximation would be the simpler formula:
$$V = A + nP$$
where n was chosen to make the value nP equal to $\dfrac{P - rA}{\cdot 33}$. This would explain the rough-and-ready method of valuing practice goodwill on the basis of n years' purchase of net fees; we can assume that n too might be fairly uniform as between different practices.

The Economist's Cost Concept
and Business Problems

By J. R. Gould

Lecturer in Economics,
London School of Economics.

ECONOMISTS have strongly criticised the methods by which cost accountants prepare figures to aid businessmen. The main attack has been directed against the accountants' concept of cost; in particular, economists have criticised the use of historical costs, the attempts to allocate joint costs, and the apparent lack of appreciation of the significance of the distinction between fixed and variable costs.

The inadequacies of the accountants' concept of cost have been easily exposed by the use of simple arithmetic examples. Less successful has been the attempt to persuade accountants that the concept of opportunity cost, which figures so prominently in economic theory, is the relevant one for many problems. The fault does not lie all on one side. Although some accountants might be accused of carrying conservatism to excessive lengths, economists may not have been sufficiently clear in their expositions of the opportunity cost doctrine to carry with them those to whom the idea is unfamiliar. To assert that the true nature of costs is contained in the opportunity cost theory, and that the definition of cost is the value of the sacrificed alternative, can be dangerously misleading—because it might be taken to advocate the rigid application of a rule rather than to promote the better understanding of the nature of problems of decision-making.

I shall argue that the opportunity cost doctrine is best viewed as a method of approach to a class of problem, rather than simply as an injunction to use a particular definition—indeed, opportunity cost is useless for the process of calculating the respective merits of alternative plans. In section I, examples will be given to illustrate the use of the concept of opportunity cost in economic theory. Section II develops a simple analysis from which is derived useful concepts of cost. This analysis is used in section III to discuss the relation between the accountant's and the economist's approach. Finally, some of the more general considerations raised by the analysis are mentioned.

218

Before proceeding, it may be as well to discuss briefly the relation between economic theory and business practice. Economists have not, in general, been mainly concerned with telling businessmen how to do their job. I refer here, of course, to the main stream of economic thought—I am not saying that economists never advise businessmen. The economist's primary task is to discover how the economy works, and in the course of this inquiry he becomes interested in certain problems that confront the firm. This close connection provides at least a presumption that the businessman may learn something useful from the analysis which the economic theorist has developed. But although the business man may expect to learn something from economic theory, he should remember that it was designed to tackle problems similar to, but not identical with, his own—and he must expect to have to make some alterations to secure a better fit for his purposes.

I

The notion of opportunity cost springs directly from what is usually considered to be the central economic problem. Professor Robbins defines economics as ". . . the science which studies human behaviour as a relationship between ends and scarce means which have alternative uses." Thus the economic problem involves choosing to which ends our resources should be devoted, and which ends to sacrifice. The problem is one of choice. The " opportunity cost " of choosing one end rather than another is the end which we sacrifice.

This fairly simple notion plays a central part in economic theory. For example, the economist is very much concerned with the study of prices and the price mechanism. The reason for this interest is largely because he sees the price mechanism as a device for solving the economic problem. Price reflects on the one hand the intensity of consumers' desires for the good, and on the other hand the sacrifice of the other goods which could have been produced with the same resources. Thus prices reflect the two sides of the basic economic problem—the ends, and the scarce resources.

By means of the price mechanism, society as a whole makes the decision on how available resources are to be allocated between the various ends. For example, a change in consumers' tastes will bring about a change in relative prices, accompanied by a new allocation of resources more suitable to the new pattern of tastes.

A rough distinction can be made between final goods, *i.e.*, those goods which are desired for their own sakes, and factors of production, *i.e.*, those goods which are used in the production of final goods. The prices of final goods are determined partly by the strength of consumer demand for them and partly by the cost of producing them. The cost of producing final goods depends on the prices of the factors of production used in producing them.

The first example of the use of the concept of opportunity cost in economic theory relates to the determination of the prices of factors of production. In its explanation of the nature of costs of production, the theory of opportunity costs provides important insights into the workings of the price mechanism.

In very rough outline the theory is this. Owners of factors of production seek the maximum reward for their services. Thus if industry A wants more labour it can bid it away from industry B. The amount an industry is prepared to pay for a factor depends on how much it can get for the product which that factor makes, which in turn depends on how much consumers are willing to pay for that product. If industry A bids away some units of a factor, say labour, from industry B, this implies that A can get more for the product of that labour than can B— in other words, consumers value the additional product of A higher than the sacrificed output from B.[1] The amount that A has to pay to bid these factors away, the costs to A, depends on the valuation that consumers put on the sacrificed alternative product of B.

For present purposes this exposition may suffice to give some grasp of the role of opportunity cost in explaining the prices of factors, and its connection with the fundamental economic problem of choice between alternatives. The cost of producing anything depends, in the final analysis, on the consumers' valuation of the opportunities forgone.

The second example occurs in the theory of international trade. The problem here is to explain why international trade takes place. Common sense suggests that different countries are not equally good at producing all commodities; and that the world as a whole benefits if countries specialise in the production of those goods which they produce efficiently, and exchange them for those goods which they produce less efficiently. The concept of opportunity cost is useful in clarifying the notion of efficiency.

Suppose that country A can produce, with certain quantities

---

[1] Strictly speaking, this is necessarily true only if the two industries are both perfectly competitive.

of land and labour, either 2 units of wheat or 1 unit of potatoes. Country B can produce, with the same quantities of land and labour, either 3 units of wheat or 2 units of potatoes. B is, in a sense, more efficient than A at producing both wheat and potatoes. At first sight, this suggests that B should produce both wheat and potatoes for itself, and has nothing to gain from trade with A. Looking at the matter in terms of opportunity costs, we get a different view. To grow 3 units of wheat, A sacrifices $1\frac{1}{2}$ units of potatoes and B sacrifices 2 units of potatoes. Thus A is *relatively* (*i.e.*, in terms of " potato costs ") more efficient in the production of wheat. Similarly B is relatively more efficient in the production of potatoes. Both A and B benefit if they concentrate respectively on wheat and potatoes, and then A exchanges some of its wheat for some of B's potatoes—at any rate of exchange between 3 wheat for $1\frac{1}{2}$ potatoes and 3 wheat for 2 potatoes.

Once again, the concept of opportunity costs directs attention to the sacrifices involved in choosing one alternative rather than another. The opportunity cost to B of securing 3 wheat by production is 2 potatoes; the cost of securing 3 wheat by trade with A is less than 2 potatoes.

We now have to ask what the businessman can learn from these examples. The answer, I submit, is very little which is *directly* applicable to business problems. To know the reason why he has to pay more for some factor of production—that consumers are now putting a higher value on the products of this factor in some other industry—may be evidence of additional insight into the workings of the economy; but it will help him very little in calculating solutions to commercial problems. Similarly, an understanding of the theory of international trade will give him no direct help in deciding, for example, what is the minimum price he should accept for some contract.

More important is the way in which economics tackles problems as fundamentally a choice between alternatives. Many business problems take this form. We can view the firm much as the economist views the economy as a whole. The firm has under its control at any one time certain resources; it can devote these to a wide variety of ends, all of which yield revenue; because of the limitation of resources, it cannot secure all the ends and must choose between them. In making the choice, it must take into account the fact that choosing some implies rejecting others. In microcosm, each firm is an economy of its own, with many ends competing for its limited resources. In the following sections of this paper, problems of choice between alternatives, and their solutions, will be more fully explored from the businessman's point of view.

II

We have seen that, in economic theory, the method of viewing problems as choices between alternatives has proved fruitful of insights. Most, if not all, of the problems which confront a businessman can be viewed similarly—if he decides to follow a course of action, this usually implies that he has rejected other courses of action; if he can follow only one particular course of action, then no decision problem exists. The class of problems of choice is wide, and it may be helpful to give a few examples: choosing the price of a product; deciding whether or not to take a contract at some specified price; deciding which of two machines to use; whether to use labour or machinery; deciding whether to make or to buy a component.

In this section the procedure will be to set up, as an example, a simple problem of choice, and then to show three forms in which satisfactory answers to the problem can be presented. It will be found that these forms of answer differ in two important characteristics. First, they differ in the type of information provided; secondly, they differ in the amount of work required for the calculation. Concepts of cost will be defined which assist *in the process of calculating* the answers. Opportunity cost turns out to be useless for this computational purpose (invaluable though it is as a general attitude).

The example is a small farmer who has to decide whether to plant his farm with wheat or barley. More specifically, we imagine that he has already decided that he will plant either wheat or barley; he has rejected other alternatives, such as planting part wheat and part barley, or leaving the ground fallow. Moreover, he has decided exactly how he would plant wheat (Plan W) if he were to choose wheat, and, similarly, he has Plan B ready in case he should choose barley.

In order to choose between the plans, it is necessary to know on what basis the farmer would prefer one plan to the other. We assume that his aim is to get rich, and that he will choose the plan which results in the most wealth for him, irrespective of the asset structure of that wealth. In other words, he will choose the plan which results in the bundle of assets of greatest monetary value.[2]

---

[2] The value of an individual asset is here defined as the sum of money which would just compensate the owner for the asset's loss. It is assumed that the value of a collection of assets is equal to the sum of the values of the individual assets. This definition and the assumption are discussed briefly in the final section.

Given the farmer's objective, the information necessary for him to make the choice can be presented in the following three ways.[3]

1. He can be told than Plan W will result in assets of value £W and Plan B result in assets valued at £B. If £W is greater than £B he chooses wheat; if less, barley. The answer enables him to make the choice and also tells him his wealth as the result of each plan.

2. He can be told by how much each plan will increase his wealth as compared with his initial capital, *i.e.*, his wealth at the time he is making the decision. His " profit " from Plan W we call £P_w, and from Plan B, £P_B. If his initial capital is £I, then £P_w = £W — £I, and £P_B = £B — £I (but the only information given to him is £P_w and £P_B, not £W, £B or £I).[4] Given £P_w and £P_B, he can make the choice according to whether £P_w is greater or less than £P_B. Note that the answers tell him how much his wealth will grow, but do not by themselves indicate his final wealth. Thus the information differs from answer 1.

3. He can be given the figure £D, the amount by which the value of the assets resulting from Plan W exceeds the value of those from Plan B. (£D = £W — £B.) If £D is positive he chooses Plan W; if not, Plan B. Here the answer indicates neither his final wealth nor by how much his wealth grows.

The three answers (1) £W and £B, (2) £P_w and £P_B, (3) £D are mathematically consistent and equally satisfactory guides for making the choice. But they *do* differ in the subsidiary information; and it is not hard to imagine that the choice between one form of answer and the other need not be trivial. For example, the farmer may be interested in his " profit " or his final wealth for the purpose of making decisions about how much he can consume.

We now turn to detailed procedures which might be used to calculate these three answers, paying particular attention to the amount of valuation involved.

1. The work involved in the first answer, calculation of £W and £B, is the prediction and valuation of the whole of the physical assets at the end of each plan. The calculation might take the following form:

[3] There are an infinite number of forms in which the information can be presented. The three forms used in this analysis enable the decision to be made immediately with no further calculation.

[4] For the purpose of making the choice between the plans, the value of £I can be arbitrary, since it affects both plans equally and thus cancels out in the solution. [(£W–£I) > (£B–£I) if £W > £B.] As we shall see, the point of stating the problem in this way is to economise on the work of valuation.

TABLE I

Values of Assets resulting from Plans W & B

		Plan W	Plan B
Land	..	£100	£100
Buildings ..	..	80	80
Machinery	..	40	45
Stock	..	40	30
Cash	..	100	90
		£W = 360	£B = 345

It is apparent that no concept of cost, opportunity or otherwise, is necessary for this formulation of the solution. Nevertheless, Table I provides a perfectly satisfactory guide to making the choice.

2. Calculating $£P_W$ and $£P_B$ need not necessarily entail all the work implied by Table I. The *changes* in the assets are what must be valued. Some of the physical assets may be common to the initial and final position; they cancel out, and so the labour of valuing them can be avoided. For instance, it may have been difficult to value the land for Table I; it may be much easier to say that, whatever the land's value, that value will not alter from the initial value as a result of either plan. Further, the farmer may avoid some of the work of valuing stock if he knows that the bulk of his stock will be the same, and that the differences will amount to, say, one bag of wheat and two bags of fertiliser. We can imagine the initial position to be:

Land	..	..	..	..	£100
Buildings ..	..	..	..	90
Machinery	..	..	..	50
Stock	..	..	..	25
Cash	..	..	..	50
					£315

Then the calculations can be restated as follows:

TABLE II

Changes from initial position in value of assets

		Plan W	Plan B
Land	..	£ 0	£ 0
Buildings ..	..	—10	—10
Machinery	..	—10	— 5
Stock	..	+15	+ 5
Cash	..	+50	+40
		$£P_W$ = +45	$£P_B$ = +30

Presumably some economists would say that the opportunity cost of Plan A is the £30 increase in wealth sacrificed by not implementing Plan B. As I shall argue in the next section, this interpretation of opportunity cost is of limited utility.

3. It is easy to see that calculation of the third answer, £D, by taking differences in the final values of the assets, may result in still further saving of work. Not only will the unchanging assets (here land) drop out of the calculation, but so will assets which change equally for both plans: here the calculation of the values of buildings (as in Table I), or their depreciation (Table II), is avoided.

The calculation of £D would be set out:

TABLE III

Differences of values of assets (Plan W—Plan B)

Land	..	..	..	.. £ 0
Buildings ..	..	..	..	0
Machinery	..	..	..	— 5
Stock	..	..	..	+10
Cash	..	..	..	+10

$$£D = +15$$

In the analysis so far, the purpose has been to establish, (a) that the solution to problems of choice between different courses of action involves evaluating the results of alternative plans according to a criterion, (b) that satisfactory solutions can be presented in forms which differ in the information they provide, and (c) that the calculations of the different answers vary in the amount of work they entail. Concepts of *cost* and *revenue* have not appeared explicitly.

Always bearing in mind that the aim is to calculate which of the plans results in the bundle of assets with the greatest value, we can adopt instead a procedure of calculation, in some respects more convenient, which uses concepts of cost and revenue. The basic difference in approach is that so far we have been posing the question in the form: what will the physical amounts of the final assets (or of the differences between the initial and each set of final assets, or of the differences between each set of final assets) be, and what will the values of these physical amounts be? The cost and revenue approach attacks the problem from the point of view that each plan involves a number of actions, each of which, taken by itself, adds to or subtracts from the value of aggregate assets. For example, hiring labour to implement a plan will, by itself, reduce the aggregate assets by the wages paid (or owed) to the labourers. The process of solution is to compile a list of all these actions, to calculate the effects of each action, and then to aggregate the effects. In our example, the actions will comprise using labour, buildings and machinery to produce wheat or barley, and then selling the produce. The results of the calculation might be set out as follows:

TABLE IIA

Changes from initial position in value of assets,
classified by type of input, etc.

		Plan W	Plan B
Depreciation			
Land	..	£ 0	£ 0
Building	..	—10	—10
Machinery	..	—10	— 5
Seed	..	—20	—25
Fertiliser	..	—10	— 5
Labour	..	—80	—80
Sales	..	+175	+155
		$£P_W = +45$	$£P_B = +30$

The calculation in terms of cost and revenues is merely an alternative classification of the positive and negative changes in the values of assets in Table II. If we inquire into the *content* of the terms " cost " and " revenue," the answer is dictated by the result we are trying to achieve, namely the differences from the initial position in the values of the assets.

Thus the analysis provides perfectly sensible definitions of costs and revenues, which are useful in calculating the answers of choice, and yet which are completely different from the definition of opportunity cost, the value of the forgone alternative.

One advantage of using the cost and revenue rather than the " balance-sheet " classification is that we can leave out transactions which merely alter the structure of assets without affecting their net value. Another advantage is that where plans are independent [5] of the rest of the business, their results can be calculated more easily.

The definitions of cost and revenue lead on to concepts of additional cost and additional revenue, which are useful in calculating the third form of answer, £D. We adopt the same classification of causes of changes in the values of assets, but now ask what is the difference between the final values of assets resulting from each plan.

[5] For a definition of " independent " see section IV, p. 232.

TABLE IIIA

Differences in final values of assets (Plan W—Plan B)
classified by type of input, etc.

Depreciation:
Land   ..   ..   £ 0
Buildings   0
Machinery   ..   ..   ..   — 5
Seed   ..   ..   + 5
Fertiliser   ..   ..   ..   — 5
Labour   0
Sales   ..   ..   +20

$$£D = +15$$

The concepts of additional cost and additional revenue are very powerful because their use may cut down the work of computation substantially. Many costs usually classed as overheads may well be constant for all plans under consideration. For example, the rent of the factory, and the costs of administration and supervision, may very well be constant for the alternatives being compared, and this approach removes the necessity of calculating these expenses. Moreover, some of the most tricky problems of valuation are completely avoided. Depreciation of fixed assets is sometimes very difficult to calculate because it often involves forecasting the future earnings of the asset. But frequently the final value of the asset is the same for each plan being considered—especially where obsolescence is a more important cause of fall in value than wear and tear—and so the task of evaluating the cost may be avoided. In Table IIIA, the costs of labour and depreciation of buildings need not be calculated because we know that they are the same for both plans.

It is true that calculating £D, while saving work, results in less information than calculating either £W and £B, or $£P_w$ and $£P_B$. However, the information suffices for the problem in hand, choosing between alternative plans; and one may doubt whether it is often so very useful to know by how much a particular plan will increase our wealth or what is the value of our assets.

To sum up, we see that the concepts of cost and revenue can be used as devices to eliminate some of the valuation involved in comparing alternative plans; and that the content of the words derives from our objective, namely the evaluation of bundles of assets which result from alternative plans.

III

In the previous section the definition of cost was derived from consideration of the nature of problems of choice, the various satisfactory answers, and the procedures for arriving at these answers. The concepts of cost and additional cost are not necessary for the solution of problems of choice—their utility lies in reducing the work of valuation involved in arriving at an answer. This analysis can be used as a base from which to discuss the approaches of the economists and the accountants.

As we saw in section II, the businessman does best if he looks upon costs simply as declines in the values of assets. We saw in section I that the economist, with the aid of the theory of opportunity costs, can *explain* why some of these costs should take particular values: market forces tend to pull factor prices into line with consumers' valuations of the output forgone. But the businessman is concerned only with the opportunities open to *him*. If some of *his* opportunities involve the purchase or sale of assets, he will see outside opportunities reflected in the conditions of supply and demand which face him in the market, and which affect the market's prices of the assets. It is these last data which, rightly used, provide the costs that he needs.

Economists have advocated the use of opportunity cost, the value of the forgone alternative, for the solution of problems of choice. In the last section, procedures were outlined which did not use opportunity cost. In a sense, the opportunity cost of Plan W was calculated when the results of Plan B were evaluated (most clearly, perhaps, in Tables II and IIA). But if we accept this interpretation of the injunction, it amounts to little more than advocating that the results of the two plans be compared; it offers no guide to the procedures to adopt in making the comparison. In a sense, the selection of the best plan and the determination of the opportunity cost occur simultaneously; the latter is not a step on the way to the former. Moreover, confusion must result from the insistence that opportunity cost is the " true " concept of cost, and that others are erroneous. Businessmen are accustomed to using " costs " in their calculations, and the substitution of opportunity cost for their own concept of cost leads them up a blind alley. Consider an accountant faced with the problem of ranking six plans in order of profitability. To work out the profit of each plan, he deducts from the revenue the costs. If— as he may think he ought to do after hearing economists speak of opportunity costs—he simply substitutes for his own notion of cost the definition of opportunity cost, he finds himself at an impasse. To rank the plans, he must know the opportunity cost; to know the opportunity cost, he must know the value of the next best alternative plan; thus to find the opportunity cost, he must rank the plans. As we have seen, the concept defined in the previous section avoids these difficulties.

But if economists are interpreted to advocate, not a particular definition of cost, but an awareness that decision problems involve choices between alternatives, then they perform a useful service. Decision problems are sometimes not posed explicitly as a choice between alternatives. They are often put in the form: should I do A (*e.g.*, accept a contract at some named price)? In order to make sense of the question, we must make explicit what is implied—should I accept the contract *rather than do something else*? Accounting practice indicates that the implied term is often ignored—the solution (" profit ") is worked out in terms of " costs " and " revenues " which ignore completely the possibilities of alternative courses of action.[6] Thus we can view the opportunity cost approach as requiring the construction of an alternative plan—as asking to what uses the resources would be committed if Plan A were not adopted.

Let us now move on to the accountant's concept of cost. Here an attack can be directed at three main targets—his use of historic cost, his treatment of fixed costs, and his allocations of joint costs.

The irrelevance of historic costs can easily be seen if we direct our attention to the object of the decision-maker's calculation—the evaluation of bundles of assets which result from different plans. Thus, if one gallon of paint is to be used in the plan, the appropriate question is, not what did the paint cost when we bought it, but how much does the use of the paint decrease the aggregate value of the assets resulting from the plan.[7] The right final value for the paint still in stock is the prediction of its worth at the date when the final bundles are valued. If the calculation takes the form of cost differences as in Table IIIA, the appropriate cost of using the paint is again the prediction.

The term " fixed costs " is used in several different ways, the most important of which refers to those costs which are the same

---

[6] The conventional accounting approach may appear to choose between two alternatives, doing A and doing " nothing." But the criticisms which follow show that the policy of doing " nothing " which is implied in many calculations is not really a feasible alternative.

[7] True, if we are comparing the costs of the two plans (one of which involves using up the paint, while the other does not) as in Table IIA, the initial values are irrelevant for purposes of choice, and may without harm be historical; provided they are the same in each plan, they cancel out (as explained in footnote 4). The only values that matter are final values.

for all plans under consideration (*i.e.*, involve no additional costs). As we have seen, the use of the method that computes additional costs eliminates the need to evaluate the fixed cost—indeed this saving of work is the method's main advantage.

Economists have often enjoined accountants to disregard fixed costs because they are not "opportunity costs." But if one wishes to calculate £P for each of a set of alternative plans, then fixed costs must be included. Although the exclusion of fixed costs would not affect the choice of the best plan (since, being by definition the same for each plan, they cancel out), nevertheless it may be desirable to know the magnitude of £P for reasons other than that of choosing between the plans. A pernicious error is likely to creep in if a clear appreciation of the available alternatives is lacking. For example, say the problem is to assess the minimum price at which to take a contract when the firm would otherwise be idle. The conventional accounting calculation of costs may appear to be an implicit comparison with doing "nothing." But if the rent of the factory is included in costs when there is no question of closing down and so avoiding the payment of rent, the alternative of taking the contract is unfairly prejudiced since the rent should weigh equally against the other alternative.

In economic theory, the essence of the distinction between fixed and variable costs is often related to the length of the planning period under consideration, *e.g.*, it is said that fixed costs become variable in the long run. We can put the distinction another way by considering what happens as the range of plans under consideration is extended. Suppose we are choosing between several possible outputs, for all of which the rent of the factory is constant, *i.e.*, is a fixed cost. If we add to the plans being considered the possibility that the factory be closed, so avoiding the rent, rent ceases to be a fixed cost in the context of this problem. Now, it is likely that one would take into account the effects over a longer period when considering whether or not to close a factory than one would when choosing only between different outputs. In this sense, there is a relation between the fixed/variable distinction and the length of the planning period. But this relation to the length of the planning period is not the crucial point of the distinction. Let us fix the planning period at one week. If we consider a set of plans for which the wages paid to labour are identical, then labour is a fixed cost. If another plan whose wage cost is different is added to the set, labour becomes a variable cost. Thus the logical distinction between fixed and variable costs depends on the equality or otherwise of the particular cost with respect to all the plans under consideration; the relation to the time period is rather the empirical one that as the range of alternatives considered is extended it is likely that longer planning periods will have to be considered.

The term fixed costs is used, perhaps rather loosely, in another sense. Actions which do not affect the value of assets are clearly irrelevant to problems of choice. Thus, suppose the firm has paid a non-returnable fee to a research association, in return for which it is entitled to request certain information at no extra charge. Clearly the action of calling for information cannot now affect the assets resulting from the plan; so there is no need to " allocate " a proportion of the fee to the plan. This kind of " cost," expenses incurred in the past, is not a cost in the sense defined in the previous section and is best referred to as a " sunk cost."

The allocation of joint costs is rather more difficult to deal with, and raises a general consideration which so far I have neglected. It is sometimes said that joint costs cannot be allocated, or cannot be allocated on a " logical " basis. But joint costs *are* allocated and the logical objection is often not made clear. Let us suppose that a single manufacturing process produces products A and B in fixed proportions. The market for A determines the price which the firm is able to get, irrespective of the quantity of A that it sells. Its discretion in pricing is limited to B. It is in this kind of situation that arguments for allocation of joint costs are prima facie not implausible. To decide on the price of B, it seems necessary to know its cost. To know the cost of B, the joint cost of A and B must be allocated on some basis. A great deal of effort and ingenuity has been devoted to devising bases of allocation which seem " fair " or " reasonable " for tackling problems essentially similar to this. But the statement of the problem is misconceived—the desirability of allocation disappears when the problem is viewed as one of assessing the effects on aggregate assets of alternative plans (prices of B). Consider two alternative prices for B. At the cheaper price for B, more B will be sold, more A and B produced, and more A sold. Thus the effect on the final assets cannot be evaluated without taking into account those associated with the increased output of both A and B, and the increased sales of A. The logical fallacy of allocation lies in the attempt to treat B as independent of A when the conditions of the problem state that A and B are interdependent. This example illustrates one kind of logical fallacy involved; and a similar argument holds good for the case of joint costs with variable proportions. Indeed, joint costs are a special case of problems where the plans are interdependent, a topic which will be discussed further in the final section.[8]

IV

In this final section, I shall discuss briefly some of the more general aspects of problems of choice. The two fundamentals of problems of choice are the alternative plans, and the criteria for choosing between them. These two aspects will be discussed in turn.

Obviously, to make an intelligent decision it is important that the alternatives to be considered should be clearly specified. We need not inquire too closely how the business man compiles his " short list " of candidates from the infinity of possible plans open to him. His imagination will suggest possibilities, but experience and intuition will lead him to exclude many of these as non-starters and unworthy of consideration. We are concerned with another attribute of the successful business man, the ability to select the best plan from those considered.

It is important to be clear about the relationships between different plans. They may be mutually exclusive, in the sense that the implementation of one necessarily excludes the implementation of the other. Thus, if we are choosing between different outputs for the forthcoming week, we cannot produce both 100 and 150 units. If the plans are not mutually exclusive they may be independent, that is, the costs and revenues of one are independent of the other plan. In this case, the two plans can be considered as separate problems, each to be considered against alternatives they might exclude. On the other hand, plans which are not mutually exclusive may be interdependent. The example of joint costs we have already considered. In general, where the costs of one plan affect the costs of another, or the revenues are related, or the costs of one plan affect the revenues of another, we have linked problems; it is necessary to include all the inter-related plans together in one plan, for the same reason that joint products must be considered together. The attempt to

---

[8] For completeness, a word should be added about the concept of marginal cost, which has proved a useful tool of analysis in economic theory. Marginal cost is defined as the rate of change of total cost with respect to output, or, in other words, the increase in total costs caused by a unit increase in output. In the terminology of this paper, each different quantity of output represents a different plan. Thus we may write the plans as $P_1, P_2 \ldots P_r \ldots P_n$, where the subscripts represent the quantities of output, and the total costs of each plan as $C_1, C_2 \ldots C_r \ldots C_n$. The marginal cost of the eleventh unit, equals $C_{11} - C_{10}$. Marginal cost is useful for deriving " decision rules," *i.e.*, short-cut methods of arriving at the answers to problems. The concept is obviously similar to additional cost, and where only two plans are being considered is identical.

isolate one of a group of interrelated plans fails because it attempts to ignore the interrelation which is a condition of the problem. The effect of the plan on the value of the aggregate assets will be calculated wrongly.[9] Interrelationships between a few plans may cause a large increase in the number of mutually exclusive plans which can be considered. For example, if it is possible to produce any or all of products A, B and C, and the results are interdependent, then the mutually exclusive plans are the combinations ABC, AB, AC, BC, A, B, and C.

Failure to appreciate the relationships between plans may lead to another kind of error, that of combining mutually exclusive actions in one plan. I have suggested that the opportunity cost approach may be interpreted as the formulation of the most likely alternative plan to compare with the plan being considered. Thus the question: " should I do A? " is to be interpreted as: " should I do A rather than B? " where B seems the most promising alternative course of action. In formulating B, the procedure might be to list all the resources used in Plan A and to ask how these resources would be used if Plan A were not adopted. In a complex problem, one might easily slip into the error of, for example, using the leather to make shoes and the labour to make handbags, when the making of shoes and the making of handbags are mutually exclusive. In other words, care must be taken that B, the alternative plan, is consistent and does not combine mutually exclusive actions. A similar sort of error may arise in the use of additional costs and revenues. Suppose Plans A, B and C are to be compared. The correct answer may be obtained by calculating the additional costs and revenues of A and B with respect to C, or of C and A with respect to B, or of B and C with respect to A; that is, one plan must be chosen as a benchmark for comparison and this must be adhered to throughout the calculation. If some costs in A are compared to B while others are compared to C the answer will be wrong.

For a clear understanding of the problem (I repeat) the alternative plans must be fully specified. For a correct answer, the criterion of choice must be the right one. The analysis of section III assumed that the farmer's objective was to choose the plan which resulted in net assets of the greatest aggregate value. This is a strong assumption which excludes the possibilities that he is not indifferent between asset structures and between different dividend or consumption policies. Moreover, it ignores the facts that plans take time to implement (interest is neglected) and that

---

[9] We may, of course, choose to neglect some interdependencies because the error is negligible relative to the saving in the work of calculation.

the predictions of the results of plans are not absolutely certain. These simplifications were deliberate, and were made in order that we could concentrate on the nature of decision problems and the development of useful concepts of cost and revenue. However, these simplifications are often in fact made by business men, so that the analysis is not without direct practical relevance.

There are two further points connected with the criterion of choice. First, it is well known that the value to a business man of a certain bundle of assets may exceed the sum of the values of the individual assets. The use of costs and revenues arrives at differences in values of different bundles of assets taken piecemeal; and the sum of these piecemeal costs and revenues may differ from the change in the value of the bundle as a whole. If the differences are important, the piecemeal approach may break down. There is little we can do beyond keeping our eyes open for these cases, and if possible making such allowances as our judgment suggests.

Second, the subject of valuation itself, which lies at the heart of the solution to problems of choice, involves something of a paradox. Earlier, I defined the value of an asset as that amount of money which would compensate and only just compensate the owner for the loss of the asset. Business men cannot realistically be assumed to have in their minds a list of their valuations of all the assets that they possess, and might reasonably ask guidance on methods of valuation. The value of the asset at the end of the plan under consideration depends on what the business man can do with it. He will not accept less for the asset than the net monetary value of the best of the plans then open to him. Thus valuation of current plans depends on valuations of future plans—and so on to infinity. As the more distant future may in general be assumed more uncertain than the less distant future, it seems as though we assume the solution to the more difficult problems to be self-evident, while the simpler problems require elaborate calculations.

The paradox can be resolved and the process become logical if it is argued that in practice there comes a point when the accuracy of the data becomes so uncertain that we might as well guess at the result as go through elaborate calculations. But given these estimates, with all their failings, we might just as well draw correct logical implications from them and eliminate at least the source of error which would arise from incorrect deduction.

This paper has attempted to derive useful concepts of cost and revenue from consideration of the nature of problems of choice. The word " cost " is used in many other connections—including determination of " income," measurement of efficiency, allocation of responsibility, and record-keeping for stewardship. There is no necessary presumption that a definition of cost which is suitable for the solution of problems of choice is relevant to these other problems—indeed such a presumption would be in direct opposition to the spirit of this paper. The appropriate definitions of costs for these problems must come from a close consideration of the nature of each of them.

Concepts of Depreciation *

By L. Goldberg
Professor of Accounting,
University of Melbourne.

IT is just fifty years ago that a Mr. Armstrong delivered a paper in England to the Northern Institute of Chartered Accountants which began with the following words: " The question of Depreciation is one upon which so many articles have been written, and so many opinions expressed, that there would not appear to be much more which could profitably be said upon the subject." [1] And in 1905 another writer—an engineer—wrote that " [Depreciation] is a difficult [item] to deal with, more particularly as it has, unfortunately, got largely into the hands of auditors and bookkeepers, who deal with it according to their own limited knowledge and entirely as a matter of account. Depreciation is much more than this, and can only be properly adjusted by an engineer who has thorough knowledge of his profession and intimate acquaintance with the particular buildings and machinery with which he is at the moment dealing." [2]

In the face of such long-standing expressions of opinion, I may, perhaps, be forgiven for feeling that I am being somewhat rash in discussing depreciation at all—not only on the count of trying to exhume, if not resuscitate a thoroughly dead topic, but also because I am trying to do so from the point of view of and with the instruments used by " auditors and bookkeepers." However, some statements of more recent vintage suggest that reconsideration of this topic may not be altogether redundant.

P. D. Leake, for example, when he wrote his *Depreciation and Wasting Assets,* stated that " the subject of Depreciation and Wasting Assets is of universal importance, and yet it has hitherto received little or no systematic attention." [3] Again, Professor Eugene L. Grant introduced a paper on depreciation with the proposition that " writers on depreciation seem to agree

---

* Based on article in the *Accounting Review*, July, 1955.
[1] John H. Armstrong, " Depreciation Reserves," *The Accountant*, August 8, 1903, p. 1014.
[2] Francis G. Burton, *The Commercial Management of Engineering Works*, 2nd ed., (Manchester: The Scientific Publishing Co., 1905), p. 280.
[3] P. D. Leake, *Depreciation and Wasting Assets*, 4th ed., (London: Pitman, 1923), p. xxiii.

on nothing except that other writers on the subject are somewhat confused." [4] And in 1952, in their book *Asset Accounting*, the two W. A. Patons (father and son) presumably considered that they could go no further than saying that " in recent years some progress has been made in the direction of wider understanding of the significance of depreciation and the importance of systematic recognition of this phenomenon in the accounts." [5]

These are but a very few of the many indications that any attempt to examine the problem of depreciation should be regarded not as an autopsy, but rather, perhaps, as a vivisection.

There exists an extensive literature on this topic of depreciation, and I do not pretend to have made anything like an exhaustive investigation; indeed, some of this literature is couched in mathematical propositions which are quite beyond my comprehension, and I freely admit that my shortcomings in this regard may very likely be reflected in what follows. Neither do I pretend that what follows is the final word—even of my own, or, perhaps, least of all my own—on the matter under discussion. In this respect I beg leave to adopt the attitude of the French writer, Jules Romains, when he said: " What I say below represents only conclusions with which I would identify myself if I were obliged to stop thinking today." [6]

The thesis in this paper is essentially simple. It is that the word " depreciation " has been grossly overworked, that it has been and is currently used in varying senses and with different connotations, so that if A uses the word in communication with B, it is likely to be not much more than a lucky chance if B understands it in precisely the same sense as is meant by A.

The case-history of depreciation is, in one sense, a case-history of a word—a word which, like so many others, has had its meaning changed, or, rather, multiplied—over a fairly lengthy period. But the purpose of this paper is to discuss some aspects of what is more than a philological question: it is part of the case-history of a concept or notion which we seek to convey by the use of a word. This notion, too, has varied and multiplied in such a way that its analysis is not by any means an easy matter.

Earlier writers on the topic frequently directed their attention towards gaining recognition for regular depreciation charges as an element to be taken into account before profit can be determined.

[4] Eugene L. Grant, " Fundamental Aspects of the Depreciation Problem." See David Solomons, *Studies in Costing* (Sweet & Maxwell, 1952), p. 292.
[5] William A. Paton with the assistance of W. A. Paton (Jr.), *Asset Accounting* (New York: Macmillan, 1952), p. 236.
[6] *I Believe—The Personal Philosophies of Twenty-three Eminent Men and Women of Our Time* (London: Allen & Unwin, 1944). p. 244.

Five brief statements may be taken as indicative of this aspect of historical development:

(i) 1876. Supreme Court of the U.S.A. in *Eyster* v. *Centennial Board of Finance*, 94 U.S. 500, 503:[7]

" ... The public, when referring to the profits of the business of a merchant, rarely ever take into account the depreciation of the buildings in which the business is carried on, notwithstanding they may have been erected out of the capital invested. Popularly speaking, the net receipts of a business are its profits ... "

(ii) (c) 1882. Richard Bithell: *A Counting House Dictionary:*

" Depreciation in commerce is mostly understood to have reference to the diminished value of coins, of bullion, or of a paper currency."

(iii) 1903. C. H. Grinling: " British Railways as Business Enterprises," *The Accountant*, February 7, 1903, p. 192:

" The notion, too commonly held, that provision for the depreciation of the plant employed by a commercial undertaking was a voluntary charge against net profits for more or less substantial reasons, was a wrong notion fundamentally."

(iv) 1917. Supreme Court of the U.S.A. in *von Baumbach* v. *Sargent Land Co.*, 242 U.S. 503, 524:[8]

" ... It is common knowledge that business concerns usually keep a depreciation account, in which is charged off the annual losses for wear and tear, and obsolescence of structures, machinery and personalty in use in the business ... "

(v) 1949. Arthur H. Dean: *Business Income under Present Price Levels*, p. 53:[9]

" ... both economist and accountant seem to agree that net income can only be determined after depreciation for the period under consideration has been taken into account ... "

The struggle to get depreciation recognised as a cost appears to have been won. Yet one can still find in current accounting literature such an echo of the 1870's as this:

> But in point of fact what happens when we write off depreciation? Do we not transfer part of the book profit which would otherwise be available, to the credit of the asset account or the separate depreciation provision account? In other words do we not decide to leave some of the profits in the business?[10]

This is, however, exceptional nowadays. But controversy still exists. The grounds have changed, and it appears now as if accountants—or some of them at any rate—have to brace themselves for an effort to restrict depreciation to being a cost. Having, over a long period, successfully advocated the recognition of depreciation as a charge against revenue, accountants are being bombarded with arguments in favour of increasing that

---

[7] Cited in Arthur H. Dean, *Business Income under Present Price Levels*, 1949, p. 56.
[8] *Ibid.*, p. 57.
[9] Published by the Study Group on Business Income, February, 1949.
[10] R. N. Elliott, " Revaluation of Assets and Issue of Bonus Shares," *The Chartered Accountant in Australia*, November, 1952, p. 312.

charge beyond what they—or many of them, at least—consider appropriate.

The aim in this paper is to sort out some of the main concepts which the word " depreciation " has been used to indicate or suggest, and to raise a few questions concerning each.

Let us admit that " depreciation " is a word which, like any other word, may quite legitimately be used with different meanings, so long as the context makes it clear what meaning is intended. The trouble is that a great deal of argument has taken place because the context has not always made it clear just which one of its multiple meanings is intended.

This brings us to the central point of the present thesis: What do we mean when we speak of " depreciation " in relation to long-term assets? There are several senses in which the word is more or less widely used in accounting and business literature, and four of these are selected for some consideration in this paper. They are:

 (i) Depreciation as fall in price.
 (ii) Depreciation as physical deterioration.
 (iii) Depreciation as fall in value.
 (iv) Depreciation as allocation of cost.

Depreciation as fall in price

Philologically, the word " depreciation " means a fall in price or a fall in value. It is desirable to distinguish between the two. In some contexts, the word is used at the present time in the sense of a fall in price. For example, the expression " depreciation of the currency " is generally intended to convey a falling of the price of a unit of money in terms of other units of measurement. This was the only sense recognised by Bithel in his *Counting House Dictionary*.

There is one instance at least in which the word is applied in this sense of fall in price in relation to fixed assets. It has been fairly common usage—subject, perhaps, to an interruption for a few years of high scarcity—to suggest that when a person buys an asset, such as a motor-vehicle, it " depreciates " by a stated amount as soon as he drives it out of the showroom or as soon as it has been subjected to a very little use. This, it is submitted, means that the taking possession of such an asset converts it from a new to a second-hand commodity and that the price of a second-hand commodity is less than that of a new commodity of the same type. It is a fall in price not necessarily accompanied by any decrease in usefulness; indeed, a motor-vehicle which has been carefully driven for several hundred miles may be a more

useful vehicle than a new one, but this is not normally considered
a virtue for the purpose of determining its price, and the word
" depreciation " appears to be used in this context to indicate
a fall in price.

Those who have read Professor H. R. Hatfield's delightful
though critical paper entitled " What they say about Depreciation " [11] may recall that he traces the notion of depreciation back
to Vitruvius, a Roman writer on architecture at the time of
Augustus Caesar. Hatfield states that Vitruvius " lays down the
rule that in valuing a masonry wall, one-eightieth of its cost
should be deducted for each year it has stood, this resting on the
assumption that such a wall has a life of eighty years. Here we
have a very clear recognition not only of depreciation, but an
acceptance of a straightline method." [12]

Now, this is ancient authority indeed, and as Hatfield
acknowledged that his observation was based on those of an
intermediate interpreter,[13] it seemed to be worth while looking
at what had been written by Vitruvius himself. The passage on
which Hatfield and his immediate authority relied has been
translated as follows:

> Therefore if anyone will from these commentaries observe and select a
> style of walling, he will be able to take account of durability. For those
> which are of soft rubble with a thin and pleasing facing cannot fail to
> give way with lapse of time. Therefore when arbitrators are taken for
> party-walls, they do not value them at the price at which they were
> made, but when from the accounts they find the tenders for them, they
> deduct as price of the passing of each year the 80th part, and so—in
> that from the remaining sum repayment is made for these walls—they
> pronounce the opinion that the walls cannot last more than 80 years.
> There is no deduction made from the value of brick walls provided
> that they remain plumb; but they are always valued at as much as they
> were built for.[14]

Now what Hatfield says is, broadly, true enough and fair
enough, but there is a little more to be said about Vitruvius.
In the first place, there is the minor point that it is not Vitruvius
himself who lays down the rule for valuation; he is reporting
it as a custom of arbitrators in assessing a valuation of party-walls
of a particular kind.

Secondly, the words used by Vitruvius are " pretia praeteri-
torum annorum singulorum," which have been rendered in the

[11] See *infra*.
[12] *Op. cit.*, p. 338.
[13] H. E. Hale, " What is Depreciation? " *Railway Age*, Vol. 86, February 16, 1929, pp. 403 *et seq*.
[14] Vitruvius, *On Architecture*, Trans. F. Granger (London: Heinemann, 1931), Bk. II, Chap. viii, 8–9. Hale has evidently used another translation which I have not located, but which is substantially the same in import.

above translation as "the price of the passing of each year" and which mean, indeed, "annual depreciation." But we might well ask: Are these words, in the context of a Roman work on architecture, intended to convey the same meaning as the expression "annual depreciation" might be meant to convey in a twentieth-century context of accounting? Vitruvius, it would seem, is citing this legal rule to illustrate the relative durability of building materials and, by such illustration, to emphasise his point that walls built of rubble should be regarded as likely to last not more than eighty years. He scarcely appears to be concerned with "depreciation" as such at all.

Further, we have to note the purpose of the calculation made. The deduction from cost was made on party walls (and there is no mention of any other kind of walls in this connection) in the course of some kind of legal action, in order to arrive at a valuation for a legal settlement. That is, the deduction represents a diminution in the price to be paid by one party to another for a particular kind of asset. This is, admittedly, "depreciation" at its philologically cleanest; it is a reduction in price. But is it what we mean by "depreciation" in modern contexts?

Depreciation as physical deterioration

The word "depreciation" is sometimes used to mean the physical deterioration of a long-term asset. This, presumably, is what Hatfield, for example, means when he states:

> One difficulty in discussing depreciation is in distinguishing between the fact of depreciation and the recording of the fact in the accounts.
> The fact itself is a physical or economic phenomenon. There is almost universal agreement that a physical asset does, in the process of use, wear out, at least to the extent of making its continued use uneconomical. The economic phenomenon which may be correlative with the physical phenomenon, but may oftentimes be independent thereof, is that with continued use of a physical asset the services which it renders tend to become exhausted.[15]

And he quotes a statement of Bowman and Percy that "depreciation represents that portion of the asset consumed in operating the business" as an example of the use by accountants of this concept.[16] (Admittedly, Hatfield regards this as "probably . . . an inept expression rather than an indication of a difference of opinion.")

Professor Bonbright, in his monumental work, *The Valuation of Property*, distinguishes impaired serviceableness as one of the

---

[15] Hatfield, *op. cit.*, p. 339.
[16] C. Bowman & A. Percy, *Principles of Bookkeeping and Business* (New York: 1927), p. 53. See Hatfield, *op. cit.*, p. 339n.

four basic concepts behind the use of the term " depreciation,"
and in relation to this he states: " In its most primitive sense,
depreciation is not a value category at all and cannot be expressed
in terms of dollars. It means simply impairment of serviceableness, or utility, or efficiency. Thus a rusty steel tool may be
said to be depreciated if the rust impairs its efficiency. By
invoking the notion of *relative* utility, one may extend depreciation
to cover obsolescence. The old reciprocating steam engine may
be just as efficient as it ever was; but as compared to a modern
turbine it may have become *relatively* inefficient." [17]

Although it is questionable whether, from a philological point
of view, depreciation " in its most primitive sense is not a value
category," it does seem practically certain that the observation of
physical impairment would historically have preceded any attempt
at its measurement—in whatever units might be employed. There
appears to be fairly general agreement that the physical basis for
depreciation accounting—whatever interpretation of the purpose,
procedure, or method of such accounting may be adopted—is
that at a certain stage of its existence an asset can no longer
be effectively used for the purpose for which it was acquired.

The " causes " leading to physical retirement of an asset
have been listed by many writers on depreciation, and it would
be wearisome and not very profitable to go over this familiar
ground. But there are one or two points in relation to this
notion of physical deterioration or impaired serviceableness
which it might be worth mentioning.

There is little doubt that a number of accountants and others,
in assessing depreciation, are attempting to measure some physical
phenomenon. It is the physical phenomenon which is the basis
of these accountants' procedures. What is the nature of this
physical phenomenon?

The known—or objective—facts relating to a fixed asset are
these:

(i) At a certain point of time an asset is acquired at, in most cases, a
known or determinable price-aggregate or cost.

(ii) Over a period of time—sometimes known at the outset, but more
frequently indeterminable at the time of acquisition—the asset is used for
the purpose for which it was acquired. (But it may be noted that an asset
such as a lease is not " used " in any physical sense.)

(iii) At the end of the period, the asset is no longer usable for the
purpose for which it was acquired. The reason may be " physical " or
" economic."

[17] J. C. Bonbright, *The Valuation of Property* (New York: McGraw-Hill, 1937),
p. 183.

Is there, in these facts, any natural phenomenon which can be designated " depreciation "?

There appears to be implied, in most discussions on these physical aspects of depreciation, a proposition that the using of an asset inevitably involves its using up. And it is often assumed that by measuring the " use " of an asset we are measuring the extent of its being " used up." It is submitted that these two factors are not necessarily identical.

It is nearly a hundred years since Sir William Fairbairn made his tests on the strength of metals. One of these, for instance, involved the raising and lowering of a load on a large wrought-iron girder. " It was calculated that the application of a single load of 12 tons would be required to break the girder, but Fairbairn found that if a load of little more than 3 tons were applied 3,000,000 times the girder would break. He concluded, however, that there existed a certain minimum load, under 3 tons, which could be applied an indefinite number of times without fracture occurring." [18] This, and subsequent tests which establish the " endurance limit " of metals, that is, the range of stress that can be applied an indefinite number of times, suggest that the notion that all long-term assets deteriorate physically in strict proportion to their physical use is somewhat naive and warrants careful reconsideration by accountants in conjunction with technical officers.

H. E. Hale cites some examples from another field. " Another example," he writes, " of a structure built by the hand of man which does not depreciate with age is the irrigation ditch. When these are first built, the leakage is generally very great and much of the water which has to be stored in large reservoirs never reaches the farms where it is needed. As the ditch grows older, leakage is reduced, owing to the growth of vegetation and the silting process, making the structure much more valuable rather than less valuable. This is probably one of the oldest types of structures built by the hand of man and has been used in all parts of the world, many of them having been in existence for hundreds of years." [19]

It is, of course, well recognised that use is not the only reason behind the " using up " of assets; decay, rust, corrosion and similar agencies make their contribution to physical deterioration. But the effects of most, if not all, of these influences can be counteracted or prevented by adequate maintenance, and some writers

[18] Wm. Alexander & Arthur Street, *Metals in the Service of Man* (Penguin Books, 1944), p. 81.
[19] H. E. Hale, *op. cit.*, p. 403.

have, indeed, interpreted depreciation in the sense of deferred maintenance. With most of these, however, the position has been that they have been concerned with the measure of deferred maintenance in monetary terms, that is, they have not interpreted " maintenance " as the physical effort of upkeep but rather as the cost of upkeep. Hence the notion of depreciation as deferred maintenance, while it may be basically related to the notion of depreciation as physical deterioration, has not, so far as I am aware, been expressly propounded in this physical sense.

Another, perhaps related, point is that many physical assets are composed of parts which can be replaced when worn out or needing repair, sometimes to such an extent that over a period practically no part of the original object is functioning in the existing " asset." As illustration, we might consider the case of an aircraft, in respect of which the keeping of meticulous records is prescribed by the regulations of the Department of Civil Aviation in the interests of safety and efficiency of operation. I recently had an opportunity of inspecting some of these records kept by one of our major aircraft operating enterprises, and, among other things, it was pointed out that each component of each aircraft was represented in the maintenance office by a card in such a way that at any time it could be known what part was in use, how long it had been in use in that or any other aircraft, when and from whom it was acquired, what repairs or modifications it had undergone, and when it was due for replacement. The only part of the aircraft which was not thus replaceable was the centre piece or fuselage—and it is conceivable that even that could be regarded as substitutable.

In the light of such information, what is meant by saying that the rate of depreciation of an aircraft is, say, 20 per cent. per annum? Is it valid, in this context, to think of an aeroplane as anything but a fictional unit set up for a peculiar purpose? And what is that purpose?

When we say that an aircraft—or a motor-vehicle, or a machine—is likely to last, say, five years, do we mean that it is a piece of equipment composed of parts, none of which will last more than five years? Or do we mean that it is a piece of equipment, of which a majority of the component parts or the principal functioning parts will last five years? And, in this case, what constitutes " a majority," or " the principal functioning parts "? Or do we mean that it is a piece of equipment composed of parts, each or most of which lasts on average five years?

If we translate the proposition into such terms as these, two questions arise:

(i) What is the factual information on which the proposition is based? Is it sufficient to warrant formulation in such terms?

(ii) If the concept of an average is used, does not the validity of the proposition depend upon the breadth of the sample examined and upon the range; that is, upon the type of average adopted and the standard deviation? Is depreciation, in this sense, then a problem of statistics?

It is recognised that in some industries and for some kinds of commodity the average usage of items of equipment is empirically established. To take the aircraft operating field again as an example, a new item is used in the first place in accordance with the supplier's recommendations, which are based upon empirical tests applied by him; and this usage may be further modified by empirical tests undertaken by the operator himself. But there are many instances in which adequate factual information relating to usage of fixed assets is not available, and there are probably also many instances in which the information, even though available in technical officers' records, is not used by accountants in any way. Further, where rates of depreciation have to be determined for income tax purposes on new types of equipment, these rates are not the result of an act of creative imagination, but are based on an examination of what are usually called " the circumstances of the case "; in other words, some sort of empirical study is made, as a result of which the rates are determined.

It is interesting to notice that, although Peel re-introduced income tax into the United Kingdom in 1842, it was not until the Customs and Inland Revenue Act of 1878 that any statutory deduction for depreciation was allowed at all for tax purposes. This Act provided that " notwithstanding any provision to the contrary contained in any Act relating to income tax, the Commissioners . . . shall . . . allow such deduction as they may think just and reasonable as representing the diminished value by reason of wear and tear during the year of any machinery or plant used for the purposes of the concern. . . ." [20] The 1842 Income Tax Act did not allow any deduction for actual expenditure on repairs and renewals for any amount beyond " the sum usually expended for such Purposes according to an Average of Three Years preceding," [21] and up to 1878 no allowance whatever was officially permitted for depreciation.[22] In

---

[20] Customs and Inland Revenue Act, 41 & 42 Vict. c. 15, s. 12.

[21] 5 & 6 Vict. c. 35, Schedule D.

[22] It should be noted, however, that " the practice of the special commissioners varied from district to district; for example . . . some commissioners permitted a general allowance for depreciation, but the majority did not." (T. R. Johnston, " Some Economic Aspects of the Law Relating to or Affecting the Measurement of the Capital and Income of Business Enterprises." An unpublished Ph.D. thesis, p. 174).

1876 the principle of this refusal was confirmed by the case of
Andrew Handyside & Co., Ltd. The company had " set aside a
sum out of their net profits, under the articles of association,
for the purpose of meeting the depreciation of buildings, fixed
plant, and machinery. The majority of the local Commissioners,
being of the opinion ' that persons in trade were equitably
entitled to write off from their profits such a sum for depreciation, and that the amount claimed was fair and reasonable,'
decided in favour of the company. The surveyor of taxes, being
dissatisfied with this decision, requested that the present case
should be stated for the opinion of the court. . . . This appeal
was tried before three judges . . . who decided that the sum so
set apart was in the nature of capital, and cannot be deducted
from the profits liable to income tax. . . . Income tax was
legally chargeable on money reserved to make good deterioration
which had already occurred and was growing, but which as yet
had not demanded actual renewals." [23] It was apparently as a
result of this decision that the deduction was allowed in the
Customs and Inland Revenue Act of 1878. Matheson points out,
rather drily perhaps, that " surveyors of taxes did not always
draw the attention of manufacturers and others to the relief and
allowances provided by this Act of 1878." [24]

Other points that might be noted, in passing, in this provision
are, first, that the allowance is for " diminished value by wear
and tear " and " depreciation " as such is not mentioned; second,
that the Act made no provision in relation to buildings; and third,
that the amount of the deduction was to be determinable by the
Commissioners.

It is interesting to note the arguments of the Colwyn Commission of 1920. One general argument which they raised was
that it was unfair to extend wear and tear allowances to other
forms of capital expenditure without making " an analogous
allowance in respect of the initial capital invested in the education
and training of a lawyer, surgeon, or workman whose earning
power is possibly of shorter duration than the life of a mine." [25]

Depreciation as fall in value

Probably the most frequently expressed interpretation of
depreciation is as a diminution in value of an asset. It seems
likely that historically the word was used in this sense before it
was applied to that of physical deterioration, which seems to

---

[23] Ewing Matheson, *Depreciation of Factories, Mines and Industrial Undertakings
and Their Valuation*, 4th ed. (London: Spon, 1910), pp. 26–27.
[24] Matheson, *op. cit.*, p. 28.
[25] T. R. Johnston, *op. cit.*, p. 181.

have been invariably expressed as wear and tear (or tear and wear) up to some time in the nineteenth century, and is often so expressed even today. Some time about the middle of last century the notion of wear and tear—or physical deterioration—and that of diminution in value coalesced in the word " depreciation." Professor Littleton notes that " depreciation receives mention as such " for the first time in a book by W. Inglish in 1861, who " says of buildings and machinery, ' In such accounts, a yearly deduction of 5 and 10 per cent. requires to be made from original cost, to allow for deterioration, or wear and tear.' In the illustrative furniture account the explanation of the entry is: ' By depreciation 5 per cent. carried to Trade Expenses.' " [26]

In the first book on depreciation, that of Ewing Matheson (an engineer), which appeared in 1884, the author remarks that " the term ' depreciation,' though not strictly accurate, was originally applied as a convenient form of expression for the phrase ' diminution of value by reason of wear and tear.' " [27]

It is interesting to notice some dictionary definitions in this connection. The *Oxford English Dictionary* contains two meanings, *viz.*, " Act of depreciating. (1) lowering of value; fall in exchangeable value (of money); (2) lowering in estimation; disparagement." Some of the senses in which the word is now used in accounting and business are perhaps extensions of the former of the meanings given, but they are applied to other categories than the monetary ones which seemed to be the main concern of the compilers of the *O.E.D.* In the supplement published in 1933 to bring it up to date there is nothing more precise to help us. The case of *Webster's* (Merriam) *Dictionary*, however, is different. Editions of this dictionary prior to that of 1943 contained meanings almost identical with those of the *O.E.D.*, but in the 1943 edition a third sense was given for the first time, *viz.*,

> " c. *Acctg.* Decline in value of an asset due to such causes as wear and tear, action of the elements, obsolescence, and inadequacy."

Further, it included the following additional entry:

> " depreciation charge. *Acctg.* An annual charge to cover depreciation and obsolescence, usually in the form of a percentage, fixed in advance, of the cost of the property depreciated. Either the book value of the pieces of property themselves is reduced (*straight line depreciation*) or a capital liability set up (*depreciation reserve*) corresponding to the total amount. If cash and investments equal to this liability are accumulated so as to be able to pay for renewals as they become necessary, a *depreciation fund* in the strict sense of the term results."

[26] A. C. Littleton, *Accounting Evolution to 1900* (New York: American Institute Publishing Co., 1933), p. 226.
[27] Matheson, *op. cit.*, p. 1.

Whether this description of a depreciation charge was supplied by an accountant or whether it represents a layman's interpretation of accountants' writings, is not known, but it can scarcely be regarded as an accurate indication of the way in which the term is used in most current accounting literature. This description has not been altered in later editions of this dictionary.

Although the trend in accounting literature in recent years appears to have been somewhat away from expressing depreciation as a valuation concept, there is evidence that the notion is still held by some accounting writers. For example, in a recent English elementary text, the following statement appears:

> All assets must be examined and valued at the end of each accounting period to discover how much loss has been sustained on them. . . . Assets such as machinery, buildings, office furniture, and motor vans, last a long time, and appear in successive Balance Sheets. . . . The fall in value of such assets is known as depreciation." [28]

There can be little doubt that the valuation concept of depreciation has been historically significant. Professor Littleton points out that in the earlier period of accounting development " even the best bookkeeping practice reflected a very simple concept of depreciation. The treatment accorded a depreciating property in the accounts was to enter it at the end of a period on the credit side ' as if sold.' " [29] He cites John Mair's *Bookkeeping Methodiz'd* as being representative of the eighteenth century and quotes his treatment of long-lived assets, which " were to be treated as mixed accounts much like a merchandise account; the inventory portion was carried forward and the remainder transferred to loss-and-gain." And he continues that " it is not certain from Mair's statement whether the ship or the house was to be shown on the credit side in closing the account at its then value or at its original cost," and he points out that in a later text Mair uses the term " value " and concludes that " if ' value ' was used then in the modern sense, any shrinkage or depreciation would be transmitted to profit-and-loss by carrying forward a decreased amount as inventory or balance." [30]

With great respect, it is submitted that there is a danger of reading rather too much into some of the earlier writers on accounting. The excerpt from Mair's book does not, in my opinion, appear to provide evidence that Mair was thinking about depreciation in any of its senses. He is, indeed, dealing

[28] A. Baston, *Elements of Accounts* (London: Gregg, 1952), p. 88.
[29] Littleton, *op. cit.*, p. 227.
[30] *Ibid.*, p. 225.

with the accounts of long-term assets—" ships, houses, or other possessions "—and his treatment is, to debit the account with " what they cost at first, or are valued at " and all charges, such as repairs, etc., and to credit it with " either what they are sold or exchanged for, or the profits [31] arising from them; such as, freight, rent, etc." [32] That is, the account is a mixed one, showing both (i) the asset cost and sale price, and (ii) revenue and charges. The charges include " repairs, or other expenses *laid out* upon them " (italics mine). Mair goes on to consider the three possible cases:

(i) If there is no entry on the credit side, the account " is closed, by being credited by *Balance* ";

(ii) If the asset is sold, the sale price is credited and the balance is the gain or loss made on the sale and is transferred to Profit and Loss;

(iii) If the credit side " contain only the freight, or rent; in this case first charge the ship, house, etc. Dr. to *Profit and Loss*, for the freight, or rent; and then close the accompt with *Balance* ".[33]

It seems clear, on reflection, that the balance of the account, in those cases (i) and (iii) where the asset was not sold, was to be the same as the opening debit, and what was transferred to profit and loss was simply the revenue and outlays recorded in the mixed account. A perusal of the illustrative accounts in Mair's work confirms this. Not only in the long-term asset accounts is the closing balance the same as the initial debit of acquisition cost, but even in the merchandise accounts, wherever there is a balance on hand at balance date, the basis of " valuation " is invariably that of acquisition cost.[34] With this treatment, there can be no question of depreciation.

It is likely, however, that the treatment was somewhat varied in the early part of the nineteenth century. By 1849, at any rate, the question of difference in valuation of both merchandise and long-term assets at balance date was recognised by at least one textbook writer, who says, in relation to his set of illustrative ledger accounts, " in Balancing the accounts of Cotton and Ship *Mars*, recourse must be had to the value on hand of the former, and to the estimated value of the latter . . . by entering these on the Cr. sides before ascertaining the Gain or Loss on these accounts." [35]

Matheson, in his treatise of 1884, recognised " various methods

[31] That is, revenue, in modern terminology.
[32] *Ibid.*, p. 225.
[33] *Ibid.*, p. 225.
[34] John Mair, *Book-keeping Methodiz'd* (Dublin, 1748 edition). See ledger accounts pp. 124–159, and especially account of Ship Britannia on pp. 126–127.
[35] C. Morrison, *A Complete System of Practical Bookkeeping* (London 1849), pp. 204–205.

of estimating the Depreciation of a Factory, and of recording
alteration in value, but it may be said in regard to any of them
that the object in view is, so to treat the nominal capital in the
books of account that it shall always represent as nearly as
possible the real value. Theoretically, the most effectual methods
of securing this would be, if it were feasible, to re-value everything at stated intervals, and to write off whatever loss such
valuations might reveal without regard to any prescribed rate. . . ."
But he is clearly aware of the difficulties. " Such a system,
however, is not feasible, and is adopted only in factories where
the trade and plant are of so simple or uniform a kind as to
allow it without difficulty. . . . The plan of valuing every year
instead of adopting a depreciation rate, though it might appear
the more perfect, is too tedious and expensive to be adopted. . . .
The next best plan, which is that generally followed . . . is to
establish average rates which can without much trouble be
written off every year, to check the result by complete or partial
valuation at longer intervals, and to adjust the depreciation
rate if required." [36]

Professor Bonbright presents two valuation concepts. The
first he expresses thus: " The phenomenon of deterioration . . .
may be responsible for a decline in value. . . . When thus used
without restriction depreciation is exactly interchangeable with
' fall in value ' and its meaning shifts with the shift in the meaning
of value itself. . . . Even those accountants and appraisers,
however, who define depreciation in terms of fall in value, . . .
ordinarily . . . limit it to those declines in value which they
attribute to certain specific causes associated with what Hatfield . . .
calls ' the irresistible march to the junk heap.' " [37] He describes
the second, which is essentially that of an appraiser, as the
difference between the present value of the old property and the
present value of a hypothetical, new property. In this case,
" depreciation is treated as a deduction from replacement cost
new, estimated as of the date of the valuation. Here the definition
' fall in value ' is quite erroneous, and the fact that it is still
current has given rise to serious confusion. Depreciation should
now refer to the difference between the present worth of the old
and obsolescent asset and the present worth of the hypothetical,
new and modern asset." [38]

When we come to ask what is this " value " that falls or
varies and just how it is to be measured, we are faced with considerable difficulty. The question of the nature of value has had

[36] Matheson, *op. cit.*, p. 35.
[37] Bonbright, *op. cit.*, pp. 183–184.　　　　　　　　　　　[38] *Ibid.*, p. 185.

much more attention from economists than from accountants, and we must look to them for guidance. The earlier economists distinguished between use-value and exchange-value, the latter of which was, broadly, measured by price. More recently, Professor L. M. Fraser [39] has distinguished four main senses in which the word " value " may be used in economics, *viz*:

    (i) cost-value, *i.e.*, normal costs of production;
    (ii) exchange-value, *i.e.*, rate of exchange, or purchasing power, or exchange equivalent;
    (iii) use-value, *i.e.*, usefulness or utility;
    (iv) esteem-value, *i.e.*, relative (subjective) importance.

He points out that these do not represent four kinds of value: " they are not different types of value (the concept), but different senses of ' value ' (the word)." [40] (I must confess I cannot understand what he means when he says there are four different meanings of a word but nevertheless only one concept. If a word has four different meanings surely it is used to communicate four different concepts; how can the word " concept " be legitimately used otherwise, unless we are going to invent " subconcepts "?)

What is meant, then, when depreciation is spoken of as a diminution of value or a change of value? It would appear that those who use the word in this way say, in effect, that after a piece of equipment or similar asset has been acquired, something happens—it deteriorates through use, or through non-use, or it becomes obsolete or inadequate, and so on—as a result of which the change of " value " takes place.

It is difficult to see how this change can apply to Fraser's " cost-value," since the cost of production of a commodity can hardly be affected by events that take place after it has been completed and put into use.

As to the second of these senses, it is submitted that the exchange-value of a long-term asset can only be positively determined at two points in its life—at its purchase and at its sale; that is, by an act of exchange. It is true that the owner of such an asset might obtain an idea of what it might be likely to bring if sold, by, say, calling for tenders; but this would be only an approximation: it would tell him what others are willing to offer for it, but in the absence of an actual exchange, it does not indicate what he would take for it, and the exchange value must be imputed, not an actual price of the commodity. Thus a fall in the exchange value of an asset is the same as a fall in price,

[39] L. M. Fraser, *Economic Thought and Language* (London: A. & C. Black, 1937), pp. 56 *et seq.*
[40] *Op. cit.*, p. 60.

and if depreciation is to be interpreted in this way it is no different from the concept of fall in price which has already been considered above.

The third sense, that of usefulness, appears to be based on the notion of physical use. A thing becomes less useful because it cannot be used as effectively as previously. Some assets, as already pointed out, may become more useful after some use. On the other hand, an asset may be just as useful in absolute terms as ever it was and yet be relatively less useful by comparison with more advanced models or substitutes or because its products have lost part of their popular appeal. This is obsolescence or inadequacy which may arise suddenly or gradually, and which is a result of factors operating altogether apart from those of physical use of the thing itself. A diminution in usefulness is surely tantamount to either physical deterioration of the asset or a change in the uses to which it is put, and if depreciation is used in this sense it amounts to physical deterioration, which we have already considered.

If, however, something else is meant, if it is nevertheless insisted that an asset can be of less " value " because it is of less use, then surely this " value " can only be esteem-value—a subjective thing which can scarcely be objectively measured. If it is argued that because it is of less use it is likely to bring less on disposal, and therefore it is of less value, then surely this " value " is exchange value, and the question of its being of less use is irrelevant—the operative concept is the market price, not its usefulness.

As an example of the kind of results arising from the valuation concept of depreciation, the Colwyn Commission in 1920 propounded the argument that depreciation of buildings may be offset by appreciation of their site: " When the question of depreciation of buildings is under consideration the possibility of the simultaneous appreciation of the site on which those buildings stand cannot in fairness be disregarded. Nor, we think, can we ignore the gradual increase in the capital value of the buildings themselves which follows from the growing prosperity of certain districts." This passage shows a confusion between a possible capital gain, through appreciation of site and structure, and a cost of a totally different character which occurs regardless of such capital gains.

If depreciation is to be used as a valuation concept it should only be with extreme care and with full regard to the inconsistencies it provides, both in theory and practice, for the unwary. As E. L. Kohler puts it, " without qualification and clear definition, including specific and operationally feasible rules for measurement, the term [value] has only subjective significance." [41]

Depreciation as cost allocation

The concept of depreciation as an allocation of cost is now so familiar as to need no introduction. Two illustrations only of the way in which it has been expressed are adduced.

In its Bulletin No. 22, issued in May, 1944, the committee on Terminology of the American Institute of Certified Public Accountants indicated its position:

> " *Depreciation accounting* is a system of accounting which aims to distribute the cost or other basic value of tangible capital assets, less salvage (if any), over the estimated useful life of the unit (which may be a group of assets) in a systematic and rational manner. It is a process of allocation, not of valuation. *Depreciation for the year* is the portion of the total charge under such a system that is allocated to the year. Although the allocation may properly take into account occurrences during the year, it is not intended to be a measurement of the effect of all such occurrences."

Recommendation No. IX of the Institute of Chartered Accountants in England and Wales, issued in 1945, expressed the matter thus:

> " Depreciation represents that part of the cost of a fixed asset to its owner which is not recoverable when the asset is finally put out of use by him. Provision against this loss of capital is an integral cost of conducting the business during the effective commercial life of the asset and is not dependent upon the amount of profit earned. . . ."

It will be noted that the American bulletin unequivocally rejects the valuation concept and at the same time censures the view that annual depreciation is necessarily a measure in monetary terms of physical deterioration or other " occurrences during the year," although it may take such factors into account. This latter point appears to be a possible, though not necessarily probable, source of weakness. What is meant by " systematic "? what by " rational "? For these are the criteria by which the validity of allocation is to be judged. Would anyone, for example, have argued that, in the days when 20 per cent. initial depreciation was allowed for taxation purposes, it was either unsystematic or irrational to allocate 20 per cent. of the cost of an asset in the first year after its acquisition and the remainder over its estimated life? And if it is rational to allocate 20 per cent., would it not be equally rational to allocate 40 per cent., or 80 per cent., or even 100 per cent.? After all, the difference

---

[41] E. L. Kohler, *A Dictionary for Accountants* (New York: Prentice-Hall, 1952), pp. 442–443.

between these cases is one of degree, which surely cannot be said to affect rationality. Or, if 100 per cent. or 80 per cent. is not rational, at what stage does the difference between reasonableness and unreasonableness occur? There is no guide on this in the bulletin. We are told that depreciation is an allocation of cost, and that this allocation may be related to " occurrences during the year." But if something *may* be done, there is also the possibility that it may not be done; and it is this possibility that is rather disturbing.

The problem may, indeed, be insoluble. For what do we know of what occurs to a piece of equipment or property during any given period? As already pointed out, the known objective facts about an asset are few. Between the points of acquisition and retirement there is, in respect of non-physical assets (such as a lease), nothing more; in respect of physical equipment there is usually a history of use (either regular or sporadic), maintenance (possibly regular but often irregular), and repair (almost always variable). So far as I know, there are relatively very few instances where adequate records of this kind of history are kept. Even the suggested forms of fixed asset registers appearing in some of the most advanced writings in accounting, while they provide for the recording of such things as additions and improvements to particular assets or groups of assets, do not appear to provide for the detailed historical recording of use, maintenance and repair, whether in monetary or physical terms.

The essential notion in the English recommendation is the same as that expressed in the American bulletin. An amount representing the original outlay less the recovery on retirement is to be apportioned over the financial periods in between. The English pronouncement is open to this comment. In their definition, depreciation is " part " of a " cost "; in a later part of the recommendation, there is reference to " Freehold buildings, plant and machinery, tools and equipment, ships, transport vehicles and similar assets which are subject to depreciation by reason of their employment in the business." It seems clear that in this latter expression " depreciation " is not being used in the way in which it was defined; it is being used here to suggest a process or something that happens, whereas it was defined as a result of a happening. Substitute the definition for the word in the later passage and the point becomes obvious. It does seem unfortunate, that in a recommendation specifically intended to clarify the nature and treatment of depreciation, the word itself should have been thus used with two different meanings.

There are other unresolved points in connection with the

concept of cost-allocation. It should be noted that the idea of allocation of cost has a wider application than this one of a periodic charge of fixed asset cost. Units of activity other than that of a period may be adopted. One might, for example, allocate the cost of a motor-vehicle over the number of miles travelled or an item of equipment over units of output; and this could be done over its effective life or over a given period within its effective life. In practice, allocation of cost is frequently made by superimposing, so to speak, one unit of activity on another, and in this procedure systematic and rational bases are normally used. But however rational the criteria for allocation may be, they are nevertheless arbitrary, in the sense that each allocation represents a selection, determined in accordance with human judgment, out of several possible criteria, some of which may be regarded as having equal validity with the one selected. It is surely desirable to recognise this element of arbitrariness, not because there is anything necessarily objectionable about making arbitrary decisions, but to avoid being misled into thinking that because something appears reasonable it therefore corresponds to objectively verifiable occurrences.

Another relevant point here is the residual return on retirement of an asset. It seems to be almost universally agreed amongst writers on this subject that the salvage or scrap return should be taken into account in determining the rate of depreciation charge. In assessing this rate there is usually only one objectively known datum—the original outlay on the asset. The period of effective life and the residual return constitute two unknowns. We are frequently reminded that an accountant " is not gifted with prophetic powers." Whose job is it, in practice, to forecast the residual return from an asset on disposal at some future date? Can the engineer do it? Can the executive manager? Can anybody? Would it not be desirable to reduce, if possible, the number of unknowns in the assessment of a depreciation charge? I wonder, too, whether, at the time and for the purpose of acquisition, the disposal return usually enters into the calculations of the person who buys the asset for commercial purposes. The assessment of this residual return on disposal at some indeterminate future time is doubly based on estimate: it involves an estimate of the period of effective life and an estimate of the movement of prices for second-hand commodities of the particular type. Would it not be equally reasonable, and perhaps more systematic, to regard such return as either (a) a windfall gain when it occurs, to be treated then as a non-operating item— as we now treat the difference between residual return and written-down " value," or (b) a set-off against the cost of the asset (if any) replacing it?

In favour of the latter treatment is the consideration that prices of new and second-hand units of the same kind ruling at the time of disposal are likely to be consistent with each other, but bear no relation to prices of several years before. And, indeed, this is not so revolutionary a suggestion as it might seem at first sight. Writers on the topic of differential costs, for example, often use illustrations in which, for purposes of determining whether replacement of an asset is desirable, the second-hand price of the existing equipment is set off against the cost of the proposed equipment and the difference is regarded as one of the significant factors in resolving the problem. If such a procedure is satisfactory for one phase of accounting endeavour, it may well be satisfactory for another. It is interesting to note, in passing, that the words " less salvage (if any) " in the American research Bulletin No. 22 were not included in the original definition in Bulletin No. 20, issued six months earlier.

Another point is the question: Why do we allocate cost at all? So far as the accounting procedures are concerned, the currently accepted reply appears to be that the cost of long-term assets is spread as part of the procedure of matching periodic revenues with appropriate charges. Admittedly, this is reasonable and practicable, but it is submitted that it is little more. Can we be sure that it would not be equally reasonable to write off the cost of a long-term asset in the first period after its acquisition— or the last? We say that this should not be done because the asset is used over the period, and, because the asset is so used, the cost should be apportioned according to the use. The services embodied in the physical—or non-physical—asset are yielded up through its use. This is unquestionably reasonable, but it is also based upon assumptions: (a) that the expected benefits will be proportional to an estimated usage rate, and (b) that it is possible to measure the benefits derived from such assets. These assumptions should be brought out into the open for critical inspection. Let us be sure that in so allocating cost we are not merely adopting a device for the purpose of evening out what might otherwise be very uneven results. Let us be sure that in following reason we do not fall into the practice of rationalisation.

There is one point more, and I can do little more than mention it, although it is the central point in current controversy. This is: What cost should be allocated? On the one hand we have those who advocate that historical cost, that is, the known original money outlay, is the amount that should be allocated. On the other hand we have those who advocate that the basis should be replacement cost and that the provision for depreciation should represent a cumulative estimate of the cost of replacing the physical asset.

I do not wish to enter into the controversy at this stage, except to suggest that the replacement argument appears to be based on the proposition that accumulated charges for depreciation are intended to provide resources for the replacement of long-term assets, so that the " real " capital shall be kept " intact." What is meant precisely by the word " real " in this context? Do the proponents of this argument intend to imply replacement by identical assets, which rather suggests a non-progressive state of affairs, or replacement by improved assets, which, to my mind, is not the same as keeping something intact? Those who advocate continuance of the use of historical cost urge the need for adequate replacement reserves in times of rising prices, in order to ensure continuity of operations.

Conclusion

The principal functions in accounting are usually recognised as being those of recording, reporting and interpreting. But underlying all these is the necessity for measuring. The problem facing the accountant is that of measuring something. He therefore needs concepts which are capable of measurement. In charging " depreciation," accountants purport to measure something. What is it?

If it is some physical event or series of events, the fact is that we don't know enough about the physical behaviour of long-term assets to consider any policy of charging " depreciation " as beyond attack. We need more " factual " data through empirical studies of different kinds of equipment: adequate plant and fixed-asset registers, more detailed than those suggested in most textbooks, would be a starting point.

In the meantime, let us try to avoid deluding ourselves and others on what we mean. If, by " charging depreciation " we mean an allocation of historical cost, let us use words (such as " cost-allocation " and " proportion of cost allocated against past revenue ") which will convey this meaning. If we mean attempting to provide resources for future replacement of assets, why not use words (such as " provision for future replacement ") which bring this meaning out? If we mean adjustment to present market costs, why not use words which say so; if we mean an

estimate of wearing out, let us indicate this clearly and unequivocally. To use a word like "depreciation" or a phrase like
" provision for depreciation " is not quite fair to ourselves or
to the readers of our reports. By avoiding the use of these
words, some of us may be compelled to examine our words and
our concepts more closely, and this, I feel sure, will promote
precision. It might mean some hard thinking for some of us,
but are not accountants accustomed to hard thinking? Or are
they?

I have tried to show in this paper that there is not necessarily a
one/one relationship between a word and its meaning. This is,
of course, obvious and should be quite unnecessary were it not
for the fact that so many writers and speakers use a word—such
as " depreciation," but there are many others—as if it had only
one meaning, namely, the one that they are imposing on it in
their own immediate context. Unless they make it perfectly
clear in which of the several senses they are using their words,
there is failure in communication between them and their readers
or listeners.

Depreciation With Special Reference to Transport *

By G. J. Ponsonby

Reader in Commerce, with special reference to Transport, London School of Economics.

THE scheme of this article is as follows. First, some outstanding causes of the depreciation in value of capital equipment and other assets are distinguished and classified. Secondly, attention is drawn to alternative aims or objects which may be adopted when determining depreciation policy, one particular aim being defined and selected for the purpose of this article. Finally, the methods of providing for depreciation which seem to follow, both from the classification of its causes and the adopted aim, are set out. Unless otherwise stated, it is assumed throughout that the general level of prices is stable, and no attention will be given to the possible effects of taxes.

I. CLASSIFICATION OF THE CAUSES OF DEPRECIATION

The principal causes of depreciation in the value of assets may be considered under four broad headings, namely:

(i) physical wear and tear resulting from use,

(ii) physical deterioration resulting from exposure to the elements, essentially a function of time rather than use;

(iii) the expiration or running out of such legal rights as leases and licences; and

(iv) the falling away over time of the demand for particular transport services provided by the assets in question. This item is, of course, usually referred to as obsolescence.

A few comments on the precise character of these four causes seem worth making.

1. *Physical wear and tear resulting from use*

This cause consists solely of such wear and tear as results from use. By reducing an asset's future technical capacity to serve, it also reduces its future earning power, and therefore its value. The reductions in the useful life or revenue-earning

* From the *Economic Journal*, March 1956.

capacity of such assets are in the nature of a " user " cost, in that they will vary with the amount of service provided. One example of this kind of depreciation is the wearing out of tyres (rubber or steel), brake-blocks or other parts of any kind of rolling stock, which results from vehicle-miles actually operated. It should be pointed out, however, that this cause is relevant for economic calculations only when opportunities exist for profitably using the assets to the point at which they are technically inefficient and require replacement because they are " worn out." For if, because of a rapid falling off of demand, the asset has to be scrapped before it is technically worn out, then it is irrelevant whether the asset is greatly worn or only partially so—apart from any possible second-hand or scrap value; the more powerful factor of obsolescence has rendered physical wear and tear irrelevant from the economic point of view.

2. *Physical deterioration resulting from exposure to the elements*

In contrast to the deterioration which takes place as a result of use, much transport equipment—notably station buildings, bridges and viaducts, road surfaces, important parts of the railway permanent way—being continually exposed to wind and weather, deteriorates with the passage of time. The extent of deterioration, and therefore of depreciation, is in this case essentially a function of time. From the economic point of view, the importance of distinguishing between (i) user-cost, and (ii) time-cost, hardly needs emphasising.[1]

3. *The expiration of certain legal rights, such as leases, patents and licences*

This cause of depreciation comes into play in many branches of industry besides transport. In transport, it arises especially in the case of the expiration of various types of licences. It is essentially a function of time, and should be treated as such.

---

[1] It is sometimes inferred that this second kind of depreciation, because it is dependent on time, can therefore be regarded as an " overhead " cost, and " independent of the volume of traffic." In a sense this is true, but only to a very limited extent and in the short run. For in the long run the magnitude of these particular time and (alleged) overhead costs depends upon the *amount of equipment exposed to the elements*, which in its turn depends for the most part upon the capacity for which provision is made. A railway may wish to maintain either large and elaborate station buildings or small and simple ones, according to the volume and character of the traffic expected. It may have much or little rolling stock, again according to the maximum amount of traffic provided for at any one time. Provision for this type of depreciation is therefore essentially in the nature of a " capacity " cost, and will remain constant only in so far as the capacity for which equipment is maintained remains so also.

4. *Depreciation in value due to changes in demand*

So far we have only considered falls in value due to changes on the side of supplying the services. There may, however, be a slackening or even cessation of demand for such services, causing corresponding falls in the value of equipment. Such falls in demand may be due to a variety of causes, which are, I think, worth distinguishing. First, technical changes within the transport industry itself may lessen demand for the services of an asset (*e.g.*, diesel traction becomes more attractive than steam); historically, this has been a most potent cause of depreciation of transport assets. Second, technical progress in other industries may cause a change in the relative prices of transport and of other competing channels of expenditure (*e.g.*, even if consumers' tastes do not alter, a fall in the price of radio and television sets tends to cause more spending on sets and less on travel to and from cinema or other public entertainment). Third, the tastes and habits of consumers may change, quite apart from relative prices; this may lead to a fall in demand for transport in general or for particular kinds of transport. Finally, demand for transport may change because of changes in the supply and location of natural resources (*e.g.*, mines or forests may be exploited to the point of exhaustion, so that the roads, canals or railways serving them become valueless).

So much for the main causes of the depreciation in value of various types of transport equipment.

II. ALTERNATIVE AIMS AND OBJECTS OF DEPRECIATION POLICY

Before discussing methods in detail, we must define the assumed aim or object of depreciation policy. For there is nothing fixed or inevitable about that; it is essentially a matter of choice. One aim, for example, might be to maintain, by means of periodic replacement, the long-run *money value* of an originally acquired asset or series of assets. An alternative aim might be greatly to enhance an undertaking's money value or revenue-earning capacity over a period of years, to " plough back " profits, save and invest. It has been a conspicuous feature of many successful one-man businesses that the owner has managed to " build up " his business out of profits. A third course might be to make no attempt either to maintain fully or to enhance (out of revenue) an asset's or undertaking's value, but to distribute net earnings, making little or no provision for the future. Let us assume that we select the first of these objectives—that is the maintenance, in the long run, of the value or revenue-earning prospects (in terms of money income) of a given asset, or series of assets, in the first of which a given sum of money was invested. If we keep to our assumption of a stable price level (including the rate of interest), this is tantamount to aiming at the accumulation, during the revenue-earning life of a particular asset, of the sum originally invested in it, less scrap value. Only sums earned over and above this amount would be available for distribution as dividends.

But that only gives us what the *total* depreciation allowance during the whole of an asset's economic life should amount to. In view of the considerable longevity (both technical and economic) of so much transport equipment, notably in the railway and shipping industries, there is the additional decision to make, that of how to spread the total depreciation allowance required over the period that elapses between the times of investment and abandonment. How much of it should be put aside after the first, second and subsequent accounting periods? It is therefore proposed to add to the first and overriding objective, that of putting aside in each accounting period a sum sufficient to compensate for the loss of value which has been sustained during that period. Thus if the capital value of the asset during an initial accounting period has fallen from £1,000 to £800, whether due to wear and tear or changed public demand, then the aim would be to put aside £200 in respect of that depreciation. So that if the aim were consistently realised, the value of the asset itself plus the value of whatever had been put aside (and possibly invested) on account of depreciation would, at the end of any given accounting period, together amount to the original value of the investment. The problem, therefore, of deciding what amount should be put aside at the end of each accounting period on account of depreciation is simply that of assessing the loss of value sustained during that period, the new (lower) value of the asset in question being based on the best estimate available of its future revenue-earning capacity. What considerations, then, should determine the amounts to be allocated to depreciation in order to achieve these two objectives? What follows is an attempt to answer that question.

III. Methods of Providing for Depreciation Consistent with Aims Defined above under II

Taking first as our accounting period the whole revenue-earning or economic life of the asset concerned, whatever that may be, then the aim would be to put aside and invest (either by

ploughing back within the undertaking or buying external securities) a sum (less scrap value) sufficient to replace the old asset
with another of no less value than the original asset. Assuming
a stable price-level, an asset bought for £1,000 would require that
sum to replace it. This is shown in Fig. 1, the line *AB* denoting
the level of the annual operating costs of the unit, and *CD*
the level of gross earnings. Let us assume that at the time of the
investment *it was hoped* that the area *CAO*, which represents the

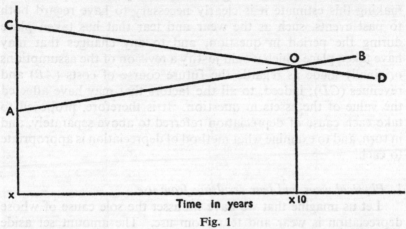

Time in years

Fig. 1

total surplus earned during the asset's life over and above
inescapable working expenses, would be sufficient to meet the
following items:

    (i) interest on debenture or fixed-interest-bearing stocks;
    (ii) full depreciation;
    (iii) dividend on ordinary shares.

Let us assume, further, that in the event of failure to earn sufficient
to meet all these three claims on net revenue, the order of priority
for payment would be strictly as given, dividends having a lesser
claim upon revenue than depreciation and interest on debenture
stocks. Thus, what is allocated to depreciation is in direct competition with dividends in the sense that the more that goes to
depreciation, the less is available for dividends. Assuming our
" accounting period " to be synonymous with that of the whole
economic life of the asset, the decision as to how to allocate the
surpluses earned arises only once. A total surplus would be
available, and it either would or would not be enough to provide
for debenture interest, adequate depreciation, and anticipated
dividend. Things being as they are, however, whereas the accounting period is usually one year only, the economic life of many
important kinds of assets may be much more than this, so that

there is the additional problem of how much to allocate on account of depreciation at the end of the first, second and subsequent years.

As already explained, given our assumptions as to the aims of depreciation policy, the appropriate sum to be set aside during each accounting period should as nearly as possible reflect the difference between the value, or future revenue-earning prospects, of the asset at the beginning and at the end of that period. In making this estimate it is clearly necessary to have regard both to past events, such as the wear and tear that has taken place during the period in question, and to any changes that may have taken place which would justify a revision of the assumptions originally made as regards the future course of costs (AB) and revenues (CD); indeed, to all the factors that may have affected the value of the assets in question. It is therefore, proposed to take each cause of depreciation referred to above separately, and in turn, and to examine what method of depreciation is appropriate to each.

1. *Physical wear and tear resulting from use*

Let us imagine that we have an asset the sole cause of whose depreciation is wear and tear from use. The amount set aside on this account depends essentially on the amount of work (often expressed in transport in terms of vehicle-miles operated) which the asset has been called upon to do. The more work done, the less technical (and in this case also the less economic) life is left for future exploitation. So long as the technicians know just how much " life " has been taken out of the asset during the period in question, there should be little difficulty in assessing how much should be set aside on this account. On the assumption that the technical efficiency and revenue-earning capacity of the asset is not affected until it is actually worn out and demands replacement, a first approximation would be to put aside sums in proportion to the life that has been used up or taken out of the asset during the period in question. A strict adherence to this practice, however, would in fact be placing an undue burden on the early years. For the value lost in an early year represents the loss of the services which would otherwise have been rendered at the end of its life, that is the present valuation of those possibly " distant " potential services only. And the present value of a service to be given at a more distant future time is less than the value of one to be given at a not so distant future time. This factor would seem to justify putting aside somewhat less per unit of service in the earlier than in the later years of an asset's life, the actual amount depending on the rate at which future earnings or benefits are presently discounted. " Pure " wear and tear due to use would seem therefore to justify an allocation per unit of service which would increase, however slightly, during the life of the asset concerned.

But in most kinds of transport equipment there are two other factors which work strongly in the opposite direction, and point to the necessity, if we remain true to our objectives, of putting aside much *larger* sums per unit of service in the earlier than in the later years of an asset's life. The first of these derives from the well-known fact that most vehicles tend to become more expensive to operate with age and as wear and tear takes its toll. In the case of most motor-vehicles, for example, in the early years of their life running repairs are relatively low, and petrol and oil consumption similarly so. But as time goes on, repairs increase and petrol and oil consumption tend to rise. Thus, even if revenues earned per vehicle-mile remained constant, " net " earnings would tend to be less in the later than in the earlier part of such assets' useful life. This case is illustrated in Fig. 2 below:

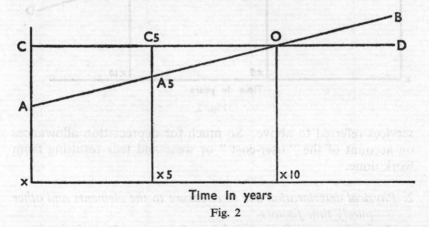

Time in years

Fig. 2

As in Fig. 1, *CD* represents the level of gross earnings over time, whereas *AB* represents the level of the costs of operating the unit. It will be observed that by half way through its useful life (at *X*5) the vehicle's prospects of earning net revenue have been reduced by far more than half. The area C_5A_5O is much less than half *CAO*, which represents the total net anticipated earnings of the asset during the whole of its life. For this reason larger sums should be set aside in the first half than in the second half of its life, and in the earlier than in the later years.

The second factor pointing in the same direction derives from the fact that the quality and reliability of the services rendered

tend to deteriorate with increased wear and tear,[1] with the result
that both the gross and therefore the net revenue earned in the
later part of its useful life may be less than in the earlier part.
This case is illustrated in Fig. 3. In this case costs are assumed
to remain stable, but the level of gross revenue falls. Again,
much more than half (or a quarter) of the asset's capacity to earn
net revenue has disappeared by half (or a quarter) way through
its life, which would seem to justify putting aside more on account
of depreciation in the earlier than in the later years of the asset's
life. These two factors operate with such force in the case of most
kinds of road vehicles as far to outweigh the case for shifting
the burden forward on account of the discounted value of future

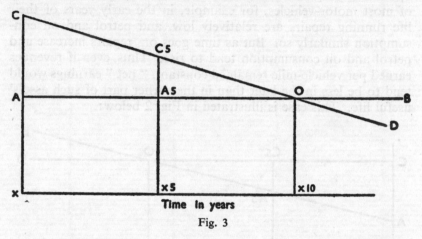

Fig. 3

services referred to above. So much for depreciation allowances
on account of the " user-cost " or wear and tear resulting from
work done.

2. *Physical deterioration due to exposure to the elements and other purely time factors*

As in the case of wear and tear from use, depreciation over
time has economic relevance only if the asset's economic life is
not terminated (*e.g.*, by fall in demand for its services) at an earlier
date than its physical end. The amount to be set aside in any
accounting period will depend essentially on the length of that
period in relation to the total time after which replacement
will be required. Thus, subject to the qualification regarding
the discounted value of the services to be rendered referred to in

---

[1] This cause of a fall in value should be distinguished from obsolescence, which
is dealt with below. It is neither due to a technical change nor to changed
demand. It derives solely from the vehicle in question giving a less good quality
of service towards the end of its life than at the beginning.

the preceding section, depreciation is in this case essentially a function of time as opposed to " user." Here again, however, the two factors tending to reduce " net " earnings in the later part of an asset's life may come into play. As the result of the physical deterioration that takes place because of time, not only may it become more expensive to operate a vehicle or maintain a roadway, but the quality of service may also decline substantially. Here again there is a strong tendency for costs to increase and for revenue to go down, in this case with the passage of time instead of with increased use. And its significance in relation to depreciation is the same. It provides both the means and the need for putting aside more in the earlier than in the later years of an asset's economic life.

3. *The expiration of legal rights such as leases and licences*

In so far as the expiration of any purchased legal rights is directly related to time, the same considerations apply to their depreciation as to other purely time factors. Although, in contrast to the last two cases, whereas regard should again be given to the discounted value of services to be rendered in a distant future, the questions of rising costs or falling revenues over time may well not arise.

4. *Depreciation due to changes in demand*

We now come to the problem of providing for such depreciation in value as occurs because of changes or anticipated changes in demand. These changes in demand may stem from at least four different sources, set out on pp. 259–261. Because so much in all these cases depends on *estimates* of future trends in demand, there are probably greater difficulties in making " correct " depreciation allowances here than in the cases already considered.

Fig. 4 illustrates the case in point. As in the other Figures, investment takes place at X. The level of the unit's working costs (excluding depreciation) is represented by the line AB. The level of revenue which was expected to be earned at the time of investment is again represented by the line CD. At the time of investment it was hoped to earn sufficient revenue out of the area CAO to meet fully this item of depreciation due to changes in demand. Given our assumption of a stable price-level, there is no difficulty about how much the *total* allocation towards depreciation should be. As regards spreading such allocations between different times, assuming that eventualities take their expected course, and that revenues fall in the manner expected, *e.g.*, along COD, it is clear that, as in previous cases already dealt with, far larger surpluses are being earned in the earlier than in the later part of the asset's life. Also a larger proportion of the asset's total capacity to earn revenue is being lost in the earlier than in the later years of its life. At the end of the fifth year, for example, its total future revenue-earning prospects (C_5A_5O) are substantially less than half what they were at the outset. This calls for much larger allocations to depreciation in the earlier than in the later years. Indeed, in the later years it would not be possible to earn anything like what it would be necessary to put aside per annum *on an average*, in order to build up the requisite and necessary amount. Of necessity, therefore, more should be put aside in the earlier than in the later part of the asset's revenue-earning life, the actual amounts per accounting period reflecting the fall in value that has taken place as the result of reduced future revenue-earning prospects.

But there is never any certainty either that demand will take the course originally forecast or indeed that the asset will earn the total net revenues originally expected of it at all. It is the effect that these *unexpected* changes in demand should, in the writer's view, have upon depreciation policy that will now be considered.

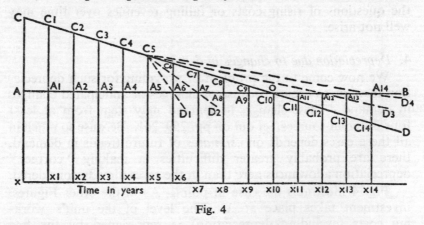

Fig. 4

Let us suppose that after the fifth year of operation the demand for the services provided by the unit unexpectedly and drastically fell off, so that by the end of the sixth year revenue had fallen below the level of working costs. This turn of events is illustrated in Fig. 4 by the level of revenue at C_5 turning downwards along the line C_5D_1. It will be seen that the results of this fall are, first, that the asset would have to be abandoned as being no longer capable of earning any surplus revenue whatever after the sixth year of operation, and secondly, that the total surplus earned by the asset during its economic life would have been reduced to the area CAA_6C_5 instead of the expected CAO. What effect should this changed demand have upon depreciation allowances? Much depends, of course, upon the time at which it became apparent that this change in demand was going to take place. Suppose, for example, at the end of the first accounting period (at $X1$) it was clearly foreseen that demand would in all probability fall off after the fifth year in the manner suggested. This changed view of the future would in itself, it is suggested, justify larger allocations to depreciation. For during the accountancy period in question, the future revenue-earning prospects of the asset had diminished substantially and a commensurate depreciation allowance should be made. Indeed, the amount of depreciation to be paid in all subsequent years might have to be stepped up substantially above the level originally planned. Were it thought, on the other hand, that demand would fall away along C_5D_2 only, it would not have to be stepped up so much. Similarly, were future prospects to improve and net revenues larger than originally planned for were now forecast (say along C_5D_3 or even C_5D_4), there would at least be justification for reducing depreciation payments below what had been originally planned and to that extent for paying higher dividends also.

In short, if, during any one accounting period, " confidence " in the future net earnings of an asset declines, that in itself would seem to justify an increase in the depreciation allowance, whether that confidence derives from revised estimates of the future course of demand or indeed of the future supply price of working costs. Similarly, if future prospects increase, smaller allocations towards depreciation are equally justified.

It has so far been assumed that the change of view of the future course of demand took place at the end of the first accountancy period (at $X1$), so that consequential adjustments in depreciation policy could be made forthwith. But it often happens that changes in demand take place suddenly and unexpectedly. Suppose, for example, the fall of demand down C_5D_1 had not been foreseen until the end of the fourth (at $X4$) or even fifth ($X5$) accounting period, then it might be too late to find sufficient revenue to replace the loss in value sustained, even if no payment of dividends were made. An unrecovered loss in value would have been sustained, and the objective of maintaining the original value of the asset would not have been achieved. Thus, the sooner any deviation from originally expected demand can be foreseen, the greater the chance of being able to make the adjustments required by that objective.

To sum up, depreciation as a cost cannot be measured in

terms of money apart from some defined objective. Given an
objective, however, then it can be determined or rather estimated
in the light of three quite different factors. The first of these is
wear and tear, resulting from use—a " user " cost. The second
is wear and tear due to exposure to the elements—essentially a
function of time, as opposed to use, though related to the maximum capacity for which equipment is provided. The expiry of
legal rights, being also a function of time, requires somewhat
similar treatment to the latter. Finally, anticipated changes in
future demand, for whatever cause, may have drastic effects upon
capital values, and therefore have a direct bearing upon what
should be set aside in respect of depreciation.

Significance of Depreciation Accounting
—with Special Reference to
Plant Replacement *

By W. A. Paton

Professor Emeritus of Accounting,
University of Michigan

THERE continues to be a great deal of sloppy thinking and careless description with respect to the subject of depreciation cost, leading at times to serious misunderstanding and questionable policies. This condition is especially noticeable among economists and financial experts who have never taken the trouble to master the fundamentals of accounting, but it must be admitted that accountants themselves have contributed substantially to the confusion. The writer believes that it is worthwhile, accordingly, to make another effort in the direction of clarification, at the level of underlying concepts and procedures, and this is a major objective of this paper.

What is depreciation cost? At bottom there is nothing puzzling or controversial about depreciation, despite the countless pages that have been written which treat the subject as something mysterious and argumentative. Depreciation is simply plant cost (or value) in the absorbed or expired stage. The periodic depreciation charge is a portion or section—in dollar terms—of the package of plant facilities employed in business operation. Depreciation is plant capacity consumed, and the slice consumed is of the same prosaic substance as the rest of the loaf.

Depreciation is explicit, out-of-pocket cost. As indicated by the above definition, depreciation is an actual, explicit cost; depreciation is not a phoney, assumed, or hypothetical charge. It follows that it is erroneous to contrast depreciation with other charges by stating that it is "not an out-of-pocket cost." It requires actual expenditure of funds to acquire the furnace just

---

* Taken, with minor changes, from *Federal Tax Policy for Economic Growth and Stability*, pp. 528–538. (Printed for Joint Committee on the Economic Report, Government Printing Office, November 9, 1955.)

as it does to acquire the coal used, and a portion of the cost of the furnace represents expenditure just as clearly and definitely as does a portion of the cost of a shipment of coal. It is true, of course, that the expenditures for coal may be more frequently recurring than the expenditures for furnaces, but one cost is no less real and valid than the other.

All costs are on same footing. There has been so much exaggeration of the special nature of depreciation that the fact that all costs of production are on the same basis, fundamentally, deserves emphasis. Periodic income accounting consists essentially of the matching of the revenues realized and recognized in the period with the associated costs—the charges reasonably assignable to such revenues. In this process there is no difference between the significance and effect of one class of charge as compared with another. If any actual cost or a part thereof is omitted, earnings applicable to stockholders' equity will be overstated, and such overstatement—if substantial—may lead to misunderstanding and unwise decisions on the part of management or other interested parties. (One very definite result of such an omission might be an increase in income taxes.) But this is just as true of the cost of employees' services or coal burned as it is of the cost of plant capacity. Each dollar of expense bears the same relation to the total revenue received and the net income realized as every other dollar so charged. The same may be said where operation results in a net loss. Suppose, for example, that the flow of revenue from customers in a particular period amounts to $90,000 and that the total of all applicable deductions (including plant cost—depreciation—of $10,000) is $100,000, with a consequent loss of $10,000. In this situation there is no point to such observations as " we broke even except for depreciation " or " we recovered all expenditures from customers other than depreciation." The actual fact is that revenues were sufficient to cover 90 per cent. of each and every type of applicable cost, including plant consumed.

Depreciation is not an optional cost, a borderline cost, a take-it-or-leave-it charge. There is nothing imaginary about plant facilities and such facilities cannot be dispensed with in carrying on operations; hence the cost of such facilities cannot reasonably be ignored or put in a subordinate position in computing income.

It is true, of course, that special problems are associated with the measurement of the portion of plant cost appropriately assignable to the revenues of the particular year or other account-ing period. A unit of plant may be regarded as a bundle of services, to be received subsequent to installation, but there may well be considerable uncertainty as to what will be the intensity of use from period to period and what will be the total time through which the particular facility will be effective. Coal is consumed in physical instalments, and this affords a satisfying basis on which to measure the amount requisitioned and burned in a particular year. The furnace, on the other hand, is used in its entirety to furnish a series of services, and it may weigh about as much at retirement as at date of acquisition. Here too, however, there has been a tendency to overemphasize minor differences. Basically it is services that are desired and received in the case of the coal pile as well as in the case of the furnace—the principal differences being the frequency of renewal and the degree of physical transformation resulting from use. Moreover, there is plenty of room for argument as to the amount of coal—in dollars—which should be charged to operations in the particular period. Coal in stock is subject to deterioration and there has been a great deal of controversy regarding the pricing-out process (in the case of all types of inventory).

" *Reserve* " *for depreciation.* Much of the confusion regarding the nature and significance of depreciation accounting no doubt originates in unfortunate procedure and bad terminology—the indirect method of crediting plant account for estimated accrued depreciation plus the use of the word " reserve " in describing the account credited. On every hand one finds examples of misunderstanding in this connection. To illustrate with one case. Some years ago a New York attorney (a very able chap) was elected chairman of the board of a certain company. He took the assignment seriously and shortly after his election spent a week at the company's office, studying the recent financial reports and other accounting data available. Just before returning to New York, he called in the controller and executive vice-president and told them that he had been carefully going over the accounts and statements and had been shocked to discover that the " reserve for depreciation " of $14,000,000 was missing. " I can't find this fund anywhere ", he told them, and then he added bluntly, and with a bit of table pounding by way of emphasis: " I've got to leave for New York but I'm coming back in two weeks and if that reserve hasn't been located by then someone is going to jail." The controller finally was obliged to take the time to prepare a funds statement covering the entire history

of the company for the chairman's examination, and even though
he was disarmed somewhat by this presentation it is safe to say
that he never clearly understood the " reserve for depreciation."

The technical accounting for depreciation literally has nothing
to do with the accumulation of funds. The " reserve " or " allowance " to which estimated plant cost consumed is conventionally
credited is simply an offset to the plant account; far from representing a fund, it measures the " hole in the doughnut ", as
Professor Hatfield put it years ago. It's a case of the use of the
sectional-bookcase method of accounting for plant cost; cost as
incurred is recorded in one section, and absorbed or expired
cost in another.   Assume, to illustrate, that a furnace costs
$100,000 and that the portion of such cost properly attributable to
operation in the first period of use is $10,000.   The indirect method
of crediting plant under these conditions may be indicated as
follows :

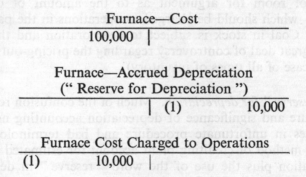

Furnace—Cost

| 100,000 |

Furnace—Accrued Depreciation
(" Reserve for Depreciation ")

| | (1) | 10,000 |

Furnace Cost Charged to Operations

| (1) | 10,000 | |

The first two of these accounts taken together constitute the
furnace account. The first section shows the total cost of the
furnace when acquired; the second shows the amount of such
total cost which has been consumed in operation; the two taken
together show the unabsorbed balance of $90,000. To label this
second section " reserve ", as is frequently done in American
practice, is of course absurd, and is almost bound to lead to
confusion—especially when this section is reported as an independent account, apart from the other section to which it is related.

In the case of the cost of coal (and other kinds of inventory),
in contrast, direct subtraction rather than offsetting is the conventional procedure. It would be quite possible, however, to
record coal consumed in the same way as plant consumed is
ordinarily booked. Assume, for example, that a company buys
a stock of coal at a cost of $40,000 and that the estimated amount
consumed in the following period is $20,000. Applying the

offsetting procedure these data would appear in the accounts as follows:

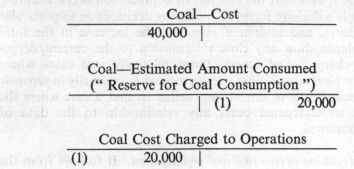

Coal—Cost

40,000 |

Coal—Estimated Amount Consumed
(" Reserve for Coal Consumption ")

| (1)   20,000

Coal Cost Charged to Operations

(1)   20,000 |

It is a fair guess that if the above were the established procedure for recording coal consumed—and especially if the title shown in parentheses were used—there would be as much confused talk about coal " reserves " and " coal replacement funds " as we find in the area of the furnace account and furnace cost consumed.

Recognising depreciation does not provide funds. Many people appear to believe that the process of depreciation accounting— accruing depreciation—automatically provides funds, and that all that is necessary to obtain more money is to accrue more depreciation. This is a completely mistaken view. Accounting is an important instrument of business administration but fortunately or unfortunately it has no magic power. Funds are provided by the delivery of product to customers at a price, not by accounting. Moreover, there is very little realism in the notion that the flow of funds from customers can be increased merely by increasing the amount of plant cost charged to current operations. No doubt there are some roundabout relationships between cost accounting and the volume of receipts from customers, but it is day-dreaming to imagine that such receipts increase or decrease automatically as depreciation cost is increased or decreased.

Moreover, the recognition of depreciation cost—plant capacity consumed—has no direct relation to what becomes of the money received from customers. Fund utilization is a fairly complex process, and the details will vary with changing conditions and changing managerial attitudes. Receipts from customers are used to pay current accounts as they fall due, including payroll, taxes, etc., to pay interest on loans, to reduce long-term debt or redeem preferred shares, to expand inventories, to acquire additional plant facilities or other noncurrent resources, to pay dividends, to build up cash backlog. In this over-all process, it is seldom if ever that the amount of depreciation accrued during the year is a decisive factor in moulding decisions as to particular expenditures, and seldom if ever will the increase in the total cash balance show any close relationship to the current depreciation charge. And among those relatively rare cases where funds for plant acquisitions are segregated temporarily in separate bank accounts, it is almost impossible to find a case where the amount so segregated bears any relationship to the data of plant consumed.

Depreciation accounting and replacement. If follows from the foregoing that the relationship between depreciation accounting and the timing and financing of replacements is by no means as close as is commonly assumed. Systematic recognition of depreciation is necessary as one step in the process of compiling the costs assignable to revenue and determining the magnitude of periodic net earnings (or loss). And the technical accounting for depreciation, in the strict sense, is in no way affected by the possibility of replacement or the conditions of replacement (except as such factors may modify service life of property in use). Indeed, depreciation accounting will follow the pattern outlined earlier even where there is a virtual certainty that the depreciating property will *not* be replaced. Take, for example, the case of a mining shaft constructed for the purpose of exploiting a mineral deposit which will be exhausted at the planned rate of extraction long before there would be any need for rebuilding the shaft. In this situation, it is necessary to recognise the depreciation of shaft periodically, in the determination of total operating cost, notwithstanding the fact that the depreciating asset will never be replaced; and the accounting procedure will not be changed in any way by the fact that no replacement is contemplated.

Importance of replacement cost. The preceding statement is not intended as an effort to minimize the importance of the process of plant renewal and the level of replacement cost. Properly interpreted as *the cost of replacing the capacity to serve represented in existing plant facilities* such cost is of outstanding significance to management. Current replacement cost is important in planning property utilization, in making departmental comparisons, in pricing policies, in determining insurable value, in setting up maintenance standards, in deciding when to retire, and so on. Indeed, in any period of rapid technological change and sharply moving prices, it is imperative that the data of replacement cost (properly defined) be made continuously available as a basis for administrative decisions. (And if the accountant isn't man enough to supply the necessary information, somebody else will have to undertake the job.)

It is important to note that the replacement cost referred to is not the estimated cost of replacing the furnace or other plant asset at the end of the estimated service life, perhaps many years in the future. It is hardly worth while even to attempt to guess what amount will have to be expended say ten years hence to replace the capacity to render service embodied in an existing facility. Those who define replacement cost in this way and then object to the use of such data in accounting are simply shooting arrows at a man of straw of their own making. The most significant fact to management—and to all others financially interested— is the *current* level of the plant cost required to carry on production. That is the cost that is reflected in new construction and equipment purchases; that is the cost that is most influential in the market process and is the most meaningful guide to decisions. As has been pointed out many times by economists, it is not what some unit of plant *did* cost but what it *would* cost currently to acquire the unit (or the capacity represented) that is significant (assuming, of course, a relatively free, competitive market structure). To refer to a homely example, a person renting an automobile recognises that in fixing the rent it is not what he paid for the car that is important but rather the current cost of cars capable of rendering the same service.

To clinch the matter, it should only be necessary to point out that a business enterprise cannot be regarded as operating successfully in a particular year unless the current flow of revenue from customers is sufficient to cover the current cost of labour and other services, the current cost of materials consumed, and the *current cost of plant capacity consumed*, as well as taxes and other charges, and provide a capital-attracting level of net earnings for stockholders. Many business enterprises, of course, do not achieve a condition of successful operation in this sense every year, and many may fail to reach this standard for several successive years (and some never reach it), but there is little room for argument with respect to the general conditions necessary to justify the conclusion that the business is being conducted successfully.

Should depreciation charges be based on current replacement cost? This brings us to the much discussed question: should periodic depreciation of plant facilities be computed as a slice of the number of dollars expended at date of acquisition to acquire the facilities, or as a slice of the number of dollars which would be required currently to replace the particular facilities (in the sense of capacity). This has always been a live subject in certain quarters but interest in it has been greatly intensified as a result of the severe and sustained advance in the level of prices in the last two decades.

Extended discussion of the matter is not feasible in this paper but a few observations are in order. As indicated above, plant capacity consumed expressed in current cost is a more significant managerial figure than plant consumed expressed in the recorded dollars at date of acquisition (so-called " actual " cost). The costs deducted from revenue to cover personal services, materials, etc., are largely current in character (having been incurred, usually, either in the period in which charged off or in the immediately preceding period), and it can be argued that a more meaningful figure of earnings results if the cost of plant consumed is also put on a current basis. In this country, however, this is not generally accepted accounting practice, and such procedure has thus far not been countenanced for income tax purposes. In the years 1946–1948, it is true, a number of prominent U.S. corporations made a start in this direction in their published income statements, but the movement did not " catch on ", in part as a result of opposition from professional accountants and government agencies, and a shift of attention to the possibilities of " accelerated " depreciation in the case of new construction and new acquisitions. There is an alternative to specific replacement cost depreciation, moreover, which produces somewhat similar results and yet can be defended as being within the settled framework of a financial accounting structure rooted in " actual cost." This alternative approach to a very real problem of measurement has long been orthodox procedure in a number of foreign countries and deserves serious consideration in accounting practice and in the measurement of taxable income in the United States. The balance of this paper will be concerned largely with this possible method of amending and improving ordinary depreciation accounting, with special emphasis on the sound determination of taxable income.

Currency debasement and accounting. The change in the price level in the last twenty years represents or reflects a change in the monetary unit employed in this country. We continue to use the old name, the " dollar," but the current dollar is hardly a close relative of the pre-war 1940 dollar. The erosion of the purchasing power of our currency, it is true, has not been as serious as the erosion that has occurred with respect to many foreign monetary units, but a decline in value of 50 to 60 per cent. is a serious change, not to be shrugged off.

This development has created a very real problem of measurement for accountants, and as yet no decisive steps have been taken to meet the difficulty. Accountants are very meticulous in their handling of accounts expressed in part in foreign currencies, and insist on careful conversion of dissimilar units to a common denominator. No accountant—or anyone else—would think of adding one French franc and one U.S. dollar together and calling the result " two dollars." And even where the same name is used, and the difference in value is slight, as in the case of the present-day U.S. and Canadian dollars, no public accountant employed by an American company with a Canadian branch would permit a financial statement to go out over his name without careful conversion of every figure originally expressed in Canadian dollars into its equivalent number of U.S. dollars. At the same time our accountants have thus far shown little or no hesitation in adding one 1940 domestic dollar to one 1960 domestic dollar, for example, and reporting the result as " two dollars," without qualification or explanation.

Correct measurement of " actual cost " of plant and plant consumed. In financial accounting the difficulty posed by the change in the value of the dollar focuses in the measurement of cost—" actual cost "—and the major problem in this area in turn is that of measuring total plant cost and cost of plant periodically consumed, as plant account is the outstanding example of a record consisting—in the raw—of an array of heterogeneous dollars. Other cost factors, in general, are renewed at frequent intervals, and hence the accounts with such factors are, for the most part, expressed at least roughly in current, homogeneous monetary units.

It should hardly be necessary to state that it is unsound measurement, unsound statistical practice, to combine unlike measuring units without a process of conversion. In the field of physical measurement the need for conversion of unlike units to a common denominator is universally recognized. Thus no one would dream of adding short tons and long tons, or metres and yards, without conversion. And in the field of financial measurement, conversion is an old story, in measuring changes in real wages, in farm prices, in exports and imports, in gross national product, and so on. Indeed about the only spot where we have persistently avoided such conversion and kept our heads in the sand—despite the efforts of many writers and special professional committees—is in the area of business accounting, especially in the matter of income determination.

To make my point entirely clear, I want to present a simple example. Assume that a building were erected with a width of 100 feet and that some time thereafter the foot was officially shortened to six inches. At this point a second building is built alongside the first of the same width (and precisely the same in every respect). This second building is evidently 200 short feet wide, or 100 long feet wide, whichever way you care to put it, and the first building may be similarly and accurately described. Now the problem arises of measuring the *total* frontage of the two buildings, in terms of the prevailing short foot. As shown by the accompanying diagram and table, it would be a sheer inaccuracy to combine the original records of width without conversion. The result of adding the unlike measuring units, 300 feet, is an arithmetic monstrosity, with no meaning whatever. The obviously correct total, expressed in short feet, is 400 feet.

TOTAL WIDTH OF TWO ADJACENT BUILDINGS

If Building No. 1 is 100 long feet wide and Building No. 2 is 200 short feet wide:

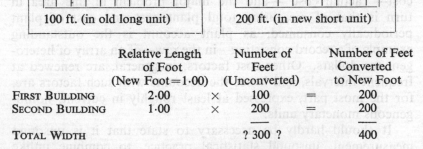

	Relative Length of Foot (New Foot=1·00)		Number of Feet (Unconverted)		Number of Feet Converted to New Foot
FIRST BUILDING	2·00	×	100	=	200
SECOND BUILDING	1·00	×	200	=	200
TOTAL WIDTH			? 300 ?		400

Now *precisely the same problem* arises in describing the total cost of two buildings originally expressed in dissimilar monetary units. Let's assume that the first building referred to above was erected in 1940 at a cost of 100,000 1940 dollars and that the second building was built in 1960 at a cost of 200,000 1960 dollars. (Construction costs have, of course, much more than doubled since 1940, but this fact is ignored for the sake of simplicity.) Under these circumstances, as shown emphatically by the accompanying diagram and table, it is a downright misstatement to allege that the total cost of the two buildings is $300,000. This figure is meaningless. One can truthfully say that one building cost 100,000 1940 dollars and the other 200,000 1960 dollars *but these figures cannot properly be combined without conversion* one way or the other. Assuming that one 1940 dollar is worth two 1960 dollars the obviously correct total of " actual cost " expressed in 1960 dollars is 400,000.

TOTAL COST OF TWO ADJACENT BUILDINGS

If Building No. 1 cost $100,000 in 1940 dollars and Building No. 2 cost $200,000 in 1960 dollars (assuming one 1940 dollar equals two 1960 dollars):

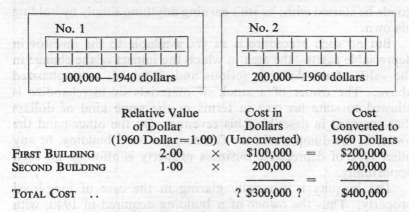

	Relative Value of Dollar (1960 Dollar=1·00)		Cost in Dollars (Unconverted)		Cost Converted to 1960 Dollars
FIRST BUILDING	2·00	×	$100,000	=	$200,000
SECOND BUILDING	1·00	×	200,000		200,000
TOTAL COST ..			? $300,000 ?	=	$400,000

And it follows that in determining the annual depreciation charge—the fraction of capacity consumed—on an *actual cost* basis, it is necessary to compute the charge in terms of the converted total to find a correct figure. Assume, to illustrate, that 4 per cent. of cost is a reasonable estimate of periodic depreciation. To take 4 per cent. of the summation of originally recorded dollars, without conversion, results in the clearly inaccurate figure of $12,000. The correct figure is either 8,000 1940 dollars (converting backward) or 16,000 1960 dollars (using the current unit as the common denominator).

It was noted above that construction costs have more than doubled since 1940. It should also be pointed out that the relation of 1940 and 1960 dollars assumed in this example does not correspond to the change that has occurred in any of the general price indexes during the period covered.

Inventory cost and plant cost. There is a major inequity in our present tax structure in that owners of depreciable assets are placed at a serious disadvantage as compared to investors in inventories of materials and merchandize. Inventories are seldom held more than a year or so and this means that in this area relatively current dollars of cost are deducted from current dollars of revenue. Morcover, through the use of the LIFO procedure authorised by Congress some years ago the process of matching current revenues with current costs is facilitated for owners of inventoriable assets. Under this procedure the taxpayer is permitted to measure the cost of goods sold in terms of the costs most recently incurred, and thus serious overstatement of income is usually avoided. The LIFO treatment rests on the view that a taxpayer is not making any money to the extent that receipts from customers are absorbed in replacing the stock of goods he started with; he isn't earning anything simply by holding his own.

But no such procedure is as yet available to the investor in depreciable assets—the area in which the impact of the change in the value of the dollar is serious and sustained, as emphasized above. The owner of a stock of materials or merchandize is allowed to state his cost in terms of the same kind of dollars that are used in describing his revenues. On the other hand the owner of the dump truck, the furnace, the hotel building, or any other type of depreciable business property is afforded no such opportunity.

The inequity is especially glaring in the case of long-lived property. Thus the owner of a building acquired in 1940, with cost recorded in 1940 dollars, is required by the present tax structure to treat one current dollar of revenue as the full equivalent of one 1940 dollar of investment. He is assumed to be breaking even when he is recovering less than half of his actual investment. This situation is unsound and unjust.

There are many cases throughout the business field where the major investment is in the form of long-lived depreciable property, and there are still many cases where the major part of the total plant capacity is represented by facilities acquired in pre-war days. The outstanding examples are, of course, found among the railways, telephone companies, and electric, gas, and water utilities, where a very large part of the total resources employed is represented by plant facilities with a typical service life of twenty-five years or more. Companies in these areas, moreover, operate with their selling prices under rigorous control. There has already been an enormous erosion of real capital in these enterprises, and if such concerns are to continue to attract private capital, under a sound capital structure, it is imperative that they be permitted to retain from revenues, not subject to tax, the funds necessary to make good the plant investment consumed in rendering service, measured in the same kind of dollars as are being received from customers.

In amending the Internal Revenue Code in 1951, Congress took a small step in the right direction with respect to home owners in providing that if an owner sells his property there is no taxable gain if the proceeds of sale are invested in another residence. This recognizes, implicitly, the point that the writer is urging: namely, that a taxpayer realizes no gain from the disposition of an asset if the entire proceeds are needed to maintain the integrity of the purchasing power invested—the *actual cost* of the property. This principle should be extended by Congress to all depreciable property, including recognition of the fact that gradual disposition of an asset through use in producing revenue over a period of years is on all fours, as far as equity is concerned, with a lump-sum disposition by sale.

One way to remedy matters—perhaps the most practicable— would be to grant a procedure akin to LIFO for the purpose of measuring periodic depreciation. This would at least tend to eliminate the favouritism shown to the investor in merchandise and materials as compared to the investor in plant facilities in the present tax structure.

Again the question of replacement funds. It should be emphasized that permitting the taxpayer owning plant facilities a depreciation deduction *based on actual cost*, correctly measured, as recommended above, would not assure the collection from customers of an amount sufficient to replace the capacity consumed when retirement of existing facilities is acquired. Correct measurement of cost will prevent the overstatement of net earnings (or understatement of losses), and likewise prevent confiscation of capital via the income tax in terms of year-by-year calculations, but correct accounting—as explained earlier—will not in itself provide the volume of revenues necessary to produce a level of net earnings sufficient to justify the description " successful operation." Moreover, where there is sustained inflation, amounting to a continuing erosion of the value of the dollar, there may unavoidably be a serious erosion of capital invested. In a competitive market there may be reasonable expectation, speaking generally, of a selling price sufficient to cover total cost correctly measured in current dollars, plus adequate earnings, but there is no reason to assume that the customer can be assessed with the additional amount needed to make up past deficiencies. It is highly desirable that cost be measured correctly in a period of inflation, and that tax deductions be based on such correct measurements, but no formula of computation—including the use of specific replacement cost as a depreciation base—can assure receipt of funds adequate to cover cost of replacing capacity when the date of retirement rolls around.

In other words, the risks of business operation are not removed by accurate annual measurement of cost and tax deductions based on such measurement.

Spreading plant cost over service life. In the foregoing, I have not attempted to deal with the important topic of estimating service life and methods of spreading total plant cost over estimated life. It should be recognized that even if correct overall measurement of depreciation, in uniform dollars, is provided for, the problem of spreading the total depreciable cost of a facility over the useful life remains. With respect to methods of spreading, it is this writer's opinion that the matter should be left primarily to the taxpayer and his accountant within broad limits. The simple straightline procedure, with service life conservatively estimated, seems to me to be adequate in many cases. On the other hand, I have no major objection to the use of a systematic decreasing-charge procedure, particularly for specialized equipment with a highly uncertain service life, as provided in the present U.S. Tax Code.

Depreciation, Income Taxes and Growth *

By Sidney Davidson
Professor of Accounting,
University of Chicago.

DEPRECIATION is probably the most discussed and most disputatious topic in all accounting. The literature on accounting theory, which we like to think is happily unencumbered by income tax considerations, is studded with depreciation references, and optimum procedures for depreciable assets are still far from settled. In his pleasing essay of a score of years ago, Professor Hatfield pointed out some thirty-six different suggested approaches to accounting for depreciation.[1] The two decades that have passed since its publication have served only to multiply the views on the subject. When income tax considerations, with taxes at their current high levels, are introduced into the scene, the controversy over depreciation becomes more heated. This paper will consider the role played by depreciation in the tax laws; the effect of accelerated depreciation provisions in the tax laws on investment decisions; and the special problems posed for the accountant by these tax provisions.

Much of the income tax controversy over depreciation stems from a basic conflict over philosophies of public finance. We can recognize two basically different views with regard to the income tax. The extreme positions are:

(1) A tax on income is an equitable means of raising revenue and the tax should be based on income determined as realistically and accurately as possible. Such a tax will certainly produce important economic effects, but to promote and preserve public acceptance of the tax, income subject to tax should be defined without regard to these effects.

* A paper given at a Stamp-Martin seminar at Incorporated Accountants' Hall, London, May 9, 1957, and published in *Accounting Research*, July 1957. Financial assistance from the John Simon Guggenheim Memorial Foundation is gratefully acknowledged. The international comparisons would not have been possible without the generous assistance of many people. Special help was received from Ralph Waller and Jacques Ruel (France), J. G. Detiger (Netherlands), Nils Norregaard (Denmark) and Professor Nils Vasthagen and Per Hanner (Sweden).

[1] Henry R. Hatfield, "What They Say about Depreciation," *The Accounting Review*, March 1936, p. 18.

(2) The tax is designed to produce revenue, but also to influence the pattern of economic affairs. Income should be defined in such a way as to make more likely certain specifically desired economic results.

There is no doubt of an increasing trend in the direction of the second position, and I must confess I am basically sympathetic to it, but with an accountant's hesitancy. However, it does present a danger that must be recognized. The Royal Commission on Taxation put the point well when it said:

> The principle of equity as between taxpayers, the principle that persons with equal incomes should bear an equal burden of tax, has been a strong foundation of the United Kingdom income tax system.... The effective collection of income tax depends in great measure upon its acceptability and that, in turn, depends upon its reputation for fairness and impartiality. This argues for finding vehicles other than the tax system to convey the state's encouragement of particular economic purposes.[2]

The problem becomes more acute if we make the reasonable assumption that the revenue needs of government are not likely to be affected by the definition of income in the tax law. Then special treatment for one group is likely to result in a heavier tax burden for all others, unless the special treatment increases the tax base, represses inflation, or produces some similar result.

This problem of special treatment has served more as a brake on the extent of action than as an absolute barrier to tax revision, and the post-war years have been marked throughout the world by alterations in the procedures for defining income for tax purposes designed to achieve specific, non-revenue purposes. Depreciation policy has been widely recognized as one of the areas in which tinkering with the definition of income may produce desirable economic effects. In fact, in almost every Western country where modification of the income tax has been attempted in the post-war years, depreciation policy has been one of the major areas of action. Some of the actions have been at least partly designed to improve income measurement, but a second look shows that every change sought, in greater or smaller degree, to influence the amount of capital formation—usually to increase it and speed up the rate of growth of productive capacity, but occasionally to restrain investment in the face of inflationary conditions.

The way these results are achieved depends on the way the three basic depreciation questions are answered:

[2] Royal Commission on the Taxation of Profits and Income, 1955, Cmd. 9474, p. 127, para. 416.

(1) What figure should be used as the depreciation base—historic cost, replacement cost, or some other variant?

(2) What time period should be used for writing-off the depreciation base?

(3) What pattern of annual write-offs should be used over this life?

On the first issue, France offers the most conspicuous example of adjustments of the depreciation base to reflect advancing prices, but Belgium, Germany, Italy and Japan have all made at least some moves in this direction. The English-speaking and Scandinavian nations have all adhered to the monetary cost base. Investment allowances may constitute a formal exception to this second statement, but since the rate of allowance is not normally linked in any specific way to changes in prices, systems incorporating investment allowances are still basically historical cost systems.

With regard to depreciation time periods, Sweden was unique in allowing taxpayers complete freedom in the setting of working lives. France, Denmark and the Netherlands allow some freedom, but Canada, England and the United States are virtually inflexible in these working-life estimates.

The greatest activity has been centred in action on the pattern of depreciation charges. Sweden permitted complete freedom in this sphere also. Canada and the United States have shifted from reliance on straight-line methods to permitting the use of the declining-balance method or some variant of it. England has experimented with various forms of initial and investment allowances, as have the Danes, the Dutch and many others.

Table 1 sets forth the provisions of several of the countries in somewhat more formal fashion. In general, the methods illustrated are the most generous provisions available for machinery and equipment.

Lines 1 to 3 illustrate the American methods to the present. Line 1 shows the traditional American straight-line method. Line 2 is an example of an arbitrary definition of depreciation life used in World War II and more sparingly since 1950—five years in this instance. Lines 8, 9 and 10 are other examples of arbitrary statements of working lives. Line 3 illustrates the nonsensical sum-of-the-years-digits method specifically recognized in the United States Tax Code of 1954.[3]

---

[3] The declining-balance method with rates twice those used in the straight-line method was also specifically recognized. Since the sum-of-the-years'-digits method shows a slightly greater amount of acceleration in almost all cases and has been more widely adopted in the United States, it is used in all the illustrations.

TABLE 1

NOTES ON TAX DEPRECIATION METHODS

(where C=original cost and n=economic service life)

	Basic depreciation rate (r)=to:	Charge, first year	Charge, second year
1. United States straight-line —old requirements ..	$\dfrac{1}{n}$	rC	rC
2. United States defence amortization	$\dfrac{1}{5}$	rC	rC
3. United States accelerated —sum-of-years'-digits	$\dfrac{1}{1+2\ldots+n}$	n (r) C	(n−1)rC
4. British declining-balance —no extra allowance	$\dfrac{5}{4}\left[\dfrac{1-\sqrt[n]{0\cdot1}}{1}\right]$	rC	r(C−rC)
5. British declining-balance —20 per cent. initial allowance	$\dfrac{5}{4}\left[\dfrac{1-\sqrt[n]{0\cdot1}}{1}\right]$	rC+·2C	r(C−(rC+·2C))
6. British declining-balance —20 per cent. investment allowance ..	$\dfrac{5}{4}\left[\dfrac{1-\sqrt[n]{0\cdot1}}{1}\right]$	rC+·2C	r(C−rC)
7. Swedish unrestricted ..	$r \overline{<} 1$	rC	0 or C−rC
8. New Swedish	·3	rC	r(C−rC)
9. Dutch	$\dfrac{1}{n}$	r($\frac{2}{3}$)C+·1C +·04C	same as Year 1*
10. Danish	$\dfrac{1}{n}$	r($\frac{1}{2}$C)+$\frac{1}{3}$($\frac{1}{2}$C)	same as Year 1†

* Investment allowance of 4 per cent. per annum continues for 5 years; $\frac{1}{3}$ C may be written-off in $3\frac{1}{2}$ years, in addition to regular charge of r($\frac{2}{3}$)C.
† $\frac{1}{2}$ C may be written off in 3 years; other $\frac{1}{2}$ C in n years.

British declining-balance methods are indicated in lines 4 to 6.[4] The difference between initial and investment allowances is illustrated by the failure to deduct the ·2C item from the depreciation base in line 6 in the second and subsequent years.

The former unrestricted and the present arbitrary 30 per cent. declining-balance method [5] of Sweden are depicted on lines 7

[4] The 5/4 factor shown on the three lines is not an essential part of the declining balance method. The Income Tax Act of 1945 authorized depreciation rates to be increased by one-quarter, presumably in response to widespread complaints that working-life estimates implicit in the former rates were too long. The assumption of a salvage value of 10 per cent. of cost at the end of normal economic life is prescribed in the law.

[5] The regulations permit an alternative method of calculation of depreciation. If book value of all plant using the 30 per cent. declining-balance method is higher than if a 20 per cent. straight-line method had been used, then book value may be reduced to the lower figure and the additional charge treated as extra depreciation. For an individual asset, use of the alternative method would be desirable in the fourth year and thereafter. Since the calculations are based on plant as a whole, however, the time when a change-over becomes advantageous depends on the pattern of asset acquisitions. In Table 2, the calculations are based on consistent use of the declining-balance method.

and 8. The Dutch have added successive increments of acceleration to their law. In 1949 it was enacted that one-third of cost could be written-off within the first five years, with this acceleration limited (by a later law) to no more than 10 per cent. of cost in any one year. In addition, in 1953 a form of investment allowance was introduced at the rate of 4 per cent. a year for the first five years of the life of an asset. The Danes also divided the cost of the asset—half being written-off over normal life and the other half over a three-year period.

Effect on investment

How likely are these various approaches to contribute to their professed goal of increasing the rate of capital formation and expanding productive capacity more rapidly? Any answer must be given cautiously because of the unsatisfactory state of our present knowledge about the way investment decisions are made, but we can generalize by saying that the methods operate, first, by affecting the desirability of investment through alteration in its relative profitability and, second, by affecting the fiscal possibility of investment by altering the supply of internal funds available to the firm.

Even though all income tax laws permit the recovery of capital (monetary capital, at least) tax free, these depreciation deductions necessarily follow the acquisition of the asset. Thus a firm makes capital formation expenditures currently, and receives in return the right to income tax deductions in subsequent years. Although the sum of these future income tax deductions is equal to the cost of the asset, their present value is, of course, less than its cost. How much less depends upon the depreciation time-period, the depreciation pattern and the rate of discount appropriate to the situation. With these factors known, the present value of these deductions can be arrived at by conventional compound interest calculation.[6]

For example, if an asset costing £100 and with a life of ten years is depreciated on a straight-line basis, £10 of depreciation a year for ten years is allowed. The present value of that series of deductions with a 10 per cent. discount rate is £61, as shown on line 1 of Table 2. That table is a summary of the present values of depreciation deductions under the several methods under consideration. There is an infinite number of present values depending on estimated working lives and discount rates:

---

[6] This approach to the tax consequences of depreciation was first suggested by E. Cary Brown in his essay on " Business-Income Taxation and Investment Incentives " in *Income, Employment and Public Policy*, Norton, 1948, p. 305.

the table merely illustrates the values for assets with ten- and twenty-year working lives under assumptions of 10 per cent. and 15 per cent. discount rates.[7] Thus the present English scheme (line 5a) of a declining-balance method with 20 per cent. initial allowance provides deductions with a present value of 77 per cent. of cost, assuming a ten-year life and a 10 per cent. discount rate, and deductions equal to 58 per cent. of cost if the estimated service life is twenty years and the discount rate 15 per cent.

Unrestricted depreciation under the Swedish system exemplifies one special feature of the calculation process. Although the full cost may be claimed as a deduction in the first year, our assumption is that the tax savings are realized as year-end annuities and thus the full cost is discounted for one period, which at a 10 per cent. rate reduces to a present value of 91 per cent. of cost.[8]

TABLE 2

PRESENT VALUE CALCULATIONS

Present value of depreciation deductions as a percentage of cost

Method	Assuming a ten-year life		Assuming a twenty-year life	
	At a 10 per cent. discount rate	At a 15 per cent. discount rate	At a 10 per cent. discount rate	At a 15 per cent. discount rate
	Percentages			
1. United States straight-line—old requirements	61	50	43	31
2. United States defense amortisation	76	67	76	67
3. United States accelerated—sum-of-years'-digits	70	60	55	43
4. British declining-balance—no extra allowance	72	63	57	48
5a. British declining-balance—20 per cent. initial allowance	77	69	66	58
5b. British declining-balance—40 per cent. initial allowance	82	76	73	66
6. British declining-balance—20 per cent. investment allowance	90	80	75	65
7. Swedish unrestricted	91	87	91	87
8. New Swedish	75	67	75	67
9. Dutch	83	71	71	59
10. Danish	72	63	63	54

[7] Discount rates of 10 per cent. and 15 per cent. were selected as being reasonable approximations of the value of internal funds to many concerns. Clearly, this rate will vary among concerns, and for some even 10 per cent. may be too high a rate and others 15 per cent. too low.

[8] This assumes assets are acquired and paid for on the first day of the fiscal year and tax payments are made on the first day of the next year. The assumption is adhered to in all cases, although there are differences in timing of tax payments among the countries and, more important, differences in the amount of depreciation that may be claimed for acquisitions made during the year. In the

If the marginal income tax rate is known, the present value of the tax reductions associated with any depreciation pattern can be easily calculated. Throughout all the examples that follow a marginal tax rate of 50 per cent. is assumed. Multiplying the figures in Table 2 by that rate gives the present value of the tax savings from the depreciation deductions. The 50 per cent. rate is approximately correct for the United States and the United Kingdom and is not too unreasonable for the other countries cited. If tax rates are higher, the present value of the tax savings is increased; if lower, decreased.

One convenient way of looking at the differences in the present values of tax saving under different patterns is to consider the differences as being akin to differences or changes in the cost of the capital assets; assets that provide tax savings of greater value effectively cost less. Thus a change to a more liberal depreciation pattern logically has the same effect as a reduction in the cost of capital assets. If we compare lines 1 and 5b in Table 2 assuming a ten-year life and a 10 per cent. discount rate, the difference between the two lines is equivalent to a difference in cost of assets of $10\frac{1}{2}$ per cent. In other words, if the selling prices of identical assets in the United States and the United Kingdom were the same in 1951,[9] the difference in the depreciation provision of the tax laws would have made British capital assets effectively cheaper by $10\frac{1}{2}$ per cent.

This analysis suggests that the British Budgetary change of April 1954, when investment allowances were introduced (line 5a changed to line 6), was the equivalent of a $3\frac{1}{2}$ per cent. to $6\frac{1}{2}$ per cent. decrease (depending upon discount rates and working lives) in the cost of machinery and plant, while the Budgetary change of April 1952, when initial allowances were suspended (line 5b changed to line 4), meant that assets effectively increased in cost by 5 per cent. to 8 per cent. Similarly, the 1954 Tax Code of the United States, which recognized the sum-of-the-years'-digits method, made it possible to reduce the effective cost of plant assets by $4\frac{1}{2}$ per cent. to 6 per cent. (line 1 changed to line 3). With any given set of demand and operating conditions, these cost changes affect the relative profitability of investment. Whether the quantities involved are significant enough to change by a

United States, for example, depreciation may be claimed for only that portion of the year of acquisition during which the asset is held; in England, on the other hand, depreciation for a full year is allowed in the year of acquisition without regard to the time during the year that the asset is acquired.

[9] In 1951 straight-line depreciation was in effect in the United States, and declining-balance with a 40 per cent. initial allowance in the United Kingdom.

material amount the volume of investment that would otherwise have been made is open to at least some question.

While present value analysis is the most logical approach to investment planning under conditions of relative certainty, there is considerable evidence that much investment decision-making introduces a prior criterion of protection against loss—that is, a criterion of early recovery of capital. This commonly takes the form of requiring that the capital asset pay for itself in a time period substantially shorter than its economic life, what is known as the " pay-off " test for investments. We can define the " pay-off " period as the time interval over which the new asset produces net cash inflows or reduces cash outflows by an amount equal to its cost. My own limited experience with American businessmen and the fragmentary empirical evidence on business practice in the United Kingdom and the United States indicates that many, if not most, decisions on whether or not to buy machinery with estimated economic service lives of from eight to twenty-five years depend on whether the machinery will pay off in two and a half to five years.

For investors who seek a protection against risk by an early return of capital, accelerated depreciation may be a decisive factor. The greater the amount of depreciation deductions that may be claimed during the pay-off period, the lower the amount of cash generated by the new investment that will be subjected to the tax and the greater the net cash contribution to the pay-off.

Table 3 shows the effect of the several depreciation methods in a simple pay-off situation. It assumes a criterion of a three-year pay-off period and columns 1 and 3 show the annual stream of net cash receipts that would be required during that period for assets with an estimated ten-year and twenty-year working life respectively. To facilitate comparison among the several methods, columns 2 and 4 relate the required revenues for each method to those under the straight-line method. This does not necessarily imply a normative function for the straight-line method, but merely a comparative one. As in Table 2, straight-line is the least generous and Swedish unrestricted the most generous depreciation arrangement, but the relative position of the other methods differs to a considerable degree, depending on the amount of depreciation deductions that can be taken during the three-year pay-off period.

Use of the pay-off criterion suggests that accelerated depreciation may have a greater effect on investment decisions than that indicated by present-value analysis. More than half of the

methods result in reductions in required revenues of more than
20 per cent. as compared with the straight-line method.

TABLE 3

PAY-OFF CALCULATIONS

*Annual net revenues required for a three-year pay-out of a £3,000 asset
assuming a 50 per cent. tax rate*

| Method | Assuming a ten-year life | | Assuming a twenty-year life | |
	Net revenues required (1)	Percentage of straight-line (2)	Net revenues required (3)	Percentage of straight-line (4)
	£	Per cent.	£	Per cent.
1. United States straight-line—old requirements ..	1,700	100·0	1,850	100·0
2. United States defense amortisation	1,400	82·4	1,400	75·7
3. United States accelerated—sum-of-years'-digits ..	1,509	88·8	1,729	93·5
4. British declining-balance—no extra allowance ..	1,422	83·6	1,613	87·2
5a. British declining-balance—20 per cent. initial allowance	1,309	77·0	1,469	79·4
5b. British declining-balance—40 per cent. initial allowance	1,197	70·4	1,325	71·6
6. British declining-balance—20 per cent. investment allowance	1,222	71·9	1,413	76·4
7. Swedish unrestricted ..	1,000	58·8	1,000	54·1
8. New Swedish	1,343	79·0	1,343	72·6
9. Dutch	1,380	81·2	1,480	82·2
10. Danish	1,350	79·4	1,425	77·0

British acceleration methods reduce revenue requirements by
from 8 per cent. to 19 per cent., as compared with the traditional
declining-balance method. There is some reason to feel these
differences are likely to be meaningful in a great variety of cases.

If accelerated depreciation for tax purposes increases the
incentive to invest, what effect does it have on the complementary
question of the financial ability of the business to invest? In a
perfect market with everyone maximizing profit potentials, this
question would never arise. Funds would always be available,
but at a price, and the firm would go on investing until the rate of
return on the intra-marginal investment was equal to the cost of
securing funds. But we know that there are discontinuities in
the supply of funds to many businesses and in their demands for
them. Many smallish businesses are unable to secure capital
from outside, most have preferred net asset structures and there

is generally a bias against resorting to outside funds. The preference for internally generated funds is found everywhere, but it is likely to be felt most keenly by the small, rapidly growing business that finds recourse to the capital markets difficult.

Even in the single-asset cases we have been considering until now there is some interest-free borrowing from the tax authorities. If we shift our attention to the firm as a whole with its complex of assets, it can be seen that in almost all cases that these are not loans but outright grants. Not only will the tax advantages of the transitional period not have to be repaid, but the steadily growing firm will enjoy ever-increasing " tax savings " under all the accelerated depreciation schemes.[10] The availability of these additional funds may be an important factor in investment decisions.

If " normal " depreciation charges are earned, they are available to finance much of the investment of a business. Only that part of investment that results in increased book value of plant gives rise to a financing problem. For a business whose expenditures for plant are growing at a steady rate of 3 per cent., the tax savings enjoyed by using as mildly accelerated a method as sum-of-the-years'-digits instead of the straight-line method are sufficient to finance between 15 per cent. and 20 per cent. (depending upon service life of the assets) of the growth after the transitional period. During the transition to accelerated depreciation, an even greater portion of growth can be financed out of tax savings. More generous acceleration methods will permit even higher degrees of self-financing.

In his excellent analysis of the Swedish economy from 1938 to 1951 under unrestricted depreciation, Professor Vasthagen shows that tax savings under unrestricted depreciation as compared with straight-line depreciation were sufficient to finance from 25 per cent. to 50 per cent. of the growth in the four industries he considered.[11]

If recourse to external finance is necessary, accelerated depreciation may make such funds easier to obtain. Most lenders seek repayment of loans made to finance equipment purchases over a period shorter than the estimated economic service life of the equipment. Accelerated depreciation permits a larger part of the cash inflow generated during the early, debt-repayment years

---

[10] See E. D. Domar, " The Case for Accelerated Depreciation," *Quarterly Journal of Economics*, February 1953, p. 493.

[11] N. Vasthagen, *Free Depreciation*, 1938–1951, Stockholm Business Research Institute, 1953, p. 162. Vasthagen relates the tax savings to total investment, but a comparison with funds required for growth seems more appropriate for our purposes.

to be free of income tax and gives an added protection to the lender.

On both the scores of increased profitability and availability of funds, accelerated depreciation comes off rather well as a factor in investment decision-making. Its importance should not be overstressed, though. Clearly, it docs not produce those technological or product demand conditions that create investment incentives. What it does do, *ceteris paribus*, is to affect the extent to which the income tax is a deterrent to investment. In this sense, it seems to offer a reasonably effective encouragement (or, if operated in reverse, discouragement) to investment and it seems likely that we will see a continued, and perhaps increased, use of acceleration devices.

Accounting effects

All signs point to accelerated depreciation methods for tax purposes remaining as a way of life in our economies characterized by high income tax rates and a striving after rapid growth. What significance will this change have for accounting?

The least disturbing effect will be found in those situations in which previous tax deductions for depreciation understated expirations of economic usefulness and similarly deficient depreciation charges had been recorded in the financial records. Acceleration may be just sufficient to put tax depreciation on a realistic basis, and book depreciation will probably follow suit. There is some reason to believe that the transition from straight-line to double declining-balance may have had this effect in certain instances in the United States.

Far more likely is the situation where the maximum depreciation deductions permitted for tax purposes are in excess of those suggested by reasonably realistic methods of income determination. Initial allowances of 40 per cent. and arbitrary five-year-life estimates for durable equipment clearly fit in this category.

When these conditions obtain, the accountant is faced with the problem of deciding the appropriate relationship between depreciation claimed on the tax return and that shown in the financial records. His freedom of choice may be limited by the national tax law, however. Denmark, France, Holland and Sweden all limit the amount of depreciation deductions on tax returns to the amount of depreciation shown in the financial records. The result in many cases has been to make tax considerations control financial reporting with a consequent diminution of the accountant's independence. Businesses have usually sought the maximum depreciation deductions legally available to them, and financial record keeping has tended to follow suit.

American tax regulations contain only one similar provision, so far as I know. That refers to the related matter of use of the last-in, first-out (LIFO) cost flow assumption for stock valuation.

Canada had a similar restriction introduced in connection with its income tax law revision of 1949. Section 1100 (4) of the revised Income Tax Regulations provided that, in order to be deductible for tax purposes, " capital cost allowances must be shown in the books of account and reflected in the statements." [12] The accounting profession and others protested vigorously and the section was amended in 1950 and finally done away with in 1954.

Sweden has had the longest experience with this type of ruling and with efforts to provide economic incentives in the tax laws. We have already considered unrestricted depreciation formerly available and there also are provisions for a write-down of stocks in trade to figures lower than one-third of cost and for optional substantial charges to income to create pension reserves. Within extremely broad limits, income determination becomes a matter of choice for the directors—they weigh the effect on taxes, the financial markets, labor negotiations and various other factors.

One Swedish business man said recently: " At the end of the fiscal period the directors have to decide how much profit to report. They consider such things as the effect that the reported profit may have on forthcoming wage negotiations, the amount of dividends they want to pay, and a proper relation between dividends and income. When the directors have determined approximately what profit they want to report, they tell the accountant to find the easiest way to adjust the books to achieve the desired figure." Another said: " We determine what profits we want to report, and then tell the accountant to arrive at the chosen figure." [13]

This situation is reflected in the wording of the auditor's report. In place of the required British statement of " a true and fair view of the state of affairs . . . and the profit or loss . . . for the year," in place of the standard American terminology in the auditor's report of " present fairly the financial position and the results of operations," the typical Swedish auditor's report contains the following paragraphs:

[12] A. W. Hamilton, " Section 1100 (4)," *Canadian Tax Journal*, July–August 1954, p. 204.
[13] John P. Shelton, " A Tax Incentive for Stabilizing Business Investment," *National Tax Journal*, September 1956, p. 232.

Our examination has revealed no reason for criticism, either with respect to the accounts and documents presented to us, the Company's accounting procedures, the inventory taken of the Company's assets, or the administration of the Company.

When judging the Company's financial position and the result of its operations during the year, due consideration should be given to the comments in the administration report on the balance sheet and the statement of income.

The comments in the administration report explain to some degree whether plant and inventory charge-offs during the period have been normal, materially greater or less than normal, and so on. As one Swedish registered accountant explained to me, every reader can then make his own adjustments of the reported income figures in the light of these comments. Income determination becomes a matter of personal subjective adjustment of published financial reports.

The lesson for accountants and others interested in reasonable financial reporting seems clear. Efforts to force financial record keeping into the tax-accounting mold are bad enough under ordinary circumstances. Accelerated depreciation for tax purposes intensifies the problem. It would seem obligatory for the accounting profession and all those interested in the effective operation of capital markets to oppose legislative and administrative action that seeks to tie financial record keeping to tax accounting.

If the accountant is not hobbled by these legal enactments, it is likely that a tax system of accelerated depreciation sufficient to encourage growth will result in a difference between the depreciation figure on the income statement and that shown on the tax return. A minimum standard of adequate reporting would call for this difference to be disclosed in the notes to the financial statements.

In countries where the figure for income after taxes is considered significant—in the United States net income after taxes is generally considered to be the most important figure in the financial statements—a substantive problem may arise when book and tax depreciation differ. The income tax charged to income for the period differs from the amount obtained by applying current tax rates to the reported pre-tax income. The difference results, many accountants say,[14] from borrowing tax depreciation deductions from future years to reduce current tax payments. They would recognize an additional current charge against income for income taxes, matched by a liability for deferred taxes. While such an action might be appropriate for

[14] See, for example, M. Moonitz, " Income Taxes in Financial Statements," *The Accounting Review*, April 1957, p. 175.

a single-asset business that foresaw continuing profits and could estimate future tax rates, for most firms such an adjustment would typify excessive conservatism. If the tax provisions with regard to depreciation methods are not altered, the mature, static business will enjoy some transitional gains that are its to keep indefinitely, and in the more typical case of the steadily growing business (growing in terms of monetary investment, at least) these " gains " will continue indefinitely, growing steadily year after year. The two necessary requirements are merely unchanged tax laws and a policy of regular investment in capital goods.[15]

Whether a regular investment policy will be maintained in the future may in some cases give rise to troublesome questions of judgment for the accountant. He may be forced to rely for an answer on expressions of intent by management rather than studying objective evidence. This state of things is always troublesome, but efforts to improve the realism of income-reporting seem to require such action regularly.

Conclusions

Tax laws with regard to depreciation have been gradually evolving for over a century. In recent years there has been a substantial shift to accelerated depreciation methods in order to promote more rapid economic growth. A plausible case can be made for the view that accelerated depreciation for tax purposes encourages investment by increasing profitability and lessening risk as well as by permitting growing firms to finance more of their investment internally. Accelerated depreciation may be expected to remain as a feature of the tax laws of those countries seeking to promote economic growth.

Such tax provision may pose problems for accountants. Where requirements are found that tax and book depreciation must be the same, the effect almost inevitably is to weaken the accountant's independence and to thwart realistic income determination. Where book and tax depreciation differ, the accountant is faced by a difficult judgmental problem of inter-period allocation of income taxes.

[15] See S. Davidson, " Accelerated Depreciation and the Allocation of Income Taxes," *The Accounting Review*, April 1958, p. 173.

Income—True and False*

By David Solomons

Professor of Accounting,
University of Pennsylvania.

No subject has occupied a larger place in accounting literature since the Second World War than the impact of rising prices. And in spite of all the attention it has received, no problem looks so unlikely to be resolved in the near future as the question of what accountants ought to do about it.

The general nature of the difficulty has been stated many times. The purchase of assets at a particular date is normally recorded on the basis of the actual money cost at that date in monetary units (pounds, say) of known purchasing power. If an inflationary rise in price supervenes, it follows that subsequent transactions relating to these assets will be recorded in terms of depreciated pounds. To add or subtract these many different kinds of pounds—some depreciated little, some much, some not at all—must give results whose significance is at the best doubtful, and at the worst positively misleading.

This is the basic problem, but it has many facets. One facet concerns the depreciation of fixed assets. How is provision to be made, in time of high prices and high profits, for the replacement of fixed assets at costs considerably above those at which the assets stand in the books? A second aspect concerns the basis of inventory valuation. Just as fixed assets have to be replaced when they are used up in production, so do stocks of goods have to be replaced when they are sold. In a period of rising prices, the cost of replacing stocks will be greater than the cost of the stock replaced. The conventional method whereby stocks are identified as the last acquired and therefore the most expensive goods still held at the balance-sheet date (in other words, first in, first out) has the effect of charging against the current period's inflated revenue from sales the cost of goods bought at lower prices in the past rather than the higher cost of current " replacement " purchases. The FIFO *v.* LIFO controversy is simply the " inflation and depreciation " problem in a different setting.

* From the *Accountants Journal*, October 1948.

It is not surprising that many more traditionally-minded accountants have been in vehement opposition to what, speaking loosely, we can call the " replacement cost " school of thought. What is surprising is that they have presented so unconvincing a case. Some of their counter-arguments are worth examination.

First, they contend, to depart from " actual cost " as the basis for matching expenditures against revenues in computing net income is to tamper with the factual nature, and therefore the truth, of accounting information. Of course, if this argument were sound, it would be decisive. But it is not sound. It mistakenly identifies " actual costs " with past costs, instead of with the present costs of producing revenue. A rise in the value of our plant consequent on a general rise in prices, and accompanied by a corresponding rise in the sales value of our product, results, no doubt, in an accretion to capital measured in money terms: but it cannot in itself result in an increased real profit from production. The receipt of higher values from sales is matched by the *sacrifice* of higher values in wear and tear of plant. The absolute profit, in money terms, will, of course, be bigger, since if, say, prices double all round, the gap between sales and current costs will also have doubled. It is because depreciation based on original cost will show profits to have more than doubled (since sales will have doubled, and depreciation will have remained unchanged) that it misleads.

A whole crop of objections against " replacement cost " accounting, as we have called it, are concerned with the book-keeping difficulties involved. If, for instance, the profit-and-loss account is debited, during the life of an asset, with depreciation amounting to more in total than the original cost of the asset, once this original cost has been written off by what credit is the depreciation debit to be offset? This is only one of many such questions which have been asked, not always so much in quest of information as to suggest how unthinkable it would be for accounting to abandon original cost as the basis for calculating profit-and-loss debits. These questions are, as a matter of fact, not difficult to answer, and we shall later endeavour to do so. But the importance which many accountants attach to them, as arguments *in themselves* against any departure from the traditional basis of accounting, is significant and disturbing. If a principle is right, mere technical difficulties of giving effect to it by means of a particular technique—in this case the technique of double entry bookkeeping—cannot make it less right. It may be that the technique needs to be supplemented. Double entry is a wonderful servant but a bad master. There are times when one is tempted to take up the cry " A plague on Pacioli! "

Again, it is said, assets may not in fact have to be replaced, or may be replaced by different kinds of assets. Why, then, emphasize the importance of charging the profit-and-loss account with the estimated cost of replacing assets now in course of being used up?

This seems to be a reasonable question, but it springs from a misunderstanding of the nature of the problem. It is true that the particular assets at present in use in a business may not in fact have to be replaced. But the *capital* represented by them must be recovered out of the gross proceeds from the business before that business can be said to have made a profit. And it is not enough merely to recover the same amount of money as was spent on the original assets if, in the meantime, that money has lost part of its purchasing power through a rise in the price-level. It is the amount of purchasing power that was originally invested that has to be recovered. To charge depreciation on the replacement cost [1] of assets, even when the assets are not going to be replaced, is simply a rough and ready way of maintaining real capital intact, and not just money capital.

A fourth type of objection is concerned with the difficulty of prophesying what future costs of replacement of assets will be, since views about the movement of prices in the future cannot be more than intelligent guesswork. How can we calculate an annual instalment of an unknown future amount? And since the future cost of replacement is not and cannot be known, is it not better to abandon the attempt and stick to historical cost as a basis for depreciation?

This argument also has an appearance of weight which is, however, illusory. It is unnecessary to provide now for the *future* cost of replacing an asset. It is sufficient if provision is made on the basis of the present level of costs. Each year, during a period of constantly rising prices, the estimated cost of replacing assets will rise, but the *value* of assets other than those, like cash and debtors, whose money value is fixed, will rise also, and

---

[1] It is not my purpose in this article to examine the various meanings to be attributed to the term " replacement cost." At least two meanings should be distinguished, *viz.*: (1) the actual cost of replacing specific assets, and (2) the number of current pounds or dollars which represent the same amount of generalized purchasing power as that originally invested in the assets at an earlier date. These two meanings will give different results whenever the buying prices of the specific assets held by the firm change more or less than the general price level has done. " Replacement cost " in the present context can have either of these meanings. My own view is that they both have their uses, but they are different uses.

broadly in the same proportion. When depreciation funds are built up, whether they are invested inside or outside the business, they are accumulated by setting aside assets. So long as these accumulated assets are of such a kind that their value is likely to move more or less in line with the asset whose replacement is being provided for, they provide a perfectly good " hedge " against unforeseen movements in the price level. If asset replacement costs rise above present levels, so, it may be hoped, will the realizable value of the assets in the depreciation fund. So long, then, as depreciation charged *now* is sufficient to provide a due proportion of asset costs *now*, future price movements can be left to take care of themselves.

Of course, it is possible that depreciation funds may be " invested " in cash or fixed interest-bearing securities, *i.e.*, in assets which will not appreciate in value however much future replacement costs rise. This means that the business has failed to hedge against future price movements, and a loss may well result. But such a loss must be looked at quite separately—it is not strictly incidental to the problem of providing for asset replacements.

The last objection which we can stop to consider—our list of objections is by no means exhaustive—is concerned with the possible distortion of the balance-sheet which may result from charging against income the cost of replacing assets used up in earning it. The point can be seen most clearly if we suppose that the price history of the years 1919–22 were to be repeated, and that a period of inflation were to be followed by a severe bout of deflation. The cost of replacing assets bought at the height of the inflation would soon be seen to be below the original cost of these assets, and depreciation based on replacement cost would fail to write off the whole of the original asset before the end of its effective life. If the matter is left here, the balance-sheet will accumulate debit balances for assets which have long since ceased to exist.

The same difficulty can be seen even more clearly in relation to current assets. Suppose that inventories at the end of a period are valued on a LIFO basis in order to charge into " cost of sales " the approximate cost of replacing goods sold in the current period. When the peak of the inflation is reached, it is the highest-priced purchases which are being written off to " cost of sales," and stocks are regarded as consisting of earlier purchases bought at lower prices. The balance-sheet may thus contain a substantial secret reserve. This is bad enough. But when inflation turns into deflation, and prices move downward,

LIFO may have the effect of writing off low-cost purchases, leaving earlier high-price purchases high and dry in the balance-sheet. Income may have been correctly stated, but at the expense of leaving current assets in the balance-sheet at anything but conservative values.

Fortunately this objection can be met. In meeting it, we shall also probably set at rest the worst fears of those who feel that in this controversy the sanctity of double entry itself is in peril.

What we need is a method of accounting which will both (a) charge against gross income the real current cost of earning that income, measured in monetary units having the same value as those in which gross income is measured, and (b) as far as possible avoid upsetting the accepted basis of preparing the balance-sheet. Such a method is not difficult to devise. In a period of rising prices, it would consist essentially, whether fixed assets or current assets are concerned, of debiting profit and loss with the *replacement* cost of assets used up, crediting the asset accounts with the *historical* cost of the expired portion of the assets, and crediting the excess of replacement over historical cost to a capital adjustment reserve. Thus, for a fixed asset, the typical entry would be:

Depreciation	Dr.	Based on replacement cost
To Asset		Expired historical cost
„ Capital Adjustment Reserve		Excess of replacement over historical cost

For inventories, the corresponding entry would be:

Cost of sales	Dr.	Replacement (LIFO) cost of goods sold
To Inventory (or Purchases)		FIFO cost of goods sold
„ Capital Adjustment Reserve		Excess of LIFO cost over FIFO cost

A simple illustration will show how this method would work out. It will also show, incidentally, how closely connected are the problems of dealing with fixed and current assets. Suppose that during a period of rising prices a business acquires a machine for £200, estimated life two years, scrap value negligible. At the end of the first year the cost of replacing such a machine has risen to £250, and at the end of the second year to £300. We will also suppose that the business during each of the two years makes a gross profit of £150; and all expenses except depreciation will be ignored.

At the end of Year 1, when replacement cost is £250, depreciation will be recorded thus:

	£	£
Year 1 Depreciation .. .. Dr. 125		
To Machine		100
„ Capital Adjustment Reserve		25

For Year 2, since replacement cost has risen to £300, we shall have:

							£	£
Year 2 Depreciation	..	..	..	..	..	.. Dr.	150	
To Machine	..	..	..	..	..			100
„ Capital Adjustment Reserve		..	..	..				50

If we now assume that at the beginning of Year 1 there were no liabilities and no assets except the machine, that sums set aside as depreciation quotas are held in the form of inventories, while *net* profits are held in cash, we can set out the balance-sheets at the end of Year 1 and Year 2 like this:

BALANCE-SHEET

	End of Year 1. £	End of Year 2. £		End of Year 1. £	End of Year 2. £
Capital	200	200	Machine	100	
Capital Adjustment Reserve ..	25	75	Inventories	125	275
P./L. Account:			Cash (net profit) ..	25	25
(£150–£125) ..	25				
(£300–£275) ..		25			
	£250	£300		£250	£300

This, however, does not complete the picture, since we have provided depreciation totalling only £275 at the end of Year 2, whilst the new machine we are about to purchase to replace the one just discarded will cost £300. At first we seem even yet to have under-provided depreciation. This has arisen because, of course, at the end of Year 1 the full rise in replacement costs could not have been foreseen. At that date only half the then replacement cost of £250 was provided, instead of half the eventual replacement cost of £300. This will not, however, necessarily mean that in Year 2 we should make up the arrear of £25 depreciation as well as provide £150 for that year. We shall see how the gap is made good, given theoretically perfect conditions, if we now turn our attention to the inventories, and apply the same accounting procedure to them that we have just been applying to the machine.

We postulated a rise in machine replacement costs of 25 per cent. in Year 1, and 20 per cent. in Year 2. In the abstract conditions posed, we can assume that the cost price of materials and the selling price of our product will have moved in the same way. In that case, the replacement cost of the Year 1 inventory at the end of Year 2 will have risen by 20 per cent. from £125 to £150: the replacement cost of the total inventory held at the end of Year 2 will thus be £300. If we suppose this to sell for £350 we can journalize the inventory realization in a way analogous to that used for depreciation above:

					£	£
Cash	.. Dr. 350	
To Sales		350
Cost of Sales (replacement cost) .. .. .. Dr. 300		
To Inventory (book value)		275
„ Capital Adjustment Reserve		25

Now, the balance-sheet will look like this:

BALANCE-SHEET

	£		£
Capital	200	Cash	375
Capital Adjustment Reserve	100		
P./L. Account: (£25 + £50)	75		
	£375		£375

We now have in cash both our net profit of £75 *and* sufficient to replace the machine at a cost of £300.

Space does not permit a detailed account of the entries which would be made for a subsequent fall in prices. Interested readers may perhaps test the theory by applying the same technique to circumstances in which assets can be replaced for less than their original cost. The outstanding virtue of the method is that during inflation it enables the profit and loss account to show as net income only what is left of gross income after real capital has been maintained intact: while it does not necessarily involve any change in the usual basis of recording assets in the balance-sheet at historical costs—that is, " actual " cost for fixed assets and first-in first-out cost for stocks. Similarly, during a fall in prices, income will not be understated through provision for replacement costs at past high levels which have ceased to apply. At the same time we obviate the great defect of the straightforward LIFO method of dealing with inventories that, in a period of falling prices, balance-sheet values thereof may be well above current values and, during an inflation, well below them.

The very conservativeness of this method lays it open to one serious criticism. By retaining the historical cost basis for fixed assets in the balance-sheet, during an inflation we keep such asset values understated and so, consequently, the capital employed will also be understated. So although income is right, its relation to capital is wrong. This is easily remedied, at least in principle. We need a further journal entry at each balance-sheet date, writing up the book value of fixed assets by the percentage by which replacement costs have risen, and crediting the write-up to capital adjustment reserve. In the above example, at the end of Year 1, replacement costs have risen by 25 per cent., so the book value of the machine is written up by 25 per cent. As this journal entry is merely for the purpose of balance-sheet adjustment, it is reversed immediately after the balance-sheet date, and a fresh adjustment made in the next balance-sheet, if necessary.

The urgency of the problem which we have been examining is naturally proportional to the instability of the value of money; and in so far as the advance in the price-level has slowed down recently, the need for reform of traditional accounting methods is less clamant than it was during the forties and fifties. Yet the problem posed by changes in the value of money remains perhaps the greatest challenge which faces the accounting profession today. Because any change in traditional accounting methods is bound to have far-reaching social, economic, and political consequences, accountants are naturally reluctant to move. Yet failure to find a solution is having no less far-reaching consequences. Our innate conservatism makes these easier to accept, for they have been with us a long time and we are familiar with them. But we should not be misled into thinking that they are not there.

Depreciation—To Measure Income or to Provide Funds for Replacement ? *

By Carman G. Blough

Director of Research of the American Institute of C.P.A.'s.

As a premise for entering into a discussion of the subject that is before us this afternoon, it may be assumed that everyone here is fully aware of the fact that during the past twenty years we have been cursed with inflation, and that there is every reason to believe that it is likely to continue for years to come. It may also be assumed that all of us are seriously concerned about the dangers of inflation.

It is not necessary to document the assertion that the conventional accounting concept of depreciation has been one of allocating costs. This was clearer to the layman in the days before the " reserve for depreciation " account came into being than it is to some today. At that time it was quite common, in making the charge for depreciation, to carry the credit directly to the asset account, on the grounds that the charge represented a portion of the cost of the asset being written off. Possibly the use of the so-called " reserve for depreciation " account to reflect this reduction has confused the uninitiated into thinking of it as something set aside for replacement. While I understand that the idea of using replacement values in computing depreciation has been proposed in one way or another for several hundred years, it has never made much headway. Here in the United States, until just a few years ago, most of the discussions with respect to the proper treatment of depreciation were directed toward the determination of the most reasonable method of allocating the costs of facilities to the revenues produced by them. In other words, our accepted conventions clearly treated depreciation as an essential factor in the measurement of income.

Accordingly, the discussion of this subject should be aimed at whether, in the future, depreciation should be considered to be a measure of income or a provision for replacement. Possibly

* From the *N.A.A. Bulletin*, August 1959.

it is unfair to even consider this question literally, since few of the advocates of price-level adjustment actually support the proposal that adjustments should be made in the accounts to provide for the actual replacement of the assets when they have to be replaced. However, it would seem appropriate to at least mention why so few actually support a provision for an anticipated cost of replacement. Undoubtedly, it is because so many weaknesses exist in the concept of providing for replacement. Only a few need to be named.

For example, whose crystal ball is to determine very far in advance what the replacement cost of any long-life asset will be, how can anyone determine the equivalent of a replaced facility when there are so many changes in technology and improvements in machines that make them far more efficient than their predecessors, and who can foresee whether the nature of the business will not change in such a way that there will be no actual replacement of particular facilities? Furthermore, replacement costs in some areas have gone down while the general price level has gone up. Of what value would an income statement containing charges for depreciation to provide for replacement really be when any estimates of the amounts needed would be so impossible to make and to verify? The question answers itself.

Again, depreciation provides no funds. They must come from the revenues of the business, and the charge for depreciation neither increases nor decreases the amount available to purchase new equipment. Of course, if there are revenues to offset the depreciation, an amount equal to the depreciation allowed for tax purposes is left entirely to the business. However, even such amounts will not be available for the replacement of assets unless the funds received as revenue are, in some way, set aside for that purpose. Making charges to income and setting up reserves for depreciation give no assurance of funds for replacement. Conversely, funds set aside for replacement will be available for that purpose whether charges have been made to depreciation or not.

Much more could be said along this line but, since the literal interpretation of the topic actually sets up a straw man, it seems unnecessary to spend more time in knocking him down by showing additional reasons why accounting for depreciation as a provision for replacement is both impossible and provides no funds.

Price-level adjustment—why depreciation only?

What then is the real question that merits our consideration? Basically, it would seem that the real controversy inherent in this subject is, " Shall the amount charged for depreciation in arriving at income be based on original dollar costs without adjustment for price-level changes or shall there be an adjustment of costs to give effect to the change in the purchasing power of the dollar?"

As in all matters in which judgment is involved, precedent must continually be re-examined to determine whether it is still applicable. Accordingly, the mere fact that our accounting has always based depreciation on actual dollar costs does not mean that it must always be so. Even though, throughout history, the purchasing power of every monetary unit has fluctuated significantly, the fact that there has been an obvious change in the purchasing power of our dollar gives ample reason for again exploring the possibility of developing concepts of accounting that will be more useful under such changing conditions.

Before going any farther, let me say that I do not disagree, in principle, with those who advocate price-level adjustments for all transactions affected by inflation, whether set forth in financial statements or not. I do seriously disagree as a matter of consistency, logic, and fairness with all those who limit their adjustment proposals to depreciation. However, though I acknowledge the soundness of complete adjustment as a matter of principle or theory, I do not feel that it is practical at this time. How far must inflation go before it would be practical? I do not know but it would have to be far enough for its significance to be understood by many more than understand it today.

In 1936, Dr. Henry Sweeney presented a plan for doing a complete job of price-level adjustment in his book entitled *Stabilized Accounting*. Again, in 1954, Professor Ralph Jones of Yale, with the help of several assistants, including Dr. Perry Mason, who is now my associate at the Institute, completed a study for the American Accounting Association which was published under the title *Price Level Changes and Financial Statements*. In it the financial statements of four corporations ranging from very large to moderate in size were fully adjusted for price-level changes.

Both studies were well considered and clearly constitute means of carrying out a sound, theoretical, overall adjustment. However, few persons have shown much enthusiasm for adopting either of them as standard procedure. What this probably signifies is that, in general, business men are not yet ready to move over to a wholly different concept of income than that with which our entire society is familiar.

The matching of costs and revenues is basic in our whole economy and affects every transaction in which profit or loss is determined, whether it is ever accounted for or not. The farmer who buys ten acres of land for $1,000 and sells it ten years later for $1,500 figures that he has made a profit of $500 because he has matched the revenue from the sale with the cost which produced it. He does not decide whether he has made a profit or not on the basis of any adjustment of his cost for price-level changes. The man who purchases ten shares of stock in a corporation for $500 and sells them ten years later for $700 figures that he has made a profit of $200, whether he intends to invest in other stock or not, and regardless of the fact that the $700 he got might buy much less than the $500 would have bought when he invested it.

Maybe these people are wrong. Certainly they have not made a profit in purchasing power but they have in dollars and that is how most human beings think and have thought, even when the monetary unit was a bead or a pound of cotton.

To shift the thinking of the American public, including most businessmen, as to the meaning of profit is likely to take a pretty severe jolt. It is only logical that some have argued that, in the face of this reluctance to adopt the whole adjustment program, we should at least take the step on depreciation. Accordingly, let us turn to that problem and see whether there is any fairness, consistency or logic in dealing with it alone.

One does not have to be too smart to recognize the fact that, to maintain the capital of a business in these days in terms of capacity to produce goods and render services, substantially more dollars must be reserved out of the revenues of the business than the amount that is charged to depreciation based on the dollars originally expended for such capacity in the form of buildings, machinery, and equipment. It does not follow, however, that the amount necessary to maintain that capacity, over and above the dollars originally invested, should be accounted for as a cost of current production. Inflation is a leech that sucks at businesses and individuals alike. If costs are to be adjusted to give effect to the deterioration of the purchasing power of the dollar in one type of business, consistency and logic require that it be done in another.

If the concept of business income is to be changed in such a way that depreciation costs will be adjusted because of inflated price-levels, it will be completely inconsistent with the concept relating to other transactions affecting business income. To be consistent, for example, a company would have to step up the charge for insurance on a five-year policy on which the premium was paid in advance and a company with a leasehold would have to increase its charges to rent for any prepayments on the lease. Indeed, any time accrual accounting requires charges or credits to income in a different period from that in which payment is made or received; adjustment would be required if there were a change in the price-level in the meantime.

Suppose a company has, for years, carried a million dollars worth of Government bonds to assure itself of ready working capital; to have the same treatment, it would have to recognize and account accordingly for the fact that the million dollars it can get for those bonds now may not buy more than half of the goods or services that it would have bought when it was put into the bonds ten years ago. Conversely, if a company has twenty million dollars of bonds outstanding which it issued ten years ago, it can pay off that obligation by using dollars which have only one-half of the purchasing power of the dollars that were received when the money was borrowed.

Supplementary data for managerial decisions

A business management responsible for the continued operation of a going concern has to make decisions as to whether it will withhold from stockholders some of the dollars currently reported as profits though ultimately needed to replace existing assets, or whether it will distribute them and rely on the acquisition of new capital at a later date to finance the continuance of the business on a higher price level. Of course, if funds are retained, there must be some recognition of the fact that, with continuing inflation, they must be placed where their purchasing power will not deteriorate as it would if left in dollars.

The need for managements to make financial decisions, however, does not necessarily require any departure from currently established accounting procedures. Managements can make any analyses of the effects of changes in the price-level that they consider useful for their own guidance. There are many other uses to which financial statements have to be put. Security holders and prospective security holders have to make decisions whether to buy, hold, or sell securities, income taxes have to be levied, rates of regulated industries have to be fixed, long- and short-term credit grantors have to make judgments, and various kinds of property rights have to be fixed between parties, all on the basis of financial statements. The adjustment of depreciation alone will not solve their problems, and departure in this one respect from the concept of cost that is widely understood would surely confuse many, and lead to false conclusions as to the extent of the adjustments for inflation in the statements as a whole.

The fact that our conventional method of determining income does not recognize changing price-levels does not mean that information concerning the effects of inflation would not be desirable. Supplementary statements or analyses, designed to show the effect of changes in the purchasing power of the dollar, might be very helpful to many users of the statements. The American Institute of C.P.A.'s and the American Accounting Association have long urged their use.

Is productive capacity involved?

One big question in this whole matter is why has there been so much agitation for changing the method of determining profit where depreciable assets are concerned, and so little concern for other areas affected by inflation? The answer given is that this must be done or the productive capacity of our country will decline and deteriorate to the detriment of us all. But how is adjusted depreciation to prevent this? Certainly not by a change in accounting alone. Presumably it boils down to the expectation that, if no profits from operations are recognized until the purchasing power of the dollars originally invested in depreciable assets has been maintained, there will be less taxes to pay, less demand from labor for increased wages and less demand from stockholders for dividends. Undoubtedly, this would be good for those with large amounts of depreciable property. However, as far as any saving of taxes is concerned, it would clearly be at the expense of other taxpayers. But do the owners of depreciable property deserve such special consideration?

In a period of rapidly rising prices, it is the person who has invested in productive, physical assets who benefits most from the inflation. Competitors can enter this field only by investing at higher costs and, since they must have higher prices in order to make a return on the higher investment, the owner of the lower-cost plant can raise his prices accordingly. He may have to pay more to replace his facilities later but he will have earned more with which to replace them.

But what happens to the one who loans his capital to this owner of productive physical assets? His interest rate is not changed, so he gets no more income from his investment than he would have had there been no change in the purchasing power of the dollar. Yet every dollar of interest he receives buys less and when the debt matures, he is paid off in dollars of less purchasing power than the dollars he originally loaned. The owner of the productive facilities to whom he loaned those dollars, in turn, not only gets the benefit of increased dollar income from the assets the dollars bought but is able to pay off his debt in dollars of far less purchasing power than those he originally borrowed.

Assume that, during the period of the loan, the purchasing power of the dollar decreased 50 per cent. and that the creditor had loaned $10,000. The dollars he had loaned were worth $20,000 in the purchasing power of the ones he got back, but he got back only $10,000. Have these depreciation adjustment advocates been concerned about his $10,000 loss? No. Then why should the borrower of the money who invested in a $10,000 machine be allowed to deduct the cost of $20,000 in arriving at his determination of profit? Advocates of price-level adjustments of depreciation respond that the man who invested his money in bonds did so with his eyes open, that he made a deliberate choice of a fixed income and, therefore, he has no basis for complaint when the tide turned against him. Why is there any less concern for him than the man who made his investment choice knowing full well that his depreciation would be calculated on the dollar costs he invested?

Ah, taxes!

Unfortunately, much of the agitation for this depreciation adjustment springs from the desire to reduce taxes. The surveys conducted by the American Institute of C.P.A.'s in both 1948 and 1957 disclosed that over half of those who advocated disclosure or adjustment of depreciation for price-level changes were not in favor of it unless it were to be allowed for tax purposes. It may seriously be questioned whether more than a small fraction of those who advocate adjustment of depreciation would do so if there were no tax reductions to be hoped for by it. Certainly, if there should be such a reduction of taxes to owners of depreciable property, the rest of us will have more to pay. The Government will get taxes somewhere and, with the increased rates that would certainly follow, even those whose taxable income was decreased might find little reduction in their taxes.

If, as a matter of public policy, it is necessary to make a special allowance to owners of depreciable productive facilities in order to save the nation, then that argument should be made, straightforwardly, to the Congress and let it act accordingly. The petroleum industry did not argue that percentage depletion should be considered a proper accounting cost in computing income and should therefore be allowed by Congress. What it did was to represent to Congress that, as a matter of public policy, it would be necessary to allow some such inducement in order for the owners of depletable assets to be willing to exploit them for the well-being of the economy and the country as a whole.

But is this kind of public policy so necessary to maintain productive capacity? A lot of figures have been quoted to show that depreciation charges have been grossly inadequate in relation to the amount necessary to replace the depreciating facilities. However, it should not take any statistics to convince anyone that, in a period of rapidly rising prices, this would be inevitable. Also, extensive figures are quoted to show how much obsolete plant there is in operation. Any experienced accountant knows that there has always been a lot of obsolete machinery and equipment kept in production. Is there anything to prove that these obsolete facilities would have been junked and new ones acquired if the company had been allowed to compute depreciation on the basis of adjusted price-levels? There seem to be no statistics on the matter, but it is pertinent to ask whether the proportion of obsolete facilities has not been much greater during periods of falling prices than it has been during periods of rising prices. Also, it would not be startling to most people who have observed many plants over a long time to be told that there was a larger proportion of the productive plant that was obsolete during the rapidly rising prices of the twenties with their low tax rates than there is today with our high tax rates.

Please do not misunderstand me; I am just as interested in having the productive plant in this country efficiently maintained as anyone else. On the other hand, I do not want to see a plea for special consideration for one group of taxpayers at the expense of others on either accounting grounds or statistical grounds that are developed on biased bases. As the old saying goes, what is sauce for the goose is sauce for the gander.

And labor relations? Stockholder relations? Enterprise?

Turning now to the second reason for adjustment, any representations that a company is not able to pay additional wages because profits are not properly determined unless depreciation is adjusted for the change in the purchasing power of the dollar are not likely to be very convincing in labor negotiations. Labor leaders understand the accounting procedures involved and will surely call such a change a subterfuge. It has been amply demonstrated that the *per capita* output of labor is not due to labor's increased efforts but to the increased amount and efficiency of capital with which it can work. Furthermore, if a company is not able to retain enough out of earnings to take care of the increased cost of replacing productive facilities, labor will not have facilities with which to earn the wages they now get. These facts should be far more persuasive in labor negotiations than a change in accounting procedure.

As to the need to convince stockholders, with proper explanations they should not be slow to grasp the fact that the management has to retain sufficient funds to replace the company's productive facilities. What they often do question, and properly so in the opinion of many, is the right of management to retain enough profits, not only to maintain the capital investment, but to materially expand the business.

The growth and success of our country, economically, has been due to its freedom of competition. People were free to risk their money and make profits or take their losses. Unfortunately, high tax rates have done much to discourage the risking of capital for profit, but let us not take away the inducement to do things better and more economically. There has been a great deal of inflation, yet many things cost less today than they did ten or twenty years ago. New processes and new inventions, improved facilities, more efficient organization, to name only a few, have accomplished much. Possibly it would cost two or three times as much to build a machine like the machine that was bought fifteen or twenty years ago, yet, for only a little more than such a machine would now cost, an improved one can be bought which will produce three or four times as much, and with only a fraction of the labor requirement.

Comparisons of dollar costs do not tell the whole story by any means. Obsolescence is created by improvement. Improvement is brought on by competition and competition is generated by the need to do things better at less cost.

There has been too much interference with the natural growth of our economy by the Government either giving special favors or exercising undue restraints on some groups at the expense or to the benefit of others. Let us not add this one to the list.

A possible political blunder

In conclusion, let me raise the question as to whether business would be well advised to press for an adjusted cost in computing depreciation for tax purposes. What better campaign material would a political demagogue want than to be able to harangue the people that business has been given the privilege of using this special method of calculating its taxable profits? He would not have to be very skilful to explain that the poor widow who bought a $75 Government bond ten years ago and cashed it in today for $100 would have to pay a tax on a profit of $25, whereas, if she had been allowed to calculate her profit the same way as the company with depreciable assets would be doing in regard to depreciation costs, she would be allowed to deduct a loss. Even the most untrained taxpayer could understand that the $75 she invested in the bond ten years ago had a purchasing power equivalent to $150 today and, since she received back only $100, she would have a $50 loss if she were allowed to adjust her costs for price-level changes. Is there any one who is advocating price-level adjustments of depreciation for tax purposes who would like to see the public relations problem that such a situation would most certainly produce for industry?

Depreciation—To Measure Income or to Provide Funds for Replacement? *

By Paul Grady

C.P.A., New York

THE answer to the question, " Is the purpose of depreciation to measure income or to provide funds for replacement? " rests more upon a point of view than upon the fact that there is any necessary conflict between the two objectives. Since both of your speakers are certified public accountants, we shall have no difficulty in agreeing that the primary accounting purpose of depreciation is to measure income. If a financial vice-president were on the panel he would undoubtedly say, " If you accountants provide an adequate charge to properly measure exhaustion of the productive capacity of facilities, I will manage the funds in such a way as to take care of replacements."

It is doubtful that your program committee expected us to spend the afternoon searching for possible conflicts between the accounting and financial purpose of depreciation. On the other hand, evidence was available that the two panel members hold somewhat different views on economic depreciation. This results from the fact that neither Carman Blough nor I can qualify as having been members of the " silent service " with respect to the impact of price-level changes on property exhaustion costs in the period since World War II. Accordingly, it may be useful to establish the major areas of this subject in which we agree and the principal points on which we hold different views.

Points of agreement

We are in agreement on the following points:

1. That political and economic developments in the United States during the past quarter of a century have resulted in the creation of mechanisms having a strong bias towards inflation.
2. That at the present time the principal cause of inflation is the magnitude of the money income generated in the process of production and available for expenditures

* From the *N.A.A. Bulletin*, August 1959.

317

by the people. Wage increases in excess of labor's
share of the increased productivity arising from technological improvements necessarily result in further spirals
of the price-level. The problem is further aggravated
by the manipulated money system predicated on a
spending philosophy, and reflecting the inability to
make the sovereign government amenable to proper
discipline in its own affairs.

3. That the following definition of depreciation accounting,
   taken from the *Terminology Bulletin* of the American
   Institute of Certified Public Accountants, is acceptable:

   Depreciation accounting is a system of accounting which aims
   to distribute the cost or other basic value of tangible capital
   assets, less salvage (if any), over the estimated useful life of the
   unit (which may be a group of assets) in a systematic and rational
   manner. It is a process of allocation, not of valuation. Depreciation for the year is the portion of the total charge under such a
   system that is allocated to the year. Although the allocation
   may properly take into account occurrences during the year,
   it is not intended to be a measurement of the effect of all such
   occurrences.

4. That depreciation in itself does not provide a flow of
   funds to take care of property replacements. The flow
   of funds must come from the gross sales or revenues
   which the company receives for its products or services.
   The same amount of funds would be available to the
   company regardless of whether or not any charge
   is made for depreciation. Accordingly, it is clear that,
   as a matter of accounting, the charge for depreciation
   or property exhaustion is necessary in order to obtain
   a proper statement or measure of net income.

5. That the funds available from the income stream are
   greatly affected by the impact of the present high rates
   of Federal income taxation. Since depreciation deductions are allowed only on historical cost, it is necessary
   for a corporation to include $2.08 in the selling price
   of its products if it is to retain $1.00 to cover the
   excess of replacement costs of fixed assets over original
   cost of equivalent productive capacity.

6. That an acceptable estimate of current dollar cost of
   depreciable properties owned by business corporations
   is approximately $85 billion in excess of cost at the
   dates of acquisition or construction. The portion of
   this economic cost applicable to a current year is
   estimated at about $6 billion.

7. That we subscribe in substance to the following findings in Chapter 9 of *Accounting Research Bulletin* No. 43:

The Committee recognizes that... in reporting profits today, the cost of material and labor is reflected in terms of " inflated " dollars, while the cost of productive facilities in which capital was invested at a lower price level is reflected in terms of dollars whose purchasing power was much greater. There is no doubt that in considering depreciation in connection with product costs, prices, and business policies, management must take into consideration the probability that plant and machinery will have to be replaced at costs much greater than those of the facilities now in use.

... The committee recognizes that the common forms of financial statements may permit misunderstanding as to the amount which a corporation has available for distribution in the form of dividends, higher wages, or lower prices for the company's products. When prices have risen appreciably since original investments in plant and facilities were made, a substantial proportion of net income as currently reported must be reinvested in the business in order to maintain assets at the same level of productivity at the end of the year as at the beginning.

... Stockholders, employees, and the general public should be informed that a business must be able to retain out of profits amounts sufficient to replace productive facilities at current prices if it is to stay in business. ...

Point of disagreement

While the foregoing findings clearly recognize the impact of inflation on depreciation, the Committee on Accounting Procedure reached the conclusion that no basic change in the accounting treatment of depreciation was practicable or desirable under the conditions then prevailing. The committee gave its full support to the use of supplementary schedules or explanations for disclosure of the effects of inflation on property exhaustion costs. It was also indicated that " should inflation proceed so far that original dollar costs lose their practical significance, it might become necessary to restate all assets in terms of the depreciated currency, as has been done in some countries."

Our principal disagreement is related to the validity of the committee's conclusion under present conditions. Mr. Blough believes that the conclusion of the committee, initially reached in *Accounting Research Bulletin*, No. 33 in 1947, and reiterated in Chapter 9 of *Accounting Research Bulletin*, No. 43 in 1953, remains valid. He does not believe that inflation has proceeded far enough in the United States to cause original dollar costs of fixed assets to lose their significance as the basis for measuring property exhaustion for purposes of determining periodic income.

I believe that inflation has proceeded in the United States to such an extent that failure to recognize current price levels in the measurement of depreciation costs results in a serious over-statement of net income for those companies having substantial fixed capital investments. This overstatement of net income, in my opinion, is in itself an important contributing factor to inflation since it stimulates demands for wage increases in excess of labor's share of the greater productivity arising from techno-logical improvements. It necessarily follows that I believe the conclusions in Chapter 9 of *Accounting Research Bulletin*, No. 43, should be revised in order to remove the road-block to recognition of economic depreciation in income taxation and in accounting.

Reasons for revising Chapter 9 of Bulletin No. 43

My principal reasons for urging a revision of the conclusions in Chapter 9 are:

1. They are inconsistent with the substantive findings expressed in the chapter.
2. They apply to the timing of recognition rather than the principle, and the judgment in regard to such timing and significance is erroneous.
3. Accounting exceeds its proper scope in creating a road-block to changes in business practices to meet the problems of inflation.
4. The overstatement of income resulting from original cost depreciation is in itself inflationary.
5. Dangerous erosion in productivity will result from failure to recognize economic depreciation.

These points are dealt with, briefly, in the following paragraphs.

The passages of the findings of the committee, previously quoted, recognize the reality of cost of productive facilities in current dollars and the necessity of retaining such costs out of profits if an enterprise is to stay in business. The conclusion that no basic change in accounting for depreciation is practicable or desirable clearly is not consistent with these findings.

The findings referred to, together with that part of the con-clusion stating that " should inflation proceed . . . it might become necessary to restate all assets in terms of the depreciated currency . . ." demonstrate that the conclusions relate to the timing of recognition of depreciation costs in current dollars rather than the principle of recognition. The committee seems to grant that, when original-cost dollars have lost their significance, it might become necessary to do something about it in the primary financial accounts. Since our monetary unit has lost 60 per cent. of its purchasing power in a period of twenty years, it seems to me that the point for recognition of price-level changes has been passed. Judgments of timing and significance necessarily will vary among individuals. Since the current dollar cost of depreciable properties is now about $85 billion in excess of original cost and the portion of such cost applicable to a current year is about $6 billion, it is respectfully submitted that the judgment as to timing and significance expressed in the conclusion is no longer valid.

Historical cost accounting is predicated upon the postulate that changes in purchasing power of the monetary unit may be ignored. The Special Committee on Accounting Research of the American Institute of Certified Public Accountants commented as follows on postulates:

> Postulates are few in number and are the basic assumptions on which principles rest. They necessarily are derived from the economic and political environment and from the modes of thought and customs of all segments of the business community. The profession, however, should make clear its understanding and interpretation of what they are, to provide a meaningful foundation for the formulation of principles and the development of rules or other guides for the application of principles in specific situations. Also, the Institute should encourage cooperative study with other representative groups to determine that its understanding and interpretation of the postulates are valid and to provide a forum which will command sufficient respect to bring about a change in the postulates when any of them become outmoded.

Adherence to the conclusion of Chapter 9 goes beyond interpretation of a postulate and prevents other segments of the business community from bringing about the changes in business and tax practices which are necessary to meet the problems of inflation. In my opinion, this is not within the proper scope or function of accounting.

It is widely recognised that, at the present time, the principal cause of inflation is the magnitude of money income generated in our economic system and available for expenditures by the people. Any wage increases beyond labor's share of the increased productivity arising from technological improvements necessarily result in further spirals of the price level. If anyone doubts that the size of reported corporate income plays an important part in stimulating wage demands, I suggest they study the recent series of advertisements by the United Steel Workers of America. All of these make prominent use of the reported income of the largest steel company. In the full-page advertisement I have here, Mr. David J. McDonald (president of that trade union) emphasizes that labor costs in 1958 are about the same proportion of each sales dollar as they were in 1952. He then invites an examination

of the dollar net profits of U.S. Steel, $143 million in 1952 and
$301 million in 1958, and points out that profits have doubled.
Mr. McDonald does not disclose by footnote or otherwise that,
if depreciation costs were stated in current dollars, the reported
profits in 1958 would have been cut in half. I am not suggesting
that he is to be criticized for not doing so, because he is carrying
on his part of an economic contest over the division of the fruits
of production. I do suggest, however, that an accounting bulletin
which prevents the statement of plant exhaustion costs in current
dollars, comparable with other costs, must bear a share of the
responsibility for further inflation. The current wage contest
in the steel industry makes it clear that supplemental disclosures
are not adequate to prevent the inflationary consequences of
overstating net income.

The final reason for urging a revision of the bulletin is that we
are courting dangerous erosion in productivity by failure to
recognise economic depreciation. The allowance of original
cost depreciation ignores the real economic cost, and thus
effectively imposes a substantially higher rate of income taxation
on those companies which have substantial investments in fixed
assets. If such companies are to recover the added current dollar
cost of property exhaustion through income, they must, as
already noted, charge their customers $2.08 for each $1 excess of
current cost over original cost. This is a hard way to accumulate
the capital required to merely stay even. The disparity between
cost of replacement and the original cost of facilities causes
postponement of replacement of over-age facilities, because a
greater operating expenses advantage is required to provide
a satisfactory rate of return on the higher capital cost of the new
facility. This lag is a degenerative economic force by lessening
demand for capital goods and by delaying improvement in the
rate of increase in productivity. If we continue to ignore economic
depreciation in income taxation and in accounting, it is my view
that we will jeopardise the needed modernization of productive
facilities—the essential arsenal in the economic battle with the
Communists. We have the word of the State Department that
this economic battle is our greatest danger.

Alone in holding to historical cost basis

In concluding my remarks, I should like to point out that the
extent of enthronement of historical cost in our Institute pronouncements is unique in the world. We sometimes like to
regard accounting as a universal business language, but I know
of no country other than the United States where recognition of

property exhaustion costs in equivalent current monetary purchasing power would require an exception in the opinion of the
independent auditors. Examples of recognition of economic
depreciation, in some manner, in the accounts may be found in
the published reports of Unilever, Limited, N. V. Philips Lamp-
works, Imperial Chemical Industries, Limited, Algemcne Kunst-
zidge Unie N. V., The Electricity Authority and Boards of
England and Wales and The Gas Council of England, Scotland
and Wales. The accounts of these enterprises carry adequate
disclosures of the basis on which depreciation and fixed assets
are stated, and the opinions of the independent auditors contain
no qualifications regarding the departures from historical costs.
A survey of several hundred reports disclosed six reports of
enterprises in the United States in which depreciation costs were
expressed in current dollars. The reports of the independent
auditors necessarily stated that the practice was contrary to the
conclusions of Chapter 9 of *Accounting Research Bulletin*, No. 43,
but also contained further wording supporting the practice as a
prudent measurement of business income. The position of the
bulletin in regard to current costs of property exhaustion is
contrary to the accepted use of current costs of inventories under
the " LIFO " method in the measurement of income. The new
Accounting Principles Board has an unusual challenge and
opportunity to resolve this most important accounting problem
of our generation. May its members be blest with wisdom,
courage and statesmanship in carrying out their task.

Depreciation Policy and the Price Level*

By George Terborgh

Research Director, Machinery and Allied Products Institute, Washington, D.C.

I. NATURE OF THE PROBLEM

To the accountant, an investment in plant or equipment is a prepaid cost, to be charged to operations and recovered to cash over the serviceable life of the facility. It is the object of depreciation policy to allocate this cost to successive periods of time or units of production by some systematic procedure calculated to complete the process by the time the asset is retired.[1] Though we may quarrel with some of the methods used, the general principles and purposes are correctly stated—subject to one proviso. The total of charges over the service life should recover the cost of the asset *in dollars of equivalent purchasing power*.

Ordinarily depreciation recovers simply the number of dollars originally committed to the asset, regardless of differences in their purchasing power. This is satisfactory enough in periods of relative stability in the price-level, but can be seriously, or even ruinously, inadequate during and after periods of inflation. Under such conditions we cannot assume that " a dollar is a dollar." If we invest 100-cent. dollars and recover later only an equal number of 50-cent dollars we have lost one-half of our capital, whatever the books may show. To hold otherwise is to take the shadow for the substance.

Hypothetical case

Consider an example. A machine costs $10,000 and is given a life for depreciation purposes of 10 years, the annual charge being therefore $1,000. Shortly after it is acquired, however, there is a 50 per cent. rise in the general price-level, so that the

---

* The first part of this article is based on a Pamphlet issued by the Machinery and Allied Products Institute in 1947. The postscript is based on the *Review* of that Institute for April 1961.
[1] If substantial salvage value is anticipated, the schedule of depreciation charges may be adjusted to recover only the excess of cost over salvage.

subsequent annual recoveries represent a diminished purchasing power. Considering the dollars originally invested as par, or 100 cents, we can describe the situation as follows:

Year of Service	Depre-ciation Charge	Index of Prices Date of invest-ment=100	Purchasing Power of Depre-ciation Charge ($1000÷ index 100)	Number of Current Dollars required to Equal 1000 Original Dollars ($1000 × index 100)
1	1000	110	909	1,100
2	1000	130	769	1,300
3	1000	150	667	1,500
4	1000	150	667	1,500
5	1000	150	667	1,500
6	1000	150	667	1,500
7	1000	150	667	1,500
8	1000	150	667	1,500
9	1000	150	667	1,500
10	1000	150	667	1,500
Total	10,000		7,014	14,400

The owner of this machine is likely to assume that he has made full provision for recovery of the capital consumed during each year, yet if he looks behind the fiction that a dollar is a dollar he finds at the end of the service life that the total of depreciation, *measured in purchasing power at the time of the charge*, is only 70 per cent. of the original investment. He may or may not have recovered the balance from net earnings, but certainly he has *not* recovered it via depreciation. So far as that reliance is concerned, he has dissipated nearly one-third of his original real capital. In the meantime he has understated costs of operation over the life of the asset by the equivalent of 2,986 original dollars or 4,400 current dollars, and has overstated net income by a like amount, with whatever consequences these miscalculations may have had for managerial policy.

Object of depreciation policy

The ideal object of depreciation policy is to recover each year a sufficient number of *current* dollars to equal that year's capital consumption in terms of *original* dollars. In our hypothetical example, the charge for the first year should be $1,100 and for the last eight years $1,500, the total for the service life being $14,400. This number of current dollars is necessary, given the time-distribution of capital consumption and the price changes in the case, to recover a purchasing power equal (at the time of recovery) to the $10,000 originally invested.[2] Superficially it looks like

---

[2] Straight-line depreciation is assumed here because of its popularity and simplicity, without necessarily implying that we approve it. The principle holds equally for any other method.

over-depreciation, but it is not. *It yields a result in real terms identical with that accomplished by aggregate charges of $10,000 in a period of stable prices.*

Failure to recognise this problem has led repeatedly, under conditions of extreme inflation, to wholesale dissipation of real capital. But at least there is one advantage to a runaway inflation that does not attach to the 50-per-cent. variety: it eventually forces corrective action. When the amounts yielded by depreciation on original cost become palpably absurd in relation to real capital consumption, something *has* to be done. With a mild inflation such as we have had, on the other hand, it is possible to stand pat, with consequences that are deleterious but not disastrous. That industry can still " take it " seems to us, however, an insufficient excuse for inaction.

II.   THE MEASURE OF PURCHASING POWER

We have said that the object of depreciation policy is to recover each year enough current dollars to equal that year's capital consumption in original dollars. But how are the current dollars and original dollars to be commensurated? What is the criterion of their purchasing power?

The measure most commonly invoked, when it is proposed to adjust depreciation for inflation, is command over the same kind or kinds of goods that are currently undergoing depreciation. It is self-duplicative, or reproductive, purchasing power. Thus, for example, the power of this year's accrual on a steam shovel bought five years ago is reckoned by reference to the change in the price of the same shovel in the interval. If there has been an increase of 30 per cent., it takes 130 current dollars to equal 100 original dollars. Or, to put it otherwise, the dollar of recovery is worth 78 cents in the dollar of acquisition.

Practical difficulties

This reckoning of specific, or self-duplicative, purchasing power has not only serious practical difficulties; it is dubious from a theoretical standpoint. Consider the practical angles first. Capital goods are rarely replaced by new ones identical with themselves; indeed, replacement typically occurs because better goods have become available. After a facility has been in service a few years it is usually problematical to get price quotations on an exact replica, a superior product, sometimes radically different, having superseded it. Under these circumstances it is difficult, and may be impossible, to say what part of the cost of the currently available replacement represents an equivalent of the original facility in physical or functional terms, and what part represents superiority.

There is another practical difficulty. Depreciation accruals (or rather, the funds they make available when earned) are rarely, if ever, earmarked for exactly the same items or types of items that generate them. Thus, for example, accruals in a metal-working plant on lathes, milling machines, drills, presses, conveyors, etc., ordinarily go into the same pot for reinvestment. It is obviously pointless to attempt to measure the purchasing power of lathe accruals over lathes alone, much less that of accruals on particular types and sizes of lathes over their current counterparts. The measurement must relate rather to the whole complex of capital goods financed from the common pot. Thus, the purchasing power of accruals in an automobile factory would have to be reckoned against the cost of metal-working plant and machinery generally, while in an electric power plant it would be computed with reference to the cost of the special types of equipment and structures used in that industry.

Even if we derive our price comparisons from groups or classes of assets rather than from an individual item, the same problem of measurement remains, though in less acute form. Since most components of a group of replacements are changing in character from year to year, it is usually difficult, and often impossible, to trace the current replacement cost of the physical capacity originally embodied in the existing assets. It is equally difficult, therefore, to make a satisfactory adjustment of current depreciation to secure a self-duplicative purchasing power equal to current capital consumption.

Theoretical objections

But these are practical considerations, not matters of principle. Suppose we have a facility whose physical capacity or function is clearly measurable in standard units, so that it is possible at any time to gauge exact replacement cost. The question remains whether this is what we really want. In our opinion, it is not. The proper measure of purchasing power for our purpose is not power for self-duplication; it is power to command goods and services generally.

This proposition may be clarified by an illustration. Let us assume that the facility referred to in the preceding paragraph is an electric generator of 50,000 kilowatts capacity. Let us assume further that the replacement cost of this much capacity falls by one half while the general price level remains constant. Should

depreciation charges on the existing installation likewise be cut
in half? So reduced, they will still be sufficient for physical
self-duplication, but they will be only half enough to recover
the *general* purchasing power invested in the present unit at
acquisition. Which of these conflicting criteria should govern?

If the object of depreciation policy is to perpetuate a given
amount of *physical capacity* from one mechanical generation to
another, regardless of its value, then the accrual on the generator
should be cut one half. If, on the other hand, the object is the
recovery of the *capital invested* in the asset, there should be no
reduction. In our view, the goal is recovery of capital, not
physical replacement of the asset. *Depreciation policy has nothing
to do with the subsequent expenditure or re-investment of the
funds recovered.* If it is a lathe that is being depreciated, the
charge is properly the same regardless of whether the funds are
spent for another lathe, a milling machine, a typewriter, a loco-
motive, or a trip to Europe. It is the same for an enterprise
under liquidation, with no re-investment, as it is for a growing
concern.

If this view is correct, it follows that specific replacement or
reproduction cost is irrelevant to the adjustment of depreciation
policy, and that we must rely on some measure of *generalized*
purchasing power. We have still to ask, however, whether it is
purchasing power over capital goods or consumers' goods.

Capital goods v. consumers' goods

There are advocates of each alternative. It is argued on the
one hand that since capital recoveries are more likely to be
re-invested in capital goods than in consumers' goods we should
measure their purchasing power by reference to a general index
of capital goods prices. On the other hand, it is urged that consumption is the ultimate end of economic activity, and that
from the standpoint of an individual the ownership of capital
goods is significant only in terms of the future consumption it
makes possible.[3] To preserve real investment in the form of
capital goods, therefore, it is necessary to preserve the exchange
value of the latter in terms of consumers' goods. It is necessary,
by the same token, to measure capital consumption in dollars
of constant purchasing power over consumers' goods.[4]

Fortunately, it is unnecessary to quarrel over the theoretical

[3] The future consumption aimed at may, of course, be that of the owner's survivors.
[4] A pioneer in the development of this view (though not in precisely these terms)
was Henry W. Sweeney. See, for example, " The Maintenance of Capital,"
in the *Accounting Review*, December 1930; also his discussion in *Stabilized
Accounting*, 1936.

issue, since in practice we get broadly similar results whether we gauge changes in the size of the dollar by reference to its command over capital goods or consumers' goods—provided we use comprehensive price indexes in both cases. The average cost of all capital goods (construction and equipment) is up by about the same ratio as the consumers' price index. It makes little difference which index is taken. We will settle for either, or a combination of both.

Time reference of measurement

The adequacy of each year's capital recovery must be appraised by reference to its purchasing power at *the time*. What happens to the *future* value of the recovery depends on what is done with the funds. If they are held in cash, it will be one thing; if they are invested in inventory, it will be another; if they are put into plant and equipment, it will be still another. In any case the result is immaterial. Depreciation policy cannot be held responsible for what happens to the purchasing power of capital recoveries *after* they are made.[5]

III. METHODS OF ADJUSTMENT

Whatever the measure of purchasing power, the procedures for adjusting current depreciation charges are the same. Basically they are of two types, one providing for continuous adjustment, the other for a one-shot adjustment only.

Continuous adjustment

The continuous adjustment calls for a comparison of the purchasing power of the dollar *each year* with its purchasing power at the time the assets were acquired. The year's depreciation charge, computed as usual on original cost, is then adjusted

---

[5] This observation has an obvious bearing on an argument heard occasionally, that the total of depreciation charges over the life of an asset should have a purchasing power *at the time of its retirement* equal to that of the original investment. The contention appears to rest on the notion that these charges are accumulated and conserved in cash to buy a specific replacement for the asset under depreciation, hence that the crucial moment for gauging their adequacy is the moment of retirement. As a practical matter, replacement (when it can be physically identified) is almost never financed from depreciation accruals on the particular facility replaced, these accruals being currently re-invested, as a rule, *while the facility is still in service*. For this reason the moment of retirement has ordinarily no greater practical weight or significance for depreciation policy than any other moment in the life of the asset. Even when depreciation accruals are held in cash or equivalent until retirement, however, we still insist that if they yield for each year enough current dollars to equal that year's capital consumption in original dollars, they are doing all that can properly be asked. The decision to hold them until retirement is a free choice of the owner, hence he must accept the responsibility if there is an erosion of their purchasing power in the interval.

for the change in the size of the dollar so as to yield a purchasing power equal to that of the unadjusted charge in original dollars. Let us illustrate. An equipment account contains depreciable assets costing $1,000,000, the annual depreciation rate being 10 per cent. The price index stood at 103 for the year of acquisition and is 162 for the current year. Adjusted depreciation for the year is $100,000 × 162/103=$157,281.

When the components of a property account were acquired in different years, the process of continuous adjustment becomes more difficult. For a strict application of the method, it is necessary to compute a weighted average acquisition price index, as follows:

Year	Amount Acquired	Price Index for the Year	Amount × Price Index
1	$100,000	90	9,000,000
2	50,000	95	4,750,000
3	400,000	100	40,000,000
4	250,000	110	27,500,000
5	200,000	105	21,000,000
Total	$1,000,000		102,250,000

$$\text{Weighted average index, } \frac{102,250,000}{1,000,000} = 102.25$$

Theoretically, this computation should be repeated every time an asset is retired from (or added to) a composite account. While this difficulty may be handled in practice by ignoring small changes in composition, or by rough estimates, continuous adjustment of temporally heterogeneous accounts is a rather fussy business. To avoid laborious calculations, it is desirable, therefore, that such accounts be broken down by year of acquisition, thus making each group of assets homogeneous as to age. Depreciation on each group can then be adjusted by a simple comparison of the price index for the current year and for the year of acquisition, as indicated above.

Single adjustment

There is another way to proceed, less accurate and flexible, but much simpler, namely, by a flat one-time adjustment designed to allow only for the inflation already accomplished, leaving adjustment for further inflation, if any (or for deflation) to the future. There is much to be said for such a one-shot correction, made on a uniform, across-the-board basis. If the general price-level, whether measured in capital goods or in consumers' goods, is somewhat more than 50 per cent. above that of acquisition date, future depreciation accruals on these assets can be conservatively supplemented by a flat surcharge of 50 per cent.

A one-shot treatment of this character has, of course, a disadvantage not found in the continuous adjustment: it gets out of line as the price-level changes. It is obviously a rough-and-ready remedy, predicated on the assumption that the price-level is not likely to change substantially from here out, and that we are making a non-recurrent adjustment for past changes only.

Alternative accounting treatments

A one-shot correction can be accomplished with or without writing up the amounts at which fixed assets are carried on the balance-sheet.

There is something to be said, certainly, for translating these balance-sheet figures into dollars of present purchasing power.[6] The conversion yields, among other things, a more realistic statement of net worth, a truer picture of the rate of profit on worth, and a better measure of the equity cushion for borrowing and other purposes. On the other hand, it may lead to difficulties where assessments for state and local taxes are tied to balance-sheet figures, as well as to arguments with the Securities and Exchange Commission and other regulatory agencies.

If it is decided to write up assets by say 50 per cent., there should be an increase by this ratio of both the gross property account and accumulated depreciation, with a credit to capital surplus for the net increase (also 50 per cent.). This done, no other adjustment is necessary. The application of the same depreciation rates to the expanded base will yield automatically the 50 per cent. increase in current charges that it is the prime object to achieve, and will close out the account at the same time it would otherwise have been closed.[7]

[6] Since the book figures presently carried represent *unamortized cost* rather than *value*, the conversion yields simply unamortized cost in dollars of present general purchasing power, by no means identical with the current value of the particular assets as determined by appraisal. There can be no doubt, however, that the converted figures would be nearer to appraised value in most cases than the existing entries, which record unamortized cost in dollars of original purchasing power.

In his study entitled *Depreciation Policy and Post-war Expansion* (Brookings Institution, 1946) Lewis H. Kimmel considers and rejects the idea of revaluation of fixed assets on the ground that the appraisals required would be too difficult and time-consuming (p. 48). What we are discussing is not an appraisal of specific asset values, which would indeed be time-consuming, but simply a flat per cent. increase of existing book values to reflect the loss in the *general* purchasing power of the dollar, an adjustment that can be made by a stroke of the pen.

[7] In commenting on asset write-ups for this purpose in the twenties, George O. May has this to say (*Financial Accounting*, p. 93):

"Many of the write-ups of fixed properties between 1920 and 1930 were efforts to reflect the change in the value of the monetary unit in the subsequent depreciation charges against income. So long as these write-ups were based on reliable evidence and the resulting credits were excluded from income and from earned surplus (so that the rule against including unrealized gains in

In the absence of a realignment of the balance-sheet, it is necessary to treat the 50 per cent. increase in current depreciation as a special surcharge and to handle it separately from the normal charge, only the latter being credited to the depreciation reserve.[8] By this segregation the normal writing off of cost is undisturbed, proceeding *as if* recovery were being made in original dollars, and leaving the surcharge to offset the error in this assumption. This method, consistently applied, should yield the same annual charges provided by the write-up of the depreciation base itself.[9]

IV. THE TAX ANGLE

Whenever there is a discussion of adjusting depreciation policy for the shrinkage in the dollar, the view is likely to be expressed that there is little point to the proposal unless the adjustment is allowed for tax purposes. While we do not subscribe to this view, as will appear later, tax is certainly important.

If we were dealing here merely with a question of principle, the answer would be clear. Once it is recognised that capital is fully recovered only when the recovery is equal to the original investment *in terms of purchasing power*, an adjustment of depreciation deductions to compensate for the shrunken dollar appears a matter of simple justice to the taxpayer. Again, if we were to consider simply the economic justification, the answer would also be clear. A larger depreciation allowance would increase the volume of funds for the renovation and expansion of productive facilities. If we are right in the belief, supported elsewhere,[10] that we are chronically under-mechanised in America

income was not infringed) there was ample theoretical and practical support for them. If the verdict upon them is made to depend on whether they were reasonable in the light of the circumstances when the entries were made, such write-ups must be held to have been fully justified."

[8] The surcharge may be credited to a special reserve, to be transferred to capital surplus when the asset is retired, or it may be credited to capital surplus as accrued. The latter course seems to us at once simpler and more sensible. Since the asset has not been written up, there is no need for any special reserve for over-valuation; the regular depreciation reserve, properly based on original cost, suffices for that. In reality, the surcharge becomes a part of equity, and it may as well be recognised as such currently, without waiting for the asset to be retired.

[9] There is one difference in the results from the two procedures, however, which appears in the computation of capital gains from the disposal of partly depreciated assets. When the depreciable base is written up, such capital gains are reduced, being reckoned from higher book values. To put the other method on a par in this respect, it is necessary that remaining book values at the time of disposal be written up 50 per cent. in each case before computing the gain. This adjustment does not understate the true gain; on the contrary, it is essential to its proper determination. For the gain can be properly figured only when the dollars of acquisition and the dollars of realisation are of like purchasing power. What the adjustment does is to convert the still unrecovered dollars of acquisition into an equivalent number of current dollars.

[10] *Business Investment Policy*, Machinery and Allied Products Institute (Washington, 1958).

by comparison with what current technology can provide and sound economy can justify, the provision of increased funds for reinvestment through an adequate tax recovery of past investment should give a salutary stimulus to productivity.[11]

Unfortunately, it is impossible to rest the decision on these grounds alone. There are certain objections to the proposal from the standpoint of the tax authorities, and others from the standpoint of industry. Let us begin with the former.

Government objections

The principal objection to legislation along this line lies in the fact that putting depreciation on a purchasing-power basis singles it out for special treatment in a tax structure left otherwise on a current-dollar basis.[12] The assumption that the dollar represents the same magnitude at different periods of time is deeply imbedded in tax policy and practice, hence a universal adjustment for changes in its purchasing power would necessitate a complete overhaul of the tax system. What is more, it would result in intolerable complications.[13] As a practical matter, therefore, the choice is between special treatment for depreciation where the technical problem is simple (assuming a one-shot adjustment) or continuance on the present original-cost basis.[14]

Despite the objection in principle to such special treatment of depreciation, a number of countries have resorted to it for over-riding practical considerations. To prevent the taxation of real capital recoveries as income, with the resultant erosion of productive investment, they have brushed aside the discrimination argument to grant relief for depreciation alone. Instances are France and Italy, where decrees of August 1945, and March

[11] The tax saving from adjusted depreciation, as we have seen, would be about $600 millions a year for corporations alone.

[12] We refer to " legislation " because it would clearly be required to effectuate the proposal. The present Internal Revenue Code requires (with a few special exceptions) that " the basis of property shall be the cost of such property." Even if there were no such specification in the Code, however, it is exceedingly doubtful if administrative officials would depart, without an explicit legislative directive, from the time-honoured practice of limiting depreciation to original cost.

[13] Adjustment would be called for wherever the calculation of income or deficit, gain or loss, depends on the comparison of dollars paid out (or received) at one time with dollars received (or paid out) at another. Since the reckoning of business profit or loss involves characteristically the commensuration of various flows of dollars separated by different time intervals, the attempt to adjust across the board would involve prohibitive effort and inconvenience.

[14] The adjustment could take either of the forms described above: (1) a tax-free write-up of 50 per cent. on pre-war assets and their accrued depreciation reserves, yielding a 50 per cent. increase in the amount recoverable from future depreciation charges; or (2) a tax-free surcharge of 50 per cent. on depreciation accruals as presently computed, with no asset write-up, the surcharge to continue until the account is fully reserved by the accumulation of the regular charge.

1946, respectively, authorised the writing up of depreciable assets to approximately their current value, and the subsequent recovery tax-free of depreciation on the written-up values. There are earlier precedents in Germany, Austria, and other countries.[15]

Industry objections

The first objective is simple. " If industry gets a tax-free increase in depreciation allowances after a period of rising prices, the government can properly ask a cut in these allowances after a period of falling prices. The adjustment can work both ways." Although a substantial decline from the present price-level seems improbable, it cannot be ruled out as an impossibility. However slender the hazard, it is something to consider.

The second objection is also simple. " Suppose corporations do save $600 millions a year through a tax-free increase in depreciation. The government has to have the revenue, and is likely to get it by an increase in the corporate tax rate sufficient to make up the loss." The answer, so far as there is one, turns largely on whether the revenue loss is in fact made up in this way. If it is, the net result is a redistribution of the same corporate tax burden, to the advantage of enterprises having heavy depreciation charges—generally, of course, those with heavy capital investment. While this should have some advantage (apart from the greater theoretical equity) in stimulating demand for capital goods, it is evident that unless the total tax burden is reduced, a good part of the benefit from increased depreciation is lost.

A third objection, though widely made and hence deserving of attention, is in our opinion misconceived. " The whole

[15] Thus, for example, the Austrian legislation of 1922 and 1923 twice permitted corporations to write up fixed assets to current value, and to recover the new value through depreciation charges. These adjustments were followed by another, in 1924, when taxpayers were required to re-appraise their assets and liabilities in a new monetary unit, the fixed-asset values thus established being likewise recoverable through depreciation. A similar provision was applied in Germany in 1924, following the introduction of the new gold mark. The German inflation also provides an example of the tax-free surcharge, the legislation of 1921 providing that:

" In determining operating profit and net profit for income tax purposes for the years of 1920 to 1926, it is permitted to set aside tax-free, reserve funds to allow for the excess of the prospective replacement costs of the durable capital assets over their common value."

Following the passage of the statute just cited, the Supreme Financial Court of the Reich observed:

" At an earlier phase it was possible for the Supreme Court to take the stable currency of pre-war times as a starting point. However, for the war years, and even more so for the post-war era, the effect of the progressive depreciation of the currency must not be disregarded. As far as possible, existing laws should be interpreted so as to prevent the disbursement in the form of dividends, as well as the taxation, of fictitious profits which appear only as a result of the declining value of the currency. Otherwise, enterprises would be forced to consume their capital in a manner harmful to the whole economy."

approach is wrong. What industry needs is not a scheme to adjust depreciation for fluctuations in the value of the dollar; it is greater discretion in fixing rates on the original-cost basis." We have always advocated greater latitude in the determination of depreciation rates for tax purposes, and shall continue to do so,[15a] but this would not solve the problem under discussion: the recovery tax-free of the *purchasing power* invested in assets. The still undepreciated balance of original cost could be charged off at twice the present rate without coming any closer to achievement of this objective. This requires, not faster recovery of original cost in terms of dollars, but rather a recovery, whatever the rate, in terms of purchasing power.

Tax allowance on balance

When we cast up the pros and cons of purchasing-power depreciation for tax purposes, it is evident that there is a good deal to be said on both sides. Though after a more drastic inflation than we have had, the advantages would undoubtedly outweigh the objections in America, as they have elsewhere, after a relatively mild inflation the merits of tax relief limited to depreciation alone are in our judgment debatable.

V. THE MANAGEMENT ANGLE

While the adjustment of depreciation admittedly loses much of its value if disallowed for tax purposes, the question remains whether management is justified in adopting it for its own accounting in the absence of tax benefit. We believe it is.

A proper accounting of depreciation is essential to correct determination of costs, and consequently, of net income. The overstatement of profits inherent in original-cost depreciation not only gives the impression to the public, including employees, that the enterprise is making more than it really is; it is likely to lead to dividend payments that would not occur if the true facts were recognised. Moreover, the understatement of costs may lead to the under-pricing of the product.

Some management objections considered

The point is frequently made that selling prices are controlled by competition, and that the charging of higher depreciation by a single company can therefore have no effect upon its revenues. This may be true, in the main, when the reform of depreciation

---

[15a] Sweden has granted corporate taxpayers, subject to certain limitations, the privilege of " free " or fully discretionary depreciation.

accounting is limited to one concern in an industry, but it does not follow that its adoption generally would be likewise without influence. With the entire industry aware of its real capital recovery costs, and with each firm attempting individually to retrieve these costs from sales, the answer might be different.

Another objection, closely related, runs as follows: " If the general adoption of increased depreciation for costing and pricing should result in better prices and increased revenues, all the gain would go to the common stockholders, with no benefit to preferred stockholders (assuming they are already getting their full dividend) or to bondholders. It is the latter who need adjustment for the effects of inflation." It is true that inflation tends to worsen the relative position of those whose claim against, or share in, an enterprise is fixed in terms of dollars. It is true also that the correct computation of depreciation does nothing to remedy this condition. But that is hardly a legitimate ground for criticism. We cannot properly condemn good depreciation policy for failing to do something it is not supposed to do. All that can reasonably be asked of it is the recovery of the purchasing power originally invested, without reference to how the benefit is divided.

The next objection is of special interest to manufacturers of productive equipment. " If industry raises its depreciation charges, it will lower its reported profits by the same amount, and will consequently curtail its dividend payments. This reduction of profits and dividends will discourage capital investment at the same time that the enlargement of depreciation charges stimulates it. The result may be no net gain at all." But why not apply this argument more broadly? If under-depreciation is conducive to the expansion of investment, why not abolish depreciation (except for tax purposes) entirely?

Profits and dividends are, of course, essential if corporations are to raise outside capital, either by direct borrowing or by security flotations. The question here, however, is not whether industry should make profits: it is whether it should *overstate* them. We think not. In the first place, investors who buy securities on the strength of these exaggerated profits are being misled. Once they catch on, they will discount the securities on the basis of their true earning power, *after* adequate provision for capital consumption. In the second place, it will be obvious when we consider managerial behaviour that a billion dollars of capital recovery, labelled as such and retained for reinvestment, will generate more capital expenditure than a billion dollars of such recovery, erroneously labelled profit and paid out to stockholders. Management will spend money in the till when it will not go out and raise it from the public.

VI. POSTSCRIPT, 1961

The vigorous upsurge of prices following the Second World War touched off a lively controversy over the resultant inadequacy of depreciation charges. This controversy, which engaged academicians, management, the accounting profession, and government agencies, extended over several years and generated a sizeable literature.

Throughout the debate, U.S. federal agencies concerned with regulation of accounting practices—the Internal Revenue Service, the Securities and Exchange Commission, the Federal Power Commission, the Federal Communications Commission, the Interstate Commerce Commission, and others—stood uncompromisingly for original-cost depreciation.[16] The accounting profession (in its official pronouncements at least) went only so far as to suggest annotations to accounting statements—the " footnote " solution. Management might thus append its estimate of the inadequacy of original-cost depreciation, but the notation would have no effect on the accounting results. As for management itself, where it took an interest in the issue it was uncertain what to do.[17]

The great illusion

These largely negative results of the great debate may be attributed in part to an illusion shared by most of the participants. It was assumed that the wartime and post-war inflation had about run its course, and that, if nothing were done about the under-depreciation problem, it would gradually shrink and disappear.

How wrong this assumption was we can now see in retrospect. The chart on p. 338 shows the movements of two price series, one an index of the prices of *capital goods* (plant and equipment), the other an index of the prices of *all* privately produced goods and services.[18]

[16] There has been one exception to this solid front, though it does not involve the regulation of accounting practices. The Department of Agriculture has long used current-dollar depreciation in computing the production expenses of farmers.

[17] This uncertainty was enhanced by the experience of a leading steel company, which undertook to charge price-adjusted depreciation on its own books (not for tax purposes), only to be attacked by the combined forces of the Securities and Exchange Commission and the New York Stock Exchange.

[18] The ' 'deflator " of the private gross national product.

Since 1947–49, when the debate was most active, the capital goods price index has risen by 50 per cent., the general index by 28 per cent. Clearly, inflation did *not* end with the post-war readjustment.

CHART 1

Indexes of the Prices of Business Capital Goods, and of All Privately
Produced Goods and Services

(1960 = 100)

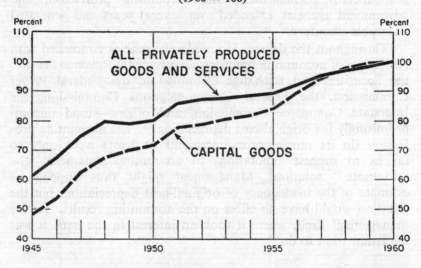

We may add in passing that the more rapid rise of the capital goods index is in our opinion largely, if not wholly, a statistical illusion. It reflects the upward bias of this index relative to the general index, the bias being due to the more rapid rate of product improvement prevailing in the capital goods area. (Since the index prices units of equipment, not units of capacity or performance, the price of the latter may be falling while that of the former is rising.)

Revival of interest

The gradual realisation by executives and accountants that the basic assumption of the early debate was false has led to a revival of interest in the issue after several years of quiescence.

Interest has been particularly marked in industries like steel that constructed a substantial volume of facilities under certificates of necessity during and after the Korean war, and later suffered a drastic cutback of capital consumption allowances with the exhaustion of amortisation. Quite naturally, this cutback has prompted a new look at normal depreciation.

CHART 2

Ratios of Current-Dollar to Historical-Cost Depreciation, for All American
Business, Using (A) An Index of Capital Goods Prices, (B) An Index of the
Prices of All Privately Produced Goods and Services

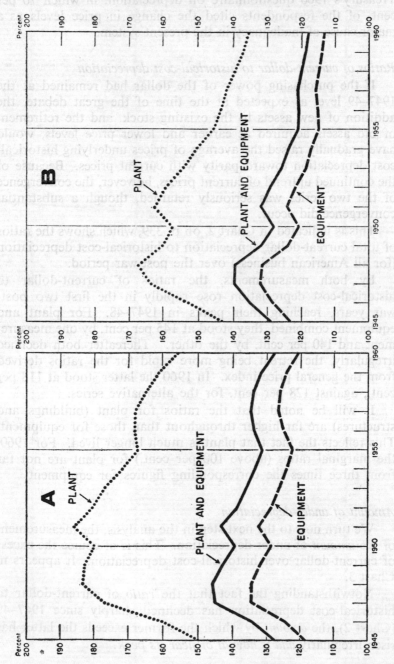

This has not been, however, the dominant factor in the revival of interest. The revival is broadly based. The latest evidence may be found in the preliminary tabulation of the U.S. Treasury's 1960 questionnaire on depreciation, in which 70 per cent. of the respondents cited the change in price levels as a major cause of inadequacy in the present system.

Ratios of current-dollar to historical-cost depreciation

If the purchasing power of the dollar had remained at the 1947–49 level as expected at the time of the great debate, the addition of new assets to the existing stock, and the retirement of old assets acquired at earlier and lower price levels, would have gradually raised the average of prices underlying historical-cost depreciation toward parity with current prices. Because of the continued uptrend of current prices, however, the convergence of the two series was seriously retarded, though a substantial convergence did occur.

This is indicated in Chart 2, on p. 339, which shows the ratios of total current-dollar depreciation to historical-cost depreciation (for all American business) over the post-war period.

By both measurements, the ratios of current-dollar to historical-cost depreciation rose rapidly in the first two post-war years, reaching their peaks in 1947–48. For plant and equipment combined, they stood at 145 per cent. by one measurement and 140 per cent. by the other. Thereafter both declined irregularly, the retreat being more rapid for the ratios derived from the general price index. In 1960 the latter stood at 118 per cent., against 128 per cent. for the alternative series.

It will be noted that the ratios for plant (buildings and structures) are far higher throughout than those for equipment. This reflects the fact that plant is much longer lived. For 1960, the marginal ratios (above 100 per cent.) for plant are not far from three times the corresponding figures for equipment.

Amount of under-depreciation

We turn now to the next step in the analysis, the measurement of the *amount* of under-depreciation. This is of course the excess of current-dollar over historical-cost depreciation. It appears in Chart 3.

Notwithstanding the fact that the *ratio* of current-dollar to historical-cost depreciation has declined sharply since 1947–49 (Chart 2), the *amount* by which the former exceeds the latter has risen irregularly *and is now at or near its peak*.

CHART 3

Amounts by Which Current-Dollar Depreciation Exceeds Historical-
Cost Depreciation, for All American Business, Using (A) An Index
of Capital Goods Prices, (B) An Index of the Prices of All Privately
Produced Goods and Services

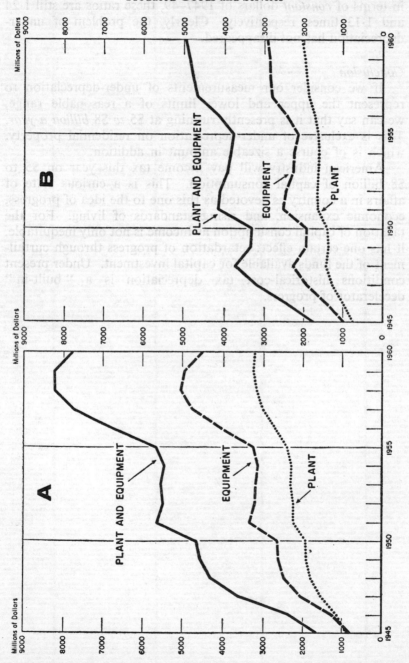

Under-depreciation in 1960 (for plant and equipment combined) was 1·86 times the 1947–49 average by one measurement (with the capital goods index) and 1·45 times by the other. Even if we restate the deficiency (which is, of course, in current dollars) in terms of *constant* dollars of 1947–49, these ratios are still 1·24 and 1·13 times, respectively. Clearly, the problem of under-depreciation has not disappeared.

Conclusion

If we consider our measurements of under-depreciation to represent the upper and lower limits of a reasonable range, we can say that it is presently running at $5 *to* $8 *billion a year*. This is exclusive of under-depreciation on residential property, which is of course a sizeable amount in addition.

American industry will pay income tax this year on $5 to $8 billion of capital consumption. This is a curious state of affairs in a country as devoted as this one to the idea of progress, economic expansion, and rising standards of living. For the taxation of capital consumption as income is not only inequitable, it has one certain effect: retardation of progress through curtailment of the funds available for capital investment. Under present conditions historical-cost tax depreciation is a " built-in " decelerator of progress.

Accountancy in the Modern State [*]

By Henry Smith
Vice-Principal, Ruskin College, Oxford.

I

THE ordinary layman must learn with surprise that before the war it was the official business of nobody to measure or estimate the national income, and that only the disinterested labours of economists and statisticians, in their private capacity, served to penetrate the gloom surrounding what is, after all, the sum total of " everybody's business." The strangeness must be the more pronounced because for decades it had been becoming increasingly important for the incomes of individuals and corporate bodies to be defined with the maximum of precision. As income tax became more steeply graduated, more discriminating between different classes of income, more carefully adapted by the system of allowances to individual capacity to pay, so it became more necessary to state with clarity the magnitude and composition of that to a share of which the state laid claim. Large as this might loom in the eyes of the citizen, however, it was only the fringe of the problem. An increasing proportion of the income of the community was coming to be earned corporately, through the activity of companies. Now the simplest form of this type of organisation, when once it has passed beyond the stage of partnership, presents a host of problems relating to the definition of its income and to the explanation of its financial position to its amateur and absentee proprietors. With the development of the holding company, too often showing in its published accounts only the net income accruing from the combined activities of its subsidiaries, the gap between the " owner " and his property tends to become so wide that he does not know from what part of it his income is derived, and thus, *ipso facto*, cannot control it.

It is mainly with the two tasks indicated above—the definition of the income of the individual for tax purposes, and the definition of the income of corporate bodies for the information of

[*] Part I of this article appeared in the *Political Quarterly*, April 1947. Part II was written in 1961 for this edition of *Studies*.

their proprietors—that the development of the profession of accountancy has been associated. Of the former, there is little to say; the Commissioners of Inland Revenue have in their employment accountants as able as those in private practice: a body of tacitly accepted " case law " has inevitably developed and it is to be doubted if the activity of the profession in this field has had any great effects upon its social standards. (One only grieves to think of two bodies of able men being employed in such a manner that, from the point of view of the national income, they cancel out. In the economic field, too, the essence of tragedy lies in the conflict of the virtuous.)

The latter, however, is an entirely different matter. It is hardly an exaggeration to say that the normal company director regards himself as so much better a judge of the policy of his company that he can and should decide (within the law) with what information it is safe, in their own interests, to provide his shareholders. And, in a word, the directors engage the accountants and determine their remuneration. Now, as a body, accountants are honourable men, and maintain a rigorous professional standard: the question of distortion or concealment of truth does not arise in any crude form. But, inevitably, the profession accepts the attitude of the directors, and, where the law and the custom of accountancy permit of a greater or a lesser revelation, choose the latter. The question of where the line may legitimately be drawn between concealment and justifiable simplification is often, however, a delicate matter. It is in this field, both in business practice and, occasionally, in a court of law, that the really eminent accountant is called upon to deliver a judgment. He has thus, to a marked degree, become the custodian of the moral standards of the business world.

This conclusion was forced upon the writer in the course of duties undertaken during the war, which involved placing considerable limitations upon the activities of businessmen: controlling their profits, directing their activity, securing their co-operation in the field of distribution and, in short (largely by permitting them to make generous profits in some branches of activity, while preventing them elsewhere), ensuring that their conduct was in conformity to the directives laid down by the British Government. A technique of this character naturally raised innumerable questions which were essentially moral or ethical in their character. To what rate of profit was a manufacturer entitled who had, before the war, made a large gross profit and spent most of it in advertising, when he could now sell all he made at more than the pre-war price, with no advertisement? Was it *right* to spoil his post-war goodwill by letting the consumer have the product at cost of production plus a reasonable net profit? What net profit, the residue of the pre-war gross profit, or some rate introduced *ab ovo*, was *just* or " reasonable "? What claim had the distributor to a share in the total supply of some commodity in short supply, because he had handled it before the war, when the supply was so low that no justice to the consumer could, because of the limits of physical divisibility, be secured? Should, in such circumstances, the consumer be expected to pay the cost of an elaborate nation-wide allocation scheme which would result in each retailer getting enough for some 5 per cent. of his customers?

To all these questions, and a thousand more, the general directive—that the minimum of disturbance to peacetime channels and customs of trade should be introduced—gave no answer at all. When the solutions natural to an economist were proposed they were, almost without exception, rejected, usually on the ground that to subject businessmen to the equivalent of " perfect competition " would cost the Ministry concerned their goodwill and co-operation, and would indeed be neither fair nor in accordance with the directive, because they were not accustomed to such conditions. Finally, in most cases where the problem resolved itself most nearly into a question of right or wrong, the authority of the accountant was invoked, and in the main accepted, as the interpreter of the moral code of the business world.

It is therefore of paramount importance that we should understand what are the standards which the accountant applies in such cases. His judgment, it must be remembered, falls mainly upon two points: the definition of ownership and the adequacy of information. In so far as the latter is concerned with company accounts, it is, in fact, one aspect of the former. Ownership implies control: control is not possible without adequate information. In the immediate future the people of this country are going to become the owners of a very substantial proportion of the industrial property of the country. The extent to which that ownership is real will depend upon what the accountants tell them. The following examples, therefore, may indicate what we may expect.

Lord Plender, in his Jubilee Address on behalf of the Institute of Chartered Accountants in 1930, has defined the role of the accountant in the present economic fabric adequately and concisely: " Today a chartered accountant's experience is not limited to the auditing of accounts, nor is his practice confined to that class of work only; but he is able, through the knowledge he obtains in dealing with the undertakings that come under his observation, to advise boards of directors, private manufacturers, merchants and others, on financial and business questions generally, on administration and costing, and he assists largely in amalgamations and in the adjustments of capital arising in a reorganising of business. No company issues a prospectus containing a statement of profit without a public accountant reporting on it. . . . The liquidation of companies, the office of receiver and manager, and that of trustee in bankruptcy or under deeds of assignment are, as a rule, in the hands of a qualified public accountant. They also act as arbitrators or umpires in cases where profits and the value of shares are to be determined."

The previous year, Mr. George O. May, in a paper presented in New York to the International Congress on Accounting, reviewed the functions of public accountants in the light of the tendency towards mergers and consolidations which had been manifest during the preceding decades, and which had been accompanied by a marked diffusion of the ownership of corporation stock. " The services of the public accountant may take one of two forms: the first, and I trust the most common form, should be giving sound advice to those responsible for the reporting and financial policies of the corporations, and dissuading them from any accounting policy which might be unjust to any group of persons having a legitimate interest therein; the second, when the first fails, protecting the interests of those who may be adversely affected by action of the management by insisting on a proper disclosure of what has been done. . . . The legal position has become so unsatisfactory that accountants, guided by sound principles and the best opinion of the day, must assume responsibility in approving or disapproving practices admittedly not illegal."

Sir Harold Bellman, speaking in April 1938 to the London and District Society of Incorporated Accountants, explicitly accepts the responsibility indicated by the previous statements. " For centuries the Church was the chief critic of business methods—the grand, ethical censor, as it were. Since the Church largely abandoned this role there has been no effective centralised substitute . . . it is now possible to discern a groping towards a condition of business which has a broad ethical justification. . . . This consideration, for instance, colours a good deal of recent discussion regarding advertising. Thus this influence today, as far as the accountant is concerned, is in the wider rather than the narrower ethical obligations."

Finally, Mr. P. D. Leake, addressing the Leeds and District Chartered Accountants Student Society in 1931, is quite definite in his claims: " Accounting science is the science of finance; the whole art of adjusting money matters: the assessment of value for money and the just price. Its aim is always the attainment of equilibrium and the fair exchange, and thus our science is concerned, *inter alia,* with the money factors inherent in the production and right distribution of wealth arising out of human effort. Accounting science is, in a word, the science of equity. . . . Modern accounting science must directly concern itself not only between individual and individual, but between bodies of employers and bodies of employed, and also between individual and state, individual and municipality, and between nation and nation."

It seems clear that the profession of accountancy, from the previous quotation, is not unaware of the moral authority which it wields. What is its code of morality? In the days when economists performed the hieratic function they sought authority from the concept of the public good, which they identified with the result of the interplay of self-seeking interests. Even in the time of the " classical " economists this involved a certain selection of evidence, and some slight illogicality: today it is manifestly impossible. The accountant, however, by training, and of necessity, takes a narrower view. It is his function to hold the balance equitably between individuals possessed of definite property rights, behind which it is not his function to peer.

But this " uncritical " attitude is inevitably strongly biased in favour of the *status quo.* Property rights may attach to the goodwill of a firm producing a spurious patent medicine, or to that engendered by the creation by skilful advertisement of a fictitious reputation for a standard product. A monopoly exploiting the consumer has an earning record which entitles it to an appropriate valuation. What criterion is to be applied when, as is most likely, firms in industries due for nationalisation possess an earning record into which an element of monopoly enters? This may not be as flagrant as in the examples quoted above, but, still may, thanks to past conservative legislation, be not unappreciable (*e.g.*, in most firms in the steel industry).

The *a priori* expectation that the standard of the accountant would be the uncritical acceptance of existing rights to income, albeit after most careful definition and exhaustive scrutiny, seems to be borne out. For example, Mr. Leake, quoted above, goes on in the same address to suggest, " Taxation should be used to raise the revenue needed for the common good, and not as a means of distributing wealth." A suitable fiscal code, he explains, could be brought about by abolishing graduated taxation, and introducing a flat rate of income tax without a downward exemption limit. He continues, in a manner reminiscent of Harriet Martineau, to concern himself as in duty bound with the relations " between bodies of employers and bodies of employed," stating, somewhat erroneously, that some 80 per cent. of the costs of industry consist of wages and salaries, and continuing—" those entitled to what we call profits . . . either take the profit or bear the loss. And the losses are generally due to the fact that the professed partners have been paid in the form of wages and salaries more in amount than has been produced. When these things are better known, wage-earners will become helpful and sympathetic, rather than antagonistic to their employers." It is difficult to discern here any concern beyond the completely uncritical definition of existing property rights. This is no doubt an extreme example of an ultra-conservative point of view, but it is interesting in that it illustrates the inevitable tendency for professional concern with the definition of rights to income arising out of property to lead to the denial of any other rights to income *except* those arising out of ownership. Is this point of view altogether unrepresentative of the profession? Unless it is, then if too much influence is allowed to accounting opinion our programme of nationalisation promises to be expensive. The point is of sufficient importance for further evidence to be desirable.

Lord Plender in 1932, in " Some Observations on Company Balance Sheets," provided an adequate example of the type of reflection which has earned the accountant his authority. " Directors should not necessarily regard legal requirements as their only guide in submitting accounts. There are occasions—many, in fact—when directors should, in the shareholders' interests, go much further. The primary considerations which should influence directors in the form in which a balance-sheet is presented . . . are firstly, the interests of the company's business as such, and secondly the reasonable requirements of shareholders whose interest is that of a permanent or semi-permanent investor." In the course of this paper, however, he expressly denies that the statistician has any claim that balance-sheets should be so framed as to provide him with data, *i.e.*, denies that the activities of a business are of any concern to any but the legitimate investor. The same attitude finds expression very clearly in an article by Mr. Stanley W. Rowland (" Some Modern Difficulties in the Measurement of Profit " in *Some Modern Business Problems,* ed. Plant, 1934.) ". . . the accountant does not regard an undertaking as accountable to *society* for the maintenance of the physical amount of earning power which an economic system has committed to its charge: on the other hand, he prepares an account between the undertaking and its *proprietors* of the money capital adventured by them and committed to the administration of the directors."

Two important points emerge from the consideration of these statements. First, the distinction between the interest of the " business as such " and the reasonable requirements of the shareholders. It is difficult to see what, apart from the interest of the shareholders (the interest of the public, and of the employees having, by definition, been excluded), the interest of the business as such can be, apart from the interest of the senior executives and directors. Second, the denial of the right of society to an interest in the affairs of an industrial undertaking merits consideration. This throws an interesting light on the operation of nationalised industries, apart from the question of their acquisition. Will the accountant, become civil servant, regard the executive chiefs as he does boards of directors? Will he have regard to the interest of " the business as such " in distinction from the views of the shareholders? Will he consider the public as the " shareholders " or only as " society "? The school in which he had been trained may make him a good servant to a rigidly formulated code, but seem to render him a dangerous person to entrust with the interpretation of policy.

II

The first half of this article stands almost as it was written in 1947: it reflected the wartime experience of the writer, and was possibly a not unreasonable expression of where a fair body of economic opinion, as it then was, stood with regard to accountancy, as it then was. During the fourteen years since, the author has taken part in various public inquiries into commercial practices in Britain and outside, has had something to do with the formulation and enforcement of the law concerning restrictive practices, and has seen something of economic reconstruction in Germany and economic planning in India. Some of these activities have brought him again into close contact with accountants, some have led him away from them. Meanwhile both accountancy and economics have been changing and developing. In a life fully occupied by just failing to keep pace with the changing theory and practice of his own side of the social sciences, much of what has been going on in accountancy has, of necessity, escaped him. Equally of necessity, therefore, what follows must be regarded as no more than the superficial impressions of a preoccupied amateur.

In general, what seems to have emerged from this period has been a very considerable assimilation of the points of view of the accountant and the economist. This has been due to a series of forces, some arising out of the internal development of economic and accounting techniques, some (in so far as the exogamous and the endogamous can be distinguished) from external influences to which both have been subjected. These can roughly be grouped as follows.

First, the effect of inflation. The slow inflation of prices in the Western world since 1945, following upon the general under-estimation of the economic cost of fighting to the point of unconditional surrender, has made it clear to accountants that capital is more than a sum of money once invested in a deteriorating physical asset and due to be recovered before its earning capacity is exhausted. Admittedly the majority of accountants adhere to historical cost as the foundation of depreciation policy, but certainly not because it has some absolute foundation which other approaches lack. Both in Britain and the U.S.A. historical and replacement costs have their advocates, with practice dominated by the former, but it is employed only as a basis upon which to build estimates of additional necessary provision. A view which seems typical of contemporary British accountants is that of F. Sewell Bray, addressing the Incorporated Accountants in 1951. " Income as we all know is devoted to consumption expenditure, and saving, which at bottom wealth implies a stock of *real* assets . . . it should not be difficult to see that income is equal to consumption expenditure plus saving and that fundamentally saving is resolved in asset forming (or if you so prefer, capital) expenditure which constitutes an addition to wealth. I think this gives rise to a formal principle of accounting design which is expressed by a set of fundamentally related accounts, one to measure periodic income, two to show its transfer and disposition, three to explain the applications of retained income or saving, its effect on wealth or capital charges, and four to measure and portray those resources which together make up the wealth of an entity." Nearly twenty years of rising replacement costs have clearly made their mark on accountants. At the same time economists, who have been talking about inflation for a very long time, have I think been more influenced in their thinking than many of them perhaps realise, not by the slow inflationary attrition of assets (of which Fisher was warning the world in 1900), but by the dramatic collapse of the German monetary system after defeat, the succeeding economic chaos, and the even more dramatic resurgence of the German economy after the currency reform. The picture of economic reality which its monetary mirror creates can be a distorted and misleading image in certain cases; but the distortion can be corrected or even eliminated. When the mirror breaks all is darkness. Mrs. Joan Robinson, an economist somewhat left of centre, writes in *The Accumulation of Capital*, " The distinction between capital and income is rooted in moral ideas. Morality is neither rational nor irrational; it operates, so to say, in a different dimension . . . to be viable over a long run, in peaceful conditions, an economy must be impregnated with the peasant's morality: this is pre-eminently true of an industrial economy where production capacity consists largely of a stock of long-lived equipment which must be maintained by repairs and renewals, and which can function only in an environment in which the rules of the game in respect to property, trade and the financial system are accepted and maintained in working order." Inflation has brought economist and accountant closer together.

Second, the Keynesian revolution in economics has given birth to the science of social accounting. Economists now know what it is they must quantify if they are to have their eyes on the determining factors in the growth and stability of the national income. And the techniques used in building up the national income estimates, and in separating out the significant categories within it, are, those of the accountant, adopted with very little alteration. One may here quote M. P. Fogarty, the fifteenth chapter of whose *Economic Control* contains what is probably the best short description of the contemporary relations between economist and accountant which is now available. ". . . social accounting has bridged the gap by facing the economist with data like those of the accountant and bringing the accountant right into the traditional field of the economist . . . social accounting data have been rapidly built up but are still far from complete. The specialists in this field overlap with those in econometrics and are still comparatively few. The art they practise is new. . . . But social accounting has already grown far enough to prove not only that the logic of accountancy and econometrics [1] is the same, but also that it is possible to combine their actual procedures in a system which uses the methods and experience of traditional accounting (including its newer developments)

[1] The science of statistical observation of theoretically-founded concepts.

to answer the more fully thought-out questions which the econometrician poses." Indeed the division of economics into macro-economics, concerned with framing questions concerning economic growth for the social accountants to answer, and micro-economics, concerned with the pricing policies and cost problems of individual groups within the economy, has had the curious result that, of those concerned with the latter branch, some have been tending to abandon the true interests of the economist in the general good either for an excessive concentration upon detail (" small castles, easily defended," to quote a recent historian of the Crusades on the work of his contemporaries) or for a complete acceptance of the individual interests of entrenched groups in the economy which recalls the attitude of an earlier generation of accountants. But it is much safer to blame this upon the terrifying magnitude of the statistical data with which the economist is now confronted, in the first case, and the increasing difficulty (to which reference is made below) in quantifying influences which cannot readily be given a monetary value, than upon contamination by contact.

Third, one may, at least in Britain, place the problems which have arisen out of the conduct of the nationalised industries. At the outset it may be said that the accounts of all the nationalised industries leave little to be desired in what they tell the " shareholder." Where difficulty has arisen is in the manner in which clear explanation of price policy has been lacking. This is not a matter in which full accounting information is of much help. Economists have been somewhat divided over the question of whether average or marginal costs should be the basis upon which prices ought to be fixed: in general, opinion is fairly strongly in favour of the latter, except in the case of industries with long period increasing returns, but even here the application of the principle need not involve permanent subsidy if a system of charging what the traffic will bear is introduced, so that consumers contribute to fixed costs according to their ability to pay. Most economic criticism of the nationalised industries is based upon two points: first, the public should be able to check on the reasonableness of the costs they are called upon to meet; second, when publicly owned industries fail to cover their costs (except purely by accident, which may happen to many a privately owned concern) the public ought to be able to refer to and if necessary criticise the instructions which the industry has been given. The latter point is put most clearly by Lewis in an article in the *Political Quarterly* for April/June 1950. " We have now considered . . . circumstances which may justify a public corporation in making either a profit or a loss. They all have this in common—namely they raise issues of public policy which are independent of the particular industry, and of whether it is being run by a public corporation or not. If any of these arguments is valid, it is equally valid for private enterprise. For the issues are issues not of industrial management but of public policy. It follows that in each case the decision whether a profit or a loss is to be made is a decision not for the management of the public corporation but ultimately for Parliament." It would appear therefore that the ball is back in the court of the conventional if up-to-date accountant. To deal with the first type of criticism we must overlap the next section of this article, which deals with the development of cost accounting.

This I have placed as the fourth main reason for the assimilation between the two sciences. This branch of accounting has passed far beyond the stage at which its concern was the proper allocation of overhead costs within a single firm. One may in this context quote the Preliminary Report of the Research Committee of the Incorporated Accountants, which appeared in 1950. " The changed perspective of accounting to which we have referred, looks upon *production efficiency* as best expressed in the relation between output actually produced and that which should have been produced. The measurement of this relationship required the ascertainment of some homogeneous unit with which to measure production and some standard basis for calculating what has been produced . . . there is always the problem to be considered of whether what is measured is the efficiency of the operator or the efficiency of the standard setter." Here is an approach which is almost identical with that adopted by the economist when thinking of alternative costs. This recognition of similar objectives, and of the employment of similar concepts, leads indeed to the borrowing of tools. E. A. Lowe, writing in *Accountancy* in April 1959, says " much more attention might well be directed to statistical techniques at present considered to be out of the accountant's field." His subject was the accounting needs of management. Stafford Beer addressing the Conference on Management Accounting (held jointly by the British Institute of Management and the British Productivity Council in 1956) urges the possibility of utilising the economist's tools of marginal cost and his technique of linear programming. It follows that accountants are developing the methods which economists claim will be needed for the external and independent evaluation of the efficiency of nationalised industry.

Fifth among the influences of reconciliation are to be placed the effects, both in Britain and the U.S.A., of the long struggle to restrict monopolistic practices where they are harmful, to limit practices artificially restricting free competition, and to control the group of natural monopolies which have come to be labelled " public utilities." Attempts to define the public interest in this field turn in fact upon the clear statement of the magnitude and the source of profit. Here the change in British company law following upon the report of the Cohen Commission, and the operations of the U.S. Securities and Exchange Commission, has given a lead to accountancy which, upon investigation, seems to consist mainly of enforcing the wider utilisation of techniques independently inaugurated by progressive accountants. As the law regarding monopoly and restrictive practices in the U.S.A. has developed, emphasis has been increasingly laid on the misuse rather than the possession of monopolistic powers. This gives more scope for the accountant than is the case in Britain, where the attenuated powers of the Monopolies Control Commission seem of less importance than the work of the Restrictive Practices Court, operating against a code of allowed pleadings rigidly defined by Parliament. To quote Lemke, writing in *Accounting Research* on the development of public utilities accounting in U.S.A.: "These monopolies are controlled in various respects: in particular, income is restricted by setting rates for service at a level which should yield a fair return on their investment, measured in various ways. Presumably the consumer is safeguarded if the monopoly does not earn an abnormal income as defined by the applicable laws, and the public utility is protected if it is allowed to earn a fair return on its investment. . . . Accounting is thus required to give effect to a philosophy of regulation. It serves as a vehicle for carrying out policy or as a tool for making regulation effective. It is to be doubted whether there is any attempt consciously to create accounting principles in a broad sense, in spite of the fact that public utility accounting is often accused of doing so." This is, from a different angle, complementary to the argument of Lewis, quoted above, that there should be no special economic (or accounting) principles applicable to public enterprise which are not equally applicable to private business.

To summarise, therefore, it would seem that the part which the accountant plays in the modern state of mixed private and public enterprise, heavy state expenditure on both capital goods and services, acknowledged public responsibility for the maintenance of a reasonable level of employment, and organised public economic information—a definition which fits both Britain and the U.S.A.—shows a most remarkable power of adaptation to change, if the opinions quoted in Part I are in any way representative of what was then contemporary practice and theory. Lemke may again be quoted: " The accountant is essentially a manufacturer of information. Just as many industrial manufacturers are insulated from the final consumer, so in much the same way the accountant meets a derived demand. He must either anticipate what the final product should be in order to be saleable, or merely supply the parts for the user to adapt to his own purposes." The pattern of demand has changed. Even the basic enduring demand for clear statements of income for tax and dividend distribution has come to involve the accountant, like the economist, in trying to penetrate behind the veil of money. The needs of public accountancy, the necessity for standard cost investigations as checks on the efficiency of large-scale private and public concerns, have called into being new techniques much closer to those traditionally associated with the economist. At the same time many of the things which economists in the past would perhaps have liked to attempt to quantify and incorporate into the policy of public enterprise—the consumer's surplus, the difference between public and private costs and revenues— have come to be recognised as unquantifiable above the level of the politician's guess or prejudice. The quantities which most contemporary economists seek to establish, incomes, income distribution, trends of growth, relationships between capital accumulation and the growth of output, involve them in work in those fields where the techniques of the econometrician, the statistician and the accountant become almost indistinguishable.

Soviet Accounting and Economic Decisions *

By Robert W. Campbell

*Associate Professor of Economics,
Indiana University.*

THE purpose of this contribution is to inquire into the relationship between Soviet accounting and the economic problem of rational choice among alternatives. The question we are asking is: " Do Soviet accounting practices permit correct economic decisions, or do they constitute an obstacle to economic efficiency? " The rationale for this question is that accounting is ultimately the main source of information concerning the costs of alternatives, and it is the comparison of the costs of alternatives that is at the root of all economizing.

This is a somewhat restricted and artificial point of view from which to examine Soviet accounting. The most important function of accounting is to provide information for control purposes rather than for decision-making purposes. Economic use of this information is really only a by-product of the process. This is probably even more true in the Soviet economy than in the U.S. economy, and the emphasis of all Soviet accounting literature is on the control functions of accounting. When Soviet accountants set out to define the functions and scope of accounting they do not even include the function of facilitating economic rationality. The writings of Soviet accountants are barren of any concern with the implications of their practices for economic calculation. That the question is raised at all betrays the prejudices of a " bourgeois economist " rather than the preoccupations of the economists and accountants of the Soviet Union. Consequently the effect of accounting practices on economic decisions in the Soviet economy is a very elusive one to deal with. Ours must be an oblique sort of inquiry. We cannot just mine the Soviet sources to find instances where Soviet economists have concluded that their accounting has led them to wrong decisions. Rather

---

* This article, and the Comment by Herbert S. Levine that follows, appeared in *Value and Plan*, ed. Gregory Grossman (Berkeley and Los Angeles: University of California Press, 1960). That book contains full references to Russian works cited, here omitted.

we must analyse given accounting rules to see whether they accord with theoretical ideals of the cost concept, and then hope that we can find real-life situations where incorrect cost concepts will mislead planners into errors of choice.

How does accounting affect economic decisions? It will probably be helpful to distinguish two aspects of the problem. (1) In some instances the data of cost accounting may serve directly as criteria on which economic decisions are based. Soviet economic discussions are full of examples where technological alternatives are accepted or rejected on the basis of relative costs. The question is whether the bookkeepers are following rules in generating these data which are relevant to the problem. (2) Any attempt to discuss economic calculation in the Soviet economy leads inevitably to the question of the meaningfulness of Soviet prices. The theories and actual practices of Soviet price planners are still an obscure part of our picture of how the Soviet economy works, but it is clear that one of the basic criteria used in determining prices is cost of production—and cost of production means cost data provided by accounting. So cost accounting may impinge on decision making at one remove, through its influence on pricing. There are, of course, enough other peculiarities in Soviet price-setting practices to overshadow or perhaps offset errors in cost accounting in individual instances. For example, the omission of interest and rent, the variegated profit pattern, and the general failure to consider value from the demand side may offset accounting errors, or may swamp them quantitatively. These questions we ignore here and are concerned with cost-accounting errors alone as one independent influence on pricing. One other preliminary point: It is clear that economic decisions in the Soviet Union are often not based on any appeal to a concept of rationality at all. Thus it may be irrelevant whether the costs and prices we are so preoccupied with are correct or not. But there are enough situations where Soviet planners do seek to satisfy some criterion of efficiency to justify the rationale of our discussion.

General deficiencies of Soviet cost accounting

It is unnecessary to discuss here all the ways in which Soviet accounting rules fail to measure accurately the sacrifices involved in producing given outputs.[1] But the main deficiencies of Soviet cost accounting in this respect can be summarized as follows:

---

[1] A more detailed discussion of the correctness of Soviet cost-accounting principles may be found in my doctoral thesis, *Soviet Cost Accounting* (Harvard University, 1955).

(1) Soviet depreciation accounting is very inexact. Incorrect valuation of assets and inaccurate rates of depreciation mean that depreciation charges are a poor estimate of the costs of capital consumption. (2) Allocations of current expenditure among individual kinds of output are made inaccurately or incorrectly. Soviet accountants accumulate large amounts of expense in general overhead accounts and then distribute these crudely among shops, sections and products. Certain outlays are never charged against the cost of output. Allocations may be according to mechanical formulas with little attempt to trace the actual benefits of outlays to specific products. Soviet planners try to value joint products by appeal to accounting rather than to economic concepts. (3) The general quality of Soviet accounting is low in the sense that it is too aggregative. The flow of expense through the plant is poorly traced, so that often costs of individual kinds of output are not ascertainable, costs of separate processes are never determined, and so on.

The effects of depreciation errors

Soviet charges for depreciation are a shortweight measure of the costs of capital consumption because fixed assets are under-valued and because the rates are based on unrealistically long conceptions of service life. One way in which these errors may affect economic decisions is by distorting the structure of prices. Distortions arise partly from the fact that rates are not uniformly low, but are differentially understated from branch to branch and from enterprise to enterprise. This deficiency has long been acknowledged by Soviet writers, but only recently, as a result of an intensive review of the whole question of depreciation, have statistical data for demonstrating it become available.

If the rates of depreciation are too low, then at the time of retirement not all the original value of assets will have been recovered in depreciation charges; assets will be shown on the books as not completely depreciated. Under Soviet accounting rules the amount of such unrecovered value is determined at the time of retirement of assets, and the loss involved (sometimes the gain) is written off the capital accounts directly and is not reflected in costs or in profit and loss. Thus the computation of losses on liquidation has always been a routine entry, required in the enterprise accounts by the logic of double entry, but not looked upon as an important economic statistic in itself. But now that the Russians have raised the issue of the adequacy of depreciation policy they have been studying these data for the first time, and have published the results for some ministries.

Table I, column 1, shows the per cent. of original value of fixed assets recovered through depreciation at time of liquidation. Usually these are averages for three recent years, so that abnormal annual variations are excluded. They are still not necessarily an accurate measure of how the rate of recovery is proceeding on assets still in use, but even so they may be taken as a rough indication of the relative understatement of rates in different branches.[2] In column 2 are listed the percentage shares of depreciation in total outlays on production in these same branches of industry. These two sets of figures can then be used to compute an index of what costs of production would have been (with reported costs taken as 100) if the rates were set high enough to

Table 1

COST DISTORTIONS FROM INADEQUATE DEPRECIATION CHARGES

Branch	Per cent. of original value of assets recovered through depreciation charges	Depreciation as per cent. of total production costs	Index of costs corrected for depreciation
	1	2	3
Coal industry	25·8	6·3	118·1
Oil industry	72·3	11·9	104·5
Electric stations	63·6	16·8	109·6
Construction material ..	51·0	5·35	105·1
Lumber, woodworking, etc.	44·7	3·4	104·2
Light industry	76·0	1·03	100·3
Textile industry	73·5	1·0	100·4
Food products	61·4	1·33	100·8
Meat and milk	60·5	1·54	101·0
Fish industry	54·9	3·69	103·1

The figures in the table are averages for 1952, 1954 and 1955.

eliminate losses on liquidation. These indexes are shown in column 3. As the table shows, relative costs of separate branches are noticeably distorted. One doubts that these distortions will lead to any seriously wrong decisions. But the important point is that if there is this much variation between such aggregated units as ministries, there must be much more significant distortions at the level of the enterprise, where the variance among rates is greater. It is primarily here that distortion may enter.

The distortion caused by incorrect rates may be increased (or perhaps offset) by the heterogeneous valuation of assets. Fixed assets are shown on the books of Soviet enterprises at

[2] Note that many of the most important branches of industry, such as machine building, metallurgy, chemicals, are not included here. This probably means only that data were not available for these branches, not that liquidation losses were insignificant in them.

original cost, so inflation has led to great variations in the value of identical assets on the balance-sheets of different enterprises. Furthermore, there are certain kinds of outlays which are never capitalized as assets, and the relative importance of these in different branches varies. The most notable of these uncapitalized investments is prospecting expenses in the extractive branches of industry. The possible magnitude of the error here is illustrated by the oil industry. It is stated that the total expenditures by the Ministry of the Oil Industry on geological work and exploratory drilling (for some unspecified but apparently recent year) was 4 billion rubles. Since these expenditures do not give rise to any specific enterprises it is hard to know how to assign them, and so they are neither capitalized nor charged as current costs in the accounts of enterprises. The gross value of output of this ministry in 1955 (in 1955 prices) was only 15·8 billion rubles. In petroleum refining, moreover, raw materials and fuel (largely petroleum) made up 85·7 per cent. of costs. Using this as a crude guide to eliminate double counting, we conclude that the net output of the ministry was no more than 9 billion rubles. Perhaps not all exploration expense is rightly chargeable to current year output, but at any rate it is clear that the omission of exploration outlays means a marked understatement of the cost of oil.

It is impossible to specify concretely what wrong decisions have flowed, or will flow, from this cost-accounting error, but it seems highly likely that there will be such wrong decisions. Consider, for example, two important areas of technological change that the Soviet planners have recently been discussing, namely, the change-over of the railroads to diesel fuel and the expansion of synthetic chemicals output on the basis of petroleum raw materials. There are cited wonderful cost advantages of plastics versus other kinds of materials, and the advantages of using petrochemical rather than agricultural raw materials as the basis for these products. This may well be a rational technological change, but it is easy to believe that calculations in individual instances will be confused because of a false notion of the cost of petroleum. Certainly at the margin of substitution the issue will be confused. As for modernizing the railroads, the costs of diesel fuel will be attractively, but misleadingly, low because of these cost omissions. There are further elements of confusion here. Diesel fuel may be priced too low, but at the same time some prospecting costs have been omitted from the costs of coal, and the rates of depreciation are even less adequate in the coal than in the oil industry. Perhaps these errors will neatly cancel out so that the cost data will correctly mirror national economic sacrifice of the two alternatives. But this optimistic possibility is hard to accept on faith.

A second general area where Soviet depreciation accounting may lead to wrong decisions is in replacement policy; the depreciation practices probably introduce a bias against the correct amount of replacement. There are two distinct mechanisms at work here. The first operates through the Soviet procedure in making replacement decisions. When Soviet writers formulate the replacement decision in any clear way, they nearly always treat it as a choice between two alternatives. The cost of producing with the old machine is compared with the cost of producing under a replacement variant. Most Soviet writers on this subject hold that the unamortized value of the assets replaced should be included as one of the costs of the replacement variant. The approach itself is incorrect and will result in a bias against replacement, although the accountants are not to blame here. But the accounting practices aggravate the error. Given rates that are too low, many existing assets will be shown on the books with an overly large part of their value unrecovered by depreciation charges, and so the replacement variants will be burdened with the accounting errors of previous years.

This bias may be strengthened by another peculiarity of Soviet depreciation accounting. The Soviet concept of depreciation is somewhat different from that in Western accounting practice. Depreciation charges are supposed not only to recover funds for the replacement of assets, but also to provide funds for their " partial " replacement, that is to finance major repairs (called capital repairs) during the life of the asset. The portion of the charge intended for replacement is removed from the enterprise and used to finance centrally planned investment. The portion designed to cover costs of capital repair is left at the disposal of the enterprise, but its expenditure for this specific purpose is controlled by having it segregated in the " special account " of the enterprise in the State Bank (*Gosbank*, the one big bank that supervises transactions and controls the use of funds by Soviet firms). When the funds are used to finance capital repair, the expenditure is in the first place charged to the asset account; later, this amount is written off from the asset and also from accumulated depreciation.

Given the serious inflation that has occurred during the life history of many assets of Soviet enterprises, it turns out that the capital-repair rate, applied to the original cost of the asset, does not provide enough funds to pay for capital repair at present price levels. What the Russians have done is to leave the over-all depreciation rates about the same, but increase the share going for capital repair, particularly in older enterprises. And in many years they have provided additional funds for capital repair through budget financing. So in older enterprises it may happen that capital repair carried out on a given asset is nearly as great as its original cost.[3] Since these expenditures are used to reduce the depreciation shown in the accounts, it may appear that a very old asset is virtually undepreciated. Indeed, the older an asset is, and the more it has been repaired, the more likely it is that it will appear to be totally undepreciated. These are the beginnings of a vicious circle.

The second mechanism by which replacement will be discouraged is the segregation of the replacement funds and the repair funds. Theoretically there is no reason why this should discourage replacement. If the decision-maker always made a rational choice between replacement and repair, and then was able to get funds to carry out that decision, the accounting segregation of repair and replacement allowances would not interfere with correct decisions. But in reality the constraint of availability of funds will probably dictate the decision. The plant manager's own funds, those in the special account in the Gosbank, are not unrestricted; the Gosbank will let him spend them only for purposes of capital repair. And given the fact that the other funds have already been extracted from his enterprise and put under the control of central planners, he may well have a hard time winning them back for his particular investment project. His local acuity of vision may be overruled by decision-makers higher up who probe blindly with aggregate indicators in search of efficiency in capital allocation. So he will have to repair the machine rather than replace it, and the capital of this economy will be directed to repair and other investments where the productivity of capital is less than in this particular replacement possibility.

Recently bank control over repair funds was somewhat loosened, presumably to eliminate this kind of bias. In 1955 the Gosbank was authorized to let the plants use the funds of the special account for modernization of equipment. This widens somewhat the range of decisions the plant manager may make in this area, but still exerts a bias against scrapping old equipment and replacing it with new.

---

[3] It sometimes happens that the total expenditure on capital repair has been greater than the original cost of the asset, so that deduction of these expenditures from depreciation would leave the depreciation account with a debit balance !

Joint-product situations

In joint-product situations Marxist theory leaves Soviet cost theorists adrift; joint products constitute a case *par excellence* where cost-of-production theories of value must founder. The responses of Soviet accountants to joint-product cases take two main forms: (1) allocation of costs on some " technological " but irrelevant basis, and (2) valuation of some of the outputs by comparison with the costs of products they can replace, and assignment of the rest of the outlays to the main products. The first is totally wrong, the second bears some resemblance to a productivity- or opportunity-cost approach to the determination of value. The opportunity-cost approach is sound as far as it goes, but the Soviet situation does not provide for the quantity reactions that would finally determine optimum prices and outputs. For instance, one author describes the following situation. In meat packing the principle implies that hides should be valued at the cost of hides obtained from other sources of supply. But it turns out that in some meat-packing enterprises this would make the value of hides greater than that of the meat! The price setters shrink from this absurdity, and set prices on packer hides much lower than prices on hides from other sources. But this is no great contribution to economic rationality. They should value the hides at their opportunity-cost (*i.e.*, at the same price as would have to be paid to get hides from an alternative source), and then make whatever adjustments in prices, output, and sources of supply for all units the cost data seem to call for.

Decisions connected with joint-product situations may arise in a narrower context—one which does not set in motion such a chain of successive reactions and adjustments. In this situation the problem may be set up in such a way that the accountants and price setters never have a chance to confuse the issue. This possibility is illustrated in a remarkable article on the " effectiveness " of using heat exchangers to generate steam from by-product heat of open-hearth furnaces used in steel-making. There is a question whether the steam shop should pay for the heat, and if so, what the value and therefore the price of the heat should be. The author says that the heat should be paid for (see below) and tries to figure the value of the heat by the opportunity-cost approach. He explains that we cannot simply allocate the cost of fuel burned in the open-hearth furnaces between the two processes on the basis of the ratio of calories sent to the heat exchanger to total calories. First, as an engineer, he is quick to note that the thermal efficiency of the heat exchanger is less than that of the traditional boiler, and so we must compensate the steam shop for accepting the worsened ratio of fuel input to steam output (both measured in calories). He also says that the cost per calorie of heating fuel is less than the cost per calorie of technological fuel, and raises the question, " Which is the appropriate price ? " At one point he says that the steam shop has the alternative of buying cheap calories in the form of heating fuel, and so for the steam shop the value of calories from the open hearths cannot exceed this limit (even though these calories cost the open-hearth shop the higher price). But he seems dubious about this argument, and advances several other rationalizations (all irrelevant). But this effort marks the boundary of his understanding. He fails to follow the approach to its logical conclusion and allow for the other disadvantageous input-output ratios of the heat-exchanger alternative. (He does say that they exist.) So he figures a value for heat that makes the cost of steam by the heat-exchanger process higher than for traditional boilers.

But he redeems himself in the end by pointing out that the question of effectiveness must be decided in a national-economic perspective. Inputs are being saved in the total process, and it matters little whether these savings are assigned to steel or steam. But as a practical afterthought he says that in the accounting the savings should be assigned to the open-hearth shop— the steam shop should pay for the heat. This will permit a lowered accounting cost for steel, and so enlist the support of the open-hearth shop for the innovation. He apparently thinks that the power structure in the combine is such that their support is more important than that of the heat shop. This is a useful reminder that rationality in economic decision-making embraces not only the mode of analysis applied to a problem, but also the institutional and motivational structure.

One of the most important joint-product examples in the modern economy is petroleum refining. There are many decisions that may turn on the price of various petroleum products, and if joint-product cost allocations made by accountants are going to influence economic decisions, here is where we might expect to find examples. The discussion of this possibility will have to be mostly an exercise in deductive reasoning, but it may still suggest some conclusions.

Petroleum refining is a variable-proportions case in which rational magnitudes for total output, proportions between products, and prices, will be determined by a complicated interaction of marginal costs for all products and the marginal productivities or utilities of the products as reflected in the levels and elasticities of demand. In the United States the importance of private automobiles means a large and inelastic demand for the light fractions. Increasing marginal costs of light products, obtained by deeper refining of a given amount of crude, requires that a large total of crude be refined, and the result is large supplies of heavy fractions. The nature of demand for them is such that low prices result. Against this background it is surprising to find that although the large demand for gasoline for private automobiles is absent in the Soviet market, the Soviet price structure for refined petroleum products is essentially the same as the U.S. price structure.[4]

It is not clear where the Soviet price structure comes from. I have seen no explicit discussion of how Soviet oil producers set prices. But it does not seem possible that they adopt any careful analysis of productivities. It seems much more likely that the price structure simply reflects the cost data generated in Soviet refineries. Methods of computing costs in petroleum refining have gone through considerable changes, but at the present time are more or less as follows. Output is divided into " main products " (mostly light fractions) and " by-products " (generally the heavier fractions). In a given process, such as straight distillation, the heavy residuals are valued at the price of crude or something less, and are subtracted from the value of raw materials going into the process. The remaining cost of raw material plus processing costs are then assigned to the main products in proportion to weight. This procedure continues through various stages of processing, and at the end results in cost figures for the various blending stocks. When these are combined into final products, the result is inevitably low costs for fuel oil and diesel oil, and high costs for lighter products.

In view of the Soviet demand situation, one wonders whether this cost-based price structure (if that is indeed what it is) is an appropriate one. It may be suspected that it values light fractions too highly and heavy ones too cheaply in view of their relative productivities. Can we conclude that the Russians have been misled into overemphasis on heavy petroleum fraction technologies? This would be a difficult assertion to support. Indeed it might be just as easy to find indications that the opposite has been true. It is conceivable that planners have failed to respond to the misleading prices.

This analysis is too vague to demonstrate that an error has been made, but it suggests a paradox which must inevitably

---

[4] See, for instance, the ruble-dollar price ratios given in Norman M. Kaplan and William L. White, *A Comparison of 1950 Wholesale Prices in Soviet and American Industry* (Santa Monica: The RAND Corporation, 1955).

confound our reflections on what constitutes rationality in the Soviet economy. The total score may not suffer if some of the cues in this game of pool are a little crooked—many of the players suffer from astigmatism. Or, to reformulate this paradox in more strictly economic terms, if the system gives rise to one irrational act, then over-all rationality may require others to make decisions which would be irrational if all were acting rationally. For example, if by some error the most productive uses of diesel fuel are not exploited, then we would not want a price system that reflected the potential productivity of diesel fuel and so led to decisions against the next-best uses.

Automation

Automation offers another concrete example of the influence of accounting on economic decisions. Much has been said in the Soviet press in recent months about the " effectiveness " of automation. The principle of automation is accepted, but there seems to be some dispute about what kinds of automation are effective and how far to carry the use of automatic equipment in individual situations. Obviously the correct sphere of application of automation and the optimum degree of automation will require close figuring. How may cost accounting introduce confusion into this decision?

There are many complaints that automation is discouraged by incorrectly high prices on the necessary equipment because the underlying cost calculations are inflated. Especially now, with the regionalization of administration, there are situations in which individual enterprises can exercise some control over their prices. Under the new system of regional economic councils (called *sovnarkhozy*) these councils propose prices for some of the output of enterprises in their regions for approval at higher levels. For some kinds of output the *sovnarkhozy* apparently have the right actually to set prices. There are also situations in which the buyer enters into the negotiations.

There is a great temptation to try to get exaggerated prices approved. This is not so much for profits, as for easier fulfilment of the output target. New items do not have " constant prices " and so they are counted in output at the " temporary prices " set in the manner described. The enterprise will certainly be partisan for higher prices, and the way it may hope to get them is by submitting exaggerated estimates of what cost will be for a new product. If these are purely prospective cost estimates, then it is not the cost accounting rules that are at fault, but it may be that misleading costs of actual output are used to bolster the estimates.

The *sovnarkhoz* planners are perhaps willing to connive at such price setting, but even if they are not, it may be difficult for them to determine real costs *ex post* as a basis for adjusting the temporary prices. Even if the prices are set first on the basis of cost estimates " *s potolka* " (pulled off the ceiling) the enterprise will try to rationalize these calculations after the fact and defend the original prices by exaggerated cost reports. It is stated that plants do try to drag out the period of these temporary prices for a longer period of time than the law envisages, and falsify their cost accounting. Many writers say that the reason for poor control of prices on the part of the superior organs is that they do not have good enough cost data from the enterprises to enable them to do a good job.

People on the other side of the automation controversy suggest that accounting rules may lead to overemphasis on automation. One author, for example, holds that failure to include obsolescence in the depreciation allowances will exaggerate the advantages of technical progress. His reasoning is not explicit, but he seems to be saying that the costs of the more capital-intensive, more specialized, and more rapidly changing new equipment will be underestimated relative to older technologies.

Another interesting article poses the following situation where the prevailing accounting procedures will give an unusually favorable view of automation. Suppose that in a given plant the question arises whether to automate a certain process. Costs under the new variant are estimated to see whether it is economically justified relative to the old process. Costs consist of labor, materials, depreciation, and the important item of overhead. Soviet procedures for dealing with overhead have traditionally been poor. A great variety of expenses are charged to this account, and are then distributed almost always in proportion to wages. So, says the author, if the bookkeeping department is asked to determine the cost of output under the new variant, the highly automated process, which uses relatively little labor, will be charged little overhead. So the costs of this variant look low, even though much of the overhead (*i.e.*, electric power, repair, and so on) is for the maintenance of the automatic process.

The peculiarities of depreciation accounting pose difficulties in automation decisions. For example, the First State Ball-bearing Factory is an automated plant, but the cost of bearings produced in it was much higher than in traditional plants. Therefore, some considered this plant an example of mistaken automation. But others maintained that the decisive element in the cost comparison was the depreciation charge—2 rubles and 45 kopecks per bearing in the automated plant, 15 kopecks per bearing in traditional plants. They argued that this difference is largely fictitious. The older plants have equipment acquired in the 'thirties, much of it from abroad, which is accordingly valued on a completely different basis than the equipment of the new automatic factory.

Specialization and cooperation between enterprises

One of the important tasks which the new *sovnarkhozy* are supposed to solve is the working out of a rational pattern of specialization and cooperation between enterprises. Seen from the position of a high-level decision maker the question is whether to have certain components or parts produced in the plants where they are used or to set up a specialized plant or shop to supply many outside customers. If the latter is decided, there arises the question of the scale on which the specialized producer should operate. Seen from the perspective of the plant manager, the question is whether to buy this part or component or to produce it in his own plant. One difficulty in analysing this problem arises from the fact that it is not clear at which level such a decision is to be made. There are indications in the management literature that it may be made by the plant manager or by the high-level official, or there may be some sharing of the decision. Thus it is necessary to analyse the results of using cost data in both cases.

Seen from above, the problem is one of choosing the optimum size for units performing specialized tasks (such as casting, stamping, production of fasteners, tools, and so on). Here the authority should ask how the delivered price to users will vary with variations in the size of plant and in average length of haul. One of the ingredients of the analysis is thus an envelope cost curve for the production of this item. Our question is whether a cost curve based on reported costs from different sized plants will give an accurate picture of this curve.

In this practical example it may be that many points on the curve will be for shops of existing plants rather than for independent plants. What peculiarities of Soviet cost accounting would militate against accuracy here? Obviously errors in allocating general plant expenses and shop expenses, and the allocation of the costs of services of subsidiary shops, might produce distorted cost data. It is likely that the planners would get some normal-looking cost curve in spite of such errors, and any errors would surely not be so great as to lead them to the conclusion that there should not be specialization. But the important problem is just how much specialization, and the final decision will be made with reference to some small section of the curve, where the errors might be important.

This example also illustrates what is probably a valid generalization about any decision based on cost data, made at relatively high levels. Here the planners will be using enough cost data from enough different plants so that errors in individual plant accounts may be offset by other errors elsewhere; the resulting averages may be valid as a basis for general policy decisions. Once such a general policy is laid down there may still be enough discretion left to decision makers at lower levels to enable them to take account of individual circumstances. In this particular instance, the individual plant manager may still have something to say about whether his plant will buy the part from a specialized plant or make it.

How a plant manager should make such a decision is discussed in an interesting book by A. V. Fortunatov. Briefly, Fortunatov's approach is as follows: Suppose that our plant is now making a part, should it be purchased instead? This depends on which alternative is cheaper. The cost of buying is easily determined, but the question of what it costs us to produce the item is more complex, and is measured by what would be saved if we did not make it. Such savings would be the cost of direct labour and materials, and, for overhead, those items which are variable. Fortunatov recognizes that ceasing to make the part will not reduce fixed costs in our plant. He also says that a 3 per cent. profit should be added to these savings before the cost of making is compared with the cost of purchasing. In his thinking this does not seem to be a charge for capital or any other cost, but simply an allowance for the fact that the price of the purchased part is higher than actual costs in the other firm. He wants to avoid the mistake of keeping the process in our plant if *cost* (as contrasted to price) in the other plant would be less than our costs. Fortunatov frequently admonishes the planners to whom his book is addressed to enhance efficiency from the national-economic point of view rather than just to obtain the cheapest costs in a single plant.

These are not particularly subtle ideas to us, although they strike me as sophisticated against the background of most Soviet economic analysis. The question here, of course, is whether the cost-accounting data provide an adequate foundation for such analytical subtlety. I doubt it—there are a number of features of

Soviet cost accounting that would make it a weak reed to lean on in making such a decision.

To begin with, there are no doubt many plants where the cost-accounting department would be unable to tell the planner what the costs of the component in question were. The accounts might simply not be kept with that degree of fineness. Further, if it did report a figure, there might be good reason to question its accuracy, because of the crudities described earlier. Suppose, for instance, that this is an old plant with undervalued assets; then the depreciation portion of costs will be low relative to that underlying the price quoted for the other plant. Or it is possible that the particular part is burdened with too much shop expense. If the process of making this part is relatively unmechanized, it would be charged outlays really incurred on behalf of other outputs, produced with more highly mechanized processes.

Furthermore, the decision maker has to distinguish between fixed and variable costs.[5] I think it is correct to say that as a general rule Soviet accounting thought and practice has not done much to distinguish fixed and variable costs. The cost-accounting classifications are not particularly oriented to this distinction. As a matter of fact the official instructions on the calculation of costs do not make this distinction at all, and the official forms on which reports of costs are made are not designed to separate fixed and variable costs. The usual distinction in Soviet accounting texts is between direct and indirect costs, which is not the same thing. However, there are many situations in which even the most bureaucratic routinist must separate fixed from variable costs, as in drawing up the cost plan for an expanded output programme, and in analysing fulfilment of cost plans. So in almost any practical handbook on planning or analysis of enterprise work, this distinction is made. The writers often suggest breakdowns of the official categories of expense into fixed and variable. The point we want to emphasize here, however, is that these distinctions are largely conventional and inaccurate, because they are made on the basis of a classification not oriented toward this problem. Soviet authors point out that the accepted conventions or branch instructions cannot hold for all cases and one author reports an empirical investigation

---

[5] This distinction is important for many other economic decisions, though it is hard to find examples where Soviet planners use it. In the electric-power industry, correct distribution of the total load among stations requires resort to the concept of marginal cost, and there are fairly good discussions of this point in some sources. But it is not clear what relationship the marginal-cost figures have to cost-accounting data.

which indicated that the accepted conventions in his ministry were seriously inaccurate.[6]

Finally, the decision maker has relied on the price of the other plant, less an estimated profit, to measure the national-economic costs of the purchasing alternative. This price may be a very poor estimate of national-economic costs. The divergence between price and national economic cost may arise for reasons outside cost accounting *per se*, but there may well be some connection. Under the present decentralization of planning and control, enterprises are now acquiring some freedom to influence their own prices, largely through manipulation of cost-accounting data in suggesting price projects for approval. (They have apparently always had some such freedom, particularly with respect to such unstandardized output as semifabricates in machine building.) Hence inaccuracies and falsification in the cost accounting of the potential supplier may also confuse the issue. As explained earlier, it may be that the cost accounting in the other plant is so poor that it is impossible for the supervising organ to verify costs and control prices suggested by the other plant.

Assortment decisions

One of the decisions that Soviet planners must make is the allocation of a given output program among a group of producing plants. The superior organ has a total output program, and must decide how to distribute the individual kinds of output among enterprises to meet the plan. In making this decision, the superior organs are guided partly by relative costs in different plants. But I doubt that these are really solid decisions. A certain plant may report costs for one output which are lower than those of other plants, and relatively high costs for other outputs. But it is possible that these cost differences are only reflections of errors in cost allocation. If the planners at a high level expect a cost reduction from this more " rational " allocation of output, they will be disappointed. What the accounting department often does in light industry is to calculate the costs of different sizes, grades, sorts, and outputs by distribution of expense in proportion to planned cost calculations or according to norms of some kind. Or it may not determine costs for separate kinds of output at all.

It seems likely that this situation will arise more frequently with the shift of enterprises to the *sovnarkhozy*, because the *sovnarkhoz* in any region has acquired a group of plants with

---

[6] One major exception to the generalization about the lack of concern with fixed and variable costs is in the cost accounting of the railroads.

accounting heritages from diverse ministries. There was likely to be comparability in accounting rules within ministries, so that variations in costs of individual outputs would be defined by variations in equipment, location, nature of the process used, and so on, rather than by variations in accounting rules. But the *sovnarkhoz* has inherited plants producing similar outputs from many separate jurisdictions, which do their accounting on the basis of old ministerial patterns which may have been diverse. The classification of expense, the rules for allocation, and so forth, are different.

It appears from Soviet discussions that there are many situations where Soviet plant managers retain some discretion in deciding on their output assortment. This may be either because the assortment is not specified in the plan, or because there are no effective sanctions imposed for failure to meet a clearly specified assortment plan. Therefore, the assortment decision is also affected by the actions of people using cost data at the level of the enterprise. How do Soviet plant managers use cost-accounting information to make these decisions, and with what implications for rationality?

Writers on price policy often speak of encouraging plant managers to produce the desired kind of output by manipulation of prices so that some outputs are more profitable than others. The plant managers are supposed to emphasize the more profitable output in order to have higher profits, more easily fulfil the output plan, and have a better cash position and so more maneuverability. But the accounting is often in such a state that managers are unable to determine which the most profitable outputs are, and so the planners find that the lever with which they are trying to manipulate subordinate behaviour is pushing against thin air. This picture does not necessarily conform with our picture of the Soviet plant manager's playing a shrewd game of arbitrage among the various constraints of his plan, but it is probably true nevertheless, and suggests another question. When the manager does engage in this kind of arbitrage, what is the result? It seems possible that the cost data at his disposal are not accurate enough to permit him to choose the most profitable selection of outputs. But this does not necessarily mean that national-economic efficiency would be affected. If the constraints are rational, then failure to meet them would interfere with efficiency, but of course they are not necessarily rational.

Conclusion

Enough examples have been adduced to show that there is an interaction between cost-accounting practices and decisions by planners. Thus misleading cost data can easily result in incorrect decisions. To place these errors in proper perspective, it is important to reiterate that even if cost data are seriously in error, they may be barren of consequences. For many decisions the cost figures may be perfectly adequate, and there are many decisions that will not be determined by cost data anyway. It is likely, however, that the impact of these errors on decision making will increase as time passes. The decentralization of administration must mean more freedom of choice at the lower levels, more recourse to cost data and prices as guides to decision making, and hence a wider field for the errors flowing from inaccurate cost data.

Soviet Accounting—Comment

By Herbert S. Levine

Professor of Economics,
University of Pennsylvania.

Professor Campbell, in his article on pages 356–373 above, has admirably demonstrated some of the inadequacies of Soviet cost-accounting practices for the purposes of rational economic decision making. His presentation is twice blessed. First, it is clear and concise. He has chosen carefully from the wealth of information contained in his thesis (where the interested reader can find points in detail) and has added to it judiciously. Second, he does not overstate the importance of his case. Both fore and aft, he warns of its limitations—limitations which include the fact that many economic decisions are not based on costs and prices; that other deficiencies of Soviet price formation may be more important sources of distortions than errors in cost accounting; that even when far from perfect, cost calculations may still often point in the right direction.

As I read Campbell's paper, though, I had a feeling of familiarity. With certain changes, important though they might be in particular cases, much of what he says is similar to attacks levelled at Western accounting practices. Campbell asks, do Soviet cost-accounting practices permit correct economic decisions, and do they provide correct information concerning the costs of alternatives? Economists in the West have been asking this of Western accounting practices for a long time. Thus, the question comes to mind: is the major part of Campbell's fire directed against Soviet practice specifically or against contemporary cost accounting generally, even as it is practised in the West?

This is not to suggest that if important similarities in the two accounting systems are found, then Soviet accounting will be proved to be a superior implement, leading to rational economic decisions. Not at all—Campbell's point stands: Soviet accounting is in many ways a poor implement. But if the similarities are found, then Campbell's case can be viewed in a different perspective. For then, if one pursued the point (which I will not do here) questions could be raised about the rationality of economic decisions in the West—decisions which are based on Western accounting practices—and some observations on comparative rationality and irrationality could be made.

Let us then first look briefly into the historical development of cost accounting (in the West).

Cost accounting was developed initially as an aid in measuring income, that is, in financial reporting. More precisely, it was used to value inventories. Then, in order to speed up the costing process, a system of standard costs was developed.[7] Soon it was realized that by investigating the variances between standard and actual costs, some insight into the efficiency of operation could be acquired and a measure of control attained. Thus, a second function, cost control, arose. In improving cost accounting as an instrument of control, the attempt was made to limit the costs assigned to a responsibility center, to those over which it had some control. This, recently, has led to a splitting up of fixed and variable costs and to a concentration on variable costs. And from this, a third function, economic decision making based on marginal accounting, is at the present time being developed.[8]

Thus, cost accounting has not been static. In the past it has mainly performed two functions: estimation of income and control of operating expenses. It is only recently that managerial accounting for decision-making, called "the new frontier" by Professor Earley,[9] has been developed.

As a result of this historical orientation it is generally claimed that cost accounting has been a poor tool for decision making. Basically the argument runs as follows: Accounting data accumulated for income- or cost-control purposes obliterate the distinctions so necessary for decision making between average and marginal costs, and between past and future costs.

In the Soviet Union, the primary function of accounting is cost control. As a consequence, decision making suffers. Accounting "does not serve two masters well."[10] But are conditions so different in the United States?

Let us look for a moment at a few of the examples discussed by Campbell.

[7] T. Lang, "Concepts of Cost, Past and Present," reprinted in D. Solomons, *Studies in Costing* (London: Sweet and Maxwell, 1952), p. 85.

[8] See J. S. Earley, "Recent Developments in Cost Accounting and the 'Marginal Analysis'," *Journal of Political Economy*, LXIII: 3 (June, 1955), and "Marginal Policies of 'Excellently Managed' Companies," *American Economic Review*, XLVI: 1 (March, 1956).

[9] Earley, *op. cit.*, p. 229.

[10] J. A. Beckett, "A Study of the Principles of Allocating Costs," *The Accounting Review*, XXVI: 3 (July, 1951), 228.

Depreciation

First, Campbell states on p. 358 that depreciation rates are inadequate because they " are based on unrealistically long conceptions of service life." He then uses column 1 of Table 1 to indicate the degree of insufficiency of those rates.

I do not challenge the claim that depreciation rates are insufficient. But the Table is not a good measure of the mistakes in estimating service life. As Campbell later explains (p. 361), the inadequacy of the rates is aggravated during inflation by the deduction of capital repairs valued at current prices, from accumulated depreciation. In the absence of inflation, the original rates (if planned to recover original cost over a realistically estimated life, and also to meet capital repairs) could result in the asset being completely depreciated at the time of retirement; but inflation, by raising the cost of capital repairs to above the original estimate, would reduce the accumulated depreciation to less than the asset's original cost, and so make the rates seem insufficient. When the rates are in fact insufficient in the first place, the deduction of capital repairs in a time of rising prices will exaggerate the insufficiency. Faults in the Soviet handling of capital repairs are thus more of a " replacement cost *versus* original cost " problem than a depreciation rate problem. One may argue that the main cause of trouble is failure to revalue fixed assets when prices are changing. This may be so, but it should be kept in mind that the original value method is used not only by the Russians but is also a canon of American practice.

Second, and perhaps more important, straight-line depreciation is a poor method for the purpose of filling the categories of economic theory. The economist would like to match inputs with outputs. There is no " perfect " way of doing this in accounting for depreciation,[11] but in general an accelerated method would be better than a straight-line one, for an asset " contributes " more to production in its early years. Thus, some economic distortion in the Soviet Union results merely from the use of straight line. Before 1954, straight line was also the predominant method in the United States. This is less so now that accelerated methods are permitted for tax purposes. But now there is greater diversity in depreciation methods. Therefore, because of this use of different depreciation methods by different firms, certain cost distortions arise in the United States which are similar to the

[11] See F. and V. Lutz, *The Theory of Investment of the Firm* (Princeton: Princeton University Press, 1951), pp. 6–8. Other problems, such as estimating the economic life of an asset, make accounting for depreciation an economically arbitrary matter.

distortions caused in the Soviet Union by unequal depreciation insufficiencies.

Replacement

Campbell points out that in the Soviet Union decisions will be biased against asset replacement due to the inclusion of book value of the old asset as a cost of the new, and due to the exaggeration of book value resulting from the deduction of capital repairs from accumulated depreciation. Strange though it may sound to economists, this situation is often duplicated in the United States. First, reversing order, contrary to what Campbell appears to imply, it is quite common practice in the United States to subtract capital repairs from accumulated depreciation (on the grounds that it is depreciation " made good "). Second, contrary to what most would tend to think, it is not uncommon business practice to add the book value of the old asset to the cost of the new.

Joint products

As Campbell clearly states, the only rational way to price joint products is with reference to demand conditions. The technology of complete jointness precludes the separate variation of each product and thus the allocation of correct economic costs is impossible. In addition, " in many cases, technically variable proportions become in effect economically fixed proportions. If the proportions between several products can be altered only by incurring large fixed costs, or if the proportions can be altered only in large steps, we approach the true joint-cost case—at least for substantial ranges of output." In contemporary economies, where multiproduct firms are prevalent, this poses a serious problem. And in economies where prices are cost-based the problem is extremely serious.

In the West, the primary impact of the problem of jointness falls on regulated industries. An article in the *Harvard Business Review* illustrates the irrationalities which result from different methods of assigning joint costs to natural gas and oil. But also to the extent that unregulated industries base prices on joint costs assigned by " rules of thumb," or adjust joint-product assortment to market-determined prices by using fully assigned joint costs, this irrationality also arises.

On the other hand, the Russians do not rely exclusively on cost-pricing methods of joint products. In a few fields cost assignment is by the revenue method (implying other than cost methods of pricing).

The example of petroleum is interesting. The present Soviet system of cost assignment was adopted in preference to a previous coefficient system, because the previous system overvalued the lighter fractions in relation to diesel oil and led to relatively greater production of lighter fractions than desired. Thus the new system was designed to encourage, relatively, the output of diesel oil—clearly a rational intention (in the context of the Soviet economy). Perhaps this indicates that the Russians realize the rational way of pricing joint products is primarily from the demand side, and that they attempt to achieve " rational " prices by adjusting the cost-assignment method. This is a rational *administrative* procedure when the system insists costs be used as the price base, but it should not be assumed that these assigned joint costs are *economically* rational—that they are true marginal costs.

Automation

Campbell points out that when deciding whether to automate a process, costs for the two systems (the automated and the non-automated) are calculated, including an important overhead charge which is assigned in proportion to wage cost. This irrationally favours automation.

But it is also prevalent American policy to allocate overhead in proportion to wages. According to a 1946 study made by the OPA, about 70 per cent. of the firms in the machinery industry (which were studied and which had cost-accounting systems), allocated overhead in proportion to labor cost, and only about 4 per cent. in proportion to machine time. Of course, it is possible that automation decisions were based not on accounting data but on special studies. Still one wonders how many irrational automation decisions, similar to the Russians', might have been made here.

Specialization and co-operation

Campbell states that a Russian manager, in order to decide whether to " make or buy " an input, has to distinguish between fixed and variable costs. Campbell doubts whether this can be done since accounting conventions do not call for such classifications.

This, too, is a problem which plagues American practice, and a major one at that. One economist, writing in 1948, stated: " The businessman, if not the economist, has accepted the accountant's miracle of converting fixed cost into variable cost." An accounting specialist, in 1945, said that the necessity to separate indirect costs into fixed and variable " has been recognized by some cost accountants, but ignored by most of them." And the Committee on Research of the National Association of Cost Accountants, in advocating the new methods of "management accounting" wrote in 1953: "The breakdown of costs into fixed and variable categories . . . has been limited to a few companies until quite recently. . . . The accountant, as an expert on costs, should be able to take the lead in this process of education."

Low quality of product costing

Lastly, Campbell's discussion pointed out that often a firm's cost data are so bad that it cannot distinguish its most profitable output. The sheer low quality of Soviet cost accounting, has perhaps its analogue in the fact that many firms in the United States have no product cost-accounting system at all, and that where they do exist they vary greatly from firm to firm. In the 'thirties, for example, a study of the paint industry showed a range of variation in the reported costs of identical items of 500 to 600 per cent. No doubt the quality of American accounting has improved greatly since then, but it is probably still a good deal worse than most people think.

To summarize this section, let me quote from Earley's 1955 article on management accounting: " Accounting analysis should be designed to provide control and evaluation of specific operations and policies and help guide management in ' choosing among alternatives,' functions which ' conventional ' accounting performs very imperfectly." This " imperfect performance " is the crux of Campbell's attack on Soviet accounting practices. As we have seen, the attack can also be applied to American accounting at least as it was practised until the last few years and even as it is practised now in most firms.

An interesting problem, then (putting it in accounting terminology), would be to investigate the variances of Soviet accounting actualities from " ideal " accounting standards. What part of the Soviet variance is due to its deviation from American practice (upon which it is substantially patterned) and what part is due to American deviation from the " ideal " standard?

A second interesting problem would be to investigate possible causes of deviations in the two systems, for example, accounting for premia [12] in the Soviet Union and accounting for tax benefits in the United States.

---

[12] Management personnel in Soviet firms are rewarded with monetary premia for fulfilling and overfulfilling their established plans. These premia form a substantial part of management's income. Therefore, the demonstration of plan fulfilment is often one of the objectives of accountants in Soviet firms.

In conclusion, what might lie ahead for Soviet cost accounting? Campbell speaks of the possible irrationalities which might result when, under decentralization, managers and planners make more decisions based on cost data. But is it not possible that cost-accounting methods for decision making will improve: first, because of the increasing need for such data and second, because of the model which is now being developed by " management accounting " in America? The current developments in electronic data-processing methods will help improve the quality of Soviet cost accounting.

I have, in this comment, not tried to dismiss the deficiencies of Soviet cost-accounting practices. They exist, they are important, and they must be seriously considered in any discussion of economic rationality in the Soviet system. We should remember, though, that parallels exist in the West. There is merit in judging Soviet performance against Western ideals, but there is also merit in judging it against Western realities.

Factors that Influence Accounting Principles *

By George R. Catlett
C.P.A., Chicago

ACCOUNTING has been created and developed to accomplish various desired objectives and, therefore, it is not based on fundamental laws or absolute precepts. Since accounting has evolved over many years through trial and error, it should be continually improved on a basis that is responsive to the requirements of those groups in our society who use the end product—financial statements.

The purpose of accounting and of financial statements might be stated as follows: to fairly reflect all material and significant facts in the light of current economic and social conditions in such a manner that these facts are most useful, meaningful and fair to the affected segments of our society (such as stockholders, managements, creditors, employees, governmental agencies, customers and potential investors) for the purpose of exercising judgment and making decisions.

The accounting profession has a tendency to over-emphasize precedent and to view its problems in retrospect. While history is an interesting record of human experiences, analysis and discussion of the past are helpful only to the extent that they are of assistance in performing a more useful service. Therefore, a continuous reappraisal of accounting principles in the light of both current circumstances and past experience is necessary.

Considerable emphasis has been placed on the "general acceptance" of accounting principles. The viewpoint that this is not necessarily the best test of such principles was discussed previously in another article.[1]

Changes in economic and social conditions have had some effect on accounting principles and their application, but in this area the accounting profession has too often looked backward rather than forward. When comparison is made for the last twenty-five years between improvements in accounting and in

---

* From *The Journal of Accountancy*, October 1960.
[1] " Relation of Acceptance to Accounting Principles," *The Journal of Accountancy*, March 1960, pp. 33–38.

other fields, the former suffers in comparison with scientific research, with production, marketing and distribution methods, and with management techniques during this era of atomic power, electronic computers, jet airplanes, color television and wonder drugs. Accounting principles, as reflected in practice, have not kept pace during this period with the needs of our system.

The suggestion has sometimes been made that the term " accounting principles " is misleading and creates the wrong impression, because it indicates a precision that is not actually present. This term could be changed, but there does not seem to be a better alternative, and any substitute that would convey the idea that there is less of an authoritative basis for accounting might not adequately serve the desired purpose. While admittedly some confusion exists in terminology, the real challenge to our profession is not a revision of words or the clarification of definitions, but the development of underlying postulates and concepts.

What are some of the factors, in addition to " general acceptance," that have had an important influence on accounting principles? They might be classified as (1) conservatism, (2) consistency, (3) disclosure, and (4) governmental regulation.

Conservatism

Conservatism (which results in resolving doubts in favor of understating assets and current income and overstating liabilities and current expenses) is a philosophy or attitude, and not an accounting postulate or principle. Conservatism has generally been considered by the profession to be a prime virtue, and it has had some very subtle and far-reaching effects on accounting. It is inherent in such principles and practices as (1) valuing inventories at the lower of cost or market, (2) anticipating losses but not anticipating gains, (3) carrying property at original cost less depreciation or depletion, when fair value may be considerably higher, and (4) reflecting investments in unconsolidated subsidiaries at cost, when underlying book value is greater.

Conservatism is only relative, since what may be conservative to one person may be non-conservative to someone else. Also, what is conservative to a creditor may be misrepresentation to a selling stockholder.

Accounting many years ago was naturally conservative since it was essentially on a cash basis, or was primarily for completed ventures. As the need has grown for the measurement of numerous transactions in various stages of completion, the problems have increased tremendously, but some of the obsolete accounting has been retained.

In the case of family-owned companies, the managements may be interested in ultra-conservatism, which results in keeping net assets and net profits as low as possible, for various reasons, including those related to income and inheritance taxes. Creditors, such as banks and insurance companies, have generally preferred conservative statements with emphasis on liquidating values. This situation still exists to some extent, but there has been a trend away from conservatism with the advent of professional managements, wide and constantly changing stock ownership, and the shift in interest of creditors to earning power and away from liquidating values.

Conservatism has also been one of the reasons for the wide variety of alternative accounting practices that are all considered to be " generally accepted." An analysis of such practices will indicate that many of them reflect different degrees of conservatism. This is illustrated by the following examples:

1. The LIFO method of inventory costing, as compared with the FIFO method.
2. The charging of research and development costs to expense, by industrial and natural resource companies, as compared with capitalizing such costs.
3. A full accrual of pension plan costs as compared with a partial or minimum accrual.
4. The completed-contract method for construction companies as compared with the percentage-of-completion method.
5. Recording the accelerated depreciation allowed for Federal income tax purposes as compared with straight-line depreciation.

Managements frequently select from the alternatives on the basis of the degree of conservatism they prefer, rather than on principle or to reflect the actual facts.

Conservative accounting may result in a non-conservative income statement at a later time. Costs and expenses that are incurred for the purpose of producing income in subsequent years, are in many instances charged off currently because of conservatism or because there may be no positive indication that they will be recovered. Thus costs may not be matched with revenues that are produced as a result of such costs.

Operating loss carry-forward credits for income tax purposes are generally not recorded as assets, primarily because there may be no assurance that the credit will be realized. The credit when actually realized is usually added to income of that year, rather than what would seem to be the preferable approach of taking it directly to earned surplus as a retroactive adjustment of the prior years in which the losses occurred. As a result, the net income of a current year may be doubled because of losses in prior years. In such a case, conservatism in the balance-sheet may result in a much higher degree of non-conservatism in the income statement.

One of the principal arguments used against the accounting recognition of the change in the purchasing power of the dollar is that this would result in an upward restatement of assets, which is unthinkable because of the fiasco in the 1920s involving appraisal write-ups. On the other hand, the lack of recognition of increased costs due to price-level changes related to property and other assets, in my opinion, has resulted in overstated profits, which is certainly not conservative.

A proper degree of caution and prudence in accounting is desirable and necessary, since an uncontrolled lack of conservatism could be disastrous. However, conservative practices in some instances may misrepresent the facts as much as non-conservative practices.

Consistency

The standard form of auditor's opinion states that the accounting principles have been " applied on a basis consistent with that of the preceding year." Consistency is important if comparisons of statements are to be made from year to year and if trends are to have any significance. Material changes in the application of accounting principles may be made by a business from time to time, and the fact that such changes are made, as well as the effect thereof if practicable to determine, is generally disclosed.

Some accountants take the position that the choice among various alternative practices is not as important as the consistent application of the practices selected. However, this almost results in the viewpoint (whether fully realized or not) that it is all right to be wrong, as long as you are consistently wrong. While the distinction between alternative practices may not always be as clear-cut as " right " and " wrong," not all such practices present the facts in a manner that is equally satisfactory.

The profession might well consider Emerson's statement, " A foolish consistency is the hobgoblin of little minds, adored by little statesmen and philosophers and divines."

Consistency is a desirable attribute in accounting, but it

does not represent a principle, and it should not be used as an excuse to justify unsound practices.

Disclosure

Financial statements and the related footnotes should disclose any significant information necessary for a proper understanding of the position and results of an enterprise.

The concept of adequate disclosure of significant data is, of course, commendable. However, in some instances, this has resulted in many complicated footnotes that are technically correct, but not particularly informative or understandable to the average reader.

Disclosure has been used to some extent by accountants as a protective measure. In some cases, unsound practices have been justified on the basis of disclosure. In other cases, footnote coverage of significant facts has been considered a substitute for appropriate adjustment of the accounts. This line of reasoning was expressed in 1932 as follows:

> The more practicable alternative would be to leave every corporation free to choose its own methods of accounting within the very broad limits to which reference has been made, but require disclosure of the methods employed and consistency in their application from year to year.[2]

In general, the above philosophy is still being followed by the profession.

Many problems arise over the timing of the recognition of income and costs between years. Mere disclosure of the practices selected from possible alternatives that might have a significant effect on net income for individual periods is of questionable value. With the wide publicity given " earnings per share," and the use of information by an increasing number of stockholders and others not well informed on accounting, additional emphasis is required in the direction of simplified and sound statements. It should not be necessary to read and understand the fine print of voluminous footnotes or technical parenthetical comments before knowing whether the figures in the statements are reliable and really mean what the reader has a right to assume they do.

Disclosure is necessary for reporting, but should not be used improperly as a crutch to lean on and as a justification for alternative practices.

---

[2] Quoted from letter dated September 22, 1932, written by the American Institute's special committee on co-operation with stock exchanges to the Committee on Stock List, New York Stock Exchange.

Governmental regulation

Governmental regulation, both by laws and by administrative action, has had a significant influence on accounting principles. Such regulation can be classified in two general categories: (1) levy of taxes, and (2) safeguarding the public interest.

The Federal income tax statutes and regulations have had an effect on many accounting practices. Some company managements (1) prefer for simplicity to keep their accounts on the same basis for both financial accounting and tax purposes; (2) believe that use of a different method in their accounts might jeopardize a favorable basis for tax; and (3) are influenced to such an extent by high tax rates that this overshadows other aspects of accounting.

While in some respects accounting for the determination of income taxes may not accord with sound principles, the accounting required for tax may be desirable for raising tax revenues, for encouraging the development of natural resources and selected industries, for assisting small business, and for many other reasons. However, the profession must recognize that tax statutes and regulations are not intended to establish sound accounting principles, and do not necessarily reflect sound accounting principles.

Governmental regulation to safeguard the public interest has related primarily to such matters as (1) rates and prices to be charged customers, as in the case of public utilities; (2) management of the public's funds, as in the case of banks, savings and loan associations, trust companies and insurance companies; (3) information to be given to the public in connection with the sale of securities; or (4) corporation formation and certain corporate activities. It is appropriate that the responsible agencies should require reports and other data in the administration of the law.

The profession should make every effort to work with the regulatory agencies to narrow the gap between accounting principles prescribed by them and sound accounting principles. This will take time. In the meantime, those accounting practices that are prescribed for regulatory purposes should not, merely because they are prescribed by a government agency, control the determination of sound accounting principles for other purposes.

Conflicting interests in our society

Statutes are enacted for social, economic or political purposes. Such laws establish the facts to be accounted for and may affect the results of the application of accounting principles, but laws do not necessarily establish or determine proper principles. Furthermore, it will be most unfortunate if accounting principles and practices are ever legislated by our political representatives as is presently being done in the case of insurance companies. If the profession determines and follows sound principles, it will have a much better chance of retaining the right to determine such principles.

Financial statements are used by various segments of our society (such as stockholders, managements, creditors, employees, government, customers and potential investors). Each of these has, in varying degrees, conflicting interests. At one time, ownership and management of many companies were closely related and the family business was common. But the trend is now toward professional management (with relatively small stock ownership) and toward wide dispersion of stock ownership.

Also labor organizations have grown much stronger and claim to have a direct interest in the financial reports of companies with which they bargain. Governmental bodies in the field of regulation have increased their authority. Many millions of potential investors are being urged to invest in business. An interesting aspect of this problem is that many persons have more than one interest; as an example, employees are often customers and may also be stockholders.

The accounting profession has the responsibility of developing principles that are useful and fair to the various groups with conflicting interests and that can be defended when challenged.

Importance of uniformity

With conflicting interests such as these, it is not easy to establish accounting principles that meet the tests of maximum usefulness and fairness. A balance must be achieved. While financial statements may take several forms or include various degrees of detail, it is essential that the basic accounting principles be the same for all enterprises organized for profit and for all industries. The application of such principles would vary to some extent, depending upon the circumstances.

Determination of accounting principles

Influences which have little to do with accounting principles have played a dominant role in determining the practices followed. The existing philosophy in this regard is based on a self-perpetuating circle of logic that accounting principles are accepted because they are sound and they are sound because they are accepted. This results in " the tail wagging the dog," since many practices are justified merely on the basis of acceptance (custom), which is given more weight than the fairness of the presentations that result.

Is it possible and practicable to determine objective standards against which to evaluate sound accounting principles? In my opinion, such objective standards can be developed. Actually, the major problem facing the profession is not whether this can be done, but how and when the objective can be accomplished.

Sound accounting principles are not scientific laws or absolute rules, and do not represent perfection. " Sound " is used in the sense of well-founded, reliable, logical and fair. Accounting is not a science and, therefore, cannot be treated as one. Whether the term " accounting principles " is preceded by " generally accepted," by " sound " or by nothing is not particularly important. What is important is that the principles *be* sound. If sound principles are determined, they quite likely will be generally accepted.

Up to the present time, there really has never been an adequate basis or foundation for accounting principles. The conclusions expressed in accounting literature and committee bulletins have been merely those of individuals expressing their own viewpoints that reflect their personal experiences. Authors have developed accounting postulates and principles as a rationalization to support what was already occurring.

The report of the American Institute's special committee on research program dated September 1958 included the following statement:

> The broad problem of financial accounting should be visualised as requiring attention at four levels: first, postulates; second, principles; third, rules or other guides for the application of principles in specific situations; and fourth, research.

The postulates are the antecedent conditions or essential prerequisites to principles. The principles must meet the tests of the postulates, and the practices must be supported by the principles. This framework of accounting standards and guides must be developed in that order. Then the profession for the first time could have " sound accounting principles." There would still be room for judgment by individual accountants in applying these principles in specific cases. However, CPAs would have the responsibility of properly relating accounting practices to the standards established. Primary attention then could be given to " fair presentation " and CPAs would not need to be distracted by arguments as to degrees of acceptance or whether conservatism, consistency and disclosure are more important than principles.

All phases of business are rapidly becoming more international in scope. Each country has it own laws, customs and conditions, but accounting principles are not entirely nationalistic in nature. " General acceptance " has almost no meaning or significance on an international basis at the present time. " Sound accounting principles " would be both a term and a general concept that could be understood by accountants everywhere.

The American Institute is the only non-governmental organization with any chance of determining sound accounting principles and having them generally recognized. The Institute's Accounting Principles Board, with its assigned mission and with its research staff and project advisory committees, has an outstanding opportunity to be of service to the profession and the business world.

A question may exist as to whether companies and governmental agencies, such as the Securities and Exchange Commission, would accept a determination of principles by the Institute. If the principles are properly determined and documented by sound reasoning, they will be difficult to disprove or ignore. Some company managements and trade associations would complain about the Institute imposing a " strait-jacket " without the authority to do so. However, they would find it most difficult to argue effectively against sound principles objectively determined.

General acceptance of bulletins

An example of how industry has followed a pronouncement occurred after Accounting Research Bulletin No. 44 (Revised) was issued by the American Institute's committee in 1958. Prior to that time, many companies were deducting accelerated depreciation for income-tax purposes and using straight-line depreciation in their accounts, but some of these companies were providing for the deferred tax and some were not. If this bulletin, which properly recommended deferred-tax accounting, had not been issued, the two alternative practices with widely varying results would have been followed indefinitely, and CPAs would have continued to give opinions that both practices were " generally accepted." There was criticism of this bulletin from some company managements, but within about a year after issue it was being followed by almost all companies except some public utilities. (With respect to public utilities, the bulletin provided that deferred-tax accounting is not required " if it may reasonably be expected that increased future income taxes, resulting from the earlier deduction of declining-balance depreciation for income-tax purposes only, will be allowed in future rate determinations.") The conclusions in this bulletin, but for the exception relating to public utilities in some situations, are sound and cannot be challenged effectively.

So long as a wide variety of alternative practices is " generally accepted," they will be used. The attitude of many managements is that they are not interested in pioneering in accounting principles, and do not want to do anything that has what they consider an adverse effect on their statements unless other companies are following similar practices. Therefore, some independent organization must take the lead, since recommended improvements must precede general acceptance.

Neither the American Institute nor any of its committees has chosen to take unilateral action with respect to accounting principles. They have preferred to rely upon the subsequent general acceptance of any pronouncements. This approach may have been necessary in the absence of an overall guide to serve as a general basis and point of departure for the solution of problems. However, accounting controversies cannot be satisfactorily settled on an item-by-item basis without the proper relationship being established to a well-conceived set of objective standards, since such problems continue to recur in different forms faster than they can be concluded. Under such circumstances, the pronouncements offered as solutions merely become a series of disconnected and unsupported personal preferences of the committee members.

The American Institute, representing CPAs who have a serious public responsibility, should be able to consider the viewpoints of all segments of our society in arriving at fair and sound conclusions. It is recognized that CPAs cannot compel their clients to follow accounting principles they espouse. On the other hand, clients cannot insist that CPAs give opinions that statements " fairly present " the financial position and results of operations unless the CPAs actually have such opinions.

An objective approach with sufficient effort and determination is almost certain to be successful, if the interests of all segments of our society are given adequate consideration. Sound principles could represent a framework of professional standards that would become generally accepted, because of merit and not because of custom. The risk involved in a positive and constructive course is far less than in not assuming the necessary leadership.

Are Accounting Principles Generally Accepted?*

By Leonard Spacek
C.P.A., Chicago.

Acceptance by whom?

One of the first questions that comes to mind in thinking about this problem is " who should do the accepting—that is, by whom should our accounting principles be accepted? " The fact that the public has used the financial statements prepared on the basis of what we choose to label generally accepted accounting principles, does not confirm public acceptance of these so-called principles any more than the existence of the rigged TV quiz programs proved their public acceptance before the public learned of their deception.

Illustrations of this non-acceptability to the public can be found whenever accounting principles become factors in lawsuits. But aside from court cases, which usually involve technical features of controversy, there are numerous illustrations of non-acceptance in Press reports, such as the following comments in the August 1, 1960, issue of *Forbes Magazine*:

> In every year since 1955, whether or not its sales volume was temporarily trending up or down, the company has been able to increase its earnings. There are so many ways of accomplishing this by mere bookkeeping tricks that financial specialists are wont these days to view any such performance skeptically. So many costs can at option legitimately be anticipated or deferred, expensed or capitalized, that no corporate earnings figure is now regarded by sophisticates as absolute and objective. Windfalls such as those deriving from favorable market prices for a commodity can have a pleasant but misleading effect on stated earnings; so can variations in the rate of remitted dividends received from foreign subsidiaries.

As a profession, we have ignored the necessity of developing and stating the reasoning as to why accounting principles should be accepted by the public, just as the networks failed to tell the public the basis of their quiz programs. When this reasoning is stated, the public will then say whether it is valid. If it is not valid, disapproval will come quickly.

* From *The Journal of Accountancy*, April 1961.

391

Until we as a profession tell the public why the principles of accounting should be accepted by the public, the public cannot be expected to know the meaning of the certified statements.

In nearly all cases where accounting principles come under scrutiny, it is where something unfortunate has happened. Therefore, until we have demonstrated the fairness of the accounting produced by accepted principles and used, we are not in a position to ask the public to accept the application of these principles in our reports. But even more important to everyone, until the profession properly develops and publicly supports, on an authoritative basis, the reasoning necessary to establish acceptance of the principles used, we are in no position to tell the public why our accounting principles should not be held responsible when something goes wrong in financial reporting. It is the job of firming up the principles of accounting, by clearly stating the reasons for their existence, that has been ignored.

Uniformity and progress

In reviewing the comments with respect to accounting principles that have come forth in the last three years, I note that they have largely been defensive. Among them was the argument that uniformity was a strait-jacket, a bar to progress. But so far as I know, not one single treatise has been presented to show the fairness of the various financial statements that would result from the application of *alternative* accepted principles to a given set of facts. No one has defended a single set of specific alternative principles by contending that both were fair, and by advancing sound reasoning in demonstration of that fairness.

If uniformity is basically bad, is it unreasonable to ask why not one of our professional leaders who holds this view has come forth (1) with a specific case where uniformity would result in damage or (2) with a case where the alternative principles now followed would produce rightful advantages for all the segments involved? If we are to continue such alternatives, our need is for the reasoning and proof as to how we can justify them, other than by merely showing that they are followed in other instances.

Is flexibility useful?

The objection has also been voiced that uniformity would eliminate flexibility in accounting principles. But to my knowledge, not one person has attempted to show where flexibility in the choice of alternative principles of accounting would result in financial statements that were fair to all segments of the business community. The arguments were only that flexibility was good, *per se*, and that the elimination of flexibility was bad, *per se*. Yet with respect to no single set of facts to be accounted for was the theory of flexibility applied and reasoning advanced to show why the " flexible " results were proper or fair.

Assuming for the moment that flexibility of principles is needed for a transition period to permit improvement in principles, would not the proof of this contention demonstrate its merit by eventual elimination of the less desirable practices? If flexibility would produce such improvement, could it not be illustrated? Yet examination of the record shows that the alternative methods of accounting for intangible drilling costs (either by expensing them currently or by capitalizing and amortizing them) are each as old as the other. The alternative treatment of deferred income taxes is as old as the laws that permitted deferral of the taxes. The alternative treatment of pension costs is as old as the requirement that pensions be paid. Flexibility, as such, has not brought improvement; in fact, the less desirable practices have tended to drive out, or at least to retard, acceptance of the good.

It is easy to prove the fallacy of the contention that flexibility is a good influence on accounting. Flexibility has been used as an excuse to prevent improvement, not to advance it. Improvement in accounting principles comes from demonstrating the unfairness on financial statements of accounting under existing principles, and then establishing new ones (or eliminating alternatives) which do not produce such unfairness.

Uniformity and experimentation

Still other accountants have argued that elimination of alternative principles would prevent experimentation. But no one has produced or illustrated a single experiment in the choice and application of accounting principles that would have been prevented by the elimination of alternative principles.

In my opinion, the present array of accepted principles applicable to a set of facts retards the adoption of improvements. Any accounting principle can and should be changed when analysis of the reasoning underlying it shows that it fails to give a fair presentation of the facts.

The use of alternative principles as a basis for experimentation is the very antithesis of what would ordinarily be assumed as a fact from the presence of the word " accepted " in the phrase " generally accepted accounting principles." No one would guess that the word " accepted " embraced " experimentation "; even to suggest such a possibility would indicate lack of integrity.

Such an idea would be equivalent to a doctor planning a medical experiment on a patient while he is on the operating table. The very thought is a chilling shock to a professional man's integrity. Ordinarily the reader of financial statements would assume from the phrase " accepted principles " that no experimentation was involved, but that definite rules were applicable to each transaction. If the phrase were to be truthfully and clearly stated, it would read something like this, "in accordance with one or another of the generally accepted alternative accounting principles." Even this clarification would prevent any experimentation outside the bounds of the accepted alternatives. A concept that alternative principles permit the adoption of additional alternatives would worsen an already intolerable practice.

So far as I can see, no one has demonstrated any merit in non-uniformity, flexibility and experimentation in accounting principles. Of course, this does not prove that merit cannot be demonstrated. I do not believe it can; but then maybe others can do it. The only support advanced thus far for alternative principles is the contention that accounting principles cannot be defined because they must be flexible, must permit experimentation, and must not inhibit new ideas. Standing alone, these are all generalized contentions that are without merit or proof of their truthfulness.

Perils of the present position

The opportunity of examining our principles is still within our hands, if we choose to take advantage of it before we are forced to do so. The initiative is still ours. We have taken the first organizational step through the establishment of the Accounting Principles Board.

But until this Board acts, we should ask ourselves, " What are the consequences of the lack of authoritative support for accounting practices which we cannot support as fair? " In reasoning out the answer to this question, we will find that the consequences are *misrepresentations*. We should then ask, " When do such misrepresentations by members of our profession become problems for us? " It is easy to find the answer to this question, too. It is when these misrepresentations get our members into trouble; when the spotlight shines on a particular practice that was unjustified in the first instance; when we could not bring forth reasoning acceptable to the public to justify our practices.

This " hard-way " process of finding our trouble spots is no different in accounting than in any other activity. TV quiz shows were accepted practice until the limelight exposed them.

They were like misrepresentations made through accepted accounting principles. They were known by the individuals involved. The participants knew the shows were misrepresented, but the practice was justified in their minds because other similar shows were doing the same thing. Prearrangement was, therefore, rationalised as being accepted practice. The authority was not what was *proper* practice, but what was *accepted* practice. There was no law that said quiz shows could not be prearranged.

This same kind of reasoning was used by the American Institute's committee on professional ethics in attempting to justify the non-compliance of the usual type of auditors' certificate on railroad financial statements with the Institute's Professional Conduct Rule 5 (e). This rule, as you know, requires the auditor to direct attention to any material departure from generally accepted accounting principles. But the usual audit certificate on railroad statements makes no reference at all to *generally accepted* accounting principles; it refers only to conformity with accounting principles prescribed or authorized by the Interstate Commerce Commission. The ethics committee made no specific finding that the accounting followed by railroads was right or in accordance with generally accepted accounting principles. The committee's decision that the usual railroad audit certificate is not a violation of Rule 5 (e) was not made on the basis of reasoning; it was made rather on the basis of presumption and custom—*i.e.*, what most accountants and the railroads were doing, not what they ought to be doing.

In the recent case of the irregularities in the Sister Kenny Foundation,[1] the auditors allowed management a high degree of non-uniformity, flexibility and experimentation in reporting fund-raising costs for a nine-year period. For some of the years, the amount of funds raised by the campaign was shown net, without disclosing costs, which were very high in relation to the funds received; for other years, the funds received were reported gross, and an expense item was shown for the fund-raising costs, but it included only a part of such costs; the rest was effectively buried in other amounts. At no time during this period was there a clear statement of the funds received from the campaign and the cost of obtaining them. As a result, the public was not adequately informed and contributed millions of dollars for charitable purposes that were siphoned off for non-charitable uses. Even with all of the criticism that might now be levelled at the accounting followed, it is doubtful that such unsupportable practices would have come to light if there had not been a

[1] *The Journal of Accountancy*, April 1961, p. 72.

simultaneous allegation of waste and unlawful diversion of funds.

This case is a clear example of the consequences of not having authoritative standards of accounting that were required to be imposed; it is an illustration of the absence of discipline in the application of accounting standards. In so far as the accounting and reporting practices followed were concerned, they did not meet standards of accountability that were acceptable to the public. They did not meet the disciplinary test of fair reporting demanded by the various segments of the public. Had sound principles for financial accounting been established by the profession on the objective standard of fairness to all segments of the public, it is doubtful that such consequences as occurred in this case would have been allowed to develop, at least to the same extent.

The profession has not set up the means by which to judge whether the accounting being followed in a given case is proper. It is hoped that thought now being given to the problem of substandard practices will provide a way for bringing such matters before appropriate Institute or state committees, and that the members who performed the accounting that is under scrutiny can be required to bring full information before such committees. This would enable the profession to hold the information in confidence, and at the same time permit the performing members to be admonished and instructed as to where their accounting did not conform to proper standards. Authoritative statements of sound accounting principles and practices will, of course, have to be developed as a basis for judging whether or not the accounting under consideration was substandard.

No decision of material consequence in accounting is final until it is decided rightly; and this applies to the decisions of the Accounting Principles Board and all of the American Institute committees which issue authoritative pronouncements. Those who would swing such pronouncements in the direction of support for their own viewpoints and practices, irrespective of the rightness or soundness thereof, are only seeking to delay the day of reckoning. Make no mistake—that day will come. Let us hope we do not wait until Congress gets around to specifying what that day is.

Accounting Principles Board

Now how should the profession go about doing what must be done to establish sound principles on a solid foundation of objective standards?

The new Accounting Principles Board has been established and provided with a research staff. The plan for the Board was conceived by the special committee on research programme, in a spirit of earnest desire to meet this pressing need. Also the Board was conceived with the idea that its members would be open-minded and unprejudiced; that they would establish sound principles on the basis of the fairness of the accounting that would result; and that objective reasoning as to fairness to all segments of business would be the criterion of the Board's decisions.

The plan calls first for the determination and establishment of the basic postulates (or objective standards, as I prefer to call them) as the foundation on which the principles are to be formulated. The postulates are to be supported by reasoning derived from the economic and political environment and from the modes of thought and customs of all segments of business. Then, a fairly broad set of co-ordinated accounting principles is to be formulated on the basis of the postulate foundation.

The program contemplates that practitioners and other interested parties will submit briefs giving their views and reasoning on the research projects. This will require every public accountant having convictions on any principle or project under consideration to file a memorandum supporting the views held, so that others may examine them and may present their own views and reasons. The Board will fail in its task if the basis for its pronouncements is generated solely within itself. This approach would merely provide the means for insulating the viewpoints of the Board from professional analysis. It would be the cowardly approach—it would prove the lack of independence of those who do not file briefs stating and arguing their own views, but who at the same time, refuse to accept the views of those who do file with the Board. On that basis the Board's efforts would be of little import.

Basic standard of fairness

The objective standard or basic postulate underlying all accounting principles is simple—it is that of " fairness "—fairness to all segments of business.

If the manner in which this objective standard of fairness is reasoned out for each accounting principle adopted by the Board, then that principle will be accepted by the public. We should be able to take any balance-sheet or income statement, and explain for every principle applied why it produces fairness in those statements. Then and only then will the ostensible needs for non-uniformity, flexibility, non-rigidity and experimentation in accounting principles be viewed in their true light, as diversionary generalizations without meaning or purpose. Improvements are the result of action taken to meet the needs of the public; they do not result from defense of the *status quo*.

Costing Terminology *

By J. Kitchen

F.C.A., National Coal Board, London.

SINCE its earliest days, the Institute of Cost and Works Accountants has been anxious to prepare " a terminology suitable for cost accounting purposes." From the beginning, those concerned have been aware of many difficulties, and the Institute has been properly deliberate in dealing with the problem. In the event, two terminologies have been compiled and published, the first (issued in March 1937) having recently been superseded by a second, the Institute's *Terminology of Cost Accountancy*, published in April last year.[1]

It seems to be universally accepted that adequate definition of terms is essential to useful discussion. But the proper role of definition is not easy to apprehend, and it is an immediate question whether definitions which take the form of authoritative pronouncements are always desirable.

The present article attempts some discussion of this problem. Even philosophers think definition a far from simple matter, and no accountant should venture a consideration of it without apology. Nevertheless, before terminological problems in cost accounting are discussed, some attention will be given to the role of definition in science generally.

Definition in general

It will be convenient to follow a distinction which is sometimes drawn between two kinds of definition. On the one hand, there is a class of definition which reports how a particular word has been used in the past by a particular person; definitions like these are sometimes called *lexical definitions*. On the other hand, there is a class of definition which says how a word will be used (or ought to be used) now or in the future; definitions like these are sometimes called *stipulative definitions*.[2]

---

* From *Accounting Research*, February 1954.
[1] *Terminology of Cost Accountancy*, published by the Institute of Cost and Works Accountants. 24 pages. Price 2s. 6d. net.
[2] See Richard Robinson, *Definition*, Oxford, 1950, where these two kinds of definition are clearly identified and discussed.

(a) *Lexical definitions.* Lexical definitions record usage, and usage is a matter of history. " We are," as Mr. Robinson says, " explaining the actual way in which some actual word has been used by some actual persons." [3]

At first sight, recording usage seems to be an easy process, and we might expect that the definitions in a good dictionary would be lexical definitions. But to record all usage is too severe a task, and selection in the interests of shortness alone involves a judgment, even though the lexicographer may take every care to minimise the influence of his own preferences. The *Oxford English Dictionary* records in a preface that its " basis is a collection of some five millions of excerpts from English literature of every period . . . represented by a selection of about 1,800,000 quotations actually printed." What is clear is that lexical definitions can hardly ever be perfect, and in particular that they can seldom be brief.

(b) *Stipulative definitions.* The scientist who identifies a new strain of bacteria will choose a name by which to refer to it, as will the pharmaceutical chemist who isolates a new drug, or the explorer who discovers a new mountain or cape. Such a process of naming is stipulative definition.[4] The name which is chosen is itself without significance. It is without importance whether our mountain is called " K.2," or " Mount Godwin Austen "; it is the same mountain, and it is the mountain that matters, not the name. Of course, once our mountain is named, we shall find it convenient if other people, referring to our mountain, call it by the name which is familiar to us. But all that is really necessary is that people should make it clear to which mountain they are referring.

It may, perhaps, be necessary to emphasise that a stipulative definition can have no " truth-value "; it is not a statement which can be said to be " true " or " false "; it is merely a statement of intention, an exhortation or a command. Professor Popper explains the process as follows [5]: ". . . the scientific view of the definition ' A puppy is a young dog ' would be that it is an answer to the question ' *What shall we call* a young dog? ' rather than an answer to the question ' What is a puppy? ' "

---

[3] *Op. cit.*, p. 35.

[4] Definitions which involve the giving of a name to something are perhaps more often called *nominal* definitions. But all the definitions here considered are *nominal* definitions as the term is generally (more widely) understood, and the term " stipulative " is used in this discussion to point the contrast from lexical definition.

[5] K. R. Popper, *The Open Society and Its Enemies*, 2nd ed. (Routledge and Kegan Paul, 1952), Vol. 2, p. 14 (italics in original).

Professor Popper is saying that the important part of the definition is the second part (here " a young dog ") rather than the name (here " puppy ") which is chosen; and that it is with the second part alone that science is really concerned. He adds: " Questions like ' *What is* life? ' or ' *What is* gravity? ' do not play any role in science." Suppose an actuary says " Let the symbol $a_{\overline{n}|}$ indicate the present value at compound interest of an immediate annuity-certain of 1 payable annually for a term of n years "; here he is stipulating that *for the purpose of the discussion on which he is about to embark* the symbol $a_{\overline{n}|}$ is to have the meaning he has given it. But, equally, our actuary could use any other symbol; all that is needed is that he should make his intention clear. Likewise, if an economist says—as Alfred Marshall said in his *Principles of Economics* [6]—" . . . the term *Quasi-rent* will be used in the present volume for the income derived from machines or other appliances for production made by man "; this, too, is a stipulative definition. Marshall chose a term which could be used conveniently to refer shortly to certain specific forms of income which he discussed. The term chosen did not affect the argument, and the definition had no " truth-value," though a statement that " *Marshall used the term ' quasi-rent ' to mean* . . ." would have a " truth-value," and would be no longer a stipulative but a lexical definition.

(c) *The unimportance of stipulative definitions.* Though stipulative definition is the kind of definition with which science is the more concerned, stipulative definitions themselves are comparatively unimportant in scientific discussion. Marshall himself said [7]: " The use of technical terms at starting adds nothing to knowledge: but it puts familiar knowledge in a firm compact shape, ready to serve as the basis for further study." Professor Popper has said [8]: " . . . science does not use definitions [*i.e.*, stipulative definitions] in order to determine the meaning of its terms, but only in order to introduce handy shorthand labels . . . all definitions [could] be omitted without loss to the information imparted . . . our language . . . would lose, not precision, but merely brevity." [9]

[6] 8th ed., p. 74.
[7] *Op. cit.*, p. 130.
[8] *Op. cit.*, pp. 14–18.
[9] It will be useful to quote Professor Popper at some length. He says (*ibid.*): " How then do the sciences make sure of the meanings of their terms? Various replies to this question have been suggested, but I do not think that any of them are satisfactory. The situation seems to be this. Aristotelianism and related philosophies have told us for such a long time how important it is to get a precise knowledge of the meaning of our terms that we are all inclined to believe it. And we continue to cling to this creed in spite of the unquestionable fact that

Standardisation of terminology

While the methodologists make it plain that all are free to
stipulate, and that it is not important if different writers use the
same word to mean different things (provided they stipulate
clearly what they *do* mean), obviously it is a nuisance when
arguments are unnecessarily complicated by linguistic problems.
The case for a common language is overwhelming, and among
intelligent people we may expect a selection to take place naturally
between differing usages, to save trouble by the adoption of that
usage which seems the most sensible, and which appeals to a
majority. This kind of natural selection amongst usages is going
on all the time. It is with problems raised by conscious efforts
to speed up the process that we are here concerned. Individuals
may surrender some of their freedom of choice to a central
authority, recognising its right to say that certain usages are
approved and others not. They will do this where they think
that the advantages outweigh the disadvantages, and in many
cases the balance will be clear. The zoologists, who have to
make provision for very large numbers of new terms every year,
have an international organisation to collect and publish lists

philosophy, which for twenty centuries has worried about the meaning of its
terms, is not only full of verbalism but also appallingly vague and ambiguous,
while a science like physics which worries hardly at all about terms and their
meaning, but about facts instead, has achieved great precision. This, surely,
should be taken as indicating that, under Aristotelian influence, the importance
of the meaning of terms has been grossly exaggerated. But I think that it indicates
even more. For not only does this concentration on the problem of meaning
fail to establish precision; it is itself the main source of vagueness, ambiguity,
and confusion.

" In science, we take care that the statements we make should never *depend*
upon the meaning of our terms. Even where the terms are defined, we never
try to derive any information from the definition, or to base any argument
upon it. This is why our terms make so little trouble. We do not overburden
them. We try to attach to them as little weight as possible. We do not take
their ' meaning ' too seriously. We are always conscious that our terms are a
little vague (since we have learned to use them only in practical applications)
and we reach precision not by reducing their penumbra of vagueness, but rather
by keeping well within it, by carefully phrasing our sentences in such a way
that the possible shades of meaning of our terms do not matter. This is how
we avoid quarrelling about words.

" The view that the precision of science and of scientific language depends
upon the precision of its terms is certainly very plausible, but it is none the less,
I believe, a mere prejudice. The precision of a language depends, rather, just
upon the fact that it takes care not to burden its terms with the task of being
precise. A term like ' sand-dune ' or ' wind ' is certainly very vague. (How
many inches high must a little sand-hill be in order to be called ' sand-dune ' ?
How quickly must the air move in order to be called ' wind ' ?) However,
for most of the geologist's purposes, these terms are quite sufficiently precise;
and for other purposes, when a higher degree of differentiation is needed, he
can always say ' dunes between 4 and 30 feet high ' or ' wind of a velocity of
between 20 and 40 miles an hour.' And the position in the more exact sciences
is analogous. In physical measurements, for instance, we always take care to
consider the range within which there may be an error; and precision does not
consist in trying to reduce this range to nothing, or in pretending that there
is no such range, but rather in its explicit recognition."

of names, and these lists are accepted (though not always without question) as determining a standard terminology. The botanists make similar arrangements. Scientific societies have co-operated, too, to recommend symbols, signs and abbreviations for use in scientific publications, and conscientious writers and lecturers endeavour to employ these so as to make life easier for students.

It is important that the advantages which it is sought to achieve by standardisation should be seen to be real ones. Sometimes, the benefits will be obvious, and standardised definitions—as with descriptions of dangerous drugs—may be given legal force. At other times the case for standardisation may seem to have no more content than an aesthetic craving after tidiness, to be outweighed by the slightest concomitant disadvantage.

Standardisation is clearly an artificial process, and evidently has more in common with stipulation (it is, in fact, stipulation by authority) than it has with the natural process of selection among usages which it is designed to supersede. Accordingly, while standardisation has many virtues, it must be expected to combine the disadvantages of ordinary stipulation with any additional disadvantages which authoritative stipulation may involve. It is easily seen that too much stipulation is always likely to put a burden on writer and readers alike, since not only are there additional definitions to be wrestled with, but there is always a fair possibility that the stipulator himself will depart from his own rules. It is apparent, too, that stipulation is likely to be particularly troublesome when it conflicts with the sense in which a word is customarily used; while to borrow from Mr. Robinson once more [10] the " emotional dimension of meaning " which many words possess " is not amenable to re-definition by stipulation." Mr. Robinson also draws attention to the risk that re-definition by stipulation may involve a process of degeneration, which will leave us " without means of indicating an important distinction which could be indicated by the word in its previous sense." [11]

It is clear that disadvantages like these are likely to be more serious if the stipulation is authoritative, simply because the new usage will then receive wider and less critical acceptance. Clearly, too, where terms have a wide variety of uses, confusion may result during the inevitable period of adjustment before the standardised definition is established. But the present writer is indebted to Professor Popper for clarification of the supreme disadvantage which stipulation by authority is likely to involve where the

[10] *Op. cit.*, p. 77.
[11] *Op. cit.*, p. 82.

terms in question are of the kind used in theoretical discussion. The disadvantage appears because, when attempts are made to standardise the usage of such terms, it is almost certain that the definition chosen will involve the acceptance of a particular theoretical point of view, since any particular term is likely to owe its origin or its significance to the use made of it in formulating some theory. Accordingly, unless this point of view can easily be recognised, those who adopt the standard terminology will adopt the particular point of view it expresses, unthinkingly, without notice, and without criticism; with disastrous results for future progress in the subject.

It is, therefore, of the utmost importance that the theoretical bases on which standardised terms rest should be made explicit. The following paragraphs offer some consideration of the 1952 *Terminology* of the Institute of Cost and Works Accountants in the light of the foregoing remarks.

The current terminology of cost accountancy

The current *Terminology* of the Institute of Cost and Works Accountants is clearly stipulative in intention. It contains 182 definitions, all of them brief. Most are limited to twenty or thirty words; none has more than sixty. They are grouped under eight main headings, with an ingenious system of cross-references. There is also an alphabetical list of terms.

The scope of the 1952 *Terminology* has been restricted by comparison with the previous publication, and terms which " do not specifically relate to cost accountancy " have been excluded. The voice of authority thus makes itself heard over a narrower field; it is to be regretted that it makes itself heard so clearly. There is a ring of finality about the reference, in the preface to the present edition, to " terms now officially defined," in spite of an acceptance (copied from the introduction to the 1937 *Terminology*) that living languages must evolve and develop. Though the 1937 publication also threatened intending examination candidates who might fail to recognise a new orthodoxy, it was more tentative and persuasive in approach than its counterpart of 1952, whose preface tersely states: " As far as students are concerned *Terminology of Cost Accountancy* will come into operation after the June 1952 examinations, when all examination questions set by the Board of Examiners will be worded in accordance therewith. Candidates therefore will need to acquire a thorough knowledge of these terms and definitions, to enable them not only to understand the questions they have to answer, but also to express their answers in orthodox language."

It is this hardening of attitude, as well as the announcement of a wider research project for a terminology of management accounting, which makes some review of the function of definition by authoritative pronouncement seem desirable.

Standard definitions may be unnecessary

Mr. Robinson places at the head of his list of rules for stipulative definition [12]: " The supreme rule of stipulation is surely to *stipulate as little as possible.*" This obviously applies especially to authoritative stipulation.

The dropping of some terms, defined in 1937, from the current *Terminology* of the Institute of Cost and Works Accountants has already been mentioned. The improved arrangement of the 1952 *Terminology*, whereby terms are grouped under main headings, has brought together a number of other definitions which could well, one would think, have been omitted on the ground that they are already dealt with in the established literature, if not in a completely uniform way, then at least without risk of serious confusion. The twelve " price " definitions, the nine " depreciation-methods " definitions, and the nine " cost-rates " definitions might be taken as examples.[13]

It may be that in the current *Terminology* the sections containing definitions on standard costing and budgetary control are justified on the ground that it is in these directions that the development of costing techniques is at present most rapid. But the Institute has already put out its own introductory publication on standard costing and budgetary control,[14] and the existing literature on these subjects in Britain and America is by no means negligible. Perhaps the *Terminology* serves its most obvious purpose in providing a list of standard names for, and definitions of, a number of the variances which it is the function of standard costing systems to throw up.

The *Terminology of Cost Accountancy* accepts, in its introduction, that no list of terms can be comprehensive and final

[12] *Op. cit.*, p. 80 (italics in original).

[13] *Terminology of Cost Accountancy*, pp. 14–17. To deal individually with these definitions would take too long. But one must doubt any pressing need for including definitions such as those distinguishing between " simple average price " and " weighted average price." Again, the inclusion of definitions for nine well-known text-book methods of calculating depreciation can perhaps best be supported on the ground that the short names given in the *Terminology* to the various methods are particularly handy labels. Handy they are, in fact, but probably the only label which is not already completely familiar, namely, the " repair reserve method," might be criticised as hardly incorporating the happiest use of the word " reserve."

[14] *An Introduction to Budgetary Control, Standard Costing, Material Control and Production Control*, April 1950.

and that terminology " must evolve." Nevertheless, the publication of a list having the backing of a recognised authority is in itself an act which must inhibit the evolution of terminology, and this (if there were no other) would be a sufficient reason for keeping official stipulation to a minimum. But beyond this, unnecessary standardisation burdens the student and irritates the expert, who is tempted to reject tools for which he has felt no need. The new *Terminology* has, in eighteen months, received only slight notice in the professional journals; and Mr. Gossman, in a letter to *The Cost Accountant* [15] when the *Terminology* had been in circulation for six months, could say to the author of the only review article published: " Mr. Rivers may rest assured that practically no managers, and very few cost accountants, have read the pamphlet." However unrepresentative such a comment may be, the fact that it was made at all must seem a poor reward to the anonymous authors of the document, who worked hard to accomplish what they did.

But Britain is not the only country where a costing terminology has recently been received with some half-heartedness. In New Zealand, where students and practitioners were faced with textbooks from all over the English-speaking world, a glossary was compiled and published [16] of 755 cost accounting terms, which were reduced to 204 standard definitions. But presumably practitioners were slow to abandon familiar usages, and new textbooks continued to arrive, vitiating the tidy classifications. Whatever the reasons, we find a member of the standards committee urging practitioners, two years later, to " give consideration to the Code " and to " spare just a little time to consider ways and means of using the Code." [17]

There is much wisdom in these words from the (American) *Journal of Accountancy* [18]: " We should bear in mind that no code of terminology will be useful, no matter how appropriate it may seem to its author, unless it can be, and is, generally *understood, accepted and used* by those interested. . . ."

The compilers of the *Terminology* of the Institute of Cost and Works Accountants have deliberately not attempted to include equivalent terms because of the impracticability of relating the different " shades of meaning of the many terms in common use in an industry, trade or district." In fact, the collection and

---

[15] Vol. 31, No. 5, October 1952, p. 167.
[16] *New Zealand Standard Specification No.* 520, N.Z. Standards Institute, Wellington, 1947.
[17] W. G. Rodger, " Standardised Accounting Terminology," *The Accountants' Journal* (of New Zealand), Vol. 27, No. 10, April 1949.
[18] Walter L. Bradley, " Terminology and Forms of Financial Statements for Co-operatives," *Journal of Accountancy*, Vol. 79, No. 4 (my italics).

publication of a series of lexical definitions on these lines might be very illuminating as a basis for a comparative study of costing practice. But the size of the task compels sympathy with the authors of the present work.

Standard definitions may mislead

If the suggestion can be made that standardisation of terminology may be unnecessary where terms already receive substantially uniform treatment, may not the criticism equally be put forward that, where terms are variously used in the established literature, attempts at " standardisation " by means of bald pronouncements alone may run the risk of turning students' text-books into jungles of confusion?

Let us look at a trivial example. The current *Terminology* distinguishes carefully between " apportionment " and " allocation." The intention seems to be that " allocation " should be reserved for directly traceable costs, while " apportionment " should be treated as importing the idea of the arbitrary division which must be made when indirect costs are distributed. The *Terminology* does not award a special signification to " allotment," using it for both cases.

This distinction between " allocation " and " apportionment " has much to recommend it, and its adoption would be convenient. But the *Terminology* ought, in fairness, to explain that all three terms are used interchangeably by writers in Britain and the United States (though it must be admitted that the reader's task is often made more involved by the variety of ways in which the words are qualified through the addition of, for example, " primary " and " secondary "—an embellishment which the Institute of Cost and Works Accountants has done well to avoid). Thus the Institute of Chartered Accountants in England and Wales entitles its most recent publication on *indirect* expenses [19] *Notes on the Allocation of Expense.* The earlier *Developments in Cost Accounting* (1947) used " allocation " and " apportionment " to mean the same thing. The American *Cost Accountants' Handbook* (ed. Lang) [20] says: " In practice, the terms allocation, proration and distribution are used more or less synonymously," and elsewhere it uses " assignment " and " apportionment " similarly. The Institute of Chartered Accountants speaks of " primary allocation " as expressing " the attribution of expense to headings which indicate the kind of expense—headings such as those commonly used as titles of nominal accounts, for example,

[19] November 1951.
[20] *Op. cit.,* p. 954.

lighting, rates, water, advertising, stationery, and so on."
" Secondary allocation " for them means allocation to " specific
departments, or to cost centres." [21] This last the *Cost Accountants'*
Handbook [22] would call " primary distribution," reserving " secondary distribution " for the reapportionment of expense from
service to producing departments; others (Blocker, for example [23])
think of secondary distribution as " the allocation of overhead
cost to units of production or sale." It would be tedious to
go on. Meanwhile in a different sense, the British Institute of
Management [24] speaks of material as being " allocated " when
it has been earmarked or reserved for a particular production
order. T. H. Sanders uses the word " apportioned " in this
sense.[25] No doubt an extreme example has been taken, but it
does seem that here at any rate, though different words are used,
the actual risk of misunderstanding is small in any particular
case. Confusion is unlikely unless uniformity of usage is expected.
Greater uniformity would be convenient, but it is by no means
vital, and it is certainly questionable whether standardisation can
usefully be attained by mere publication of definitions without
explanation.

But the fact that problems of standardisation may be trivial
must not be allowed to blind us to more serious dangers. These
are most apparent where attempts are made to lay down, without
explanatory comment, brief standard definitions for some of the
very complex concepts which are of fundamental importance
both within the field of cost accountancy and beyond it. Most
people agree that " cost " is a meaningless concept unless some
qualifying word or phrase is employed. If economists fall into
the habit of thinking of the word " cost," used without qualifications, as relating to " opportunity " cost (the cost of the
opportunity forgone in applying resources), they cannot complain
if cost accountants think of it (so used) as referring to " original "
or " historical " cost (the money value expended in acquiring
resources). But they can and should criticise an official definition
which attempts to restrict " cost " as a concept to original cost,
as the 1952 *Terminology of Cost Accountancy* does [26]; and their
complaint should be made as much on behalf of students of cost
accounting as on their own. It is to the freshest and most original

---

[21] *Notes on the Allocation of Expense*, pp. 6 and 7.
[22] *Op. cit.*, p. 958 *et seq.*
[23] *Cost Accounting* (2nd ed., 1948), p. 164. Blocker, too, uses " allocation "
and " apportionment " interchangeably, as do standard English texts by Wheldon
and Bigg, and as also does Ryall, *Dictionary of Costing.*
[24] *Stock Control and Storekeeping* (1952), p. 14.
[25] *Cost Accounting for Control* (1934), p. 85.
[26] *Op. cit.*, p. 10. " Cost: The amount of expenditure incurred on a given thing."

minds in both fields that we must look for more light on cost theory and cost accounting. But new light is unlikely to dawn in minds conditioned from the beginning of their studies to accept a single narrow point of view. It may be that the compilers of the current *Terminology* intended no more than to abandon the over-condensed definition of 1937,[27] and that they substituted a more limited concept because that alone would allow their ingenious cross-reference system to work intelligibly. But without explanation, and without direct reference elsewhere in the *Terminology* to the idea of cost as " sacrificed alternative," the present " official " definition is unfortunate.

No less unfortunate is the definition of " marginal cost," which has degenerated into " prime cost plus variable overhead." [28] It seems a pity that this blunt instrument should be substituted, without a word of explanation, for the concept so well established in economics. Such a duplication of terms, one of which bears the hall-mark of authority, surely places an unfair burden on students. Again, the chief danger is to the young student, who may fail to distinguish between the two ideas and end by understanding neither, or—what is worse— may get the impression that he flirts with the more subtle at his peril.

The truth is that the whole concept of cost, like value, is one of great complexity, and attempts to explain it, comprehensively and exhaustively, in a few words are over-optimistic. Professor W. J. Vatter, whose chapter, " A Re-examination of Cost Accounting," appears in J. J. W. Neuner's *Cost Accounting,*[29] sums up the situation when he says: " Arbitrarily defining the word ' cost ' is a useless procedure; what we need to acquire is an understanding of the group of associated ideas—a ' thought-pattern '—if we are to understand what we mean by ' cost.' In other words, we need to understand the *concept* ' cost,' not to define the word."

Brevity and ambiguity

Brevity is a desirable feature in definitions, but it runs the risk of putting ideas in a straitjacket. Too great an anxiety for shortness can easily lead to over-simplification and ambiguity.

[27] *Costing Terminology* (1937), pp. 4–5. " Cost " is defined as the money value of " real cost," which is: " The efforts expended, the utilities consumed, the risks incurred and the abstinence endured in providing a commodity or service, expressed as such. . . ." This definition at least attempts to be comprehensive. But such a condensed statement can never have been intelligible except to those for whom a definition of " cost " was unnecessary.

[28] *Op. cit.,* p. 13.

[29] 3rd ed., 1947, p. 735.

Alfred Marshall used to say: " Every dogma that is short and simple is false." To explain both " depreciation " and " obsolescence " in thirty words is impossible, though the *Terminology* attempts it.[30] The danger is again to the young student who at the beginning of his studies may be given the impression (and given it by the highest authority in his profession) that these concepts are simple. Would it not be wiser—and more interesting —to hint at some of the questions begged by an expression like " intrinsic value "? [31] And does not the definition of " expense " (" the cost of services provided to an undertaking and the notional cost of the use of owned assets ") likewise raise more problems than it solves?

It is no criticism of the compilers to recall some words of Dr. Johnson taken from the preface to his *Dictionary of the English Language*: " When the nature of things is unknown, or the notion unsettled and indefinite, and various in various minds, the words by which such notions are conveyed, or such things denoted, will be ambiguous and perplexed." Dr. Johnson, however, was saying this about definitions which no one was under any obligation to accept.

Accounting terminology in the U.S.A.

It will be convenient at this point to notice how the problem of securing an increased understanding of terms, together with something like uniformity in their employment, has been tackled by two professional organisations in the U.S.A.

After some abortive attempts in the early 1930s, the American Institute of Accountants formed a Committee on Terminology in 1940, under the chairmanship of Mr. George O. May. This committee was constituted from the membership of the Institute's Committee on Accounting Procedure, and (having particularly in mind previous failures) it approached its work with great caution and humility. It undertook the discussion of a number of terms in common use by the public, which had also a specialised usage in accounting, as well as the consideration of a few purely technical terms developed by accountants and unfamiliar to the public. This discussion was to be " *more extensive than mere definitions and might perhaps include suggestions for modifications of present practice, with the object of minimising misunderstandings.*

---

[30] *Op. cit.*, p. 11. " Depreciation " is defined as " the diminution in the intrinsic value of an asset due to use and/or to lapse of time." " Obsolescence " is " the loss in the intrinsic value of an asset due to its supersession."

[31] By comparison, the space allotted (a full page) to definitions of methods of calculating depreciation must give the impression that methods are important and complex, while depreciation itself is an easy concept to grasp. Is this wise?

Such a discussion might not only be circulated in the profession, but brought to the attention of the publishers of general dictionaries with a view to recognition of the special usages in the new editions of such works." The committee added: " A question may no doubt be raised whether all such uses are necessary or expedient or whether some should be abolished." [32] The Committee on Accounting Procedure was to approve the reports of the Committee on Terminology for presentation to the Council of the Institute, and to authorise their publication, though the reports were not to represent formal pronouncements of the Committee on Accounting Procedure.

Between 1940 and 1944, about a score of words or expressions were discussed (usually at considerable length) in published Research Bulletins. In practically every case a definition was eventually attempted, but the qualifications with which those set out in the Committee's third published report were introduced are significant: " In the section which follows, the several definitions of specialised accounting uses of terms suggested in this or previous reports are brought together, and there are given also the dictionary definitions which come closest to them of any that the research department has discovered. The latter are included for comparison only, and are not necessarily approved. In some cases they are obviously defective. *It should be clearly understood that the Committee's definitions are to be read in connection with the discussion which has preceded them and are not comprehensive nor exclusive of other uses.*" [33]

Though its own recommendations are bound to carry much weight by reference to its members' status in the profession, the creditably democratic attitude of the A.I.A. Committee on Accounting Procedure is illustrated elsewhere by its practice of giving, after every formal recommendation, details of the majority (never less than two-thirds) by which it was adopted, together with the names of members dissenting or " assenting with qualifications "; dissentient views are then usually set out.

After 1944, the Committee on Accounting Procedure (directly and through another Sub-Committee) continued the May Committee's full and painstaking word-by-word discussion of terminology, and undertook in some cases further consideration of differing views. The American Institute seems to have felt throughout that understanding of the concepts discussed was more vital than agreement on formal definitions. Accordingly,

---

[32] A.I.A. *Accounting Research Bulletin*, No. 7 (special), November 1940 (my italics).
[33] A.I.A. *Accounting Research Bulletin*, No. 9 (special), May 1941 (my italics).

the chief function of the various Research Bulletins was educational. Uniformity in the employment of terms was not expected to be achieved by decree. Such an attitude acquires particular significance when it is recalled that the Institute's concern was chiefly with financial accounting terms where the interests of shareholders, creditors and the public might seem to demand more uniformity than would be required in cost or management records used mainly within a single firm or industry.

The views of the American Accounting Association seem to have been somewhat similar. Introducing the 1948 revision of its *Accounting Concepts and Standards Underlying Corporate Financial Statements*, the Executive Committee of the Association said [34]: " The basic objective has been *to stimulate the continued study and discussion* of accounting standards. . . ." Even so, there was criticism from a later president of the Executive Committee who called for presentation of minority reports, adding, " Surely the statement as it stands must be the result of many compromises of differences of opinion." [35] Also in 1952, the Association's Committee on Cost Concepts and Standards published a report [36] " with full awareness of its tentative nature." This report offered some two dozen definitions, together with comments and explanations.

Conclusion

By way of conclusion, we may recall that we have stressed the comparative unimportance in scientific discussion of definitions of the kind which comprise the current *Terminology of Cost Accountancy*. An individual author is entitled to use words as he pleases, provided he makes it clear—and sometimes he may have to do this by means of a special definition—how he intends to use them in any given context. Though the convenience of a common language is unquestioned, and though we agree that words should be responsibly used, the paramount requirement (that people should make themselves understood) does not involve that particular words must always be used in a particular way. The importance of the meaning of terms may be exaggerated. Precision should be sought rather by keeping well within the " penumbra of vagueness " which inevitably surrounds all our words, and " by carefully phrasing our sentences in such a way that the possible shades of meaning of our terms do not matter."

Where usages differ, selection of a generally preferred usage

---

[34] *Accounting Review* (October 1948), Vol. 23, No. 4, p. 340 (my italics).
[35] *Accounting Review* (April 1950), Vol. 25, No. 2, p. 138.
[36] *Accounting Review* (April 1952), Vol. 27, No. 2, p. 176.

will take place naturally. But sometimes individuals will wish—with the aid of a central authority—to speed up the process of selection, especially where the number of terms involved is very large, or the subject to which they relate is developing very rapidly. Such stipulation by authority is not without disadvantages and foremost among these is the risk that clear and original thought may be inhibited in the degree that authoritative definitions receive unthinking acceptance, to the extent that they set an official stamp on some particular dogma, or in so far as they lean towards over-simplification and ambiguity. That official definitions, hammered out by compromise in committee, are likely to suffer some loss of precision in the process of adoption seems obvious. More than this, however assiduous the committee, and however learned its members, it is impossible to foresee all future needs. Definitions can be propounded which will be appropriate in many contexts, but definition becomes more difficult with every demand for an extension of applicability. To coin definitions which will be appropriate in all circumstances must be impossible unless the terms in question are of quite trivial significance. In particular, it is unlikely that highly complex ideas can be conveyed comprehensively in a very few words. Brevity in definition—though desirable—may be suspect.

Official definitions are no more than arbitrary decisions about words; they should not imply that knowledge is other than uncertain and incomplete. It is, accordingly, the more important that the discussions out of which authorised definitions have emerged should be published,[37] so that their origin and purpose can be understood. In so far as American practice seems to fulfil these requirements, it could with advantage be followed in this country.

Nothing that has been written above should be interpreted as an attack on the compilers of the *Terminology of Cost Accountancy*, or, indeed, on any particular definition. Those who serve on research committees have a hard and thankless task. The *Terminology* is a worthy attempt to set out concisely a large number of difficult ideas. Criticism would be unnecessary were this document published as the work of a fallible individual. It is the implied infallibility of authority which (despite disclaimers) is dangerous.[38]

---

[37] Other considerations apart, publication of the discussions would enable more value to be derived from the considerable educational facilities which the local organisations of bodies like the Institute of Cost and Works Accountants provide.

[38] By contrast, Professor Kohler's lengthy *Dictionary for Accountants* (Prentice-Hall, New York, 1952, pp. 453) may be welcomed as a frankly personal contribution in this field.

Recommendations on Accounting Theory [1]

By W. T. Baxter

Professor of Accounting,
London School of Economics.

I. *The need for a review*

Various societies of accountants have now for some years been issuing official statements on our profession's problems. What I have mainly in mind are of course the "recommendations" and "bulletins" published by the Institute of Chartered Accountants in England and Wales, and by the American Institute of Certified Public Accountants. These started to come out in quantity soon after Hitler's War, and they now add up to a substantial volume covering a long list of subjects. Their influence on accounting and auditing is great, and is likely to become greater. So some review of this development seems not out of place.

Almost every accountant must find the recommendations exceedingly useful in his day-to-day work. They provide him with a code of rules on all sorts of difficult points (notably where the law leaves awkward gaps); and they save time, thought, and worry. They have also served the general public well by raising the quality of published statements.

In view of these benefits, it may seem churlish, and academic in the worst sense, to attack the recommendations. Nevertheless I shall try to argue that at least in one aspect (which could be changed) they are doing a great disservice. And many other accountants—even if they do not share my feeling that the recommendations have already gone too far—may perhaps like to discuss how much further the process of recommending can with propriety go. Where is the limit? Are we to look forward to the day when every detail of our work has been dealt with? Should our goal be—as high authority has hinted apropos the question of price levels—super-recommendations by a massed assembly representing *all* the professional bodies?

Another reason for airing the matter is this. Some accounting societies have so far made few or no recommendations. Their

[1] Based on an article in *The Accountant* of October 10, 1953.

members may well have some feeling that the omission betokens lack of zeal and public spirit. They should recognise that a policy of official silence has in fact much in its favour. However, this most emphatically does *not* mean that inertia should be lightly excused, or that accounting societies need take no part in furthering knowledge. On the contrary, they should do everything in their power to encourage education, debate and research. For instance, they could give great help by setting up much-needed scholarships (perhaps to be awarded on the results of the professional examinations) to enable their brilliant young men to study further.

II. *Scope of the review*

A recommendation tends to contain three types of ingredient:

(1) A description of the given problem;
(2) A reasoned discussion, often based on fundamentals, on how best to solve the problem; and
(3) The recommended solution.

It is mainly (2) that seems objectionable. For here the accounting society weighs intellectual principles, analyses the *pros* and *cons* of the alternative arguments, and decides that one view is better than the others; in short, here authority tells us what is true. Is it wise for any group of men to say what is " true " or " right " in matters of theory?

By " theory " I mean the attempt to explain, in terms of fundamentals, what accounting is and what it tries to do; I thus assume that accounting is a branch of knowledge, like law or physics, with basic principles that are worth exploring. (One might use phrases like " scientific laws " instead of " principles " or " theory," but that would suggest work among test-tubes. Other phrases, employing " abstract knowledge " or " scholarly learning," might sound a bit pompous. On the whole, " theory " seems the neatest word to cover what we have in mind.)

The distinction between (2) and (3) can best be seen by contrasting our recommendations with a set of *working rules*, for instance the Companies Act or the Football Association's rules of play. Such rules are a framework designed to make something run smoothly; unlike the recommendations, they consist only of (3), and do not start off with a discursion into the philosophy of, say, companies or football. The test of a good law is that the institution works well; it is not educational but practical.

Consider, for instance, the problem of how assets should be dealt with in a balance-sheet. When a writer on accounting tries to show us the best method, he probably builds up his case by discussing and judging various theories. But when a law says that company accounts must show the values in such-and-such ways, it does not analyse all the theories and then tell us which satisfies logic. It merely issues orders. It tells us *what*, and perhaps *how*, but not *why*. So we can obey this kind of law without feeling that we are being forced to accept a particular theory, and that our freedom of thought is being lessened. Besides, few citizens of a lively democracy grow up believing that everything in their laws is sensible; we hear much criticism of laws, and we accept that we have the right—indeed the duty— to try to repeal or reform bad laws.

Of course, even the answers to *what* and *how* can be influenced by theory. Normally the makers of a law must have some theory in mind when they draft it. A legislature may even be forced to choose between scientific theories, *e.g.*, public health law assumes that the views of Pasteur and Fleming are right. But the choice is made merely so that hopeful lines of development can be tried without delay, and should not imply that the official seal of approval has been put on any theory; if the experiment fails, it can be promptly scrapped without loss of face. Legis- lators who went further—to the point of explicitly endorsing a theory—would exceed their function, and would indeed be threatening our freedom of thought. Similarly, if an Act of Parliament includes definitions, these are not meant as revelations of final knowledge, but only as tools for making effective the particular set of rules; a judge may even hold that the definitions in one Act do not apply in the context of another Act on a dissimilar subject.

An obvious corollary seems to follow. When rules are pre- scribed for published accounting statements, they should not only avoid *why*, but should be chary about *how*. The stress should be on *what*. Authority can set minimum standards of disclosure without dragging in much theory; if it prescribes methods— particularly in the context of valuation—it must inevitably choose between theories. A terse list of minimum requirements, such as is given in the British Companies Act, works well and leaves honest men tolerably free to think and experiment. It provides a floor, not a ceiling.

Our views on recommendations may thus depend on whether we look on them as law or research; we may indeed regard a rule in (3) as useful, and yet object to its preamble in (2). In many cases, the tenor of the recommendations suggests that contributions to both theory and law are the aim. Whatever the intentions of their framers, there can be little doubt that they have been accepted by wide audiences as official and definitive pronouncements on theory.

We shall thus restrict the scope of our review to the parts of recommendations that pronounce on theory, or imply adoption of a theory, and shall say little about the other parts that proffer rules for minimum action on technical problems. Likewise we are not concerned with recommendations that adopt a different pattern, or deal with non-technical problems. They may for instance be concerned instead with *public policy*. A professional body sometimes advises its members to follow a common policy on questions that have little to do with the intellectual content of its members' work. For instance, it may make statements on " professional ethics," fees, registration by the state, and so forth. Such types of advice should be judged by standards quite different from those useful in our present review. If, for example, a body of architects or lawyers advises its members to charge a uniform scale of fees, or pay its assistants a standard wage, we judge the issue in the light of our views on the benefits or otherwise of economic monopoly; if it commends integrity to its members, perhaps we merely wonder whether it is not preaching to the converted in most cases, and wasting its breath in the rest.

Again, a recommendation may deal with *definitions* and *uniform practice*. To some extent these can be handled in ways that avoid theory—in which case they too fall outside our discussion. But such matters infringe on theory more often than might be supposed; and so we must give a little space to them.

One other matter should be made clear. Our review will make its point better if it omits all discussion of whether individual recommendations on theory have in fact been right or wrong. What is said here is thus not meant as criticism of any recommendation's content. Indeed, we may for our present purpose agree that every word in every recommendation seems entirely true; and yet we may think that a policy of making recommendations on theory will, in the long run, be disastrous.

III. *Origins of recommendations*

I should like to admit that, when official statements on accounting principles were first published, I was enthusiastic about them. My doubts have arisen since, on seeing how the new venture has developed.

Looking back, one remembers certain features in early statements that have unfortunately not usually been copied since. Consider the *Statement on Accounting Principles* of 1938. It was published by the American Institute, to whose members it was commended in a foreword; but it bore the names of three distinguished authors—Messrs. Sanders, Hatfield and Moore—who had been formed into an independent committee to do this bit of writing (and who were not even members of the Institute). Under such an arrangement, the Institute was plainly doing its duty to foster discussion, and yet was itself not taking sides. That kind of procedure goes far to disarm criticism.

Since this venture, the trend has been for the statements to be drafted by committees much more closely linked with the sponsoring body, and for the latter to back the conclusions in a much firmer way. The American Institute, for instance, set up its own Committee on Accounting Procedure to issue research bulletins. Bulletin No. 1 explained the aims and methods. It stressed the growth of corporate organisation, and therefore the social importance of good accounts; and it noted that there " has been a demand for a larger degree of uniformity in accounting." The committee stated that its rules were not intended to have retroactive effect; also they may be subject to exception, but " the burden of proof is upon the accountant clearly to bring out the exceptional procedure and the circumstances which render it necessary."

This has perhaps a somewhat mandatory ring. But the American bulletins have in fact used two safeguards that make their tenor less authoritarian: the members of the drafting committee are named in recommendations, and any member who disagrees with the majority is entitled to have the fact of his dissent recorded in the document. At least one American committee has had the courage to say bluntly that an earlier pronouncement by itself now seems wrong.[2]

The Institute of Chartered Accountants in England and Wales announced its first recommendation as follows:

> " The Council has requested the Taxation and Financial Relations Committee to consider and make recommendations to it on certain aspects of the accounts of companies and it is proposed from time to time to publish approved recommendations for the information of members. It is, of course, a matter for each individual member to consider his responsibility in regard to accounts presented by directors, but it is hoped that the recommendations to be made will be helpful to members in advising directors as to what is regarded as the best practice."[3]

These words are as modest and cautious as anyone could wish. They show how undogmatic the original plan was; and

---

[2] *Accounting Problems Arising from Devaluation of Foreign Currencies*, Research Department, American Institute of Accountants (1949).
[3] *The Accountant*, December 12, 1942, p. 354.

they suggest that the Council did not foresee the eventual scope of the recommendations, or the deference with which they would be treated.

IV. The case for recommendations

It would be ungenerous not to set down at length the good that has been done by the recommendations. Their benefits have obviously been great.

Recommendations have been so widely accepted that they have in fact acted very like a supplement to the law. What we may call extra-parliamentary control can often eke out statutes in a useful manner, particularly at the experimental stage; the rules of a stock exchange are another example of such control. In England, the early recommendations did much to prepare the way for the 1948 Companies Act, and indeed have in fact been absorbed into that Act. In America, the interplay between the Institute's bulletins and the S.E.C. regulations clearly is close; and the absence of a counterpart to the Companies Act enhances the bulletins' value as a code of standards.

The recommendations may thus serve as private forerunners and reinforcements to the law. Their record in this work has on the whole been excellent—notably in procuring full, frank, and consistent accounts.[4] The auditor has special cause to be thankful for them; the task of persuading his clients to comply with high standards in published accounts is sometimes delicate, and the recommendations have greatly strengthened his hand. They have also aided the analyst by fostering uniformity.

Though the recommendations have been less successful in the realm of theory, they have yielded some benefits. As each recommendation is first suggested, amended, and then adopted, undoubtedly it gives rise for a time to discussion and interest. Again, many of us used to deplore the fact that our profession's leaders never could spare time to write about their work; whatever the faults of the new system, it does prompt these men to tell us a great deal about what they think, and what they regard as usual practice.

We thus have cause to feel grateful to the drafters of recommendations; and this review should on no account be construed as an attack on them. Obviously they have devoted much time and

---

[4] Some other writer may like to examine the question of what safeguards (if any) are needed if a private group is to make rules, almost with the force of law, that affect non-members. Already one company has felt impelled to try to stop publication of a statement (alleged to have been prepared without normal opportunities for hearing objectors) that seemed likely to damage the company's borrowing status: *Appalachian Power Company* v. *A.I.C.P.A.*, 268 Federal 2nd 844 (Court of Appeals for the Second Circuit).

care to their task, and have been prompted by a high sense of public service. If harm should in the end come from their work, the blame should attach more to disciples who have accepted their teaching too eagerly, and have invested it with an *ex cathedra* quality that could not perhaps have been foreseen.

It is not unusual in human affairs for a thing to be started with the best intentions, and yet to develop aspects that threaten harm. My plea is that we should now review the good and bad alike, and see whether we cannot guide future growth in directions that are wholly good.

The recommendations' benefits are clear and present. Their ill results are hypothetical, and will show—if at all—in the future. Moreover these ill results are suggested by experience in other fields of study; and conceivably accounting is unlike these in nature and difficulty. If accounting differs from other subjects in its nature, then the arguments that follow may be weakened. But I see no reason to think that it is different.

V. The case against recommendations

The case against official recommendations on theory is threefold. First, men do not always become better at research when they work as a group. Second, if authority takes direct part in the pursuit of truth, it may hinder rather than help. Third—and most important—there are no sure signs by which truth can be recognised.

The first objection need not keep us long; admittedly it is not always a strong factor. To judge from experience in most fields of learning, men tend to do their best research when left to their own devices. There are many exceptions; a large team of chemists may be the quickest means of dealing with a laborious task, and a government committee may be admirable at sifting evidence and assessing opinion. In general, however, thinkers are apt to be hampered by close connection with a team or with a powerful institution. The link may curb initiative, or bring a need for diplomacy and compromise. The welfare of the institution may seem more important than truth; thus the authorities of the Church could not deal fairly with the ideas of Copernicus and Galileo because these ideas clashed with official pronouncements of the past.

The second objection is much weightier. It is an indirect way of saying that freedom is necessary for progress. " Freedom " here means the absence, not merely of crude tyranny, but also of benevolent authority that makes us respectful to some ideas and hostile to others. Man should be able to think freely and without bias, so that the stream of new ideas can flow strongly; and he should be able to discuss and experiment freely and without bias, so that all ideas can be criticised and tested with rigour. If authority intervenes—by joining in the quest itself or by giving its *imprimatur* to some favourite idea, let alone by making attacks on personal liberty—the chances of progress are lessened. Men cease to think so freely—whether from fear, or powerful pre-conceptions, or belief that others can do the job better; and therefore the stream of new ideas dries up. They cease to discuss and experiment so freely; and therefore criticism loses its edge, and ideas are not put to a stern test.

This train of reasoning leads to the third objection. How can we tell what is true? Even the objective tests of the laboratory are not final (and pronouncements on accounting must surely be based on discussion, and so be far from objective). Under strong criticism, many ideas soon prove false. Others satisfy all immediate tests, yet should be accepted as tentative only, for they, too, are likely to show flaws as the years go by. Even after an idea has survived triumphantly for centuries, some critic may shatter it, or else show it to be capable of improvement. Einstein was able both to generalise Newton's theory and to correct it for conditions that had not previously been considered. No human being—however distinguished—can certainly foretell which idea will become a casualty. As Bacon says: " Truth is the daughter, not of Authority, but of Time."

The root of the matter, surely, is man's fallibility. Only if we believe a statement to have divine inspiration can we treat it as beyond doubt.

It may be helpful to ask why learned bodies do not in general issue official solutions to questions puzzling their members. Why, for instance, does the Royal Society not organise a team of Fellows to solve this or that intractable problem of physics? All three objections suggested above are relevant to the answer. The Fellows may perhaps feel that they work better apart. Their training in science has made them sceptical, and more apt to test and attack than to defend ideas. They have learnt from the experience of centuries that their " laws " can never be regarded as final. If the Society gave official approval to theories, its members would probably soon be rent by a schism between an orthodox and a dissenting party; and sooner or later (the chances are) the Society would be proved wrong, and would be forced to utter an embarrassing recantation.

Similarly, official recommendations by an institute of engineers would have to be framed with some care. Assume, for instance,

that it advised its members to build bridges in a uniform way,
based on the best current knowledge. For a while, standards
might well be raised. But research would in time point to better
bridges; nonconformist bodies of engineers would be free to
build these, while the orthodox would be denied the fruits of
advancing science.

Exactly what do we mean by " authority " in this context?
A wide sweep should be given to the word; it here includes all
forces that can give weight to some ideas at the expense of others.
Privilege is bad for ideas as for men; only if they can jostle one
another in a democratic way is the best likely to reach the top.

Authority may thus rest (at one end of the scale) on prestige
only, and (at the other) on power. Occasionally the brilliance of
a single thinker can cause his views to be treated with deference.
A close-knit school of able thinkers may well dominate opinion
to an unhealthy point—even if they lack organisation and can
impose no sanctions. The harm becomes vastly more formidable
when the authority controls education, or can mould adult
opinion. It reaches its worst when authority has total power.
In its extreme forms, we are all agreed that it is evil—and that
the evil persists whether or not the views that it promulgates
happen to seem true or false.

Happily, we are here concerned with authority at its mildest
and most benevolent. Nevertheless, we may wonder whether,
in the realm of mental freedom, even a slight degree of control
must not lead to harm.

VI. *Training and innovation*

With our recommendations, the basis of authority is of course
mainly the prestige of the bodies concerned. But this is of a high
order. We all know in what respect such a body is held by the
bulk of its members. Moreover, its drafting committee will
include many of the profession's best-known men. It gives the
recommendations its whole-hearted backing and much publicity.
In consequence, the issue of a new recommendation is treated
as a matter of great moment by the accounting Press; this attention
is fitting, though one could wish that the notices were a shade
less passive and fulsome.

The recommendations must therefore have a considerable
influence on the thought of the mature accountant. On the
immature mind—that of a young man in training—their impact
must be deep. They are given conspicuous place in his textbooks
and correspondence courses, and so play a large part in moulding
his views when he is still impressionable and uncritical. They

naturally appeal to the feebler type of teacher, who finds it easier to recite an official creed than to lead a brisk argument. Even before the days of recommendations, accounting textbooks and teachers preferred in general to state facts rather than explore theories. Their main concern was painstaking description of normal practice; scant space was accorded to the reasoning behind the practice, and next to nothing was said of controversy. This dull and sterile approach has now been made far more likely. If an official answer is available to a problem, why should a teacher burden his examination candidates with other views? Further, the body that gives the answers also controls the examination. A young man has thus good cause for minute and respectful study of its statements. And his question paper does not often include such items as: " Discuss Recommendation No. —. Set out the grounds for supposing that its reasoning is (a) correct, and then (b) fallacious; and give your own views on this point."

Thus the recommendations tend to rob our young men's education of its power to enrich and stimulate. On such a spare diet, they may perhaps still train well enough to master the techniques of today. But their minds will be less fit to solve the new problems of tomorrow; and such fitness is no bad test by which to judge an education.

Recommendations must also to some extent cramp the mature accountant's thought. They relieve him of responsibility for intellectual decision—a state that is comfortable, but hardly stimulating. They may hinder him if he wants to try out new ideas or make experiments. In America, one important experiment has already been stopped because it offended " accepted accounting principles " as set forth in a bulletin: the S.E.C. compelled the U.S. Steel Company to amend 1947 depreciation figures based on the current price level, and so prevented all further experiment in this field by companies under S.E.C. control.

Even where there is no legal prohibition, recommendations could endanger a thoughtful auditor if they were used as evidence in lawsuits. Consider for instance a case that hangs on questions of auditing theory—say, the valuation of stocks and wasting assets when price levels change. Suppose that a company follows the advice of an auditor who sincerely believes a recommendation to be wrong; that the company thereafter runs into financial trouble, and that it sues the auditor for negligence. In such a case, the determining test would probably be the standard of behaviour followed by good professional practice. Hostile counsel would treat the recommendations as powerful evidence, and could make the most damaging use of the auditor's deviation.

The defence might have some difficulty in proving that many conscientious but inarticulate accountants still regard the issue as open to argument. A judge or jury might well be swayed decisively by the recommendations, and give a verdict against the auditor.

An analogy is tempting. Suppose that the medical profession's first dislike of antiseptic surgery had crystallised in a hostile recommendation; that one of Lister's patients had died; and that the deceased's relatives had brought a suit for negligence. What would have been the effect on surgery?

Such cases must inevitably crop up sooner or later. Where an auditor is faced with this risk, the temptation to play safe—by abandoning his independence of judgment—is very great. Yet a pliant attitude in such matters is scarcely compatible with the dignity of his profession.

VII. Other kinds of recommendations

Section II suggested that there are some kinds of recommendations which may seem to avoid theory, but in fact are apt to be entangled with it. Let us consider these briefly:

(a) *Definition.* If precise and uniform meanings can be given to our terms and figures, then doubtless we shall be able to exchange ideas with more ease and clarity. Also, accounting data will be more consistent. (The Royal Society *has* set up a standing committee to make recommendations on the symbols, signs and abbreviations used in scientific publications.)

Standard definitions are, however, not without their drawbacks. If speech is made rigid, it cannot evolve to meet new needs. There may be a clash between the ordinary and the technical use of a word. Both the American and the English Institutes have pointed out the ambiguities of " reserve " (which in everyday speech can mean something quite different from its sense in a balance-sheet), and have tried to restrict its meaning helpfully; yet even this restricted use may still bewilder rather than enlighten the public.

Further, words are seldom quite neutral in the battle between ideas. With " goodwill," for instance, the ordinary meaning stands out so strongly that it obtrudes when we are trying to unravel the technical concept, and thus colours our understanding of " goodwill " in accounts. Again, choice of a definition often demands a choice between ideas. For example, any definition of " depreciation " is almost sure to be tendentious.

Thus an official link between a word and an idea is likely to bias our minds. What is almost as bad, some definitions have an air of finality that checks inquiry, and leaves students with no exciting sense of being explorers in a great and unknown territory.

(b) *Standard practice.* Uniformity in presentation of published data (minimum content and method of layout) has strong arguments in its favour—provided it neither cramps honest business nor begs ideas. If a choice between words or methods clearly is arbitrary and free from any pretence of research, it is not likely to damage future thinking or to act as a straitjacket; for example, whether traffic keeps to the left or right of the road is an arbitrary matter, and uniformity yields a gain in convenience, so no one regards a standard rule as an attack on freedom. Therefore, when we are attracted by uniformity, a good test is perhaps this: if a decision between possible terms or practices can be reached by tossing a coin or pulling words from a hat, then uniformity is unlikely to do harm.

However, it is one thing to say that such-and-such items must be shown and explained, and quite another to say how their size must be calculated. The size of the figures is a matter of valuation theory; and, as is shown by our hot debates on such matters as depreciation, income measurement, asset valuation, and the effects of changing price levels, this is certainly an area in which we are far from knowing where truth lies. Rules for standard practice should not prescribe valuation methods. Even rules on how items should be grouped in a balance-sheet may impinge on principle; thus, if they say that allowance for deferred tax must be shown in (or out of) the owners' capital group, they are in effect forcing us to swallow a particular view on the valuation of capital.

Perhaps " standard " should here mean " usual," *i.e.*, what is normal but not necessarily right. For convenience, the reader of published accounts should be able to rely on their compliance with standard practice—unless he is given clear warning to the contrary, and (where this would not mislead) a note of what standard practice would have shown. An accountant should always reserve his right to depart from the standard, on giving notice, if he thinks the standard does not fit the particular case, or the reader's current needs, or his own views on theory.

(c) *Legal opinions.* Counsel's opinions, given at the request of an accounting society and sent out to its members, are not usually classed as " recommendations." To round off our review, however, we should ask ourselves how such statements fit into our reasoning.

The opinions do not seem so dangerous as recommendations on theory, on two grounds.

First, no wise man tries to be expert in everything; outside his own province, he can to some degree accept ideas from others without sapping his mental independence. *Second*, as we noted in Section II, the law does not pretend to state absolute principles. When a lawyer is trying to find what is " true " or " false," he is mainly concerned with the arbitrary—though no doubt exacting— task of interpreting words (especially those in statutes) according to the intentions of their users and the rules of his craft.

VIII. Conclusions

If the above arguments are sound, where do they lead us? Perhaps the recommendations that should be made on recommendations are:

(a) Official statements on accounting cover a number of very different things, which are often hard to separate. They include:

> Working rules, *e.g.*, for company reports.
> Guidance on professional policy.
> Definitions.
> Suggestions for uniform accounting.
> Legal opinions.
> Abstract theory.

None of these is without its pitfalls. However, given due care and caution, the risks seem worth taking—except in the case of theory. Official quests for the abstract are apt to bear little fruit and to run into great hazards. No human being, however impressive his trappings, knows what the truth is.

(b) Recommendations should not only confine themselves to rules for action, as contrasted with principles, but should stress this restriction in their scope. For instance, if a recommendation suggests a definition of "current assets," it might expressly disclaim any attempt to elucidate principles, and describe the rules as being based merely on convenience or custom.

(c) The more concerned a statement is with theory, the stronger is the case for not treating it as an official recommendation. A group of distinguished accountants who have debated a subject, and who wish to help us by announcing their conclusions, would not have the least trouble in finding a publisher.

(d) A recommended " standard practice " should be explained in terms of normal behaviour—something that the user of published accounts can take for granted if nothing to the contrary is said. The accountant, acting in good faith and with due warnings, should feel free—indeed obliged—to vary the practice when he deems it unsuitable. Final responsibility should still rest on the accountant's own judgment; where possible, the rule should be cast in the form of minimum standards, thus leaving room for improvement.

(e) The objections to a recommendation become much less marked if it is described as the work of certain named persons. We all know that individuals can err; we all tend to look on institutions as infallible. Therefore recommendations should—following the American example—be signed by the men who approve the final draft.

(f) A dissenting opinion at once adds a valuable extra dimension, making the recommendation far more useful as an aid to the mind. Therefore great pains should be taken to foster and express minority views.

To conclude. Recommendations by authority on matters of accounting theory may in the short run seem unmixed blessings. In the end, however, they will probably do harm. They are likely to yield little fresh knowledge; "the best test of truth is the power of the thought to get itself accepted in the competition of the market." [5] They are likely to weaken the education of accountants; the conversion of the subject into cut-and-dried rules, approved by authority and not to be lightly questioned, threatens to reduce its value as a subject of liberal education almost to *nil*. They are likely to narrow the scope for individual thought and judgment; and a group of men who resign their hard problems to others must eventually give up all claim to be a learned profession.

---

[5] Dissenting opinion of Judge Oliver Wendell Holmes in *Abrams* v. *United States*.

The Case Law Relating to Company Dividends *

By B. S. Yamey

Professor of Economics,
London School of Economics

IN the company dividend cases, the courts have had to decide both whether particular categories of " abnormal " gains may be included in the calculation of the amount available for the payment of dividends, and also whether particular categories of losses and declines in asset values are to be deducted before striking the balance available for distribution to shareholders. This article is largely concerned with British decisions affecting the negative items in the calculation. This emphasis is dictated by the fact that the decided cases have rarely turned on the admissibility for dividend distribution of realised capital gains and other non-recurrent profits. In the two leading cases on this point it was held that the profit arising out of the sale of a portion of the company's business,[1] and the proceeds of the recovery of a debt which had been considered valueless at the time of the company's formation,[2] could rank as divisible profits, taking all the circumstances into account. This generous attitude was confirmed in an unexpected context when it was decided that premium moneys received on the issue of share capital may be utilised to swell the dividend fund [3]; the Companies Act of 1948 (s. 56) has since reversed this position, following the recommendation of the Cohen Committee on Company Law Amendment (Cmd. 6659 of 1947, para. 108). The judgment in the *Ammonia Soda Co.* case of 1918 suggests, moreover, that an unrealised increase in the value of a fixed asset may in certain circumstances enter into the calculation of divisible profits.[4]

Nowhere in the succession of Companies Acts can any direct reference to the nature of the dividend fund be found. The

---

* This article is the main part, somewhat revised, of an article, " Aspects of the Law Relating to Company Dividends," in *The Modern Law Review*, Vol. 4, No. 4 (April 1941), pp. 273–298.
[1] *Lubbock* v. *British Bank of South America* [1892] 2 Ch. 198.
[2] *Foster* v. *New Trinidad Lake Asphalte Co.* [1901] 1 Ch. 208.
[3] *Drown* v. *British Gaumont Picture Corporation, Ltd.* [1937] Ch. 402.
[4] *Infra*, p. 439.

legislature has thought it unnecessary or unwise to lay down definite rules or even general principles for the computation of the fund. It has been left to the judges to settle the questions which were bound to arise. The judges, however, could not or were not disposed to devise rules without attempting to justify them by reference to the supposed intentions of the legislature, on a matter on which it had never expressed its opinion. It was believed that its views on dividends could be divined from the tenor and general provisions of the Acts. And history has shown that a reading of the Acts could suggest different intentions on the part of the legislature to different judges.

A single unifying idea runs through the decisions in dividend cases before the year 1889. This idea was premised on the view that the provisions of the Acts regarding the capital of a company, and more especially its reduction, made it clear that the legislature would have frowned upon any dividend payment which would have left the company with a sum of assets less, in value, than its nominal paid-up capital. It was argued that the paid-up capital of a company could be used only for the furtherance of the declared objects of the company, and these did not include the return to the shareholders of the capital they had subscribed. Moreover, the statutory ban on the reduction of capital, except under the strict supervision of the courts, was held to imply that it was not legal to reduce the capital by returning it to the shareholders, without safeguards, in the guise of dividends. The argument is clearly stated by Jessel M.R. in *Re Exchange Banking Co.* (*Flitcroft's* case) [5]: " A limited company by its memorandum of association declares that its capital is to be applied for the purposes of the business. It cannot reduce its capital except in the manner and with the safeguards provided by statute and, looking at the Act 40 & 41 Vict. c. 26, it clearly is against the intention of the legislature that any portion of the capital should be returned to the shareholders without the statutory conditions being complied with. A limited company cannot in any other way make a return of capital, the sanction of the general meeting can give no validity to such a proceeding, and even the sanction of every shareholder cannot bring within the powers of the company an act which is not within its powers."

In formulating this doctrine the judges were primarily concerned with the protection of the creditors of a company. Continuing his judgment, Jessel M.R. said: " One reason is this—there is a statement that the capital shall be applied for the purposes of the business, and on the faith of the statement,

[5] (1882) 21 Ch.D. 519 at p. 533.

which is sometimes said to be an implied contract with creditors, people dealing with the company give it credit. The creditor has no debtor, but that impalpable thing the corporation, which has no property except the assets of the business. The creditor, therefore, I may say, gives credit to that capital, gives credit to the company on the faith of the representation that the capital shall be applied only for the purposes of the business, and he has therefore a right to say that the corporation shall keep its capital and not return it to the shareholders."

The desire to see that the creditors' security, the capital, was not frittered away by its repayment to the shareholders either as dividends or in any other way, excluded almost every other consideration. In *Re Alexandra Palace Company* [6] the court would not be swayed by the contention that it was necessary to pay preference dividends out of capital in order to ensure the continuation of the company's operations. In *Trevor* v. *Whitworth* [7] (not a dividend case) the argument that the reduction of the company's capital by the purchase of its own shares was legitimate, being a question of " domestic management and the object being to keep the company a family concern ", was dismissed by Lord Herschell's statement that even where " it was considered for some other reason desirable in the interest of the company to do so . . . the result to him (the creditor) is the same."

It appears, therefore, as if company directors in the period before 1889 were confronted by a rigid rule forbidding any dividend payment which would have left the value of the remaining assets below the company's paid-up capital. However, it would not be correct to suppose that the early statement of the law was free from ambiguity, or that in practice it must have led to results which it may appear to indicate. The rule that paid-up capital has to be maintained intact may be interpreted to mean that the company's assets, if sold for cash, should realise an amount at least equal to its paid-up capital. Or it may mean that the value of the assets to the continuing enterprise should be at least equal to its paid-up capital. " Value " is a word of many meanings, and there is no hint in the series of decisions as to which " value " of the assets had to be maintained intact. The difficulty was apparently overcome by accepting the accountant's conception of valuation, [8] which already in this early period was markedly different from any layman's idea of valuation. Thus

6 (1882) 21 Ch.D. 149.
7 (1887) 12 App.Cas. 409.
8 See, for example, *Re County Marine Insurance Co.* (1870) 6 Ch.App. 104.

the " value " of assets such as plant and machinery, land and buildings was taken to mean their cost to the company; fluctuations in the market values of these assets were ignored, though it was becoming customary to write off, as depreciation, the cost of the asset over its expected useful life.[9] The accounting " value " of an asset could exceed or fall short of its market value, or the price which a continuing enterprise would have paid for it. By attaching a specialised meaning to the " value " of a company's assets, some of what might have been regarded as undesirable consequences of a strict interpretation of the legal doctrine were avoided. The acceptance of accounting valuation conventions may help to explain why accountants were satisfied with a rule which superficially seemed to be opposed to some of the basic practices of accounting.[10]

Any rule which makes the payment of dividends contingent upon the maintenance of the remaining assets above a certain level (in this case the paid-up capital) has the disadvantage that the " values " of some assets are never anything more than estimates which subsequent events may falsify. Thus in *Re Mercantile Trading Co.* (*Stringer's* case)[11] the decision hinged upon whether it was proper for a company to have paid dividends on the faith that a debt incurred by the Confederate Government during the American Civil War was valuable. Events proved that the debt was worthless; but the court held that an estimate made in good faith was acceptable, and pointed out that almost every balance-sheet contained estimates.

Before 1889, the " capital maintenance " rule was not thoroughly tested in any of its possible points of weakness. There was no clear-cut case before the courts where a dividend was paid out of the excess of current receipts over current payments, despite a decline in the value of the company's assets.[12] The matter was brought to a head in the case of *Lee* v. *Neuchatel Asphalte Co.*[13] which marked the end of the early doctrine and paved the way for the development of a fresh approach.

In this case the plaintiff's counsel contended that, in declaring a dividend, the company could not ignore the decline in the value of its principal asset, even though its articles of association apparently permitted it. In the lower court, Stirling J. accepted

[9] See F. W. Pixley's *Auditors: their Duties and Responsibilities* (1st ed., 1891), and Dicksee's *Auditing* (1st ed., 1892), for a description of accounting practice.
[10] See, for example, editorial in *The Accountant* (1887), p. 474.
[11] (1869) 4 Ch.App. 475.
[12] *Davison* v. *Gillies* (1880) 16 Ch.D. 347n. is a case in point, but it was decided according to the special articles of the company, and not according to the general law.
[13] (1889) 41 Ch.D. 1.

the evidence for the defendant company that the value of the
asset had in fact increased and not declined. He merely reaffirmed
the earlier series of decisions, and did not dispute the contentions
of the plaintiff's counsel. It was in the Court of Appeal that
Lindley L.J. sowed the seeds of the new doctrine, after Cotton L.J.
had delivered a somewhat confused judgment. The Court of
Appeal's pronouncements were made on the assumption that
there had been a decline in the value of the asset.

Lindley L.J. based his views on the indisputable fact that the
Companies Acts contain no direct reference to the payment of
dividends. " There is nothing at all in the Acts about how
dividends are to be paid, nor how profits are to be reckoned."
Again, " The Companies Acts do not require the capital to be
made up if lost. . . . If it is said that such a course involves
payment of dividends out of capital, the answer is that the Act
nowhere forbids such a payment as is here supposed." Whereas
the judges previously had construed the legislature's silence to
mean that its intention was clear from the Acts as a whole, and that
therefore a specific ruling was unnecessary, Lindley L.J. inferred
from its silence that it did not wish to impose on the business
world its own opinion concerning an essentially business problem.
Regarding the calculation of profits, he said: " All that is left,
and very judiciously and properly left, to the commercial world.
It is not a subject for an Act of Parliament to say how accounts
are to be kept; what is to be put into a capital account, what
into an income account, is left to men of business." Business
men were to be the judges on business matters. In the particular
case before the court, business men, the directors, had thought
it fit to pay the dividend, and as there was no suggestion of bad
faith, it was not for the court to interfere.

In addition to the desire to leave technical business matters to
business men, Lindley L.J. wished to avoid any ruling which could
fetter the " legitimate " activities of companies. The appellant's
argument that capital should be maintained at all costs was
dismissed because, if adopted, it would " in my judgment, paralyse
the trade of the country." He also stated: " It appears to me
that the proposition that it is *ultra vires* to pay dividends out of
capital is very apt to mislead, and must not be understood in
such a way as to prohibit honest trading." If the validity of the
proposition were granted " you find yourself landed in consequences which the common sense of mankind would shrink from
accepting."

The appeal judges did not formulate any new theory of
dividends; but by their approval of the practice of ignoring

declines in the value of a company's property they demolished the existing " capital maintenance " theory of the dividend fund. By condoning this accounting practice, by dismissing the previous interpretation of the Companies Acts, and by expressing the view that accounting matters should be left to businessmen, the stage was set for the promulgation of new criteria for judging the legality of dividend payments.

One may expect that accountants would have welcomed the decision with its message that business matters were to be left to business men, because accountants, as a profession, represent a very responsible section of business opinion, especially on matters of accounts. But the decision met with a storm of disapproval from accountants, despite the opinion of the law journals that the decision was in accordance with the " principles of business." [14] An editorial in *The Accountant* declared that " the principles it lays down are simply startling and as they are directly applicable to all colliery and other mining concerns, the danger to be apprehended from their general adoption is neither fanciful nor small." [15] The same journal later denounced the judgment as " the most mischievous which has ever been given in relation to company matters," and as being " entirely against the almost universal practice of accountants." [16] It seems that accountants felt that it was they, and not " men of business ", who should have been designated as arbiters of company accounting practices.

However, the decision was not entirely as straightforward as contemporary opinion had interpreted it. In the *Lee* case the asset in question was of a particular kind—a " wasting " asset. Also, there was no evidence that the wasting asset had decreased in value, though the appeal judges argued on the assumption of a loss in value. Some of the doubts were removed by the 1892 case of *Bolton* v. *Natal Land and Colonisation Co.*[17] where the decline in the value of the asset, land, was held to be irrelevant for the calculation of the dividend fund. But as land itself is an asset in a class of its own, the law was not yet altogether clear.

The case of *Verner* v. *General and Commercial Investment Trust* [18] established the new doctrine more firmly than ever. Here the company, an investment trust, in one year had receipts in excess of its current payments. But this " profit " was completely overshadowed by a slump in the value of the company's

14 See *Law Quarterly Review*, Vol. 5 (1889), p. 221, and *Law Journal* (1889), p. 353.
15 *The Accountant* (1889), p. 89.
16 *The Accountant* (1889), p. 149.
17 [1892] 2 Ch. 124.   18 [1894] 2 Ch. 239.

assets, the securities in its portfolio. The payment of a dividend in such circumstances was contested.

In the lower court, Stirling J. pointed out the radical alteration in the law occasioned by the *Lee* decision. He correctly showed that his decision in the particular case would depend upon whether the earlier doctrine or the *Lee* doctrine were operative. Being bound by the decision of the Court of Appeal, he had to sanction the dividend payment, though he made the proviso that his decision might have been different had the company been " an ordinary trading company—if, for example, the object of the company had been to carry on the business of a stockbroker, and the investments had been the ordinary stock-in-trade of that business."

In the Court of Appeal, Lindley L.J. approved of Stirling J.'s decision. He shunned any " hard and fast rule which would prevent a flourishing company, either not in debt or well able to pay its debts, from paying dividends so long as its capital sunk in creating the business was not represented by assets, which would, if sold, reproduce in money the capital sunk." He reiterated the arguments of his judgment in the *Lee* case, and made a statement of the new rule (which we shall call the *Lee* rule), which was to become the classic and always-quoted pronouncement of the doctrine: " Perhaps the shortest way of expressing the distinction which I am endeavouring to explain is to say that fixed capital may be sunk and lost, and yet that the excess of current receipts over current payments may be divided, but that floating or circulating capital must be kept up, as otherwise it will enter into and form part of such excess, in which case to divide such excess without deducting the capital which forms part of it will be contrary to law." The rule envisaged the division of assets into two classes: fixed assets, which are permanently retained by the company and not intended for re-sale; and floating or circulating assets, which the company does not intend retaining for any length of time, but which have a short life-cycle of acquisition, disposal (or conversion and disposal), and replacement. Declines in the value of the former as well as expenditure on their acquisition need not be deducted from current receipts when calculating the dividend fund. But any devaluation of the latter or any expenditure made on their purchase has to be treated as a diminishing item.

The Accountant's comment on the judgment was that the court's rulings " are indeed fearful and wonderful; but there is —and has often been—a wide distinction between the authorised interpretation of statutes and the principles of sound account-ing." [19] The creditors' safeguard contained in the earlier version of the law was greatly weakened. [20]

Any doubt as to the scope and meaning of the *Lee* rule was dispelled by *Re Kingston Cotton Mills Co.* (*No. 2*). [21] Here Vaughan Williams J. held that, in accordance with the Court of Appeal decisions, the depreciation in the value of the fixed capital (mill property) could be ignored in the declaration of a dividend. Part of the judgment reads: " I have only to follow the principles laid down within them [the *Lee* and *Verner* cases] provided I think that the facts of the present case are governed by those principles. It is true that the present case is not the case of a company formed to work a necessarily wasting property as was the case in *Lee* v. *Neuchatel Asphalte Co.*, nor the case of an investment company as in *Verner's* case; but I think that this case falls within the principles of those two cases read together." [22]

In 1899 a new problem appeared before the courts [23]: in calculating the dividend fund for any particular period, is it necessary to subtract the losses of previous periods? The pre-ceding cases had laid down that losses of fixed capital could be ignored altogether, unless the particular articles of association stipulated otherwise. But suppose the loss in a previous period represented a deficiency of that period's receipts as against the expenditure on *circulating* capital?

In *Re National Bank of Wales, Ltd.*, [24] the facts appertaining to the disputed dividend payments were that dividends had been paid out of the current net receipts while losses on account of

---

[19] *The Accountant* (1894), p. 176.

[20] A practical effect of the decision in the *Lee* case is illustrated by some develop-ments reported by Lee, the plaintiff in that case. He tells how two companies which were in the process of reducing their capital according to the special provisions, and subject to the special safeguards, of the Companies Acts, promptly abandoned their capital reduction schemes when the decision was published (letter in *The Accountant* (1889), p. 178).

[21] [1896] 1 Ch. 331. In *Wilmer* v. *McNamara* [1895] 2 Ch. 245, decided in the previous year, the *Lee* rule was interpreted to cover depreciation of goodwill and of leaseholds.

[22] The *Lee* rule, strictly interpreted, implies that there is no need to allow for ordinary depreciation of fixed assets. This interpretation seems to have been followed in the *Kingston Cotton Mills* case. Indeed, the late Lawrence Dicksee, writing in 1928, said: " It would appear doubtful as to whether the law compels *any* company to make provision for depreciation, before declaring dividends out of its earnings." (*Auditing* (14th ed., 1928), p. 271). On the other hand, business opinion today would insist that depreciation ought to be provided for. And it is likely that the business view would now prevail in any dividend liti-gation involving ordinary depreciation. The business view of depreciation has been accepted in other cases not concerning dividends, *e.g.*, *Glasier* v. *Rolls* (1889) 42 Ch. 436; *Re Crabtree, Thomas* v. *Crabtree* (1912) 106 L.T. 49.

[23] But see footnote 38 below.

[24] [1899] 2 Ch. 629.

bank advances made to impecunious clients in previous years were ignored. The reasoning behind Wright J.'s judgment is obscure, but apparently the view was taken that the losses were losses of circulating capital which had to be made good before dividend payments could be resumed. The Court of Appeal, where Lindley, then Master of the Rolls, read the judgment of the court, reversed the decision. The court was unwilling to countenance any ruling likely to fetter " men of business." " It may be safely said that what losses can be properly charged to capital, and what to income, is a matter for business men to determine, and it is often a matter on which the opinions of honest and competent men will differ. . . . There is no hard and fast legal rule." It seems as if the court wished in this way to escape from the consequences of what seemed to be its pre-viously-enunciated rule that losses of circulating capital could not be ignored.

This decision which, in effect, permitted the results of any period's trading to be considered in isolation without reference to the company's previous fortunes, did not find favour among all accountants. One of the foremost members of the profession, Sidney Dawson, wrote: " The leading cases . . . since 1889 . . . suggest that questions which presumably were very properly and judiciously left to the commercial world and shareholders to settle—questions which were being settled and the results codified by a consensus of opinion—have been reduced to a financial ' go-as-you-please '—with an undecipherable minimum of prin-ciple—by the quinquennial decisions of the Court of Appeal." [25]

The *National Bank* case was taken to the House of Lords.[26] As all the parties concerned acquitted the respondent of all " moral obliquity," the discussions on dividend questions were regarded as irrelevant for the decision. The sole reason why the problem of dividends received any consideration at all, was that the Lord Chancellor wished to dissociate himself from some of the earlier judicial pronouncements on the subject. He doubted " whether such questions can ever be treated in the abstract at all," and he foresaw that in any particular case " many matters will have to be considered by men of business, which are not altogether familiar to a court of law." He was impressed by the fact that rigid rules may prove to be a great inconvenience to companies. " People put their money into a trading company to give them an income, and the sudden stoppage of all dividends would send down the value of their shares to zero and possibly

[25] *The Accountant* (1899), p. 892.
[26] Reported as *Dovey* v. *Cory* [1901] A.C. 477.

involve its ruin." Lord Macnaghten was even more emphatic in his denunciation of definite rules: " I do not think it is desirable for any tribunal to do what Parliament has abstained from doing, *i.e.*, to formulate rules for the guidance and embarrassment of business men in the conduct of business affairs."

It is not easy to appraise the net effect of the dividend discussion (one cannot call it a decision) in the House of Lords. It is not clear whether it was intended as a repudiation of the Lindley " fixed capital, circulating capital " formula on the ground that any rule was undesirable. The discussion was further confused by Lord Davey's contribution. Accepting in the main the *Lee* rule, he disagreed with the decision of the Court of Appeal because in it " the learned judge appears to me to have departed " from his (Lindley's) earlier statement of the law. However, though it did little to clarify the main problems, the House of Lords' deliberations confirmed a dominant trend in the decisions since the *Lee* case. The principle, first enunciated in that case, that business matters are the province of business men, was reaffirmed in strong terms by the highest tribunal. In the future the well-worn phrase that " capital must be kept up " could be countered by citing not only the decisions of the Court of Appeal, but also the statements of the noble Lords.[27]

Accountants, business men and lawyers, who probably expected a more positive statement from the House of Lords, must have been disappointed at the meagreness of the " decision." Nevertheless, some of the fears of accountants were allayed. *The Accountant* wrote: " Still, the ground has been greatly cleared by the removal of what all our readers must have felt to be an entirely incorrect general statement with regard to the matter, and it is now apparent that any case that may hereafter come before the courts will be decided on exactly the same lines as those which ordinary business men would adopt in dealing with the same question." [28] Apparently it was believed that the *Lee* rule, which to them was unpalatable, was to be superseded by

---

[27] *Lawrence* v. *West Somerset Mineral Ry.* [1918] 2 Ch. 250, shows how firmly the doctrine of capital maintenance has been rejected. The railway company leased its property to another concern for a rental which enabled it to pay interest to its bondholders and a dividend to its ordinary shareholders. The lease ran till 1919; but several years before that, it was clear that the value of the property had fallen appreciably (traffic on the line having been discontinued). The rental was, however, being received annually, and in 1918 the bondholders asked the court to restrain the payment of the ordinary dividend on the grounds that the payment of the dividend and the imminent termination of the lease would have left grossly inadequate assets to repay the bondholders in the event of dissolution. The court refused to intervene, because the dividend was not being paid out of capital in the legal sense, but out of the divisible profit.

[28] *The Accountant* (1901), p. 876.

an arrangement where responsible business opinion, including accounting opinion, would be called in, in every case, as arbiter.

Bond v. *Barrow Haematite Steel Co.*[29] was the first case to be decided after the House of Lords' discussions. The company owned the leases of mines producing ore for smelting. The mines were flooded, as a consequence of which the leases were surrendered, blast furnaces pulled down and some workers' cottages sold. A dividend payment was urged by a preference shareholder on the ground that the losses arising out of the flooding of mines and miners' cottages could be ignored in the calculation of the dividend fund. The defence was that these losses had to be taken into account because the losses were incurred on mining, which was not the company's main business but was carried on to provide a supply of raw material for the main smelting activity.

Following the lines suggested by *Dovey* v. *Cory*, Farwell J. correctly stated that "the real question for determination, therefore, is whether there are profits available for distribution, and this is to be answered according to the circumstances of each particular case, the nature of the company, and the evidence of competent witnesses." The defendant company called witnesses, including the eminent accountant, F. W. Pixley, who expressed the opinion that the losses could not be ignored, but had to be deducted from the company's earnings. On the evidence it is clear that the judge's decision that there were no divisible funds was in accordance with the view favoured by the House of Lords, and approved by *The Accountant* in the previous year.

However, Farwell J. apparently was not wholly satisfied with this argument, and in his judgment he declared that his opinion coincided with that of the experts " inasmuch as I think that the money invested in these items [mines, etc.] is properly regarded in this company as circulating capital." He therefore came to the same conclusion whether he followed the House of Lords, or whether he followed the Court of Appeal's *Lee* rule. His judgment has been criticised by many authorities, including the contemporary *Accountant*, on the ground that the losses were losses of fixed capital, and not of circulating capital.[30] It is

29 [1902] 1 Ch. 239.
30 See *The Accountant* (1902), p. 153; Scrutton L.J. in *Ammonia Soda Co.* v. *Chamberlain* [1918] 1 Ch. 266; Halsbury, *Laws of England* (2nd ed., 1932), p. 392n. An asset is generally considered to be a circulating asset if it is acquired for use as raw material or stock-in-trade as distinct from use as equipment. Such an asset usually is not held for long by the firm, as it is re-sold (with or without conversion) after a relatively short period. For this reason, a circulating asset is often looked upon as one normally held for a short period. In the *Bond* case, the mines, etc., were held to be circulating assets by Farwell J. because to him they served in this smelting company the same purpose as a stock of

plain that the learned judge, as well as accounting opinion, was still thinking in terms of the *Lee* rule, and that the evidence of competent business and accounting witnesses was not necessarily the deciding factor. The House of Lords' warning not to treat the question in the abstract had been forgotten. Moreover, *The Accountant's* denunciation of the decision because " the requirement that ' circulating capital must be kept up ' would be impracticable if extended so as to require every mining company to show value for all the money that it had ever spent upon acquiring and developing its property " suggests that the line of decisions since 1889 did not perhaps diverge so greatly from the practices of responsible accountants as some of their criticisms may lead one to believe.

A more recent case where important aspects of the law have been discussed is *Ammonia Soda Co.* v. *Chamberlain*.[31] In the first years of its existence the company had suffered trading losses, but eventually its operations showed successful results. The early losses had been offset in the accounts by writing-up the value of the company's property, as ascertained by a valuation which, it was held, had been made in good faith. Dividends were paid and disputed. The case turned on whether it was proper to include the unrealised increase in the value of the property in the computation of the divisible profits. If this were held to be improper, the dividend distribution would nevertheless be in order if it were held that it was unnecessary to deduct prior trading losses from current trading profits.

On the first point, an eminent accountant, Sir Woodburn Kirby, gave evidence that " it was contrary to all principles of commercial accountancy to write up the value of a fixed asset and apply the surplus so obtained to meet a deficit on trading." Peterson J. refused to accept this view. " If an agricultural company has land under which valuable coal reserves are discovered, it is difficult to see why it should not be allowed to show in its balance-sheet the increased value of its lands." He also indicated the peculiar consequence of accepting the accounting point of view. The company could not pay dividends. But neither could it have a capital reduction scheme sanctioned, because its paid-up capital was in fact represented by equivalent

already-mined ore—a stock which would be circulating capital. His critics, however, seem to have taken the position that the mines and ancillary buildings were not assets held for only a short period, and hence were fixed, not circulating, assets. The two criteria, which usually give the same answer, in this case gave two different answers.

[31] [1918] 1 Ch. 266. See also *Stapley* v. *Read Bros., Ltd.* [1924] 2 Ch. 1.

assets. Once again a matter which, according to the House of Lords, should have been left to business men, was settled by the court in opposition to the views of some acknowledged experts who gave evidence.[32]

On the second point, the learned judge stated that: " Where a company has made losses in past years and then makes a profit out of which it pays a dividend . . . such a dividend is not paid out of paid-up capital. If it were, the paid-up capital would be still further reduced by the payment. In fact the assets representing the paid-up capital remain the same or of the same value as before the payment of the dividend." [33] This ingenious argument, which places the results of each period's trading into watertight compartments, virtually means that any item of loss is irrelevant to the size of the dividend fund except in the period in which it is incurred. The corresponding rule that profits may not be carried forward from one period to another could be supported by an argument analogous to that used by Peterson J.; but it would scarcely be to the taste of men of business or accountants.

The Court of Appeal was in full agreement with the ruling of the lower court. In addition, Scrutton L.J. reverted to the *Lee* rule in unambiguous terms. He respectfully brushed aside the objections of the House of Lords against that rule by saying that " one requires a much clearer expression from the House of Lords . . . before one can treat a decision of the Court of Appeal as overruled."

Even accounting opinion had at last approved of a legal decision, partly because of its undoubted lucidity (as compared with its predecessors) and partly because it " is likely to be convenient in practice." " It would often be a very great convenience if directors felt fully justified in declaring dividends out of profits earned as soon as a company has really ' turned the corner,' and begun to make profits, instead of feeling compelled in the first instance to apply all profits made towards the making up of past losses." [34] It is interesting to compare this comment with that which was provoked by a similar decision in 1899.[35]

[32] The court's dilemma should be noted. Against Sir Woodburn Kirby's evidence was the fact that the body of shareholders, which included " commercial men," had approved the writing-up of the asset, and that the company's auditors, " admittedly experienced chartered accountants," had certified the resulting balance-sheet.

[33] " Before the payment of the dividend " presumably means at the beginning of the period in which the trading " profits " were earned.

[34] *The Accountant* ,Vo l.57, p. 418.

[35] *Supra*, p. .436.

In concluding this review of the case law on divisible profits, reference should be made to the idea, which appears in some judgments, that considerations of equity as between different classes of shareholder should be given some weight. An interesting example is *Dent* v. *London Tramways Co.*,[36] which was decided in 1880, before the *Lee* rule was propounded. It is necessary to go back to the earlier case of *Davison* v. *Gillies*,[37] concerning the same company. Here the payment of an *ordinary* dividend was restrained because depreciation had been ignored and the articles of the company were held to imply that depreciation reserves had to be created. In *Dent's* case the payment of a *preference* dividend was urged on the grounds that, according to the articles, preference dividends were " dependent upon the profits of the particular year only." There was expert evidence of the existence of profits for that year, in the sense that the value of the net assets at the end of the year was higher than at the beginning of the year, though still below the issued capital of the company. The plaintiff's claim was upheld by Jessel M.R. partly because of the special proviso of the articles, but largely because to have decided otherwise would have caused a fairly obvious injustice: " The argument for the company amounts to this, that inasmuch as they have improperly paid to their ordinary shareholders very large sums of money which did not belong to them, they, the company, are entitled to make good that deficiency by taking away the fund available for the preference shareholders to an amount required to put the tramway in proper order. When the argument is stated in that way, it is clear that it cannot be sustained." [38]

The *Lee* case is another example. Here Lindley L.J. advanced as one of his subsidiary reasons for rejecting the contention that capital should be kept up, the fact that " putting it into plain language, he [counsel for the appellant] is asking us, at the instance of the ordinary shareholders, to break faith with the preference shareholders."

The difficulties involved in the adjudication of the conflicting interests of different classes of shareholders are clearly brought out in *Verner* v. *General and Commercial Investment Trust*.

---

[36] (1880) 16 Ch.D. 344.

[37] (1880) 16 Ch.D. 347n.

[38] Mr. J. L. Weiner in his " Theory of Anglo-American Dividend Law," *Columbia Law Review* (1928), p. 1052, is of the opinion that *Dent's* case decided the question, " May a company declare dividends out of the profits of the particular year despite past losses ? " in the affirmative. But it seems to be more reasonable to regard it as having decided in the negative the question, whether past errors in favour of the ordinary shareholders may be allowed to prejudice the interests of the preference shareholders. The preceding case of *Davison* v. *Gillies*, decided by the same judge, refutes Mr. Weiner's contention.

Counsel for the appellant urged that " the rights of preference
shareholders must be considered as well as those of creditors."
He argued that if dividends were paid despite a loss of capital,
there might be insufficient assets left in the case of dissolution,
and the prior claim of the preference shareholders in the winding-
up assets would be of little value. Stirling J. however, pointed
out that if no preference dividends were paid unless capital was
kept up, the effect " would be to preserve the capital of the company really for the ultimate benefit of the deferred [ordinary]
shareholders "; the argument being that on dissolution, if the
capital had been maintained, the ordinary shareholders would
be repaid their original contributions after the preference shareholders' claims had been met. Now, paradoxically, both these
arguments may be sound. Either course may be more beneficial
for the preference shareholders, depending largely on the amount
in every year that would be available for the ordinary shareholders as dividends, and on the extent of the capital loss.[39]
The question of dividend distributions bristles with such problems;
and the issues have not been considered systematically by the
courts.[40]

[39] A simple example may clarify the point. One investment company with a
nominal capital of £100 has 50 6 per cent. preference shares of £1 each and £50
in ordinary shares. The preference shares rank before the ordinary shares
in the event of a winding-up. The company exists for two years. Its investments
depreciate by £50 to £50, and on dissolution realise that amount. The current
net receipts (*i.e.*, gross receipts less working expenses) are £3 in each year.
  (i) If dividend payments are not permissible where capital is lost, then the net
  receipts will accumulate within the company, and on dissolution the assets
  will realise £56, of which the preference shareholders receive £50, and the
  others £6.
  (ii) If dividend payments are legal, the preference shareholders would receive
  two annual dividends of £3, and their capital, £50, would be repaid on
  dissolution. The ordinary shareholders will receive nothing either as
  dividends or on dissolution. Clearly a permissive rule is more advantageous to the preference shareholders.
    Assume now that another company has the same capital structure.
  Its assets depreciate to £40. The current net receipts in each year are £5.
  (i) If the dividend payments are not permissible, winding-up assets would
  yield £50, all going to the preference shareholders.
  (ii) If the payments are legal, and dividends are paid up to the hilt, then in
  each year the preference shareholders receive £3, and the ordinary £2.
  The £40 on dissolution goes to the preference shareholders, who in total
  receive £46 out of the £50. Clearly a restrictive rule in these circumstances
  favours the preference shareholders.
[40] Another illustration of some of the complexities may be found in the two cases in
connection with the liquidation of the *Smyrna and Cassaba Ry.* In the first
case ([1895] 2 Ch. 265), the application of the *Lee* rule was contrary to the interests
of the ordinary shareholders. In the second case ([1895] 2 Ch. 596) its application
worked in their favour.
See also footnote 27, above, for a further illustration.

The Greatest Accountant in the World *

By John McCarten
of The New Yorker.

THE year 1938, which saw the trial and conviction of Richard
Whitney, and the suicide of Philip Musica, also marked the end
of another unorthodox financial career, which was, in its own
way, greater than either Whitney's or Musica's. Whitney came
to grief because he was a misguided man, Musica because he
was a rogue; our hero, Raymond Marien, was neither. It is
hard to find exactly the right word for him. Perhaps it would
be best to call him an artist whose medium was the bookkeeper's
ledger. His *chef d'oeuvre*, which won him the awed respect of
the nation's best financial minds, was the creation on the books
of the Interstate Hosiery Mills, Inc., of $1,900,000 in totally
non-existent assets—a structure without foundation which stood
up sturdily for four years, and in the end fell only because of an
accident. It cost Marien much toil and brought him no profit.
His only motive, as far as anybody can discover, was the creative
urge that is in every true artist, his only reward the knowledge
that he had wrought a master-work which others of his craft
would admire for years to come. The S.E.C. investigators who
had the task of untangling the intricacies of Marien's fictional
ledgers are unanimous in proclaiming him the greatest accountant
they have ever known. Probably he is the greatest accountant in
the world.

The Interstate Hosiery Mills maintains sales offices in New
York City and a manufacturing establishment in Lansdale,
Pennsylvania. Until recently its accountants were the local firm
of Homes & Davis. In 1931, Homes & Davis assigned to supervision of the Interstate account one of their best men, Raymond
Marien. He had been in their employ for two years. A slight,
clerkish man in his late thirties, with a long nose and intelligent
eyes magnified by rimless spectacles, Marien produced an
impression of conservatism and utter reliability. Several of
Homes & Davis's clients liked him so well that they always asked

* From *The New Yorker*, December 16, 1939. Reproduced by permission of the
author. Copyright 1939 by The New Yorker Magazine, Inc. (formerly the F.-R.
Pub. Corp.).

especially to have him put to work on their books. He made an equally good impression on the Interstate executives. Marien was endlessly painstaking: he insisted that Interstate install a Protectograph system, to guard against possible raising of cheques, and he would keep the comptometer operators up all night searching for an error. He was human, too. Once, when one of the Interstate bookkeepers was about to be dismissed for a small mistake, he wrote a letter to the president of the corporation urging him to " temper justice with mercy." In a few years Interstate came to regard Marien almost as an employee of its own, and entrusted him with complete control of all its accounting matters.

Most of the Interstate executives made their headquarters in New York; only the secretary worked in Lansdale. The company had no comptroller. Marien supervised the Lansdale bookkeeping staff in making out the semi-annual certified statement of Interstate's financial position. He also supplied the New York office with an unofficial monthly report, spending several days by himself in Lansdale in the preparation of " work sheets " from which, after his return to New York, he would draw up formal reports. By 1934, Marien was the sole contact between Lansdale and New York, as far as bookkeeping was concerned. In Lansdale was the raw material of prosperity—the plant, the thread on hand, the boxcars full of Interstate stockings going out to the four corners of the nation. In New York there were the abstract financial statements, the gratifying statements that proclaimed, month by month, that the depression was over. And there was Raymond Marien, a sober, thoughtful fellow driving back and forth between New York and Lansdale, a bulging briefcase on the seat beside him. The Interstate secretary, working in Lansdale, took care of the payrolls, the bank balance, and the collection of accounts; it was no part of his duty to break down and re-check the semi-annual reports of Marien.

Whenever a man does something remarkable, the reporters approach his neighbors and ask if they knew that they had a remarkable man in their midst. Usually the neighbors are obliging: yes, he did this and that strange thing, they relate, or he acted " different " and mysterious. Marien seemed an ordinary enough fellow, however, and the people who knew him in his daily life can throw little light on his character. He lived in an apartment in Sunnyside, Long Island, with his wife and their three adolescent children. The family lived well on his salary, which was a hundred dollars a week. They did the things other families in Sunnyside did. In the summer, Mr. Marien would come home early from the office, load the family into the Chevrolet and take them to Jones Beach. He took a paternal interest in the fact that his son played first base on a neighborhood ball team called the Long Island Owls, and even helped the boys draw up a schedule of games with other local amateurs. Once in a while Mrs. Marien and the children would go to a movie, and Mr. Marien would have some of the men from the office in for an evening of beer and poker—always for conservative stakes.

Mr. Marien was a domestic man—domestic to a fault, almost, if that is possible. He kept his clothes pressed and in good repair, and performed the same services for his wife. Now and then he would bring home a length of goods and a pattern, and make a dress for her. He was admittedly a better cook than Mrs. Marien, and sometimes, when he got home early, he would delight the children by stirring up a batch of cream puffs. But he was apparently an average man except for these mild eccentricities and the fact that he had on the top of his head a large, bald bump, as big as a golf ball, the result of an injury suffered in his youth.

Beginning in 1934, Interstate stock went up. Within the next four years it almost doubled in value, going from 21 to 40. It paid dividends of nearly a million dollars, and there were some fine bonuses for the officers. Secure in the eyes of Dun & Bradstreet, and favoured by market analysts and tipsters, Interstate Hosiery was one of the happiest little corporations in the country. And back of all this bustling prosperity stood the inspired accounting of Raymond Marien.

In February 1938 Mr. Harold Greenwald, secretary of Interstate, had a telephone call at his Lansdale office from a clerk in the First National Bank of Lansdale. " Just wanted to tell you that we got your letter too late to do what you wanted us to," the clerk said.

" What letter? " asked Mr. Greenwald.

The clerk explained. " The letter you sent to the bank asking us to have this month's canceled checks forwarded to Mr. Marien in New York instead of to you."

Puzzled and faintly alarmed, Mr. Greenwald asked to have the letter sent around to him. It was a forgery. Then he looked at the batch of canceled checks, which had already arrived at his office, and found the reason for the letter. His signature and that of the assistant treasurer of Interstate had been forged on two cheques totalling $801·75. The obvious deduction was that the forger of the cheques and the letter was Raymond Marien. If the letter had reached the bank in time, Marien could have certified their correctness and filed them away, covering up, probably successfully, all evidence of his small crime.

The Interstate officials, confronted by evidence that Marien had gone astray, were grieved and annoyed, but no more. To a corporation as magnificently secure as Interstate, the loss of $801·75 was nothing. They simply thought it was sad that their trusted accountant had fallen from grace, and they were annoyed because a board meeting was to be held soon, and now who was going to prepare the statement of their profits? Finally they decided to report the matter to Marien's employers, Homes & Davis, with a request to have the prosecution delayed until after Marien had drawn up the statement.

This was an unusual request, but Homes & Davis saw no harm in it. They gave Marien time enough to prepare the Interstate report. Then they confronted him with his forgeries and after he confessed to them they fired him. At Interstate's request, another man was sent to Lansdale to check back over his books before the company released its statement. The new man naturally took with him all the balance-sheets Marien had presented to the Interstate officials in New York. It was the first time during Marien's regime that the New York figures had been checked against the Lansdale figures, and it was brought about not by any obvious flaw in Marien's bookkeeping but by a purely extraneous forgery.

In the week that followed, the missing $801·75 was forgotten. The Homes & Davis operative discovered that the New York books, on which Interstate had been paying off, bore only the sketchiest relation to reality. For almost four years Interstate had been basing its salaries, dividends, bonuses, and general financial policy on balance-sheets which Raymond Marien had just made up out of his own head.

The drawing up of the profits statement was put off and Marien was immediately lodged in the Tombs on a charge of forgery. The Attorney-General's office and the S.E.C. got to work on an investigation of Marien's books, expecting momentarily to find evidence on which they could bring charges of fraud, grand larcency, or something equally serious. It never materialized. They discovered, in a general way, what Marien had done. He had dreamed on to Interstate's books a round $1,900,000, or almost one-sixth of its total capitalization. But they couldn't find a satisfactory motive. Marien hadn't profited, except for the eight hundred-odd dollars. When questioned, he said that he had forged the checks to make up for a bad month at the race tracks. He also admitted that the discrepancy between the

New York and Lansdale books was all his doing. His reason?
" Overwork," Marien said. " Nervous strain."

Overwork might more reasonably be accepted as the result
rather than the cause of Marien's hocus-pocus with Interstate's
finances. The work involved was just about five times what it
would have been had he been keeping honest records. To
conjure up the imaginary assets, he had had to introduce similarly
fictitious figures in the profit-and-loss statement, the surplus
statement, and the various other sources from which the balance
sheet was drawn up. Interstate's Lansdale office kept its plant
inventory on a quantity basis, and in translating its figures into
dollars and cents for the New York books Marien had seized
the opportunity to inflate them. The " prime cost of sale," the
cost at the factory of producing merchandise, a figure intricately
arrived at by bringing together such factors as labor, depreciation,
and costs of material, gave Marien a chance to deflate costs, thus
increasing the assets. There are some items on a balance-sheet
which are fluid and not subject to immediate verification, such as
" checks in transit." All these had burgeoned under Marien's
touch. In 1937, for instance, Interstate had really operated at
a small loss, but this was swallowed up in Marien's books. Thus:

	New York books	Lansdale books
Cash	$ 386,073	$ 151,839
Accounts receivable	1,263,543	561,605
Inventory	1,840,393	936,034
Profits	582,541	−56,759
Total assets	$4,859,508	$3,382,558

This is a radical simplification of Marien's accomplishment,
which was a stupendous job of bookkeeping, imaginative and
daring in scope, and carried out with minute attention to detail.
In order to deflate manufacturing costs, for example, Marien
not only had to falsify the overhead expenses but lower the book
cost of raw silk and other materials by inventing all kinds of
favourable transactions with both the throwsters and the commission knitters with whom Interstate dealt. He apparently
knew more about the hosiery business than anybody else in it,
and it was a simple matter for him to describe in orderly columns
of figures the economic adventures of a strand of silk from the
time it left Japan until it was woven into an Interstate stocking.
It is impossible for a layman to comprehend all this completely.
Even the investigators from the S.E.C. and the Attorney-General's
office were baffled. Marien, in his cell in the Tombs, would

admit that he had fudged such-and-such an item in his books, and the investigators would be unable to correct it without his help. Marien enjoyed expounding his financial theory and practice, and the federal accountants, even those who were not assigned to his case, used to go down to the Tombs to hear him questioned, as a matter of professional education. " That man did things with figures that would make Einstein look like a schoolboy," one of them has said.

Marien was held nine months in the Tombs, awaiting trial on forgery charges, while the Attorney-General's office tried to build up a criminal case based on his juggling of the Interstate books. Attorneys, psychiatrists, and probation officers investigated him from every angle, unearthing much that was enlightening but nothing that hinted at a criminal motive, or even a selfish one, beyond the paltry $801·75. It was discovered that Marien held four shares of Interstate stock, but not even the professionally suspicious investigators could bring themselves to believe that this gigantic manipulation arose out of a desire to boost the value of four shares of stock. There was never any evidence of collusion with any of the Interstate officials.

Interstate apparently just couldn't believe what had happened. Marien had given them sound advice about financial policy and procedure; he had even been offered the post of comptroller and had refused. He had been offered bonuses—Interstate had been happily offering almost everybody a bonus—but had declined, except on one occasion, when an order on Saks-Fifth Avenue was diplomatically proffered as a Christmas present for Mrs. Marien. The investigators were, as they say, baffled; if there was no motive, what was the explanation of the crime?

For a touch of low-comedy relief, there was the plight of the other clients of Homes & Davis who had insisted on the services of Marien. Were their profits, too, no more than the whim of an eccentric auditor? One can imagine the corporate blood pressure rising, the sleepless nights of executives. It turned out, after investigation, that all was well except with Interstate. The other books that Marien had audited were accurate to the last penny.

The investigators dug up the life story of this remarkable man. He was born in Canada, of French-Canadian parents. Erasmus Marien—he changed to Raymond after he left school—was something of an infant prodigy. At the age of fourteen, he entered the University of Montreal, where he took both an A.B. and a civil engineering degree. After his graduation, he was employed during the war as a testing engineer by the Imperial

Ministry of Munitions. This job lasted until 1919. Shortly afterward, he forsook the Dominion in rather a romantic fashion, eloping with Grace Kingsland, daughter of a vice-president of the Canadian National Railways. They came to New York, and Marien got a job with Price, Waterhouse & Co., the largest firm of accountants in the world.

It was not until 1925 that Marien first revealed any impatience with orderly business procedure. He then forged checks totaling $16,000 on the New York account of one of Price, Waterhouse's clients, the D'Orsay Perfume Company, of Paris. He made no attempt to cover up the forgeries on the company's books—just went on writing checks until there was no more money in the bank. With the police on his trail, he fled to Paris and threw himself upon the mercy of the company, which showed itself willing to forgive him. However, this love feast was interrupted by extradition proceedings. Marien was brought to New York and tried. His attorney could only point out, by way of extenuation, that Marien had not spent the money on dissipation but merely to raise his family's standard of living. Marien was found guilty, sentenced for an indefinite term to the county penitentiary, and released after six months.

At this point, the chronicler must step out of the role of interpreter. We are dealing with an inexplicable happening. Marien's rehabilitation is surely one of the most startling on record. How an accountant convicted of forgery could, in a few years, without changing his name or leaving the city where he committed his crime, re-enter his profession and rise again to a position of responsibility is a mystery. The Attorney-General, the S.E.C., and (unofficially) all the firms which have occasion for the services of an accountant were passionately curious about this, but they got little satisfaction. Marien's talent for forgery, abetted by listlessness on the part of the city probation officers, gives us the pattern of his procedure, but the details are lacking. The city lost track of Marien, and he forged credentials which were accepted by a reputable firm of accountants. After this and several intervening accounting jobs, in which he gave complete satisfaction and received bona fide letters of recommendation, he landed with Homes & Davis.

While Marien was in the Tombs he was questioned almost daily by the Messrs. Pierce Bradley, then of the S.E.C., and Ambrose McCall, Assistant Attorney-General of the State of New York. Neither of them could shake his story that it was simply " overwork " which had led to the Interstate prank. Marien used to amuse himself by writing letters to Bradley, pointing out that McCall knew little or nothing, to his way of thinking, about accounting and finance; he would also write to McCall, asking him how he ever expected to complete his investigations, hampered as he was by Bradley's colossal ignorance. It was a pretty situation: a man lodged in jail for something that the authorities were certain was a crime, unwilling or unable to help them define it or put a name to it. Marien astonished his fellow prisoners by fixing up an application for a writ of habeas corpus which looked, so faultless was his penmanship, as if it had come from a legal stationer's shop. The writ was denied, but Marien received orders for the same sort of document from half a dozen other prisoners.

Committed to Bellevue for a routine observation, Marien made an excellent impression on the staff. The report, signed by Dr. Karl Bowman, is flattering. " He is an individual of superior intelligence," it says in part. Dr. Walter Bromberg, psychiatrist for the General Sessions Court, made a gallant attempt to explain the inexplicable. Marien, said Dr. Bromberg, had become emotionally involved with Interstate Hosiery Mills. There existed a fantasy of identification. " People working for a large corporation often allow their personality to be absorbed within the larger structure of the corporation, and in that way gain ego-satisfaction in their work. . . . This more or less childish fantasy of aggrandizement made him anxious to have the company appear to be doing excessively well."

In the end, since nobody could find out what crime, if any, Marien had committed when he monkeyed up the Interstate books, he was tried simply on the forgery charge. He received a sentence of two and a half to five years, which, with good behavior, can amount to less than two. He entered Sing Sing in November 1938. The prison psychiatrist rated his I.Q. at 165, and got him a job on the teaching staff. This I.Q. rating is very high. One of the smartest prisoners in Sing Sing, Richard Whitney, who is also on the faculty, has a rating of 138. Mrs. Marien is philosophically taking the bad with the good, and supports herself by working as a waitress. Her oldest son has a job out West, and between them they make enough to take care of the younger children. Her father wanted her to forget Marien and return to Canada, but this she refused to do. " When you marry a genius, you have to be prepared for anything," she told an interviewer recently.

The story has a not unhappy ending. Interstate proved to be sound enough financially to withstand its sudden deflation. A bonus totaling $145,000 had just been paid out when Marien's activities came to light, and before that the company had distributed over $150,000 on the strength of Marien's reports. The officers, as a matter of good will, have repaid all these bonuses since Marien was discovered. The stock, after being suspended from trading pending the S.E.C. investigation, is back on the boards, doing as well as could be expected. On the whole, the affair has had no untidy effect on the lives of widows and orphans. Mr. Bradley, now retired from the S.E.C., says he plans to recommend Marien for the best job available when he is released. Properly supervised and restrained, he thinks, Marien should prove invaluable to any organization. " That man," he says with heartfelt admiration, " can make a prime-cost-of-sales sheet look like something by Rembrandt."

The Case of the Royal Mail *

Sir Patrick Hastings
Barrister, London, deceased

LORD KYLSANT was the chairman of the Royal Mail Steamship Line, and Mr. Moreland was a partner in one of the largest and most respected firms of accountants in the world. Lord Kylsant was a man who, until the moment of his trial, was universally acclaimed, not only as a great shipping magnate, but as one of the most respected figures in the country. He had been made a peer in 1923. He was a Grand Cross of the Order of St. Michael and St. George. He was the Lord-Lieutenant of the County of Hereford West. He had been president of the Chamber of Shipping of the United Kingdom and of the London Chamber of Commerce. In fact, his whole career had been one of personal triumph and achievement.

Mr. Moreland stood equally high in the opinion of all who knew him. Not only was he one of the heads of a great profession, but he was a gentleman whose private and public life had earned the respect of everyone who knew him.

On July 20, 1931, these two gentlemen stood side by side in the dock at the Central Criminal Court, charged with publishing balance-sheets of the Royal Mail Steamship Company which were false and fraudulent. It was alleged against them that they had wilfully deceived the shareholders by representing that the company was in a very prosperous condition when they knew that it was on the verge of ruin.

The Royal Mail Company owned one of the largest shipping lines in England and, like many other similar concerns, had undergone periods of violent fluctuation in its financial condition. During the period of the First World War, it had made extremely large profits, and with commendable foresight the board of directors had placed a large portion of those profits to reserve, with the object of being in a position to meet any possible liability to income tax and excess profits tax. At one time, these reserves had accumulated to an amount exceeding two million

---

* From *Cases in Court* (London, 1949), the reminiscences of Sir Patrick Hastings (1880–1952).

pounds, and after all the requirements of the Revenue had ultimately been settled there remained in their hands over a million pounds, which could be used as the directors thought proper. During the years 1921–25, the profits of the company had largely decreased, and the directors had decided to use some portion of their accumulated reserves for the purpose of increasing their annual profits, and no complaint was made at the trial of the method by which a portion of those reserves had been so utilised.

It was in respect of the years 1926 and 1927 that the trouble arose. In 1926 the company applied to the Treasury to extend the period during which certain repayments were due from the company to the Treasury, in respect of loans which had been made. The Treasury thereupon desired an inquiry to be made into the financial affairs of the company, and for that purpose appointed an accountant to look into their books. It was as a result of that inquiry that the prosecution was commenced. It is, therefore, necessary to see exactly what was the position of the company in the years 1926 and 1927—what the balance-sheet purported to show, and what were the true facts.

The balance-sheet showed that in 1926 there was a trading profit of £439,000. The Government inquiry discovered that, so far from there being any trading profit for the year, the company had in fact been running at a loss, and the way in which the alleged profit was arrived at was by crediting the accounts with £750,000 drawn out of the tax reserve, and that in fact instead of a trading profit of £439,000, the company had really incurred a loss of about £300,000. In consequence of this discovery, the Treasury maintained that the balance-sheet was fraudulent, and decided to institute criminal proceedings against Lord Kylsant, as chairman, and Mr. Moreland, as auditor. Sir John Simon, K.C., and Mr. Singleton, K.C., were instructed to represent Lord Kylsant, and I and Mr. Stuart Bevan, K.C., represented Mr. Moreland.

At the outset, the case appeared to be a very difficult one, and it was necessary to make some very careful inquiries, not only as to the practice of preparing balance-sheets generally, but also as to the precise figures in this particular case.

Of Lord Kylsant I saw but little, but I was supplied with information as to his views on the matter. According to his understanding of shipping business, he took the view that great fluctuations in the earnings of shipping companies were only to be expected, and gave no indication of the true financial position. His experience had taught him that periods of prosperity occurred in regular cycles, and it was necessary, from a business point of view, to accumulate large reserves in prosperous years, in order that in leaner periods the company should be able to draw upon them to make up the losses which might well have been anticipated. He pointed out with considerable force that, unless this course was adopted, an untutored body of shareholders, being faced with a sudden drop in their annual profits, might well fall into a panic, which would be unfair alike to them and the investing public; and, generally speaking, he justified everything that appeared in the balance-sheet on that basis. He moreover maintained that his company had employed the best possible firm of accountants as auditors, and that he relied on them to see that the balance-sheets were properly prepared. There was a further point on which Lord Kylsant very naturally relied, although I personally never thought quite enough weight was attached to it at the trial, that he was supported by a board of directors of the highest position, some of them very eminent lawyers, and no one of them had ever queried the propriety of what was being done.

From the outset, it was apparent that the main burden of this part of the trial would fall upon those representing Mr. Moreland, and it was to him that we looked for a more thorough elucidation of the facts. Although Mr. Moreland was no doubt an admirable accountant, as a client he was a little trying. Being completely conscious of his own integrity, he treated all the allegations made against him with supreme contempt, and absolutely declined to recognise the very grave position with which he was faced and the danger in which he stood. Moreover, being a devoutly religious man, he was convinced that a divine interference would necessarily decide the issue, a view which, although no doubt satisfactory to him, was a little trying to his harassed and even exasperated legal advisors.

However, in the end, we were able to get a clear view of the facts, particularly the manner in which the 1926 balance-sheet had been prepared. Apparently the accounts were prepared in the office of the Royal Mail, and the balance-sheet in its proposed final form was then submitted to Mr. Moreland for his certificate and approval. Mr. Moreland was, of course, aware that the revenue reserves had, to some extent, been utilised to increase the profits for some years prior to 1926, and said that such utilisation was quite usual and proper. In the year 1926, inasmuch as it was proposed to utilise so large a sum as £750,000 to change an admitted trading loss of £300,000 into a declared profit of £400,000, Mr. Moreland considered that the time had arrived when some indication of that fact should be given to the shareholders.

When the draft balance-sheet was submitted to him in 1926, Mr. Moreland, in dealing with the profit, himself wrote into the draft the words " including adjustment of taxation reserves." He did this entirely of his own initiative, and he stated that those words were the ones usually employed by accountants, to give notice to shareholders and anyone who might be concerned with the declared profit that such profit had only been arrived at by a utilisation of reserves. Lord Kylsant had nothing whatever to do with the words which Mr. Moreland inserted in the balance-sheet, but he made no comment upon them, and the final balance-sheet, as published, contained Mr. Moreland's addition.

This information immediately made it apparent that the whole defence must necessarily turn upon the one question, whether or not the words used by Mr. Moreland were well recognised in accountancy circles, and were sufficient to give notice of the manner in which the trading loss had been turned into an apparent profit. From that moment, every effort was made to obtain balance-sheets in other companies, certified by accountants of the highest position, in which a similar phrase had been used in similar circumstances. Whether or not this accountancy practice was to be commended was, in our view, wholly immaterial. The charge we had to meet was a charge of dishonesty, and if it could be shown that Mr. Moreland had merely adopted the customary practice, it would be very difficult for anyone to accuse him of dishonesty. Infinite labour had been expended by the solicitors instructing me in obtaining instances of such practice, and, before the preliminary hearing, I had been provided with a pile of balance-sheets with which to cross-examine the distinguished accountants who were to be witnesses for the prosecution.

The great difficulty with which we were then faced was whether or not to disclose our main defence at the preliminary hearing. If we cross-examined the accountants at such an early stage, no doubt each would endeavour to draw great distinction between the cases in which he had used such a phrase and the case of the Royal Mail. Thus we had to decide whether or not it would be wise to let them know in advance what our line of defence would be, while at the same time gaining an opportunity of finding out what distinctions could be raised against us. Conversely, should we leave the point entirely until the hearing at the Central Criminal Court? As subsequent events proved, we were well advised in adopting the former course.

The preliminary hearing took place at the Guildhall before the Lord Mayor, when the first important witness was Sir William McClintock, the head of the well-known firm of accountants bearing his name. In front of me were piles of balance-sheets, some of them having been audited by Sir William himself, and it was fairly obvious that the cross-examination was likely to be prolonged. Upon my first question directed to the main point of the defence, namely that the actual words " including adjustment of taxation reserves " were precisely the words customarily used by wise accountants in similar circumstances, the magistrate adopted what was to my mind a most extraordinary and unprecedented course. He refused to allow any of the questions, calling them irrelevant. Sir Phené Neale was then Lord Mayor and the senior magistrate in the City of London. He was also a solicitor, and perhaps a little over-conscious of his own importance, but how in the world he took upon himself to reject, at a preliminary inquiry, a cross-examination which was obviously based upon the considered opinion of a large number of somewhat eminent counsel has always passed my comprehension. His ruling necessitated an immediate decision. I saw at once that the defence might in the end benefit extraordinarily by reason of the course he had adopted. I rose in my place and stated that, having regard to his ruling, no one of the counsel present could possibly take any further part in the hearing before him, and in a procession we all left the court. I should imagine that such an event has never previously occurred in the Guildhall, and Sir Phené may well have regretted his ill-advised and perhaps hasty decision.

I immediately communicated with the Attorney-General, and obtained from him permission for my solicitors to interview the prosecution's witnesses, in order to obtain from them a statement of their views, which we had been prevented from obtaining at the preliminary inquiry by the Lord Mayor. There was only one witness whom we really desired to see, and that was Lord Plender, perhaps the doyen of accountants. He also in the past had verified balance-sheets containing words substantially similar to those complained of in the present case. Accordingly a very carefully prepared questionnaire was submitted to him, with a view to obtaining his agreement with the principles on which we so strongly relied. As was only to be expected in the case of a man such as Lord Plender, the replies were absolutely frank and, in our opinion, entirely satisfactory. It was upon the material supplied by Lord Plender that our defence was mainly based.

The trial took place on July 20, 1931, at the Central Criminal Court before Mr. Justice Wright and a jury. No doubt the atmosphere which prevailed at the time was none too friendly towards the defendants, and the court was packed with onlookers, most of whom had suffered severely.

From the exposure which had, of course, taken place in consequence of the preliminary proceedings, I could not help wondering whether the distinguished accountants who were to be called by the prosecution were a little unhappy that they had not been already asked to give a little more explanation of the prevailing practice as to certifying balance-sheets, as by this time they were of course aware of the information in our possession. They must also have known that we ourselves were in a position, in case of necessity, to call into the witness box the heads of their own profession to give evidence in support of the suggestions which we had already made to Lord Plender. We, upon our part, were gravely anxious in case Lord Plender himself should in any way qualify the answers which he had already given to us; accordingly our pile of balance-sheets was given a prominent place upon the desk before us.

The case was opened by the Attorney-General, who appeared for the prosecution, and as I listened to his speech, I could not help wondering if he too would not have been better served if the defendants had been allowed to outline their defence before the Lord Mayor; once or twice it seemed to me that he had been completely misinformed as to what the defence was going to be. There were two charges against the defendants: the first was based upon the alleged fraudulent balance-sheets, and in that both Lord Kylsant and Mr. Moreland were implicated; the second was against Lord Kylsant alone, and in that I took no part. It was on the first charge that I felt the Attorney-General had been somewhat led astray. After outlining the facts and figures, he made this specific allegation against Mr. Moreland: " the phrase ' adjustment of taxation reserves ' was a phrase quite deliberately prepared and selected and chosen as a phrase which would convey nothing whatever to the mind of the ordinary person, but at the same time would enable anyone to say in case the need thereafter arose, ' Oh! but all this is covered by the phrase " adjustment of taxation reserves." ' It betrays, members of the jury, on my submission to you, an uneasy conscience about what was being done."

It was upon that very point that Lord Plender had been questioned, and it was upon Lord Plender's answers to those questions that the defence relied. The Attorney-General was

right in thinking that to be the whole basis of the prosecution;
if Lord Plender's evidence turned out to be what we anticipated,
could that prosecution be maintained?

Lord Plender himself was the first witness called before the
jury, and his evidence for the prosecution was merely formal.
It was upon his cross-examination that everything depended.
I never remember to have approached a cross-examination with
more anxiety, and inasmuch as the questions and answers formed
the basis of the whole defence I have recorded them in full.

" Lord Plender, is it quite a usual and a proper thing for
companies to set aside large sums against their liability for
excess profits duty and income tax? "

" Yes."

" If they were not required for the next year, could they
properly be brought back into profits for subsequent years? "

" That would be quite a regular credit."

" In many cases, would they not be disclosed in a profit and
loss account as having been brought into credit? "

" Sometimes no reference is made, but, generally speaking,
it will be found that an indication is made that some transfer
has been made."

" Do I understand you to mean by that that if the secret or
inner reserves are used for that purpose, there might properly
come a time when an auditor would say that some indication
should be given to the shareholders that those transfers are being
made? "

" Yes."

" Are there not many cases in which a reserve of this kind is
made into the credit of the year's profit and loss, and no mention
is made that reserves have been called upon? "

" There are such cases."

" Is it done by firms of the very highest repute? "

" Yes."

" Is it your view that no exception could be taken to that
practice? "

" As a principle, no exception could be taken."

" Might there come a time when the auditor would say:
' Now if these reserves are to be used again, some indication
must be given to the shareholders that the profit and loss account
is augmented by transfers from the excess profits duty reserve '? "

" Yes."

" Are there common phrases used by auditors to indicate
such augmentations in one or other of these forms: ' Excess
profits duty adjustment,' or ' after adjustment of reserves for

excess profits duty,' or ' taxation adjustment,' or ' adjustment of taxation reserve ? ' "

" Yes."

" Are all these phrases commonly used by auditors to indicate transfers to the profit account from taxation reserve ? "

" That is so."

" And those transfers, according to the facts of any particular case, might be either small or large ? "

" Yes."

" That being so, if you saw such words as those which I have described in a profit and loss account, would you understand from them that there had been a transfer from an excess profits duty or other reserves, which might be small or large ? "

" Certainly."

That was all we could have hoped. Mr. Bevan's relief was quite as great as mine. When I sat down he whispered, " That has done them! "

Whether or not anyone in court immediately realised the importance of those answers, I never knew. Certainly the action of Sir Phené Neale had prevented the prosecution from learning what was our real defence, and it may be that the answers of Lord Plender took them by surprise. The judge seemed to take comparatively little interest in them at that stage of the proceedings. But those answers were vital, and what was of equal importance to us was that the Attorney-General asked no questions in re-examination of Lord Plender to minimise the effect of the evidence he had given. But what was still more remarkable was that none of the subsequent witnesses for the prosecution were ever invited to express a view in contradiction of Lord Plender's, and, in our view, the propriety of Mr. Moreland's conduct was completely established by the accountancy evidence given by the Crown.

After that evidence how was it possible to contend that Mr. Moreland had deliberately prepared that phrase in order to hide an uneasy conscience ?

As Lord Kylsant justly contended that he had nothing whatever to do with the wording of this suspicious phrase, and that he relied in that respect entirely upon his accountants, the main burden of the defence fell upon Mr. Moreland, and whatever else he might succeed in doing, I did not envy the Attorney-General his task of trying to establish criminal dishonesty against Mr. Moreland. As I called Mr. Moreland into the witness box, anything less fraudulent in appearance it would be impossible to imagine. His demeanour was precisely as it had been upon the first occasion when I had seen him. He treated any allegation made against him with supreme indifference, and regarded his accusers almost with good-natured contempt. He accepted full responsibility for the wording of the phrase " adjustment of taxation reserves," which he said was perfectly well-recognised throughout the entire profession of accountancy to indicate exactly what had been done. He stated that those words gave the fullest notice of the inclusion of moneys previously reserved for taxation, and it was perfectly open to anyone interested in the accounts to ask a question as to the extent to which they had been so utilised.

Although he was cross-examined at some length, he declined to budge one inch from his original statement. When asked about his interest in the company, he said that he had no interest financially or otherwise, except his auditor's fee, which was, of course, shared with the many partners in his firm, and which, after payment of tax, resulted to him in a benefit of only £20.

If any jury could have convicted kind old Mr. Moreland of fraud, my faith in juries would have been gravely shaken. Many of the heads of his profession followed him into the witness box to give evidence on his behalf, all of them stating that, if called upon to do so, they would have signed the balance-sheet exactly as Mr. Moreland had done; and upon that note the evidence closed. The judge summed up at length, no doubt by reason of the importance of the case and the many complexities in which we had been involved. As I listened to him I began to feel that he had been, at the end, very deeply impressed by the defence we had put forward, but he must have recognised, as we all did, the tremendous amount of public prejudice which existed at that time against anyone connected with the Royal Mail Company. The jury retired and were absent for some hours. The period of waiting while a jury is considering its verdict is one I have always hated. In this case I hated it more than ever; I was so determined that my client should be acquitted, and the jury were out so long. All the devoted band of most skilful lawyers who had worked so hard, and had helped me so much, shared my anxiety. Nerves began to fray and tempers became short; Mr. Moreland alone maintained his attitude of confidence almost amounting to indifference. That same attitude which had exasperated us so much during the preparation for the trial now became intolerable, and when it was found to have extended to Mr. Moreland's own domestic hearth it became more than those instructing me could bear. While the jury was still out of court the telephone rang from Mr. Moreland's home; somebody wanted to speak to my solicitor. He hurried to the telephone, deeply distressed that there was still no news. A sweet and gentle voice addressed him: " Could you kindly tell me if Mr. Moreland is likely to be late for dinner? " That was the last straw. " Yes, Madam," he replied, " I should think about twelve months late." But he was wrong. When the jury came back into court, they returned a verdict of Not Guilty, and both Mr. Moreland and Lord Kylsant were acquitted.

Unhappily for Lord Kylsant, that was not the end. Against him alone there was a further charge based upon the issue of debentures in the same company, and in that charge I was merely an onlooker. My client Mr. Moreland was no party to that indictment, but Lord Kylsant was convicted and sentenced to a term of imprisonment. As a mere observer my opinion is completely valueless, but I was never completely satisfied of the justice of that conviction. I was very sorry for Lord Kylsant.

Fraud*

By E. E. Spicer

*Professional accountant,
deceased, London*

EVERY practising accountant is constantly on the lookout for
fraud, but seldom comes across it. This is due to two causes.
In the first place most people in this country are inherently
honest, notwithstanding anything which the Rev. Stephen Collins
and other righteous men may say to the contrary; and secondly,
the system of internal check, in large and well-regulated concerns,
is such as to render it unlikely—in the absence of collusion—
for fraud to remain undetected for any length of time.

It must be admitted, however, that there are still a few dishonest people in the world, and that in many of the smaller
business houses it is quite impossible to institute anything
approaching a watertight system of control. Thus the practising
accountant can never relax his vigilance, but must ever assume,
for his own protection, that fraud is " winking " at him round the
corner.

The young practitioner, who successfully unravels a fraud,
is apt to experience a sense of elation, which, though pleasing
to his vanity, may nevertheless lead him into an indiscretion.
A very natural desire that his astuteness should be recognised
may cause him to seek out his client before his pulse has resumed
its normal beat and before he has had time to don a black tie.

The older practitioner will never be guilty of a psychological
error of this nature. He will realise that a client who is the victim
of fraud is likely to view matters through a somewhat jaundiced
eye and to accept the discovery of the fraud very much as a matter
of course. The accountant should thus suppress outwardly
all trace of inward exaltation and assume a countenance expressive
of sympathy rather than of satisfaction. He should remember
when talking to his client that it is part of an auditor's normal
duty periodically to examine the system of internal check in
operation and to report in writing regarding any weaknesses
which may exist. More particularly should he do this in cases
where it is impossible to institute a really efficient system owing
to the smallness of the administrative staff.

Thus, following the successful detection of a fraud, the
auditor's first action should be to acquaint himself with the

* Based on an article in *Accountancy*, July 1951.

circumstances which rendered the fraud possible; to ascertain why it had not been detected earlier, either by himself, or internally, under the system of control in force, and to ask himself cold-bloodedly and honestly whether he has, in any way, failed in his duty. He should also consider very carefully whether there is anything in any of the reports which he has submitted in the past, dealing with the system of internal check, which has a direct bearing on the case under consideration.

By this time he will doubtless be in a proper frame of mind to discuss the fraud with his client, and will be able to answer at least some of the questions which are likely to be addressed to him.

It is at these moments that the supreme value of written reports on the system of internal control becomes apparent. A client will rarely admit having received oral warnings, and even when forced to acknowledge that a discussion did take place at a particular hour on a particular day, his recollection of what was said may differ surprisingly from the auditor's notes, made—be it understood—on the very day of the interview. A written report, however, affords incontrovertible evidence, which may prove of the utmost importance to the auditor in the event of a charge of negligence being preferred.

It is clear, therefore, that too much importance cannot be placed on these periodic reports, and obviously the more up-to-date they are, the greater will be their value. It must not be supposed, however, that they are written merely to relieve the auditor of responsibility. Their main object is to protect the client by reminding him that an audit does not necessarily guard him from loss by fraud, nor does it necessarily render certain the detection of fraud, which is actually being perpetrated.

The practising accountant should ever bear in mind that an employee who sets out to defraud usually endeavours to acquaint himself, as far as possible, with the exact scope of the audit. From this it follows that the auditor should not only vary the programme of work performed, but also should endeavour to avoid giving the employee valuable information, as a result of the system of " ticking " adopted. It rarely happens, in an audit of any size, that every item is checked, but it is certainly undesirable that a dishonest employee should know, for a certainty, that only those items which are ticked have, in fact, been checked. The auditor should therefore adopt, to a limited extent, a system of checking without ticks and should inform his client of his reasons for so doing.

There are some frauds which cannot be detected, save by

some fortunate chance, owing to the weakness of the internal system of control, and it is not always easy to convince one's client of this fact. Hence the importance of warning the client and in cases where such warnings are disregarded, of repudiating responsibility for any fraud which may, in consequence, take place.

Let us take an example from our notebook.

In this particular case a firm of professional accountants were employed to write up the books dealing with the household expenditure of a well-known peer, who entertained largely. From the point of view of the accountants, the system adopted placed too much reliance on the honesty of the head servants, and recommendations were made to tighten up the control. These, however, were rejected as likely to cause difficulties, and in consequence the accountants wrote stating that they could assume no responsibility for the accuracy of the prime records on which the final accounts were based.

Illustration one

After leaving the university in the summer of the year 1897, Mr. Greatheart was articled to a firm of professional accountants in London, and one of the " cases " entrusted to his care, during the last year of his articles, was the writing up of the household accounts of the great and wealthy Lord Panbury of Ewick.

At the beginning of each month, Mr. Greatheart presented himself at the house in Park Lane and received from the butler, the coachman, the chef and the aged housekeeper, their respective cash books showing the amounts which each had received and disbursed during the preceding month. The cash payments were supported by receipted bills and tradesmen's books, and the cash receipts were checked against the sums which Lady Panbury had advanced during the month. The balance in hand or over-spent was brought down, and cheques were drawn sufficient to provide each servant with a reasonable working " float." The total expenditure for the month was then analysed under appropriate headings and duly recorded by Mr. Greatheart in the household books of account.

It was freely admitted by Lord Panbury that the system was theoretically faulty; but in practice it worked well, and as all the four servants in question had served the family for many years and were regarded as thoroughly trustworthy, it was decided not to effect any changes, notwithstanding the lack of internal check emphasised by the accountants.

Mr. Greatheart carried out his arduous duties in his lordship's study, and punctually at one o'clock luncheon was served by the footman at a side table, under the eagle eye of Mr. Cole, the butler, who graciously took it upon himself to uncork, with appropriate ceremony, a bottle of very excellent claret.

Now, on one exceptionally warm afternoon in the summer of the year 1900, Mr. Greatheart—having enjoyed a hearty lunch and demonstrated, in no unmistakable manner, his appreciation of the wine—experienced an unaccountable feeling of drowsiness, and fearing lest he might be discovered asleep in his chair, decided that a drive twice round the park, in a swift-moving hansom cab, would be the treatment which the doctor would recommend for his particular complaint. In order to justify the expense of the cab, and to provide a *raison d'etre* for any apparent dereliction of duty, in the event of the unexpected appearance in Park Lane of one of the partners of the firm, he slipped into his pocket a few of the coachman's receipted accounts.

Those who are old enough to remember that most delightful of all horse-drawn vehicles, the hansom cab, will not be surprised to learn that, after one single journey round the Park, Mr. Greatheart's feeling of faintness, due to overwork, had completely disappeared, and instead of repeating the circular tour, he ordered the driver to proceed forthwith to the establishment of that well-known firm of corn chandlers, Messrs. S. Beddow & Sons. On arrival, he informed Mr. Beddow that Lord Panbury had questioned the price charged for oats, which had risen somewhat steeply during recent months, and requested an explanation. In reply, Mr. Beddow stated that he had not the honour of serving his lordship, and when confronted with one of the receipted accounts, declared that it was a bare-faced forgery.

Mr. Greatheart thereupon returned to the office to report the discovery of the fraud to his firm, and on the following day, in the presence of Lord Panbury, interviewed the coachman.

After some little hesitation, a full confession was extracted from the guilty man. A brother-in-law, engaged in the printing trade, had supplied the headed account forms; and Reynolds, the coachman, having filled them up with imaginary items, at full West End prices, while feeding the horses himself on the cheap, had pocketed the difference.

Mr. Greatheart received the hearty congratulations of his firm, but did not deem it necessary to refer to the claret.

Reynolds, the coachman, after receiving a severe " dressing down " by Lord Panbury, was given a second chance, in view of his long service with the family and the fact that in size and girth he rivalled the Lord Mayor's coachman, a circumstance which was regarded as very important; while Mr. Greatheart

was requested to " keep his eye in the future on the stables,"
whatever that might mean.

Thus, from time to time, prior to taking luncheon, Mr.
Greatheart visited the stables, chatted with the groom in charge,
smelt the oats as he allowed them to trickle slowly through his
fingers, examined the horses' hoofs and went through the ritual
normally followed by persons claiming a knowledge of horse-
flesh.

On one such visit, he asked the groom, very casually, how
many horses were still in London. The groom replied that the
number was four and that the others had been sent down to
Ewick some six weeks previously.

Now Mr. Greatheart had that very day drawn a cheque in
payment of the farrier's account, and he remembered that there
had been a charge for fitting twenty-one horseshoes during the
second half of the preceding month. The question which puzzled
him, therefore, was how twenty-one shoes could be attached to
the legs of four horses in one week, and, being unable to solve
the problem mathematically, he decided to interview the
farrier.

It was the blacksmith who had actually shod the horses who
eventually provided the clue to the mystery, by remarking that
perhaps Lord Panbury's coachman had borrowed one or two
of the horses from the milkman, and had received privately some
consideration for his courtesy.

Thus, for the second time within a space of four months,
the coachman, was—by lucky chance—detected in fraud, and
although Lady Panbury pleaded on his behalf with her husband,
emphasising the impossibility of finding another coachman who
could carry, with such conviction in the park, so vast an extent
of waistcoat, Lord Panbury decided that an example, however
painful, must be made, and in consequence Reynolds was dismissed
forthwith, without a character.

In dealing with fraud, the young practitioner should bear in
mind that whereas it is easy to accuse a man of fraud, it is by
no means so easy to prove the man guilty and obtain a conviction
in a court of law. Our criminal laws are exceedingly tender
towards the wrongdoer, and not only is he invariably given the
benefit of any possible doubt, but he may, though obviously
guilty, escape punishment as a result of some legal technicality.
Moreover, an accusation which cannot be proved may result in
heavy damages against the party making the accusation.

Let us choose a few examples to illustrate the truth of these
weighty words of friendly advice.

Illustration two

The old and trusted manager of a small and prosperous private limited company unhappily developed heart trouble at the comparatively early age of fifty-seven, and it became evident to the directors that if his life was to be prolonged it would be necessary for him to take matters very much more easily in the future than he had done in the past, and therefore he was asked whether he could find an experienced assistant, whom he could trust, and who could, under his general supervision, take over the main burden of the management, thus enabling him to regulate his activities strictly in accordance with medical advice.

These arrangements were made and for two years everything ran very smoothly. The assistant manager did all in his power to relieve the manager of anxiety and very rapidly acquired an intimate knowledge of the business. In fact, so loyally did he apparently perform his duties that on the death of the manager the directors did not hesitate to appoint him to fill the vacancy and to extend to him the same wholehearted confidence which they had reposed in his predecessor.

But, "alas for the innate sinfulness of the seekers after the mammon of unrighteousness," as remarked by the Rev. Stephen Collins, when the facts in the case were brought to his attention.

From the very day of the old manager's death, his successor embarked on a series of frauds, involving fictitious purchases, wage manipulations, false returns inwards, etc., all of which were rendered possible owing to the inevitable lack of internal check. These frauds remained undetected for nearly three years, and were only discovered as a result of certain investigations, conducted with great assiduity by the chairman of the company personally.

The directors regarded the breach of trust as so flagrant that a prosecution was essential and in due course the manager found himself in the dock at quarter sessions. The main witness for the prosecution was the chairman, since he was the only director who had taken active steps in unravelling the fraud, and he gave his evidence in chief in a very quiet, restrained and convincing manner.

Counsel for the defence then rose to cross-examine, and his first request was to see the minute of the directors, authorising the prosecution by the company. The minute book was produced and counsel's attention was directed to page 179 thereof. The chairman was then asked how many directors were needed to form a quorum.

Now, the chairman remembered that only he and one of his

fellow directors with the secretary had been present at the meeting in question, and so without a moment's hesitation and in all good faith he answered that the number was two.

Counsel then started laboriously to examine the minute book, page by page, in an endeavour to find a resolution on the matter. Failing in his search, he inquired of the chairman what Table A had to say on the matter.

The chairman, having spent the bulk of his life as an officer in the Indian Army, knew no more about Table A than he did about the co-efficient of brass, and appealed to the learned judge for an explanation. The judge, however, ruled that a sufficient amount of time had already been wasted on the matter, and as no copy of Table A could be found in the court, the evidence of the chairman on the point must be accepted as correct.

The trial thereupon proceeded, and in due course a verdict of " guilty " was recorded, and the manager was sentenced to six months' imprisonment, with hard labour.

On the journey back to London, Mr. Greatheart, who had been a silent spectator throughout the proceedings, informed the chairman that on page 1 of the minute book there was a resolution to the effect that any three directors would form a quorum. The learned counsel had scrutinised every page except the first. Had he chanced to examine that page, the whole case would have collapsed on the technicality that the resolution to prosecute was invalid.

Let us now take another example from our notebook. The case which we have chosen does not deal with a class of fraud which normally an auditor can be expected to detect, because secret commissions do not pass directly through the books of account. It must be remembered, however, that an employee who accepts a bribe is morally, if not legally, as guilty of fraud as is the man who robs the till. He is, in fact, stealing his principal's money, because whatever he receives illicitly in this manner will—sooner or later—be added to the firm's expenses, or deducted from the quality of the goods purchased.

It is hardly necessary to remark that if a fraud of this nature be suspected and the auditor is consulted, he should refuse to act, save in close co-operation with the company's legal advisers. This does not mean that he should be a silent spectator and allow his imagination to run to seed. The professional accountant should never play second fiddle but should always be in the limelight. It means that he should take no important step without the full approval of the lawyers—and he does this for his own protection.

Illustration three

The directors of a great multiple store had collected what they deemed to be conclusive evidence that their chief buyer had accepted substantial secret commissions, and so certain were they that this was the case that they summoned him to the board-room, and after closely questioning him for nearly two hours, informed him that they could reach no other conclusion than that he had betrayed his trust and accepted bribes.

The man, of course, denied the charge, and when asked to explain how it came about that he was able to spend money so freely and to live so extravagantly on his salary and commission, replied that he had discovered a system of betting which had proved highly successful.

He was then asked to produce his bank pass-book, but this, at first, he steadily refused to do, remarking that his private affairs had nothing whatever to do with the company. Eventually, under what amounted to a threat of criminal proceedings, he agreed, very reluctantly, to submit his pass-book.

An examination of this disclosed that substantial sums had been paid into the account, apart altogether from his normal salary and commission, and bearing in mind all the circumstances, the directors decided that while they would refrain from prosecuting, they could no longer continue his employment. They therefore informed him that his service agreement would be cancelled and that they would pay him, in full settlement, three months' salary in lieu of notice and a fixed sum of £250 on account of commission.

This offer was indignantly refused. In due course, the buyer started an action against the company for wrongful dismissal and claiming heavy damages for defamation of character. In his evidence, he produced his betting cash book, together with detailed records of all his betting transactions from the start, which statements had been prepared and audited at the appropriate dates by a well-known firm of professional accountants.

All the bets were made with the totalisator, and at the end of each day's racing, instead of cashing his winnings in the ordinary way, he obtained from the totalisator a cheque, made payable to his order and crossed " Account Payee only, Axminster Bank Ltd. Not Negotiable," avoiding in this manner all risk of being robbed of a large number of £1 notes. He was thus able to show exactly what bets he had made on each day's racing, and exactly how much he had made on each race, and finally he was able to prove that the amounts paid into his account— apart from small sums representing net winnings on comparatively unlucky days—were represented by cheques issued to him personally by the totalisator. Even the small sums of cash paid into the bank were fully explained in the cash book, and could be vouched by reference to the totalisator records.

His evidence—which was fully supported by the professional accountant—was so exact and the statements submitted were so detailed and so clear, that all cross-examination proved unavailing and in the end the buyer won his action and was awarded substantial damages.

And yet, in spite of all the evidence, the buyer was as guilty of having accepted bribes as Wainewright, the poet, was guilty of having murdered Helen Abercrombie because she had very thick ankles. What perhaps was even more remarkable was that he had never, throughout his whole life, made a bet either with a bookmaker or with the totalisator.

These facts came to light some years after the death of the buyer (who was killed in a railway accident on the Continent), thus enabling us, at long last, to reveal the truth about this strange case.

The buyer was a man of intelligence who held the view that an individual who embarks on a course of action condemned by honest men should assume—right from the start—that sooner or later he will most assuredly be caught napping. He decided, therefore, that he must always have a complete answer to any charge of accepting bribes, and that successful betting on the totalisator, provided it could be supported by cast-iron evidence, constituted the most convincing way of accounting for a rapid accession of wealth. He recognised that he must act with caution and spend a little money if necessary to ensure the best results, and thus adopted the following procedure.

All bribes, which he accepted—and he only accepted large ones—were, of course, paid in £1 notes. Armed with these notes, he went " to the dogs." He made the acquaintance of a man who willingly agreed, for a small consideration, to buy up winning tickets from people waiting their turn in the queue to collect their winnings at the totalisator, and in this manner was able to convert his £1 notes into winning tickets of an equivalent value. All he lost by the transaction was the small commission paid to his " friend " of doubtful morality, who knew better than to worry his head about the intricacies of high finance.

Having collected the requisite number of winning tickets and having made exact notes regarding the names of the dogs running and the dividends paid out by the totalisator on winners, he exchanged the tickets at the totalisator for a cheque drawn to his order and crossed, and, on the following day, paid it into his account with the Axminster Bank, Lombard Street.

Periodically, with the object of giving a touch of artistry to his imaginary betting transactions, he paid into the bank small sums in cash, entering into his betting cash book a series of winnings, less losses, which equalled the cash paid in.

He never took the smallest risk in any of these matters, and he avoided every short cut. He never entered in his cash book, the name of a dog which had won or lost on a day when he was not actually present to watch the race, and he took great pains to be in a position to prove by outside evidence that he had in fact been " to the dogs " on every day that a record of a win or a loss appeared in his cash book.

His records showed that he had started betting in a small way and had only gradually increased his operations. This was done purposely to avoid any difficulty in having to explain how he had come by the initial capital to enable him to start betting heavily. Later, he made a point of carrying on his person a reasonably large sum in £1 notes, which rendered unnecessary frequent withdrawals from the bank.

Altogether he exercised such care and foresight that he was able eventually to turn the tables on the company with whom he had been employed; deceive a court of justice into awarding him a substantial sum by way of non-taxable damages; and finally so to " fox " a reputable firm of professional accountants as to convince them that the detailed statements of betting transactions, which from time to time they had prepared from the buyer's records, checked with the official records of the totalisator and certified, were, in fact, true and correct summaries of betting activities, which actually never took place.

The employment of professional accountants from the very start of the operations to enable the buyer to prove a falsehood at any time, in case of need, was unquestionably a " touch." At any rate, it completely knocked the directors of the company off their balance when they got to know about it, and it certainly went far to convince the court.

There was another " touch " which should not be overlooked. The buyer recognised full well that if the suspicions of the directors regarding his honesty were at any time aroused, his future with the company would become impossible. His object, therefore, in such circumstances, must be to force the directors to accuse him of dishonesty and to dismiss him from their service, so that he might be in a position to bring an action against the company for defamation of character, and to succeed as a result of his carefully worked out alibi. He wanted the directors, therefore, to demand the production of his pass-book but obviously it would have been inartistic to comply with their wishes (which coincided with his own) too quickly. The indignant refusal, which was his first apparent reaction to the proposal, constituted the second noteworthy " touch."

Do not these subtle and delicate " touches " raise to the sublime, actions which otherwise might appear merely coarse, sordid and vulgar?

Our next example is introduced to illustrate the fact that, when dealing with cases involving fraud, secrecy is all-important.

As " Women, generally speaking, are generally speaking," it is perhaps safer to employ strong silent men as far as possible. More particularly is this important where fraud is suspected, and tests are being tried out with the object of obtaining proof. In such a case a misplaced word, a loosely-worded letter or an incautious move may result in far-reaching and terrible repercussions. All hasty decisions should be avoided, and legal advice should be sought before action is taken.

The particular example which we have selected is certainly unusual in that everything turns up bewitchingly at the end, like Mrs. Grundy's nose. Moreover, comedy, tragedy and romance are all beautifully blended and all the actors in the little drama live happily ever afterwards.

How differently the story might have ended! There are some to whom even now the mere thought of what might have been, produces a sensation of excruciating mental torture.

Well may it be said, with apologies to Dr. Johnson:

> It left a dream, at which the Board grew pale,
> To point a moral or adorn a tale.

Illustration four

Some years ago, Mr. Greatheart was asked by his friend Mr. George Osborn whether he could recommend a suitable person to take the place of his private secretary, who was leaving to get married. Now, by a curious coincidence, the actuary of the insurance company of which Mr. Greatheart was a director, had, that very morning, spoken to him about his sister, who was seeking such an appointment. The lady in question, by name Miss Laura McIntyre, was a graduate of London University; had qualified as a Chartered Secretary; spoke French fluently and was an expert shorthand-typist. She was thirty-two years of age, attractive looking but not dangerously beautiful, and altogether it seemed as if Providence had ordained that she should become the private secretary to George Osborn, Esq., chairman of Osborn Bros., Ltd., the wholesale paper merchants of Upper Thames Street, London, with branch houses in all the leading cities of England and Scotland.

An interview was accordingly arranged, at which Mrs. George Osborn (who held strong views regarding private secretaries) was present, and in due course, with her full approval, Miss McIntyre was informed that she could start her duties at the commencement of the following month. The appointment proved a great success, and for nearly a year Mr. Greatheart could never meet Mr. Osborn without having to listen to enthusiastic eulogies regarding Miss McIntyre's amazing tact, unusual abilities and strict attention to business. In fact, so overwhelming was his praise, that Mr. Greatheart could not help wondering whether Mrs. George Osborn's judgment of secretaries had not, on this occasion, proved faulty.

And then, one morning towards the latter part of September, Mr. Greatheart received an urgent summons to attend a special board meeting of the directors of Osborn Bros. Mr. Osborn opened the proceedings by informing Mr. Greatheart that for some months past some of them had felt doubtful regarding the honesty of Mr. Wilfrid Summerhaven, the manager of their Manchester branch, and in consequence it had been decided that Mr. Cullross, the director responsible for the Northern branches, should visit Manchester and Liverpool before proceeding to Edinburgh and Glasgow. This had been arranged, and during the past six weeks Mr. Cullross had conducted a very close investigation into the stock records and other matters connected with the company's business without, however, in any way arousing the suspicions of the manager.

In the meanwhile, he, Mr. Osborn, assisted by two of the junior directors of the company, had worked out a somewhat elaborate scheme, in the nature of a trap, which they thought might be tried out, with the object of testing the manager's honesty, should Mr. Cullross deem such a course desirable. Without waiting to receive from Mr. Cullross his official report on his investigation, they had dispatched this highly confidential document by registered post the previous afternoon; but, as a result of an unaccountable lapse on the part of Miss McIntyre, the envelope had been addressed, not to Mr. Cullross as intended, but to the manager. This dreadful mistake had been discovered by Miss McIntyre herself and immediately reported by her to Mr. Osborn.

She had woken up in the middle of the night with the uncomfortable thought that she might have misdirected the envelope, and an examination of the postage book that morning had confirmed her worst fears.

Another circumstance, which, though highly satisfactory from one point of view, in no way relieved the general embarrassment, was the receipt that morning of the official report from Mr. Cullross. He had been able to satisfy himself completely regarding all the matters which had created suspicion in their minds, and had convinced himself beyond all possible doubt regarding the absolute honesty of their manager.

Such was the story to which Mr. Greatheart listened on the morning of Thursday, September 17. The advice which he gave was that Mr. and Mrs. Osborn should withdraw to Eastbourne for a long week-end, and that they should all meet again on the following Tuesday morning, by which time they might be in a position to formulate a plan of action. He suggested that if, in the meanwhile, Mr. Summerhaven came up to London, Miss McIntyre should explain that the chairman had been called away on urgent business and would not be back in town before the middle of the following week. He emphasised the fact that the legal position was extremely delicate and that it would be essential to consult with Mr. Crawley, the solicitor, and later to seek the guidance of counsel.

Thus the meeting closed on a note of melancholy apprehension, and Mr. Osborn left for Eastbourne, feeling more like a criminal fleeing from justice than the chairman of a highly respected company.

Now Mr. Summerhaven, the manager of the Manchester branch, had received the incriminating document by the first post on the Thursday morning, and his feelings on perusing it may very easily be imagined. At any rate, he caught the 10.15 a.m. train to London and early that afternoon found himself at the head office of the company in Upper Thames Street. He was received, as arranged, by Miss McIntyre in her room next to that occupied by the chairman, and the interview lasted for more than three and a half hours. There was a further long interview the next morning and even then, instead of returning to Manchester for the week-end, he decided to remain in London.

On the Tuesday morning, Mr. Osborn, looking pale and haggard, entered his office at 9.30 a.m. precisely and was met by Miss McIntyre, who handed him a bulky foolscap envelope, which Mr. Summerhaven had left with her on the previous

Friday, with the request that it was not to be forwarded, but was to be deposited in the safe pending the chairman's return to the City.

Fully five minutes elapsed before Mr. Osborn could summon up the courage to break the red seal, but when he did so he read as follows:

GEORGE OSBORN, ESQ.,
23A, Upper Thames Street,
LONDON, E.C.   September 18.
SIR,

    The enclosed document reached me in Manchester yesterday morning, the 17th instant.

    As, however, it was clearly addressed to me in error, I hasten to return it to you herewith.

    It is, I hope, unnecessary for me to state that I have not retained a copy of the document.

I beg to remain, Sir,
Your obedient servant,
WILFRID SUMMERHAVEN.

Mr. Osborn's reaction, on reading this letter, was quite remarkable for a man of his unbending and puritanical character. He experienced a strong desire to dance round the room and simultaneously to chant the doxology. Restraining this unseemly impulse with an effort, he rang the bell for Miss McIntyre, and assuming as stern a visage as his feelings of thankfulness would permit, asked her whether she was acquainted with the contents of the envelope which she had handed to him. With a slightly flushed countenance, she replied in the affirmative; but when urged to give a detailed account of the interviews which she had had with Mr. Summerhaven, remarked that she had purposely avoided taking any notes. All that she could be persuaded to say further was that Mr. Summerhaven had unhesitatingly accepted her assurance that the directors no longer doubted his absolute honesty and that, for the rest, he had acted as she would expect any true gentleman to act in similar circumstances.

When Mr. Greatheart and Mr. Crawley arrived shortly and were informed of the totally unexpected development which had arisen, the question was raised as to what action the directors should take. The majority of those present were in favour of offering Mr. Summerhaven a cheque for a substantial sum, but Mr. Greatheart advised otherwise.

He argued that a man who had refrained from taking advantage of an opportunity so unparalleled would resent any offer of money, and suggested that a frank and manly apology by the chairman would constitute the only immediate reward that would prove completely acceptable.

A holograph letter was thereupon written by the chairman to Mr. Summerhaven, asking that gentleman to meet him on Thursday, the 24th, at 12 noon of the clock.

As he was leaving the office, Mr. Greatheart asked Mr. Osborn's permission to discuss this very interesting case with Miss McIntyre on some future occasion, as he felt there was perhaps more in it than met the eye. This permission was readily granted, and about a month later Mr. Greatheart found himself chatting with Miss McIntyre over a friendly cup of tea in her cosy little office. It is unnecessary to dwell on the conversation which ensued, except to recall one little feminine outburst on the part of Miss McIntyre in reply to a seemingly innocent remark, thrown out at a venture by Mr. Greatheart:

> " Of course he was very angry with them. They suspected him of being a thief and naturally he was very indignant, but that does not justify you in suggesting that he ever thought, for one second, of trying to blackmail them. Do you seriously suggest, Mr. Greatheart, that I would consent to marry a man who could sink so low?
> " Oh my gracious, what have I said ? "

Another form of fraud, which is often difficult and sometimes impossible for an auditor to detect where the internal check is weak, is that known as " Teeming and Lading."

These frauds involve the use of money received from one set of debtors to make good cash received from other debtors, which has been misappropriated. Constant adjustment as between various debtor accounts is thus inevitable, if the fraud is to remain undetected, and this should be impossible where an efficient system of internal control is in operation.

Loose-leaf ledgers often provide a valuable aid to the wrong-doer in this class of fraud, and the auditor should therefore endeavour to see that there is a strict control on the issue, from stock, of the loose leaves.

In practice, teeming and lading frauds must eventually be discovered internally, because, like systems of gambling which involve ever-increasing stakes, a limit is reached beyond which the system cannot easily be extended. In the meanwhile, however, the aggregate amount misappropriated may be considerable.

The accounts of charitable institutions offer considerable scope for making the contribution of one anonymous donor serve as an acknowledgment of similar contributions received from other anonymous donors. This is a form of " teeming and lading " and it is often necessary to suggest very special precautionary measures to guard against such frauds.

Another type of fraud involves the fraudulent use of chemical ink erasers, whereby the dates on documents may be altered, thus enabling them to be used as vouchers in support of fraudulent cash payments. The only effective safeguard against such frauds is the use of a machine which perforates the date of payment, and thus prevents an improper second use of the voucher.

Let us select from our notebook a simple example which illustrates the above remarks.

It causes us very deep distress to be forced to choose a case involving the misappropriation of ecclesiastical funds, but we have searched in vain for an equally convincing example dealing with secular funds.

Illustration five

The Rev. Stephen Collins was often heard to remark that whereas financially his labours were inadequately rewarded, spiritually they had been abundantly blessed.

He was wont to point, with undiluted thankfulness, to a small band of zealous lay-workers, headed by Mr. and Mrs. Samuel Bergler, who were ever ready and eager to perform tasks calculated to lighten the heavy burden carried by their dear vicar. Mr. Bergler in particular was regarded by Mr. Collins as a shining example of the ideal parishioner. Amongst other positions, he occupied that of treasurer of the church, and the enthusiasm with which he carried out his arduous duties won for him the wholehearted praise, not only of Mr. Collins, but also of the churchwardens. His accounts were prepared with meticulous care, and at the end of each year were audited by Sir Ambrose Whiting prior to submission to the parochial church council.

Apart from the main church account, there were numerous other subsidiary accounts, including the Church Restoration Fund, the Organ Fund, the Sunday School Fund, the Pew Rent Fund, the Church Missionary Fund, the Clergy Stipend Augmentation Fund, the Winter Relief Fund and several others. Each fund was a self-contained unit with a separate banking account, cash book, petty cash book, counterfoil receipt book, etc. The books were written up by Mr. Bergler in his best copperplate handwriting, and everything possible was done to simplify the work of the auditor, Sir Ambrose Whiting.

In fact, so easily and quickly did that gentleman complete the work, that he took the very next opportunity of informing

Mr. Greatheart that in his opinion auditing was mere child's play and that he was convinced that it must be far more profitable than banking. He inquired of Mr. Greatheart whether by any chance he was on the look-out for a young and energetic articled clerk, not more than seventy-five years of age, and, if so, what premium he would charge! In reply Mr. Greatheart congratulated him warmly on the rapidity with which, apparently, he had mastered the whole science of accounting, and stated that he would dearly like to be afforded an opportunity of studying his methods, at close quarters, on the occasion of the next audit of the church accounts. Sir Ambrose smilingly promised to give him this unique opportunity (realising that he would thereby be relieved of much tedious detail work) but suggested that neither Mr. Collins nor Mr. Bergler should be informed of this arrangement beforehand, as Mr. Greatheart was not *persona grata* with either of the gentlemen.

Ten months later Mr. Greatheart received a brief note from Sir Ambrose stating that he would expect to meet him at the house of Mr. Bergler on the following Thursday morning at 9.30 a.m. of the clock.

It is unnecessary to describe the elaborate programme of work which Sir Ambrose had drawn up and which was duly carried out. Everything, as usual, appeared to be perfectly in order and he had actually taken up his pen to append his signature as auditor to the various accounts, when Mr. Greatheart remarked that he would like to count the aggregate cash in hand on all the accounts, which, if his arithmetic were not faulty, amounted to £274 18s. 2d. Poor Mr. Bergler went white to his very collar stud, but pulling himself together with a supreme effort, said that he had produced the cash once and was quite certain that a gentleman of the standing of Sir Ambrose Whiting would not wish to trouble him to bring up all the separate petty cash boxes a second time from the safe on the ground floor. Mr. Greatheart replied to this little outburst by reminding him that the maximum sum in cash which they had counted at any one time was £34 8s. 4d., and as £274 18s. 2d. was a somewhat large sum to retain overnight in the house, he, at any rate, would like to satisfy himself that it was still intact. Sir Ambrose acquiesced, adding that the cash must be regarded as a single unit and checked as such.

Eventually Mr. Bergler had to admit that there was a grave shortage, and falling on his knees, begged Sir Ambrose not to ruin an unfortunate man who had found himself temporarily in financial difficulties. All the cash he could produce amounted to £37 2s. 8d., including a somewhat worn half-crown dated 1878, which Mr. Greatheart had noted very particularly as forming part of the balance contained in no less than seven of the individual petty cash boxes which had been produced for their inspection.

Mr. Greatheart then asked Mr. Bergler whether he had robbed the church of any further money, a question which occasioned a second outburst on the part of the unhappy man, and which even Sir Ambrose regarded as being unnecessarily cruel in the circumstances. Mr. Greatheart, however, produced from his pocket case five receipts for anonymous gifts of £1 each, and requested to be shown the particular counterfoil receipt book from which they had been detached, which had not been produced to them while conducting their audit.

At first Mr. Bergler declared that they were forgeries and that he had never seen the money; but when Mr. Greatheart informed him that these sums had been contributed, at his suggestion, many months previously by five of his friends, with a specific request that they should be entered in the list of donations as " anonymous contributions," and when, moreover, he produced the actual envelopes in which the receipts had been enclosed, bearing the names of his five friends in his, Mr. Bergler's, own handwriting, the guilty man collapsed for a second time. Notwithstanding the admission of guilt, it was some time before Mr. Bergler could be persuaded to produce the special counterfoil receipt book which he kept specially for the benefit of persons who contributed suitable sums anonymously. When, however, he did so, it became apparent that he had indulged in this form of petty fraud over a long period of years.

Mr. Greatheart then stated that he would retain all the vouchers and all the cash books, so that he might subject them to further scrutiny. This examination revealed the illuminating fact that several of the payments alleged to have been made during the current year were identical in amount with similar payments made during the preceding year, and inquiries at the shops in question established that the dates originally placed on the receipts had cleverly been altered by means of chemical ink erasers to enable the vouchers to be used a second time. On the preceding year's audit, Sir Ambrose had merely used an ordinary lead pencil for ticking.

The pew rent cash book also revealed irregularities going back several years.

Most of the regular church members paid their pew rents either quarterly or half-yearly; to save them the trouble of sending the money by post, special envelopes were provided and placed in the pews on the appropriate dates. The envelopes were then dropped into a special offertory box near the church door, and collected by the treasurer.

In order to test whether Mr. Bergler had accounted for all the pew rents actually received, Mr. Greatheart arranged for a printed slip to be sent to each seatholder in the name of Sir Ambrose Whiting, marked " For purposes of audit only," asking them to state:

(a) The amount of the annual pew rent payable—
(b) Whether payable quarterly or half-yearly—
(c) The date when the last payment was made,

with the further request that the slip, when filled in, should be returned to him in the enclosed, stamped envelope.

From the information thus obtained, Mr. Greatheart was able to prepare a complete pew rent register, and a comparison of this with the pew rent cash book revealed that a number of those who actually paid quarterly, were entered in the cash book as paying half-yearly only, and only half of the total amount received from these individuals was accounted for by Mr. Bergler. There was, of course, no fixed pew rent, the principle being to extract the biggest sum possible from each seatholder. The individual amounts therefore varied considerably.

When the Rev. Stephen Collins was informed that irregularities had been discovered, he could not credit his ears, and though terribly shocked at the very thought of any shortage in the cash, refused to believe that Mr. Bergler could be guilty not only of fraud, but worse still of sacrilege, and was convinced that a satisfactory explanation would be forthcoming. When, however, he was told that the fraud embraced not only the main church accounts and several of the subsidiary funds (including the Church Missionary Fund) but also the Pew Rent Fund, which formed part of his own stipendiary emoluments, his righteous wrath knew no limits, and he insisted that Mr. Bergler should be handed over forthwith to the regulators of the law. He also murmured something which sounded to Mr. Greatheart suspiciously like " liability of the auditor."

After Mr. Greatheart had completed his investigation and had ascertained, as accurately as circumstances would permit, the full extent of the defalcations, Sir Ambrose Whiting handed over a cheque for the full amount, with the exception of that portion applicable to the Pew Rent Fund. He resigned his position as auditor, and at the meeting of the parochial church council proposed a resolution whereby in future the accounts should be audited by professional accountants at a fee to be agreed. He further suggested that Mr. Greatheart should be asked to undertake the work, and although the resolution was bitterly opposed by the Rev. Stephen Collins, who exhibited unusual warmth on this occasion, it was carried by a substantial majority.

As he was leaving the church hall, Sir Ambrose whispered to Mr. Greatheart that he no longer experienced any desire to be articled to him.

It may be asked how it came about that Mr. Greatheart had requested each of his five friends to send a donation of £1 for the Church Missionary Fund, to be recorded in the printed list of donations as an anonymous contribution.

It was, of course, a shot in the dark, which on this occasion hit the mark. Mr. Greatheart argued that, at any rate, it was a cheap way of testing Mr. Bergler's honesty in the handling of £1 notes.

To be perfectly frank, Mr. Greatheart had never liked Mr. Bergler, who was reputed to suffer from dyspepsia and a catarrhal infection of the throat. He regarded him as a sanctimonious hypocrite, with a red nose and a gin-and-bitters cough.

And so we come to the end of another chapter.

If we have succeeded in convincing the young practitioner that the first duty of an auditor is to study the system of internal check, our object has been fulfilled. If, on the contrary, we have merely bored our readers with our constant re-iteration of the truism, we bow our heads in shame and accept the verdict of Cicero that:

" Old age is by nature somewhat talkative."

Let us by all means cultivate a sense of proportion, and end as we began by admitting that fraud is rare and that honest actions do not normally constitute " news."

If we suspect all men of being rogues because one dishonest man has robbed us, we shall be following in the footsteps of the Rev. Stephen Collins, who nowadays finds:

Tongues in trees, books in the running brooks,
Sermons in stones and FRAUD in everything.

Business Accounts and How to Read Them*

By Sir Thomas Keens

Professional accountant,
deceased, London

You will notice that our title is not " Balance-sheets and How to Read Them." That subject is important and might very well occupy our attention for an evening or more, but my own topic is even wider and therefore more difficult to compress.

Let us clear up at the outset a matter that is the source of a good deal of misunderstanding. You will hear all sorts of accounts loosely described as balance-sheets. Thus, when the Chancellor of the Exchequer makes his annual budget statement, the newspapers usually describe it as the annual balance-sheet—which, of course, it is not. The annual account of receipts and payments it may be, but it is certainly not a balance-sheet. What, then, is a balance-sheet? Strictly speaking, it is not an account at all, but a summary of the balances left on the books after the preparation of a profit and loss account. On the left-hand side it contains liabilities and capital, on the other side the assets, the balancing figure being the undistributed profit or accumulated loss.

Obviously, the purpose of the balance-sheet is to show the value of the undertaking to the proprietor or proprietors. That seems fairly simple, but in practice there are complications. Distinguishing, as we should, between fixed and floating assets, the valuation of the latter must, in the first place, be reasonably accurate. I use the word " reasonably " because every valuation, except that of actual cash, is in the nature of an estimate which may be falsified by the course of events. In some countries even the cash item is subject to the same conditions, but with our more stable system this risk may be disregarded. As to the fixed assets, these are usually stated on the basis of cost, less depreciation, no attempt being made to give the actual realisable value of these assets. The reason for this is that such assets are not primarily held for realisation, but really represent the machinery for creation of profits which will not be broken up

* *The Accountant*, June 15, 1935.

in the normal course of the business in its present form. Because of this system of valuing all fixed assets at cost, less depreciation, the question of depreciation is an important one, and it may also be desirable to make special appropriations in respect of obsolescence, particularly in good times. With these preliminary observations, we turn to the practical side of our talk together, although I shall have some remarks to make on the balance-sheets of public companies at the close of my address.

The usual method of approaching our subject is for the speaker to recommend, first, a preliminary survey of the practical side of the business in question; secondly, a detailed analysis of the profit and loss account in relation to turnover, and, lastly, a consideration of the balance-sheet items. On this occasion, however, I suggest that an alternative method of diagnosis should be followed, namely, that we should consider the various diseases with which a business may be afflicted, with particular reference to the ways in which the onset of these ailments will first be indicated in the financial records of the typical concern. In this way we shall be able to use our figures as they should be used, that is, not as dead records, but as living and growing guides to future policy.

I. *Turnover*

As we all know, the chief " killing disease " in the business world is declining sales. Although many of us are directors of industrial undertakings, it is not the primary task of an accountant as such to concern himself with management, and our sphere is thus usually confined to the early detection of elements of weakness which, if allowed to develop, may perhaps imperil the whole business. In the first place, then, it is necessary to keep a watch on the progress of sales month by month, or even day by day, so that we may know long before the end of the year what is the general trend of the business. For this purpose a graph of monthly sales is most useful, particularly if we show also the cumulative total to date and the moving annual trend, together with the corresponding curves for the previous financial period. In this connection, it is important to watch not only the value of sales but also the volume, since it is so easy to think that sales are increasing when all that is happening is that the selling price has risen. Our records should therefore include figures as to the number of units sold, and there should be available statistics as to changes in selling prices.

In some businesses it is very necessary to break up the sales figure between various departments or commodities, so that the individual trends may be seen. In laundry accounts, for example, one sometimes finds that a consistent total turnover may mask a decrease in fully-finished services which has been compensated for by increases in the machine-ironed services. This is important if one of the departments happens to be relatively more profitable than the other, as in this case. A further point in connection with sales is the standardisation of products, where substantial economies can sometimes be obtained without loss of output. We may also analyse sales under geographical areas, while watch may be kept on the number of new accounts opened. In some trades it is desirable to go a step further and see how our sales are comparing with the total output of the industry, if ascertainable, so that we can see whether we are holding our position in the trade. In the majority of industries the figures are not ascertainable, but at least we should have an approximate idea as to the general condition of the trade as a whole, so that we can form an opinion as to whether variations in our turnover are due to factors peculiar to our own business or to the locality, or whether similar variations are being experienced throughout the whole industry.

II. *Expenses*

The second chronic disorder is excessive expenses. How are we to tell from the accounts of businesses with which we are connected whether this is happening? There are perhaps three main tests:

(1) We can compare each item of expense in the profit and loss account with the corresponding figure for the past two, three or more years.

(2) Each item of expense may be expressed as a percentage of the sales total or as cost per unit.

(3) We may subject each item to a detailed analysis since, to quote Sir Josiah Stamp, "Economies . . . are only secured by an attack on a multitude of items of expenditure and a review of the simplest function. . . ." To take wages as an example, we should have figures relating to the numbers employed, the staff functions, the overtime charges, and the labour charges in relation to the turnover of each department.

In connection with this question of expenses, it is important that profit and loss accounts should be prepared at reasonably frequent intervals, so that excessive expenditure may be discovered at once and not lie undisclosed until the annual accounts are prepared. In all except the smallest businesses, monthly profit and loss accounts and cash summaries are of the greatest value, and here the benefits of recent developments in mechanical accounting are being mainly experienced.

III. *Working capital*

What is our next ailment? It is, I think, shortage of working capital. This is an ever-present danger which may come upon even a prosperous business quite unexpectedly, particularly in times of rapid expansion. How may we detect the preliminary symptoms so that the necessary arrangements may be made before the need for capital becomes urgent and dangerous? From our ordinary balance-sheet we can, of course, learn much by watching the ratio of current assets to current liabilities. If we find that year by year the item creditors is growing faster than the total of debtors, stock and bank balances, we may well suspect that before long the business will be short of working capital. It is also possible to have a graph prepared showing our total liquid resources each month as a guide to the most convenient times for capital developments, hire-purchase instalments, credit policy, purchases of stock and dividend payments. Further we can have before us each month a cash summary disclosing the disposal of our liquid resources. But, in addition, it is desirable that every large company or firm should prepare a budget of estimated receipts and payments for the next three, six or twelve months. The figures cannot, of course, be strictly accurate, but at least they can be intelligent anticipations, and the path before us will thus not be wholly uncharted and unconsidered. There can be no doubt but that the system of budgetary control is receiving more and more attention.

IV. *Stocks*

Closely allied to the question of working capital is the kindred problem of stock turnover. I need not say how essential it is for the health of every business that capital should not be locked up unnecessarily in stock, and the control of stock turnover rates is perhaps the most important element in the success of most manufacturing and distributing businesses. On this topic, it is not for an accountant to dogmatise, since the practical needs of a business are best known to those in intimate touch with its daily life, but there are certain types of records which may be of assistance to the managers of a business.

    (1) Following the technique of cost accounting, figures may be kept as to the turnover in each principal line of stock, so that purchasing policy may be guided accordingly.

(2) Graphs may be drawn showing monthly sales and purchases curves on one chart, so that the danger of making purchases far in advance of sales may be avoided.

(3) Over a period of years the annual rate of stock turnover may be closely watched. This figure is, of course, obtained by dividing the average stock total into the turnover (*i.e.*, sales at cost price) for the year. For example, if our average stock is £5,000 and our sales (reduced to cost price) total £50,000, we are turning over our stock ten times each year. If comparative figures are available for similar concerns in the same trade, a useful comparison may often be made.

V. *Debtors*

The next chronic disease with which we have to deal is the locking up of capital with " long-winded " debtors. Every business man has his own method of dealing with these troublesome people; and I need only suggest one or two financial indices which may sometimes be useful in this respect. In the first place, we can compute the average length of credit which is being allowed by dividing our sales figures by the average debtors' total. If, for example, we find that with sales at £100,000 per annum our debtors average £25,000, the average allowance of credit is one-quarter, *i.e.*, three months. Over a period of years some interesting trends may often be detected in this way. The second method is very simple, and consists of taking out the trial balance of debtors' ledgers in three columns, used respectively for debts not overdue, debts overdue up to three months, and debts overdue beyond that period. The poor payers are thus distinguished and our three separate totals give us some idea of the general position.

VI. *Plant*

There may be another unhealthy feature present in the accounts, concealed in that item " Machinery and Plant at cost, less Depreciation." How can we tell from our records whether excessive, over-valued, or obsolete plant is included? There is really no substitute here for practical knowledge of the details of production, but certain financial data are important. For example, we should have a plant register showing the cost of each item or class of item, and the depreciation written off thereon. We can also compare the value of production by a given plant in successive periods with the cost of that plant, and we can watch expenditure on repairs. It frequently happens, for example, that an old van is kept in use when a new van would fully justify itself by reduced charges for repairs, but here again practical knowledge is essential. Similarly the question of the general efficiency of the plant and the decision as to whether some machines shall be scrapped in favour of newer and more efficient ones is a matter for the management or proprietor. In my experience, the question of internal transport and hauling of goods is of the greatest importance. The difference in costs between an ill-designed and equipped factory or warehouse and one where the problem has had full consideration and suitable equipment provided is considerable.

VII. *Miscellaneous matters*

So much for the major items of business accounts. There are also a number of minor abnormalities, to one or two of which reference may be made. There is first that interesting wasting disease associated with the law of diminishing returns. Shortly, what happens is that a successful business goes on increasing year by year until one day it goes past its proper economic size and ever afterwards every successive " dose " of capital yields a less than proportionate return. Take the example of the laundry quoted above. You may find that after your turnover has gone past £500 a week you are getting increased, instead of diminishing, percentage costs, because of lengthening deliveries or increasing depot charges. How can we tell when the danger point is being approached, so that we can think about building a new laundry instead of enlarging the old one? In most cases we shall eventually have to prepare a detailed computation of standing and fluctuating charges, but there is one guide which can be used here with great advantage. It is this—what is the trend of net earnings expressed as a percentage of the true capital employed, *i.e.*, the total of share capital, reserves and profit-and-loss balance? The point about including reserves and profit-and-loss accounts balance with the capital is important, since if we are retaining money in the business in this way instead of paying it out in dividends, we ought to be earning something on it; if we are not, there is possibly something wrong, and it may be that this law of diminishing returns has commenced to operate.

The final trouble to which reference may be made is that of badly organised capital. The capital structure of a company may be unsatisfactory for many reasons, and it is only possible o lay down a few general rules:

(1) If the business is speculative, a large proportion of the capital ought normally to be in ordinary shares.

(2) Interest on debentures and other prior charges should not be unreasonably high.

(3) The terms of repayment on debentures and redeemable preference shares should be within the capacity of the company.

(4) Voting rights must be reasonable.

(5) The capital structure of the company must be sufficiently elastic to allow of future development; for example, by the issue of additional debentures, if new assets are acquired.

VIII. *The balance-sheets of public companies*

The question of capitalisation brings us finally to the published balance-sheets of large companies. So far we have dealt mainly with moderate-sized companies or businesses where we were in a position to obtain inside information; what of the large public company where we have only the published balance-sheet to guide us? At what factors should we look, for example, when we are thinking of buying shares on the Stock Exchange?

I suppose that we all look first at the general circumstances of the business in relation to such matters as management, possible markets, advertising policy, monopolies, possible competitors, substitutes, promotion profits, and the like. Then we turn to the last few annual reports, and look in particular at the following matters:

(1) The trend of disclosed profits.

(2) Dividend declarations and earnings retained in the business.

(3) The amount of liquid resources.

(4) The character of the company's investments, if disclosed.

(5) The net assets available for shareholders, excluding fictitious assets.

(6) The " gearing " of the capital, *i.e.*, what proportion of the total is in ordinary shares.

Let me emphasise, however, that in the purchase of shares for investment, the purchaser is buying income. It follows that the profit-and-loss account is more valuable as a guide than the balance-sheet. The profit-and-loss account should be a full statement of the company's activities; where it is not, the investor encounters serious difficulties. The best accountancy practice has always been in advance of legal requirements, and I have little doubt that the accounts of public companies would be more informative if the public would make up their minds that fuller information was really desirable and that they would support the auditor of a company on the occasions, happily rare, when he finds himself compelled to report specially to the shareholders.

The Interpretation of Accounts

By Bertram Nelson
F.C.A., Liverpool

I. THE PURPOSE OF ACCOUNTANCY

A LEADING article in *The Accountant*, after reviewing an address on factory accounts, concluded that, " the final accounts of a merchant are too often looked on by the accountant as a reflection of the *books*, whereas they should be a properly contrived representation of the *facts*."

You will appreciate where the essential distinction lies. Accounts, you will see, are to be regarded as a factor of control of present policy and not merely as a summary of past book-keeping entries. Three principles may be distinguished in this connection:

  (i) Accounts must keep pace with the business. For example, even in the case of small concerns, monthly or quarterly accounts are usually desirable, in addition to the annual financial statement.

 (ii) Accounts must adequately reflect the realities of the business: they must " strike below the surface." Thus in a trade where prices fluctuate violently, it may be expedient to include, in the accounts prepared for the management, figures as to the volume of sales as well as to their value.

(iii) As much attention must be given to the interpretation of accounts as to their preparation. In this connection, I believe that in many cases auditors would do well to supply not only a formal report on the accounts which they have examined, but also a more detailed memorandum, for the information of the management, on the trend of the business over a period of years and on elements of strength and weakness.

In illustrating these three principles, I want to talk more about methods of feeling the pulse of a living business than of post-mortem operations based on balance-sheets. Balance-sheets, you will appreciate, are in any case rather dangerous documents, since the position of a concern at the date of balancing may be wholly unrepresentative of its typical state: huge bank balances at December 31 may, at other times of the year, be sunk in stock which is only liquidated at Christmas, with a result that the balance-sheet at that date is quite unrepresentative of the average condition of the business. We start, therefore, with the trading and profit-and-loss accounts:

II. ACCOUNTS AS A MEASURE OF EFFICIENCY

Sales

The most exciting way of watching the progress of sales throughout a financial period is the " Z " chart. A single sheet of graph paper is used for three separate sales charts. The bottom line of the " Z " at the foot of the sheet is the graph of monthly sales, the middle line running from the bottom left-hand corner of the sheet to the top right-hand corner is the graph of cumulative sales, and the top line is the moving average trend chart. This moving average trend graph is really the most valuable part of the whole method, and it is quite simple to compute. For the year 19x7, for example, we should commence by taking the total sales for the twelve months to January 31, 19x7, to give us our January figure. For February, we should take this January figure, add on February 19x7 sales and deduct February 19x6, thus arriving at a total for the year to February 28, 19x7. Each month, in future, we should add on the new month's figure and deduct the sales for the corresponding month last year, thus eliminating seasonal fluctuations. The resultant graph shows the pulse-beat of a business extremely well, in a readily understood form.

It is often necessary, however, to go further than this and to trace variations in such items as—Sales classified by departments, commodities and geographical districts; sales per employee, per van, etc.; outstanding orders at the end of each month.

In considering sales, it is necessary to have regard to the volume as well as the value of turnover, so that due allowance may be made for price variations. Figures which may be of value here are—Total turnover in units (*e.g.*, tons or passenger miles); amount of average purchase per customer; changes in the prices of standard articles, expressed perhaps as an index which may be applied to total turnover to reduce sales over a period of years to a common basis.

Expenses

The first step in considering expenses is, of course, to arrange the trading or manufacturing account and the profit-and-loss account in a suitable functional order. We can then apply the following tests—

(a) The obvious method is to compare this year's figures with those of the previous few years, remembering that it is not sufficient to look merely at variations over two years. The ideal procedure is to take the totals of each group over as long a period as nine or ten years, so that the long-term trend may be appreciated.

(b) If there have been no great variations in prices or stock, it may also be useful to compare the ratio of the expenses items to sales, either by percentages or by the use of semi-logarithmic graph paper.

(c) Next, items may be analysed individually. Wages, for example, may be considered in the following ways: Numbers employed in each department, with particular emphasis on indirect labour; wages in each department, expressed as a percentage on turnover; overtime per department, per foreman, or per worker; labour turnover rate.

(d) Time does not permit us to consider standard costing methods, which are, of course, of growing importance in relation to the control of the expenses of a manufacturing business.

Net profit

We come now to the net profit. Here I want to draw your attention to a method exemplified in the following balance-sheets, covering a period of three years (000's omitted).

You will see that the business in question shows steadily increasing profits and has paid successive dividends of 6 per cent., 7 per cent., and 10 per cent. The position appears to be satisfactory, but let us apply the net profits test by working out the ratio of net profits to the average total capital employed, *i.e.*, the sum of share capital, reserves, and profit-and-loss account balances (the mean between the opening and the closing figures being taken each year). From the table at the foot of the balance-sheet, it will be seen that, in the first year, we earned 22·9 per cent. on the capital employed, but that, in the third year, the percentage was only 18·5 per cent., a serious deterioration. I shall refer later to the reasons for this decrease, but, meanwhile, would ask you to note the value of this method of expressing the net profit rate. Without this test, the deterioration in the position would have been masked by the large sums retained in reserves.

Other methods of testing the net profit figure are to work out

BALANCE SHEETS

						Year	
					1	2	3
					£	£	£
Current assets:							
Bank	..	..	..	..	18	8	10
Debtors	..	..	..	..	22	32	45
Stock	..	..	..	..	10	15	20
					50	55	75
Less Current liabilities:							
Creditors	..	..	..		52	61	83
Tax	..	..	..	..	4	6	7
					56	67	90
Net working capital		..	..		−6	−12	−15
Subsidiaries	..	..			50	50	50
Fixed assets:							
Plant	..	..			75	100	120
					119	138	155
Share capital, etc.:							
Ordinary shares	..	..		100	100	100	
Retained earnings	..	..			19	38	55
					119	138	155
Sales (credit)	..	..	..		200	208	216
Gross profit	..	..	..		67	69	72
Net profit	..	..	..		25	26	27
Dividend	..	..	..		6	7	10
Capital employed (average of opening and closing net assets)		..	..		109	128	146

RATIOS AND PERCENTAGES

			Year	
		1	2	3
Earnings:				
Gross profit: % of sales	..	33·3	33·2	33·3
Net profit: % of :				
Sales	..	12·5	12·5	12·5
Average capital employed	..	22·9*	20·3	18·5
Ordinary capital	..	25·0	26·0	27·0
Sales:				
Average credit allowed to debtors	..	1·0* month	1·6 months	2·1 months
Average stock turnover	..	17·7* times	11·1 times	8·2 times
Ratio of sales to average plant	..	3·2	2·4	2·0
Ratio of sales to average capital employed	..	1·8	1·6	1·5
Financial position:				
Ratio of current assets to current liabilities ..	.. ..	89·3%	82·1%	83·3%

* The year 1 figures assume:

	opening capital was	£100
	opening debtors ,,	12
	opening stock ,,	5
	opening plant ,,	50

the number of times the preference dividend and prior charges are covered, or to compute the percentage of profit going to each class of shareholders and to reserves. A careful watch should, of course, be kept on the trend of increases or decreases in net profits over a series of years.

Stock

Most successful businesses attach special importance to stock control. Detailed and continuous stock records are really essential as a basis of such control, but a rough check may be applied by working out the annual rate of stock turnover, *i.e.*, by dividing the total sales reduced to cost price by the average stock. In the example before you, it will be seen that the stock turnover rate, worked out in this way, has fallen from 17 to 8, this indicating that part of the deterioration already noted is probably due to excessive or obsolete stock. Another useful method is to prepare graphs showing monthly variations in stocks and sales, so as to reveal whether too large a stock is being carried in preparation for future sales.

Plant

Expenditure on plant may also be related to sales in the manner shown in the table above, the figures in that case indicating that the plant is increasing much more rapidly than sales. Statistical control, however, cannot in this case be a substitute for active and intelligent management.

Debtors

A parallel case arises as regards debtors, where the average term of credit may be calculated approximately by dividing sales for the period by the average amount of debts uncollected. A valuable subsidiary check is to take out the trial balance of the debtors' ledger in three columns, showing respectively debts not overdue, debts overdue up to three months, and debts overdue beyond that period.

III.   ACCOUNTS AS A GUIDE TO FUTURE POLICY

Future turnover

Business forecasting in practice depends upon an intelligent budget for a comparatively short future period of perhaps six or twelve months, based upon market surveys, past experience, and general business prospects. In addition, there is a tentative and experimental technique based upon the general theory of the analysis of a time series. Briefly, the sales of a business for the past twenty or more years are set out and then corrected for variations in prices. The resultant figures may be used to find two main factors:

(a) The long-term trend.

(b) Cyclical and irregular variations.

The long-term trend may be ascertained very approximately by a graph, moving averages, least-squares, compound interest curves, semi-averages or other mathematical devices, which defy short description. Having arrived at the trend, however, it will be seen that any excess or deficiency in our yearly figure over or below that trend represents the other factor—cyclical and irregular variations. In some cases, there is a pronounced cycle over perhaps nine years and future probabilities may be estimated in some degree on this method. The procedure is, however, very tentative and much reliance cannot usually be placed upon past experience as a guide to the future.

Expenses

In addition to the detailed survey of future expenses which is usually necessary, assistance may be obtained by the use of Gantt Charts, which may be employed with advantage where one wishes to watch the relationship between monthly budget estimates and actual expenditure.

DEVELOPMENT BUDGET (Small Business)

	Year		
	1	2	3
I. Normal increase in cash resources through profits			
Add Depreciation			
Deduct Income tax			
Dividends			
II. Present commitments:			
Hire-purchase instalments ..			
Increased credit to debtors ..			
Additional stock			
Repayment of bank overdraft			
Replacement of plant, vans, &c.			
III. Suggested essential developments: Machinery, plant, buildings, &c.			
IV. Balance: *Surplus* for development or *Deficit* to be met by bank overdraft, new capital, extended credit, &c.			

Maintenance of working capital

The next matter of importance is the maintenance of an adequate reserve of working capital. For small businesses, a sufficient test will be imposed by a computation on the lines of the Development Budget shown on page 495.

A more detailed treatment may, however, be necessary in certain cases, particularly in a hire-purchase business. One method is shown below.

Estimate of Working Capital Requirements

(manufacturing company selling on hire-purchase terms)

	Jan.	Feb.	Mar.	Apr.	May	June	July	Aug.	Sept.	Oct.	Nov.	Dec.
1. Estimated number of machines sold	10	10	15	20	40	50	60	20	40	40	50	30
2. Payments:	£	£	£	£	£	£	£	£	£	£	£	£
Works cost..	100	90	140	190	350	440	530	200	360	360	440	280
Administration, &c.	100	100	100	100	120	120	120	120	120	120	120	120
Selling	50	50	70	80	100	100	100	60	60	60	60	60
Collection and bad debts	—	—	30	40	50	60	60	70	60	60	60	60
Total	250	240	340	410	620	720	810	450	600	600	680	520
3. Receipts:												
Cash sales	40	40	60	80	160	200	240	80	160	160	200	120
Credit collection	—	30	70	120	180	300	450	640	700	820	950	1,080
Total	40	70	130	200	340	500	690	720	860	980	1,150	1,200
4. Deficit: (Initial circulating capital needed)	210	170	110	210	280	220	120					
Surplus								170	260	380	470	680
5. Cumulative deficit	210	380	490	700	980	1,200	1,320	1,150	890	510	40	(+640)

In this estimate, it will be seen that the maximum is reached in the seventh month of trading, when £1,320 is needed. This figure is therefore the working capital required.

Finally, useful guidance may be obtained by comparing the ratio of current assets to current liabilities over a series of years, any deterioration in this respect being, of course, a danger sign.

Financial policy

In conclusion, it may be added that, in most businesses, it is desirable to prepare a graph showing monthly bank balances for guidance in such matters as the purchase of new plant, the fixing of dividend dates, stock purchasing, and credit policy.

All these tests will probably appear to you to be very complicated. Let me therefore suggest that one of the best ways of testing their utility is to apply them to some business with which you are closely connected, and to concentrate each month on one specific aspect of the accounts, so arranging your programme as to cover all the points during the course of the year. At each monthly meeting there should, of course, be the " Z " chart, showing the progress of sales, together with a monthly profit-and-loss account and a cash statement. When these have been considered, you can next turn to some item selected for special consideration. In January, for example, it may be wages analysis, in February sales, and in March debtors. In this way the interest of clients may be maintained, and the accounts may become the flexible instrument of interpretation which they should properly be in the hands of the accountancy profession.

Financial Statements for Published Reports[*]

By William Blackie

C.A., Vice-President,
Caterpillar Tractor Company, Illinois.

This article was first published in 1947, with the 1946 statements of
Caterpillar Tractor Co. as illustration. The article and company
report had considerable influence in developing the modern form
of report. Some recent comment by Mr. Blackie is now inserted (*in
italics*), and the company's 1960 figures are here used as illustration.
—*Editors.*

Introduction

This article presents a summary of the considerations underlying the form and terminology of the financial statements of
Caterpillar Tractor Co., as contained in the annual report. It
is prompted by the fact that innovations in the company's financial
statements, particularly in 1944, attracted considerable attention
and have been acknowledged as an influence upon revised forms
adopted by many other companies in their published reports.
This being the case, it seemed appropriate to make public the
thinking behind the actions of Caterpillar Tractor Co., thereby
providing opportunity for those who may wish it to disagree,
to agree, or preferably to improve upon the efforts of that
company.

In this way there may perhaps be developed a greater
uniformity of expression among reporting companies, to the end
that financial statements which purport to convey approximately the same information do so in approximately the same
way. The general reader should not be confronted with major
differences of form or terminology which do not reflect material
divergencies in substance; and although Caterpillar Tractor Co.
is itself creating some of these present differences in form and
terminology, it is doing so in a sincere belief that the purposes
of financial statements can be better served by some departures
from traditions which do not seem to have been very successful.
It is hoped that other companies and their professional accountants
will go on to develop the subject further.

[*] Published in the *Journal of Accountancy*, March 1947.

Grateful acknowledgment is made to the company's independent public accountants and to George O. May for their helpful interest in these efforts to carry out a thought which Mr. May himself expressed many years ago: " There is no need to revolutionize or even to change materially corporate accounting; but there is room for great improvement in the presentation of the conclusions to which accounts lead. The aim should be to satisfy (so far as is possible and prudent) the investor's need for knowledge, rather than the accountant's sense of form and respect for tradition."

Historical background

In accordance with the by-laws of Caterpillar Tractor Co., it is a duty of the directors " to present at each regular annual meeting of the shareholders, a full statement or statements showing in detail the assets and liabilities of the corporation and generally the condition of its affairs." With these words fresh in mind, the company's first annual report, for the year 1925, presented (1) a balance-sheet with independent accountants' opinion thereon, (2) about 500 words of comment, and (3) a list of the directors and officers. It complied fully with the spirit and intent in which the by-laws were written, and it was typical of the times.

In 1929, when the company had acquired a few years of background, there were added to the report (4) a historical summary of the balance-sheets at the end of each year, (5) a comparative statement of income and expense, (6) an analysis of surplus account since inception, (7) a dividend history, and (8) a listing of the gross addition to plant and equipment during each year. This was the first time our shareholders had been given an opportunity to see a statement of operations or to reconcile the changes in surplus account from year to year. The merits of such a development were, however, quickly apparent. Each year thereafter the historical summaries were expanded to include another year; but until 1937 the reports remained somewhat terse and visually rather unattractive.

By 1937 business was again on the upgrade, but the intervening depression years had brought about many changes. The greatest of these was, perhaps, in the mode of thinking of a large proportion of the population which had either suffered from economic distress or from the fear of it. In such circumstances there was naturally some doubt about the efficiency of the private-capital-enterprise system, and in such a state of mind there were fertile opportunities for the culture of new ideas which might somehow seem to promise something better. In economic thinking, there developed the idea that man might become master of his economic destiny if he could shape the course of events rather than be shaped by them.

The idea, of course, is one which should be pursued—and maybe, someday, progress will be recorded. The missionaries who had been saving us from ourselves had (and have), however, left us not only with all the old troubles but also with some new ones. With the prospect of a return to better times, there arose a tidal wave of labor disputes. In 1937, for the first time in its history, the operations of Caterpillar Tractor Co. were shut down by a strike.

In the battling out of these labor disputes, on both the national and local fronts, the employee became the target of a verbal barrage which hit from all directions. Labor's main objective was organization, and it fired with a rifle while industry spattered back with the less penetrating buckshot of economic fact. In the words of one Josh Billings it became apparent that: " It ain't ignorance that causes so much trouble; it's folks knowing so much that ain't so."

These events naturally impressed upon industrial management the need for a greater understanding of the private-enterprise system and of the part played in competitive capitalism by each unit of business. There followed, just as naturally, a realization that published company reports could be made to serve a broader purpose than had previously been the case. To achieve increased effectiveness they would, however, have to be made more attractive, not only to shareholders but also to employees and the public at large. They would first have to be opened and then read. The Caterpillar annual report for 1937 was, therefore, expanded from the previous 6 x 9 inch, 10 page, collection of words and figures, to an attractive 8 x 11 inch, 22 page, arrangement of data and comment with graphic and pictorial illustrations. For the first time the report was addressed to both shareholders and employees and was furnished to every employee of the company. It was also furnished to the members of what are deemed to be the opinion-forming groups in communities near our plants.

With this broader approach to the use and function of the annual report, there arose a need not only to glamorize the report and popularize the comment, but also to present the financial information in such a way as to evidence the genuine desire to disclose more fully and to explain more clearly. In an effort to achieve this, the formal or conventional financial statements for 1937 were supplemented by what were called " explanatory " statements of (1) assets and liabilities, and (2) income, expenses, profits, and dividends, in which the conventional accounting titles for the various items were expanded in descriptive comment to indicate in more everyday language the nature or content of the item.

At that time, major consideration was given to the matter of terminology, but it was also recognized that there was need for an improvement in form. The explanatory balance-sheet at the end of 1937 was, therefore, presented in a single-column form in which liabilities were deducted from assets. The explanatory income statement for that year also presented a variation from conventional form in that all costs and expenses were deducted from all income to arrive at an amount which was described as: " a balance which was retained in the business and used for expansion of employment during the year."

The reports for the next six years carried further refinements of the ideas developed in 1937, and continued to receive wide acclaim. The approval came, however, largely from accountants and other businessmen. While we thought we had made a little progress, we were not satisfied that we were reaching the mass audience which was our main objective. In preparing for the 1944 report, we therefore again made a major reappraisal of the problem.

The problem

Primarily, our job was to make the *results* of a somewhat technical process reasonably intelligible to an ordinary citizen who was neither blessed nor handicapped with any special training. But note that we were concerned with the *results* rather than the process. The art of accounting did not, therefore, have to be obscured by the technique of bookkeeping. To be sure, the beauties of any form of art can best be understood in the light of technical knowledge of the process by which it is produced; but a high degree of appreciation and attraction can, nevertheless, be experienced by those who lack the technical background but still have ears to hear and eyes to see.

These, then, were not to be statements of accountants by accountants for accountants. They were to be plain statements of informed opinion, uncompromising in their truthfulness— which, for this particular purpose, means that, within the limits of accepted accounting principles and of our very human abilities, they were to rest on judgments and estimates divorced of fancy and prejudice. And where such a presentation might possibly be misleading (as is always possible even with informed opinion and intellectual integrity), there would have to be clarifying interpretation. Without sacrificing any of these great attributes for mere popularity, the statements also had to be stripped of distracting trivia, confusing " prescription " language, and diverting complexity of form. There would be no purpose in giving the drivers of the economic train a power plant so complicated that absorption with the gadgets would leave no opportunity for a look at the tracks.

The statements were, furthermore, to bear the stamp of approval of independent accountants, whose audit would embrace underlying detail which, although essential to the determination of totals, need not be shown in the published statements. The purpose of such independent examination and opinion was, of course, to give assurance that, subject to the usual proper qualifications in the opinion, the statements were fairly presented.

At the same time we wished, if possible, to eliminate the somewhat embarrassing admission of deficiency implied by our use of *two* statements—the one conventional and the other explanatory. So we set about trying to compile a single set of financial statements which would be accounting-wise proper, and yet readily convey to the lay reader a reasonably correct comprehension of just what the statements were meant to convey.

And what were the statements meant to convey? We thought we knew. Colloquially:

    (1) How are we doing?—in terms of
        (a) What did we get in?
        (b) What did we do with it?
        (c) What's left?
        (d) How is it left?
    (2) Is that good or bad?
and, these being relative terms, we interpolate—
    Is that better or worse?—
so that those who choose to do so might possibly guess at a conclusion—
    (3) Where do we go from here?
We had therefore not only to give the facts, but to give them in such a way as would help the adolescent reader view them with a sense of proportion and perspective.

In approaching the problem, it was natural that we should attempt to appraise, first, those matters which seemed to give the general reader the most difficulty. In this connection, I use the word " seemed " because we have found it very difficult to obtain from those without some accounting training a reasonably clear understanding of just where the troubles lie. This, of course, is to be expected. We nevertheless gathered some fairly definite impressions: that one of the troubles with the balance-sheet was that it balanced, that something called " surplus " was plugged in to make it balance, that " capital " was grouped with the liabilities rather than with the assets, that reserves did not seem to be reserves in the usual sense of the word.

The statement of financial position

With these points for a start, we tried to place ourselves in the position of the untrained reader looking in, rather than the trained accountant looking out. The fundamental difference seemed to be that while the latter knew his debits from his credits, the former was blissfully ignorant of such subtle distinctions. Double entry—which, as a mode of thinking, is perhaps the trained accountant's greatest asset—had created an equation which could only puzzle the layman left to wonder why the sum of the things on the left was always the same as the sum of the things on the right. His own affairs, he hoped, would never get into such a sorry state of unprogressive equilibrium. But trial-balance thinking did not have to be extended from the general ledger to the published financial statements; and the general public did not have to be subjected to the seductive technicalities of the system. So we attempted to destroy some of the undue influence which double-entry bookkeeping has had upon the presentation of results (and upon financial accounting as a whole) by adopting a single-column form, in which liabilities were deducted from assets to arrive at the total owner capital invested in the business. This form (modified slightly over the ensuing years) is shown at Statement 2 of the report (page 504).

By this change of form, we killed two or three birds and cut a couple of Gordian knots. Surplus and capital were still there, but they no longer arose like a black-market thumb to balance the scales.

First of the questions prompted by this arrangement was whether all the liabilities should be deducted from all the assets, or whether there should be an intermediate step—not only to recognize the conventional segregation of so-called current assets and current liabilities, but also to place these two groupings in juxtaposition. In favor of the " total " treatment was its greater simplicity. This method would also have been more consistent with the " going-concern " basis upon which the statements are presented, since it would not have involved a somewhat artificial distinction between deferred charges for inventories and for plant and equipment—neither of which can have any going-concern utility without the other. Use of the " total " treatment would, furthermore, have permitted ready avoidance of labels such as " current," " net current " or " working "—with their counter-implications that items not so described were perhaps lower on the scale of accounting worthiness.

STATEMENT 2

CONSOLIDATED FINANCIAL POSITION DECEMBER 31, 1960

Current assets:
Stated on basis of realizable values:

Cash	$ 17,380,257	
Receivable from customers and others	66,938,553	
	84,318,810	
Stated on basis of cost using principally " last-in, first-out " method:		
Inventories	227,116,780	
		$311,435,590
Deduct: Current liabilities:		
Notes payable to banks by:		
Parent company	51,000,000	
Foreign subsidiaries	25,268,302	
Payable to material suppliers and others	54,770,482	
United States and foreign taxes based on income	26,275,467	
		157,314,251
Net current assets (statement 5)		154,121,339
Bond discount and expense, etc.—cost allocable to future operations		3,050,118
Buildings, machinery and equipment—balance of original cost allocable to future operations (statement 7)		264,145,086
Land—at original cost		10,017,610
Investment in Caterpillar Credit Corporation (at cost, plus retained profit. See notes)		8,846,857
Patents, trade-marks and other intangibles—at nominal amount		1
Total assets less current liabilities		440,181,011
Deduct:		
Notes payable—3⅜%, due 1964–1972	35,000,000	
Debentures—4½%, due 1962–1977	65,000,000	
		100,000,000
Net assets		$340,181,011
Ownership:		
Preferred stock—4·20% cumulative:		
178,595 shares of $100 par value		$ 17,859,500
Common stock:		
27,172,968 shares of no par value	$125,296,260	
Profit employed in the business	197,025,251	
		322,321,511
		$340,181,011

See notes on page —

Editors' note: Statement 6 gives the same figures, along with those of the three preceding years.

Nevertheless, we adopted the alternative treatment whereby the conventional current items were grouped, and a balance struck, to arrive at what we first called " working capital " but now prefer to describe as " net current assets " (because the earlier term was more a definition than a logical derivative of the process). The complication, we felt, was not too great for most of those who might attempt to understand the statement; and such treatment would, presumably, be helpful to accountants, bankers, investment analysts, and others in the habit of thinking in terms of " current " relationships. Loan agreements and other credit instruments commonly called for the maintenance of net current assets as determined in accordance with accepted accounting principles which had not (yet) rejected the " current " classifications. This method, furthermore, lent itself to a comparative summary in which the changing relationships were brought out more clearly than would otherwise be the case.

In this part of Statement 2 it will also be observed that we adopted a somewhat unusual presentation to bring out the differing bases upon which the assets have been valued. While the statement of financial position reflects useful totals, it should nevertheless be thoroughly understood that these totals are composed of elements which are not homogeneous. Recognition of this fact is, in our opinion, fundamental to any proper interpretation of the statement, and it is particularly important that lay readers realize the limited extent to which current realization or replacement values find a place among the conventional and historical bases for asset accounting. We have, accordingly, shown the cash items and receivables on the basis of " realizable values," thereby defining that particular realm of thought, and at least creating the presumption that the things outside such limits are stated on some other basis.

In the earlier presentation, inventories were " Stated on basis of approximate cost or market, whichever lower." Since then the impacts of inflation and income taxation have had their proper influence upon accounting enlightenment, and inventories are now " Stated on basis of cost using principally ' last-in, first-out ' method."

Before leaving the current position, it might be well to comment on the matter of inventories, on which we were taken to task in one of the accounting periodicals. We had not disclosed the all-revealing secrets of the segregation of raw materials, work-in-process, and finished goods. In our inventories, we have scrap metal and pig iron with which to make our own grey-iron castings; we have also purchased castings and forgings which are machined through two to twenty operations to produce piece parts; we have purchased steel in bars, channels, strips, shapes and sheets which are cut, stamped, welded into other forms; we have purchased finished parts which may be either incorporated in assemblics or sold individually as replacement parts. Where does " raw " become " in-process " or " finished "? We do not know—and unless the reader is cognizant of whatever classification we might happen to choose to adopt, how could any portent of the segregation be appraised? Furthermore, for purposes of operating management, we do not think we need the segregation badly enough to warrant the cost of evaluating the many thousands of requisitions effecting transfers between the usual inventory subdivisions. (Instead, we have what we find to be much more useful—a segregation of material, labor, and manufacturing overhead in inventory.)

Continuing with Statement 2, our treatment (or mistreatment) of depreciation is perhaps of interest. We wished, first, to avoid the words " reserve " and " depreciation," each of which has in accounting a specialized meaning not likely to be apparent to the uninitiated. In ordinary language, a reserve is something stored or held back for future use (like nuts in a squirrel's nest)— and to leave anyone with the impression that a reserve for depreciation conforms to that definition is to mislead. " Depreciation " also is a misnomer. In the colloquial sense, it relates to a lessening of value without regard to cause. Our method of computing depreciation—that most generally used throughout industry— made no attempt to measure changes in value or degrees of physical exhaustion within an accounting period. We merely distributed in a systematic manner the cost of the facilities over the number of accounting periods for which the facilities might reasonably be expected to have an effective service life. The process was clearly one of allocation and not of valuation.

So we term the annual charge: " portion of cost (of facilities) allocated to operations " (Statement 1, page 513), and the reserve: " portion of cost allocated to operations to date " (Statement 7). And since this latter exhibit gives the details, we deem it better to show in the statement of financial position only the net balance of " cost allocable to future operations." Statement 7 gives the major classification details necessary to a reasonable understanding of the subject.

STATEMENT 7

CONSOLIDATED BUILDINGS, MACHINERY AND EQUIPMENT AT DECEMBER 31

	1960	1959	1958	1957
Original cost:				
Buildings	$146,904,927	$133,532,480	$122,176,724	$113,890,334
Machinery and equipment	246,281,876	209,821,563	175,934,995	152,439,880
	393,186,803	343,354,043	298,111,719	266,330,214
Deduct:				
Portion of original cost allocated to operations to date shown:				
Buildings	27,696,318	22,410,760	17,640,408	21,701,924
Machinery and equipment	101,345,399	80,022,045	69,752,487	60,193,490
	129,041,717	102,432,805	87,392,895	81,895,414
Balance of original cost not allocated to operations to date shown (statement 6):				
Buildings	119,208,609	111,121,720	104,536,316	92,188,410
Machinery and equipment	144,936,477	129,799,518	106,182,508	92,246,390
	$264,145,086	$240,921,238	$210,718,824	$184,434,800

Note: Whenever the cost of any unit of buildings, machinery and equipment has been fully allocated to operations, such cost is eliminated from the accounts.

In a fine shading of semantics, we believe that, by the use of " cost allocated," we have lost none of that idea of an orderly, rational method which accountants have thought (or hoped) was conveyed by the word " depreciation."

Under the impact of rapidly changing price levels, Caterpillar, like many other forethinking companies, became more acutely aware of the dangerous distinction between provisions for depreciation based upon original costs, and the need to preserve capital investment and earning capacity by replacing " fully depreciated " assets at much higher costs. Neither those in power in professional accounting nor income taxation were, however, prepared to face up to the seriousness of the matter, and to appreciate the significance of both accounting and taxation as more than processes of reporting or collecting—the former traditionally in mere bookkeeping measures expressed as money; the latter, as always, in real, hard currency. As a " disclosure " which might, at least, draw attention to this query in acceptance of a practice held to be " in conformity with generally accepted accounting principles," Caterpillar qualified

the word " cost " by prefacing it with the adjective " original."
Caveat investor!

This brings us, in Statement 2, to the sum of net current assets plus other assets—before deducting long-term liabilities—and we confess failure to reach any happy expression which would seem to describe this balance more aptly than no description at all. (*This failure gnawed sufficiently to produce in later years a current usage of " total assets less current liabilities." The need for help is still felt.*) With a call for help we will, therefore, pass on to the net difference between all assets and all liabilities—and how to label it. To describe it as capital stock plus surplus would defeat our entire purpose, and would smack of alchemy. Net worth, a value concept, was of course unacceptable. So, having revised our thinking to favor " net current assets " for the description of that balance, we concluded that the final balance could best be described as " net assets "—a term which would seem to be reasonably understandable to most people who have both possessions and creditors.

And whence did these good things come? From contributions received from shareholders and from profit not disbursed as dividends. So, in selecting a phrase to lead the reader from the net assets to their source of origin, we resisted temptations towards " evidenced by " or " represented by " in favor of " derived from " capital stock and profit. In doing so, however, we realized that we were adopting terminology which could not be universally applicable—as, for example, when profits have been incorporated into legal capital by stock dividend or other appropriate action. We were not, therefore, wholly happy with our solution, even though it was applicable in our particular case.

In preparing the statements for 1947 the matter was, accordingly, given some more consideration, as a result of which " source of net assets " emerged as the most appropriate phrase to convey the idea of derivation from contributory sources and, at the same time, be consonant with a title which had been chosen for the analysis of capital stock and retained profit. *Then, in 1949, this title gave way to " ownership equities "—for reasons which, on later thought, were deemed to be in conflict with the original intention to avoid esoteric terminology. So, in 1957, the equity accounts were collected under the one heading: " Ownership."*

At this point, it may be of interest to note that our 1944 restudy led us to a stronger recognition of the fact that, in our position, a paid-in capital surplus was not wholly compatible with a common stock " without nominal or par value." By appropriate action early in 1945, paid-in surplus was, accordingly, transferred to common stock account—with hygienic benefits upon the whole presentation.

Later introduction of a preferred stock required that the original capital stock be distinguished as " common." At the time of this change, the common shares were given a par value of $10 in order to reduce the federal tax levied upon the proceeds of sale of shares which, if they had no par value, were then deemed for such tax purposes to have a nominal value of $100. This unprincipled flaw in federal taxation has since been remedied by levying the tax upon market rather than nominal values, and unpenalized freedom was thereby restored to take advantage of the American concept of shares without par value. The appropriate reversion was duly made in 1959, and recognition was then given to our idea that paid-in capital of any kind should be incorporated in equity capital represented by shares of no par value.

The beneficial effect of this simplification is perhaps best illustrated in Statement 3; and it might be worth drawing attention to the easy distinction now possible between capital obtained through the contribution of cash or other assets, and capital derived from retained earnings, including appropriations into formal capital.

For our purpose, the term " surplus "—even if " earned "— was thoroughly objectionable. As far as possible we intended to use words in their popular everyday meaning and, despite its special accounting connotation to the initiated few, " surplus " inevitably conveyed to the general reader the idea of too much, more than enough, a lot of corn in a lot of bins, or left-over war material. In search for a substitution, thoughts naturally turned to such alternatives as " undistributed profits " and " profit invested in the business." " Undistributed," however, seemed to convey an idea that maybe the profits would be distributed— when, of course, they could not be; and " invested " seemed to create a possible question of purchase or other acquisition of capital stock—a common implication of the term. " Reinvested " we rejected since it seemed merely to compound the trouble over " invested " by raising a time element. " Kept " had perhaps only the disadvantage that it was too crudely simple; " left " had a strong appeal; and " held " seemed to be more acceptable when it was spelled " retained." So we used " retained "— until we encountered sufficient objections from our " relations " people, who thought that the term failed to connote the " putting to use " inferred by " invested." So we changed to " employed."

STATEMENT 3
OWNERSHIP

CAPITAL STOCK, PREFERRED

Year			Total in capital accounts
1949	Sold 250,000 shares, $100 par value, for cash	$ 25,000,000	
1951–60	Retired 71,405 shares	7,140,500	$ 17,859,500

CAPITAL STOCK, COMMON

Year		Number of shares	Amount paid in for stock	Profit employed in the business incorporated in capital accounts	Total in capital accounts
1925–26	Issued at incorporation for net assets of predecessor companies	1,625,000(1)	$ 12,320,380	$ —	$ 12,320,380
1928	Issued for net assets of Russell Grader Manufacturing Company	86,127	2,518,416	—	2,518,416
1929	Sold for cash	171,113	8,305,981	—	8,305,981
	Balance	1,882,240	23,144,777	—	23,144,777
1949	Exchange of two shares of $10 par value common for each share of no par common	1,882,240	—	14,500,023(2)	14,500,023(2)
	Balance after stock split	3,764,480	23,144,777	14,500,023	37,644,800
1951	Issued for entire capital stock of Trackson Company	54,000	2,202,000	—	2,202,000
1952–55	Sold under stock option plan	38,372	1,743,609	—	1,743,609
1953–54	Issued as 4% stock dividends	311,785		16,932,671(3)	16,932,671(3)
	Balance	4,168,637	27,090,386	31,432,694	58,523,080
1955	Issued one additional share for each share outstanding	4,168,637	—	24,849,660(2)	24,849,660
	Balance after stock split	8,337,274	27,090,386	56,282,354	83,372,740

Year	Item	Shares	Amount	Incorporated in capital accounts	Amount at end of period
1955–59	Sold under stock option plan	192,038	7,395,376		
1956	Sold for cash	500,000	33,175,000		
1956	Issued for entire capital stock of Englehart Manufacturing Company	20,000	1,017,849		
	Balance	9,049,312	68,678,611	56,282,354	124,960,965
1959	Exchange of three shares of no par value common for each share of $10 par value common	18,098,624			
	Balance after stock split	27,147,936	68,678,611	56,282,354	124,960,965
1959–60	Sold under stock option plan	25,032	335,295		335,295
		27,172,968	$69,013,906	$56,282,354	125,296,260

PROFIT EMPLOYED IN THE BUSINESS

Year	Profit	Appropriations — Dividends	Incorporated in capital accounts	Amount at end of period
1925–56	$387,925,561	$197,885,210	$56,282,354	$133,757,997
1957	40,012,023	22,453,965	—	151,316,055
1958	32,239,831	22,492,024	—	161,063,862
1959	46,517,987	25,213,575	—	182,368,274
1960	42,580,335	27,923,358	—	197,025,251
	$549,275,737	$295,968,132	$56,282,354	197,025,251

Source of net assets (statement 2) $340,181,011

(1) At incorporation, 260,000 shares of common stock were issued for net assets of predecessor companies. In February 1926, those shares were increased to 325,000 shares by a five for four stock split effected in the form of a 25% stock dividend. In December 1926, a conversion of five shares for one share increased the issued shares to 1,625,000.

(2) Excess of par value of shares outstanding after stock split over amount carried in capital accounts prior to the stock split.

(3) Market value of stock at date issued as 4% stock dividends in 1953 and 1954.

And having done these things to the old balance-sheet, we decided we should no longer call it a balance-sheet. We recognized, of course, that the term had become somewhat institutionalized to connote a financial summary of assets and liabilities even without the balancing feature; and we realized also that, while we had eliminated one equation, we had set up another in showing that " net assets " constituted an accounting for, and was therefore *equal to*, share capital plus profit employed in the business. Nevertheless, we felt that we had departed sufficiently from the conventional form to warrant departure from the conventional title—and that, in any case, the term " balance-sheet " could be improved upon.

We first ruled out " condition " in a possible title for the statement—on the grounds that it conveyed ideas of realizable value and, possibly, liquidation. This left us with " position " as the best alternative we could think of—and recalled to mind that several years ago the public accounting profession had standardized on that description in its opinions on corporate statements. At the same time the profession had discontinued use of the qualifying adjective " financial "—on the grounds, I believe, that it was thought to be a factor contributing to the fallacy that the balance-sheet presented realizable values. Nevertheless, we felt that the title would not be as helpfully descriptive if the adjective were omitted and we, therefore, adopted " financial position."

We have recently received an interesting suggestion favoring " accounting position." Some consideration might also be given to the idea of " statement of stewardship " or " stewardship position."

The statement of operations

Turning next to the statement of operations, we decided that our former practice of deducting the separate elements of cost and expense to arrive at a series of consecutive sub-totals was not only arithmetically confusing but tended to convey an erroneous impression as to their incidence and importance. In all our thinking, we proceeded from the premise that the presentation was to reflect a " going-concern " basis; and this being the case, there could be no question regarding the relative necessity of the expenditures, since they were all to be deemed equally necessary for the operation of the business and all deductible from income before arriving at any figure which could be considered to be profit. We therefore deducted a total of all costs and expenses from sales income, to arrive at profit for the year as shown in the statement of operations for the year—Statement 1 in the set of financial statements accompanying this article.

In approaching this phase of the problem, we attempted to make such a presentation as we thought would be most helpful to most readers; and we felt that this could best be achieved if we were to follow natural, homogeneous classifications applicable as far as possible to both the peanut vendor and the billion-dollar corporation. Thus we show one total of all materials, supplies and services purchased, and another total for all

STATEMENT 1

CONSOLIDATED RESULTS OF OPERATIONS YEAR 1960

Sales		$716,038,220
Costs:		
Inventories brought forward from previous year	$206,372,118	
Materials, supplies, services purchased, etc.	383,502,386	
Wages, salaries and contributions for employee benefits	244,041,656	
Portion of original cost of buildings, machinery and equipment allocated to operations (depreciation and amortization)	28,314,300	
Interest on borrowed funds	7,454,938	
United States and foreign taxes based on income	31,352,201	
	901,037,599	
Deduct: Inventories carried forward to following year	227,116,780	
Costs allocated to year		673,920,819
		42,117,401
Profit of Caterpillar Credit Corporation ..		462,934
Profit for year—consolidated		42,580,335
Add:		
Profit employed in the business at beginning of year		182,368,274
		224,948,609
Deduct:		
Dividends paid in cash during year:		
Preferred stock—$4·20 per share ..	761,866	
Common stock—$1·00 per share ..	27,161,492	
		27,923,358
Profit employed in the business at end of year ..		$197,025,251

See notes on page —

Editors' note: Statement 4 repeats the figures of Statement 1, and adds those of the preceding three years. It also gives, for each year:

	1960
Profit percentage of sales	5·95%
Profit per share of common stock	$1·54
Cash dividends per share of common stock ..	$1·00

employee compensation. The general reader is thereby given information which seems more likely to be of interest than the figures in the alternative grouping, so-called manufacturing costs segregated from commercial overhead (especially when the basis of segregation is unknown). The latter grouping is probably more generally used for internal management and, for such purposes, may well have greater value. This would be especially true where there are separate groupings of all the costs passed through inventories, and of all the costs excluded from inventories. But internal management has available all sorts of classifications which would be either too confusing for general consumption or too revealing for competitive consumption.

This point is worth pausing on—for there are always outside critics who feel thwarted when they do not have as voluminous detail as they think would enable them to walk on common ground with the internal management. It should, therefore, be understood that published statements for general public consumption cannot reasonably be of the same nature as the many varying and detailed analyses available internally. And we do not believe that the general reader wishes to be given a mass of necessarily complex information, which might delight the expert analyst but would certainly confuse and confound the reader whom we are trying most to reach. We accordingly selected, from the alternatives, what we thought would interest rather than repel most readers.

Our inclusion of income taxes in the total deducted direct from sales has met with expected opposition—and unexpected support. The United States federal income tax—levied on the corporation as such—is neither a sales tax upon the customers nor a personal tax upon the shareholders. There is, of course, a statutory concept of taxable income, but we felt we could no longer subscribe to such a contradiction as " profit before income taxes." Neither did we wish to foster any ideas that lower tax rates would necessarily mean higher profits. Tax rates, we believe, have an influence upon every aspect of " doing business "—on costs, prices, volume, and profits; and profits have a bearing on taxes.

We are also stubbornly old-fashioned in clinging to a belief that the Federal Government is still meant to be the servant of the corporation—not the master. It contributes no capital, shares no losses, has no equity in the net assets, and is not an equity holder; we could not, therefore, consider the payment for federal protection (which, in a broad sense, should be the sole purpose of government) to be an allocation or distribution of profits among owners. It is a payment for services rendered—often very badly and always at a very high cost—but presumed to be services which, over the long term, enhance or at least preserve business opportunities.

An objection sometimes raised against our treatment is that income taxes are not suitable for the determination of costs or prices of individual products. We, however, feel there is no necessary relationship between the treatment of taxes in the income statement and for such other purposes. In our detailed analyses of operating results by product, we do allocate income taxes, and this serves our purpose satisfactorily.

In our treatment of inventories in the operating statement, we decided in 1946 to revert to showing the opening and closing balances. Theretofore, we had reported only the net change in the inventories from beginning to end of the year, in the belief that we were bringing into sharp focus a factor of great significance. Whether the dollar amount of change be large or small, we believe it important to consider the effect of production in excess of sales, or sales in excess of production. This is particularly true when a substantial volume of costs does not pass through inventories, and where the results from manufacturing and the results from selling are, accordingly, of separate significance. Proper appraisal of the inventory position at the end of the period would also seem to require understanding of the changes in inventory in relation to sales trends.

Nevertheless, the fact remained that adding decreases in inventories to costs, or deducting increases in inventories from costs, was a point of major confusion among all but the expert—and we decided that the expert could figure out the change with his own pencil rather than ours.

The purpose of applying the change in inventories to costs is, of course, to adjust costs *incurred* during the year to costs *allocated* to the year. Failure to appreciate this appeared to be the main reason for the trouble with our earlier treatment. It therefore seemed desirable to attempt to bring out better the underlying reason for either treatment, and this we are now doing by adopting a sub-title for " costs allocated to year "—as shown in Statement 1.

An interesting exception has been taken to our use of the term " profit " on the grounds that it conveys a sense of finality—of marking a terminal point in operations. We had no such connotation in our minds since we knew, and thought most others realized, that profit is a transitory, illusory will-o'-the-wisp—here today and gone tomorrow (with the tax collector getting in somewhere between). The thought has also been expressed that " profit " has acquired a stigma—as something left over, without apparent social justification—and that this could be overcome by using alternatives such as " earnings " or " income." We had almost the opposite approach—that profit and the system which makes it possible arc things with honor, and that their honor can best be defended by meeting the challenge offered by financial statements.

And having done all these things to the statement of profit and loss, we decided that once again the technical jargon of accounting had created some difficulty. The statement might be one of profit or one of loss; it could hardly be one of both. The essential was its purport to describe operations. It seemed therefore simplest and clearest just to title it " results of operations "—and so we did.

We then made one further rearrangement to recognize the fact that most readers look first at the statement of operations and then proceed to the statement of financial position. We placed the former before the latter.

Editors' Note: The other statements in the published report are:

Statement 4. Consolidated results of operations. Items as in 1; covers 1957–1960.

Statement 5. Consolidated source of net current assets. See opposite.

Statement 6. Consolidated financial position at December 31. Items as in 2; covers 1957–60.

The next page is headed " Significant Trends since incorporation April 15, 1925." It is a table with columns for:

Year. Sales. Profit (amount; percentage of sales; per share of common stock). Cash dividends on common stock (amount; per share). Materials, supplies, services purchased, etc. Wages, salaries and contributions for employee benefits. United States and foreign taxes based on income (amount; percentage of sales). Land, buildings, machinery and equipment purchased. Depreciation and amortization. Average number of employees. Number of shareholders of common stock at year end. Year.

The horizontal lines show each year's figures under the above headings, from 1925 onwards.

A final page of figures gives the results of the Caterpillar Credit Corporation.

Conclusion

In reaching all our conclusions, it was our purpose to preserve the financial statements as an integral part of a report of stewardship—but we approached the problem with a broadened concept of what is meant by stewardship. In the course of events, our responsibility, like our company, had expanded; and over the years there had been growing in us a social consciousness which has become more impelling than our legal obligation. We had come to realize that, in the words of an early *Accounting Research Bulletin*, " The test of the corporate system and the special phase

STATEMENT 5

CONSOLIDATED SOURCE OF NET CURRENT ASSETS

	1960	1959	1958	1957
Additions to net current assets:				
Operations—				
Profit for year	$ 42,580,335	$ 46,517,987	$ 32,239,831	$ 40,012,023
Portion of original cost of buildings, machinery and equipment allocated to operations (depreciation and amortization)	28,314,300	28,012,113	27,710,165	21,849,366
Capital assets sold or scrapped	343,169	672,265	289,371	296,661
Common stock issued for cash under stock option plan	248,223	1,944,646	1,117,186	1,544,225
Net proceeds from sale of debentures	—	—	—	63,915,438
	71,486,027	77,147,011	61,356,553	127,617,713
Reductions of net current assets:				
Cash dividends paid	27,923,358	25,213,575	22,492,024	22,453,965
Land, buildings, machinery and equipment purchased	53,160,844	59,061,108	54,567,848	73,563,234
Increase or (decrease) in deferred expenses	1,320,679	70,134	(162,047)	329,915
Investment in Caterpillar Credit Corporation	462,934	419,006	536,724	2,227,368
Preferred stock purchased	503,500	1,137,000	1,500,000	890,000
	83,371,315	85,900,823	78,934,549	99,464,482
Increase or (decrease) in net current assets during year	(11,885,288)	(8,753,812)	(17,577,996)	28,153,231
Net current assets at beginning of year	166,006,627	174,760,439	192,338,435	164,185,204
Net current assets at end of year (statement 6)	$154,121,339	$166,006,627	$174,760,439	$192,338,435

of it represented by corporate accounting ultimately lies in the results which are produced. These results must be judged from the standpoint of society as a whole—not from that of any one group of interested parties."

But if the results are to be judged in a test of the corporate system, then there must be a common ground of understanding between the results and the judges. And this common ground must be achieved on trust derived from honest and effective reporting. More people are forming opinions on things economic and political, and they must have more information in more understandable form if the opinions are to be well founded. And unless the opinions are reasonably well founded, we shall suffer the consequences, for it is the essence of our particular form of government that, right or wrong, the will of the majority shall prevail.

If, therefore, we not only tell the accounting truth, *but tell it well*, we shall be laying the sound foundation for that further progress which, in our happy form of disturbed society, can come only with the consent of self-governing people learning to govern themselves by learning to think for themselves.

Reporting on the Flow of Funds*

By Maurice Moonitz

*Director of Accounting Research,
American Institute of Certified
Public Accountants New York.*

I

IN the conduct of an enterprise, management has two major financial tasks of importance to accountants, namely,

(1) to operate the enterprise profitably; and

(2) to finance the activities of the enterprise and to keep it solvent.

In the case of non-profit activities, the statement of the first task should be modified to indicate that management is charged with making the enterprise perform within its prescribed limitations, such as a budgeted amount of expenditures.

With respect to the first task, accounting has done a good job. That is to say, the necessity of a formal report on the results of operations is widely recognized, and the numerous problems involved in its preparation have received close and earnest attention among all groups and at all levels. With respect to a report on the way management has discharged its second task, our performance is less satisfactory. It is true, of course, that both the flow of funds into and out of an enterprise, and the effects of its financing activities, are recorded in the books, but a formal statement or report is typically not prepared.

The statement of the sources and the applications of funds is an attempt to report on the second task of management, to fill a gap usually left open in the typical published report. The statement is, therefore, a supplement or addition to the conventional battery of statements, not a substitute for them in whole or in part. Assertions, for example, that a funds statement is better or worse than an income statement are unfortunate. The two statements have different functions; both suffer from attempts to set them up as rivals.

The need for a statement to report changes and movements not clearly reflected in the balance-sheet and the income statement

---

* From the *Accounting Review*, July 1956.

has long been felt. In the U.S.A., the attempt to construct such a statement is usually dated from the publication in 1915 of William Morse Cole's *Accounts: Their Construction and Interpretation*. In that book, Cole described his " where-got-where-gone " statement. But progress was slow. In 1929, Myron M. Strain wrote in his *Industrial Balance Sheets* (p. 132), " The statement of application of funds had best be described, as it is one of the most useful of accounting statements and deserves frequent use; but it may be dismissed briefly, because it does not get it. This exhibit details the sources from which all the funds used during a fiscal period were derived, and describes the uses to which they were put. It is a striking and significant interpretation of the changes that have taken place in financial position between two periods." Hector R. Anton, in the October 1954 issue of the *Accounting Review*, has published a report, "Funds statement practices in the United States and Canada." Anton notes that, according to his survey, 68 per cent of the companies involved used a funds statement in some way or other, but that only 19 per cent included such a statement in annual reports to stockholders. In other countries, the publication of such statements is rare.

The two managerial tasks under discussion are, of course, related. It is sufficient for present purposes merely that they are not identical. As a matter of fact they tend to merge into a single problem or task over the entire life of an enterprise, or, as a practical approximation, over a substantial time period. That is to say, over the long pull, a profitable concern will also be a solvent concern, although the reverse proposition, namely, that a solvent concern will also be profitable, is manifestly not true. Over a relatively short period of time, however, profitability and solvency are almost independent of each other, sometimes almost antagonistic goals. Numerous cases are at hand in which enterprises expanded rapidly and profitably, but with a tremendous strain on working capital in the form of over-extended receivables, swollen inventories, top-heavy current debt, and a marked shortage of cash. Similarly, other cases exist of concerns which are unprofitable for several years on end, yet actually improve their debt-paying ability in the process of contraction. The apparent paradox of profitability and solvency moving in opposite directions is not new, nor is it real in the sense of persisting indefinitely. But in the short run, the two attributes pose two distinct problems; it is helpful to prepare accounting summations of them at frequent intervals.

To follow the point just made as to the relationship between profitability and solvency, we comment on the functions performed by the balance-sheet and the income statement. The initial balance-sheet of a newly formed concern is usually also a good statement of funds—it reflects among the assets the results of the applications of funds acquired from the sources listed among the liability and proprietary items. Since operations have not commenced, the problem of profit measurement does not arise. As a practical approximation, even a balance-sheet prepared a little later on will also serve as a statement of funds. For example, this would be true in the case of a company with an extended development period during which little or no revenues arise, followed by an operating period in which additional development work was negligible. But at some relatively early point after operations have begun, the balance-sheet, standing alone, begins to lose its function as a funds statement.

At the other extreme, an income statement for the whole life span of an enterprise would serve as the backbone of a funds statement covering the same time-interval. It would not be complete, because, to the revenues (sources) and expenses (applications) we would have to add at least (a) the long-term borrowings and repayments, (b) the issues and redemptions of capital stock, and (c) the dividends declared. But the combination of the items just listed would produce an eminently satisfactory funds statement, without the intervention of a balance-sheet. Notice that even the depreciation charge becomes an application of funds in this statement, because over a long enough period of time the summation of depreciation charges approximates quite closely the actual investment in the corresponding assets. As in the case of the balance-sheet, some practical approximations can be introduced. For example, an income statement covering fifty years, supplemented by data on long-term financing and on charges and credits to surplus, would undoubtedly be acceptable as a funds statement. But as the period covered by the income statement was shortened, the need for adjustments or modifications of some kind would begin to be felt in order to convert the income data into funds data.

As a consequence, neither the balance-sheet nor the income statement taken alone will give the story of the financial flows for the relatively short periods of time (one year, five years, ten years) covered in reports submitted to stockholders or prepared for top-management. But these considerations with respect to the two conventional statements as potential exhibits of the flow of funds are worthwhile for two reasons, (1) they indicate why a separate statement of funds is ordinarily desirable or even necessary, and (2) they indicate the limited but by no means rare cases in which one of the conventional statements will double in brass and serve the purpose of a complete reporting on management's performance of both tasks.

II

According to Anton [1] " in essence, funds analysis is the study of the flow of funds into the business unit and the uses for which such funds flow out during the same given time period." *External* transactions, then, are involved; so-called internal transactions (transfers, amortizations, and accruals) do not constitute part of the funds flow. This emphasis is both proper and important; in fact it constitutes the first principle underlying the statement. All the examples of funds statements that I have seen that are internally consistent, logical, and useful make this distinction in some form or other.[2]

To help visualize the problem, a classification of financial flows is attached as Exhibit A. Basically sound, the classification is not put forward as being necessarily the best one that can be devised. Its purpose at this point in the discussion is to make fairly concrete the kind of thing we are talking about. A good funds statement, then, would include some or all of the items included in this classification; it would exclude other kinds of items found in accounting statements. For those who like to play with permutations and combinations, this classification is material for your recreation. Just by way of illustration, let us take the conventional form of funds statement as it has appeared in some annual corporate reports, that is to say, a statement accounting for variation in net working capital. Such a statement would show explicitly items 1, 2, 5, 6 and 7, if at all material, under sources as well as under applications; these items might be shown " broad " or " netted." Items 4 and 4 (a) under both captions would be combined in a net source of funds from operations (*i.e.*, profit before depreciation and other " nonfund " charges to operations); item 3 would probably not be shown at all but instead would be buried in net working capital itself.

---

[1] Hector R. Anton, *A Critical Evaluation of Techniques of Analysis of the Flow of Business Funds.* Unpublished Ph.D. dissertation, University of Minnesota, 1953.

[2] The importance for funds analysis of the distinction between external and internal transactions is emphasized heavily by Louis Goldberg, " The Funds Statement Reconsidered," *The Accounting Review*, October 1951, pp. 485–491.

If it has escaped attention, one other characteristic of the classification should be stressed. Each item in the classification constitutes part of a " flow," a movement, and refers to the amount received, for example, from customers during a given time period. None of the items is a balance on hand at any point of time. The scheme is therefore incomplete because it does not tie into anything. But it can be made complete (in the logical sense) by relating it to a " funds balance " at beginning and end of period; this can be done in several ways. One form which appears satisfactory is appended as Exhibit B.

Before the formal, technical problems of the statement are discussed, a word of caution may be in order. It is easy to become overly enthusiastic about the funds statement, an enthusiasm not justified by the capabilities of the instrument. True, the funds statement does supply information not otherwise available in conventional statements, but remember that it " reverses the accruals " and ignores " internal transactions." Therefore, in at least one respect it is a cruder device than an income statement or a balance-sheet. The " cash-profit " approach of some discussions of this problem can easily be overdone, and raise more issues than it resolves.

The positive uses of the funds statement and the reasons for the recent upsurge in its popularity are interesting. For one thing, the recent inflationary movement, associated with a high level of business activity and high tax rates, has posed financing problems on a scale so large as to constitute really new problems to business. A statement of source and application of funds becomes useful in explaining why a net profit of a million dollars is not identical with an increase in funds of the same amount, available to increase dividends or raise wages. For another thing, the rapid changes of prices in an inflation make comparisons of income statements difficult; a flow of funds analysis may help by submitting a more elementary, less sophisticated type of statement. Finally, a further use, widely employed by economists, and one in which accountants ought to develop an interest, is to reveal " distributive shares " in the output of a concern or an industry—how much " take-home pay," for example, does labor actually get, how much do the suppliers get, how much to creditors, stockholders, government, etc. Properly handled, a statement of funds is better adapted to the dissemination of this type of information than the conventional income statement with its highly abstract, sophisticated cost allocations and estimates, and its completely different orientation.

III

We now proceed to the more formal aspects of the topic. Foremost among the problems involved is that of a fairly precise definition of " funds." A definition is necessary not only to satisfy the niceties involved, but also to assist us in the preparation of the statement and in the resolution of new or difficult problems. A definition of funds provides this assistance by supplying a framework for the whole project, giving us a beginning and an ending balance into which the fund flows must fit or be reconciled, and thereby leading to a second " principle " by which to decide whether or not to include a given financial event.

The conventional statement of funds, as it has appeared in published annual reports of the last ten or fifteen years, will serve as a starter. Simply on the basis of frequency of appearance, little doubt exists that " funds " in these reports are defined as identical with " net working capital," that is to say, the difference between current assets and current liabilities. This definition has the virtues of simplicity and of reliance on other widely used concepts, namely, current assets and current liabilities. These virtues we will stress at the moment; its defects will be revealed later.

Certain consequences flow from the definition. First of all, it establishes the content of the statement of funds—the statement must explain the change, increase or decrease, in net working capital during the period under review. Secondly, and perhaps of more importance, it provides the basis for consistent and logical answers to any question that may arise with respect to the inclusion or exclusion of a financial event, because any external transaction that increased net working capital is, by definition, a " source " of funds, and any external transaction that decreased net working capital is, for the same reason, an " application " of funds.

For example, under this conventional definition of funds, a stock dividend (in Britain, an " issue of bonus shares ") should not be reflected in a " funds " statement, because a stock dividend does not involve any net working capital account in either its debit or its credit aspect. By contrast, a cash dividend, when declared, is an application of funds because it results in a credit to dividends payable or to cash, either of which reduces net working capital, and is therefore a part of the funds flow. Similarly, a dividend in kind, if it is payable in some current asset, also reduces net working capital and belongs in the funds statement. If, however, it is payable in a non-current asset (for example, the shares of a subsidiary corporation) no working capital account is involved; as a consequence, that transaction is not logically a part of the funds flow.

The definition also helps resolve questions with respect to amounts to be reflected and their classification, as well as to the type of event to be included. Suppose, for example, that a substantial portion of plant is sold for cash at a loss. Ordinarily, the financial effect of this transaction will be reflected in the appropriate property accounts, their related depreciation allowances, and in an account reflecting the loss on sale of property. It may also involve offsets to income taxes. Two points seem clear enough, (1) the event provided funds, and (2) the amount to be reflected in a funds statement is the amount by which net working capital increased, in this case, the amount of cash received on the sale. But this amount is no longer reflected in a single account; therefore the bits and pieces of the transaction, as they are distributed through the property accounts, the depreciation allowances, the loss account, and possibly the related tax effects, should all be combined into one figure to show the increase in net working capital, the " source " of funds.

But the definition of funds as identical with working capital apparently possesses certain disadvantages. Symptomatic of these is the experimentation with " cash flow " statements in published annual reports. For example, United States Steel and American Phenolic have presented two funds statements, one of conventional type, consisting of a schedule of changes in working capital during the year, and the other purportedly showing the flow of cash in and out of the business. These two statements, as published in the 1952 report of American Phenolic Corporation, are appended as Exhibit C.

A record of cash receipts and disbursements, with the receipts classified by origin (*e.g.*, from customers, issues of capital stock, borrowings from banks, etc.) and the disbursements by object of expenditure (*e.g.*, to suppliers of materials, employees, stockholders, bondholders, etc.), while useful in its own way, and undoubtedly a form of " funds " statement, probably is overly narrow. A better balance would be achieved if funds were defined somewhere between the narrow extreme of cash and the broad extreme of working capital; a useful middle point is the concept of " net money assets available for disposition." Concretely, this concept consists of the sum of cash on hand and in banks, marketable securities held as secondary cash reserves, and current receivables, less the current liabilities that will be paid by quick assets in the near future. In brief, funds become identified with cash on hand plus cash in process of collection minus checks in process of being written. Where bank financing is important, as in the American Phenolic case, bank loans can be excluded from the category of " funds " and treated as a source or application.

A comparison of the conventional definition of funds with the one proposed above will indicate that the only major difference between the two is the treatment of inventories. Under the conventional definition, inventories are included as a part of net working capital, *i.e.*, the funds balance itself. In the proposed definition, inventories are treated as a source of funds, when they are sold to customers, and as an object for the application of funds when debts are incurred to move them from the materials stage through process and into finished goods. This latter treatment seems more in accord with the function of inventories in a going concern. Of course, when the " inventories " are in reality indistinguishable from receivables, they should be classed with the purely financial items; the reference here is to the output of a gold or silver mine, or the work done on a cost-plus-fixed-fee (C.P.F.F.) contract.

Regardless of the definition of " funds " adopted, certain types of financial events that ought to be included will be omitted, unless the first principle previously enunciated is invoked—that we are dealing with external transactions. The type of transaction that is likely to be left out, if attention is focussed too narrowly on the definition of funds, is the barter deal or the deferred-payment transaction. Take the case of a building acquired for 10 per cent cash and 90 per cent first mortgage bonds. Whether funds are defined narrowly as cash, or less narrowly as " net disposable money assets," or broadly as net working capital, only the 10 per cent down-payment results literally and directly in a decrease (application) of funds. Still, the whole event is important, and, under the first principle, should be reflected by showing an application of the full amount of the purchase-price of the building and a source of funds equal to the bonds accepted by the vendor. When the bonds are retired, the statement for that period should show an appropriate application of funds to retire long-term debt.

A rationale in the form of a presumed hypothetical intermediate cash transaction is theoretically satisfactory. Under this explanation, the event is treated as though the bonds were issued for cash, and the cash used to buy the building. But this type of explanation leaves the way open for other hypothetical interpretations which may not be so acceptable, and furthermore, is unnecessary. It is better, with any definition of funds, to refer back to our first principle, namely, that we are dealing with relationships between the concern and the outside world, and include these barter deals and deferred payment arrangements explicitly, rather than by the back door of hypothetical intermediate transactions.

Certain other problems arise. Non-cash gifts and subsidies, for example, have no impact on funds; yet the amount involved may be material, and the reporting may be essential to full financial disclosure. These gifts and subsidies should be included as (a) funds provided by the donor and (b) applied to the object received. Gifts or subsidies in the form of cash do increase funds, however defined, and will appear in a funds statement.

An example of this type of problem comes to mind. A hospital, newly formed, acquired equipment for cash, and then was reimbursed for its actual expenditures by a governmental agency. In this form, no difficulty arose in the preparation of a funds statement—the hospital had clearly applied funds to acquire equipment; the hospital had clearly received funds from an outside source when it was reimbursed for its earlier outlays on equipment. But suppose the governmental agency had acquired the equipment itself and made the gift (subsidy) to the hospital in kind. No cash (or other fund account) would have been involved on the hospital's records. Yet it seems clear that the two forms lead to identical results; the substance should prevail in the preparation of a funds statement, as in the case of any other accounting report.

One additional observation may be useful. Notice that we are not concerned with the classification of a gift or a subsidy as an increase in capital or in earnings, or in neither. We are concerned solely with the fact that a financial event occurred involving the entity and an outsider; when we report that event, we have fulfilled the requirements of a funds statement. In the related but not identical problem of income measurement or the reporting of financial position, the question of the proper classification of a gift or subsidy as between capital and income will have to be faced. But not in a funds flow analysis.

Another problem is the treatment of depreciation and other amortization. No extended analysis of this warhorse is necessary; instead a few observations will be made. First, the application of funds to the depreciable or amortizable item is reported in the period of its acquisition. Second, depreciation itself is omitted from the funds statement because it is a cost or expense, properly recognized in the measurement of income, which does not require the application of funds, however defined, in the current period. Third, any attempt to show depreciation as a " source " of funds is awkward, unnecessary, misleading, and just plain wrong. The reference here is to the widespread practice of adding back depreciation to the net profit figure to get the amount of funds provided by operations. This is a work-sheet adjustment, and does not belong in a formal statement. The figure we are after, and that we usually get by this adjustment, is the amount of funds provided by operations *before* deducting a non-fund item such as depreciation expense. Fourth, the depreciation adjustment may be incomplete in a manufacturing concern—a considerable amount of depreciation may be tied up in inventories, and ought to be reversed.

Another problem is the tendency to want to reverse the entries for estimated bad debts. Except where funds are defined as cash, and the funds statement accordingly becomes a report of cash receipts and disbursements, this type of reversal is not warranted. Current receivables are a part of funds; the allowance for bad debts is an attempt to reflect those receivables on a net collectible basis, and should therefore be left alone in a funds analysis. Perhaps the difficulty arises when the analyst recognizes quite correctly that the charge to income for bad debts is not an application of funds. But the proper treatment in this instance is not to reverse the entry as a non-fund adjustment, similar to depreciation. Rather the charge to income should be interpreted as a revenue deduction item, a correction of an otherwise over-stated revenue account. If the bad debts debit is so interpreted, and it is the correct interpretation, no difficulty on this score will be encountered in the preparation of a funds statement.

A loss on the conversion of any funds item constitutes an outflow of funds, a diminution in the " pool " of homogeneous elements; as a consequence the loss would usually be classified as an " application " of funds. For example, assume that marketable securities, held as a secondary cash reserve, and reflected in the books at their cost of $100,000 are sold this period for $95,000. Assume also that in this same period a theft of $5,000 cash takes place, without recovery of any sort. Each loss of $5,000 represents an " outflow " of funds, and should be so reported, even though the events themselves were unplanned and undesirable. The related case of a gain on the conversion of a funds item is clearly an inflow of funds, classified usually among the sources.

The treatment of inventories as a source of funds or an object of their application has already been urged, primarily on the basis that inventories, in the usual case, are too important to be buried in a net working capital figure, and require substantial outlays to move out to customers.[3] The sales figure is of course identical with the funds provided by customers during the period. The application of additional costs to process the inventory during the current period can be calculated by a simple formula, namely, the cost of goods sold plus the difference between the ending and the beginning inventories. In the case of the so-called actual cost systems, this formula will always hold regardless of the method of inventory pricing employed, whether cost or market, first-in, first-out, last-in, first-out, or average cost. The formula yields a total figure; it will not give the breakdown of the costs among labor, materials, supplies, etc.

In the case of a standard cost system, the formula just given will also hold, provided the variances are closed out at the end of the period to inventories and to cost of goods sold. If the variances are instead carried direct to income, the formula, as it stands, will calculate funds applied *at standard*, which is presumably not satisfactory in a funds analysis. Consequently, the formula should be expanded to include " plus or minus the standard cost variances."

As the last problem to be discussed, consider the situation when a previously non-current item becomes current, without an actual transaction with an outsider. Specifically, consider the case of the current portion of a serial bond issue (normally classed as a long-term loan). Each year a new series is detached from the long-term debt and placed among the current debts, indicating payment in the near future. In a funds statement, this amount is treated as an application for the same reason that a dividend declaration is so treated, namely, that payment in the normal course of events is automatic in the short-term. As a consequence, the pool of net disposable money-assets or of net working capital is diminished. In either case, we have a clear case of an event giving rise to a decline in funds.

IV

In the process of preparing the funds statement, several methods are available. Vatter, of the University of Chicago,

---

[3] Where the finished goods or merchandise is virtually as good as cash the conventional inclusion of inventories in the funds total is satisfactory. In addition to inventories of precious metals and costs tied up in C.P.F.F. contracts, inventories of commodities for which a highly organized spot and futures market exists would qualify for inclusion. The case for inclusion is especially strong if these types of inventories are stated at net realizable value instead of at cost, because cost does not, except by coincidence, measure the inflow of funds from the holding of highly marketable inventories.

has proposed the derivation of data from direct posting to T-accounts.[4]

Others have stressed the desirability of inserting a summary analysis of non-fund accounts in audit working papers, thereby also obtaining directly the necessary data, as under Vatter's proposal, but without the intervention of actual accounts. This procedure is illustrated in Finney and Miller, *Principles of Accounting: Intermediate*, and in Holmes and Meier, *Intermediate Accounting*. The most widely used method, however, is the process of adjusting changes derived from comparative balance-sheets, as supplemented by an analysis of income and retained earnings.

If this procedure is followed, the same technical problems arise regardless of the definition of funds. These may be summarized as follows:

(1) Reverse the differences in account balances representing transactions not involving funds (example: the depreciation entries).

(2) Reinstate any transactions involving funds that are suppressed in the usual accounting process (example: sale of a non-current asset).

(3) Combine and reclassify the remaining items to bring the bits and pieces of funds data together.

In the worksheet itself, the funds analysis should be quite detailed, to insure that no important aspect of the financial flow has been omitted, overlooked, or underestimated. But in the statement itself, similar items should be judiciously combined and grouped, important aspects played up, and minor, inconsequential flows thrown into a " miscellaneous " or " all other " category. No one would disagree with the basic soundness of these common sense rules of presentation of data. But a related problem lurks in the background on which there is no unanimity of opinion or of practice—the extent to which similar sources and applications should be set off against each other. For example, all would agree that if X Company borrowed $1,000,000 from each of three different banks, we would meet all the niceties of disclosure and relevance if we reported a source of funds of $3,000,000 from bank borrowings; no one would insist that we ought to spell out the three separate borrowing operations. But suppose during the same period, X Company also paid off $1,500,000 of other bank loans. Should we now report a source

---

[4] Wm. J. Vatter, " A Direct Method for the Preparation of Funds Statements," *Journal of Accountancy*, June 1946, pp. 479–489; also see " Correspondence " in the September 1946 issue of the same *Journal*, pp. 256–257.

of funds of $3,000,000 and an application of funds of $1,500,000, or should we be content with the disclosure of a net source of funds of $1,500,000 from bank borrowings?

Of more substance is the treatment of the funds flows generated by operations—sales to customers and wages, materials, etc. A single source from operations, calculated by adding non-fund charges to net profit, is found in most published analyses of changes in net working capital. But this practice may be omitting data on significant changes. Notice, for example, the difference in mode of treatment of the operating items in the American Phenolic data, attached. In the statement of changes in working capital, funds provided by operations are shown conventionally in two figures, net profit for the year, and provision for depreciation. In the statement of cash receipts and disbursements, however, the influence of operating items is reflected under receipts, in one item, sales; and, under disbursements, in four items (specifically, materials, supplies and services; salaries and wages; taxes; and interest). The recommendation here is to set forth a statement more along the lines of American Phenolic's " cash flow " than along its working capita analysis. Fundamentally, the point being made is that we should guard against unwarranted inferences as to causal relationships, particularly when an application of funds is subtracted from an important source of funds, and the difference only then set forth in a formal statement.

Part of the difficulty here stems from the fiction that the funds statement is an attempt to explain what became of the profit, and that accordingly the tie in must be with the net income figure. But even a casual examination of published funds statements will reveal that (a) they display sources and applications of funds beyond those connected with operations, and (b) they tie in with net working capital, or cash, or some other concept of funds, but not with net profit. No one can ever tell what became of net profit, a calculated magnitude, the difference between revenue and expense. We can tell a great deal, however, about the inflow of funds generated by sales, by borrowings, by issues of shares, and by other means; and about the outflow of funds for the services of employees, of suppliers, of lenders, of stockholders, etc. The influence of income measurement is strong; it has obviously dictated the central position of the income statement. It has less obviously but nevertheless just as certainly dictated the form and content of the balance-sheet. To judge by published statements, it has also influenced the form and content of the funds statement. But the proper function of a funds statement is not to tell us more about the income generating and income measuring processes, but rather to disclose data on the related but nevertheless distinct task of financial management.

Exhibit A
Financial Circulation—A Classification

Funds are derived from
1. Contributions of stockholders;
2. Long-term loans, *e.g.*, mortgages, bonds, equipment contracts;
3. Short-term loans supplied primarily by commercial banks;
4. Sales to customers. This class includes reduction of inventories;
4 (a). Government subventions not included in 4, above, such as subsidies to airlines, steamship companies, etc.;
5. Disposal of non-current investments;
6. Disposal of plant, property, and equipment;
7. All other sources, *e.g.*, gifts.

Funds are used to
1. Cover dividends and redeem shares of stock;
2. Services and retire long-term debt;
3. Service and pay short-term loans;
4. Cover operating costs, such as labor, materials, supplies, etc. This class includes increase of inventories;
4 (a). Pay taxes not included in 4, above;
5. Acquire non-current investments;
6. Acquire plant, property, and equipment;
7. Cover all other applications, *e.g.*, loss by embezzlement.

Exhibit B
X COMPANY
FUNDS STATEMENT
For period from............ to..........

		Sources	Applica-tions
Funds, beginning of period		xxx,xxx	
Fund changes during the period:			
I. Net funds from operations (profit or loss as adjusted for non-fund items)—See Note		x,xxx	
II. Funds transactions with stockholders			
Dividends paid			x,xxx
Investments		xx,xxx	
III. Funds transactions with long-term creditors			
Sale of bonds		x,xxx	
Retirement of bonds			xx,xxx
IV. Funds transactions, involving plant and inventories, etc.			
Plant, intangibles, and investments ..			x,xxx
Decrease in inventories		xx,xxx	
Totals		xx,xxx	xxx,xxx
Net increase (decrease) in funds (See Schedule A) [Not reproduced]			xxx,xxx
Funds, end of period			xxx,xxx

Adapted from Hector Anton, *op. cit.*, p. 107.

NOTE.—Anton concludes that, on balance, a reflection of net funds from operations fits in most closely with current practice and its apparent objectives. My own preference is for more detail, at least to the extent of revealing sales and the major operating costs. But in either case, the classification and form illustrated above will serve the purpose.

Exhibit C
AMERICAN PHENOLIC CORPORATION
Statement of Changes in Working Capital

	Year ended December 31	
	1952	1951
Working Capital—Beginning of Period	$ 2,904,385	$ 3,845,476
Funds Provided—		
Net profit for year	$ 1,279,290	$ 941,868
Provision for depreciation	541,786	367,411
Proceeds from sale of fifteen year 4⅞% sinking fund notes	2,000,000	—
Sundry, net	201,879	50,971
Total funds provided	$ 4,022,955	$ 1,360,250
Funds Applied—		
Additions to plant and equipment	$ 1,050,481	$ 1,673,326
Provision for sinking fund including payment of long-term loans	969,049	232,950
Dividends declared	380,532	320,016
Increase in prepaid expenses..	21,326	75,049
Total funds applied	$ 2,421,388	$ 2,301,341
Net increase or decrease in working capital	$ 1,601,567	$ 941,091
Working Capital—End of Period	$ 4,505,952	$ 2,904,385

Statement of Cash Receipts and Disbursements

Cash Balance—Beginning of Period	$ 1,295,109	$ 800,424
Receipts—		
Sale of merchandise to customers	$36,456,101	$24,355,836
Bank loans, including $3,200,000 " V " loan ..	—	3,950,000
Sale of U.S. Government securities	—	1,185,315
Refund of prior year's Federal income taxes and renegotiation		45,261
Long-term 4⅞% loan	2,000,000	—
Sundry	101,575	110,941
Total receipts	$38,557,676	$29,647,353
Disbursements—		
Materials, supplies and services	$21,229,937	$19,106,502
Salaries and wages	8,312,128	6,572,904
Taxes, including purchase of U.S. Treasury tax savings notes	4,195,700	1,205,563
Plant and equipment	1,050,481	1,673,326
Dividends	360,408	320,000
Retirement of bank loans and " V " loans ..	1,450,000	—
Debentures purchased, including deposits with Trustee for retirement of long-term loans ..	978,825	170,411
Interest	254,733	103,962
Total disbursements	$37,832,212	$29,152,668
Net increase in cash balance	$ 725,464	$ 494,685
Cash Balance—End of Period	$ 2,020,573	$ 1,295,109

Company Accounts and the National Economy

By Harold Rose

Director of studies, course in industrial financing, London School of Economics.

A SET of accounts is a statement of the relationship between a business and the outside world. In drafting a profit and loss account or balance-sheet, the accountant is therefore tracing a thread in the fabric of our economic life—even though the accounts of any one business normally form only a minute part of the national economic picture. The accountant may therefore pause to consider in what way the results of his labours have been affected by broad economic trends or, to put the link rather differently, in what way a set of accounts reflects the general course of economic events. He may also consider how far the accounts before him are typical in this broader context.

At the same time the economist, who is looking at the same picture from the opposite and usually more distant standpoint, may well derive a clearer insight into the interaction of economic forces by examining the accountant's handiwork. The contribution of both accountant and economist to our understanding of the national economy can be heightened by a review of company accounts in the aggregate.

Statistics of company finance

In an advanced economy, like that of the United Kingdom or U.S.A., companies (or, if you will, " corporations ") are the predominant form of economic organisation, outside the fields of personal service, agriculture and, perhaps, retail trade. In such an economy the experience of the company sector therefore constitutes a major part of the experience of the country as a whole. But the extent to which company reports are available for examination will depend on the legal and other requirements concerning publication. In Great Britain, for example, there were approximately 320,000 companies having a share capital registered at the end of 1959. Of these, however, only some 11,000 were public companies, compelled by law to file their balance-sheet with the Registrar of Companies. Accounts which can most readily be studied are those of companies with a Stock Exchange quotation, and the number of these in Britain amounts to some 5,000 (together with some 20,000 subsidiaries).

In one respect, at least, this limitation does not destroy the value of an aggregate of published accounts, for quoted companies, in most industries where the company form is typical, cover the major part of output, employment and income. In Britain, quoted companies account for about four-fifths of the total profits recorded by all companies, both public and private, in manufacturing industry; in the case of construction, and of the distributive trades, on the other hand, the proportions are smaller, at approximately one-quarter and two-fifths respectively.

A combined appropriation-of-income account for the whole British company sector is included in the annual national income accounts. Statistics of quoted company accounts in the aggregate are analysed each year in *Economic Trends*, an official publication of the Central Statistical Office.[1] These are presented so as to show changes in the pattern of finance and the uses to which finance is put, and cover companies engaged mainly in manufacturing, construction and distribution. Usually aggregate tables only are published; but tables for each of twenty-two industrial groups can be obtained on application to the Board of Trade, and so the accountant can attempt a comparison between the accounts he is preparing and those of the industrial group in which they fall. Aggregate balance-sheets and profit and loss accounts, in industrial groups, are also compiled by *The Economist*[2] and published in a series appearing in each successive quarter of the calendar year. A more detailed examination of company accounts in the post-war period has been carried out by the National Institute of Economic and Social Research,[3] and an analytical commentary on various aspects of the results has been compiled by a number of economists.[4] In this article, advantage has been taken of all these sources.

Quoted and unquoted companies—some differences

Although aggregate company accounts are available only for quoted companies, the national income statistics throw light on some of the differences between these and the accounts of

---

[1] See, for example, *Economic Trends*, No. 86, December 1960 (Her Majesty's Stationery Office, London).
[2] See, for example, *The Economist*, April 29, 1961.
[3] *Company Income and Finance* (London: National Institute of Economic & Social Research, 1956).
[4] *Company Income and Finance*, ed. Brian Tew & R. F. Henderson (Cambridge University Press, 1959).

unquoted companies; for, as the national income accounts cover the whole company sector, certain aspects of unquoted companies can be derived as a residual. Of these, the most important concern the ways in which companies finance the growth in their assets.

If we consider investment in physical assets alone—*i.e.*, in fixed assets and stocks (inventories)—we find that a much higher proportion of investment is financed from internal sources (retained current income plus depreciation charges) in the case of unquoted companies, as Table 1 indicates:

TABLE 1

BRITISH COMPANY SAVING AND INVESTMENT

	1949–53 *Average*		1954		1956		1958	
	Quoted	*All*	*Quoted*	*All*	*Quoted*	*All*	*Quoted*	*All*
Saving* .. £m.	538	1123	719	1424	793	1710	889	1641
Investment† .. £m.	609	941	779	1058	1257	1535	954	1397
Saving as percentage of investment .. %	88	119	92	135	63	111	93	117

* Saving:
  Quoted Companies: Balance retained in reserves *plus* depreciation provisions *plus* additions to future tax reserves *plus* " other " net receipts on capital account.
  All Companies: Saving before providing for depreciation and stock appreciation (excluding saving of financial companies) *plus* net borrowing from tax reserves *plus* capital transfers (net receipts).
  Investment:
  Quoted Companies: Expenditure on tangible fixed assets *less* surplus on disposal of fixed assets *plus* increase in value of stocks.
  All Companies: Gross fixed capital formation at home *plus* increase in value of stock.
  Source: *Economic Trends*, December 1960 (H.M.S.O. London).

The statistics of Table 1 allow only the broadest of comparisons to be made, especially as the two sets of figures are not exactly comparable, in that investment in physical assets overseas is excluded from statistics relating to " All Companies," thus exaggerating the extent to which unquoted companies are self-financing. Nevertheless, it remains a strongly probable implication that, as far as the unquoted company sector *as a whole* is concerned, internal sources finance a higher proportion of investment than in most quoted companies.

Two reasons can be presented for this. The first is that the rate of growth of unquoted companies is probably lower on the average than that of the quoted sector. As a result, the ratio of investment to income is probably lower in unquoted companies, so that, even if they distributed the same proportion of their income as quoted companies, their retained income would still be relatively large in relation to their investment. In other words, part of the difference between the two sets of figures in Table 1 can be explained by the relatively low investment, rather than the high saving, of unquoted companies. The difference, so to speak, is to be found in the balance-sheet rather than in the appropriation account.

Nevertheless, if we could examine their profit and loss accounts, we should probably find that unquoted companies do retain a relatively high proportion of their income. Several factors would account for this. The first is that the owners of a small family business may hope to minimise the weight of surtax on their personal incomes by keeping dividends low— a course of action that cannot, however, be taken far without incurring the hostility of the tax authorities. The second is that the relatively young business often has to retain income in order quickly to pay off debts to the initial providers of its finance. The third and probably most important reason is that the unquoted company, because of its legal status, cannot easily raise long-term capital from external sources, so that it is forced to rely more on retained income if it is to grow.

The very limited access of the unquoted company to external long-term finance may have several consequences that make it necessary not to interpret Table 1 in too homogeneous a fashion. The financial disadvantage of the unquoted company may have the effect simply of retarding its growth, keeping its investment low. Secondly, within the group of unquoted companies as a whole there must be many whose retained income falls far short of the increase in assets that seems profitable. This will naturally be true of quoted companies as well, but the difference is that unquoted companies will be less able to turn to long-term external capital in order to finance their expansion. They are obliged to rely much more on short-term finance, and they will usually be found to be larger borrowers from the banks, in relation to their size, than are most quoted companies. Young unquoted companies, in particular, also will often rely to a disproportionate, and perhaps dangerous, extent on the receipt of trade credit.

Company income and its appropriation before and since the war

The national income accounts make possible a broad survey of the way in which company income as a whole is appropriated from year to year. A long historical sweep may be par cularly revealing, in showing the effect, for example, of changes in the levels of taxation and prices over the years. Since the war, there has been a persistent rise in prices, and the proportion of gross company income taken by tax, while varying from year to year, has been considerably higher than in the pre-war period. In Table 2, both trends can be traced.

TABLE 2

BRITISH COMPANY INCOME AND ITS APPROPRIATION

	1938* £m.	1949 £m.	1959 £m.	% Increase since 1938	
				1949	1959
Trading profits earned in the U.K.†	548	1443	2414	163	341
Trading profits earned abroad†	106	207	301	95	184
Non-trading income	239	340	774	42	225
Total Income† ..	893	1990	3489	123	291
Less:					
Debenture interest, gross‡	61	28	90	−44	48
Preference dividends, gross‡	121	103	108	−15	−10
Miscellaneous interests and dividends, gross‡ ..	66	85	240	29	264
	248	216	438	−13	77
Leaves:					
Available for taxation and ordinary shareholders	645	1774	3051	175	373
Of which:					
Taxation, including overseas taxes	129	842	1054	553	717
Ordinary dividends, gross§	368	391	781	6	112
Retained income, net ..	148	541	1216	266	715

Source: National Income and Expenditure Accounts (H.M.S.O. London).
* The figures for 1938 relate to some companies that were nationalised in 1949 and are therefore excluded from the table in 1959.
† After statutory depreciation allowances.
‡ In this table, income tax deducted from payments of interest and dividends is treated as falling not on companies but on the recipients of the interest and dividends, so that interest and dividends are shown gross, before deduction of tax. The figures of taxation recorded here can be regarded, therefore, as falling only on undistributed income. Total U.K. taxation accruing on company income, including income tax on interest and dividends, was £256m. in 1938, £981m. in 1949, and £1208m. in 1959.
§ Mainly building society interest and dividends; co-operative society dividends.

Table 2 shows some of the effects of post-war inflation, particularly on the ordinary shareholder. The latter has benefited from rising business activity and prices in two ways. The increase in profits before tax since pre-war years has been substantial; and this increase in money profits, together with the usual process of redemption, has greatly reduced the proportionate weight of interest on debentures and other loan capital, and of dividends on preference shares. Thus the ordinary shareholder has received benefits from inflation in the form of a continual reduction in the degree of capital gearing (or " leverage," to use American terminology).

Company capital structures, including reserves, are very much lower geared than before the war, so that companies can withstand a much larger proportionate fall in profits before ordinary dividends are endangered. This improvement in the security of ordinary dividends—which cannot be discerned simply by calculating the number of times dividends are covered by available equity earnings—has played its part in raising the status of the ordinary share as an investment, especially in the eyes of large institutional investors, which are usually concerned with the continuity of dividend income. However, because low capital gearing has enabled the ordinary share market to withstand shocks more easily, it has also helped to weaken the force of government policy when the threat of inflation has made credit restriction necessary: it has become more difficult for the government to restrict, or make more costly, the supply of finance into the market for new ordinary share issues.

The increase in profits, together with the relatively static behaviour of prior charges, has naturally resulted in a substantial increase in the amount shown in Table 2 as " available for taxation and ordinary shareholders." Those shareholders were, however, prevented from receiving the full benefit, owing to the increase in company taxation after the war.

Moreover, the needs of company finance, in a period in which high dividends were discouraged by government policy (including a discriminatory tax on distributed profits) led to a fall in the proportion of available earnings after tax that was distributed to shareholders. The burden of company taxation can thus be seen to have fallen on dividends rather than on retained profits, at least in the decade after the war. More recently, however, as opinion has grown more favourable to dividend increases, the proportion of earnings distributed has increased; but it still remains lower than before the war, probably because investment in new assets is higher in relation to the level of net company income.

The balance-sheet and the national income accounts

Whereas the national income accounts include a composite income and appropriation account of the company sector, they do not include an aggregate balance-sheet. This is partly because these accounts revolve round the concept of income, or net value added in production, of which company profits form a part; and partly because it would be difficult to draw up for the economy as a whole something that would correspond to a " national " balance-sheet. It might not be so arduous a task, admittedly, as far as the country's foreign assets and liabilities are concerned; it is the assets and liabilities within the country that cause real difficulty.

Many problems would arise if we tried to evaluate consumers' capital goods, roads, natural resources, and so on. Another problem is that company accounts themselves do not distinguish between overseas and domestic claims. Yet another is that the cross-balance of assets and liabilities between the firms themselves would present both conceptual and practical difficulties. Simple aggregation might not be particularly meaningful, for example, where some companies have bank loans when others have positive cash balances. A consolidated balance-sheet, as opposed to a simple aggregated account, would eliminate assets and liabilities that found their counterpart within the company sector itself, just as the cross-items between members of a group cancel out in standard consolidated accounts.

Nevertheless, certain items of a consolidated balance-sheet, were one available, would fit readily into the national statistics. The national income, or national product, consists basically of consumption expenditure plus investment. That is to say, part of the national product is used up within the year, while the remainder augments the nation's assets; and the latter part would fall, of course, within the " national " balance-sheet. As far as the company sector is concerned, we could envisage a consolidated balance-sheet along the following lines—

1. *Physical Assets*
       At home   ..   ..   —
       Abroad   ..   ..   —
                                                      _____
         Total physical assets   ..   ..   —
2. *Financial Assets*
       Home (sums owed by non-company sector,
         net)   ..   ..   —
       Abroad (sums owed by foreigners, net)   ..   —
         Total financial assets   ..   ..   _____

         Total physical and financial assets ..   —
3. *Less Long-Term Liabilities, etc.*
       Home (long-term liabilities to non-company
         sector)   ..   ..   —
       Abroad (long-term liabilities to, and minority
         interest of, foreigners)   ..   ..   ..   —
         Total ..   ..   _____

4. *Gives Net Company Assets* owned by domestic
   non-company shareholders ..   ..   ..   --
5. *Obtained thus*
   Share capital owned by domestic non-com-
     pany shareholders ..   ..   —
   Capital reserves and retained earnings attri-
     butable to domestic non-company share-
     holders   ..   ..   —

—

In this scheme, cross-items between companies are eliminated, leaving physical assets and financial balances due by the non-company sector and foreigners. Britain has considerable overseas assets, but against these must be set the mainly short-term liabilities to foreigners that arise because of the role of Britain as an international banking centre, as well as the interests of foreigners in companies operating in this country. The increase in physical assets in any year, plus the increase in *net* overseas assets, form part of the country's total capital investment for the year, which in turn forms part of the national income; domestic financial claims cancel out, and so do not increase national income. The increase in *net* overseas assets constitutes foreign investment, which, for the country as a whole and in the absence of international gifts, is identical with any net surplus in the nation's balance of payments on current or income account. If the country has a surplus of exports over imports, the result must necessarily be an increase in the country's foreign assets or a reduction in its foreign liabilities.

An aggregate company balance-sheet

Whereas a consolidated balance-sheet for the company sector would probably be almost impossible to prepare, aggregate balance-sheets, from which cross-items are not eliminated, are available for the majority of British quoted companies. Those for the years 1956–58 are reproduced in Table 3. They reveal a number of points relevant to our understanding of general economic affairs.

The first is that internal sources (retained income plus depreciation) finance a high proportion of physical investment for these companies as a whole; reference to Table 1 records that this ranged from 63 per cent. in 1956 to 93 per cent. in 1958, the proportion being particularly high in this latter year because the addition to stocks, a volatile element, was then relatively small. It is true that, in considering the adequacy of self-finance, the need to finance " paper " assets must also be borne in mind. The process of growth requires the acquisition of investments

TABLE 3

AGGREGATE BALANCE-SHEET *

(Manufacturing & Distribution)

	1956	1957	1958
Number of Companies †	2960	2879	2808
	£mn.	£mn.	£mn.
Fixed Assets			
Tangible fixed assets, net	5035	5676	6317
Goodwill	293	279	269
Trade investments	286	314	358
Investments in unconsolidated subsidiaries	38	26	44
TOTAL FIXED ASSETS	5651	6296	6988
Current Assets			
Stocks and work in progress	3999	4215	4216
Trade and other debtors	2649	2824	2901
Marketable securities	478	498	530
Tax reserve certificates	228	210	225
Cash	659	658	709
TOTAL CURRENT ASSETS	8013	8405	8581
Less Current Liabilities			
Bank loans	450	497	509
Trade and other creditors	2153	2304	2372
Dividends and interest due	189	201	215
Current taxation	748	750	733
Provisions	108	114	114
TOTAL CURRENT LIABILITIES	3647	3866	3944
Net Current Assets	4366	4538	4637
Total Net Assets	10017	10834	11625
Less Long-term External Liabilities			
Long-term loans	1053	1218	1313
Minority interests	343	349	390
TOTAL	1396	1567	1703
Shareholders interest in Net Assets (Net worth)	8620	9268	9921
Represented by:			
Issued Share Capital:			
Ordinary shares	2829	3062	3407
Preference, etc., shares	955	960	967
TOTAL	3784	4023	4374
Reserves			
Capital and revenue reserves	4235	4637	4972
Future tax reserves	601	608	575
TOTAL	4836	5245	5547
Total Capital and Reserves	8620	9268	9921
Notes:			
Outstanding contracts for capital expenditure	711	660	550
Accumulated depreciation on fixed assets	2363	2576	2954

* Quoted companies engaged mainly in manufacturing, distribution, construction, transport, and certain other services (excluding agriculture, shipping, property and finance). Comparability between the three years has been obtained by eliminating the effect of changes in the number and composition of companies. The figures for each year quoted relate to companies' accounting years finishing in the twelve months up to April 5 of the following year shown.
Source: Economic Trends, December 1960 (H.M.S.O., London).
† Plus approximately 15,000 subsidiaries.

in other concerns, and an increase in net trade credit extended and in net liquid assets; this can be discerned in Table 3. In the years covered by the inquiry carried out by the National Institute of Economic and Social Research,[5] the years 1949–53, these acquisitions amounted to the equivalent of one-fifth of gross company saving.

Secondly, the sources of external finance are to be found mainly in the new issue market, and only to a small extent in the form of bank loans, as Table 4 shows in detail.

TABLE 4

BRITISH COMPANIES—SOURCES OF FINANCE

	1949–53 average		1956		1957		1958	
	£mn.	Per cent.	£mn.	Per cent.	£mn.	Per cent.	£mn.	Per cent.
Ordinary shares ..	61	7	157	11	242	16	155	12
Preference shares ..	10	1	9	1	28	2	10	1
Long-term loans ..	60	7	114	8	156	10	87	7
Reserves retentions (including depreciation provisions) ..	497	54	813	56	846	54	930	73
Additions to future tax reserves ..	46	5	−13	−1	14	1	−34	−3
Bank loans	16	2	73	5	48	3	14	1
Other sources	228	25	309	21	220	14	111	9
Total ..	918	100	1,462	100	1,554	100	1,273	100

From *Economic Trends*, H.M.S.O. 1960.

One consequence of this has been to render more difficult the application by the Government of a disinflationary financial policy, which can influence the supply of finance through the new issue market less closely than through the volume of bank credit. This difference has become even more marked in recent years, for, owing to the growing popularity of the ordinary share as an investment in the post-war conditions of full employment and inflation, the proportion of new issues in this form has increased. It is more difficult for the authorities to restrict, or make more costly, the flow of funds through the medium of ordinary share issues, for this flow depends on the degree of investors' optimism, whereas the cost of fixed-interest finance can be closely influenced by the Government's interest rate policy.

The increase in bank loans can be seen from Table 4 to have

[5] Tew & Henderson, *op. cit.*

provided a surprisingly small part of the flow of external finance to quoted companies.[6]   The work of the National Institute of Economic and Social Research, moreover, shows that in the years 1949–53 overdrafts were important only in the finance of relatively small and slow-growing concerns. The proportion of companies with *some* bank overdraft may be high, but the size of overdrafts was small, as against their net assets, in the case of the larger firms. The relatively unimportant part played by bank loans in company finance was one reason why the Government's attempt in 1955–57 to check inflation through the banking system was so unsuccessful; the authorities seemed to be unaware of the facts of company life in this period. The picture today, however, might be somewhat different, as removal of all controls from bank lending (towards the end of 1958) has resulted in a considerable increase in bank advances as a whole—76 per cent. between the end of 1958 and the end of 1960—so that bank loans now play a more important part in company finance.

Even so, as long as finance through the new issue market is readily available on terms acceptable to business men, restriction through the limitation of bank advances cannot be of much value (though, for one reason or another, individual firms may find it difficult to obtain sufficient bank credit or new issue finance, especially if the authorities apply direct restrictions, of a quantitative or qualitative nature, on either channel of finance). British experience of the nineteen-fifties, moreover, shows that financial restriction may be weakened still further by changes in another section of the balance-sheet, namely, in trade debtors and creditors.

Most manufacturing businesses give more trade credit than they receive; the difference is related to the " net value added " in production—most of which consists of immediate cash payments of wages and salaries. Some manufacturing firms are no doubt net receivers of trade credit, but these are probably small firms whose behaviour can properly be described as overtrading. Retail firms, on the other hand, are often net takers of credit, in so far as they sell mainly for cash; if we exclude hire-purchase, probably the majority of retail distributors will be found to be net takers of trade credit in the narrow sense.

It will be observed from Table 3 that trade debtors and creditors are considerably larger than bank loans. Changes in

---

[6] The volume of bank finance provided by discounting bills of exchange (which are included in " trade and other creditors " in Table 3) is extremely small. At the end of 1960, the London clearing banks held commercial bills with a total value of less than £150m; the greater part of these were probably drawn in connection with the finance of foreign trade.

the flow of trade credit, therefore, may be important in determining the level and pattern of company finance, even though changes in the *net* amount of trade credit outstanding may be relatively small; the position is shown in Table 5.

Trade credit is one channel by which liquidity is diffused more evenly over the whole company network. When business activity is increasing, or when additional finance is needed because of a rise in prices, firms that are short of funds may seek to conserve finance by taking somewhat longer to pay their suppliers; the latter may be obliged to grant longer credit because of competition, or because pressure on slow payers may be costly and ineffective. Thus firms that are short of funds may use the mechanism of trade credit to limit the extent to which they have to turn to the banks or to the new issue market, and this is likely to be the case particularly in years when the volume of stock-building is high.

Firms from which additional trade credit is taken will naturally be made correspondingly *less* liquid. But the mechanism has usually worked, on balance, to augment company liquidity as a whole; companies which have recourse to additional bank finance or to the new issue market are usually those in the best position for doing so, and the finance that they obtain eventually finds its way, at least in part, to the firms most in need of it, via the network of trade credit. The mechanism has thus tended to weaken restrictive credit policy.

At the same time, company balance-sheets show that the company sector has tended to become somewhat less liquid, in the aggregate, in recent years. Company holdings of liquid assets, whether presented on a " gross " or " net " basis (that is, after deducting " quick " liabilities), have not kept pace with the growth of business turnover. The reason is that the economy as a whole was excessively liquid at the end of the war, a legacy of wartime finance; thereafter the effect of Government policy has been to prevent the quantity of money from keeping pace with the increase in the money value of the national income. Because the public's holdings of money are now smaller in relation to their expenditure, it has become increasingly expensive for companies to replenish their liquidity by long-term borrowing from the public—that is to say, interest rates have risen.

The gradual erosion of company liquidity can be traced in Table 6. Total liquid assets did not rise between 1954 and 1958; and net, or surplus, liquid assets actually became a negative figure; in the process, the gross liquid " backing " for the flow of trade credit also declined, as a proportion of the level of trade

TABLE 5

THE GROWTH OF TRADE CREDIT IN THE QUOTED COMPANY SECTOR 1948–56

(Manufacturing, Building & Distribution)

	No. of Co.'s	Bank Loans		Stocks		Debtors		Creditors		Ratio of Debtors to Creditors	Net Trade Credit Given	
		Level £mn.	Change £mn.	Level £mn.	Change £mn.	Level £mn.	Change £mn.	Level £mn.	Change £mn.		Level £mn.	Change £mn.
1948	2,709	212		1,885		1,136		961		1·18	175	
1949	2,704	226	+ 14	2,021	+136	1,248	+112	1,036	+ 75	1·20	212	+37
1950	2,766	260	+ 34	2,295	+274	1,426	+114	1,191	+155	1·23	271	+59
1951	2,865	368	+108	2,944	+649	1,744	+282	1,456	+265	1·20	288	+17
1952	2,909	331	– 37	2,969	+ 25	1,811	+ 67	1,461	+ 5	1·24	350	+62
1953	2,879	288	– 43	2,961	– 8	1,911	+100	1,528	+ 67	1·25	383	+33
1953	2,933	294		2,987		1,903		1,459		1·30	444	
1954	2,892	315	+ 21	3,212	+225	2,120	+217	1,636	+177	1·30	484	+40
1955	2,842	372	+ 57	3,579	+367	2,416	+296	1,870	+234	1·29	546	+62
1956	2,960	450	+ 78	3,999	+420	2,637	+221	2,074	+204	1·27	563	+17
1957	2,879	497	+ 47	4,215	+216	2,811	+174	2,223	+149	1·22	588	+25
1958	2,808	509	+ 12	4,216	+ 1	2,877	+ 66	2,277	+ 54	1·26	600	+12

Sources: 1948–53 *Company Income and Finance 1949–53*, National Institute of Economic & Social Research (annual figures "linked" year to year, the difference in coverage of quoted companies being adjusted by changes in net assets; Debtors and Creditors include "non-trade" items).

1953–55 *Economic Trends*, February 1958, H.M.S.O. ⎱ (Comparable Parent-Company Groups;
1956–58 *Economic Trends*, December 1960, H.M.S.O. ⎰ Trade Debtors and Trade Creditors only).

The figures have been compiled, in the case of the period 1948–58, from company accounts with accounting periods ending between April 6 of the year in question and April 5 of the following year.

credit outstanding. How far the operations of companies will be affected by this gradual diminution of liquidity, and how far this development will increase the efficacy of a restrictive credit policy, is open to debate. But a continued examination of company accounts in the aggregate may provide a valuable indication of the direction of events.

TABLE 6

SURPLUS LIQUID ASSETS

£mn.

	1949	1953	1954	1955	1956	1957	1958
Cash	591	835	847	732	659	658	709
Tax reserve certificates ..	188	238	306	249	228	210	225
Marketable securities ..	294	355	349	476	478	498	530
Total liquid assets ..	1073	1428	1502	1457	1365	1366	1464
Less:							
Overdrafts and loans ..	220	294	316	378	450	497	509
Taxes due	497	652	653	684	748	750	733
Dividends and interest due	95	138	165	183	189	201	215
Total " quick " liabilities	812	1084	1134	1245	1387	1448	1457
Surplus liquid assets ..	261	344	368	212	−22	−82	7

LIQUIDITY RATIOS

	1949	1953	1954	1955	1956	1957	1958
Total liquid assets as % of creditors	106·4	97·9	90·3	75·6	63·4	59·3	61·8
" Immediate " assets*/ current liabilities ..	1·17	1·23	1·23	1·19	1·10	1·08	1·11

* Liquid assets *plus* trade and other debtors.
Source: Economic Trends, December 1960 (H.M.S.O., London).

United States Statistics

In the United States more comprehensive data on company finance are available. Statistics on the " Sources and Uses of Funds " in the corporate sector are published by the Department of Commerce, for all corporations other than banks and insurance companies. As in the case of the United Kingdom a gradual reduction in the degree of liquidity can be traced over the post-war years. For example, at the end of 1946 corporate holdings of cash and U.S. Government securities were almost as large as total corporate current liabilities. By 1955 this ratio of liquid asset holdings to current liabilities had fallen to under 50 per cent. and by the end of 1960 to 37 per cent.

In addition to annual data, quarterly financial statistics are published for manufacturing corporations by the Securities and Exchange Commission and Federal Trade Commission jointly (Quarterly Financial Reports for U.S. Manufacturing Corporations). These can be used to illuminate the impact on company finance of cyclical fluctuations in business activity more clearly than can annual figures. They show, for example, the changing course of liquidity over the business cycle—the improvement in the early stages of the upswing, when profit margins are high but expenditure on fixed assets low, and the gradual deterioration towards the end of the boom, when margins narrow and capital outlays increase.

Monthly Analytical Reports—
An Aid to Small Companies Too! *

By Robert E. Newberg

*Assistant Treasurer and Controller,
Delavan Manufacturing Company, Iowa.*

Introduction

During the past decade, many middle sized and large firms have recognized the need for a monthly (or period) report to top management, analysing financial results as compared with forecast and with prior periods. Too often the accountants in a small firm assume that this type of report is needed only in big companies. They therefore devote their efforts to accumulating data, and the extent of their reports to management may be a profit and loss statement and balance-sheet with supporting schedules. It is then left to management to make comparisons with forecast and prior periods, and to analyse the deviations. The accountant who limits his reports to these standard statements is passing up a real opportunity of service.

This paper presents the efforts made by the financial division of a small (400 employees) manufacturer of precision metal products to supply monthly analytical reports that would be a real aid in appraising performance and guiding decisions.

The approach

The first step was to take a critical look at existing reports. A review of operating statements showed a two-page (down to the penny) report for the month (and a similar report at the end of each quarter, giving the year-to-date figures). These statements, along with a detailed two-page balance-sheet, constituted the monthly report to management.

Our analysis led to these conclusions:

> (1) As a historical record, these reports are excellent and serve a purpose.

* From the N.A.A. *Bulletin*, July 1958.

    (2) As an analytical report they fall short because:

        (a) No comparison is provided, and, without a " yard-stick," there is nothing with which to measure success or failure.

        (b) Vital figures are buried among the insignificant, due to down-to-the-penny detail.

Our decision was to continue the detailed reports for reference and for historical records, and to establish a monthly analytical report. The analytical report was to highlight the significant figures for the month and the year-to-date, make comparisons between actual, forecast and prior periods, and explain deviations.

There are three prime requisites for a worthwhile report:

    (1) Timeliness;

    (2) Readability;

    (3) Importance;

The first, timeliness, meant that the monthly report must be issued before the information becomes ancient history. Fortunately our closing was usually completed each month by the fifth working day, which allowed us to complete and issue our report by the seventh working day.

Readability is deemed to be of paramount importance. To the non-accountant (and maybe even to accountants) vital facts regarding operations may be overlooked if the figures are presented merely in a long column. Figures stand out if highlighted with editorial comments and supported by graphs and charts. The rounding of figures to a significant point also aids in readability; pennies are irrelevant and should be dropped and, in larger companies, the hundreds also. We decided to round figures to the nearest dollar. The length of the report is also a factor in readability. The report must be long enough to cover the significant points, but not so long that it fails to hold the interest. We attempt to limit our analytical report to three or four pages of editorial comment plus the condensed statements and a graph on sales.

The third prime requisite, importance, calls for decision on which facts and figures are significant enough to be included. In determining these and also their order of appearance, we went to those who were to receive the report (president, vice-president, general manager, and vice-president sales) and asked them what they would like in the report. They suggested that they would like a quick recap containing, for the month and year-to-date, a comparison with forecast and the same period of last year of the following:

(1) Sales;
(2) Gross profit;
(3) Gross profit ratio to sales;
(4) Net earnings before taxes;
(5) Net earnings (before taxes) ratio to sales;
(6) Net earnings after taxes;
(7) Net carnings (after taxes) ratio to sales.

This, then, gave us about three-fourths of our opening page, presented as follows:

ANALYSIS OF OPERATIONS AND FINANCIAL POSITION

From: Financial Division Subject: November 19■7 Operations

To: Board of Directors Date: December 9, 19■7

YEAR-TO-DATE—Significant Figures

	19■7 Forecast	19■7 Actual	19■6 Actual
Sales	$3,965,000	$4,111,913	$3,276,410
Gross Profit	776,900	813,112	682,746
Ratio to Sales	19·6%	19·8%	20·8%
Net Earnings before Taxes	401,500	431,493	373,746
Ratio to Sales	10·1%	10·5%	11·4%
Net Earnings after Taxes	197,800	212,159	184,441
Ratio to Sales	5·0%	5·2%	5·6%

NOVEMBER OPERATIONS—Key Information

	19■7 Forecast	19■7 Actual	19■6 Actual
Sales.	352,850	421,877	293, 85
Gross Profit	73,650	90,820	59,521
Ratio to Sales	20·9%	21·5%	20·2%
Net Earnings before Taxes	36,970	46,106	28,780
Ratio to Sales	10·5%	10·9%	9·8%
Net Earnings after Taxes	18,203	22,589	14,273
Ratio to Sales	5·2%	5·4%	4·9%

One method we use to attract attention to a particular item is to rubber stamp an arrow towards the figure we deem of vital importance.

To keep our reports from becoming too stereotyped, every

few months (usually at the end of a quarter) we present three key figures for the year-to-date in graphic form. The opening half-page then appears somewhat as follows:

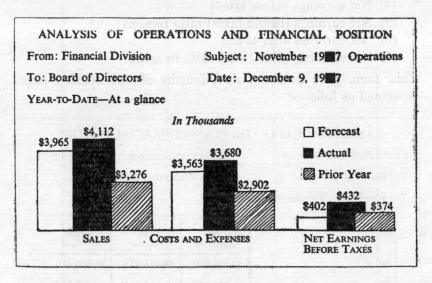

ANALYSIS OF OPERATIONS AND FINANCIAL POSITION

From: Financial Division Subject: November 19▮7 Operations
To: Board of Directors Date: December 9, 19▮7

YEAR-TO-DATE—At a glance

In Thousands

☐ Forecast
■ Actual
▨ Prior Year

$3,965 $4,112 $3,276
$3,563 $3,680 $2,902
$402 $432 $374

SALES . COSTS AND EXPENSES NET EARNINGS BEFORE TAXES

Management also asked to have several balance-sheet figures on the first page. They wanted to know total assets, how this compared with a year ago and with forecast, how much we had invested in fixed assets before and after depreciation, what our working capital is, and the total of stockholders' equity along with the book value per share of stock. These figures (see below) comprise the balance of the cover page.

FINANCIAL POSITION—compared with forecast and a year ago

	November 30		
	19▮7 Forecast	19▮7 Actual	19▮6 Actual
Total Assets	$1,395,000	$1,446,592	$1,116,712
Fixed Assets (Cost) ..	625,000	642,073	491,437
Fixed Assets (Net of Depreciation)	400,000	417,244	321,372
Working Capital	478,000	475,445	278,201
Stockholders' Equity ..	598,000	612,359	450,200
Book Value per Share of Stock	79·73	81·65	60·03

This completes the highlighting of the key figures. We next move to some of the important details. This may take several different forms. Occasionally we present each segment under its own heading, and compare actual with forecast and prior year (if pertinent). We normally cover: sales (by product line and, if significant, by major product within the line), cost of sales or gross profit ratios (with the same sub-divisions as sales) and expenses (by major items).

Our most frequent manner of presentation is to break down the total deviation from forecast into its various parts. (We consider the forecast a more important guide than prior year figures even though we use the latter for reference.) We then give the dollar amount and per cent. of variance, along with brief reasons for each of these parts:

---

(2)

NOVEMBER OPERATIONS—resulted in net earnings before taxes of $46,106. This is $9,136 (24·7%) over the forecast and $17,326 (60·2%) ahead of the comparative month of 19█6. The breakdown of this $9,136 favourable variation is as follows:

			Over (Under) %	Forecast $
SALES of $421,877 were substantially over forecast:				
Product Line " A "	up	20·7%	$28,140	
Product Line " B "	up	0·7	820	
Product Line " C "	up	98·4	28,510	
Product Line " D "	up	15·0	11,557	
Total Sales are up over forecast by—			19·6	69,027
COST OF SALES are also up from forecast because of:				
Increased volume	up	$54,504		
Change in product mix	down	(283)		
Decreased costs	down	(2,364)		
Total Cost of Sales exceed forecast by—			18·6	51,857
EXPENSES were in excess of anticipated. The major items of increase were:				
Advertising	up	88·3%	$3,972	
Sales travel	up	47·6	1,353	
Commissions	up	20·6	1,583	
All other	up	6·7	1,417	
Total Expenses over by—			23·0	8,325
NON-OPERATING (net) varied only slightly, in dollars, from forecast:			(64·7)	(291)
NET EARNINGS BEFORE TAXES OVER FORECAST BY			24·7%	$ 9,136

This completes page two. Our next step is to analyse the year-to-date operations. Again we vary the manner from month to month. Sometimes it is similar to the one illustrated above. Other months the analysis is by segments as mentioned on page 553. This, then, is the basic pattern we follow:

(3)

YEAR-TO-DATE—details:

SALES of $4,111,913 are $146,913 (3·7%) over the forecast and 25·5% ($835,503) ahead of the same eleven months of 19■6. The breakdown by major product is as follows:

	January thru November		
	19■7 Forecast	19■■7 Actual	19■6 Actual
Product Line " A "			
Product # 1	$ 513,000	$ 539,542	$ 589,669
Product # 2	172,000	168,713	148,527
Product # 3	220,000	189,029	83,217
Product Line " B "			
Product #10	1,065,000	1,137,012	1,296,421
Product #11	555,000	636,902	16,199
Product Line " C "			
Product #20	356,000	349,817	298,192
Product #21	237,000	164,503	163,306
Product Line " D "			
Product #31	225,000	246,312	181,327
Product #32	197,000	216,498	157,319
Product #33	89,000	99,220	71,398
Product #34	336,000	364,365	270,835
TOTAL SALES	$3,965,000	$4,111,913	$3,276,410

Attached is the analysis of sales in graphic form. Please note the effect of November operations on the twelve month moving average.

The sales graph shows the average monthly sales by product line during the previous five years, and a twelve month moving average for the current year. The advantage of the twelve month moving average is that it irons out seasonal fluctuations, and thus gives a trend line. The calculation of the twelve month average is made by taking total sales for the last twelve months and dividing by twelve. This graph is drawn on a translucent paper and is easily brought up to date by drawing in the information for the new month and rerunning on an Ozalid machine:

SALES (Exhibit "A")
(In thousands of dollars)

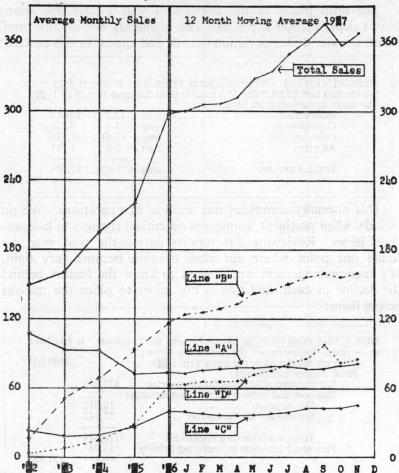

The balance of the third page and a portion of the last might be devoted to an analysis of gross profit ratios as compared with forecast and actual:

GROSS PROFIT RATIOS for the year-to-date average 19·8%. This is slightly above the forecast of 19·6% but approximately 1% below the comparative period of 19■6. The decline from the ratio of 20·8% appears to be small, but the dollar amount, when applied to 19■7 sales, amounts to $42,000.

It should be pointed out that the price increases in product lines " A " and " D " are bolstering our margin—please note the November gross profit ratios of the product lines on the November operating statement. There are four major factors in the decline in our gross profit ratio this year as compared with 19■6:

  (1) *Our direct labor* average hourly rate for the first eleven months of 19■7 is $2·28 as compared with $1·99 for the same period of last year.
  (2) *The overall burden rate* has risen this year by 9·2%.
  (3) *Price increases* effective October 1, 19■7 in product lines "A" and " D " have helped to offset the increased basic rates.
  (4) *Improved production methods* have also aided in combating the profit squeeze.

The third phase of the analysis of year-to-date operations covers departmental expenses. The highlights are usually brief, unless a major dollar deviation occurs, and appear in this pattern:

DEPARTMENTAL EXPENSES total $386,024 — $7,024 (1·8%) over the forecast and $73,428 (23·5%) greater than the same period of 19■6. The major deviations from forecast are:

Sales travel	..	..	..	over	15·2%	$3,615
Commissions		..	..	over	3·8	3,236
Office payroll	..	..	..	under	(2·6)	(1,588)
All other	..	..	..	over	0·8	1,761
TOTAL EXPENSES	..	..		over	1·8%	$7,024

This normally completes our analysis of operations. We do include, when pertinent, comments on critical changes in balance-sheet items. Reviewing our reports during the past year, we found one point where our cash position became very tight. We knew management would want to know the factors behind the decline in cash, and this is our effort to place the reasons before them:

OUR CASH POSITION in March became the " tightest " it has been in — years—following are the underlying factors:

Cash on hand and in the bank Jan. 1-■7 ..			$107,924
Funds became available by:			
Net earnings after taxes for the quarter	$51,670		
Plus non-cash items deducted from earnings:			
Depreciation	16,012		
Income tax for the quarter	52,942		
Total available thru operations ..	$120,624		
Plus small increases in operating liability	11,037		
			131,661
Total funds available			239,585
Funds expended as follows:			
Increased investment in receivables ..	63,512		
Additional machines and equipment purchased	37,420		
Payments made on the new addition ..	43,419		
All other asset investments increased ..	3,992		
Total additional investment ..	148,343		
Payment made on 19■6 Income Tax ..	89,327		
Total funds used			237,670
Net cash before 90 day note			1,915
Funds borrowed on a 90 day note Mar. 21-■7 to give us funds sufficient to pay invoices and other cash expenditures ..			50,000
Cash on hand and in the bank Mar. 31-■7			$51,915

Along with the monthly analysis, we include a condensed balance-sheet (exhibit " B ") and operating statement (exhibit " C ").

(Exhibit " B ")

CONDENSED BALANCE-SHEET
November 30, 19■7

	Forecast	Actual	Nov. 30th 19■6	% Incr. (% Decr.)
ASSETS:	$	$	$	%
Current assets:				
Cash on hand and in bank ..	90,000	117,312	84,312	39·1
Accounts receivable ..	375,000	426,817	313,740	36·0
Inventories	485,000	440,549	356,661	23·5
Total current assets ..	950,000	984,678	754,713	30·5
Fixed assets:				
Cost	625,000	642,073	491,437	30·6
Less Depreciation reserves ..	225,000	224,829	170,065	32·2
Net fixed assets ..	400,000	417,244	321,372	29·8
Other assets:				
Prepaid expenses	25,000	26,712	21,210	25·9
Other	20,000	17,958	19,417	(7·5)
Total other assets	45,000	44,670	40,627	10·0
GRAND TOTAL ASSETS	$1,395,000	$1,446,592	$1,116,712	29·5%
LIABILITIES AND STOCKHOLDERS EQUITY:				
Current liabilities:	$	$	$	%
Accounts payable	80,000	106,219	78,420	35·4
Mortgage payable—due in one year	15,000	15,000	15,000	—
Federal income taxes ..	160,000	172,597	186,873	(7·6)
Accrued liabilities	217,000	215,417	196,219	9·8
Total current liabilities	472,000	509,233	476,512	6·9
Long-term liabilities:				
On buildings and equipment	325,000	325,000	190,000	71·0
Stockholders equity:				
Capital stock	75,000	75,000	75,000	—
Earnings retained:				
Current year	197,800	212,159	184,441	15·0
Prior years	325,200	325,200	190,759	62·0
Total stockholders equity	598,000	612,359	450,200	36·0
TOTAL LIABILITIES AND STOCK-HOLDERS EQUITY ..	$1,395,000	$1,446,592	$1,116,712	29·5%

(Exhibit " C ")

OPERATING STATEMENT
November 19■7

	MONTH			YEAR-TO-DATE		
	Forecast	Actual	19■6	Forecast	Actual	19■6
SALES:						
Product Line " A " ..	$135,750	$163,890	$115,630	$ 905,000	$ 897,284	$ 821,413
Product Line " B " ..	110,250	111,070	92,000	1,620,000	1,773,914	1,312,620
Product Line " C " ..	29,800	58,310	23,840	593,000	514,320	461,498
Product Line " D " ..	77,050	88,607	62,415	847,000	926,395	680,879
Total Sales ..	$352,850	$421,877	$293,885	$3,965,000	$4,111,913	$3,276,410
COST OF SALES	279,200	331,057	234,364	$3,188,100	$3,298,801	$2,593,664
GROSS PROFIT..	73,650	90,820	59,521	776,900	813,112	682,746
Ratio to Sales	20·9%	21·5%	20·2%	19·6%	19·8%	20·8%
EXPENSES						
Selling:						
Payroll	5,250	5,375	4,107	51,100	52,612	40,690
Travel	2,840	4,193	2,615	23,700	27,315	19,412
Advertising ..	4,500	8,472	3,750	50,200	51,189	33,815
Commissions ..	7,700	9,283	6,388	85,575	88,811	70,707
All Other	590	615	415	6,825	8,178	7,958
Total Selling ..	20,880	27,938	17,275	217,400	228,105	172,582
Administrative:						
Payroll—Executive	7,000	7,050	6,410	76,300	76,915	69,300
Payroll—Office ..	5,850	5,820	4,242	59,900	58,312	46,279
Travel	500	1,147	715	5,000	4,630	5,319
All Other ..	750	837	626	8,000	7,752	7,401
Total Administrative	14,100	14,854	11,993	149,200	147,609	128,299
General Expense ..	1,250	1,763	1,172	12,400	10,310	11,715
Total Expenses ..	36,230	44,555	30,380	379,000	386,024	312,596
OPERATING EARNINGS ..	37,420	46,215	29,141	397,900	427,088	370,150
NON-OPERATING						
Income	800	1,013	712	12,100	13,317	11,715
Expense	1,250	1,122	1,073	8,500	8,912	8,119
NET EARNINGS BEFORE TAXES	36,970	46,106	28,780	401,500	431,493	373,746
PROVISION FOR INCOME TAXES	18,767	23,517	14,507	203,700	219,334	189,305
NET EARNINGS AFTER TAXES	18,203	22,589	14,273	197,800	212,159	184,441
Ratio to Sales:						
Before taxes ..	10·4%	10·9%	9·8%	10·1%	10·5%	11·4%
After taxes ..	5·2%	5·4%	4·9%	5·0%	5·2%	5·6%
GROSS PROFIT RATIOS:						
Product Line " A " ..	24·9%	25·2%	24·0%	24·0%	24·3%	25·2%
Product Line " B " ..	18·7	18·1	17·9	18·3	17·6	19·0
Product Line " C " ..	20·1	19·6	20·2	20·1	19·7	21·1
Product Line " D " ..	17·2	20·3	16·8	16·9	19·6	18·9

Conclusions

We fully realize that a monthly analysis, such as ours, can only " touch the surface." However, the phases analysed but briefly in each report frequently raise further questions from a member of top management (or the financial division), which lead to a detailed special analysis. Our experience, over three years, leads us to say " Yes, monthly analytical reports are a real aid to management in small companies too !! "

The Budget Comes of Age *

By James L. Peirce

Vice-president—finance,
A. B. Dick Company, Chicago.

ANY technique of management reaches maturity when, after its earlier mistakes have antagonized human beings sufficiently, it emerges with a new outlook and practice that is in harmony with basic motivations. Budgeting now seems to be undergoing this metamorphosis. Out of the disturbance it has created is appearing a calmer, more orderly, more positive approach.

It is my purpose in this article to add to the spreading view that budgeting rests on principles which have more in common with concepts of human relationship than with rules of accounting; and that, if these principles are applied, successful practice is inevitable.

There is no doubt that thousands of management people are well grounded in budget practice and derive from it a sense of balance and direction. No businessman who has had extensive experience with an ably managed budget system appears to doubt its value. But there are many more thousands who are so confused on the subject that it might indeed be better for them to discard their budgets entirely than to continue as they are. Surveys have shown that in some quarters budgeting is about as popular among foremen as a layoff, and stress the damage from the misuse of budgeting.

Some executives freely admit the shortcomings of their budget practices, and acknowledge that they could be remedied by the application of more intelligent human relations. If it is as simple as that, then why cannot budgets be made a welcome and productive feature of business without delay? The answer, I think, is that the problem is not such a simple one—just as human beings are not simple, and just as the science of human relationships is not simple.

How shall we go about the task of instilling revitalized ideas in place of negative or short-sighted attitudes?

We can accomplish nothing until we face up to the fact that many of us have acquired a defensive approach to the subject

* From *Harvard Business Review*, May–June, 1954.

through painful experience. People generally do not like budgets. Foremen are people first and supervisors second; so are department managers and top executives. Budgets represent restriction. They are in the same category as school bells and Monday mornings.

If from the very beginning of our careers we had been told, with accompanying evidence, that budgets were a help to us, affording us guidance, stability, and strength, as well as keeping us out of innumerable troubles, our responses would by now be quite different. But what was our actual experience? Have not many of us been introduced to budgets when the budget was blamed, rightly or wrongly, for our failure to get a raise in pay? Have not many of us become acquainted with the budget only as a barrier to spending what we felt was necessary for better equipment or performance? Is it surprising, then, that budgets are associated in many minds with paucity and niggardliness rather than with planning and direction?

Attitudes—the key

Good attitudes are the key to successful budgeting. When the attitudes of people toward each other are generous, understanding, and based on mutual respect, any technique adopted to further performance is apt to be successful. When attitudes are dominated by distrust, criticism, and recrimination, any such technique is likely to fail. In such cases, by a strange twist of human nature, the budgets and those who defend them bear the brunt of the blame for errors entirely unconnected with budgets.

Budgeting is a trained, disciplined approach, which recognizes the need for standards of performance to achieve a result. Hence it must be built on a base of good organization; otherwise, favorable attitudes have no chance to operate. But at the same time it lives in an atmosphere of perpetual adjustment to the needs and capacities of people. It thrives on such fundamentals as recognition of accomplishment, consideration for the rights of individuals, fair play—in other words, enlightened relationships.

Motivation for budgeting. The first consideration should be the motivation for the budget system. Why have one at all? Is the budget a part of a system of over-all planning, with the aim that all concerned may have a measure of the amounts to be spent, and action may be by design rather than by expediency? Or is the budget a pressure device designed to goad people into greater efforts? It takes a little soul-searching to determine honestly which of these concepts represents the position of a particular management.

Both concepts are prevalent. They may be symbolized by two wooden sticks—one neatly divided into thirty-six one-inch spaces, and the other sharply pointed at one end. The yardstick, symbolising the planning concept, may be used, for example, by a foreman to establish standards of performance and cost, and to measure actual results in relation thereto; in this sense, it is a tool used by the foreman and his boss in partnership. The pointed stick, a symbol of the pressure type of budget, is found only in the hand of the superior, turned menacingly toward his foremen or workers. The yardstick elicits the voluntary effort of men to do their best work. The pointed stick forces a reluctant and minimal performance.

There is plenty of evidence that the yardstick concept will not diminish the yield from the budget tool in terms of cost reduction. It has been shown again and again that high costs which stubbornly resist all efforts of the pressure type will melt away under the warmth of an approach which is attuned to our basic responses. The attitude to be adopted here is an enlistment of all concerned in a common effort, with a complete explanation of objectives and methods.

Planning—the foundation

Although budgeting can be separately applied to any unit of the business, it is far more effective when it rests on an integrated plan for the entire operation. In the proper sense, it is only one phase of planning. When planning has been adopted, budgets emerge of necessity.

The presence or absence of intelligent planning is reflected to a surprising degree in the effectiveness of the people who are asked to operate with a budget system. And this means all the people—from top executives to production-line workers. Individuals are usually more intuitive than we realize. When a budget is built on sound planning, they respond to that fact without always knowing why.

Meaning of planning. As used in this discussion, *planning* refers to the predetermination of a course of action in such detail that every responsible unit of the firm may be guided thereby. It includes sales forecasting, production scheduling, expense budgeting, and estimating of manufacturing costs and inventory levels. It involves making advance decisions concerning new products, merchandising methods, material procurement, and labor rates. In short, planning implies facing problems and making decisions about them *ahead of time* (subject to later revision if necessary). The planning period is usually a year where operations are concerned, longer for financial and developmental activities.

These decisions are frequently so hard to make in advance that they border on the impossible. Yet they insure a reasonable net profit as no other method can. And on this planned net profit figure—the apex of the planning structure—depends our ability to attract new capital as needed and to compensate management and shareholders.

Effect on people. Let us examine the effect of the planning process on the people involved in it. In particular, we might first consider the impact on administrative people, for their outlook in the long run determines the attitudes of the larger non-administrative group. What is the planning technique doing to foremen, department managers, division heads? Is it building up or tearing down their confidence in their company's future? Is it affecting favorably or adversely their independence of thought, their self-assurance, their capacity to understand and rely on those around them?

It seems self-evident that planning alone does not afford the entire answer. If administrators are already exhibiting " good morale " the chances are that the installation of planning can do them untold good; with proper explanations, the management can hold forth the legitimate promise of better accomplishment, greater satisfaction, more confident operating, and, ultimately, opportunity for increased compensation. If, on the other hand, management is struggling with a discordant staff, perhaps suffering from the blight of fuzzy organization lines or other impediments to good work, it might be better to defer planning and control until it has put its house in order. Too frequently a well-designed budget system has collapsed after being superimposed on a faulty base of administrative personnel policy. Then the budget is discarded, and all concerned return to their bad habits.

Control—the complement

But there is another phase of budgeting which tests the fiber of men even more than planning. I am referring to control, which is the eternal complement of planning. Neither one is useful without the other, and to budget even the smallest unit of a business implies the presence of control also.

Budget abuses. It is in control that the colossal mistakes of budgeting are made. It is here that the amateurs censure their subordinates for exceeding budgets, without realizing that they themselves are to blame for inadequate training. It is here that men become so frustrated under maladministered budgets that they resort to all sorts of tricks to conceal actual results, and pad their budgets to give themselves breathing room. It is here that staff men usurp authority, merited pay increases are denied because of budget limitations, and tales are carried up to the top under the guise of budget reporting.

The list of abuses could be prolonged indefinitely. There are many wrong ways to exercise budget control. There is only one right way. Let us then discard the negative approach, since the assertion of an affirmative truth will dissolve all counterfeits.

Control might be quickly and simply defined as a disciplined effort to follow a plan or explain deviations from it. The effort referred to takes the form of self-discipline—voluntary, unified, and cooperative. Deviations from plan are permissible, if they are deliberate, foreknown, and authorized. If they are apparently beyond anyone's ability to prevent—as for instance a failure to reach budgeted sales volume—at least they are spotlighted as early as possible, and management has the chance to take whatever action is indicated. Control is simply the modern form of the old formula, " management by exception."

It is, of course, at the point of deviation from the budget that most of the human problems are born. This is, by design, the central point in the entire system—the moment which demands explanation, instruction, decision, argument, or even discipline, as the case warrants—the flash-point for management action.

Common sense departures. It should be evident that the effect of control on people is commensurate with their training and conditioning for it. If they understand thoroughly the meaning and uses of control, they will view it in the light of common sense. They will neither resent it nor be awed by it. They will turn it to the constructive use for which it is intended, and it will become an aid rather than an obstacle.

Perhaps the best way to clarify this common sense approach is to examine a typical situation in which a manager wishes to make what he believes to be a desirable expenditure not covered in his budget. This problem is encountered daily, and solved without friction by managers equipped with knowledge of budget principles and skill in their application. The following case is a good illustration:

The case of a sales promotion manager who is also responsible for advertising. Having been instructed to prepare a budget, he has first carefully completed his sales promotion and advertising plans for the coming period, basing them on discussions with the sales vice-president and others responsible for policy and sales objectives. After constructing an acceptable plan, he has converted it into dollars in the form of a budget, which has been approved.

Because he has prepared this budget himself, he is thoroughly familiar with it. It is supported with adequate detail. He feels confident that plan and budget are as nearly right as he can make them.

Furthermore, he knows the implications of accepting this budget as his guide to operations. It is not to be exceeded without approval. It is a commitment that must be honored, and he well understands its importance to the company, his associates, and himself.

Nevertheless, he senses in the attitudes surrounding his budget an element of flexibility. If conditions change, the budget will be altered, either upward or downward. He is not uneasy about this prospect. He is simply alert to recognize such a situation if it should develop.

Now let us suppose that an opportunity is presented to exert extra pressure on a certain market, and it appears that a special direct-mail campaign, supplemented by some local newspaper advertising, will yield good sales results. He knows enough not to throw the whole idea aside simply because it is not provided for in his budget. He has already a clear understanding with his " boss " about what to do in such cases. So he goes about preparing a report, including proposed action, cost, and anticipated results; and he presents this report, knowing that it will be given proper consideration, even though it represents expenditure beyond budget limits.

How simple this miniature study in budget attitudes! How mature the responses governed by common sense! And yet how often common sense is violated! Is there any reason not to extend this frank approach to the foreman who sees a need for maintenance expenses or a merit increase not embraced in his budget? The frictions, frustrations, and other evils supposed to be inherent in budgets must all be susceptible to eradication in the same sensible manner.

Essential prerequisites. All this presupposes, of course, that the supervisor in question enjoys a satisfactory relationship with his immediate superior. It also rests on clear-cut organization lines and the disposition to delegate authority along with responsibility.

Further, the accounting principles used must be well tested, and the accounting administration of high caliber. Strict honesty must govern the determination of the content of budgets. Nothing confuses budget operation more than the charging of costs over which the supervisor has no control, unless such items are set out separately and so labelled.

A last important requisite is understanding of the make-up of the budget. Flexible factory budgets especially can be complicated and subject to dispute. The factors used must be clearly explained, with full recognition of their weaknesses. If an item—such as machine repairs, for example—is in fact neither wholly fixed nor wholly variable, and yet must be treated one way or the other for budget purposes, the shortcomings of the resulting budget figure should be conceded frankly. If scrap and rework costs are subject to dispute between foremen, the situation must be talked out in an air of give-and-take. No plant management should encourage or permit embittered arguments between foremen on such a matter.

Cost reduction—the goal

The attitudes we have been discussing should add to, rather than detract from, the effectiveness of budgets in the field of cost control. Most firms operate, in good times and bad, under the pressure of relentless competition, which forces them to devote ceaseless effort to cost reduction. It is perhaps this circumstance more than any other that has given impetus to the spread of budgeting. And it has doubtless given rise to the abuses falling under the general heading of " pressure."

The usual tone of the complaints in this category is that budgets are used only as a hammer on costs (and at the same time on people), and particularly that budgets are constantly being tightened and compliance enforced indiscriminately. The impression received by a supervisor in this situation is one of constant insistence on better and better performance, continuous blame for failure to meet the budget, and complete absence of credit for his good work. The budget becomes purely a pressure device, against which he must defend himself or lose his job.

The only effective cure for such a distorted outlook is to substitute, as rapidly as possible, a " let's do it together " attitude

for the shortsighted " you do it or else " attitude. The latter may
have gained more ground in a plant or office than the management realizes. To correct this attitude may take time and patience,
but it is never impossible to blank out negatives and substitute
positives in human thinking.

Cost reduction drive is a feature of the competitive system
and is admittedly responsible in large measure for high living
standards. Budgets can be used for such stimulation without
enslaving people. They furnish the standard from which to
explore cost-savings possibilities. They provide the measure of
yield from improved methods. But the attitude surrounding
them must be right.

Incentives, true and false. This line of thought runs directly
into the question of incentive. What incentive does a production
supervisor have to reduce costs? The incentive supplied by threat
is negative and, in the long run, ineffective. Direct money
incentives, correlated to budget factors, claim some merit but,
as we shall see, are fraught with problems. The true incentives,
it is at last becoming clear, are those usually referred to as
" intangible," supplemented by wages carefully determined and
sympathetically explained.

Let us examine for a moment the possibilities of direct money
incentives. Some companies use and defend them—and we can
have no quarrel with success. The line of reasoning on which
they are based runs something like this: " If simple piecework
can be an effective incentive for the workman, then the same
principle can be applied to the foreman. We will provide a
bonus and include in it a factor measuring success in complying
with the budget. Savings against the budget benefit the company
and, at the same time, provide funds for rewarding the foremen."

The fallacies in this reasoning begin to appear early in the
process. They arise from two sources: (a) from the almost
insurmountable difficulty of setting a completely fair and acceptable budget for this purpose, especially in the light of unfore-
seeable changes in operating conditions, and (b) from the tendency
for the foreman to emphasize budget performance to the detriment
of necessary action. It is a temptation to defer maintenance
when the need is not urgent and the expenditure would reduce
one's own pay check.

As the foreman grows to the stature of a manager, as he
becomes more able to carry responsibilities (and this is the goal
of enlightened management today), the problems become progressively tougher. The experienced foreman is conscious of

the importance of cost reduction. He is also conscious of the need to spend money. He is likely to resent being rewarded for unwise penny-pinching as much as being penalized for exceeding his budget when the need is evident to everyone.

To a foreman properly informed and aware of his role as a part of the management team, the real incentive is the satisfaction that comes from knowing that he has given his best effort, evidenced by suitable recognition both financial and in the manner and words of his superior. There is nothing better to assure the success of a cost-reduction program than a foreman with a real comprehension of objectives, needs, and policies.

Management support—the need

One of the rocks on which many systems founder is the lack of top-management support. This is a strange commentary on a management group which, in America, is generally supposed to have reached the acme of sophistication in the motivation of people. Nevertheless, examine any limping, half-hearted budget system, and note how the " chickens come home to roost " in the president's office.

Even more surprising, it frequently turns out that the top man does not really understand the planning and control concept and the attitudes that make it work. Consequently his allegiance to it is tentative and lukewarm. He constantly questions the methods used and is instinctively distrustful of results. This frame of mind permeates the organization. It bolsters opposition to the budget and weakens its proponents. No budget system can realize its potential value without the unqualified support and understanding of top management.

Controllers' mistakes. There is another enemy of successful budget practice which may well cause more of the friction between budgets and people than all the other errors put together. I refer to the misconception on the part of controllers, budget managers, accountants, and other staff people concerning their part in the process.

When a controller takes operating personnel to task for exceeding the budget, he is inviting trouble of the worst kind. His correct course is to report the situation to operating management and, if necessary, to the president, using the same figures and terms in each case. The problem then rests with the president and his operating subordinate, which is exactly where it belongs. It should be discussed and acted on in the direct line organization. No controller should permit himself to be placed in the position of representing the president in such matters.

The same principle applies to all staff people concerned with coordinating the budget system, whether they report to a controller, treasurer, or factory accountant. There is impressive evidence that over-zealous budget people have caused a great deal of mischief, practically all unnecessary. They cannot be blamed individually, of course, for the failure of management to provide the principles needed for good budget practice. The remedy is in the eradication of faulty notions concerning staff and line.

One of the first steps is to insist that each manager or foreman establish his own budget. He knows best his potential performance and the extent to which he can commit himself. He may enlist expert help, of course, from the budget man, but under no circumstances should the budget man establish the budget, nor should the foreman be permitted to feel that this is happening. The penalty for violating this rule is the sacrifice of the sense of responsibility that locks a man securely to a budget when he knows it is his own.

Another misconception of budget men is that they are almost solely responsible for cost reduction; that they alone are expected to seek opportunities for cost savings, such as excessive waste, dispensable overtime, carelessness in handling tools, and so on. In some cases, they have apparently been told to report such instances to a factory superintendent or even to top management rather than to the responsible first-line supervisor. It is difficult to conceive of a practice that violates more completely the basic principles of good relations.

Line organisation. This medieval mess will clear itself up once management has established that the line organization is responsible for cost control—fully and absolutely. Using a familiar type of organization, let it be clear that the vice-president of manufacturing is charged with the manufacturing cost reduction campaign; he delegates this work as he sees fit to plant managers, and they in turn to factory superintendents, who then look to the front-line men, the foremen.

The controller and budget men still fit into this picture importantly:

(1) They are equipped to establish and co-ordinate the budget system, with all the tools of accounting and cost analysis.

(2) They should be able to teach the operating people how to use it.

(3) They should provide timely and intelligible reporting on performance against budget.

The attitude which should govern the staff people is one of maximum helpfulness to the line personnel. Only in this way can the budget man gain the foreman's confidence. If he finds cost-saving ideas, they should be volunteered promptly to the foreman for what use the latter can make of them. The budget man's own superior should be adept enough to detect a skilful job—and one primary evidence will be satisfactory relations with operating personnel.

Conclusion

The steps to be taken to improve budgeting depend, of course, on the mistakes an organization has been making. A searching self-examination would seem the first move. Having identified the practices which most clearly abuse budget principles, management will find that the corrective steps will present themselves.

Summary of principles. Here, for your convenience, is a summary of points to be considered by any management wishing to establish its budget on a sound foundation:

(1) Establish your budget system on the highest possible level of *motivation.* To be specific, this means using it as a means for setting standards of performance, for measuring actual results, and for guiding management to satisfactory achievement; and not as a pressure device to goad people into greater efforts. Accept this as a part of the philosophy of your company. Think about it, talk about it, make it a reality. A budget program cannot be advanced to the stage of maximum fruition without this step.

(2) Anchor your budgeting firmly to *planning.* The budget is not the plan; it is merely the statement of the plan in the language of figures. First turn the thinking of your people to planning; then ask them to prepare budgets for their plans.

(3) Establish the meaning of *control,* and then put it into practice. In particular, this requires the manager of each department to establish his own budget. Top management may not be able to approve as high a figure as he asks for, but can reach agreement with him over what he is expected to accomplish and what it will cost. Thereafter he is responsible for planned performance. If he finds it necessary to exceed the budget, he should discuss this action with his superior and ask for advance approval. A budget is neither to be considered sacred nor to be taken lightly. Managers will respond with better attitudes when they understand that the budget permits them to control their own operations.

(4) Insist on a *clear-cut organization.* A budget system cannot thrive without it. Each department should have a responsible manager, vested with authority commensurate with his responsibilities. He should know both to whom he reports and who report to him. A searching organization audit may be needed.

(5) Arrange for good, common sense *accounting* and complete, simple and prompt explanations of the content of the items. This requires an accounting staff that is more concerned with operating facts than techniques of balancing the books. No supervisor should

in his budget have any item which he does not control. If your house is not in order in these respects, almost any amount of effort is justified to put it in shape. And this will cost more money initially than you expect to pay, in terms of staff salaries and, perhaps, outside consulting services. The cost is usually well justified.

(6) Use your budget as a *cost control* tool—to be placed in your foremen's hands, not held as a club over their heads. To implement this rule, it may be a good idea to design an educational programme; meetings attended by line and staff supervisors may prove effective. Cost reduction must be an effort toward a common aim.

(7) Insure the active participation of *top management*. The budget program cannot succeed otherwise. If you are the president, and question how well you measure up to this requirement, examine your thinking critically and ascertain which of the points in this article, if any, arouse resistance in your thought. Discussion with a controller other than your own may afford a fresh view. In any case, set aside the time to explore the subject fully and to practice budgetary control in your daily affairs. If you are a controller, your course in enlisting top-management support is one of patient teaching, until your case is won.

(8) See that the *controller* and his staff express the correct attitude for the responsibility they undertake with budgets. It is the controller's job to establish, maintain, and coordinate a budgetary system—in fact, a complete system of planning and control. But his work must be accomplished through authorized management. He must not enforce his instructions or issue orders. He and his staff must produce, report on, and interpret information. He is wholly a staff executive, and his only honors stem from the confidence of his associates.

I have refrained from specifying the manner in which these ideas might be made known, or "sold," to the administrative groups. The task is the most challenging project the controller is privileged to conduct, and it gains momentum as he enlists the support of management at all levels. The method of carrying on this unremitting campaign varies from company to company, but there is a tendency to rely largely on daily contacts. The controller and his staff—all the budget men and cost accountants—spread the idea in their working conversations. Relatively few companies hold regular meetings for this purpose.

It is interesting that the eight steps listed have their roots deep in personnel administration—that each one reflects a problem involving people.

Measuring the Productivity of Capital *

By Joel Dean

Professor, Columbia University, New York City.

THE president of one of our largest oil companies, who was pushing through a program of drastic decentralization of management, stated recently that the last thing he would delegate would be decisions about capital expenditures. This is understandable because capital expenditure decisions form the framework for a company's future development and are a major determinant of efficiency and competitive power. The wisdom of these corporate investment decisions, therefore, has a profound effect upon a company's future earnings and growth.

From the standpoint of the stockholder and of the consumer, capital expenditures are the principal bulwark against the seemingly endless progression of wage increases. From the standpoint of labor, capital expenditures are the basic economic source of future wage advances, since they embody the creative forward strides of advancing technology. Finally, capital expenditures, both by their aggregate size and by their cyclical timing, have a great deal to do with the character of the economy as a whole, and thus with the government's role in maintaining stability.

Management program

Farsighted judgment is an essential requisite for wise decisions about capital expenditures. But such judgment, to be sound, must be based on analysis of all the facts, many of them extremely technical and complex. In particular, top management needs an objective means of measuring the economic worth of individual investment proposals, in order to have a realistic basis for choosing among them. The basic measure of economic worth is the productivity of capital, which means its power to produce profits. The purpose of this article is to suggest better ways of making that measurement.

Need for specialized skills. Unfortunately, the problem of managing capital expenditure has not generally been attacked

* From *Harvard Business Review*, January–February, 1954.

with the kind of thorough and objective analysis that has paid such big dividends in other management areas. I have made a study of the capital expenditure methods of some fifty large companies. These are all well-managed companies so far as production, engineering, and marketing methods are concerned. But on capital expenditures they show widespread failure to measure the investment worth of individual proposals, lack of defensible objective standards, and distorted dedication to procedures and paper-work. In other words, when it comes to capital expenditures, they are still forced to play by ear to a distressing extent.

The development of an effective system for managing capital expenditures requires a complex combination of disciplines: (a) application of economic theory; (b) knowledge of financial mathematics, which most of us acquired in our apprenticeship days but have forgotten long since; (c) economic forecasting; (d) techniques for projecting the amount and timing of outlays and receipts; and (e) techniques of control through comparison of actualities with projections. Top management clearly needs technical help. No executive, even if he had the time to analyse each capital proposal, could be expected to have all the necessary disciplines at his command; they can only be gathered together by a team of specialists.

Ten elements. This article concentrates on the measurement of the economic worth of individual investment proposals. But we must remember that, though this is likely to be the critical element, it is only one of many components in a well-rounded programme of capital management. Exhibit I, describing the ten components of a complete programme, may serve to put this particular element (No. 4 in the exhibit) in its operational setting.

Exhibit I.

Ten Components of a Capital-Expenditure Management Program

A realistic way to see how these elements tie together is to trace the biography of a single project, such as a proposal to invest $10,000 in a fork-lift truck and pallets for mechanizing materials handling in a warehouse.

1. *Creative search for profitable opportunities.* The first stage is the conception of the underlying profit-making idea which is to be embodied in the capital facility, in this case the fork-lift truck. Turning up profitable opportunities for investing is in part a by-product of good management. But this cannot be depended on to provide the plethora of enticing capital proposals that constitute the raw material for good management of capital expenditures. Inadvertent opportunities should be supplemented by an active program of seeking out and investigating opportunities.

Competition is a great creator of investment opportunities, as when equipment manufacturers vie with one another to make facilities obsolete. Comparisons of costs, earnings, and facilities with those of rivals often suggest productive avenues for investment. One company has for several years being going over its entire product line, surveying product design and components with the aim of reducing costs by changing design, substituting materials and processes, and reconsidering past buy-or-make decisions.

2. *Long-range capital plans.* The second stage in the life-cycle of our fork-lift truck proposal is to see whether it conforms with long-range dreams of development.

Because today's capital expenditures make the bed that the company must lie in tomorrow, today's decisions must be based on assumptions as to what tomorrow will be like. For example, decisions on warehouse facilities need to be made in the light of an overall, long-range plan for the number and general location of distribution facilities needed for the future. Some companies have detailed plant and equipment targets. Others are content to draw up their plans in broad brush strokes, leaving the details to be worked out and adapted as the program is implemented.

To provide consistent bench marks for proposals, it is necessary to have *some kind of plan*, no matter how tentative.

3. *Short-range capital budget.* The next hurdle our project must take is that of getting on to the one-year capital budget. Listing a project in this budget should not mean that the expenditure is authorized but only that it is approved—such *approval* indicating that the project is considered sufficiently timely and promising to warrant careful study for the coming year.

The short-run budget has several purposes. One is to force operating management to submit the bulk of its capital proposals early enough to give top management an indication of the aggregate demand for funds. A comparison of the capital requested with the available supply will help in weighing the desirability of outside financing or the need for cutbacks. Another purpose is to stimulate thinking about the program early in the game, so that there will be a reasonable amount of time for analysis.

4. *Measurement of project worth.* The next stage is *justification* of the fork-lift project on the basis of a financial and economic analysis of its investment worth. To permit an objective ranking of projects, this analysis needs to be summarised in a single measure of productivity. This is the critical component of capital management, and will be discussed fully below.

5. *Screening and selection.* Next, our project must pass the screening tests set up to compare this proposal with rival projects. Screening standards should be set in the light of the supply of cash available, the cost of money, and the attractiveness of alternative opportunities. If our project survives these tests, the expenditure is *authorized.*

6. *Control of authorised outlays.* The next stage is *control* of the outlays authorized for acquisition (or construction). Controls are needed to assure that the facility conforms to specifications, and that the outlay does not exceed the amount authorized. A system for the prevention of overages will keep estimates of investment amount " honest."

7. *Post-mortems.* To preserve the integrity of estimates of earnings, and to provide an experience base for improving such estimates in future, a post-completion audit of the earnings performance of our fork-lift truck is needed. Without some comparison of projections with actual performance, estimates might be inflated to the point of making a joke of the entire capital-rationing system.

One company recently instituted an audit of all major projects that had been put into service in the preceding year. On a third of these projects it was found that the earnings had been overestimated by an average of 25 per cent., including one new product investment aggregating several hundred thousands of dollars which was rendered obsolete by a competitive development two weeks after it went into production. On another one-third of the projects, the available data were found to be inadequate to the task of checking on the estimates. This points up the need for a system of record keeping which will permit competent audits.

8. *Retirement and disposal.* Management's responsibility for a project ceases only when the facilities have been disposed of. The usual expectation is that the asset will be retained throughout its economic life, so that it will be virtually worthless at the time of disposal. In a dynamic economy, however, economic life projections are necessarily imprecise. Specialized assets may come to have more value to others than to the company itself. To take proper action when the future earnings value falls below the asset's market value requires an analysis focused on disposal.

9. *Forms and procedures.* An effective system of control must in any large company be implemented by specialized forms, written project analyses, and routines of approval, which are tailored to the company's needs. This paper work, though a nuisance, is essential to smooth operation.

10. *Economics of capital budgeting.* Good estimates of rate of return require an understanding of the economic concepts that underlie sound investment decisions, as well as ability in estimating techniques. Such understanding can be achieved only through special training.

Are profits controlling? As we turn to our main concern—measurement of capital productivity—we must face an underlying question: To what degree are investment decisions actually controlled by profit considerations?

Concern with capital productivity of course implies that the company's goal is profits. But in many cases money-making is a secondary objective. Often the primary goal is strategic—to maintain or increase the company's share of the market, to achieve growth in sales volume or number of employees, or simply to build reputation and status. Often capital expenditures capture and embody this kind of motivation in the form of corporate monuments made " just to become the kind of company we want to be." I am thinking of welfare and prestige investments like gymnasiums, country clubs, and palatial offices.

A corporation is not single-minded. It is composed of groups and individuals whose interests conflict. The concept of management as arbiter among employees, customers, and stockholders can lead to capital expenditure policies and commitments that stray from the directional beam of productivity. Not that this is necessarily wrong. But, at least, when a company does let such goals as welfare or prestige govern, it ought to know the cost. The only way to find out this cost is to determine the profitability of capital projects and see how much profit is being passed up in order to build such corporate monuments. The cost of prestige, then, is the amount of earnings forgone by departing from a pattern of investment ruthlessly directed at profit maximization.

Even where money-making does dominate, the theory that a company tries to maximize its profits needs some qualification. Much more prevalent is what can be described as the doctrine of *adequate profits*. Of course, when profits are inadequate, the stockholder's power does come into play, and capital expenditures are likely to be oriented toward profit maximization. But so long as the company is making adequate profits, the drive to have all capital expenditures selected on the basis of profit maximization is blunted.

Thus I am well aware that making maximum profits is often not the sole or even the dominant goal. But that does not lessen the importance of being able to measure the productivity of capital. Moreover, my viewpoint here remains that of the missionary rather than the anthropologist; as in other applications of managerial economics, the objective is to help executives improve policies, not simply to report practice (or malpractice).

Yardsticks of investment worth

To measure a project we must have the right kind of yardstick. Just what should a good yardstick do?

The productivity of capital can be indicated in several ways, but the central requirement of a good yardstick is that it should measure what the proposed outlay will do to net earnings, and do this in a way that permits realistic comparison of one proposal with another. What we seek is a measuring rod which will help decide, for example, whether a $5,000 project that will earn $2,000 a year for three years is more attractive than a $60,000 project that will earn $10,000 a year for ten years.

A good yardstick should summarize in a single figure all the information that is relevant to decision and none that is irrelevant. It should be applicable to all types of proposals, and should permit appraisal in terms of a single set of standards. Also, it should provide an index that is relatively simple to compute; once the basic data have been assembled, the operating people should be able to measure the project's worth easily and without any need to explain how they do it. Finally, the yardstick should permit simple adjustments to allow for ranges of uncertainty in the earnings estimates, since one of the facts to be taken into account is man's inability to see very far into the future with any great precision.

How do the three most commonly used yardsticks—(a) degree of necessity, (b) payback period, and (c) rate of return—stack up against those criteria?

Degree of necessity. The degree of urgency of the project— that is, the extent to which it cannot be postponed to later years— is one kind of yardstick for assigning priorities. For example, a railroad might put a power crane replacement ahead of a repair shop modernization because the old crane had broken down and something had to be done about it immediately, whereas the repair shop could wait.

Degree of necessity has a place in capital budgeting. Some investments must be made to meet requirements imposed by government. Grade-crossing eliminations for railroads, sanitary facilities in food-processing plants, and smoke-control installations are examples. Other investments clearly must be made if the company is to remain in business, *e.g.*, replacement of a washed-out section of a railroad's main line. In these cases, the alternative is such that its adoption would have a catastrophic effect. Projects of this nature seldom bulk large in a capital-expenditure program.

A serious defect of degree of urgency is that it fails to measure productivity. A plant-modernization project may be highly postponable; but if it can produce annual savings which will yield 30 per cent. on the added capital tied up, it is to be preferred to a less postponable but less profitable project. Replacement of a workshop destroyed by fire may seem completely unpostponable, whereas actually the company might find its profits enhanced by subcontracting the operations performed in the destroyed facilities.

Moreover, the degree of urgency is not a measurable quantity. Proposed projects cannot be assembled and arranged in a single priority ladder; acceptance standards cannot be set up to choose wisely among projects submitted on a necessity basis.

The most serious result of accepting or rejecting proposals on the basis of urgency is that the budgeting program is likely to degenerate into a contest of personalities. The biggest share of the money will go to the division heads who are the most eloquent or most persistent, rather than to those who have taken the time and effort necessary to make an objective appraisal. The result is that all projects come up for review in an atmosphere of haste and emergency, with full scope for the arts of persuasion and exhortation. Not only will projects whose desirability is dubious be pushed through, but also a large proportion of investments that would yield big savings and high profits may be put off.

Payback period. The yardstick of payback period—that is, the number of years required for the project's earnings to pay back the original outlay—is unquestionably the most widely used measure. Payback is superior to postponability, since it takes into consideration the projected gross earnings, and has certain other uses.

> Payback can serve as a coarse screen to pick out projects that are so clearly desirable as to require no refined rate-of-return estimates, and to reject quickly those projects which show such poor promise that they do not merit thorough analysis. In addition, it may be adequate as a measure for companies with a high outside cost of capital and severely limited internal cash-generating ability in comparison with the volume of highly profitable internal investment opportunities. If a shortage of funds forces the company to accept only proposals which promise a payback period after taxes of two years or less, the use of a more refined measure might not affect the list of accepted projects.
>
> It also can be useful for appraising risky investments where the rate of capital wastage is particularly hard to predict. Since payback weights near-year earnings heavily and distant earnings not at all, it contains a sort of built-in hedge against the possibility of a short economic life.

For most firms, however, payback is an inadequate measure. It is a cash concept, designed to answer the single question of how soon the cash outlay can be returned to the treasury. As such, it fails in three important respects to provide a satisfactory yardstick.

> (1) Payback tends to overweight the importance of liquidity. No firm can ignore liquidity. But most can achieve it by means that are more direct and less costly than sacrificing profits by allowing payback to govern the selection of projects.
>
> (2) It ignores capital wastage (*i.e.*, depreciation). By confining analysis to the project's gross earnings (before depreciation) it takes no cognizance of its probable economic life.
>
> (3) It fails to consider the earnings after the initial outlay has been paid back. At the end of the payback period, the company has just

got its bait back. How much longer the earnings will last is what determines the profitability of the investment. A three-year payback project may yield a 30 per cent. return on average investment if it has a long life, but only 12 per cent. if its life is four years, and no return at all if just three years.

In short, because payback does not reflect all the relevant dimensions of profitability, it is neither inclusive enough nor sensitive enough to be used as the measure of investment worth.

Rate of return. Measurement by means of rate of return relates the project's anticipated earnings to the funds which will be tied up. Rate of return embodies the concept of *net* earnings after allowing for capital wastage. Neither degree of necessity nor payback period uses this concept, since payback is measured in terms of gross earnings, and urgency does not consider earnings at all.

Two projects, each of which shows a three-year payback, may differ greatly in the length of time for which they will produce earnings. Take this case:

> Certain refinery equipment that showed a three-year payback actually became obsolete and was replaced in less than three years. This project's rate of return, therefore, was less than zero, despite what appeared to be a very satisfactory payback. In contrast, a pipeline that had the same three-year payback kept on earning (and promises to continue for twenty years more); clearly its rate of return was much higher.

Capital wastage—that is, loss of value over time—is of vital importance in the appraisal of a proposal. Productivity should be measured by earnings over the whole life, even though estimates of the distant future may be subject to wide margins of error.

Because rate of return considers the full life of an investment, correct comparisons of the value of projects can be made. Proposals can therefore be arranged in a ladder of priority, even where they seem to be of the same urgency or to have the same payback period. Moreover, the fact that projects may differ widely in character does not impede comparison. New-product investments can be compared with cost-reducing projects; or a proposal this year can be compared with one which will not be ready until next year.

Better standards of rejection are made possible by rate of return. A firm's cost of capital—say, 15 per cent.—can be used to determine the proper rate of cutoff on the ladder just discussed, *i.e.*, the minimum acceptable profitability of a proposal. This not only provides an objective, defensible basis for acceptance or rejection; it also aids top management in delegating authority, by providing bench-marks for personnel down the line to use in killing off the worst propositions before they have gone far up the chain of command.

Finally, rate-of-return rationing is likely to produce more earnings for stockholders, since it directs funds to their most profitable use by measuring productivity of capital and comparing it with a relevant standard.

Making rate-of-return estimates

Two problems arise in the application of this yardstick. The first concerns the empirical projections needed to get the three determinants of worth: (a) earnings, (b) life, and (c) amount of capital tied up. The second problem (discussed later) is how to combine these determinants in an index of profitability.

Ten fallacies. The part of this measurement problem which is most often muffed is the job of getting a clear idea of just what needs to be estimated. Why should there be any problem in clarifying the concepts for rate-of-return measurement? The nature of the difficulties and their importance can be seen by looking at ten common fallacies:

1. "*No alternatives.*" Perhaps the most common mistake in analysing a capital proposal is failure to consider any alternatives. There are always alternatives, and their systematic analysis is the bench-mark for estimating both the investment and the earnings of a capital project. What will happen if the requested investment is not made measures what the company will get out of it if the investment is made. If, as usual, there are several alternatives differing in the amount of investment required, earnings estimates should logically be built up-on the smallest investment alternative which is acceptably profitable. Alternatives which require greater investment are preferable to this one only if the *added* investment over this amount produces enough *added* earnings to yield a satisfactory rate of return.

2. "'*Must*' *investment.*" Closely related is the " must " investment fallacy. The common conviction that certain equipment replacements are indispensable implies that management has no alternatives. True, the alternative is sometimes so catastrophic that it is academic. But even in such a case the reason for making the investment should not be that it is urgent or indispensable, but that its profitability is terrific measured against the catastrophic alternative. Thus the rate of return from replacing a burnt-out pump in an oil pipeline may be astronomical; the investment is small, and its earnings are the profits from the whole line, since the only alternative is a complete shutdown.

High-profit investments of this nature are rare. Skeptical study of supposed " must " investments will reveal alternatives to many of them, and will show that some are neither necessary nor even acceptably profitable.

3. " *High strategy*." Another fallacy is the notion that some projects are so pivotal for long-run welfare that they possess high strategic value which overrides mere economic considerations, and lifts their evaluation into a mystic realm beyond the ken of analysis. For example, the dogma that an integrated oil company should own 75 per cent. of its crude oil sometimes precludes analysis of integration investments.

It is true that some capital expenditures do have benefits which are hard to measure because they are diffused over a wide area of activity, or stretch over a protracted time. And there are some investments which must be made on almost pure faith (*e.g.*, a new research center). Nevertheless, the idea that there is such a thing as strategic value not ultimately rooted in economic worth is demonstrably wrong. If a contemplated investment produces results that do not have economic value, then directors and stockholders should question its wisdom.

4. " *Routine replacement*." This fallacy maintains that scheduled periodic replacement of facilities is a practical and inexpensive substitute for an analysis of the desirability of individual replacements. For example, many fleet owners replace motor-trucks on a routine basis (*i.e.*, after a certain number of years or a certain number of miles), without determining whether the added net earnings from replacing this or that old truck are an adequate return on the added investment. Routine replacement has the virtues of simplicity, orderliness, and predictability. But vintage retirement will not produce as profitable a pattern of investment as will a capital-earnings plan.

5. " *Prediction is impossible*." Scoffers maintain that since the future cannot be predicted with accuracy, it is futile to try to guess the useful life of a proposed facility, or to project its earnings beyond the first year. The consequence of this fallacy is an unwillingness to define concepts in a way that will force explicit projection. People try to duck out by proclaiming that " with a four-year payback, it doesn't matter " or by embracing " unfair " Bureau of Internal Revenue depreciation rates.

The basic mistake is refusing to recognize that forecasting, though difficult and subject to error, is nevertheless necessary in appraising the worth of projects. Prediction, whether or not it is done consciously, lies at the heart of any judgment about a proposed investment. Usually it is better to *know* what is being done.

6. " *Fair share of overhead*." A common error is to use allocations of current overhead instead of estimating the added costs that will be caused by the project. Such cost-proration confuses problems of equity with problems of consequences. This is illustrated by a question frequently raised: Should a new product line, acquisition of which is being contemplated, carry its full share of the overhead now borne by mature products, or should it get a free ride? Neither of these suggested solutions is correct, at least for estimating project earnings. Old overheads do not matter—only new overheads. What is needed is not a reallocation of past overheads but a forecast of how future overheads will increase by acceptance as opposed to rejection of the project. This cost increment is wholly unaffected by the conventions of apportionment of common costs.

7. " *Free ride*." A related fallacy errs in the opposite direction. It holds that new products or added volume are " plus business " in the sense of incurring negligible additional costs. This " free ride "

fallacy leads to the conclusion that earnings from expansion investments are almost equivalent to their revenue. There is something to this notion; long-run incremental costs are often smaller than fully allocated average costs. But they are larger than short-run marginal costs, and never negligible.

While short-run marginal costs are relevant for operating decisions, long-run added costs must be used for investment decisions. Herein lies the peril of the " free ride " fallacy. What, for instance, are the earnings from an added gasoline service station when existing pipeline and bulk plant capacities will just take that added volume? If only the marginal cost of using this bulk-movement capacity is included, rate of return is high. But continued normal growth will soon force expansion of the bulk-movement capacity; the new service station brings this time that much closer. If the full cost of this expansion is included in estimating lifetime earnings, the return of course shows up as much lower.

8. " *Carrying charge*." The practice of charging the earnings of all projects with an interest cost might be called the " carrying charge " fallacy. Usually this charge is computed by applying the company's short-term borrowing rate to the capitalized portion of the original investment. This approach has the virtue of recognizing that money is not costless, even where no entry is made in the accounts. It has, however, two defects: (a) it uses the wrong cost of money, since high-cost equity capital is left out, and (b) it introduces cost of money into the capital-management program in the wrong way. Instead of subtracting carrying costs from individual projects, it is better to use cost of capital as a cutoff rate to select acceptably profitable projects.

9. " *Book value*." Determination of the investment amount looks so easy that it is often done wrong. Bookkeeping is the root of error here. Accounting conventions that are indispensable for financial reporting give the wrong steer for estimating a project's investment base. The test of what should be included in the investment amount is not how it is handled on the books, which bears only on the tax effects of the proposal, an important but quite separate issue. The test is whether or not the outlay is necessary to produce the stream of earnings contemplated in the proposal.

The " book value " concept excludes outlays that are expensed (rather than capitalized) from the amount of the investment. Take a proposal to convert an unused portion of a building into a sausage factory, requiring $100,000 of capitalizable machinery plus $150,000 of expensed repairs. The pretax investment amount is the whole $250,000; after deflating the expensed portion for 50 per cent. income tax rates ($150,000 minus $75,000), the after-tax investment amount is still $175,000. But the book value is only $100,000.

Book value also gives bad guidance for propping up, transferring, or abandoning existing assets. The book value of an existing asset is based on historical cost less depreciation. For investment decisions, its value should be determined by what the company can get for the asset or what the company can do with it in its next best internal use, rather than by the figures that happen to be on the books.

10. " *Taxes don't matter*." There is a surprisingly widespread conviction that adjustment for income tax is academic. This " taxes don't matter " fallacy assumes that the worth of a project is obscured (rather

than revealed) by allowing for tax effects, and that the ranking of capital projects will be the same whether or not they are deflated for taxes. This beguiling notion is wrong in two respects: (a) In order to apply standards such as the company's outside cost of capital, it is necessary to measure rate of return after taxes, rather than before taxes. (b) The impact of taxes differs depending on the time shape of the project; and the after-tax ranking of proposals differs significantly from their before-tax ranking. For example, the tax effects of accelerated amortization can convert a border-line project into a highly profitable one.

Positive concepts. Having looked at these ten fallacies, we are in a better position to formulate positive concepts of what needs to be estimated.

A correct estimate of earnings must be based on the simple principle that they are the total *added* earnings or savings from making the investment as opposed to not making it. The proper bench-mark for computing earnings is the *best alternative* way of doing the job; comparison will indicate the source and amount of the added earnings. Project costs should be unaffected by allocations of existing overheads, but should cover all the changes in total overhead (and other) costs that result from the investment, and nothing else—nothing that will be the same regardless of whether the proposal is accepted or rejected.

The estimate should be based on the best available projections of future volume, wage rates, and price levels, over the economic life of the proposed facilities. Because earnings vary in time shape, and because this will affect the rate of return, the estimates should reflect variations in the time trend.

In estimating the life of an investment, consideration must be given to (a) physical deterioration, (b) obsolescence, and (c) the possibility that the source of earnings will dry up before either of the first two factors becomes operative.

Interest on investment should not be deducted from earnings. Charging interest increases the complexity of the rate-of-return computation without adding to the information it provides. Earnings should be stated after income tax, for only in such form are they relevant for capital attraction and dividend payment.

The appropriate investment base for calculating rate of return is the added outlay caused by the adoption of the project (as opposed to rejecting it and adopting an alternative which requires less investment). The entire amount of the original added outlay should be included in the investment amount, regardless of how it will be treated in the books. Any tax benefit from expensing certain items rather than capitalizing them should be reflected. Repairs which would be made whether or not the proposal is adopted should be excluded, because they are not caused by it.

If the proposal involves a transfer of facilities from another part of the firm, the opportunity cost of these facilities (the amount forgone by using them this way rather than another) should be added to the amount of investment. If the opportunity forgone is merely to sell the facilities for scrap, then this will indicate the value to set on the transferred assets.

The amount of the investment should also include any additional working capital or other auxiliary facilities. Research and promotional expenses to get new products rolling or to develop new methods or to expand business are no less investments than plant and equipment.

Calculating rate of return

Once the basic estimates of project earnings and investment have been made, there are two major ways of combining them into a rate-of-return measurement. One way—which can be called the " accounting method " because it is closely related to many of the concepts used in conventional accounting procedure—computes rate of return as the ratio of (a) the project's earnings averaged over the life of the proposition to (b) the average lifetime investment. The other—which can be called " discounted cash flow "—computes rate of return as the maximum interest rate which could be paid on the capital tied up over the life of the investment without dipping into earnings produced elsewhere in the company.

Accounting method. A characteristic of the accounting method is that it has many variants, each of which produces a different rate of return for any one proposal. One set of variants comes from diverse concepts of the investment amount (*e.g.*, the original outlay, $100,000, versus the average amount tied up in the facility over its life, $50,000). Another source of variants is the diverse concepts of earnings. Earnings can be either gross or net of depreciation, either before or after taxes. They can be for the first year only or the average for several years. This variety produces a tremendous range of results. But they all fall into the category of accounting method, provided the final result is a ratio of earnings to investment.

This shortcoming can be minimized only by arbitrarily standardizing on one variant of the method, and making all computations according to this standard.

A more serious drawback to the accounting method is that it is insensitive to variations in time patterns. By taking an annual average of net earnings over the life of a project, it ignores earning trends.

The worth of an investment is affected by the time shape of its lifetime earnings, because near money has greater economic value than distant money. For example, an oil well has a strikingly different time shape than a service station. A well which comes in as a gusher trails off to a pumper. In contrast, a service station in a new area has a rising curve of earnings, and is likely to show post-operative losses in the first year or so. Failure to reflect these time-shape disparities leads to wrong decisions.

The effect of time shape on economic worth is especially great when the company's cost of capital is high, or when the forgone earnings on projects that are passed up are high. Only a firm whose projects are roughly similar in time shape and in life can ignore this feature. For such a firm, the added accuracy of the discounted-cash-flow method probably does not justify the transitional pain and effort required to install the system. But any firm with projects that vary significantly in either time shape or longevity has an important stake in using the most sensitive rate-of-return method available.

Discounted cash flow. The mechanics of the cash-flow method consist essentially of finding the interest rate that discounts future earnings of a project down to a present value equal to the project cost. This interest rate is the rate of return on that investment. Exhibit II illustrates the way in which rate-of-return

Exhibit II.

Cash-flow method of computing rate of return illustrated
(Machine costing $2,200 with anticipated life of five years and no salvage value at the end of that time)

Year	Gross earnings before depreciation	Present value of earnings discounted at		
		18%	20%	22%
1	$200	$184	$182	$180
2	600	458	446	432
3	800	510	486	462
4	1,200	640	596	556
5	1,200	534	488	448
Total	$4,000	$2,326	$2,198	$2,078

can be determined under the cash-flow method for a cost-reducing machine which costs $2,200, and has an anticipated life of five years with no salvage value at the end. In this case, an interest rate of 20 per cent. is found to make the present value of the future earnings stream equal to the present cost of the machine, so 20 per cent. is the rate-of-return.

Conceptually, this method is based on the principle that in making an investment outlay we are actually buying a series of future annual incomes—ranging in the example in the exhibit from $200 the first year to $1,200 by the fourth and fifth years. We have an investment in each of those incomes, an investment which compounds in value through time until its own year arrives and it materializes in cash earnings. Thus, for example, the $596 present value of the fourth year's earnings at 20 per cent. is the amount that would have to be invested at 20 per cent. now to yield $1,200 gross earnings during the fourth year ($596 compounded at 20 per cent. for three and a half years—since the $1,200 would begin to come in at the beginning of the fourth year).

The basic simplicity of the method is brought out by this illustration. Earnings are stated as gross cash receipts, *i.e.*, total receipts less cash operating outlays and tax, but before depreciation. Depreciation enters the determination only through its impact on taxes, as a side calculation. The main calculation takes care of it automatically—because the correct interest rate discounts the gross earnings to equality with the initial capital cost; the rate measures return on investment *after* annual provisions for repaying the principal amount. Thus, using the figures on the top row of Exhibit II, the first year's gross earnings of $200, discounted at 20 per cent. per annum for six months, give a present value of $182; this $182 may itself be looked on as return of investment outlay (or as the capital in the yearly instalment received from annuity, or as the depreciation quota), and $18 as net income.

The method is simplified by the fact that there is no need to make a decision on which base to use (*e.g.*, original outlay, average investment, and so on), nor is there any need to enter interest as a cost. Once the data are gathered and set up, there is only one rate-of-return answer possible, and it can be arrived at by straightforward working of charts and interest tables.[1]

Net superiority of discounted cash flow. The accounting method does have the advantage of familiarity and transparency. Although education would be necessary to get everyone to standardize on one method of averaging earnings and investment,

[1] But multiple solutions become possible if there is a negative cash flow during the life. See James H. Lorie and Leonard J. Savage, " Three Problems in Rationing Capital," *Journal of Business*, October 1955.

the idea of computing a simple ratio by dividing one number by another is familiar to anyone who went beyond the second grade.

The discounted-cash-flow method admittedly is less familiar. While a method similar to this has been widely used throughout the financial community for computing bond yields, insurance premiums, and rates on leased facilities where even small errors may cause serious loss, it is new in its application to the measurement of productivity of capital-expenditure projects in industry. Hence the job of explaining it to the bookkeeper and the clerk will require time and effort. But its appearance of complexity is deceptive. Once the basic method is understood, it is simpler and quicker to use than the accounting method.

Another deterrent to its use is the fact that it does not correspond to accounting concepts for recording costs and revenues, so that special analysis is necessary to compute a post-mortem on an investment. But this seems minor in comparison with its imposing superiorities:

(1) The discounted-cash-flow method is economically realistic in confining the analysis to cash flows and forgetting about book allocations. The books, although valuable for other purposes, are irrelevant for the task of measuring investment worth.

(2) This method forces guided thinking about the whole life of the project and concentration on the lifetime earnings.

(3) It weights the time pattern of the investment outlay and the cash earnings so as to reflect real and important differences in the value of near and distant cash flows.

(4) It reflects accurately and without ambiguity the timing of tax savings, either from expensing part of the investment outlay or from writing off capitalized costs over the life of the investment—something quite difficult to do by the accounting method.

(5) It permits simple allowances for risks and uncertainties, and can be adapted readily to increasing the risk allowance over time.

(6) It is strictly comparable to cost-of-capital ratios, so that decisions can be made quickly and safely by comparing rate-of-return and the value of money to the firm.

Special forms and procedures to implement these principles need to be tailored to the particular conditions of the individual company. Above all, good capital-expenditure management must operate in an enlightened intellectual environment throughout the firm; all the personnel should understand the economics of capital expenditures and the measurements and controls which a sound program entails.

Statistical Inference and the Accountant's Discretion[*]

By H. C. Mackenzie

Statistics Department, National Coal Board, London.

IT is possible to distinguish two separate fields of application of statistical method in accounting. One is concerned with the use of techniques such as regression analysis and programming, in costing, budgeting, planning and pricing problems. A classical example of this is Lyle's *Regression Analysis in Factory Operations*.[1] That author showed how statistical relationships between cost and output can be used to separate fixed and variable elements in direct costs, to provide a criterion for cost control, and to estimate marginal cost. The object of applying this and other types of mathematical or statistical model is to obtain, for management, information about costs and prices which is not, in general, obtainable by conventional accounting techniques. The second field is concerned with the application of the principles of sampling to the work of accountants in their fiduciary and auditing capacities; in particular, to that part of their work which involves the valuation of large and varied quantities of product, materials or transactions, or which calls for the testing of an accounting system by means of sample checks. This paper is concerned with the latter line of development; that is, it considers the sampling, and consequent inferential, problems which occur in the professional work of auditors and accountants, and the possible role of modern statistical methods in accounting and auditing practice.

It should be noted that, although this paper was written mainly on the basis of observation of professional auditing,

---

[*] This paper was written while the author was in the Department of Economics, University of Bristol. Acknowledgments are due to several American accountants and statisticians (Professor Richard Cyert, Carnegie Institute of Technology, Professor H. Arkin, City College of New York, Professor R. Clay Sprowles, University of California, Mr. H. J. Davidson of Touche, Ross, Bailey and Smart, and Mr. E. F. Schumann of H. Deare & Company) for providing reprints of published and unpublished articles and case studies, and for some helpful private communications. This does not necessarily mean that they agree with my views or approach.

[1] 2nd ed., edited by L. H. C. Tippett (Edinburgh, 1959).

no attempt has been made to distinguish rigidly between what is done by external and by internal audit. The evolution of auditing in general, and the developing relationship between external and internal auditor in particular, are such that the distinction is a matter of debate (and perhaps choice) even within the profession itself. This article does not offer a blueprint for the development of accounting. It merely suggests that, in one particular field of auditing, that of sample testing, some rethinking, and probably setting of standards, is necessary in the light of modern statistical developments.

The status of statistical problems in auditing

A suitable point of departure is a passage from Dicksee's *Auditing* [2]:

> ... the auditor may take advantage of the existence of a good system of internal check to relieve himself of the labour of examining every separate entry. It would be a mistake, however, to suppose that a mere random selection of entries for detailed examination may be substituted. The " test " ought to be more scientific than that. The items to be tested ought to be so chosen that they cover the whole field to be examined, or in other words, they ought to be, in the statistical sense, fair samples of the whole group. A little consideration will show that the " spread " of the sample ought to take into account the fact that there are (a) entries relating to transactions of various kinds; (b) different officers engaged on various sections of the work; (c) at all times throughout the year. These three elements should accordingly be given full weight in the selection of samples, so that all the classes of entries are fairly covered and so that every officer's work comes under due consideration, having further regard to the fact that the honesty and efficiency of these officers ought to be tested over the whole period covered by the audit.
>
> A danger connected with test audits must be mentioned. If there be 10,000 entries and if every one be examined, the discovery of one error would (unless the circumstances were exceptional) be a very small affair. But if the 10,000 should be subjected to a one per cent. test, then the discovery of one error would be very serious indeed, for it would lead to the inference that there are probably 100 errors in 10,000. Where the percentage of items checked is very small, there is an obvious weakness in such an inference, and attention is called to the point in order to remind auditors to use the most careful discretion in fixing the statistical standard to be observed in their tests.

This passage, written many years ago in what is now a standard auditing manual, can be taken, with one or two qualifications, as a simple statement of the two basic concerns of sampling theory and method, the interrelated problems of sample selection and interpretation. To the statistician, it is a

---

[2] Ed. Magee, B., p. 34.

starting-point for study of the proper use of samples as a source of information about the whole set of individuals or items from which they are taken. To the accounting profession, on the other hand, the statement has generally, and until fairly recently, been regarded as complete in itself. There is hardly any indication in British accounting literature about how statistical " fairness " of samples is to be achieved or statistical standards of inference set and observed. Traditionally, it is at the discretion of the accountant or auditor. A more recent textbook, for example, by A.C. Coomber, in a section on audit tests, states that, the accountant " having satisfied himself that the system is efficient, the selection of ' samples ' for testing purposes requires some thought. Care should be taken, for instance, that all sections of the work under consideration should have an equal chance of being examined." This, however, is the total extent of his contribution to the problem of sample selection. Dicksee's words, of course, were written before the major developments in statistical method of the last thirty years.[3] It is only in the last decade that accountants, principally in the United States, have begun seriously to explore the statistical implications of test-checking, the possibility of value estimation by sample, and the potential contribution of modern statistical theory to these aspects of accounting. In the following paragraphs, it is proposed, first, to consider some of the implications of Dicksee's standards, secondly, to discuss some of the objections which have been raised by accountants to a more rigorous application of statistical criteria, and, finally, to review some of the developments which have already taken place in this field.

Two illustrative examples

The issues involved in Dicksee's statement may be clarified by a preliminary discussion of two simple examples.
Example 1. The checking of advertising stock.

This example concerns a large manufacturer of perishable consumer goods who does a lot of advertising. A considerable amount of the work of audit clerks consists of checking entries on " vouchers " relating to various items of stock in the inventory. The vouchers are numbered consecutively and filed in binders, each binder containing vouchers, *i.e.*, certificates signed and

---

[3] Writing today, an accountant as aware of statistical problems as Dicksee evidently was, would not have referred to " *mere* random selection," in view of the importance of the principle of randomisation in securing statistical " fairness "; nor would he have referred to the smallness of the *percentage* checked when the " obvious weakness " in the inference arises from the smallness of the *number* checked.

countersigned by the men doing the physical check, for stock kept at one store or branch. The detail shown in each voucher for advertising stock, for instance, consists of a dissection by type of advertising, the product advertised and the advertising item, the supplier, type of stock (reserve or working), quantity, price, value and total, and, finally, the certification of stock count, price insertion, and extensions and additions. The stock is not usually checked physically by the auditor, although he satisfies himself that stock-taking procedures are reliable. The audit of advertising stock therefore has three main purposes: (a) verification of the total value of advertising stock, (b) verification of extensions, and (c) verification of the correctness of the prices used. The first of these, which ensures that items included in the balance-sheet correspond with a properly vouched record of the physical stock-taking, is carried out by a complete check. The remaining two, which require the time-consuming operations of checking arithmetic and referring to independent evidence such as invoices or price-lists, are carried out by a 10 per cent. check. In a recent audit, there were, in all, vouchers for 2,055 items of stock, divided among the various branches as shown in Table I, excluding high-value stocks which were checked completely. A systematic sample of one in ten yielded a sample of 206 allocated between branches in the same proportions. Since the entry in the balance-sheet related only to total stock, the records were treated together for the purpose of sampling and checking. Nevertheless, since each binder referred to a different branch, it is obvious that some importance is attached to the location of any erroneous entries as well as to the total number of such entries found. If, in the course of the audit tests, errors or irregularities are discovered for which satisfactory explanations are not found by the clerks, these are reported to the principal, who decides what further action to take. Leaving aside the question of what constitutes an error and how important it is, it is clearly relevant to the auditor, in considering what is reported, to know the statistical implications of the 10 per cent. sample.

Dicksee's standards can be applied in the following way. Assume that if 1 per cent. of the stock vouchers contain an error of a certain kind, it is a serious fault which calls for some action or qualification by the auditor. Such a situation would, for instance, be implied by a distribution of errors such as appears in the third column of Table I.

In order to discover the presence of error at all, it is necessary to find at least one erroneous voucher. The answer to the following question is therefore relevant to the auditor's assessment: assuming

(a) that the presence of as many as 1 per cent. faulty entries is serious enough to call for some action, and (b) that there *is* this proportion of error, what are the chances that at *least* one error will be discovered by checking a 10 per cent. sample?

TABLE I

(1) Branch	(2) N	(3) M (·01 N)	(4) n=(·1 N)	(5) P_n (O)	(6) 1–P_n (O)
A (H.Q.)	689	7	69	0·441	0·559
B	153	2	15	0·789	0·211
C	247	3	25	0·705	0·295
D	272	3	27	0·710	0·290
E	179	2	18	0·788	0·212
F	297	3	30	0·708	0·292
G	129	2	13	0·778	0·222
H	89	1	9	0·876	0·124
	2055	(23)	206	0·070	0·930

N=number of items in stock; M=number of errors; n=size of sample.

In other words, if the unknown error rate is large enough to warrant some action, what are the chances of discovering the presence of error with a sample of the chosen size? The answer in this case is given in the last column of Table I, which shows, for the various locations, the probability (*e.g.*, 559 or 55·9 per cent. for sub-population A), of finding at least one incorrect voucher when the set of vouchers for that location contains as many as 1 per cent. incorrect.

To understand the basis of calculation of this probability, it is necessary to consider the various possible outcomes of a sample check. Given M erroneous vouchers—*i.e.*,

$$\left(\frac{M}{N} \times 100\right) \text{ per cent.}$$

in a population or sub-population of N, a sample of size n may contain from O to M (if M is less than or equal to n) erroneous vouchers, and from o to n (if M is greater than n). The latter case is not considered here. When the sample is to be obtained by random (equal probability) selection,[4] the actual *number*, say x, of erroneous vouchers that will be found is uncertain,

[4] This is taken to mean that, subject to the condition that a voucher, having been drawn once for the sample, is not eligible for subsequent selection, all eligible vouchers have an equal chance of being chosen, and when selection begins all possible combinations of n items are equally probable. To non-statisticians, it may seem unnecessary to state the obvious as the condition included in this definition seems to do. In fact, the condition involves a rather important point in sampling, and in the present example determines the probability distribution of the variable being considered.

but the *probability* of finding in the sample any specified number x is determinate, and dependent on N, M, and n. In statistical language, the number x is a hypergeometric random variable, with probability distribution:

$$P_n(x) = \frac{\binom{M}{x} \binom{N - M}{n - x}}{\binom{N}{n}}$$

i.e., the probability of finding x erroneous vouchers is the product of the number of ways [5] of choosing x items from M and the number of ways of choosing n − x items from N − M, divided by the number of ways of choosing n items from N. For instance, the probability of finding no erroneous vouchers in a random sample of 69, taken from a population of 689 vouchers in which there are seven incorrect, is given by

$$P_{69}(o) = \frac{\binom{7}{0} \binom{682}{69}}{\binom{689}{69}} = \cdot441,$$

and the chance of finding at least one is $1 - P_{69}(o)$ or $\cdot559$. Similar calculations for each branch and for the stock as a whole are shown in Table I.

Consider, now, the implications of those results in relation to Dicksee's requirements for audit tests, " fair " or scientific selection, and statistical interpretation of results. The method used for selection of vouchers was systematic, or quasi-random; that is, selection of every nth voucher from randomly arranged binders. This is a standard selection procedure in such tests; if careful consideration and investigation disclose no reason to believe that special kinds of voucher occur at intervals of n, or of multiples of n, it may also be treated statistically as a random procedure. Thus the method of selection can be regarded as satisfying the scientific requirement.

The extent to which Dicksee's second requirement is met is not so clear. It is first of all necessary to be more specific about the objects of the test. These were, as already indicated, (a) to verify extensions, and (b) to verify the correctness of prices used.

[5] *i.e.* $\binom{M}{x} = \dfrac{M (M - 1) \text{——} 2 \cdot 1}{(x.x-1.\text{——}2 \cdot 1) \, (M-x) \, (M-x-1) \text{——} 2 \cdot 1}$ = the number of ways of taking x things from M. For example, $\binom{6}{2} = \dfrac{6.5.4.3.2.1}{2.1.4.3.2.1} = 15$, *i.e.*, there are 15 ways of selecting 2 things from 6. There is 1 way of selecting o items from M.

Since the extensions were carried out at individual branches by their own staff, it follows that the stock at each branch may be considered as a single population. Prices, however, were fixed at a central office and communicated to the various branches. In the tests for pricing errors, therefore, the whole set of vouchers can be regarded as a single population. The table states that if there are as many as twenty-three (or just over 1 per cent.) incorrect vouchers in the population of 2,055, the probability of finding at least one with a sample of 206 is about ·93, or 93 per cent. Since none were found, the inference is that the population as a whole is relatively free from error, that there are fewer than 1 per cent. of the vouchers with price errors. If incorrectness also includes extension errors, the same conclusion applies to total stock. It does not, however, apply to the individual branches, since a higher error percentage in any one of these could still leave the overall figure at less than 1 per cent. With a 10 per cent. sample, the chance of discovering the presence of error in the vouchers from say branch H, if the error percentage is 1 per cent., is only ·124 or 12·4 per cent. Taking a 10 per cent. sample thus leads to a variety of different results for the individual branches, ranging from 12·4 per cent. for branch H, to 55·9 per cent. for branch A; that is, the implied statistical standards vary from branch to branch according to the number of items in stock. However, the effect of a 1 per cent. error rate in any branch on the total picture (and this is what the auditor is essentially concerned with) is also dependent on the number of items in stock in that branch. Assuming that major errors, if any, are discovered by a complete check of items over a specific value, the presence of 1 per cent. incorrect extensions in branch H, with eighty-nine items, is of much less consequence than 1 per cent. in branch A with 689 items. Furthermore, extension errors, unless they are deliberate, may well tend to cancel out, and so are less serious than pricing errors, which may involve questions of principle. Therefore the statistical standards used in verifying extensions need not be so rigorous as in verifying prices. Thus, since no errors were found, the auditor achieved, in this instance, a reasonably high degree of assurance that the vouchers, and, by inference, the stocks considered as a single group, were correctly priced and valued. There was, however, no such degree of assurance for the individual branches, nor was there a consistent level of assurance maintained for each branch. This conflicts with Dicksee's criteria of giving due consideration and fair cover to all classes of entry and every officer's work.

The conflict arises because the auditor sets his test procedures *without reference to statistical standards.* The typical British auditor, if questioned about this, would give one of two answers. If he were sophisticated enough, he would admit that the proposition is true, but state that the use of statistical standards would bring no important gain, if indeed, they could really be applied. Otherwise, he might say that " experience " has shown 10 per cent. to be the best figure for this particular job. These answers will be considered in the next section, but in the meantime, let us suppose that in the above example the statistical standard for verification of prices was satisfactory, while that for extensions in individual houses requires some modification, namely a more consistent though less rigorous standard of testing for each branch.

Such a modification may be achieved statistically in one of three ways, by relaxation of the permissible error level of 1 per cent., by a reduction of the confidence level required in the tests—represented in the example by the 93 per cent. chance of discovering at least one error, if there are 1 per cent. errors present—or by a combination of both; for instance, by increasing the permissible error level to 5 per cent. and decreasing the confidence level to, say, 85 per cent. instead of about 95 per cent. as in the implied standard for total stock. The auditor, in other words, would determine his sample size in such a way as to make approximately 85 per cent. the chance of finding *at least* one error if there are 5 per cent. present. Such a relaxation gives sample sizes n for each branch as shown in column (5) in the following table.

TABLE II

(1) Branch	(2) N	(3) M (Error rate=5%)	(4) P_n (o)	(5) n	(6) (n in 10% samples)
A	689	34	·15 (=1–·85)	37	69
B	153	8	·15	31	15
C	247	12	·15	35	25
D	272	14	·15	33	27
E	179	9	·15	33	18
F	297	15	·15	34	30
G	129	6	·15	34	13
H	89	5	·15	27	9

Thus, for verification of extensions, the sample of items at branch A under the 10 per cent. rule is almost double what is necessary under the relaxed standards, while the sample sizes at the remaining branches are all too low. The total amount of checking required is increased only from 10 per cent. to just under 13 per cent.

There is, of course, the additional labour of determining sample sizes on a valid statistical basis, and of making specific rules about permissible error and acceptable sampling risks. To this extent, introduction of statistical sampling methods may result in some extra work.

Example 2. Testing customers' statements of account.

Introduction of statistical standards will not always lead to increased testing. Application of the above principles to another test suggests that the sample was larger than was really necessary. In this case, tests were made on the state of customers' accounts at the last credit period in the financial year. Sales to retail outlets are here dealt with under a system roughly as follows. Salesmen call on customers on specified days at five-weekly intervals. The salesman takes the customer's orders, possibly receives payment for the previous order, and transmits them to his head office, which checks the customer's credit position and authorises dispatch of the order if the position is satisfactory. The customer is also sent an invoice, and the amounts dispatched and invoiced—which are not necessarily the same—are entered on a continuous record of transactions. Since calls are made at five-weekly intervals, the customer has, in effect, five weeks possible credit. No goods are authorised for customers who have not paid for the previous order, unless there are special circumstances. The statements are kept on cards in a file arranged according to the day of the salesman's call, or call-days. The financial and physical transactions recorded in these statements are the core of the company's business. From the auditing point of view, therefore, it is essential that they should be up to date at the end of the year, *i.e.*, that there are no or few uncollectible accounts. Furthermore, there is a presumption that if the account is live at the end of the year, the customer's other transactions during the year were satisfactorily completed. The proposition to be tested is therefore that the call-day file contains only " live " accounts at the date of audit.

There are, let us say, 50,000 customers, or roughly 2,000 cards for each call day. It is physically impossible to audit all the cards. The usual procedure is to examine all the accounts for one call-day, and check (1) that a statement of account or invoice was sent to the customer towards the end of the financial year, (2) that payment was made within the five-week period, and (3) if no payment was made, that there is good reason to believe that the account is collectible. Although the bulk of the cards is likely to pass the check immediately, a considerable amount of work arises out of the small number of exceptions, and a major advantage of sampling is that it reduces the burden of this work.

A justification for taking one call-day as the sample is that, although it is recognised to be a " chunk " rather than a random sample, the arrangement of cards and customers in a call-day is itself the result of a random process, and that, by taking a particular call-day, the auditor ensures that accounts from *all* salesmen are included in the sample. Whether this is a valid argument or not depends partly on the particular situation, and it is not proposed to discuss it here. If the accounts were re-arranged by salesmen and call-days, however, a sample could be designed which would satisfy the requirement of randomness and include accounts for all salesmen.

Obviously no auditor would feel very happy about giving an unqualified certificate if he thought it possible that as many as 1 per cent. ($=$ 500 customers) of the customers' accounts could be uncollectible. On the other hand, as long as he relies on a sample to give him information about the population, there is some risk attached to the auditing process. As an illustration, suppose that the auditor would regard as many as 100 unexplained exceptions out of the 50,000 customers as a serious situation calling for qualification of the certificate or some other action. If there were 100, in fact, the sample of 2,000 would be expected to yield four and the chance of finding at least one would be 98·2 per cent. If the sample were reduced to 1,500, the expected number would be three and the chance of finding at least one would be 95 per cent. Any increase of the sample size over 2,000 would give only a marginal improvement, and a 10 per cent. (or 5,000) sample would more than double the work without a corresponding increase in the degree of assurance. With a reliable control system in operation, on the other hand, the auditor could afford to reduce the sample to 1,500 in spite of the slight additional risk, thereby cutting out about a quarter of the work.

Some general implications

Consideration of these examples suggests a number of comments on the use of sampling by auditors. It may be argued that little can be said on the basis of a sample of two, but these examples illustrate reasonably well the normal approach to test-checking. Furthermore, with certain qualifications, they show that the amount of testing actually carried out is not unreasonable statistically, given that the statements of auditing requirements, *e.g.*, the serious nature of a 1 per cent. error rate, are acceptable. Other examples could have been chosen which would not have emerged so well from a statistical critique, but the purpose of this article is not to show that auditors use bad samples. It is rather to focus attention on the fact that methods are available whereby they can supplement their experience by introducing objective standards and procedures, and that there is a strong case for suggesting that the wide discretion with respect to the extent of sample testing, which is vested in the auditor as an individual, ought to be tempered at least by recognition of statistical standards by the profession.

To a statistician, one of the paradoxes of accounting practice is the contrast between the great attention to detail in searching for satisfactory explanations of test-check exceptions, and the almost complete neglect of the problems of sample selection and adequacy. It is a common practice simply to choose some " reasonable " percentage of items to check, often 5 or 10 per cent. The claim that " experience " has shown this to be the best does not bear very close examination. An auditor's certificate is generally its own guarantee. Consequently, few questions have arisen in the past simply because the auditor does not have to justify his sampling procedures or sample sizes. Two competent auditors may, in fact, adopt completely different standards for exactly similar situations, and still claim that they are using their " most careful discretion." Perhaps it is only fair to say that two statisticians might do the same. The latter, however, could be called upon to justify their claims with reference to certain generally accepted principles of sampling and statistical inference.[6] At present, the former could not. The American accounting profession have been aware of this paradox in professional standards for some time, and a committee of the American Institute of Certified Public Accountants is at present actively studying the general role of sampling.

It is evident from the examples that, although he does not use statistical criteria in planning tests, the auditor cannot escape the fact that statistical standards are implied in the use of samples. The universal use of a 5 or 10 per cent. sample is a very simple and convenient solution to test-checking problems, but it can vary considerably in its statistical implications. The proposition in the first example that " there are fewer than 1 per cent. extension errors in the stock vouchers for this branch " has clearly received very different levels of substantiation in

[6] *Cf. Statistical Problems of the Kinsey Report.* A searching critique of Dr. Kinsey's methods by a specially appointed Committee of the American Statistical Association.

Branch A and Branch B. A low level of substantiation in one subsection may be relatively unimportant by itself, but ultimately the audit is an integration of the individual propositions, and therefore of the individual levels of substantiation.

The case for wider use of statistical standards of sampling in auditing and accounting practice is thus not that it is necessarily an economising device, although in the United Kingdom it would probably lead to elimination of much laborious detail in checking postings and vouchers. The principal advantage of the introduction of statistical standards is the gain in control over an audit which would accrue from using reliable and defensible methods of sample selection, and objective standards for the amount of testing. A great deal of auditing effort now goes into inspecting the transactions of very large organisations. General accounting methods and procedures have developed with the growth of these organisations, but sampling methods in auditing have changed hardly at all, except where modified by case law, or under the compulsion of changes in the nature of its material. Yet one of the important problems facing the auditor of a large company is to secure adequate control over the large volume of routine testing which he has to delegate. Judicious use of valid statistical techniques would go a long way to help in solving this problem. As an illustration, consider the case of a large engineering department which has recently introduced a new system of recording its purchases. The work of ensuring that the system and records are reliable devolves on two audit clerks. At the introduction of the new system they were required to do a considerable amount of checking—a complete check of every second month's records. As the system settles down and the initial problems are overcome, the records become more and more reliable, until at a certain stage the clerks are finding, perhaps, fewer than ·05 per cent. errors. By this time, however, the practice of checking six months per year is written into the agenda, and the issue of reducing the amount of test-checking has become an issue of changing the agenda. At the same time, it is the audit clerks who know about the records, but it is the principal who has to decide whether to change the agenda. In this sort of situation, the provision of a set of statistical standards, in the form, say, of some simple rules and tables, would have enabled a decision to reduce test-checking to be taken by the clerks, subject to a short report to the principal. The advantages would be, first, that the clerks would be relieved as soon as possible of much unnecessary routine work, secondly, that they would have a greater degree and feeling of responsibility, and thirdly, that the auditor would still be in control of the operation. If the clerks were not felt to be responsible and capable enough for such a decision, there would be no guarantee that the work was adequately performed anyway.

Accounting objections

At various times, accountants have raised objections to the application of statistical principles to auditing problems. Some of these objections arise out of misunderstandings of statistical principles by accountants, and of accounting principles by statisticians. Others raise real difficulties which may require the development of special statistical techniques if they are to be overcome.

It is not proposed to deal at any length with the problem of misunderstandings, but two examples illustrate the directions in which they may occur. In an article in *The Journal of Accountancy*,[7] Mr. H. P. Hill examined the contribution of statistical sampling methods to auditing problems and gave a number of instances where the application of statistical principles seems to be wrong.[8] One of these is concerned with the auditor's criteria for deciding on the extent of testing. Among these is his " professional valuation of what the system should produce," or, to put it another way, the " existence of potential for trouble." Mr. Hill quotes a passage from the work of a statistician, the essence of which, to another statistician, is that the more errors there are in a set of accounts, the smaller the sample required to establish that the accounts are bad. The passage is not so clear to a non-statistician, however, and Mr. Hill's comment is: " At first blush, this argument sounds valid, but can he mean that if the accountant judges internal control to be bad, he should not use a larger sample? " The key to this apparent contradiction is simply that a bad system of internal control does not necessarily mean a set of erroneous accounts. It does mean that the auditor must rely less on the system and more on the test-check; that is, he must reduce the sampling risk he is willing to take, or increase the chance of discovering error if it exists. In doing this, he will automatically increase his sample. This does not invalidate the statistical proposition that, given this chance, the higher the true level of error, the smaller the sample required to detect it. Later, in a discussion of random

---

[7] " An Accountant Looks at Statistics," April 1958, p. 57.
[8] An effective but general answer is given by Professor H. Arkin, of the City College of New York, in the same issue.

sampling, Mr. Hill draws on the experience of a Department of Internal Revenue, which, having originally used a random procedure in choosing individuals for tax investigation, dropped it in favour of a more selective procedure. The change was an obvious and proper one to make, but, in using it in a *statistical* argument, Mr. Hill misses the point. Random sampling techniques as used by statisticians are applicable to situations in which the characteristics of a population are unknown, but are to be inferred or estimated from the sample. No claim is made in respect of any other objective. The purpose of selection in the case quoted was to secure tax payments from individuals, and *ought* therefore to have been biased towards persons more likely to have undisclosed incomes.

Some of the accountants' objections have arisen, however, out of genuine conflicts between statistical and accounting desiderata. A frequent point of conflict, for instance, in an annual audit, is whether to choose records for one complete month or a series of samples for all months. Clearly the latter complies with Dicksee's recommendation that " the honesty and efficiency of these officers ought to be tested over the whole period of the audit." On the other hand, opting for a single month may possibly bring the considerable advantage of reconciliation with an independent check-total, for instance, with a bank statement. In some cases—the call-day example is one—there are other reasons for choosing a particular period, *e.g.*, the importance of end-year accounts, and the fact that live accounts at that time may contain implicit confirmation of the completion of earlier transactions. In other cases, particularly in internal and independent audits, where staff are employed full time, it is reasonable to suppose that a continuous random sample check, in addition to providing a more defensible sampling procedure, could secure improved control of the quality of accounting work. Clerks will often relax after a once-a-year check, even though it is known that the following month *may* bring another. Random sampling may not be universally the best procedure, but the " reconciliation " argument is not sufficient to justify its rejection.

Another objection sometimes advanced is that accountants and statisticians do not mean the same thing by " proof." Exactly what the difference is, is not very clear, but the nature of the objection is summed up in the following passage [9]:

[9] Mautz, R. K. " Reliability of Audit Evidence," *Journal of Accountancy*, May 1958, p. 60.

Rather than requiring sufficient evidence to establish the financial statement assertions as true or in error, they [some auditors] act on the assumption that if they gather a reasonable amount of evidence and find nothing wrong, then all must be well.

Mr. Mautz is here not writing only about sample tests, but about audit evidence in general. In this and other articles,[10] he shows that financial statements are a series of propositions to be proved, and that the required proof is not in any way different from other kinds of proof: " a reasonable investigation that uncovers no reason to doubt the proposition effectively supports it. It has been tested and found not false; in effect, it has been proved ' true.' " This is exactly what the statistician means by testing a hypothesis. Since, then, auditing " proof " in test-checking is the same as " statistical " proof, the key word in Mr. Mautz's first passage is " sufficient." He suggests, however, that the absence of rules of admissibility for evidence in auditing leaves an auditor with no guides for screening evidence other than his own judgment and training. A major advantage of using statistical standards is that they provide an objective guide for one important aspect of screening, statistical evaluation of the sample.[11]

Statisticians themselves have to some extent given grounds for valid objections. Except where it includes the actual preparation of financial statements, auditing is essentially an acceptance procedure, in the sense that the purpose of an audit is to enable the auditor to reach a decision about the acceptability (or otherwise) of a set of financial statements as a fair representation of a company's financial position. In some of the earlier applications, therefore, statisticians adopted without modification standard techniques of acceptance sampling, already used in industry. This approach overlooked two important differences, however. The first is that a test check of a particular set of records is part of a much wider complex of auditing activities, and that consequently statistical sampling techniques, if not properly integrated into the general programme, can at best only be applied to limited areas. Since there are complex inter-relationships between different audit steps, this problem of integration is of considerable importance. Very little impression has so far been made on it, although work is going on.[12] The

---

[10] *e.g.*, " Evidence, Judgement, and the Auditor's Opinion," *Journal of Accountancy*, April 1959, p. 40.

[11] Perhaps it should be made clear that in these articles Mr. Mautz discusses auditing principles and not, explicitly at any rate, statistical sampling.

[12] For instance, by a team of accountants and statisticians at the Carnegie Institute of Technology.

second difference is that while standard acceptance sampling techniques envisage an automatic and well-defined method of making decisions from sample results, the auditor's action on uncovering a number of exceptions is not easily stated as a routine. This is partly because the relationship between auditor and client is different from that usually found between the agents in an acceptance sampling arrangement. It is also because his action may depend on a number of factors which cannot be specified in advance, such as the stage of the audit, the implications of the fault for the audit as a whole, whether the exceptions are errors of principle, failures of internal control, or trivial clerical errors, and whether they consistently point in one direction. Thus the problem is not merely one of deciding whether to accept, examine more fully or reject a set of accounts.

Clearly, the question of how to define an error or exception is also involved, since a discrepancy of, say, 10s. in an account of £50,000 is trivial in magnitude, but serious in nature if it signals a breakdown in internal control. For this particular difficulty in acceptance sampling, the accountant himself is partly to blame, because of his general haziness about the exact propositions [13] that samples are supposed to test, and his consequent application of uniform sample checks for all kinds of error.

The inadequacy of the orthodox acceptance sampling approach has been recognised in recent years by some of the leading statistical writers in this field.[14] Attempts have been made to develop other ways of applying statistical principles to auditing problems, for instance, by using samples to estimate error levels, and by using the concept of discovery sampling. The latter, a modification of which was used in the examples given in the earlier section of this paper, is one of the more promising developments. As originally proposed, it was associated with the need to give the auditor a reasonable chance of locating major faults, such as failures in internal control or manipulations of accounts.[15] The central idea is that sampling procedure and sample size are chosen so as to provide a specified (by the auditor) degree of assurance of finding at least one example of the fault if it occurs with a prescribed minimum frequency. Application

[13] A well-stated proposition would imply a sufficiently well-defined specification of error. A good discussion of error definition is to be found in K. F. Schumann, " Use of Sampling Procedures in Internal Auditing," *N.A.A. Bulletin*, December 1957.

[14] Vance, L.L., " A Review of Developments in Statistical Sampling for Accountants," *Accounting Review*, January 1960; Arkin, H., " Statistical Sampling in Auditing," *New York C.P.A.*, July 1957.

[15] Arkin, *op. cit.*, p. 467.

of the concept has been elaborated more recently,[16] and suitable tables are now available.

Sampling and estimation problems

Statistical inference is concerned with estimating the properties (parameters) of populations, *e.g.*, averages and total values, as well as testing the validity of propositions about them. The emphasis on the latter aspect of statistical inference in accounting in the preceding pages, however, has been deliberate, since application of statistical standards to estimation has already achieved some degree of success, possibly because the advantages are more obvious, being mainly a reduction in the cost of estimation.

A number of case studies have been published in the professional journals [17] and other applications are known to have been successful. In one instance,[18] the introduction of sampling reduced the number of man-hours for an inventory count from the 200 straight-time, 360 overtime needed for a full 100 per cent. count, to 260 straight-time for the sample count. Other examples of estimation reported have included valuation of physical inventory, estimation of uncollectibles or associated variables, and the settlement of intercompany transactions. There is little doubt that this particular kind of application of statistical inference will become much more widely used, especially in cases where a physical check of inventory is made quickly at close of year.

There are, however, two problems which still may cause difficulty. One arises from the nature of accounting data. The individual items in an accounting population, such as the values of items of stock, tend to have an extremely skew distribution,[19] so that for sample estimation, it is essential at least to separate high value from low value items. Where this cannot be done, the sample estimates may be critically affected by the spread of values. Efficient estimation, in fact, can best be achieved when the population is divided into fairly homogeneous strata for sampling purposes. The most successful applications have made

[16] Arkin, H., " Discovery Sampling in Auditing," *Journal of Accountancy*, November 1960.

[17] *e.g.*, Rudell, A. L., " Applied Sampling Doubles Inventory Accuracy, Halves Cost," *N.A.A. Bulletin*, October 1957; Cyert, R. M., Hinckley, G. M., Monteverde, R. J., " Statistical Sampling in the Audit of the Air Force Motor Vehicle Inventory " (Forthcoming).

[18] Obrock, R. F., " A Case Study of Statistical Sampling," *Journal of Accountancy*, March 1958.

[19] S. F. James, " Some sampling problems in connection with accounting records," *Applied Statistics*, June 1956; Mackenzie, H. C., " Statistical Sampling in Accountancy," *The Accountant*, October–November 1958.

use of some form of stratified sampling, generally by imposing on the sampling plan the condition that the more valuable items should have a higher sampling fraction. This, of course, is the kind of condition that provides both a suitable criterion for stratification, and a satisfactory safeguard for the accountant. Preliminary sorting, or, if necessary, reorganisation of inventory records for stratified sampling, will generally compensate for the nature of the data.

The second problem is not statistical, but legal, *i.e.*, the legal acceptability of sample results in accounting. It is perhaps worth while to refer to an American case [20] in which this kind of issue was involved. In 1955, Sears, Roebuck & Co. brought a suit for a sales tax refund from the City of Inglewood in the Los Angeles Superior Court. On the basis of a probability (*i.e.*, random) sample, the amount overpaid was stated to be $27,000 $\pm$ 3,000, and a statistician gave evidence as an expert witness testifying to the reliability of the sample. The judge took the view that the sales tax was computed on each individual sale as it occurred, and that, however reliable the sample, any claim for refund must be made on the same basis, *i.e.*, the company must produce evidence of each individual transaction. The company having accepted the court's permission to perform a complete audit, the actual overpayment was determined to be $26,750·22, excluding some missing records which would almost certainly have increased it. The curious feature of the judgment lies in the fact that, while the court decision was based on an implied practice of unit-by-unit aggregation of sales tax, the sales tax auditors of the City of Inglewood, in auditing sales tax liability, were accustomed to sample the transactions of a number of days in each period and to project the result over the entire period. The plaintiff, in other words, had merely been using a method already accepted in principle by the defendant. The legal ruling, on the other hand, was based on the argument that sampling techniques, though well established in principle and practice, had not been so established in courts of law, and that the legal requirements of the sales tax did not appear to admit of statistical determination. It may be that a different judge would have interpreted the law in a different manner and accepted the sample estimate, thus opening the way to legal admissibility of evidence from random samples in auditing as in

[20] Sprowls, R. C., " The Admissibility of Sample Data into a Court of Law: A Case History," *U.C.L.A. Law Review*, February 1957.

other allied fields.[21] There is little doubt, however, that such an outcome would be greatly facilitated by official recognition by the accounting profession of the role which random sampling techniques could play in providing efficient, accurate and relatively cheap estimates for auditing and financial purposes.

The meaning of discretion

It is hardly possible to doubt that, given an open-minded outlook on the subject by accountants, and a willingness on the part of statisticians to co-operate in developing suitable concepts and methods, the application of statistical principles can provide an important addition to the store of auditing techniques. The accountant's objections, relevant or otherwise, and the misdirected efforts of the statistician are both part of a necessary process of learning and adapting. Why, then, is the profession rather reluctant to take a closer look at the possible implications of test-checking methods and the relevance of accepted statistical standards? Perhaps the answer lies in a fundamental misunderstanding of what the statistical argument is about. It is felt by many accountants that what is being recommended is an abdication of responsibility. Thus it is possible for an accountant to say that " the mathematical approach based upon probabilities has much to commend it, but it has not been widely adopted and in any event cannot displace the auditor's judgment, if only in interpreting the results." [22] The whole point of statistical sampling is not to *displace* the auditor's judgment, but to *sharpen* his judgment by providing him with better tools than he has so far used. The technique and the extent of testing the individual transaction are, of course, purely auditing matters. The method of selection of transactions and the number of transactions to be checked are statistical as well as auditing problems. The auditor, however, using his discretion, has traditionally brought no statistical criteria to bear. Thus, although a number of writers state, like Mr. Irish, that " the object (of selecting samples for test-checking) is to select a representative sample without intruding bias," there are none who follow this to the logical conclusion that for practical purposes the only definition of an unbiased sample is a sample selected by an *unbiased procedure*. From this flow the statistician's requirements for *objective* sampling procedures. Again, on sample

---

[21] *Cf.* Deming, W. E., " On the Presentation of the Results of Sample Surveys as Legal Evidence," *J. Amer. Stat. Ass.*, December 1954; Kecker, " Admissibility in Courts of Law of Economic Data based on Samples," *Journal of Business*, *Univ. of Chicago*, April 1955.
[22] Irish, R. A., *Auditing* (Australia, 1957), p. 196.

size, Mr. Irish offers the following advice: " Each case must be decided on its own merits, though, as a broad guide, it may be said that an exhaustive test of a sample equivalent to 10 per cent. of items or of, say, one month in a year, will usually be much more than enough to show whether the internal control is reliable." How this proportion is arrived at, or what " merits " would lead one to use a different proportion, is not discussed.

It is precisely this haziness in the auditors' judgment which the adoption of a fairly simple principle would clear up. This principle is that the auditor, when he uses sample evidence (as opposed to, say, cross-check evidence) for judging a set of accounts or an internal control system, should focus his attention on the degree and kind of error which would lead him to qualify the certificate, and the risk he is prepared to take of making a wrong judgment. It is true that this principle would require the auditor to state the degree of assurance he requires in terms of a precise probability, say a 90 per cent. chance. Such an exact statement would be unfamiliar and perhaps rather frightening initially, but once accepted and brought into common use, the advantage of having a firm, objective method of fixing standards for sample sizes would be apparent. Further, even when such standards are used, the auditor would still bear in mind the past history of the account, the personalities involved, the soundness of internal check, and other factors on which his examination is normally based. Indeed, it is precisely his view of these matters, together with the importance of the particular accounts, which would enable the auditor to assess the degree of tolerable risk and the consequences of error. The sample check does not take place in a vacuum. If *no* error can be tolerated, the auditor cannot rely on a sample.

This procedure is, in fact, the most effective one that is open to the auditor. It takes into account the " merits of the case " and relates the latter, through his judgment about acceptable risks, to sample selection and size. He does not need to rely on rule-of-thumb suggestions such as the 10 per cent. sample.

In conclusion, it is worth noticing some of the results [23] of one of the few serious investigations of the applicability of statistical principles to auditing. As a result of a major project carried out in the U.S. Air Force, it was reported that the Auditor-General was especially impressed with the usefulness of the statistical methods for combining the audit results from a number

[23] Monteverde, R. J., " Better Audits Through Statistical Sampling: U.S. Air Force shows the Way," *Quarterly Review* of Touche, Niven, Bailey & Smart, August 1958.

of bases, and the fact that through the use of the objective methods of measurement available from statistical sampling, and the uniform sample sizes, it was possible to make objective comparisons of results. At a lower level, participating auditors found that the obvious random selection of items gave them more confidence in the audit, while at the same time they could obtain reliable results from significantly smaller samples of items than they would normally have used.

Of course, the initial effort required if accountants are to re-examine and re-evaluate test-checking practices in the light of modern statistical methods may be greater than the importance of test-checks in auditing warrants. This view, however, is hardly consistent with Dicksee's injunction to auditors to use their most careful discretion in setting appropriate statistical standards.

Statistical standards are generally accepted whenever inferences have to be made with the help of samples. The question that the accounting profession has to ask itself is whether it can continue to interpret the auditor's duty to use his discretion as a valid reason for ignoring recent developments in statistical standards and methods.

Automatic Control and Computing in Industry *

By R. H. Tizard

Fellow, Churchill College, Cambridge

RECENT scientific and technical developments have led to the idea of a " second industrial revolution " and to the invention of a new word—" automation." These words are not well defined, mean different things to different people, and have given rise to fruitless arguments. This paper will discuss some of the background to these developments, which are in fact leading to a revolution in industrial techniques.

They are based essentially on two concepts, of " feedback " and of " digital data processing," parts of a general science which has also been christened with a new name—" cybernetics "—defined by its author [1] as the science of control and communication in the animal and the machine.

Roles of electronics and of mass-production machines

Before discussing these concepts, we must mention two aspects of industrial innovation which, whilst of great importance in practice, are not of fundamental theoretical significance as is sometimes supposed.

Electronics is playing such a major part in new developments in industry that it is often thought of as being the principal factor in the new revolution. In fact, however, it is only one tool in the practical realisation of the new techniques. With its advantages of very high speeds of operation, and flexibility in design and construction, it has made so many schemes realisable, which by any other means would be impracticable, that it is certainly an essential feature of the revolution. Yet it is not fundamental, and many systems operated by mechanical means, by pneumatics and by hydraulics, exhibit the same principles of action.

---

* An address delivered on May 31, 1957, at the twenty-eighth national cost conference, in London, of The Institute of Cost and Works Accountants.
[1] Norbert Wiener, *Cybernetics* (New York: John Wiley & Sons, 1948).

Consideration of existing applications of electronics in industry will show that it is used in three main roles:

(i) In a process in which the electrical or electronic nature plays a fundamental role, as in induction heating.

(ii) In the control of a process, as in machine-tool control.

(iii) In the processing of data, as in the use of an electronic computer for " office-work."

This paper will be concerned only with the last two, which are closely allied.

Automation is a word frequently used to cover new developments in mass-production machinery, in particular " transfer " machines consisting of a collection of special-purpose machines linked together by automatic transfer of the work-piece between them in the required sequence. Such machines are no more than an extension, although an extremely important one, of the mechanisation techniques which formed the first industrial revolution. There is nothing fundamentally new in them.

Open-loop control. Suppose that we wish to heat a house to a constant interior temperature, despite the vagaries of the weather outside. We might do this by considering all the factors which effect loss of heat from the building—the outside temperature and humidity, the strength and direction of the wind, whether the sun is shining and whether a window is open. By theoretical considerations, and by experiment, it would be possible to work out just how much heat would be lost by any combination of values of these factors. Then by measuring all the factors and carrying out this calculation we could automatically regulate the furnace so that the flow of heat into the house exactly balanced the heat loss, and kept the internal temperature constant.

Such a scheme would only work if we knew the exact effect of all the factors, and could measure them and make the calculations with great accuracy. It would clearly not, in this example, be practicable, although such a method is used for control in simpler cases. It is known as " open-loop " control, and does not employ " feedback ".

Closed-loop control based on feedback. A better method of controlling the temperature of a house is the one which is used in practice, generally known as a thermostatic system. Here we measure the variable that we want to control, the internal temperature of the house, and use this measurement to increase the supply of heat if it is too low, or to reduce it if it is too high. Even apart from the comparative simplicity of such a scheme, it appears to be the ideal method of control, for the effects of external changes are completely counteracted without any pre-knowledge of their effects or even of their existence. Unlike the open-loop system, it would still work even if an unexpected disturbance occurred, such as the sudden appearance of a hole in the wall.

Such a system is known as " closed-loop " control, and is said to be actuated by " feedback ". The significance of these words appears on a slightly closer analysis.

It is convenient to suppose the existence of a temperature " setting " (which does in fact exist in practice, although its physical form is not always apparent), corresponding to the constant temperature which we wish to achieve, known as the " desired temperature." By subtracting this from the measured value of actual temperature, we obtain the " error " in tempera-ture. The error is used to decrease the heat supply if it is positive (actual temperature too great) or increase it if it is negative. Thus the temperature controls the heat supply, and the heat supply of course controls the temperature, and so we have a " closed-loop " system.

By analogy particularly with servo-mechanisms, which are identical in principle, the temperature setting or desired value is known as the input, and the actual temperature as the output, of the system. The term " feedback " is used to indicate that the output is fed back for comparison with the input, in order to effect control.

The reason for using the term " open-loop " for the previous type of system is now apparent, for in this the heat supply affects the internal temperature, but the internal temperature does not affect the heat supply.

Instability in feedback systems. It might seem at first that a feedback system such as the one described is perfect. The slightest departure from the desired temperature will cause a change in the heat supply which is bound to correct it. Of course the change in heat supply may take some appreciable time to act, during which time the temperature will not be right. We can always mitigate this, however, by arranging that the heat supply is changed by a very large amount for a small error in temperature. But here we come up against one of the funda-mental limitations of feedback systems; the system will become unstable so that the temperature, instead of remaining constant, will " hunt " continuously from very cold to very hot and back again. This effect is due to the time lags in the system; increased heat supply does not immediately raise the temperature.

The effect may be explained in qualitative terms by considering a particular example of such a system. Suppose the house is heated by hot-water radiators fed from a coke boiler, and imagine that it has been running steadily at the desired temperature when suddenly it is upset by the opening of a window. The temperature quickly goes down and more heat is demanded by the control. The boiler is stoked up and the draught is increased, but there is no immediate effect on the water. Then the fire gets hotter and hotter and the water starts to heat up, but still the house temperature remains low. The hotter water gradually circulates to the radiators, and the air immediately around them starts to get warmer. Then the warm air circulates and gradually the house heats up, until it reaches the desired temperature and the control demands less heat.

But by now the water is very hot and the fire even hotter, and though the fire is damped right down the house continues to get hotter very rapidly. At last the fire gets cold, the water gradually cools, and the house temperature, after reaching a high peak, drops down again and eventually reaches the desired value. But now water and fire are cold, and nothing will stop it dropping further; and so down it goes to a low trough, and then starts to rise again to repeat the cycle. With an unstable system this goes on indefinitely.

Complex feedback systems. In more complicated cases, feedback systems may consist of many inter-related closed loops, and their analysis and design, to ensure stability and satisfactory operation, becomes a very difficult process involving advanced mathematical techniques. Although an extensive theory exists for certain types of system, considerably more research is needed before all aspects of these systems are really understood.

The following are a few examples of automatic feedback systems at present used in industry:

(i) Automatic control of many variables in process plant, as in a chemical factory or oil refinery. The variables most commonly controlled are temperature, pressure, flow and liquid level. The nature of these plants is such that provided the values of these sorts of variables at key points are kept constant, the product is satisfactory.

(ii) Speed control of steam-turbines, by the old-established Watts governor, and of electric motor drives as in mine-winders and rolling mills.

(iii) Control of rolling-mills to produce a given gauge of steel, by feedback from measurement of the gauge.

(iv) Grinding of ball races to a given diameter, from measurement of the actual diameter during grinding.

In the physical world in general, examples of feedback systems abound. Some of these were designed as such, whilst in others the feedback principle has only recently been recognised. In ships, the servo-driven rudder and the anti-roll stabiliser are both feedback systems. In aircraft, " George," the automatic pilot, is an obvious example, but it is not often realised that even an aircraft with locked controls is a feedback system; for its attitude in flight affects the aerodynamic forces on its wings and tailplane, and these in turn affect its attitude.

In animals, a feedback control keeps the body temperature constant, to a remarkably high degree of accuracy. The control of muscular actions, as in picking up an object with the hand, is effected by two closed-loops, one within the other; the inner loop directly controlling the position of the hand by passing on commands from the brain, and the outer loop controlling these commands from visual observation of the error between position of the hand and of the object. Recent work has indicated that animal behaviour as a whole may be explicable by postulating a complex system of closed-loops within the brain, some being closed at birth (giving inherited characteristics), and others being closed afterwards, in a pattern determined by experience and with the motive of survival (acquired characteristics).

The spread and decay of epidemic diseases, and of plant and animal populations is another example of feedback, whilst in economics not only is the system easily seen to be a feedback one, but the pre-war succession of booms and slumps brought home forcibly the effects of instability.

Digital data processing. Manufacturing processes ultimately depend on control based on measurement such as dimensions or temperature or pressure. Information obtained from these measurements has to be " processed," that is transmitted, used for computation, translated, recorded, and used for control— any of these operations being preformed either by human beings or automatically.

Contrast with analogue representation. For this purpose the data have to be represented in a suitable form, and two basic and fundamentally different forms exist, *analogue* and *digital*. In analogue representation, the value of any physical quantity is represented by a corresponding value of some other physical quantity—for instance in the normal car speedometer the speed is represented by the angle through which the needle turns.

In digital representation, the value of a physical quantity is represented in number form in the same way as numbers are written on paper, or in a similar way; the car mileometer is an example. In an electrical transmission system an analogue representation might be the value of current in a line, whilst a digital representation might be a series of current pulses whose values are immaterial, but whose pattern in time represents a number in a coded form.

Until recently, analogue representation has been used almost exclusively, except in certain simple cases such as revolution counters, because the techniques for digital representation were not available. Analogue techniques were developed to a very high state during the last war, particularly in connection with radar and gun-control.

Advantages of digital representation. The disadvantage of analogue representation lies in the limits of accuracy with which operations may be performed or the data interpreted. For instance in the example of the speedometer, even if the speed measurement were very accurate it would not be possible to read the needle position to better than say $\frac{1}{2}$ m.p.h., or about 1 per cent. The percentage accuracy of the mileometer however depends only on the number of figures shown, and would be 0·0001 per cent. for one reading tenths of a mile up to 100,000 miles. This is a good example of a case in which each form of representation is suitable for its purpose and for the accuracy actually required.

Similarly in the example of analogue representation by value of an electric current the accuracy is limited to that with which we can actually measure the current. The technical choice between the two forms often becomes one of economics. Suppose such an analogue system exists with an accuracy of one part in one thousand. To improve the accuracy to one part in ten thousand might cost ten times as much. But for a corresponding digital system the increase in accuracy would only involve increasing from three figures to four figures, at an extra cost in equipment of one-third or possibly even less. A further tenfold increase of accuracy would show an even more marked contrast.

The contrast becomes greater still in systems which involve a whole series of processing stages, such as computing or complex transmission or control systems. For in analogue systems some accuracy is lost every time the data are processed, and this sets a limit to the number of stages which are practicable. With digital systems on the other hand the initial accuracy, dependent on the number of digits used, remains unimpaired however many stages of processing are used.

Digital representation also shows great advantages when it comes to storing or "remembering" data. Data must be stored for two reasons, to fit in with the time sequence of the process being controlled, whether it be, for instance, machine-tool control or keeping customer accounts, and to enable processing to be carried out at a more convenient or economical rate than that at which data arrive or must be used. To store large quantities of data in an economical manner, the stored energy must be small, and this again makes it difficult to maintain accuracy with analogue systems.

It is these advantages of digital representation, together with the development of electronics, which have made automatic computers so widely applicable. The digital computer contains a large store for data, whilst it has very simple arithmetic units which, with minor exceptions, carry out only one operation at a time. Thus very large calculations are carried out with sequences of millions of simple operations, each one using only a minute part of the data in the store. Digital representation allows this enormous number of operations to be carried out without loss of accuracy, and the speed of electronics allows it to be done in a reasonable time.

Industrial applications. The first thought of applications of digital techniques to industry is naturally to cases of actual computation. Thus a digital computer can be applied to clerical operations which consist in greater or lesser degree of computation—*e.g.*, wage accounting—and to problems of engineering design. A second obvious application is to cases which consist primarily of data storage, as in stores control. But the biggest potential application is in conjunction with feedback techniques in the control of manufacturing processes and even of entire enterprises.

Analogies with human processes. As with feedback, digital data processing presents analogies with animal functions. In particular there is considerable controversy over whether digital computers can " think." This probably depends on what is meant by the word " think," and the argument is not a very fruitful one. However, it can certainly be said that computers are capable of taking over " mental work" and of carrying out operations in industry which are at present considered as requiring an intelligent operator.

Control of machine tools. An important application of feedback and digital techniques is in the control of machine-tools. For very large-scale mass production the conventional automatic machine-tool is appropriate. With such a machine a highly skilled operator is required to make mechanical settings each time the design of the workpiece is changed or a tool is renewed. With the new type of control no mechanical settings are required, but the motions of the machine are controlled by feedback systems usually using digital measurements of displacement of the slides.

The controlling data come straight from the design office, in the form of punched cards or tape, or magnetic tape, and contain all the designed dimensions of the workpiece, equivalent to the present working drawing, together with machining instructions. Once the designs are available in this form, the machine can produce a number of " short run " pieces of different designs just as easily and economically as a single piece over a long production run.

Control of chemical processes. Chemical processes are at present controlled by adjustment to a set of physical conditions, of temperature, pressure and so on, at various points in the plant, which are known to produce a satisfactory product under given conditions. Each of these physical conditions is maintained constant by a very simple analogue type feedback control system, usually pneumatically operated.

Automatic measurement of the actual desired qualities of the end product is seldom carried out, and the only overall feedback control is via a slow chain of laboratory analysis and plant management decision. This system is satisfactory where the raw material does not vary rapidly in quality or quantity, and where only a single product is concerned. In most plants, however, the first condition does not often hold, and there are many products and by-products, each affected in a different way by changes of plant operation, making it very difficult to assess the " best " conditions of operation.

The future of control of such plants lies in the use of a digital computer, which will be supplied with information from all parts of the plant, and from automatic analysis of the end-products and possibly the feedstock. The computations involved are so extensive as to be practicable only by digital methods, except in very simple cases. Moreover, measurements will be required at widely separated parts of the plant, and digital techniques will have advantages for transmission of the data.

Application to accounting and office work. There are now, in 1961, some 250 large or medium-sized digital computers installed in Great Britain, and the figure will nearly double in another year. Most of these are used wholly or partly for business work, *e.g.*, cost accounting, invoicing, payroll, stock control and production control. In this field, therefore, their use is now well established, and their potentialities are understood, although many optimistic predictions of earlier days have not been fulfilled.

In a computer organisation, the collection of input data, its processing, and the dissemination of results, are much more definitely separated operations than they are in normal clerical processing. To take payroll as an example, a conventional weekly wages office will be able to complete computing the pay of some employees, *e.g.*, those on holiday, on the Monday, and to carry on, during the week, computing as the input data becomes available, so that the last man's time-sheets need not be available until just before five o'clock on Friday. Because of limitations in input and output, however, a computer cannot work in this way; all the input data must be collected first, and checked, before any computing can begin. Then the computation is done and the results printed all in one operation. In consequence it is found there is very little time left for the actual computer operation, between collection of the last bit of data and the latest time for making up wage-packets; and so there is greater emphasis on both speed and reliability of the computer.

The same limitations in input and output (which will be discussed further in a later section) make it necessary for computer operations to embrace the whole of a firm's activities before an installation is really justified economically. There is a great deal of data common to, for instance, payroll and cost accounting, stock-control and production-control, and so on, and it is very costly to feed all this information into a computer separately for each operation. Data once fed in must be used for every purpose for which they are relevant.

Although on economic grounds it is often possible to justify the use of a computer by showing that it can do more cheaply operations which are at present carried out clerically, this is usually a minor feature compared with the increase in efficiency of the enterprise which can result from the ability to do, by computer, operations which are impracticable clerically, thus making more efficient use of the information available.

All these considerations mean that the installation of a computer requires a complete re-thinking of the present clerical system, and of the whole requirement for data-processing for management. Old departmental barriers must be broken down, data collection totally reorganised, and a searching appraisal made into the best ways to make use of the data. This is a very costly operation, often more costly than the installation of the computer itself and its associated equipment. Failure to realise its necessity was responsible for some early disappointments in this field, and now that its necessity is acknowledged it acts as the principal factor in limiting the rate of application.

Control of whole enterprises. The example of the chemical process may be extended to show how the use of these techniques will lead to automatic control over a much wider field. The system described will operate the plant in the best manner to produce a given combination of products and by-products. But what is the best combination? This depends on the state of the market, and the predicted future state of the market, both for products and for raw materials and also, in a wider sense, for all the commodities required to run the plant, including fuel and repairs and replacements.

This is the function of management, and is based on experience in running the particular enterprise, and a great deal of it consists of calculations, or perhaps of inspired guesses which could better be replaced by calculations. Thus the concept of a computer controlling a plant in the best way to given requirements of products can be widened to that of a computer controlling the entire enterprise, given market and other relevant data and an overall requirement as a criterion of success.

In a similar way the computer used for office-work may be visualised as extending its activities. The improvement in efficiency to be gained by better processing of the available information will come about as a result of the integration of all office-work into a single computer organisation. One facet of this will be production control, allied with the control of stocks of raw materials, part-finished and finished products; and it is only a short step from this to the integration of office-work and physical control of the manufacturing process.

In fact it may be forecast that the firm of the future will no longer be divided into " office " and " factory," and the shop-floor worker and the clerk will be the same person. In such an enterprise the computer would be concerned not only with day-to-day control, but also with " research " in the sense of such things as market forecasting, and operational research to ensure optimum use of the available resources.

The learning machine. The designer of a control system has to know a great deal about the plant or process to be controlled, if he is to avoid instability and obtain a satisfactory performance. Often, with complicated systems, obtaining this knowledge is a difficult and very costly matter. It seems possible to arrange that the controlling computer itself obtains this knowledge, or can do without it, by a process of tentative trial-and-error, in which it finds out what kind of plant it is controlling, and what actions are successful or unsuccessful in obtaining satisfactory control. Here again there is close analogy with human or animal learning.

Many possible applications, especially in business or clerical work, are hampered by limitations of machine memory or by the difficulties of communication between man and machine. For instance, a computer doing wage accounting could learn from any mistakes it made, and so not repeat them. But it would be unlikely to learn by receiving a kick from an employee, accompanied by the words " You've given me a pound short "; not because it was insensitive to reprimand, but because that is the wrong kind of reprimand for a machine.

An interesting example of the possible use of a learning machine for a clerical process has been investigated. This is the case of a computer used for the maintenance of, and reference to, an index of names. In many cases the reference must be made on the basis of inquiry data which have been misquoted, such as by the misspelling of a name, and so do not exactly correspond to any entry in the index. The object of the learning machine is to discover by experience, just as a human being does, what kinds of misquotations are commonly associated with each name.

This it can do by making trial searches of the index with variants of the name, and keeping a record of its successes and failures. Of course this process can be greatly accelerated if the machine is provided initially with knowledge of the subject obtained by human experience, and if subsequently human beings are able to assist it in its learning, in the same way as a teacher assists a pupil.

Human operator in a control loop. It must not be thought that the application of new techniques of control necessarily means that all operations will be automatic. The human operator has many advantages in certain roles. In particular, he is more versatile, both in mental and physical processes, than any machine at present conceivable. For instance an operator may be used to carry out a simple controlling operation, which in itself could be better done by machine, because at the same time he is capable of detecting danger and acting correctly to avert disaster.

Human beings are also better at certain particular functions, such as the recognition of shapes. They often take up less space and require less maintenance, and are self-propelling. And, most important, they are often cheaper, although as wages rise it may become economic to instal a machine where before it was not, provided that the cost of the machine has not risen in the same proportion.

An interesting point on the question of the comparative versatility of men and machines is that the data-storage capacity of the brain is something like ten thousand times greater than that of a present-day computer. If computers can be developed with stores of the same capacity as the brain, at a reasonable cost and of a reasonable size, there may be few limits to their application.

Limitations of machines. At a time when such a broad vista of possibilities is opening up, it may be as well to consider a few of the major limitations of machines. Some obvious ones are directly attributable to limitations of capacity and speed, and probably many more are indirectly due to them. Two examples will be discussed.

It has been mentioned that human beings are better than machines at recognising shapes. In fact, machines are very weak on this point. A machine, for instance, which could recognise aircraft, motor-cars, or even human faces, with the same facility as does a human being, is a quite impracticable proposition for the foreseeable future. But the greatest shortcoming in this respect at present is in the difficulty of communication between man and machine. A great many applications of computers to business and clerical work are severely handicapped by the inability of the computer to read documents which have been written in the normal form for human beings to read, and the corresponding difficulty that humans have in writing documents in a way which computers can read.

A start has been made on this problem by the development of experimental machines which can read typewritten or printed characters; but this is a long way from a machine which can decipher, as efficiently as a clerk can, hastily scrawled handwriting.

An example of a physical sense in which machines are completely inferior is that of smell. Whilst there are perhaps not many applications in industry for an automatic smeller, a machine which could tour a district automatically locating malodorous drains might have its points. As a rather similar example, whilst milk bottles are made automatically, filled, weighed, capped and later washed automatically, it has not been possible to make a machine which automatically inspects washed bottles and detects any which are still dirty.

Conclusion. It is hoped that this very superficial survey of some of the factors involved in new technical developments in industry may have given some idea of the underlying principles. The theme of the Industrial Revolution was the replacement of human or animal muscular power with mechanical power, and the application of invention, mainly in mechanical engineering, to supplement or replace man's physical processes. Now the theme is to replace human control with automatic control, and, mainly by electrical and electronic engineering, to supplement or replace his mental processes. Whether this justifies the term " second industrial revolution " can be safely left for each man to decide for himself.

To a technologist, engaged in the development of these techniques, it seems quite wrong that their coming should be feared. Nothing is more certain than that they will bring less drudgery, a higher standard of living, and more leisure. The trouble is that we are ill-conditioned to such a happy state of affairs, and not ready for the rate at which it is coming. Many of us, it must be admitted, like drudgery. Improvement in the standard of living takes a wholly material form which seems to involve a reduction in non-material standards as well as a profligate waste of the world's resources; and most people seem to avoid leisure as a disease, or to use it for pursuits which are appropriately named " pastimes."

The remedy lies in education, not of the present pattern, but for the world of the future; education for work which will be more creative and less routine, and which will require the highest functions of which each brain is capable; and education for life in a society which will give greater opportunities and call for greater responsibilities.

The Elementary Ideas of Inventory Analysis

By M. H. Peston

Lecturer in Economics,
London School of Economics.

IN this essay, I propose to explain as far as possible in the ordinary language of economics what the theory of inventory control is about. I shall not have explicit recourse to mathematics since my main objective is not the derivation of formulae but the clarification of ideas. It is hoped thereby to assist the non-technical economist to understand an important new branch of his subject; and also to assist the accountant by showing that his reading in economics textbooks (on the optimum combination of inputs) has direct practical applications.

Inventory control theory is a branch of the general approach to business activity called operations research. Its problems are typical of those found in operations research, and a discussion of them should throw some light on the field as a whole. In particular, a better appreciation may be reached of what is meant by the solution of a problem.

In operations research, questions both of a positive and a normative variety have to be dealt with. The end product of any investigation is the discovery of an optimum policy within a given environment. This requires a positive study of the environment to determine the set of possible actions, and the use of a criterion of choice to isolate the best action. It follows that, while in the broad sense the operations researcher is doing welfare economics, he is not spared the dual tasks of inventing theoretical investigations of behaviour and testing them.[1] He may also have an additional task, the invention of what might be called a method of selection. By this is meant a means of applying the criterion to an environment in practice so as specifically to discover an optimum policy. Since the objective of operations research is practical (and mostly quantitative) application, it is not sufficient to formulate a problem and provide general conditions for its solution. It is also necessary or at least desirable to show how in individual cases the solution can be discovered.

[1] *Vide*, G. C. Archibald, " Welfare Economics, Ethics, and Essentialism," *Economica*, November 1959, pp. 316–332.

This may be thought a trivial matter, so it should be noted that there are some problems for which no efficient method of selection has yet been found. For these the investigator must try every possibility and test it against the choice criterion. Where it is necessary to consider explicitly every alternative (or very large numbers of alternatives) in order to be absolutely certain of the optimum one, it is reasonable to say that a problem has not yet been fully solved.

Consider now the profit maximising firm of economic theory. At the most elementary level, its decision to hold an additional unit of a commodity in stock will be based on a comparison of the resulting gains (or revenues) with losses (or costs). Treating storage as an input into the process of production, the marginal revenue product of storage will be compared with the marginal cost. If the former is above the latter, it will be profitable to expand stocks; if below, to contract them.

In order to examine these gains and losses, it is necessary to understand what is meant by adding an additional unit to stocks. The firm's activities have a time dimension, and over time stocks are used up[2] and new stocks are acquired. In the present discussion the first of these will be taken as given (*i.e*, as exogenously determined), the analysis of stock control policy being related entirely to the second.

Suppose the quantity of stocks is taken to be the average quantity which the firm has on hand over time. If, for example, its stock level over time is given by the following sequence of numbers, 321 321 321 . . ., its average holding will be two units per time period. If instead its stock level is given by either of the following sequences, 432 432 432 . . ., or 54321 54321 54321 . . ., its average holding will be three units per time period; in the former, the level of the sequence (compared with the first case) is raised, while in the latter the amplitude (or maximum height) of the sequence is raised but the frequency of ordering is reduced. All three sequences are illustrated in the figures on page 623.

It may be seen, therefore, that in general the firm's stock control policy cannot be calculated solely according to the average quantity of storage. An infinite number of different time sequences could all involve the same average quantity so that a decision must be taken about the best one of these.

---

[2] The expressions " using up of stock," " the rate of use of stock " appear frequently in the remainder of the paper. They should be interpreted quite broadly as meaning that the stock is no longer available, but has been transferred for use as an input in the process of production in another part of the organisation, or has been sold.

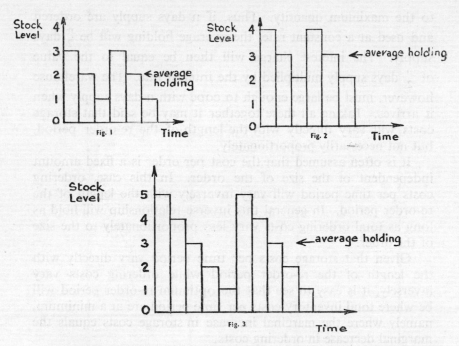

Fig. 1

Fig. 2

Fig. 3

Assume, however, that the rate of use of the commodity is given with complete certainty. The problem then becomes simply one of choosing the times at which stocks are to be replenished. This is equivalent to determining the appropriate ordering quantity, and the average quantity of stock to be held. At any point of time when an order is given the quantity ordered will be equal to the rate of use of the commodity multiplied by the interval elapsing until the next order is placed. Since there is complete certainty, no stocks have to be ordered or held except to meet the known rate of use of the commodity; thus, the ordering policy and the rate of use determine completely the time path of stock levels. It follows that the average quantity of stock is determined, and to each average quantity there corresponds a unique time sequence.

The interval between successive points of time when stock is ordered is called the re-order period. In deciding the optimum length of the re-order period two sorts of costs have to be taken into account; storage costs and ordering costs. Storage costs may include any or all of the following items: (a) interest on the capital locked up, (b) depreciation, (c) maintenance, (d) general surveillance of stocks, and (e) warehousing costs. The first three of these are increasing functions of the average quantity of stock held, but the last two appear more likely to be related to the maximum quantity. Thus, if n days supply are ordered and used at a constant rate, the average holding will be $\frac{n}{2}$ days supply. The interest charge will then be equal to the value of $\frac{n}{2}$ days supply multiplied by the interest rate. The warehouse however, must be large enough to cope with n days supply when it arrives. Taking all these together it may be said that storage costs will vary directly with the length of the re-order period, but not necessarily proportionately.

It is often assumed that the cost per order is a fixed amount independent of the size of the order. In this case, ordering costs per time period will vary inversely with the length of the re-order period. In general this inverse relationship will hold as long as total ordering costs vary less proportionately to the size of the order.

Given that storage costs per time period vary directly with the length of the re-order period while ordering costs vary inversely, it is easy to see that the optimum re-order period will be where total inventory costs per time period are at a minimum, namely where the marginal increase in storage costs equals the marginal decrease in ordering costs.

This is illustrated in Fig. IV.

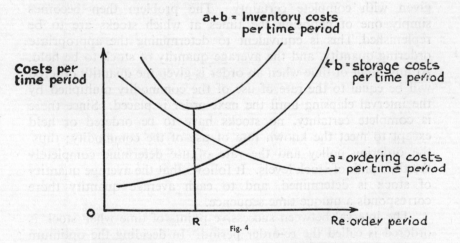

Fig. 4

The optimum re-order period is given by OR. It occurs when a + b is at a minimum, namely where the downward slope of a equals the upward slope of b.

For one elementary case a very simple formula can be derived for the optimum length of the re-order period. Suppose all storage costs vary proportionately with the average value of stocks held, while ordering costs are fixed.

Let

R=the length of the ordering period
m=the rate of use of the commodity per time period
p=the price of the commodity
i=storage costs per unit value of the commodity per time period
s=cost per order

The average value of capital locked up in stock will be $\frac{Rmp}{2}$, and this will involve an interest charge of $\frac{Rmpi}{2}$ per time period. Ordering costs per time period will be $\frac{s}{R}$. Inventory costs per time period will then be $\frac{Rmpi}{2} + \frac{s}{R}$, and these will be at a minimum when $\frac{Rmpi}{2} = \frac{s}{R}$, or $R = \sqrt{\frac{2s}{mpi}}$.

As an arithmetical example, suppose the rate of use of the commodity is 500 units per week, and its price is £2. Let the storage costs be $\frac{1}{5}$ of 1 per cent. per week, and the cost per order be £4. The formula then gives a value for

$$R = \sqrt{\frac{2 \times 4}{500 \times 2 \times \frac{1}{500}}} = 2.$$

In other words, the commodity should be ordered once every two weeks, a thousand units at a time.

If the rate of use is quadrupled and becomes 2,000 units per week, the commodity should be ordered once a week, 2,000 units at a time. The quadrupling of the rate of use leads only to a doubling of the ordering quantity.

Clearly, changes in any of the parameters on the right-hand side leads to the changes in R that common sense would expect. What might not be expected from casual analysis is the square root. In particular, this implies that the optimum ordering quantity, Rm, and the optimum inventory costs, $\sqrt{2mpis}$, increase as the rate of use of the commodity increases, but less than proportionately.

The case for holding stocks under conditions of certainty is that the storage costs incurred may be offset by the ordering costs saved. Where the first of these is very large, therefore, and the second very small, little or no stock will be held.

Another reason for holding stocks may be that the price paid for the commodity (or, in general, the cost of having it available) may vary inversely with the size of order. The most obvious example is that the supplying firm's processing costs may vary less than proportionately to the size of order, part of the saving being passed on in lower prices to the bulk buyer. Even if this were not so, however, if the buyer does not hold stocks then either the seller must hold them or the buyer must wait for the seller to acquire (possibly even manufacture) them. In either case, the price the buyer pays will contain some inventory costs. Viewing the system as a whole, therefore, a decision not to hold stocks is not the same as a decision not to pay inventory costs. Rather it becomes a question of the form in which they will be paid.

This suggests, too, that small firms need not be at a disadvantage compared with large firms in the same industry with respect to the costs of holding stocks. A large firm may buy directly from the manufacturer, and obtain quantity discounts plus the " square root " advantage of size. A small firm may buy from intermediate suppliers, also of large size, which reap the same cost savings. The position of the small firm will then be determined by the efficiency of the intermediate suppliers and their monopolistic power.

Uncertainty about the rate of use of a commodity, or about the ease with which additional quantities may be obtained, provides another reason for holding stocks. In the simple example already considered, every R time periods an amount of the commodity equal to Rm units was ordered, arrived, and was used up at the rate m, stock levels being run down to zero just in time for the next amount Rm to appear. Suppose, however, that when an order is given, it is not absolutely certain that it will arrive a fixed number of days later, or that when a quantity of the commodity arrives, it is not certain that it will be used up every day at the rate m. It may pay the firm under these circumstances to insure against unforeseen contingencies by holding an additional amount of the commodity as a buffer or safety allowance.[3]

Let m now be viewed as an average rate of use of the commodity instead of a fixed rate, so that the actual rate of use may be expected to fluctuate about m, being sometimes lower and sometimes higher.[4] If no safety allowance is held, the firm may

[3] Viewing money as a special kind of durable commodity which firms and households store, the discussion has so far been about the transaction demand for money, and is now about the precautionary demand. *Vide* W. J. Baumol, " The Transactions Demand for Cash: An Inventory Theoretic Approach," *Quarterly Journal of Economics*, November 1952, pp. 545–556.

[4] The general argument that follows applies also to the case where there are random fluctuations in delivery times.

have to take a decision about which demands on the stock are to be met, or, if it decides to meet all demands as far as possible completely as they occur, it may occasionally run out of stock. In either case net revenue will be lost. Clearly then it pays to hold a safety allowance if its cost is less than the revenue lost.

The benefit to be derived from holding an additional unit of the commodity as a safety allowance may be viewed as composed of two parts. There is the value of the extra demand for stock that is satisfied, and the likelihood of that demand occurring. If the first of these is greater than the relevant storage cost per period, it does not necessarily pay to hold a safety allowance if the chance of the order appearing is very low.

Assuming that a money value can be attached to the benefit as a whole, additional stocks will be held as a safety allowance up to the point where the marginal benefit equals the marginal cost of the safety allowance.[5] This is illustrated in Fig. V.

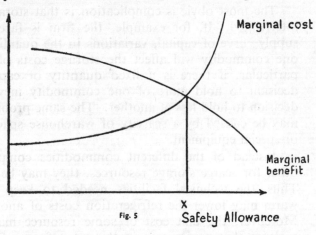

Fig. 5

The quantity O X equals the optimum safety allowance, or additional quantity of stocks which it pays the firm to hold to meet random fluctuations in the rate of use of the commodity. Once again it should be noted that the alternative to holding these stocks may be to pay a higher price to some other organisation to hold them. In general the firm has the alternatives of foregoing benefits or of incurring the additional storage costs in one form or another.

An interesting question that arises is : what happens to the safety allowance as the average rate of use of the commodity

---

[5] Marginal cost here means the addition to the total cost of storage resulting from holding an additional unit of the commodity as a safety allowance. Needless to say, in practice the firm will not necessarily divide the stock physically, calling one part stock for ordinary use, and the remainder the safety allowance.

rises, other things being equal? It may be shown fairly generally that if the rate of use of the commodity and the safety allowance increase equiproportionately, the probability of running out of stock will decline. The reason for this is the so-called law of large numbers, and from this point of view the firm is subject to increasing returns to scale.[6] Given that now it is relatively cheaper for the firm to meet random fluctuations in demand, it will vary its safety allowance in such a way that its probability of running out will be lower. Its total stocks will be higher, but, if the marginal costs of holding stocks is non-decreasing, the ratio of its safety allowance to its total stocks will be lower.

The whole of the preceding discussion has been based on the assumption that the firm is concerned with the stock control of only one commodity. Where there are several commodities to be dealt with a number of additional complications arise which are worth noting.

The most obvious complication is that storage costs may be interrelated. If, for example, the firm is faced with a rising supply curve of capital, variations in the quantity stored of any one commodity will affect the storage costs of the others. In particular, if there is a fixed quantity of capital available, a decision to hold more of one commodity inevitably implies a decision to hold less of another. The same problem of allocation may be caused by a scarcity of warehouse space, or personnel, or special equipment.

Instead of the different commodities competing with each other for scarce storage resources, they may be complementary. Thus, the technical facilities needed to keep one commodity warm may lower the refrigeration costs of another commodity. Moreover, the unit cost of some resource may decrease with scale so that an increase in the rate of use of one commodity may lead the firm to hold not only more of that in stock but more of some other commodities as well. Thus, the unit costs of heating or refrigeration may decrease with scale. Similarly, the cost of a warehouse may vary less than proportionately to size.

Another sort of complication is connected with the timing of new orders. In deciding the optimum interval between successive orders for one commodity, it may be necessary to take into account the timing of orders of other commodities. Ordering costs may vary not only less than proportionately to the

---

[6] *Vide* T. M. Whitin and M. H. Peston, " Random Variations, Risk, and Returns to Scale," *Quarterly Journal of Economics*, November 1954, pp. 603–612.

size of order of an individual commodity, but less than proportionately to the size of all commodities taken together. There may be indivisibilities of transport, for example, so that it pays a firm to use a truck of minimum size less frequently but to full capacity, rather than more frequently but partly empty. Working in the opposite direction would be scarce ordering capacity. It ought then to be advantageous to the firm to schedule its inventory operations so that they do not coincide. The point is that in either case the treatment of inventories commodity by commodity is likely to be suboptimal.

Turning now from the supply side, so to speak, to the demand side, additional interdependencies need to be taken into account. In the first place, the rate of use and, above all, the fluctuations in the rate of use of different commodities may be related. The likelihood of a specific amount of one commodity being required cannot be viewed as independent of the stock control policy being applied to another commodity. Fluctuations in the demand for nuts will not be independent either of fluctuations in the demand for bolts or of the extent to which that demand is met.

A second connection on the demand side concerns the benefit to be derived from a particular policy. The benefits to be derived from a given holding of one commodity will be determined in part by the holdings of other commodities. To take the extreme case of fixed proportions, if more nuts are in stock than bolts, the benefit obtainable from the excess is zero. Such complementaries, of course, occur in retail shops as well as the possibility of substitution, where the value of stocks of one commodity increases as the stocks of substitutes decrease.

One final complication of great interest is that the demand for the firm's products may not be independent of its stock control policy. To refer once again to retail shops, the customers' propensity to buy or to come into the shop may be affected by their expectation of the probability of getting what they want. In this way a stock control policy may become self-defeating in that a failure occasionally to meet demands may lower the whole level of demand. There is an important complementarity here too, because an inability to meet the demand for one commodity may reduce the demand for other commodities.

The list of complications may be extended almost indefinitely. From what has been said, however, the essential elementary ideas should be apparent. The most important conclusion is that inventory control theory involves allocation problems of a fundamental kind, and, in particular, is concerned with those arising from the interdependence of different commodities. A second conclusion is that while the elementary analysis of these problems can be carried out in the ordinary language of economics, this is not the same thing as saying that they can be solved in this way. Many of the complications that have been mentioned give rise to problems for which no general solution exists, and for which no practical method significantly different from trial and error has been devised for calculating solutions in practice.

INDEX

PRINTED IN GREAT BRITAIN
BY
THE EASTERN PRESS LTD.
OF LONDON AND READING